NAMES and STORIES

Emilia Dilke, by Hubert von Herkomer, 1887. By courtesy of the National Portrait Gallery, London.

NAMES
AND
STORIES

⊱―◆―O―◆―⊰

Emilia Dilke
and
Victorian Culture

KALI ISRAEL

New York   ◑   Oxford

Oxford University Press

1999

Oxford University Press

Oxford   New York

Athens   Auckland   Bangkok   Bogotá   Buenos Aires   Calcutta
Cape Town   Chennai   Dar es Salaam   Delhi   Florence   Hong Kong   Istanbul
Karachi   Kuala Lumpur   Madras   Melbourne   Mexico City   Mumbai
Nairobi   Paris   Singapore   Taipei   Tokyo   Toronto   Warsaw

and associated companies in
Berlin   Ibadan

Copyright © 1999 by Oxford University Press, Inc.

Published by Oxford University Press, Inc.
198 Madison Avenue, New York, New York 10016

Oxford is a registered trademark of Oxford University Press

Library of Congress Cataloging-in-Publication Data
Israel, Kali, 1962–
Names and stories : Emilia Dilke and Victorian culture / Kali Israel.
p. cm.
Includes index.
ISBN 0-19-512275-5
1. Dilke, Emilia Francis Strong, Lady, 1840–1904.   2. Women authors, English—
19th century—Biography.   3. Great Britain—History—Victoria, 1837–1901—
Biography.   4. Dilke, Charles Wentworth, Sir, 1843–1911—Marriage.
5. Politicians' spouses—Great Britain—Biography.   6. Women art historians—
Great Britain—Biography.   7. Women labor leaders—Great Britain—Biography.
8. Great Britain—Civilization—19th century.   9. Pattison, Mark,
1813–1884—Marriage.   10. Feminists—Great Britain—Biography.
I. Title.
PR4599.D42Z73 1998
942.081'092—dc21
[b]   98-42855

1 3 5 7 9 8 6 4 2

Printed in the United States of America
on acid-free paper

To *Arthur Lee Potts*
and to Paul Israel

ACKNOWLEDGMENTS

Names cannot come near telling the stories that enabled this book.

The life-world I have found at the University of Michigan, in and beyond the Department of History, and in Ann Arbor, made this book possible, allowing, challenging, encouraging, and enjoining me to think and rethink, write and rewrite, take chances and pleasures, over the last five years. Dear friends and colleagues have given support, hilarity, food and drink, and a life I love. These names move me: Susan Johnson, Carroll Smith-Rosenberg, Fred Cooper and Jane Burbank, Tom and Ruth Green, Martha Vicinus, Richard Candída Smith, Sue Juster, George Sanchez, Scott Spector, David William Cohen, and Gina Morantz-Sanchez. Bill and Elie Rosenberg, Kathleen Canning, David Scobey, and Sonya Rose have been especially enspiriting, entertaining, and generous, and their friendships give me great joy. Linda Gregerson and Steven Mullaney, John Kucich, Adela Pinch, and Patsy Yaegar of the University of Michigan English Department have given thoughts and warmth I treasure. The fabulous FFBs of my writing group—Yopie Prins, Liz Wingrove, and Catherine Brown— read and read and read some more, with consistently improving results, and I have learned more than I may know from their own works. The Program in the Comparative Study of Social Transformations heard two pieces of this project in draft but helped even more by providing the best possible space for ongoing interdisciplinary thought over the years. Students at all levels have allowed me to think by listening and by sharing their own work. The staff of the History Department are always smart, helpful, and right. A summer research grant from University of Michigan was crucial in enabling my research. Dagmar Herzog and Lauren Berlant have been marvelously enthusiastic readers and friends. This book would also not exist without the Michigan Theatre, the staffs of far too many cafes, the friendship and wisdom of Nick Chapman, the gardeners of Liberty Street, Shaman Drum Bookshop, and a light-filled room where names matter and stories unbend and open.

Geoff Eley gets his own paragraph: beloved friend and best actor in a multitude of supporting roles. By his example, unstinting sharing of thoughts, listening, and reading, and even more by his affection and great good humor, he has made me at least a little braver and smarter than I'd otherwise be. Among the pleasures of his friendship, moreover, is that of knowing Sarah and Anna Eley.

My debts extend back to other places where I have been educated and encouraged. I was fortunate to spend a year teaching at the University of Cincinnati where Barbara Ramusack and Joanne Meyerowitz especially were the best of colleagues and friends— challenging, funny, and encouraging. At Rutgers, where this book began as a Ph.D. dissertation, past and present faculty members, especially the late Harold Poor, Suzanne Lebsock, Carla Hesse, Martha Howell, and Victoria DeGrazia, were helpful and bracing; the Center for the Critical Analysis of Contemporary Culture allowed me to explore varied perspectives on writing about selves; I continue to learn from the work of other former Rutgers graduate students, including Polly Beals, Pamela Walker, and Joy Dixon. Daniel Harris taught me about Victorian poetry and about reading, in ways that have had a profound impact on my work, while his friendship sustained me during my early research. The members of my dissertation committee—Bonnie Smith, Cora Kaplan, and John Gillis—contributed in distinctive and irreplaceable ways and helped me see beyond the dissertation, and Judy Walkowitz was the best possible advisor; her careful, generous, and sharp readings have often transformed my work. Earlier, at Lewis and Clark College, Henry Bair, Denise Thompson, and Dorothy Berkson were teachers in the broadest sense. Robert Cruden did more than supervise an undergraduate thesis on the Women's Trade Union League; with Janet Cruden, he offered me great and lasting inspiration. Ian and Valerie Adams in Edinburgh were kind beyond any possible recompense. Earlier still, Steller, Michael Storto, the Guess family, and the taxes of strangers gave shelter and sustenance.

The research for this book was enabled by the staff of Bodleian Library, especially by Tim Rogers, who guided me to the records of the Library, which proved a rich source; the staff of the Manuscripts Room of the British Library and the Newspaper Library at Colindale; the very kind staff of the Trades Union Congress Library, London, who allowed me to use Gertrude Tuckwell's unpublished "Reminiscences"; the National Art Library, London; the Librarian of Somerville College, Oxford; the staff of the Churchill College Archives Center, Cambridge, especially Carolyn Lye; and the Probate Division, Somerset House, London. I am indebted to the Trustees of the Trevelyan Papers, Library of the University of Newcastle-upon-Tyne, for copies of some letters to Pauline Trevelyan, and to Leslie Gordon for her assistance; to the Principals and Bursars of Somerville College and St. Anne's College, who let me rooms in their colleges' properties during my Oxford researches, and to the National Portrait Gallery for providing photographs of works in their collections.

My researches in Britain would not have been possible without the kindnesses of individuals beyond institutions. Maxine Berg and John Robertson provided shelter, assistance in finding my way around Oxford (figuratively and literally), introductions, and several excellent meals; I am deeply grateful for their warm hospitality. Katherine Bradley generously shared her research on Oxford women; the Reverend Dr. V. H. H.

Green, former Rector of Lincoln College, granted me several long conversations on matters Pattisonian and kind encouragement of my work; and Oxford English Limited offered lively seminars which, mercifully, had nothing to do with anyone named Pattison. The Rt. Hon. Lord Jenkins of Hillhead took time from his schedule in Parliament to talk about Charles Dilke. The encouragement of Elaine Jordan and Leonore Davidoff of the University of Essex was deeply enabling, and their gifts included arranging for me to meet Angela John, who has given me years of friendship and encouragement, months of shelter in London, a magical holiday in Wales, the chance to enjoy the glorious Bron, and unfailing enthusiasm, for all of which I am profoundly grateful.

Leonore and Angela also allowed me to develop some early ideas in a short essay in *Gender and History*; Keith Nield and the collective of *Social History*, and the readers and collective of *Radical History Review* aided this book by their criticisms of early versions of chapters 6 and 5, which appeared in those journals. I am also grateful to the many audiences in Britain and the United States that have, over the years, given space and thought to my work. Thomas LeBien of Oxford University Press has been a model editor: understanding, prompt, intellectually engaged, helpfully critical, and, best of all, enthusiastic. Thanks also the readers for the Press, whose comments helped a great deal.

Achilles, Athena, and Rainy, and the Guys did the hard work of distraction.

Long ago, in Alaska, Art Potts made my stories possible; his name is a talisman for me. Paul Israel's gifts can't be counted: he too is my home. *Names and Stories* is dedicated to them.

CONTENTS

NAMES AND STORIES

INTRODUCTION
Genres of Life-Writing

Life Stories

After her death in October 1904, Emilia Dilke was memorialized as an "exceptional woman" by diverse mourners. Involved with the Women's Trade Union League from its foundation in 1874, Dilke had been its president from 1886 until her death; accordingly, the *Women's Trade Union Review*, the League's journal, grieved as "her colleagues in the work to which she devoted the larger part of her life and the choicest powers of her fine intellect," regretting the loss of "one . . . fitted, as few human beings . . . to fill the post of leader in a crusade against the tyranny of social tradition and the callousness of social indifference." Her funeral was attended by representatives of the Trades Union Congress and the Miners' Federation and by such trade-union luminaries as Mary Macarthur and Ben Tillett. Their testimonials spoke of trade-unionism as "[her life's] chief enthusiasm, its ruling aim and purpose." The *Review* printed letters of mourning from dozens of individuals and organizations in the labor movement along with plans for a memorial fund to support the League's work.[1] But a year after her death, an anonymous article entitled "The Art-Work of Lady Dilke" appeared in the *Quarterly Review*.[2] The writer intersperses a discussion of Dilke's eight volumes of art history with long laments that she had spent her energy on anything else. She had "sacrificed precious hours and months of a too brief life to a benevolent mission which might have been fulfilled by others," neglecting her "unique vocation."[3] Her trade-unionist and feminist work are positioned by this writer as an unfortunate distraction from more exalted intellectual labors.

Organized labor and this admirer of Dilke's art history agree on one thing: the fullness of the life. Similarly, in his "Memoir" of Emilia Dilke, her widower, Charles

Dilke, evokes a woman of wide interests and activities, although he does not represent them as conflicting.[4] Virtually on her deathbed, Emilia Dilke chats about politics as she opens a letter "from Tokio, thank[ing] her for . . . [her work] for the Japanese wounded, and widows and orphans," then "jot[s] down notes on some tapestries" recently seen, referring occasionally to thick reference books.[5] Unlike those who perceived only one aspect of Emilia Dilke, Charles Dilke contends that this life was whole, offering as evidence others' words: "She had it all—beauty, bounty of heart, high intelligence, simplicity. How could anyone not cherish this special woman, so absolutely complete and unique."[6] Emilia Dilke's greatness encompasses her femininity, her exemplary wifehood, and her public activities in politics and scholarship. Charles Dilke's memoir argues for Emilia Dilke's place in these canonical and intimate histories and contends that her multifaceted consistency was itself extraordinary: despite her "apparently distinct spheres of activity . . . [her] lives were one."[7] Charles Dilke rests his claim for the value of Emilia Dilke's life—and the value of his "Memoir"—on her status as a thoroughgoing and unified "exceptional woman." His emphasis on this rare creature's love for and happiness with him also renders Dilke an "exceptional man" by association; he proclaims, "I alone shared both lives and knew all the friends, and thus of necessity the duty [of writing her life] has fallen to me."[8]

Charles Dilke's text is not only privileged but privileging; in reading, it covertly suggests, we too can survey the whole life and gain a comprehension of Emilia Dilke. But Charles Dilke's memoir's stress on the continuity of Emilia Dilke's character contains the possibilities of narrative even as it tells its story. In its paradigmatically biographical logic, the "Memoir" insists that all the subject's qualities were visible from her childhood and youth, and that while "no influence ever ended," events and changes were subordinated to an ongoing inner being. All Emilia Dilke's activities were marked by her qualities of "overmastering sense of duty, and an unfailing courage—little short of sublime."[9] This continuous, unified, life story is morally and aesthetically uplifting, but among the letters Charles Dilke received on the publication of the "Memoir," reiterating commiserations on his loss of such a "noble," "learned," "really unique" woman, one noted his account's tendency to stasis. Reading Dilke's memoir had been like "looking at certain Greek Statues."[10]

Fixing the subject, especially in a heroic position, is generic to obituaries and family memoirs, but Dilke's "Memoir" reminds us that conventions shape biographical writing more broadly, including the obvious and highly Victorian instance of the *Dictionary of National Biography*.[11] The DNB overtly privileges the events of a life in the "public realm," but private events or emotionally revealing passages are often smuggled in, to be savored all the more for the whiff of transgression. As it happens, Emilia Dilke is among the relatively few women included in the DNB, and her entry suggests how uneasy may be the fit between the generic conventions of genre and imaginable stories, and it also signals Emilia Dilke's location in both official histories and other enticingly emotional, intimate, and gendered narratives. Dilke's entry, by Sidney Lee, is a mélange of births, marriages, deaths, friendships with Great Men—Ruskin, Browning, Prince Leopold, William Morris—and references to scandalous marriages.[12] From 1861 to 1885, Emilia Dilke had been Mrs. Mark Pattison, wife of the much older and famously embittered Rector of Lincoln College, Oxford, who was much older than she; she then married Sir Charles Dilke, a Liberal parliamentary star, just as his career was radically reorganized by a lurid sex scandal in 1885. The status of "Lady Dilke" in the cultural imagination derives from these marriages as much as from her political and scholarly work; Lee's essay wavers between slightly disreputable gossip, claims for her importance by association with famous men, and a catalogue of her contributions to knowledge and the public weal, which come across as laudable but slightly dull. Her volumes of French art history are dutifully listed but the judgment that "her critical powers were inferior to her industry" appears as if one fact among others, sandwiched between publication dates. Her fiction—two and a half volumes of short stories—is granted brief notice for "originality," while her social reform activities serve to demonstrate the fineness of her moral character. But if Lee's sketch easily, even glibly, demonstrates how tenuous are distinctions between fact and interpretation, its exclusions and incoherences—like the obituarists' and grieving widower's text—make visible the partiality of reading and writing lives.

These memorial texts—obituaries, DNB entries, and memoirs—share another feature, both banal and provocative: they must name their subject, settling on a signifier that allows easy reference in alphabetical lists. But for Emilia Dilke, names seem less to stabilize a subject than to dramatize the mobility of identity. David Lodge, writing about novels, suggests, "[f]or an author to openly change his mind about the name of a character, in mid-text, is a particularly blatant admission that the whole story is 'made up,' something readers know but usually suppress, as religious believers suppress their doubts. . . . One may hesitate and agonize about the choice of a name, but once made, it becomes inseparable from the character, and to question it seems to throw the whole project en abime, as the deconstructionists say." Lodge claims writers assume the meaningfulness of names; while it is not "customary for novelists to explain the connotations of the names they give to their characters . . . such suggestions are supposed to work subliminally on the reader's consciousness."[13] Yet if the public name under which the subject of this book died—Lady Dilke—is a rich signifier of class and gender meanings, it is also wholly inadequate. "Emilia Dilke" preserved the initial of her patronymic name—an "S." at the middle of her signature—through her marriages, according to Charles Dilke, in order to "mark her wish for some recognition of the independent existence of the woman, and in some resistance to the old English doctrine of complete merger in the husband."[14] In this narrative, a name (or at least its trace) establishes the continuity and autonomy of the self, but Lodge suggests that while names are crucial to the making of stories, naming continually threatens to give away the fictionality of stories in which readers are meant to believe. Names can be changed by choice and imagination, in secret decisions and intimate texts as well as by marital contracts, and they bear meanings beyond their legal status.

"Emilia Dilke" was christened Emily Francis Strong and known by her middle name through her childhood as the daughter of an army officer-cum-bank-manager in Iffley, near Oxford, and her days as an art student in London. Then, in her first marriage, she was Francis Pattison or Mrs. Mark Pattison, while her published works of art history and criticism were neutrally signed E. F. S. Pattison. More: in the 1870s she privately changed her first name to Emilia, a renomination made public when she remarried in 1885; by that marriage she also became Lady Dilke. Compounding and emphasizing this knot of naming and narrating, private names, pet names, nicknames, and past names continued to circulate within specific relationships even after they had been formally or publicly eschewed. Nomination and narration combine and contend: each name did work—denoted a subject in a story of professional activities, marriage, and politics—and masked other names and narratives.[15]

Names and stories constitute a character by significations and by evasions. Like her names, the partial and conflicting stories of Emilia Dilke's life freeze her *and* reveal her mobility. Emilia Dilke's names can be inserted into many stories: the histories of women, feminists, intellectuals, trade unionists, Liberals and Labour politicians, Oxonians, happily and unhappily married people, good and bad parents, writers, artists, students, critics, art historians, and actors in Victorian sexual scandals. All of these histories are important; they often intersect. In some of these stories, her character is active and "significant"; in others, she appears marginal, wrong-headed, atypical, or odd. Moreover, besides this heteronomous movement through diverse historical narratives, Emilia Dilke circulated in a variety of fictional *stories* during and after her lifetime. Stories were told about her as a person who had been made into a character. That is, a number of overtly fictional works were said to contain characters based on her. The most famous and controversial of these attributions is the character of Dorothea in George Eliot's *Middlemarch*, but other novels include Rhoda Broughton's *Belinda* (1883); Andrew Lang alluded to the story of the two novels' purported sharing of models by writing a series of fictional letters between the protagonists of *Middlemarch* and *Belinda*. W. H. Mallock's *The New Republic: Or Culture, Faith, and Philosophy in an English Country-house* (1877), Mrs. Humphry Ward's *Robert Elsmere* (1888), and perhaps her *Lady Connie* (1888) also contain characters associated with Francis Pattison, and the Pattison marriage has been suggested as an inspiration for a poem by Robert Browning. In at least one case, Emilia Dilke actively collaborated with a novelist, in Hector Malot's *Vices Français* (1887). In the twentieth century Robert Liddell's *The Almond Tree* (1938) and Betty Askwith's *The Tangled Web* (1960) tell stories that intersect with Emilia Dilke's two marriages. Michael Dyne-Bradley placed Emilia Dilke on stage in his play *The Right Honourable Gentleman*.[16] Nor did Emilia Dilke just allegedly pose for others; she wrote short stories, a disguised memoir in an essay on positivism, art history and criticism, essays on women's participation in and exclusion from economic and political life, and she participated in making paintings and photographs. In Emilia Dilke's circulation as both a cultural figure and a cultural actor, the distinction between the two grows unclear. Her public attitude to the works in which others saw her ranged from amusement to studied indifference (she claimed not to have read *Middlemarch*—an assertion even Charles Dilke doubted—and regarded allusions to it as "an unpardonable offense"), but at least one contemporary suspected a culpable process of self-imagination: Margaret Oliphant remarked caustically after a visit to Oxford that Francis Pattison "considers herself the model of Dorothea."[17]

More stories: J. E. C. Bodley, Charles Dilke's one-time private secretary and a possible author of the *Quarterly Review* essay on Emilia Dilke's art-historical writing, criticized Charles Dilke's memoir for including too much emphasis on "her labours—writing & public engagements." Charles's emphasis on Emilia Dilke's achievements was a distraction from her essence—which could be better portrayed through the inclusion of descriptions of their houses and such pathetic touches as the mourning of her dog after her death; Charles Dilke had, in Bodley's view, "let her be seen almost solely 'en representation.' "[18] Bodley's diminishment of Emilia Dilke's public and professional activities was inflected by his own politics, but it also attests a faith in the severability of Emilia Dilke's life en representation from her real—private, emotional, feminine—life, which was for Bodley the real ground of her exceptionality. Charles Dilke's memoir also drew criticism from Maria Theresa Earle, an old friend of Emilia Dilke. For Earle, Dilke's memoir failed as a "psychological study," not only as a natural effect of his love for his late wife but because Charles had failed to capture the "strangeness" of Emilia Dilke's life.[19] More recently, while writing this book, I spoke to a noted British feminist historian of working-class women, families, the state, and labor. She told me a story: when she was a graduate student, she was asked by a well-known art historian and critic what she was "working on." He agreed that her studies of working-class women were important and valuable but suggested she might enjoy a topic with "passion" (and, by implication, romance and sex) "like Lady Dilke." Setting aside the assumption that writing the history of working-class women is an unpassionate business, the ironies of this story remain dizzying. Emilia Dilke's role as a feminist trade unionist complicates the separation of "topics" presumed by the art historian's suggestion, while the suggestion that the history of women could be a gratifyingly exciting making of stories about exceptional characters echoes Bodley's and Earle's objections to Charles Dilke's memoir.[20]

My project will not satisfy the interlocutors in these stories. I am interested in the resources of stories—how they create, contain, extend, multiply, and make lives. The life of the woman who became Emilia Dilke was strange, or, put differently, exceptional. But I approach Emilia Dilke neither as a story of a remarkable individual nor as a set of representations to be "read through" for the revelation of a real self, but as exceptionally useful material for considering the relationships between lives, images, and stories. Emilia Dilke resided and survives in representations. Her life offers an extreme occasion for thinking about how a life may be caught up in texts—those that explicitly name and rename her and in imagined associations with fiction.

My work converges with several recent innovative life studies of exceptional women by feminist literary critics, especially the works of Biddy Martin on Lou Andreas-Salome, Jacqueline Rose on Sylvia Plath, and Toril Moi on Simone de Beauvoir.[21] Rose, Martin, and Moi refuse to separate "works" from "lives" and insist that their subjects cannot be severed from the texts that surround them, comment on them, criticize them, and make them into objects of knowledge.[22] These scholars also demonstrate that reading texts closely for multiple and subterranean meanings enriches intellectual history, as writings come to be understood as generated, enabled, and disabled by writers' positions in powerful institutions and discourses.[23] My overriding goal, however, is not to locate Emilia Dilke in a critical pantheon alongside other famous women, but to use her as a site for analysis of nineteenth-century Britain. I show that the texts of her life are interesting and useful for multiple modes of historical scholarship, not because they should be canonical but because they allow us to read across public and private, political and intellectual, aesthetic and autobiographical histories.

Emilia Dilke offers a series of specifically Victorian nexes to generate understanding of Victorian culture. For example, Charles Dilke's account of Francis Strong Pattison's religious development need not be read only as a true or false account of an individual's spiritual subjectivity but can be considered in relation to other stories he tells about faith and doubt, women, intellect, and love, stories that participate in wider historical projects of constructing cultural and political efficacies for bourgeois men. Other scholars have examined the circulation of images of and around Victorian "public" women like Florence Nightingale, Ellen Terry, Alice Liddell, or the Queen, whose lives were continuously refracted through multiple mirrors of contemporary texts, artworks, and fields of representation.[24] Like such women, Emilia Dilke was never "representative," but her status as representation is nearly paradigmatic because of her specificity and her fictionality, her elusiveness and scattering.[25]

Throughout this book, I write not about what people felt or thought but about what they said and wrote and did, and I write about stories about feelings and thoughts. For example, I read Emilia Dilke's stories about marriage as narratives that reveal competing and incomplete ways of representing, undertaking, or escaping marriage in nineteenth-century Britain, rather than as deposits to be excavated for truths about a specific marriage. I read and write stories of visions, angels, madness, furniture, missionaries, gin, and walls, and stories in which class, gender, nation, and empire offer violence and everyday pleasures. I do not force these texts into alignment, whether to construct a story of a singular self or to attain closure in a unified history. Rather, Emilia Dilke is a point of entry into a range of historical and contemporary issues and an incitement to consider the relations—contradictions and reversals as well as homologies and importations—of diverse political, intellectual, social, and aesthetic histories.[26]

One text by the woman who became Emilia Dilke struggles to represent a life that inhabits and confounds "aesthetic" and "political" categories; like Charles Dilke's "Memoir" (and many more recent biographies of diverse figures), it does so by emphasizing personal exceptionality. E. F. S. Pattison's 1879 *Renaissance of Art in France* concludes with a gripping account of the Renaissance ceramicist Bernard Palissy. A hero, emblem, site of mourning and loss, and figure in many histories, Pattison's Palissy is "artist and Huguenot" as well as scientist and political thinker; "the same spring of initiative energy" leads him to engage in a "search after the secrets of nature and art" and "the secrets of social and political life." Palissy brings "the same uncompromising determination" and desire to "push to the innermost centre" to spiritual, political, and artistic pursuits. As with Lady Dilke in Charles Dilke's "Memoirs", Palissy's ability to move across fields is grounded in his own character—"*opinaître*," "strong," "self-relian[t]," "outspoken," "self-confiden[t]," he is never "servile" to tradition or place. Yet Pattison's Palissy is doubly historically indicative: he is an embodiment of "national" character and, when he dies of "want, misery, and ill-treatment" at the age of eighty, persecuted and imprisoned, an epochal story ends. The brutal throwing of his body to dogs is the end of Pattison's French Renaissance.[27]

I both refuse and follow the leads given by E. F. S. Pattison's account of her polymathic Palissy. I do not attempt a comprehensive study of the works of Pattison/Dilke nor produce her as a subject whose works across genres are unified by the power of a personality. My goal is not to reconcile, to abolish differences or contradictions, nor to offer a synecdoche of a nation, era, or "Victorian women." Yet, as E. F. S. Pattison's story of Palissy provocatively ranges across genres and histories while arguing that threads of commonality surface and submerge, I move across Pattison/

Dilke's works, traversing genres—from trade-unionist speechs, to art-critical essays, to private love letters. Following these changing names offers traces of many productive and partial pasts, but Dilke's dispersal also prompts the development of a model of historical writing that foregrounds representation, narrative, figuration, and intertextual analysis. Emilia Dilke's stories offer spaces to grapple with widely troubling, as well as historically specific, questions about writing, lives, and historical knowledge, and to think about life-reading and life-writing as the examination of the stories that make up lives.[28]

Recursions and Mutations

The large structure of this book is its constant attention to stories—produced, enacted, written, circulated, recounted, read, retold, believed, and doubted. Within this frame, as in the double helix of a DNA molecule, elements recur in varied combinations, producing both repetition and mutation in twisting lines. France and Oxford; gender and class, childhood and families; pictures and ekphrasis; names and places; education, work, art, institutions, and politics; violence and pleasure; marriage, adultery, and death; style and performance—these terms and others combine and recombine, interlocking and sometimes surprising as they move across contexts and carry accumulated associations across different discourses and genres.

In 1913, Elizabeth Robins impatiently contended,

> [The] Exceptional Woman is one of our chief obstacles . . . because *she is a Drug in the Market!* I can scarcely find one of my sex whom someone has not been ready to persuade of her Exceptionalness! . . . Those who were "great ladies" by the accident of birth, or the chance of marriage; those who were successful artists, able to command a hearing— practically all who had some measure of liberty, seem to have lived in the fog of this old illusion. They were "Exceptions," not merely in opportunity or in gifts, but in the essentials which lie behind these things.[29]

The first three chapters of this book engage with "exceptional" children and young people, taking up Robins's challenge to include the production of exceptionality while also attending to the making of stories. These chapters tell family stories. Chapter 1, "On Not Being an Orphan," reads the stories about families that circulate around Francis Strong's childhood and considers the ways in which those who wrote about Francis Strong both provide stories of family heritages and separate her from her sisters and mother to endow her with the status of exceptional child. This chapter also examines Emilia Dilke's later political deployments of personal narratives about class, empire, and family life; Dilke's texts claim that such large categories are both constitutive of and escapable through individual subjectivity and adult politics. I then consider Francis Strong's and her sisters' educations. I argue that Francis's exceptionality resides in her privilege, but I also raise an elusive possibility by considering stories of uncanny psychological and physiological peculiarities and experiences, stories that enticingly gesture toward irrecuperable narratives of gender and pain.

In chapter 2, "Pictures and Lessons," I consider stories about Francis Strong making and being made into pictures and raise several themes that will recur: style, aestheticization, and women's places in institutions that both included and marginalized them. I begin by showing more fully Francis Strong's position of privilege in local communities, placing her childhood education in art in a wider cultural history of local Oxford art culture, especially Oxford's privileged relation to Pre-Raphaelitism. I then move to London for another set of stories about access to artistic resources, beginning with another family story. I read Charles Dilke's family culture as both highly privileged and as a condensation of wider developments in gender and modernity, especially the construction of a modern metropolitan masculinity that blended politics with high culture and aesthetic sensitivity, privileged heterosociality, offered resources to some women, and maintained gendered divisions. I then examine the institutions of art and education in which Charles Dilke and Francis Strong met, especially the South Kensington Art School, to map art education as a site of conflict about gender, class, and access to state resources, knowledge about bodies, and professional careers. I consider women's status as artists and their circulation as figures of art by looking at accounts that depict Francis Strong as an art student as a vivid visual and aesthetic object, an object of male patronage, and a woman artist producing female figures. Yet I conclude by considering another exceptional woman's disappearance.

Chapter 3, "Making a Marriage," while continuing the exploration of narratives of exceptionality, is also the first of two chapters organized around marriage stories. Middlemarch haunts this chapter, as a story by which some contemporaries thought they could make sense of the 1860 marriage of Mark Pattison and Francis Strong, as the story from which some of Mark Pattison's life writers have sought to rescue him, and as an instance of a wider genre of stories about young women marrying for knowledge. But this chapter begins with more family stories, this time in the register of Gothic horror. I recount some stories about the Pattison family in Yorkshire and Oxford, and read these tales of patriarchal madness, violence, faith, and the ends of education through the lenses of gender and class. The stories of Mark Pattison's marriage to Francis Strong are thus placed in a longer set of family stories, not simply in order to produce a longer psychological history for Mark Pattison but to argue that seemingly extreme stories condense more normative violences. I move from accounts of the gendered privileges and pains of education in the Pattison family to the gendered institutions of knowledge in Oxford and argue that marriage in Oxford was peculiar, exceptional, extreme, and illuminative of the structure of Victorian marriage more generally. These examinations of the local organizations of gender and knowledge form a framework for understanding the Pattison marriage beyond exceptionality, despite its notorious inscriptions in novels. But the final section of this chapter returns to fiction by examining Charles Dilke's use of Middlemarch as an intertextual guarantor of his own tales and by reading Emilia Dilke's fictional stories of seductions and of marriage as a Faustian bargain by idealistic and doomed women. I read these Dillke stories as instances in a wider genre of happy and unhappy stories about women entering unequal marriages as a route to knowledge, rather than as encryptings of the "truth" of the Pattison marriage. Throughout this chapter, education, and the lives it makes possible, is a terrain of desire in which men and women, but especially women, risk violence and death. Reading the murder in Emilia Dilke's stories of Oxford does not supercede reading caginess or confidence in other stories Dilke told about women's agency in the institutions they inhabit. Or vice versa.

Chapter 4, "Bodies," focuses on stories about bodies and bodies of stories, again moving through three sections: first, an examination of Francis Pattison/Emilia Dilke's texts about sex in marriage; second, a reading of the "adulterous" texts and tales by and around Francis Pattison's relationship with Charles Dilke and Mark Pattison's relationship with Meta Bradley; and third, a discussion of stories about Mark Pattison's death. Francis Pattison's letters to Mark Pattison narrate conjugal sexuality as an area of deep conflict, but conflict is also waged within these letters between rhetorics of self-assertion and self-punishment. In fictional stories by Emilia Dilke, too, female bodies are both vulnerable stakes and grounds of resistance. I argue that these texts suggest the usability of the language of sexual bodies in combats about gender in public and private institutions. In the second section, I consider the adulterous narratives into which two relationships were inscribed; I explore them not in order to resolve questions of sexual conduct and sexual culpability but to argue that possibly adulterous relationships were not concealed but constituted by uneven and unequal movement between rhetorics of familial relations, pedagogy, politics, comradeship, spirituality, and friendship as well as eros. The third set of stories I tell circle the dying body of Mark Pattison: Francis Pattison's texts about Mark's death; Emilia Pattison's attempts to use Mark Pattison's will to open new narrative possibilities for women; and Emilia Dilke's fictional stories about the deaths of male scholars. Although this chapter tells many stories about bodily pains as they circulated in texts, it has a comic coda: a narrative of arguments about bodies of texts, as the stories of the Pattison marriage were fought over, censored, locked up, unlocked, and made into fiction's fodder long after the sexual and mortal bodies of all concerned had been buried or burnt.

Chapter 5, "The Resources of Style," again reads scandalous Oxford stories, doubling back to stories told about Francis Pattison in Oxford and to the issues of figuration raised in chapter 2. Francis Pattison was depicted in a variety of Oxford texts as transgressive, provocative, and memorable, her "femininity" written in highly visual language. I consider these representations as emblems of tensions around the increasing heterosociality of Oxford and examine the ways in which Mrs. Pattison's figure was marked as extravagant, sexual, artificial, and evasive of local assignments of status and identity. I draw on poststructuralist feminist and queer-theoretical analyses of gender as performance in order to suggest the scandalousness of Francis Pattison's ultrafeminine enactments, but I also argue for a historically specific understanding of the uses of sexual and aesthetic style. I read the texts that depict Francis Pattison's "otherness" in Oxford in terms of class, nation, aristocracy, in relation to British constructions of France, the specific theatrical context of Oxford University, and instabilities in Oxonian economies of gender, sexuality, and prestige. Yet, after doubling back in the first half of this chapter to issues raised earlier, I look forward by considering the ways in which Francis Pattison's enactments of femininity, intellectuality, Frenchness, and aristocracy could be recuperated into conservative discourses of gender and class. I then explore the limitations on access to the resources of style in Emilia Dilke's own feminism, reading some of Dilke's texts on trade unionism and her practices of educating other women.

Chapter 6, "French Vices," continues the themes of performance, France, and scandal, and the work of feminity in narratives of class that I explored in chapter 5, while also returning to the construction of adulterous narratives and stories about sex. The widowed Emilia Pattison married Charles Dilke in 1885, just as he was named as corespondent in one of the most spectacular divorce cases of the late nineteenth century. The "case" of Virginia Crawford and Charles Dilke has been repeatedly told, worried over, and staged in a variety of texts and media ever since, but my consideration of possible adulteries again foreswears attempts to solve questions of sexual culpability and emphasizes the proliferation of stories. I discuss the stories told between and by Charles and Emilia, before and after their marriage, but then focus on the public competition of narratives by Dilkes and Crawfords, judges and newspaper writers, feminists and Liberals. I analyze the ways diverse texts construct plausibility and agency, sexual pleasure and sexual danger, and make claims about their audiences. Anxieties and hatreds of class, nation, and religion, as well as gender and sexuality, circulated through the case's stories, and each plotting of the case struggled both to contain and to draw upon crosscutting social, cultural, and political categories. I move, however, from the competion of narratives within the case to a reconsideration of the case's significance by looking at the continued political careers of both Dilkes and especially the deployments of the figure of Emilia Dilke as a victim, accomplice, heroine, or fool. As in chapter 4, I emphasize the usability of sex, this time in the production and enactment of virtuous politics in the public sphere. I conclude by examining another marriage story: Gertrude Tuckwell's account of Emilia and Charles Dilke's marriage makes the Dilke household an institution, a site of labor and pleasure, a setting for aesthetic and political activity, and above all, a happy ending that underwrites a politics of the future. I suggest that Tuckwell's story of the Dilkes also smuggles in a "marriage" story of her own in which politics and eros are joined.

The final chapter, "Renaissances," is a microcosm of the book as a whole. I read across Pattison/Dilke's art-writings to follow some crucial terms and place them in relation to works in other genres, focusing on Francis Pattison/Emilia Dilke's stories of the Renaissance as an object of historical knowledge and a site of contemporary political meanings. Pattison/ Dilke's history of art is a history of institutions that enable and confine, and her texts repeatedly thematize violence, pleasure, nature, and desire, and represent "the self" as a site of boundless knowledge. Her Renaissance's mobility and its repetitions suggest that we understand these texts as intersecting, riven, fruitful, and symptomatic, rather than concocting a figure of a unified feminist intellectual, weighing the adequacy of Dilke's art-historical scholarship, or appraising the consistency of her social thought. Endings are frequent and ambiguous in Emilia Dilke's past and projected histories and the stories told around her—and in my text as well.

Claims and Refusals

This book engages a number of ongoing historiographies, including the history of nineteenth-century feminism, the history of art discourses, and the history of Oxford. Some of my analyses—for example, of the impossible position of Victorian women intellectuals in Oxford or the competition of sexual stories in public political debates—may illuminate questions about "the economy of intellectual prestige" with obvious continuing relevance.[30] But I also hope to model historical and analytic practices usable and translatable to other places and projects, not the model of life-writing but an example of writing about the historically variable modes and materials of figuring selves and writing lives. "Emilia Dilke" is both a figure in a variety of Victorian histories and a figure of possibilities. Because this book participates in a larger scholarly conversation, I want to briefly expand on my theoretical framework, enabling readers to understand the choices I seek to enact.[31]

This book rests upon both contentions and refusals. It is not a biography or a "life" of Emilia Dilke but an examination of the stories and texts that constitute her.[32] I do not sort through texts to judge them as more or less truthful reflections of a "real" and retrievable person, but to delineate multiple representations of Emilia Dilke in their relations to each other; to Emilia Dilke's own texts; to texts in which she wrote of others' readings of her; to facts that constrain interpretation and revision; and to other contemporary and historical stories. These multiplex texts are not temporary refractions of an original person who can be reconstructed separate from the stories she inhabited.[33] Texts are not just something to read through in order to see history on the other side; what texts—novels, newspapers, memoirs, histories, criticism, and library records—do is history. Historians can read stories and past readings (including women's readings of stories about them) to understand figuration and narration as constitutive historical processes.[34]

In considering the texts that claim Emilia Dilke, including her own and mine, as complex narratives blending fact and fiction, I heed Liz Stanley's call for feminist biographers to enable readers to make visible in their text their "acts of understanding" and foreground interpretive choices.[35] I also discuss the partiality and provisionality of texts and the ways in which "evidence" was made—preserved selectively, guarded, lost, and found in institutions and discourses. No document or artifact can be considered "raw," unprocessed and unmodified by time and human agency, and I provide readers with information about the circumstances that have shaped the survival and form of my evidence and the erasures and oubliettes of archival histories.[36] The most vivid example of editorial cooking is the case of Charles Dilke's engagement books: as corespondent in a sensational divorce trial, Dilke made a notoriously bad impression by presenting in evidence diaries in which many pages were topped and tailed, had jagged edges, or even had holes cut out of the middle. He excised names and engagements, and claimed that he did so in order to "reduce the bulk" of the books. Yet if Dilke was concealing incriminating information, he did so astonishingly publicly, sometimes sitting in the House of Commons library chopping out bits of his diary and dropping the debris into the upturned hat at his feet.[37] Such performances of discretion are extreme but many of the archival materials safely housed in the Bodleian and British Libraries have been at least as deliberately transformed—letters and diaries meticulously mutilated with scissors and eraser.[38] As in obituaries and other retrospectively tactful accounts, readers may detect ghosts and undercurrents that eluded the control of their authors; we can fill in some gaps and rasurae in these pillaged texts and discern patterns of deletion, rhetorics of erasure and denial that, like photographic negatives offer historical evidence, but the contingency of textual creation and preservation are part of my analysis. Fragmented, motivated, and accidental texts make up Emilia Dilke's life.

I stress the textuality—the metaphoricity, linguistic complexity, and especially the narrativity—of the materials I read. Many scholars have noted the pervasiveness and importance of narrative as it shapes historical writing, autobiography, and biography, but my method surmises that source texts too—including "primary sources" as well as previous historical accounts—participate in and evoke larger narratives, albeit often incompletely.[39] I view diaries and private letters as sites of story making just as much as published novels or historical accounts, rather than assuming that "private" texts are more truthful or offer more immediate access to "experience" than "public" ones. In attending to narrative, I also join scholars across disciplines who argue that the powers of narrative are not limited to making textual meanings. Stories and the historically varying shapes within which stories can be told attempt "to seduce their readers into thinking and desiring in textually specified ways."[40] That is, stories are not just post hoc accounts within which we construct meaning afterward; they organize perception and delineate possible ways of thinking, acting, and being.[41] As Alan Sinfield says, "They make sense for us—of us—because we have been and are in them . . . we come to consciousness in their terms . . . certain interpretations of experience strike us as plausible because they fit with what we have experienced already."[42] "No narrative is finally capable of determining its reading subjects or of controlling precisely how it will be read," but stories offer limited and historically variable possibilities for being and action, repertoires of persons to be as well as things to think, multiple but finite "plausible" means of understanding and acting, subject positions and trajectories.[43] People enact as well as write stories they inherit, learn, are imprisoned by, recast, and renew. Most of all, stories do not arise from unfettered imagination but through powerful social institutions; narratives are not reducible to authorial intention.

Attention to narratives as a form of historical enquiry can find precedents in Victorian discourses. In an essay on her former drawing teacher, William Mulready, Emilia Dilke suggested that among the lessons she learned from Mulready was a theory of history and subjectivity. Her essay retells a scene in which Mulready narrated himself as confined and mutilated by his time:

> I think he felt that . . . a fresh tide had set in, bringing wider possibilities to English art and an encouraging stimulus of general interest unknown to the days of his youth. There were traces, too, of unexpressed regret that so much should have been missed, and of the thought that if things had been other than they were in his own time he might have come nearer to the fulfilment of his own aspirations, and those aspirations themselves might have found a wider outlook.[44]

Dilke's Mulready teaches, alongside a theory that individuals possess inherent traits, a suggestion that the shape of desires themselves may be made by the social and cultural order. Victorian concepts of selfhood were not unified, and diverse theories and rhetorics of selfhood coexisted; Victorian cultural discourses illuminatingly display tensions about the relations between selves and stories. Anthony Trollope said, "In our lives we are always weaving novels, and we manage to keep the different tales distinct." [45] *Middlemarch* itself begins with a complex prelude on the satisfactions, limitations, and necessity of stories for lives:

> Theresa's passionate, ideal nature demanded an epic life: what were many-volumed romances of chivalry and the social conquests of a brilliant girl to her? . . . Many Theresas have been born who found for themselves no epic life wherein there was a constant unfolding of far-resonant action; perhaps only a life of mistakes . . . perhaps a tragic failure which found no sacred poet and sank unwept into oblivion. [46]

In *Adam Bede*, too, Eliot wrote of the necessity of stories to make desires: "Hetty had never read a novel. How, then, could she find a shape for her expectations?" [47] Or, as Virginia Woolf suggested, "women and fiction might mean . . . women and what they are like; or it might mean women and the fiction that is written about them; or it might mean that somehow all three are inextricably mixed together." [48]

The fields of narrative within which Emilia Dilke and other historical actors were emplotted—the stories they told and the stories they enacted—were not monolithic; they include, to borrow Raymond Williams's categories, hegemonic, oppositional, alternative, and residual narratives. [49] Because they are social, narratives collide and conflict as well as reinforce and reiterate each other; some are authorized and others are not, some prestigious and others marginal. [50] Michel Foucault warned that disciplinary discourses, especially psychology or sociology but perhaps history as well, may produce life-stories in order to lay them alongside of and ratify larger narratives that are then, conversely, "proven" by the life. [51] Crudely "symptomatic" lives are the obverse of stories of exceptionality; they recall Virginia Woolf's comment when she was contemplating writing a novel about Byron: "wanting to build up my imaginary figure with every scrap I could find . . . suddenly the figure turns to merely one of the usual dead." [52] Although I place Emilia Dilke in larger narratives, for example, of class or gender, I also attend to the ways in which lives may cut athwart or be oblique to normalizing structures. [53] But the complexity and continual reformulation of hegemonic discourses do not mean their absence; as Foucault also argued, the constitutive power of discourses includes shaping resistances and counternarratives. [54]

My emphasis on narrative as a site of historical enquiry is thus different from the use of narrative in some other feminist writing, especially from the trope of *self-creation*. [55] Phyllis Rose has sweepingly represented all selfhood as a process of literary self-construction that follows the conventions of the realist novel to achieve greater or lesser aesthetic completeness: "Each of us, influenced perhaps by one ideology or another, generates our own plot." [56] Life-writing, for Rose, is therefore a matter of discerning the actions of an agency-laden self making its story, and biography is a form of aesthetic criticism: lives are to be judged by the degree to which they emulate *Bildungsromane*. [57] Rose's position is extreme, but narratives of self-making are common in feminist biographical writing. Such stories covertly posit a hidden but choice-laden self, constrained but not constituted by history, who constructs "the" self. This hidden agent is the woman behind the curtain even as the reader's attention is directed toward the visual and narrative pleasures of the Emerald City.

My aim is not to produce a story of a successful project of "self-creation" in Emilia Dilke's life but to explore the continuous, shifting, and temporary process of figuration—the ways in which historically specific discourses construct selves and stories. [58]

I offer not an account of a subject's self-production but a series of accounts of the production of a subject in sentences, stories, and accounts—acting, acted on, heroic or victimized, thinking, feeling, embracing, refusing, colluding, despairing, desiring—but not stably locatable outside of sentences and stories, not covertly exercising control or free choice, not continuous across texts and readerships. Moreover, an array of material constraints—not reducible to access to cash—limits access to stories and produces discontinuities in lives. Multiple and contradictory subject positions are made by social, economic, and political structures, and people have uneven access to narrative resources. Victorian culture was constituted and fractured by divisions, fascinated by and hostile to differences, in life and fiction. Eschewing the quest for continuity allows attention to how dis-solutions, dis-integrations, and aporias in life stories expose historical contradictions.[59]

In reading the texts of Emilia Dilke's life in a number of specific histories—the institutions of Victorian intellectual life, the tense historical relations of feminism and labor movements, debates about the relationships between art and the state, and others—I move freely across genres and discourses even while stressing textuality. I locate texts in their genres and sometimes argue that particular genres generate particular costs or effects, and I show that some discourses are more powerful than others. But I subordinate structural to intertextual analysis, tracing the movement of plot elements across genres and discourses. Emphasizing the mobility of tropes and themes, I also refuse to force judgments about priority. Rather than arguing that one discourse creates or "in the last analysis" determines another (e.g., when we notice homologies between works of art history and letters between lovers, the question to be settled is whether the "private" life shaped the scholarly or whether intellectual commitments organized intimate ties), I draw attention to historically overlapping vocabularies and textual mirrorings.

A final clarification again takes the form of a refusal. As scholars understand life-writing as selective, constructed, and textual, some follow this awareness with a foregrounded presentation of themselves, narrating their responses to their "subject"; personal and autobiographical writing has become especially prominent in recent feminist literary studies.[60] Despite my emphases on partiality and the active work of interpretation, I will not produce such a personal narrative. A modern response to an 1873 text by E. F. S. Pattison may illuminate some reasons. Pattison's review of Walter Pater's *Studies in the History of the Renaissance* was critical of Pater's scholarship (his polished phrases "are not history nor are they ever to be relied upon for accurate statements of simple matters of fact"), against which charge John J. Conlon argues that Pattison did not understand that Pater did not intend to give accurate "dates, facts, and events" but to "transform the presentation of history by writing his interpretation of it, what it means to him."[61] Setting aside the problem of knowing Pater's intentions, Conlon's elision of the foregrounding of interpretation with representing the writer's subjectivity is not logically necessary, any more than attention to the process of interpretation entails the abandonment of factual accuracy. I am less interested in the psychological processes of reading and writing life-stories than in their ideological, epistemological, and historical construction.

My reasons for refusing personal narrative are also connected to my refusal of biography. I share widely held suspicions about how "traditional" biography tends to both assume and produce its subject—the individual in the title—as exceptional.[62] I am also critical of how the appeal of biography seems to reside in—indeed, to be motivated by—a logic of identification and a claim to knowledge. Although feminist scholarship and politics explore women's diversity and sometimes conflicting histories and interests, many feminist biographies contain the implications of historical difference by constructing narratives in which historical women may be heartrendingly or inspiringly or exotically different but are nonetheless available for vicarious "experience" and knowledge through reading.[63] Life-stories of women who survive to be "known" offer reassurance of the stability of individual subjects; they also offer a chance to avoid theoretical debates about the social construction of subjectivity, representation, and narrative.[64] Kathryn Hughes's review of a recent work on the life of Virginia Woolf endorses this epistemological conservatism:

> As fiction has broken down over the past few years into fictions—slight, partial stories that make no claim to see beyond their own borders—biography has stepped forward to satisfy a lingering desire for a solid world peopled by knowable characters . . .

> Biography, then, provides many of the pleasures associated with the classic novels of the 19th century. It has none of contemporary fiction's worry about its own instability or provisionality. It sidesteps many of the debates of modern criticism and reads texts as oblique but vivid representations of the [subject's] life.[65]

Biographical texts become a refuge from postmodernity, a haven in an epistemologically unsettled world, offering a reassuring faith in the knowability of past subjective experience and the existence of unified, if mobile and adventurous, selves. Lives are discrete, long-running stories, and individuals are coherent and continuous subjects whose piquantly historical subjectivities are available for writers' and readers' retrieval. Biography offers historical narratives that deny history's weight.

I do not privilege identification or understand texts as offering access to subjectivities, and therefore I do not attempt to cajole readers into fantasies of knowledge about "me." Instead, this book takes seriously what scholars versed in the varieties of postmodernism claim to know: experience is constructed, meaning is not a hidden essence within texts but is produced by readers; surfaces, masquerades, metaphors, and images make as well as reveal meaning; selves are made and remade and unstable and discontinuous; culture matters deep down and immeasurably; we can talk neither to nor with the dead but only and imperfectly about them.[66] Taking these knowledges seriously means the reader will not end the book able to contend that she "knows" Emilia Dilke. Instead, she will know many stories about Emilia Dilke, she will know about the making and competition of stories, she will know that there is no knowledge that is not dependent on and enabled by partial and contingent readings of partial and contingent texts, by the historically variable limits of the sayable, tellable, writable, and thinkable.[67]

To borrow Caroline Walker Bynum's eloquent words, "my understanding of the historian's task precludes wholeness. Historians, like the fishes of the sea, regurgitate fragments. Only supernatural power can reassemble fragments so completely that no particle of them is lost, or miraculously empower the part to be the whole."[68] The reader can possess many narratives, some efficacious, some occluded, during Emilia Dilke's lifetime, but these cannot be filtered clean from the conditions of their production, circulation, survival, and re-presentation. Yet although I stress interpretation and problematize identification, reading this book need not be a bloodless and cold, if theoretically and intellectually proper, undertaking. Some of the texts and events I present were, in my reading, harrowing, infuriating, moving, funny, and inspiriting. Recognizing how hundreds of partial, fragmentary, biased, ignorant, mutilated, motivated, and imaginative voices, and I, produce Emilia Dilke in words displays the powers of texts to unsettle, reorganize, damage, contain, and haunt. Moreover, this book aspires to be what Bynum calls "history in the comic mode": historical writing that "know[s] there is, in actuality, no ending (happy or otherwise)—that doing history is, for the historian, telling a story that could be told in another way," and "no one of us will ever read more than partially." Such histories are not necessarily about pleasant or easy topics, but history in the comic mode refuses to forfeit the pleasurable knowledge of its own provisionality. It is history that *enjoys* the prospect of revision and continuation.[69]

In a partly and covertly autobiographical essay, "The Idealist Movement and Positive Science. An Experience," to which I will repeatedly return, Emilia Dilke warned against intellectual pursuits that attempt to "lay [truth] bare with the knife."[70] Despite the risks Dilke's text signals in conjunctions of knives and knowledge, I conclude this introduction with a metaphor for textually attentive and theoretically engaged reading that reiterates my emphasis on partiality and my claim to nonetheless produce historical understandings. It is possible to take a piece of fruit and carefully peel away a bit of skin, opening to view a bit of the flesh beneath, and to say, "here is what is not seen, here more is visible than the surface suggested." Or one can cut in half lengthwise, exposing new surfaces, and then turn again, slice crossward, and perhaps again cut open each segment; each cut reminds us that the process is endless and that there is always unseen matter between surfaces.[71] Crosswise and lengthwise cuts each display the grain, and each shows new faces and facets. Previously hidden centers and seeds come into view, perhaps hard and indigestible, perhaps with unexpected textures and colors. Each revelation of new surfaces and structures offers knowledge, but no knowledge annuls another: the whorled pit of the peach is not more true than the flesh just beneath the skin, or the caper-like seeds in the papaya more real than the yellow and green rind. This process of opening, exposing, and paying attention cannot end in reassembly, the object re-membered by invisible suturing into a whole. I undertake multiple openings and turnings of the texts of Emilia Dilke—not "her" but surviving and varied texts by and about her (including some in which we will find images of apples) and the many histories in which she is a figure. My reading and writing strive to keep visible the variety, as well as the relations, of surfaces and centers. Resisting false closure offers more, not less, knowledge and pleasure.[72]

1

ON NOT BEING AN ORPHAN

Victorian novelists notoriously relied on orphanhood to foreshadow the exceptionality of a hero's or heroine's adult life; dead or missing parents often seem a prerequisite for an interesting plot.[1] The characters for which Francis Strong has been seen as a model in George Eliot's *Middlemarch* and Rhoda Broughton's *Belinda* are orphans; Dorothea Brooke and Belinda Churchill are each under the nominal guardianship of loving but sometimes unwise older relatives and each has a single sister who is a loyal, commonsensical contrast to the imaginative exceptionality of the central character. But although the Strong family—and the Dilke and Pattison families discussed in the next two chapters—produced members whose stories have circulated in public texts and whose lives have been written as narratives of exceptional characters, neither Francis Strong nor the other "characters" whose childhoods I describe were orphaned as children.

Biographical writing often presents childhoods as preludes if not origins, but rather than orphaning the central figure, it tends to offer families as a backdrop for exceptionality, a fire in which subjectivity is forged or at least scorched, or a microcosm of "historical context." But families are never just idiosyncratic psychic configurations or instances of ideal types within schemas of broad-based demographic trends. Inscribing lives into broader family stories should not mean taking an exceptional individual and locating her in an unmediated "real" by placing her in a family. Families too tell themselves through stories they do not fully control but which are constructed within generic conventions and available languages of natural and unnatural, healthy or deviant domesticities, just as they participate in larger historical stories of the material and ideological organization of family life. Some narratives of family life are valorized or normalized, while others are stigmatized or cast as exceptional.[2]

Politics, region, specificities of religious culture, and accounts of continuity or change in class shape family narratives. I attend therefore to the production of family stories as well as the stories of individuals.

Although I will return to Emilia Dilke's essay, "The Idealist Movement and Positive Science," a partial and partially autobiographical text, Francis Strong Pattison/Emilia Dilke did not write a narrative of her life across her several names, and only a few scraps of childhood writing have been preserved in public hands. The principal texts that include accounts of the Strong family are family stories: Charles Dilke's "Memoir" of Lady Dilke, a preface to a posthumous collection of Emilia Dilke's essays and short stories, The Book of the Spiritual Life, and Gertrude Tuckwell's account of her aunt "Fussie" in her unpublished typescript reminiscences in the Library of the Trades Union Congress. Paradoxically, these accounts by husband and niece are shaped by the overriding project of insisting that Emilia Dilke was from childhood marked by qualities of mind and spirit excessive to, rather than produced by, her family. Charles Dilke's account repeatedly establishes the differences that marked Francis Strong as a girl, as if covertly worrying that Emilia Dilke's achievements would be diminished by any intimation that she was formed by her environment; Dilke's text disavows any "hereditary determinants" of Francis's talents and describes her desires and interests as rebelliously cultivated in vague defiance of her family.[3] This stress on Francis Strong's exceptionality may be read as Charles's own motivated claim to exceptionality by association, but he also participates in a multiauthored project in two senses. Dilke's texts incorporates and echoes other texts, including some by Emilia Dilke, and it collaborates with Gertrude Tuckwell's. Tuckwell's account was written long after the deaths of her aunt and uncle and perhaps was not meant for publication, but Dilke's "Memoir" and Tuckwell's "Reminiscences" overlap, even to the point of exact language.[4] Despite differences, for example, the greater command of the materiality and domestic detail of the Strong household of Tuckwell's reminiscences, both texts share and ceaselessly reiterate a project of representing Emilia Dilke as exceptional.

Charles Dilke's and Gertrude Tuckwell's texts strive to delineate wholeness and argue for an enduring and exceptional self behind all the names and changes of Emily/Emilia Francis Strong Pattison Dilke. Linking truth and excess, Dilke's and Tuckwell's texts also cagily flatter readers: by comprehending—knowing and containing—Francis Strong's continuous, consistent, and sublime character, we can show our own mirroring exceptionality, our abilities as readers to make parts into a whole. But rather than fusing Dilke's and Tuckwell's accounts with other scraps of evidence into a childhood story for Francis Strong and thereby continuing their project, I focus on reading texts at work, not only attending to the narratives they produce or covertly proffer but making their gaps and games visible. Dilke's and Tuckwell's texts, along with Emilia Dilke's own, contain many stories beyond those they explicitly tell. I will argue that the narrative effectivities of empire and class in these stories destabilize Dilke's and Tuckwell's projects of writing exceptionality by putting Francis Strong's childhood into larger histories while also drawing attention to the value of considering the production and reproduction of class and empire in family story-making. Conversely, both texts omit at least one highly interesting incident in Francis Strong's youth, which Emilia Dilke may have concealed, thereby provoking awareness that the limits of authors' knowledge are also unknowable.

Imperial Stories

The Strong family and Francis Strong's childhood could be represented as falling well within the parameters of respectable, comfortable, provincial, and unexceptional bourgeois life, less a shaping environment than a usefully subfusc backdrop for a childhood of exceptionality. Married in 1826, Henry and Emily Weedon Strong had had a son named Owen Henry and two daughters, Henrietta Frances ("Ness") and Rosa, before Emily Francis was born on 2 September 1840. Two more daughters, Marian and Ethel Rigaud, followed. Henry Strong was a retired army officer and amateur artist living in Ilfracombe, a small Devonshire resort (its population in 1841 was 3,679), albeit one offering the pleasures of fashionable society in the sea-bathing season; in the early century, Ilfracombe had had a vogue as a haunt of Romantic poets who proclaimed it the "English Switzerland" for its healthy climate and natural beauty.[5] But by 1841, Henry Strong took up a position as manager of the newly founded London and County Bank in the High Street, Oxford, under the pressure of some financial reverses. Although a retired officer and an investor in the bank, Henry's social status as a salaried employee was roughly that of George Eliot's Mr. Bulstrode in *Middlemarch*.[6] The Strong family settled in Iffley, just south of Oxford on the Thames, in a house called The Elms.[7] Owen Henry was educated for the Army and Henrietta and Rosa married while Francis was still a child, but the three younger children were educated at home and Francis grew up in a household of several children.[8]

Despite Ilfracombe's periodic access as a resort to more metropolitan cultures, in Iffley the Strong family lived in more consistently, self-consciously, and institutionalized milieux of intellectual and cultural activity, during a period of increased movement of contemporary ideas and figures between London and Oxford. Yet when Emilia Dilke wrote an extended account of her family's background, she said little about her childhood. Instead, she constructed a more distinguished heritage than my account has offered. In "Samuel Strong and the Georgia Loyalists," written for the Toronto chapter of the United Empire Loyalists Association of Ontario in 1899, Emilia Dilke vigorously produces her paternal family as a geographically far-flung microcosm of the tumultuous history of British imperial possessions.[9] Emilia Dilke's essay begins with a disavowal: she had been asked about her grandfather's connection with the American Revolution but had felt "inclined to say: 'Story, indeed, there is none to tell!' " It then flatters her immediate audience by claiming her narrative lacks "the heroic features which attract us to the annals" of the Canadian Loyalists. If her family's story is simply and plaintively one of "personal suffering and loss of fortune," Emilia Dilke's essay still goes on to recount it, disinterestedly rendering the historical record complete: "there is so little known concerning [the Southern Loyalists] . . . and so little attention has been paid to the situation of those who became 'Refugees' . . . that even the outline of one family history may have something of historical interest [and illustrate] an obscure phase of the great struggle" of empire. Dilke's essay repeats this oscillation between disavowal and assertion as it continues, positioning her as offering only fragments ("the little that I know of these things") while heaping up names and the results of obvious research.[10]

The imperialist ancestry Emilia Dilke recounts centers on her grandfather, Samuel Spry Strong (1749–1834) and his brother Thomas (1745–1811), who were American colonists in Georgia; her grandfather and great-uncle died before Francis Strong's birth and Dilke's text emphasizes that her knowledge of them derives from her father. Henry, the youngest of eleven children of Samuel Strong and Sarah Earle Hartridge Strong—widow of another Georgia landowner before her marriage to Strong—was born in England in 1794 and was probably never in the United States. His own knowledge of the family's Georgia history was indirect and derived from his father's and uncle's accounts. But if Francis Strong's colonial heritage was highly mediated, Henry passed along to his daughter a family history both prestigious and slightly raffish. The Strongs, of "Scotch-Irish extraction," having "got into some political trouble and being attainted for treason" in Britain, settled in Massachusetts "shortly after the voyage of the Mayflower," and Henry Strong told his daughter, "we had the blood of some of the first settlers in our veins." A second politically motivated round of Strong immigration to the New World followed in the eighteenth century; some members of the family moved to Virginia after "being compromised" in the Jacobite uprisings of 1715 or 1745, although Emilia Dilke claims descent from the Massachusetts branch of the family. Moreover, her grandfather and great-uncle had had a brother, Richard, who "it is said" was in the Royal Navy but combined patriotism with a whiff of piracy as a successful privateer and looter of Spanish ships. If Emilia Dilke's family story is one of imperial service, she nevertheless endows her ancestors with a history of political and physical adventure.[11]

The Strong family is more respectably loyal by the time of Francis's grandfather. Samuel and Thomas Strong "began life as land-surveyors, an occupation then followed by many wealthy men in the States," and Samuel was Deputy-Surveyor to the Crown by the time of the Revolution. Dilke repeatedly invokes the names of the wealthy Fairfax family of Virginia—William Fairfax "the early companion of George Washington," Thomas Fairfax "the sixth baron," and others—to endorse the gentlemanly status of surveying. She reiterates Samuel Strong's importance and genteel status; he "was not only an important public official" but a landowner, holding property in Augusta and a Crown grant in Savannah, and her text claims that the Strong family left permanent marks in Georgia history, through a place name in Savannah, as well as faithfully serving the Crown. This service reached its height during the American Revolution, when Samuel and Thomas Strong were "early marked out for hostility from the 'Whigs'"; Samuel Strong "never complained of having endured any maltreatment," but he suffered "a very heavy loss of fortune" and was forced to flee to England, via Canada, settling in London by 1786. Thomas Strong, however, was tarred and feathered for his views, including their publication in one or more Loyalist pamphlets, and developed a permanently nasty temper as a result. "The mere mention of America was enough to drive Thomas to fury" and his treatment was always "alluded to with a certain air of mystery and horror" and "resented as a personal disgrace" in family stories.[12]

Emilia Dilke's narrative arcs from slightly scandalous antecedents through loyal imperialism to personal suffering in the service of the Crown, but her account seems indecisive as to how to conclude. On the one hand, she emphasizes the hardships and losses borne by her family; "the sufferings of these unfortunate people . . . [were] severe" and Samuel Strong often "lamented the loss . . . of a great fortune." On the other hand, she repeatedly guards against the suggestion that her family had lost its claims to gentility and public importance. Samuel was "never in the absolutely destitute condition of many of his fellow-sufferers . . . his means were never insufficient," and his "situation as a refugee . . . [was] marked by exceptional features." After the war, Samuel Strong returned to the United States to dispose of "a large portion of his property at Augusta, where he owned a large plantation and many slaves," and his daughter Nancy and three of his stepchildren resettled in Georgia, Nancy receiving Samuel's remaining Augusta property on her marriage. Emilia's and Charles Dilke's account of the Strong family history include assertions of the Strongs' and their Hartridge half-siblings' continued importance and respectability in the United States; in later life Emilia Dilke was visited by cousins "who played a leading part in the public life of Georgia, South Carolina, and even of New York."[13] The Strong family sacrificed for their allegiance to the Tory side in the American Revolution but nonetheless preserved respectability in both countries in the Dilkes' accounts. Henry Strong's officer status and army pension gave him, at least, entrée into provincial bourgeois society and his family history of imperial service and "sacrifice" offered further guarantees of class status.[14] But Emilia Dilke's essay implies that the Strong family possessed not only the cachet of demonstrated loyalty to the Empire but some relationship to networks of aristocratic patronage, which may have bolstered their ability to recuperate their fortunes in England. "It is a curious coincidence," she writes, that her grandfather settled for some time on a Fairfax property near Leeds Castle "where . . . he had previously no connection or interest."[15]

Emilia Dilke's essay forms the basis for Charles Dilke's account of his wife's ancestry in his memoir of her and in his own unpublished memoir. Charles Dilke's redactions both disavow too much ancestral influence, periodically downplaying the Strong family's place in English history to assert Emilia Dilke's individual exceptionality ("Emilia's genius was so little of an inheritance that I found she had no distinguished persons in her ancestry unless some dashing sailors should be so accounted"), and enunciate the importance of her familial connection to Britain's imperial power.[16] Charles Dilke elaborates on the continuing bonds between Emilia Dilke and her imperial family, claiming she was a living link to her family past for younger generations and an embodiment of the history of the empire: "Cousins [from Georgia, South Carolina, and New York] used to come in the Twentieth century to see Lady Dilke; but while they looked on her aunt as a remote ancestress . . . and were separated from [her] grandfather by nine to twelve generations, my wife with an acute remembrance of her father's accounts of his father and with an elder sister living who remembered the grandfather himself, and with the portraits of the hunted Loyalists of 1774 hanging by her side, seemed to revive in living force the story of the War of Independence." Charles repeatedly describes Emilia as proud of her colonial forbears; she preserved portraits and souvenirs "from the old home at Augusta, Georgia . . . with the most sacred pictures of those she loved" and she carried around family relics.[17]

Charles's adumbration of the Strong family history endows Emilia Dilke with an honorable genealogy to set beside his own and aligns her with his own political passions for the Army and the Empire, but his text also cunningly appropriates the imperial and patriotic irreproachability of her grandfather's politics for Emilia Dilke's feminism and trade unionism. Charles Dilke claims Emilia resembled her grandfather Samuel Strong in features and "in her character [which held] a good deal of the

toughness of the fierce defenders of the lost cause of George III . . . their unconquerable physical and moral courage and their characteristic virtue of not allowing the
largeness of a majority to convince her that she was wrong."[18] Emilia Dilke's essay,
however, reveals a less reputable or democratic political history without comment:
her relatives' retrieval of their family fortune depended on their continued participation in racial slavery. Her grandfather had been a slave-owner, the land on which
Emilia Dilke's "ancestral home" stood had been given to Nancy Strong "along with
a great many negroes" by her father Samuel, and Nancy's son was "Colonel Barrett,
a well-known veteran of the Confederate army." Emilia Dilke positions her family's
slave ownership as a sign of their continued wealth and respectability, and she details
her Barrett relatives' Confederate careers—Nancy Strong's son and three of her grand-
sons were in the Confederate Army—as evidence of a tendency to courageous "devotion to lost political causes, which . . . has shown itself again and again" in the
family.[19]

Feminists from Wollstonecraft forward have focused on the ways in which children
acquire sexed and gendered subjectivities during infancy and childhood; more recently, Carolyn Steedman and others have eloquently argued that class also constitutes
children's subjectivities through disavowals and identifications, love and the need for
difference, stories, violences, and seductions.[20] The texts that represent Francis Strong's
childhood remind us that racialized imperialism may also be a subjectivity acquired
in childhood. Moreover, although the institutions of schooling and the ceremonies
and spaces of public life were unquestionably central to the production of imperialist
identities for children, the imperial and racialized subject positions increasingly produced and reproduced through the nineteenth century were not only constructed and
enacted in the public sphere. For some children, imperialism was also a family story
and a site of assumed identities and loyalties imbricated with other learned subjectivities of class and gender from an early age. Attention to the production of imperialist
children therefore complements recent feminist scholarship on the ways white British
women participated in, profited from, and shaped and were shaped by racialist ideologies and imperial projects in the nineteenth and twentieth centuries.[21]

Charles Dilke represents the young Francis Strong as sometimes choosing her political positions in direct reaction against her family's views—she "scandalized her
family by praying publicly for the success of the Russian arms during the Crimean
War, partly, I think, because everybody about her was agreed in ferocious anti-Russian
opinion"—but the grown-up Emilia Dilke acknowledged the power of childhood
"prejudices" even when claiming the possibility of grown-up transcendence.[22] An
1889 essay by Emilia Dilke on missionary activity in India represents her as sharing
in and eluding familial claims and implies that imperialist identifications were entangled with learned and loved models of class and gender. Family ties can "make us
accept unquestioningly and hold tenaciously opinions for which we have not the
slightest grounds": "I remember, when war broke out betwixt North and South, how
difficult it seemed to me to believe in the just cause and triumph of the North, simply
because I possessed an unlimited number of relations in Georgia and South Carolina,
and an aide-de-camp cousin was promptly shot."[23] "The Great Missionary Success"
narrates Emilia Dilke as moving from a position of dislike for missionaries produced
by "the accidents of early association, the chances of relationship" and enmeshed

with a family rhetoric of class; in her family's imperial culture, antipathy to missionaries was expressed by "allusions . . . constantly made in [her] hearing to the impertinence of his pretensions, to his want of birth, or wit, or learning." Francis Strong developed a "prejudiced" view that "if a missionary coud not be induced to stay at home, the sooner he fell in with cannibals the better."[24] The adult Emilia Dilke comes to see missionary efforts as valuable and selfless, and other texts by Emilia Dilke present the possibility of movement away from family loyalties and prejudices and suggestions. But Dilke's texts also suggest that such loyalties are tenacious because of their imbrication with gendered childhood experiences. During a trip to India, Emilia Dilke wrote, "I like . . . being with . . . officers its like my childish days I get on so well with them."[25] Masculinity, as represented by Francis Strong's father and other male relatives, was military in her earliest social world, and her second marriage to a prominent Liberal Imperialist, expert on Army reform, and advocate of "preparedness" renewed associations between intimate relations and British martial strength.[26]

Emilia Dilke concluded "Samuel Strong and the Georgia Loyalists" with a listing of her male relatives' service to Empire in successive generations. Henry Strong was entered in the military academy at Addiscombe—probably owing something to patronage—and commissioned in the army; he joined his regiment in India in 1809 and served for sixteen years as a quartermaster, retiring while still a young man of thirty-one.[27] Henry's brother Thomas joined the Royal Navy and rose to the rank of commander; he was eventually lost at sea, perhaps in a mutiny. Francis's own brother Owen Henry is Lieutenant Colonel Strong, and of his three sons, one is "taking out troops to the Cape" on a ship of which he is Master, another is already in Kimberley, and the third is in charge of the Medical Staff Corps of the South Rhodesia Volunteers, en route, as she writes, to Mafeking.[28] Emilia Dilke thus recounted a masculine family history, linked to the fortunes of Britain's armies in the American colonies and in India in the past, and in Africa into the new century. Her own name paradoxically marks this masculine history. According to Charles Dilke, Francis was named for a military man, her godfather and "favourite friend" Francis Whiting, killed at Cawnpore in 1857.[29] Emilia Dilke did not put the imperial roles played by the women of her family into print. Her sister Henrietta married a Lieutenant Colonel W.A. Neale, with whom she went to India; Gertrude Tuckwell suggests that Henrietta understood her own role as an extender of Empire in the moral domain, as "young, attractive" and "eager to help," Henrietta engaged in volunteer nursing of poor Indians before fleeing back to Iffley with her three children during the Indian Uprising of 1857, in which her husband was killed.[30] Francis's younger sister, Marian, died of fever in Madras within a year of her marriage to another servant of empire.[31] Emilia Dilke's published narrative of her family history is insistently patrilineal, if not wholly masculine, and it does not include stories of female distinction among either ancestors or nearer relatives.

Mothers and Margins

> What are novels? What is the secret of the charm of every romance that
> ever was written? . . . the heroine has *generally* no family ties (almost *invariably*

no mother), or, if she has, these do not interfere with her entire independence . . .

—Florence Nightingale, "Cassandra"

Dilke texts have little positive to say about mothers. Emily Weedon Strong's middle daughter bore her mother's name but eschewed it for most of her life; only two letters from her childhood are signed "Emily Francis Strong" and she was never simply Emily Strong.[32] Emily Francis Strong was differentiated from her mother by a different name—obviously, a matter of some convenience in a family—but also by a name which signified a difference that did not exist, the difference of gender. Francis Strong's name moved her away from her mother by appearing to denote a male subject. While Charles Dilke argues that Francis Strong Pattison/Emilia Dilke preserved the initial "S." of her patronymic in her married signatures as a feminist act, her initialed signature during her first marriage—"E. F. S. Pattison"—also degendered her.[33] Only some of her works bore her gender's mark clearly; some readers of her published works assumed she was a man.[34] If she preserved the initial of her father's name as a signifier of selfhood, the fate of her mother's name was more ambiguous. "Emily" was preserved and erased, reduced to the sexless cypher "E.," and then came to denote not the shared and ordinary name "Emily" but a new, exotic, self-begotten "Emilia." No longer masculine Francis but feminine-with-a-difference Emilia, vaguely Latin or Italian or French but in any case foreign, not domestic; self-named rather than dutifully filial; Emilia Pattison/Dilke's return to the name of her mother altered and supplanted it.

Marianne Hirsch has argued that the suppression or omission of maternal influence is characteristic of eighteenth- and nineteenth-century women's stories in novels. The daughter's story inscribes her own "will to difference"; "the heroine who wants to write, or who wants in any way to be productive and creative . . . must break from her mother, so as not to be identified with maternal silence." Silence is deeded over to the mother in the text, who is absent, trivial, or denigrated.[35] Hirsch's argument focuses on the occlusion of mothers in texts by women, but Charles Dilke's and Gertrude Tuckwell's accounts of the Strong family share the blurring of the figure of the mother. Even in the context of a more general refusal by Dilke's and Tuckwell's memoirs to elaborate on cultural and familial supports for Francis Strong's exceptionality, both writers emphasize Francis's distance from familial models of femininity. If Francis Strong's exceptionality is discursively emphasised on many grounds, it is utilized most urgently to stake out a place for her beyond local norms of womanhood.

No remembrances of Emily Weedon's descent survive in Emilia Dilke's published work or the archival collections of her papers; neither Tuckwell nor Charles Dilke provide Emily Weedon Strong with a genealogy, recount her class background or her premarital life. Tuckwell names Emily Weedon an "Oxford girl," but while she was probably some years younger than her husband, even her age is not clear; she survived her husband by only three years. If the Strongs' establishment in Iffley placed them in or near Emily Weedon's natal community and thus facilitated Henry Strong's entrance into local social and business circles, no detail confirms this.[36] After Henry's death, Emily left the Elms to live in Bournemouth, with or near her daughter Ethel and her family.[37] Emily Weedon probably had a more limited education than her well-travelled husband; it was certainly less official and less public. Bearing children across almost twenty years, she would have been occupied with childbearing and rearing throughout the 1830s and 1840s, and the six children who survived to adulthood were probably only a portion of Emily Weedon Strong's pregnancies and deliveries, since even privileged childbearing Victorian women endured miscarriages, stillbirths, and deaths in infancy.[38]

Emily Weedon Strong's reproductive history and her responsibility for the organization of household labor—that is, her domesticity—need not have meant her absence from published and unpublished family texts by her daughter, son-in-law, or granddaughter. The relative absence, physical and rhetorical, of women from the public sphere is not necessarily reproduced in autobiographical and biographical representations of mothers. For example, Eileen Yeo has suggested that Francis Power Cobbe's representations of her distant and unloving mother as saintly and admirable demonstrate how autobiographical and biographical material is reworked by generic conventions as well as psychological desires.[39] But Emily Weedon Strong rarely appears in texts about Francis Strong, and when she does, her dominant role is that of conservative, even repressive, but ineffectual roadblock to daughterly ambitions, especially artistic ambitions.

Charles Dilke cites Emilia Dilke's sister Rosa Tuckwell as saying that "dear mother strongly objected to [Francis] going" to London to study art in 1858. Emily worried about Francis moving about in public. Although Francis's friends allayed her mother's fears by finding Francis "a home near the schools," which Francis shared with another young woman, and both girls fell under the supervision of an older female friend of their families, Charles Dilke adds that Francis disliked this living arrangement for compromising her "strong . . . love of personal independence."[40] Charles Dilke places the emphasis not on Francis's achievement of quite exceptional freedoms—the ability to live in London and study art—nor on Emily Weedon Strong's lack of final authority in her family, but on Emily's failure to respect Francis's feelings. Emily Weedon Strong is too much and too little a mother; she is both criticized for attempting to exercise control and for failing at feminine tasks of empathy and emotional support. Similarly, during her first marriage, Francis Strong Pattison represented her mother as blind to her feelings, complaining to Rosa Tuckwell that "dearest mother fails to comprehend" her mental or physical sufferings.[41]

While Charles Dilke's memoir takes pains to distinguish Francis Strong from "hereditary" influences in favor of her own originality, it does provide information about Henry Strong's ancestry and interests and depicts him as benignly encouraging; Francis's mother's influence is more explicitly downgraded. Emily Weedon Strong functions principally as a foil to her daughter, her influence noted only to be diminished and to mark her daughter's exceptionality. Although Charles Dilke's memoir, borrowing some of its language from an essay by Emilia Dilke, claims "[Francis] was brought up under a strict High Church training. . . . When she was a child her mother used to take her to great numbers of Church functions, with a strong desire to inculcate a strict Church training." Charles's memoir then moves to undercut Emily Weedon Strong's religious influence on her daughter. Francis's flamboyant adolescent religiosity is, as the next chapter will show, central to Dilke's depiction of her as an exceptional young woman, but Dilke's text insists that this spirituality was not a form of dutiful daughterly behavior. Dilke emphasizes that Francis's religious education by her mother was not "a specially Puseyite" one, so that Francis's "original" High Church piety is a contrast to, rather than a ground of commonality with, her mother.[42] Emily Weedon Strong's religiosity is a negative model against which Francis's exceptionality can better be seen. In her 1897 essay, "The Idealist Movement and Positive Science," Emilia Dilke wrote a passage of religious autobiography that similarly deletes any detail about family religious culture as well as transferring her narrative of youthful piety to the story of a young *male* friend. This young man was brought up in the High Church but "took to heart the moral code of Anglo-Catholicism with intense fervour," exceeding his upbringing.[43]

"The Idealist Movement" generally emphasizes interior spiritual struggle in an unnoticing world, but its regendering of its protagonist more specifically dissociates exceptional religiosity from femininity. Emilia Dilke's short story "The Physician's Wife," to which I return in later chapters, includes a story of the dangers of *stories* of maternal spirituality: the young man with whom the unhappily married protagonist falls in love leaves her because he is humiliated by his position vis-à-vis her cruel husband, but he justified his departure by saying that "before all on earth, his mother was sacred to him and for her sake he would not abide there, nor could he face her with the girl at his side."[44] A mother's moral authority is dishonestly invoked to ease a man's pride, hurting another woman; the protagonist's consequent despair leads to murder and self-destruction. Another of Emilia Dilke's short stories offers a frightening tale of (super)maternal piety and its consequences; in "A Stainless Soul," the Holy Virgin, "Mary Mother," asks Jesus to give her (i.e., kill) a "fair and good" young girl of whom she has heard to serve as her attendant. When the girl is sad in Heaven because she believes herself unworthy, the Virgin sends her back to earth so that she can fulfill her desire for suffering. The ultimate Good Mother thus claims feminine virtue for her service, removes the young girl from the worldly, and ratifies pain as desirable. As it turns out, however, the girl fails her spiritual test by attending too much to feminine decorum: beckoned by "a murmur of much cruelty, of oppression, and of sin," and the cries of "one suffering grievous wrong" in need of help, the girl hesitates for fear of staining her white clothes with the "great foulness and mire of black and troubled waters." After this failure, "the sting of [her] sorrow shall be sharper than any death!"[45] In this story, Mothers claim spiritual preeminence but do not actually educate their spiritual daughters. Neither the vague valorization of suffering nor concern for feminine propriety is the training girls most need.

The theme of how mothers do and do not educate their daughters to tackle the needs of those suffering in the world recurs in another, highly complex story of moral development that Emilia Dilke told in public as an adult. In this case, although Emily Weedon Strong registers and respects her daughter's feelings, she nonetheless functions as a silent and privileged backdrop against which other women can better be seen; Emily Weedon Strong is a foil not only for her daughter. In an 1889 speech advocating women's trade unions, given to a largely labor audience, Emilia Dilke presents a tale of the awakening of her social conscience. As a little girl aged eight, Francis Strong noted the hunger of her mother's seamstress, Kitty Davis, and her eagerness to have her tea on those days when she came in to sew for the Strongs. She asked Mrs. Davis why she was so hungry, and received the reply, "Missie, if you never got a bit of meat but when your mother asked you to work for it you maybe would worry for your dinner today." At her own lunch that day, Francis asked the price of a mutton chop and begged her mother to use Francis's allowance of six pence a week to buy one for Kitty Davis. Eventually, she was allowed to visit Mrs. Davis's "hovel" and take tea with her, an encounter that, Emilia Dilke reported, impressed upon her the terrible living conditions of the working poor.[46]

Generically, this is a "princess and the pauper" story that constructs the female subject's precocious sensivity to social distress and provides an origin for a narrative of the development of social concern. It is also what Thomas Laqueur has called a "humanitarian narrative," a genre which from the eighteenth century onward came to "speak in extraordinarily detailed fashion . . . of the pains and deaths of ordinary people in such a way as to make apparent the causal chains that might connect the actions of its readers with the suffering of its subjects." Reformers tell stories of themselves being moved by individual sufferings, not "abstract wrongs"; individual cases are epiphanic and motivate action; "great causes seem to spring from the power of *a* lacerated back, *a* diseased countenance, *a* premature death, to goad the moral imagination." Laqueur follows Hume in noting how such narratives authorize the speaker's moral action in part through appropriating the experience of the suffering other, but Laqueur also links these narratives to the development of the novel and the production of an expansive, nuanced, sometimes self-congratulatory, emotional register for middle-class subjects.[47]

By 1889, working-class politics, especially increased trade-union militance, put pressure on the usability of "princess and pauper" stories to underwrite middle- and upper-class social reform. Thus, although Emilia Dilke endows Francis Strong with a history of moral self-development, in Dilke's story the working-class figure of Kitty Davis is neither a passive recipient of charity nor simply a suffering body whose display sets in motion a narrative of moral agency for a middle-class observer. Mrs. Davis is knowledgeable and vocal, rebuking little Francis and impelling her to learn about experiences she does not share. Kitty Davis tells Francis Strong that things have costs and that ignorance of the cost of things is a luxury. This story paradoxically constructs a moral lineage for Emilia Dilke by describing her child self as ignorant and rude. The insensitive litle Francis criticized Kitty Davis for lacking manners, but Davis teaches Francis that she has committed a deeper discourtesy; finally, a more respectful mutual courtesy is restored by the ritual taking of tea.

This story provides a history in which a working-class agent is the origin of *Lady* Dilke's beliefs about the importance of specific knowledge of material conditions of working-class life. Emilia Dilke ends her story less with a claim for her own special sensitivity as a child than with an emphasis on education and reformation of the self, consistent with her trade-unionist texts' repeated castigations of self-serving ignorance among the well off. The end of Emilia Dilke's story is neither little Francis's charity— her offer to donate her allowance for Kitty Davis's mutton—nor her receipt of Kitty Davis's words, but her *education* outside her own home. This ending draws attention to the presence of another female figure in Dilke's story, besides her little middle-class self and the working-class other. In Dilke's tale, Francis is not only asked to contrast earned and unearned money and to think about the chasm between the family of the Elms and the working- class woman dependent on the Strongs' employment, but to think about her mother. Emily Weedon Strong, Kitty Davis tells Francis, is not only a mother but an employer. Women—Mrs. Strong as well as Mrs. Davis—are economic agents.

Dilke's story obviously illuminates one of the quotidian and often-erased details of middle-class childhood: the visible presence of working women and the visible falsity of the ideological division between the domestic sphere and the world of work and economics.[48] Kitty Davis educates Francis Strong about the untruthfulness of ideologies in which effortless middle-class domesticity emanates from the mother's figure, by demanding that Francis recognize bourgeois domesticity as dependent on labor done by working-class women for money. Moreover, when Francis Strong takes tea with Kitty Davis, she moves outside the house of her mother: the little girl's ability to separate herself from her mother is an origin in Emilia Dilke's political self-narration. Emilia Dilke's story of Francis Strong's education in difference—the differences in minds, bodies, and manners produced by differences in social and economic positions—also covertly, and incompletely, constructs a difference between mother and daughter. But Francis Strong goes to tea with her mother's permission. Emilia Dilke's story occludes Emily Weedon Strong's enablement of her daughter, instead emphasizing Mrs. Strong's structural power as an employer and Kitty Davis's educative agency.

If the middle-class girl is able to learn from and defer to the knowledge of the working-class woman, the middle-class woman slides into the position of the Other in this story. But one more story exposes the instability of these shufflings. Emilia Dilke published a series of three "Parables of Life" in 1889, later collected into her second volume of short stories, The Shrine of Love. The first parable, "The Outcast Spirit," is unremittingly bleak, and this eerie and sad story is obviously not autobiography. Nonetheless, I want to mark its handling of the theme of mothers and class. "A girl was born of the desire that her father, the son of a great man, had unto a beggar-maid." His father disavows him, "bidding him to live as befitted one that had his liking in those of low estate," but the girl's mother, called "the beggar" in the rest of the story, is angry "for she had thought to wed her rags with wealth and ease." When the child is born, "the milk of the woman's breasts was bitter"; the child of a plebian woman suffers from her mother's thwarted desires of status and wealth. As the family suffers hunger, "the reviling of the beggar was as a sharp sword and her curses were like stones," and the girl-child is sad and silent—"undefiled" but unable to help. When her father becomes ill, he sends her to his relatives to ask for help for her, "for their name's sake," but they reject her, sneering that they have enough "kitchen wenches" already. This abrogation of patriarchal responsibility is followed by a greater maternal cruelty: when the girl returns home, "the beggar laughed, for she had it in her mind how she would make money of her daughter" by selling her. As her husband is dying, she "chinked the money" she had got in his face; he rises up with his last strength, grabs her by the hair and strangles her; then he dies.[49]

The girl's grim story continues, but obviously the tale hinges on a violent demonization of the working-class mother. When the working-class woman is also the mother, the rhetorical respect accorded Kitty Davis evaporates. Even if one reads the story as a denunciation of mothers for collusion in the sale of daughters in marriage, this narrative enlists brutal tropes of class. The "beggar" is motivated by greed in her liaison, unlike the "desire" of the father; she is a shrew and harridan, bitter and cursing, taunting and cruel. Like Marian Earle's mother in Elizabeth Barrett Browning's *Aurora Leigh* or some working-class women in W. T. Stead's "The Maiden Tribute of a Modern Babylon," she sells her daughter.[50] Her murder is not only wholly earned but is also a reassertion of the father's love for his daughter, even if fathers can only kill, not save. Even in the story's continuation, patriliny matters: the mother's family gives the daughter shelter only for a night then "harden . . . their hearts and [drive] her from their doors," while—despite their earlier cruelty—the father's family take her in, if only to immure her.[51]

I do not read this story as expressing the "true" feelings of Emilia Dilke about mothers or working-class women. It is also inadequate to say simply: under the hegemonic sway of discourses of middle-class angels in the house, evil mothers could only be figured by displacement into another class. Nor is it enough to assert: class ideologies trump gender ideologies to produce bigoted stories of working-class women as monstrous mothers. Rather, what is notable is this text's collapse of monstrosities. If the story of Kitty Davis split adult women into the strong, sharp working-class woman whose concern for material things is proper and educative and the middle-class mother who teaches feminine decorum and holds power, "The Outcast Spirit" offers an adult woman whose material desires are signs of evil rather than poverty, whose lack of concern for and failure to properly nourish her daughter, even with her "bitter" milk, is morally culpable, and whose sexualization of her daughter, rather than "normal" maternal enculturation of the daughter in gender, is grounds for murder. With adult womanhood so thoroughly inhabited by monstrosity, is it any wonder that the story ends with the daughter's self-chosen death? Or that she should remain homeless even after death, learning that for "those who have no place in life, neither is there any place in death"?[52]

In the "imperial stories" of the Strong family, I suggested, empire is a familial terrain which shapes children's subjectivities to construct and multiply heritage, exceptionality, and gender, while privileging masculinity and patriliny. In both Kitty Davis's story and "The Outcast Spirit," positions of difference for daughters and mothers are constructed through class. These imbrications of femininities and class could be powerfully useful, needed, and enormously politically volatile. In the story of Kitty Davis, learning about class offers a space for the demonstration of exceptionality, and the daughter's split from her mother opens a wider world. In "The Outcast Spirit," home is the site of class difference and of the failure to maintain class divisions; the upper-class father does not live up to his status by providing for his wife and child but the working-class mother's moneymaking activity is despicable. In this story, womanhood is singularly embodied in a mother who is angry, powerful, and, in both senses, wanting; class differences do not educate; splitting does not open space; homes can only be lost, and lost again; and the story of the exceptional daughter is a story of doom.

Sisters and Angels

In the family stories I have recounted, class is foundational to stories that construct differences among women. The story of Kitty Davis also suggests that Francis Strong could be represented as "different" and exceptional in terms of her privilege by comparison to the vast majority of girls and women. But Gertrude Tuckwell's and Charles Dilke's texts, despite their authors' public engagements in class politics, remain within the Strong family instead of moving from the familial to the socioeconomic. Moreover, neither Tuckwell's nor Charles Dilke's include vivid stories of Francis Strong's female relatives, excluding even the woman cousin who defiantly took rooms in Gray's Inn in 1887 and laughed when told, " 'Madam, the Inn does not recognize the existence of women.' "[53] Rather, Tuckwell's and Dilke's memoirs secure Francis Strong's exceptionality by emphasizing her difference from the other women in her family, not only her mother but her sisters.

The Strong girls as a group possessed exceptional privilege in access to the resources of education. While the authority of women's education remained embroiled in questions about its proper ends throughout the nineteenth century, the Strong girls had very good luck in their family, teachers, and community. In that good fortune, they resemble midcentury feminists, including members of the Langham Place Group like Barbara Leigh Smith Bodichon and Bessie Rayner Parkes Belloc, who came from families that not only shared a rich domesticity and belief in mental cultivation but aggressively supported female education and saw roles for women in Radical and rational social reform, expecting women's knowledgeable participation in local and national cultural discourses.[54]

Francis Strong, we will see, especially profited by her position in Oxford during a period of intensified art activities, but all the Strong girls benefited from their local environment.[55] Institutional barriers to female education remained high in the 1840s and 1850s, and the Strong girls' schooling predated the founding of the Oxford High School for Girls, but the sisters—unlike many Victorian girls—received a kind of Oxford education in their own home.[56] Precisely because women could sometimes quarry knowledge from the intellectual resources and cultural milieu of Oxford even while they were excluded from the official life of the University, "bluestockings" and "frank spinsters"—often sisters and daughters of dons, doctors, and parsons—circulated in local intellectual society.[57] Some worked for wages as governesses. Francis was taught by a Miss Bowdich, probably along with her younger sisters, Marian and Ethel. Gertrude Tuckwell, her sisters, and other daughters of Oxford liberals were later taught by Miss Bowdich in the late 1860s; Gertrude described the Miss Bowdich of her childhood as very devout and gentle, "terrifed of thunder . . . a darling old lady . . . with a little white cap with lace around her kind face, and a sort of bombazine dress . . . [who] always brought with her a large red book which contained the various dates . . . beginning with that of the Creation." If Miss Bowdich's persona was not that of a "strong-minded" woman, her intellectual reach was nonetheless exceptional, and as the sister of an African explorer, Miss Bowdich was another link between the Strong family in Iffley and the farther reaches of the British Empire.[58] If Gertrude's later lessons are indicative, the Strong sisters learned history, geography, arithmetic, French, and the rudiments of German from her. She also taught Francis Latin and

Greek—an unusually rigorous linguistic education for women in the 1850s, more often provided to other "exceptional" girls by fathers and brothers than by governesses.[59] By her command of ancient languages, Miss Bowdich merited the titles—"a somewhat distinguished governess" and "a notable teacher"—Charles Dilke bestowed on her.[60] According to Tuckwell, Miss Bowdich's capacities exceeded most of the Strong girls' needs, since only Francis "penetrated into the mysteries of Latin and Greek . . . with the dear old lady."[61] Tuckwell's account thus reiterates Francis's position of exceptionality while eliding her family's provision of resources and support. Charles Dilke also emphasizes the space between Francis Strong's intellectual ambitions and her educational milieux, claiming that Miss Bowdich was not in great sympathy with Francis's artistic leanings: "Miss Bowdich would have preferred more time to be given to studies in which she was herself more competent."[62] Ironically and sadly, Miss Bowdich was eventually excluded from intellectual employment by the growth of more formal women's education; Rosa Tuckwell and the other mothers of Gertrude's fellow students decided, in the late 1860s, to replace her with a younger, college-educated woman.[63]

Leonore Davidoff notes, "*between* sisters . . . siblings can provide models to be emulated or rejected. Since there is always a range of masculine and feminine behaviours and meanings available, children and young people are acutely aware of same-sex siblings as models, sometimes identifying with one another but sometimes rejecting such identifications. . . . Brothers and sisters constitute the comparative reference group par excellence. . . . In their shadow, decisions—subconscious as well as conscious—are made about life choices, even in situations where those choices are severely limited."[64] The texts of Rosa Tuckwell's life ratify and complicate the wider Strong family story of female educational privilege but also reiterate the complexity of family stories. Rosa's frequent appearances in the Dilke papers are not wholly an effect of her daughter's editorial powers. Rosa was thirteen years older than Francis but Emilia Dilke's letters suggest that she was throughout her life by far her most important sister. Francis/Emilia confided in Rosa through her first marriage and the scandal surrounding her second, Rosa and William Tuckwell entrusted the Dilkes with their daughter Gertrude, and after Emilia Dilke's death, Rosa and William lived with Charles Dilke.[65] Rosa can also be read as a model for Francis Strong in some significant choices, but the uses to which Gertrude Tuckwell puts her mother's figure in her autobiographical narrative are more complex and fragmented. As Davidoff suggests, sibling relations, including ties between siblings and their children, are also narrative sites. Gertrude Tuckwell's emphasis on her aunt's distance from family norms of femininity and from her own mother is more complicated than a "failure" to write the Strong family's exceptionality in socioeconomic privilege.

Gertrude Tuckwell's text does not provide a sustained narrative or description of her mother; her longest discussion of Rosa's life occurs extremely late in the text, following the mention of Rosa's death in 1914, and Rosa is textually marginal compared to Gertrude's father, William, who is granted numerous small narratives and repeated praise for political activities and oratorical skill.[66] More striking, however, than this favoring of one parent in Tuckwell's memoir is Rosa Tuckwell's eclipse by her sister Francis, who dominates the entire manuscript. Gertrude's treatment of her mother is profoundly ambivalent. Like Emily Weedon Strong in Charles Dilke's texts,

Rosa Strong Tuckwell is a foil and a double for Francis Strong in Tuckwell's memoir; although praised for qualities of body and spirit, Rosa is granted few virtues her sister Francis does not also possess, usually with greater vividness and intensity.

Yet Gertrude Tuckwell's story does establish Rosa as an exceptional daughter, if always less exceptional than her sister. Gertrude tells us Rosa was considered a great beauty and pursued an artistic education before her marriage. Musically talented, Rosa studied with a singing master named Torriglione in Jersey in her late teens and early twenties. This move of living apart from her parents in order to pursue artistic training prefigures Francis's art training in London, but Rosa's musical education could be rendered the more exceptional story. Although there was increased interest, after long indifference, in music as well as the visual arts in 1840s Oxford—Jenny Lind herself sang in the Sheldonian Theatre in 1848, an exceptional female voice audible in the Bodleian itself—the encouragement and permission Rosa received for independent study reveals an astonishing parental supportiveness.[67] But when Torriglione encouraged Rosa to become a professional singer, this course was vetoed, marking the line drawn by even permissive mid-Victorian parents on the display of female talent, especially in the performing arts. Anonymity was possible in art, the object separate from its maker, but music demanded the singer's bodily presence and display; public singing beyond the drawing room lacked even the acceptance given the works of women artists. The stage, even in singing rather than acting, was not an acceptable career for a young woman of the Strongs' class.[68] Jenny Lind was not only sanitized by her persona of intense piety; she was not English. Despite this larger context, and although both Francis and Rosa ended their artistic educations by marrying, Gertrude Tuckwell attributes the different outcomes of Rosa's and Francis's artistic educations to differences of personality. Rosa is described as lacking any strong leaning toward rebellion, deeply committed to her family, and mindful of the strictures of proper femininity.[69]

Rosa Strong Tuckwell may never have regretted her parents' vetoing of a musical career. She was already engaged to William Tuckwell (1829–1919) during her residence in Jersey, and Rosa's parents' support for her musical training may have rested on the prospect of an ending in conventionality. They married in 1858 and Gertrude, born in 1861, was their third child.[70] Gertrude's text assigns Rosa's marriage happiness and even slight heroism; Rosa and William endured a seven years' engagement before they could wed, since although an Oxford graduate, a clergyman with generous interests in science, education, and Radical politics, and a member of a large and respectable Oxford merchant and medical family, William was almost penniless when he and Rosa became engaged. Rosa would develop a public political role herself and enjoy lifelong access to Radical and feminist circles through her husband, sister, brother-in-law, and daughter. But Gertrude marks her mother's limits: "it cost her sometimes an effort to keep pace with [William's] intellectual development as her loyalty demanded of her" and to share a "stage of religious enthusiasm" with him.[71] When William Tuckwell accepted a living that required a move from their longtime home, Gertrude suggests that the move caused her mother pain but then hastens to remove herself from the position of judge and disavow knowledge of her mother's feelings, adding "I am not sure" and "over and over again I reproach myself lest I may have misinterpreted their decisions."[72] Gertrude emphasizes William's praise for

Rosa's feminine talent for happy family life, but Gertrude's praise for her mother's self-abnegation is ambivalent and relies in the end on her father's opinion.[73] Through Tuckwell's text, appreciations of Rosa as a loyal wife who taught her husband important lessons about family and love contend with hints that Rosa's submission to husband and social conventions was unattractive to her daughter.[74]

Gertrude recounts that her father, a schoolmaster, not only took the leading role in educating his daughters but set them on professional careers over their mother's and even their own objections. There was "a stigma" on women "who earned their living, and only the most level headed and intelligent women realised that it was an honourable instead of an undignified position"; "Mother . . . having many of the old Victorian standards could not have been happy."[75] Rosa Tuckwell herself could claim to hold "old-fashioned notions" about family proprieties that her younger sister did not share, but Gertrude Tuckwell's text implicitly separates her mother from the "most level headed and intelligent women" and aligns Rosa with Emily Weedon Strong as a nay-saying voice regarding female independence.[76] Moreover, in Gertrude's account, the task of persuading Rosa to acquiesce in her embarkation on a professional career was substantially achieved not by her father but by her aunt Francis. Gertrude's text invites the reader to compare Aunt Francis's empowerment of Gertrude's adult participation in a public world of work and politics to her mother's and grandmother's qualms; her account of her life with Charles and Emilia Dilke in the 1890s and early 1900s is the gaining of a "second family" in which young women are encouraged in independence.[77]

In Gertrude Tuckwell's text, both of the eldest Strong daughters, Henrietta and Rosa, are represented as "Victorian." When Henrietta Neale temporarily came to keep house for Gertrude and May Abraham in 1890, her perception of her duties as including chaperonage irritated the young women enormously. But Tuckwell's memoir cunningly doubles and reverses its construction of Gertrude's mother and aunt in its depiction of her feelings toward her own younger sister, Marion. Like Francis Strong, Marion Tuckwell bore a name with a masculine spelling. Like Francis in Tuckwell's and others' texts, Marion had charm; she was "a fairy thing petted by all," "very pretty, determined, and reserved," "ambitious," musical, theatrical, unwilling to put up with annoying male relatives, and sometimes a competitor for their aunt's attentions. Gertrude's text depicts herself feeling admiration and slight resentment for this younger sister, and in doing so allows the reader to imagine that Rosa might have felt toward Francis the same slight, ironized resentment, cushioned by affection and loyalty. In presenting sisterly pairs—Rosa and Francis, herself and Marion—Gertrude Tuckwell depicts women negotiating with parental pressures, making choices between conflicting allures of aesthetics, public performance, female duty, and "socially useful" work.[78]

Yet we need not rest with a story of cross-generational family transferences shaping memorial texts. Tuckwell's and Charles Dilke's "shortfalls" in locating Francis Strong in wider social and material terrains of class and gender in the mid–nineteenth century remind us that Francis Strong's education during her girlhood was probably addressed not in terms of statistical comparison to the mass of her contemporaries but in local discourses that positioned her as a special girl, an exception. If Francis Strong was allowed and encouraged to learn Latin and Greek and petted and patronized for drawing the casts in the Ashmolean Museum, her studies would have been represented as unusual exceptions to the norms of sex. If we can read her exceptionality as made possible by luck in her familial and local cultures, young Francis Strong was nonetheless almost certainly seen as exceptional in her "self." The narratives Charles Dilke and Gertrude Tuckwell imaginatively elaborated in their texts may have incorporated not only Emilia Dilke's narratives but stories Francis Strong held and considered as a child and young woman.

I am suggesting, that is, that exceptionality may have been an available subject position for Francis Strong during her childhood, and that narratives of Francis's difference from those around her need not have been only (self-)aggrandizing or (self-)idealizing but may represent ways Francis Strong made usable stories out of ambiguous childhood experiences.

The nexus of stories that most intriguingly raises this possibility reiterates and heightens all the ambiguities to which I have drawn attention and to which I will return: families as backdrops in stories of isolated figures and families as doubly producing such stories; complex and doubled mediations through multiple texts; the claims of stories to relay and to combine interior and physical experiences; disbelief in stories; narratives of pain and narratives of pain about stories refused; claims of texts to preserve the untold; pathos and irony. Charles Dilke's published "Memoir" presents some quotations from unpublished and unknown writings by Emilia Dilke, which are embedded in his text; the Dilkes' double account tells a small set of stories about complex inner experiences of painful and fearful isolation. In later chapters, I discuss Francis Strong/Pattison as an object of vision, but here Francis Strong has visions. Both Dilkes—Emilia Dilke's words and Charles Dilke's surrounding text—connect Francis Strong's childhood visionary episodes with her adult capacities, but these are also doubly family stories: Charles Dilke's text allegedly holds Emilia Dilke's words, and Emilia Dilke tells of Francis Strong's experiences of subjectivity in her family.

Emilia Dilke locates Francis Strong's first hallucination—the term is placed in inverted commas—"at the age of five or six." Francis awoke in bed in a dark room and "saw a patch of brilliant light, and in the light the figures of two or more angels bending towards me. The vision was a delight to me, I being a very devout child." Emilia Dilke contrasts Francis's calmness and acceptance of the vision to the reception given her description by her parents. Her tale was greeted by "incredulity," which she tried to meet by giving details, such as that 'the angels wore blue boots.' " Emilia Dilke construed Francis Strong's visual memory of the angels' footwear as "serv[ing] to show that the vision was perfectly distinct in all its parts," but these details did not convince her parents, and their "ridicule taught [her] to keep silence." The Dilkes' joint text thematizes this memory along the common Romantic axis of the innocent certainty of childhood opposed to the mocking doubt of adults, a theme sustained in Emilia Dilke's account of later hallucinations: "As I grew up, and every now and then made statements as to servants or friends having done things, or having been in places, the truth of which they denied, I was punished for 'lying' or 'inventing', as I believed unjustly . . . I have no doubt that I was frequently the subject of 'hallucinations.' "[79] The ridicule that met her description of angels has become a harsher chastisement, and Emilia Dilke's young self is confused and alone.

Just as in the Kitty Davis story, Emilia Dilke did not claim that Francis Strong was an exceptionally moral child, the Dilkes' story of these hallucinations does not claim Francis Strong possessed special powers of psychic perception as a child. In another story, Francis Strong even proves the unreality of her visions. During the Indian Uprising of 1857, when Francis was seventeen, "several members of [her] family" were in danger. On going to bed after an evening of family conversation about them, Francis saw in the mirror as she plaited her hair "a faint spot in the centre . . . gradually enlarg[ing] (as a grease spot spreads with heat) until the whole surface was covered, and then in the centre of this veil, came through the face of one of the near relatives . . . as plain as might have been his living reflexion." Unlike the serenity given by the angels, this vision caused "spell-bound fascination" followed by "frantic terror," but Francis's flight from the room was arrested by the recognition "there was no one I dare tell; my father would have admonished me not to be a fool: as for my mother, then in delicate health [perhaps a euphemism for pregnant], I could not venture such a matter to her, the appearance having been that of her only son." Emilia Dilke withholds the terrible secret of the vision's identity until the climax of the tale, but the story then proceeds to ironic self-deflation. Having carefully depicted her adolescent self, poised in the corridor between flight from the mirror's image and fear of her parents, she deflates the generic expectations of ghost stories. "I noted, however, the day and hour, and ascertained, six weeks later, that the relative seen had incurred no sort of danger at that date."[80]

The Dilkes' account tells of involuntary isolation and depicts Francis Strong as taught not to want the exceptionality her imagination conferred on her. Although, as in the Davis story, Francis is educated by experience, in this tale she is subject to a harsher pedagogy. The judgment of Francis's stories as "true" or "false" by those around her confines her in a grid of interpretation that betrays her and leads her to feel alone and anxious; her bitterness toward her parents is not because they rejected her visions' "truth" but because they were mocking or inaccessible. Emilia Dilke's stories emphasize her innocence and subjection to the powers of her own mind, but agency is located in whatever causes "hallucinations," not in her desires or in the supernatural. Emilia Dilke's adult words also combat her parents' labelling of her visions as "lies" and "inventions" by a mixture of rationalist, semiphysiological explanations and reminders of her childhood intellectuality. Charles Dilke quotes her as saying that she had "eyes of different focus," and "the centre of vision of the right eye deflects to the right," so that her vision tended to double or blur without glasses; "there is a moment of consciousness [on looking to the left] as the effort is made to bring the two sights together." The Dilkes thus imply that ordinary sight requires effort from Emilia Dilke and invoke these natural peculiarities of vision as contributing to her hallucinations. The language of science is harnessed to represent Francis Strong as gifted and marred by special sight, exerting an effort to be ordinary but liable to punishment when she fails. However, if her childhood and later "visual hallucinations" were facilitated by her "strong visual memory," this visual memory was "a strong ally" to whatever induced visions because she had "cultivated" it for her art studies. Intellectual/aesthetic pursuits and physiological peculiarity together produce exceptional psychological experiences.

This conjunction recurs when Emilia Dilke hints at choices and decisions in the experience of "apparitions." Probably referring to a period during her first marriage, Emilia Dilke detects potentially dangerous gratifications in visions:

> You will ask me to explain what I mean when I say that the will can affect these "hallucinations." I do not mean that at the instant of their occurence the will can do anything beyond keep the brain steady. I have, however (you must take it for what it is worth), an intimate conviction and consciousness that there was a period when physical weakness, coupled with the moral dispositions which accompany a mystic and speculative bias of mind, might have caused me (let me confess further, were near causing me) to take passive satisfaction in my own "hallucinations" instead of treating them as matter for investigation. I am conscious that in that state they were tending to become more frequent.[81]

Her mind is an ally both of her exceptional experiences and her ability to master those experiences, but she cannot control its operations absolutely, and, in the Dilkes' account, she suffers.

Emilia Dilke's suggestion of her psychological agency in receiving at least some hallucinations also suggests something more provocative: the usefulness of a set of narratable stories about one's own natural, physiological, and unchosen exceptionality. Francis Strong's hallucinations can be read as the Dilkes' organization of exceptional or quite ordinary childhood pains into tellable stories, but these stories also suggest that experiences of uncomfortable or gratifying sensations of uniqueness may be consciously or unconsciously chosen. Living stories in which one is "different" and misheard can authorize, to others or oneself, separation and movement. Suffering exceptionally, even or especially in a childhood lacking apparent hardship, could be both painful and valuable. As we know from all those orphans in Victorian novels, a childhood of misunderstanding, loneliness, and psychic isolation—neither simply experienced nor simply invented but both—was the perfect overture for an adult story of adventure and exceptionality. Children's self-figuration in available, imaginable, and desirable subject-positions—the sensitive and misunderstood child, the instrument of God, the naive inquirer—may mark out for them, not just for those who write their lives, desires and identifications to occupy and narratives on which to embark.

In offering this suggestion, I do not want to erase awareness that suffering can be both useful and real. Later chapters return to this theme, in relation to Pattison family stories of mental anguish and Francis Strong Pattison's marital stories of a suffering body. The only surviving childhood texts by Francis Strong remind us of the plausibility of stories in which exceptionality is experienced as loneliness as well as self-congratulation, difference felt as falling short of—rather than refusing—familial standards, especially standards of proper femininity. We will see that Francis Strong later wrote with relief to Rosa about foreswearing the pain of exceptionality by becoming engaged to marry. The only two surviving pieces of Francis Strong's childhood writing are also addressed to Rosa. One is a fragment of occasional verse, illustrated with a bouquet of flowers.[82] The other is a letter that accompanied a gift, apologized for its inadequacies, and positioned Rosa as an exemplar of feminine decorum and obedience. Francis promises, "My own sister I will try to be humble and quiet as I know you wish so much to see me be & a comfort to you & Mama instead of a trouble I really will."[83]

2

PICTURES AND LESSONS

Pictures haunt texts about Francis Strong's childhood. D.S. Maccoll, who knew Francis Pattison in his undergraduate days at Lincoln College and Emilia Dilke as a fellow art critic, wrote of seeing a picture of Francis Strong as a little girl, "curled up in the window of a book-lined Holywell sitting room, immersed in reading."[1] Charles Dilke's memoir claims two of "a series of original historical cartoons" in pen-and-ink by Francis as a child had "been thought by critics to be worth preservation and exhibition," but neither names the critics nor divulges the location and subjects of the drawings. Francis Strong's childhood artwork is invoked but invisible, perhaps surviving but not in public. As further proof of the claim that Francis Strong's "art turn" was "developed at an early age," Dilke's memoir cites a text about pictures—Sir Charles Bell's *Essays on the Anatomy of Expression in Painting*—which Francis bought with her "first pocket-money" at age eleven. Dilke makes the book an emblem of the continuity between Francis Strong and Emilia Dilke—it was her "most cherished possession" and she inscribed it "E. Francis Strong, 1851" and reinscribed it "Emilia F. S. Dilke, 1885" when she gave it to him as a wedding gift. Dilke also attributes Francis's embarkation on a London art education to the encouragement and support she received from John Ruskin after he saw her drawings from casts in the Ashmolean Museum, "from the skeleton and from life."[2]

Another story about a picture was told by both Dilkes. Charles Dilke recounts a story of little Francis Strong, aged nine, in 1849, sitting on the knees of an as yet pre-Pre-Raphaelite John Everett Millais. She "directed him to draw for her a spirited sketch of a cavalry battle under Stirling Castle." Charles guarantees his text by referring to his possession of physical proof: "[the picture] hangs now in my room at Pyrford

39

Rough [the Dilkes' Thames cottage] alongside her chair, and bears also on its back a portrait by her father."[3] Emilia Dilke too recalled this episode in a newspaper interview in 1893, remembering herself as a little girl demanding that Millais draw "more dead bodies."[4] These tales purportedly display Francis Strong's precocious interest in artistic representations of human anatomy as well as her high spirits, and Charles Dilke's version is positioned as proof of Francis Strong's exceptional artistic talents and passions that attracted the kindness of famous men even when she was a child. Dilke's invocations of Francis's pictures participate in a narrative of continuity, as they lead to her more formal studies of art in London as a young woman and foreshadow her adult career as a scholar of art, but Francis Strong is also presented as a memorable child, made into pictures and making pictures. A picture actually offered by Charles Dilke's "Memoir" seems to corroborate his claims of his subject's exceptionality. Dilke places a sepia photograph probably taken around 1860 as the frontispiece of *The Book of the Spiritual Life*; it is captioned with its subject's chosen name, E. Francis Strong.[5] A determined young woman looks at the camera with one very slightly raised eyebrow, her fair hair, with a high widow's peak, is arranged so it appears boyishly short. Her dark dress with white ruff collar is trimmed with a darker squared velvet ribbon, framing her pale face and faintly suggesting anachronism and theatricality. Her stance, with one arm draped across the back of a chair and the other extended, is casual and allows her to nearly fill the oval space of the photograph. Charles Dilke cited this photograph too as evidence of Francis Strong/Emilia Dilke's continuity; it shows Lady Dilke "as she was in youth" with "the courage & unconquerable spirit which was predestined to grow stronger even to the last."[6]

I want to place the continuities Charles Dilke's texts construct in a larger history, moving them from the status of evidence about an individual to evidence in the histories of art, gender, and local and national discourses and institutions. To borrow Carlo Ginzburg's phrase: "If this [text] is a . . . portrait, then its model is Boccioni's paintings in which the street leads into the house, the landscape into the face, and the exterior invades the interior; the 'I' is porous."[7] The story of little Francis and John Everett Millais is a story of a child who is exceptional, but I emphasize that she was exceptional in the privilege of a family and a local community in which artists, including fathers, paid attention to little girls.[8] Whatever pains Francis Strong may have incurred in the course of family life, these picture stories display Francis Strong's luck. She reads in book-filled rooms, receives pocket money to buy books on art and anatomy, and has friends who show her drawings to prominent critics. (Emilia Dilke herself positioned childhood relations with artists as a form of privilege that illuminates larger histories.[9]) In the second half of this chapter, I move to stories about Francis Strong's studies in art in London and explore the construction and instability of feminine figures in the histories of aesthetics and institutions; again, E. F. S. Pattison/Emilia Dilke's own later writings include these themes. Other materials and discourses I put into play in this chapter—especially stories about marriages and bodies—will also circulate through later chapters, not en route to a finished arrangement but, like Francis Strong, as figures whose recurrences and shifting relations move us across complex histories.

Artists in Oxford: Men, Women, and Girls

Charles Dilke's memoir underplays Francis's father's and her local community's provision of models, encouragement, and support for art studies. Dilke claims that while Francis's "inclination" toward art was "partly hereditary," it was "mainly personal and natural." Dilke's text admits that Francis's father "was no doubt pleased to find power of drawing in his child," but hastens to add, "this tendency was not noticed in any other member of a large family, and was pursued as a personal pleasure by this one daughter."[10] Dilke's acknowledgement of Francis's father's artistic interests is vague and cursory; even if Francis shared talents with her father, she was unique among her siblings in his account. Yet the story of little Francis Strong's urging Millais to draw her a battle suggests the simultaneous valorization of the military and the artistic in Francis Strong's childhood culture.

Military prowess, in the forms made necessary by the expansion of the British commercial empire, and the cultivation of artistic talents were equally present in Strong family masculinity. Despite his indubitably middle-class position as an Iffley bank manager and his past in the army as a quartermaster rather than a mounted warrior, Henry Strong combined, in his own figure and as in his family history, military manhood with aesthetic and commercial activities. In the Strong household, national loyalties and high cultural pursuits intertwined. The Elms milieu included men and women who practiced and patronized the arts as enthusiastic amateurs and engaged in public intellectual life alongside military men and messengers of empire. Its mixture of officer-class military histories and high-cultural and artistic interests destabilizes stereotypes of military philistinism or bank-managerial bean-counting and evoke a more complex and long-lived provincial masculinity in which bourgeois and genteel mingled and in which status and pleasures in the public sphere were not limited to the narrowly economic or political.[11] An active amateur painter, Henry Strong was involved in local artistic and cultural pursuits and provided his children with knowledge of local and national art. He showed his work in London at least once, in an 1840 exhibit of the Society of British Artists, in Suffolk Street, London.[12] He was active in Oxford art circles, acting as treasurer for an "Exhibition of Oxford Amateur Art" in 1851 that displayed eighteen paintings of his own. Most of his works mentioned in the catalogue are landscapes of Oxford and Ilfracombe, but included are some studies of Indian subjects, suggesting that his interest in art was not just a pastime of his retirement; his "Scene in Central India" was a prize auctioned for charity in the 1851 exhibit.[13] When Henry Strong's son-in-law William Tuckwell later wrote of a "growth of artistic feeling" in Oxford, "perceptible" by the late 1840s, he tactfully placed "Captain Strong, an accomplished amateur" in the company of other local art fanciers representing town and gown. Tuckwell credits Captain Strong's organization of amateur exhibitions with "[bringing] out unknown talent and [drawing] the artists together."[14] While Tuckwell may have flattered Strong's agency, Strong clearly had a role in local artistic society and contact with other amateurs and art lovers in the University of Oxford as well as the town. Other sources represent Henry Strong as attuned to other aesthetic realms as well; "[he] sang and played the flute . . . in spite of having had two fingers shot away in India," and D.S. Maccoll, probably on Emilia Dilke's authority, endows him with "keen literary tastes."[15]

Francis Strong also possessed privileged access to cultural milieux beyond the purely local. While not exactly "cosmopolitan"—a term no one would apply to Oxford in the 1830s—Oxford was indubitably an important center of intellectual life. Relations between town and gown in Oxford were less hostile than in some other periods, and local families like the Strongs and Tuckwells could form local social circuits of men and women, inside and outside the Colleges, interested in science and art, theology and politics, education and empire.[16] Moreover, the relative cosmopolitanism of the Strong household coincided with Oxford's gradual shift toward greater integration with metropolitan culture. Specifically, Francis Strong's childhood coincided with growing national interest and intense local concern with the status of art in historical and modern cultures. In the 1840s and 1850s, Oxford was a locus of the most important British artistic movement of the nineteenth century: the development of Pre-Raphaelitism. Maria Theresa Earle, who knew Francis Strong in London at the South Kensington art school, noted the extent of Francis's social range before coming up to London; Francis was "well acquainted with Ruskin and all the young pre-Raphaelite painters. I quite recall how this excited my envy."[17]

William Morris and Edward Burne-Jones did not arrive at Exeter College until 1853, but Millais was frequently at Oxford, at least from 1848, as was Charles Collins after 1850. In 1857 the famous Pre-Raphaelite corps of "[D.G.] Rossetti, Arthur Hughes, Val Prinsep from London, with Morris, Burne-Jones, J.B. Pollen and Spencer Stanhope from Oxford," assembled to paint murals in the debating hall of the newly built Oxford Union.[18] The paintings themselves were notoriously short-lived (they faded within three years), but the project was emblematic of the status Oxford had assumed as a site of artistic innovation. The Union had embraced the idea of the murals in part because the Pre-Raphaelites commanded the support of John Ruskin, whose first work, Modern Painters, was signed "An Oxford Graduate." Ruskin was bound to Oxford by numerous ties; a "gentleman commoner" of Christ Church from 1836 to 1840, he remained closely if beratingly associated with the University throughout his life. As Slade Professor of Art, he would begin an art school within the University itself, but even in the 1850s his ideas and writings shaped the design of the Oxford Museum of Natural History, that great hybrid of Victorian natural history, Pre-Raphaelite ornament, and ironwork. Ruskin's friendship with its architect, Benjamin Woodward, allowed him to "hover about" the rising building.[19] Henry Acland, Lee's Reader in Anatomy at Christ Church from 1844 and Regius Professor of Medicine from 1857 to 1890, was Ruskin's close friend, as well as an important encourager of the young Francis Strong. Acland and Ruskin's relationship formed when both men were undergraduates and was sustained by their matched enthusiasms for art and science. Acland was "Ruskin's only Oxford friend with whom there was increasing intimacy" and was Ruskin's confidant during the breakdown of his marriage.[20]

It is obviously important that several early members of the Pre-Raphaelite Brotherhood (PRB) were Oxford students, but some writers discern a deeper affinity between Pre-Raphaelitism and Oxford. Timothy Hilton attributes the special intensity of Pre-Raphaelitism in Oxford—"the most medieval of English cities"—to the "medievalising strain in Pre-Raphaelitism, as well as a new emphasis on environment," and S. Gaselee argues that there was a powerful current of aestheticized and philosophical medievalism in Oxford—"a feeling of desire to return in some things to the ideas and ideals of the Middle Ages"—predating both Ruskinian and Tractarian explorations of the middle ages.[21] Yet despite this increasingly self-conscious medieval atmosphere, Oxford as a University and a town was beginning to "modernize" in rapid and drastic ways during the mid–nineteenth century, a modernization with artistic, literary, theological, demographic, and economic, as well as institutional, dimensions. Oxford as a university town was a city of young men as well as crabbed dons and ancient cloisters; the PRB was a self-consciously paradoxical backward-looking avant-garde.[22] Moreover, Oxford included middle-class families linked to but outside the University, whose active patronage of contemporary aesthetic production included women and families as well as men in the consumption and display of art. When William Tuckwell asserted that "Art was in the air" in midcentury Oxford, he presented as evidence museums and exhibitions, the decorations of a lady's drawing-room, the "sunshade" on Dr. Acland's windows, and the omnipresence of Ruskin's books in parlors by the mid-1850s.[23]

The Victorian middle class was never unified by a homogenous attitude to art and art education.[24] For all the Evangelical or Gradgrindian stalwarts who denigrated art as frivolous, other bourgeois groups were passionately interested in private study and public display of old and new artworks and in consolidating claims to public power by demonstrations of cultural energy. Suspicion of artistic pursuits, haziness about the status of artists as professionals, Romantic admiration of the individual artistic genius, and anxiety about the status of high art in Britain in an age of industrialization, coexisted. Just as some rising segments of the middle class figured scientific and social-scientific studies as a modern pursuit, underwriting their political aspirations and claims to be makers of a modern economic world, middle-class people could imagine a social ascendancy by which middle-class sponsorship of art, both privately and through state and civic organizations, superceded aristocratic patronage.[25] But if the middle class was forging a cultural and political identity through repudiations of some aristocratic behaviors and encroachments on aristocratic monopolies, on local scales domesticities and communities that included aesthetic activities might form a shared, rather than contested, ground of sociability between bourgeois, professional, genteel, and even aristocratic, circles. Individual family cultures like the Strongs' show the concrete compatibility of military, commercial, and aesthetic activities, whether motivated by the working out of a complicated family lineage of gentility through ongoing entrepreneurial and professional careers or the appropriation of prestigious modes of public life.

The inadequacy of stereotypes of philistine bourgeoisies is clear.[26] Moreover, middle-class women's art education, in Oxford and elsewhere, expanded in relation to ongoing discourses about art as symbolic capital.[27] The Liverpool tobacco and wood-merchant-cum-shipowner John Miller not only collected PRB works himself and played a central part in Liverpool and London art institutions but encouraged his daughters' art studies.[28] Nonetheless, the development of middle-class female artistic skills and knowledge was a site of tension in bourgeois discourses. Concerns about seeming to ape the aristocracy endured, especially in stereotypes of the dilettantish (rather than publicly enriching) cultivation of artistic and musical tastes and talents by nonproductive, effeminate aristocratic men and decorative, unnatural women. Hannah More's *Coelebs in Search of a Wife* (1809) had satirized the fashionable "Miss Rattle" who "was taken to London every winter to be accomplished," learning " 'to paint flowers and shells, and to draw ruins and buildings, and to take views' . . . modelling, etching and engraving in mezzotinto and aquatinto."[29] The trope of a young woman playing at art as a part of being groomed for the marriage market could be opposed to images of bourgeois romance, honest affection, and pious partnership; many members of the bourgeoisie overtly preferred the image of the young woman with her needle and her Bible to the young lady with her piano and drawing master, even if the latter's "refinement" was covertly attractive. As Jan Marsh and Pamela Nunn note, some local arts societies excluded or marginalized women in special categories of membership in order to solidify their own status as serious, not femininely amateurish, associations.[30] However, other powerful bourgeois discourses inscribed middle-class women's aesthetic education as valuable because of women's presumed roles as arrangers of gendered and classed domestic space, homemakers, and educators of children. When William Thackeray criticized women's art education, its deficiencies were highlighted by setting them against women's destinies as mothers: "when the young ladies are mammas . . . can they design so much as a horse, or a dog or moo-cow for little Jack who bawls out for them?"[31] The problem is not women's art education per se but making that education appropriate to women's domestic roles.

Many Pre-Raphaelite women, like Elizabeth Siddall, for example, are now better known for the ways in which they circulated as images of femininity and objects of PRB men's love than for their own creative projects and ambitions, but women played numerous roles in Pre-Raphaelitism. Moreover, Pre-Raphaelite men and women alike participated in a larger project infused with gendered meanings: considering the relations between the aesthetic and daily life in an increasingly industrial society.[32] Nunn and Marsh suggest that the Pre-Raphaelite rejection of Royal Academy orthodoxies (and the Academy's training, from which women were barred) and the liberal-bourgeois ethos of merit may have encouraged women artists.[33] More certainly, the PRB valorized "sketching from nature" and other "feminine" genres; some opponents of Pre-Raphaelitism attacked it as a "feminine art," lacking "broader masculine life and temper."[34] Further, Pre-Raphaelites called for the reform of mundane spaces and daily perceptions. Domestic interiors especially should be permeated by chosen significations, composed of studied artistic meanings and effects.[35] The PRB's eloquent calls to redeem middle-class daily life by filling homes with objects designed for beauty as well as for use, carrying symbolic weight for eyes trained to properly take in meaning, offered aesthetic meanings grounded in but promising to transcend materiality. British homes could be transformed into spaces for the consumption of food for the spirit, and bourgeois women could and should be active in these processes.[36]

Domestic artistry composed by women could be a hedge against the horrors of the outer world but could also be a model for larger social transformations. Ruskin positioned properly educated middle-class women as educators well beyond their own homes, teaching other classes and participating in the organization of wider social spaces. Although *Sesame and Lilies* marks the home as a sacred and feminized place separate from the harsher world (if "the hostile society of the outer world is allowed . . . to cross the threshold, it ceases to be home . . . a sacred place, a vestal temple"), it also suggests that "woman's" gift for "sweet ordering, arrangement, and decision" extended beyond the hearth. Women's domesticity could extend to "a public work and duty" to "assist in the ordering . . . and in the beautiful adornment of the State." Since women's aesthetic influence might extend from the individual to the social household, a girl's education should not make her a mere "sideboard ornament."[37] In short, bourgeois interest in the morally useful roles of art and design authorized as well as confined female artistic ambition.

Francis Strong gained her exceptional education through Oxford circles affiliated with and shaped by these larger discourses. The household of Henry and Sarah Acland in particular introduced her to several individuals important in her later life—Pauline Trevelyan, Eleanor Smith, and Mark Pattison. More immediately, the Aclands brought Francis to Ruskin's attention; in Charles Dilke's account, Francis's drawings from the Ashmolean casts and from nature were "shown to Ruskin when he was visiting Dr. Acland, and it was he who determined her to go to South Kensington to study anatomy."[38] Dilke notes that when Francis Strong attended South Kensington, she "revived" her acquaintance with Millais. Like Theresa Earle, Dilke claims Francis's sophisticated familiarity with Pre-Raphaelites impressed her friends. But Francis Strong's artistic interests, including her studies of anatomy and natural forms, were continuous with Ruskinian and Pre-Raphaelite ideas and are coherent within specific local and national chronologies of art, gender, class, and institutionality. They reveal Francis's lucky but not wholly individual access to intellectual communities. Her older friend Pauline Jermyn Trevelyan, whom she met through the Aclands, similarly found that artistic interests and sketches from nature gave her entrée as a girl into a world of scientific and artistic thinkers including Ruskin and the geologist William Buckland. Pauline continued to participate in this heterosocial milieu after marriage to one of its members.[39]

Francis Strong's embarkation on a more formal art education in London was not a break with but an expansion of her Iffley and Oxford childhood as an exceptionally educated girl. Nonetheless, this story did not have an obvious ending. What happened when girls were no longer pets and protegées but young women? Limits remained on the public outcome of the development of female artistic and intellectual talent, if less sharply drawn for Francis's painting and drawing than for Rosa Strong's singing. Liberal Victorian middle-class discourses of cultural production and consumption advocating the aesthetic improvement of daily life negotiated, elaborated, and preserved gender differences. The assumed ending for a young woman's art education was not a career but marriage, if perhaps a marriage deferred by a formal education.[40] Women's aesthetic practices were ultimately meant to enrich the pleasures of the domestic sphere.

Indeed, marriage plots could be offered to young women as a chance to unexceptionably affirm their exceptionality by marrying exceptional men. Oxford gave models of marriages in which wives were not always as shadowy as Emily Weedon Strong; the Acland household displayed the possibility of a woman achieving a social and intellectual life of wide-ranging religious, artistic, and scientific interests by marriage to a distinguished husband. Charles Henry Pearson described both Aclands as strong partners in an Oxford marriage of intellect, piety, and purpose, noting Sarah's ability as a translater of Dante, her musicality, and her knowledge of Greek, metaphysics, and political economy, despite the disparity between Sarah and Henry Acland's public power, influence, status, and freedom. Pearson and the Aclands' daughter Angie constructed Henry and Sarah's emotional characters as complementary and depicted them as sharing profound religious beliefs and a spiritual pilgrimage. Although Sarah and Henry "diverged" in their attitudes to art—"Mrs. Acland had not real enjoyment of pictures or architecture"—Pearson claimed each "completed the other."[41] In Charles Dilke's and Gertrude Tuckwell's memoirs, however, the Aclands' roles are to testify to Francis Strong's exceptionality by appreciating her talents, not to exemplify Oxford domesticity or mark a continuity between Francis's childhood and the social world into which she first married. Nor does Dilke or Tuckwell mention another Oxford couple who offered Francis Strong patronage and a form of career counseling at the same time as the Aclands, or tell a possible story about art, marriage, and Francis Strong's refusal of the kindly sponsorship of culturally sophisticated elders.

Thomas Combe, Printer to the University of Oxford and his wealthy and cultured wife, Martha, known as "Mistress Pat," were close friends of the Aclands. The Combes were "at the very centre of the Anglican High Church party" in Oxford, instrumental in the building of the Italianate church of St. Barnabas in the Jericho district.[42] They were among the most important early patrons of the Pre-Raphaelites, especially John Everett Millais, Charles Collins, and William Holman Hunt, providing patronage, loans, and hospitality. To Hunt, they were a second family; they were "surely 'the salt of the earth' to a large circle . . . unpretending servants of goodness and nobility."[43] The Combes sought to influence the somewhat wild young PRB men in the right way to go, and Mistress Pat was an active matchmaker, seeking proper wives for the brotherhood. In Hunt's case, the Combes' moral project took two tacks: they led him to question his long and tormented relationship with Annie Miller, and they agreed he needed a wife. Hunt was "emotionally starved"; "a celibate life [was] entirely unnatural for such an energetic man." Accordingly, in late 1858 or early 1859, Mrs. Combe arranged a meeting with a suitable Oxford girl for his next visit, "Miss Strong."[44]

Hunt had sent Mistress Pat his specifications. He wanted height ("5 feet 6 or 7"), an aquiline nose, "long round neck and very beautiful . . . not more than 24 . . . not engaged . . . [and] content to live on about £500 a year. Birth and money rather a disadvantage than otherwise." Presumably Hunt was able to overlook Francis Strong's deficiencies of height (she was always considered short); he was actively wooing her during the summer of 1859 during her vacation from art school.[45] Sometime that summer, he proposed, and, very politely, Miss Strong turned him down. Francis Strong apparently pleaded that her delicate health would prevent her making Hunt the sort of wife he required, especially since he was intent upon returning to Syria, where he had painted his famous *The Scapegoat* in 1855, to paint more biblical scenes.[46] Francis may not have been enticed by Hunt's expectations of married life in the Holy Land: she would be expected to learn Arabic, shoot Arabs, camp in gutted tombs, and "stew camel steaks over smouldering dung."[47] By several accounts, Francis Strong did suffer from various illnesses, but it is hard not to suspect other reasons for refusing Hunt. She may have rightly wondered whether Hunt's affair with Annie Miller was indeed over or resented a role as a morally desirable alternative, a prize catch with proper religious views, good looks, and artistic interests.

Whatever the grounds for her decision, Francis Strong's refusal of William Holman Hunt was a refusal of the Combes' conspiracy and the narrative they proposed for her. She was not going to be Hunt's (second choice) muse and she was not going to make sure his domestic arrangements ran smoothly in the desert. She was not going to serve and inspire a great male artist.[48] She remained in London for a little time more. But if Francis Strong's escape from a plot about the proper ends of female artistic abilities makes a temporary but exhilirating story, this story also reflects and depends on larger gendered and public histories of art, patronage, and heterosocial-ity.[49] In the next section, I describe the more metropolitan terrains of London for which Francis Strong refused William Holman Hunt, where Francis Strong's contin-uation of her art studies again illustrates larger histories of aesthetics, gender, and institutionality. I begin, however, by examining some stories by and about another family, the Dilkes.

London: Art, Gender, and Metropolitan Modernity

Sloane Street: The Dilkes

Charles Dilke emphasizes that at South Kensington, Francis Strong had been his su-perior. He waffles about how well he knew her: his manuscript autobiographical notes claim, "from 1858 to 1860 I had been very intimate with a girl three years older than myself who had much influence over me—Emilia Francis Strong," but his pub-lished memoir emphasizes distance in their early relationship: "I used to be patronized by her, regarding her with . . . awe."[50] In both accounts, Dilke stresses Francis Strong's superiority to his tongue-tied teenaged self: "[I] regard[ed] her with the awe of a hobbledehoy of sixteen or seventeen towards a beautiful girl of nineteen or twenty."[51] "[H]er great talent, and power of expression in speech and writing made her a rather terrible person to a boy of sixteen when she was nineteen, and she seemed altogether to belong to an older generation than myself, and I classed her with people of an older age and rank, but still worshipped her from afar, and she was very kind to me and used to talk to me a good deal."[52] Dilke's construction of Francis Strong as above his student self had strategic value: these reminiscences lay the basis for his later account of his reacquaintance with "Mrs. Mark Pattison" but fend off readings that imagine a continuous romantic history between the two of them during their mar-riages to other people.[53] But although Dilke's memoirs are careful to display Francis Strong as an object of interest and highly visible graces to his humble self, an account of Dilke's own family and resources can illuminate the larger histories in which both young people moved. Dilke's stories of childhood, family life, and education intersect his account of Francis Strong and elucidate the resources and experiences to which Francis Strong gained access in London. A consideration of the Dilke family also reiterates themes suppressed in Dilke's account of Francis Strong: the existence of bourgeois masculinities combining earnestness and cultural sophistication; the role of local heterosocial cultures; the importance of institutions in ongoing redistributions of cultural capital; tensions between family stories and stories of exceptional individ-uals; and gender differences in possible or plausible careers. These enlaced discourses are fully displayed in the formal and informal institutions in which Charles Dilke and Francis Strong first knew each other.

The Dilke family knew Francis Strong's great-uncle Thomas, who lived nearby, but Charles Dilke places his first acquaintance with Francis in the open air of an orchard behind Gore House where both were members of the "South Kensington trap-bat club."[54] That is, Charles Dilke knew Francis Strong in the context of a metropolitan culture that extended beyond shared enrollment at the South Kensington art schools to include family and neighborhood connections. South Kensington was a school, a neighborhood, a government project; a site of art, leisure and politics; and a synecdoche for shifting modes of metropolitan modernity and the boundaries of "the public." Gore House itself was a symbol of renegotiations of public space in the early and mid–nineteenth centuries and the mingling of elites, bourgeois and aristocratic, in new institutions and projects. First the home of William Wilberforce and a space of evangelical reform, it was then owned by Lady Blessington before being purchased by the government for use in the Great Exhibition; the site is now occupied by the Albert Hall.[55]

For Charles, the South Kensington trap-bat club was probably a part of his neighborhood life—he lived his entire life at 76 Sloane Street—and it was clearly a heterosocial recreation of the children of a more specifically local intellectual and literary middle class, including the daughters of William Thackeray.[56] The Dilke family itself was a complex embodiment of London "progressive" culture—literary, artistic, highly political, cosmopolitan, and intensely interested in education, gender, and the making and remaking of a modern public sphere.[57] Charles was the privileged scion of a multigenerational household in Chelsea, "so large as to be almost patriarchal." Charles's father (also Charles Wentworth Dilke, "commonly called Wentworth") presided until 1853 over a home that included his wife, Mary Chatfield Dilke; Charles and his younger brother Ashton; Charles's maternal grandmother, Caroline Chatfield; his maternal great-grandmother, Mrs. Dunscombe; and his mother's cousin, Miss Folkard. Charles's grandfather, Charles Wentworth Dilke—called "Grand" by Charles and Ashton—moved into the Sloane Street house in 1853, a few years after the death of his wife, Maria Dover Walker, and he became the real head of the household.[58]

"Old Mr. Dilke" was a prominent public figure. As "Charles Dilke of the *Athenaeum*," he had a highly illustrious career as a publisher and was famous as a sponsor and champion of Keats. William Garrett has coined the term "an ethnos of art and literature" to denote Old Mr. Dilke's "system . . . for merging art and literature with societal good," and Charles was largely educated by his grandfather in commitments to republicanism, Romanticism, public duty, art and literature as transformative forces, historicism, and the desire for a liberal millenium.[59] The *Athenaeum* was "unusually devoted to Art," in contrast to journals like "*Blackwood's*, the *Quarterly*, the *Edinburgh*, and *Fraser's*," and had "fought outspokenly for the ideals of secular, practical, and scientific studies," the establishment of Mechanics' Institutes, and the reform of the National Gallery and the Royal Academy ("it grubs on the dark—it toad-eats the aristocracy . . . we must rattle its old bones about").[60] Charles's education stressed travel (especially to France), wide reading (he had the run of the library), frequent trips to the theatre (he remembered the French actress Rachel vividly), constant introductions to the great men of his day (e.g., Dickens, Thackeray, Prince Albert, the Duke of Wellington), and, during periods of inability to "read and work" due to illness, lessons in drawing and music. His grandfather encouraged Charles to execute "conscientious delineations of buildings visited" in their travels as "training for the eye and observation."[61] Charles Dilke later claimed to have shown no precocious interest in politics, only following his grandfather's lead until awakened to great political issues at eighteen by the American Civil War, but once awakened, he shared his grandfather's enthusiasm for William Godwin.[62]

Charles Dilke's adult texts and those of his biographers represent the Sloane Street household as one in which Wentworth Dilke is almost completely occluded as an influence on his sons. Charles Dilke was scornful of his father's interest in details and his lack of "literary power," representing his grandfather as "greatly disappointed" in Wentworth Dilke and casting Wentworth as dependent on "Grand": "My father . . . consulted his father—dependent on him for bread—in every act of his life." Charles's official biography makes no bones about Wentworth Dilke's "overshadowing" by Old Mr. Dilke, representing Charles's upbringing as a collaboration between him and Charles's mother. Shortly before her death in 1853 when Charles was ten—following the death of a third child, Mildred, in infancy—Mary Chatfield Dilke wrote her elder son a letter confiding him to his grandfather's care for his "moral education," and even entrusting young Charles, rather than his father, with her younger son.[63]

Charles Dilke's and his most recent biographer's accounts emphasize the exceptionality of his upbringing, focusing his status as the child and student of his grandfather. David Nicholls depicts Charles Dilke's unusual upbringing—especially his "nervous" illnesses, his mother's early death, and his closeness to his grandfather—as producing a skewed, if not pathological, psychological development. For Nicholls, Old Mr. Dilke's affection was "a substitute for his mother's love," and as an adult Charles would be both inclined to "over-dependent and self-sacrificing" friendships with men and "at times of personal stress" to have "a strong craving for female companionship—a dependency that would prove his undoing."[64] The Sloane Street household's arrangements of gender are disordered and lead to Charles Dilke's failure to achieve an adequate adult masculinity, which for Nicholls comprises restrained emotionality in general and an aloofness toward and independence from women in particular.

It is certainly true that Charles Dilke's formal education was unconventional for a boy of his class and political aspirations. He escaped the usual elite male sequence of day school followed by being sent away to prep school and public school, and never attended any school consistently. Tutored by a Chelsea curate in classics and mathematics, he was "half-attached" to a local day school but did the set work without attending classes regularly.[65] Dilke's own narration of his formal education represents him as exceptional by nature, not family resources, attributing his educational oddities to concerns about his particular constitution. Weak health and a tendency to "nervousness . . . led to my being forbidden for some years to read and to work, as I was given to read and work too much." Dilke represents himself as having suffered from "a nervous turn of mind, overexcitable and overstrained by slightest circumstance," and depicts himself as a child—as he would as an adult—as unusually sensitive, emotionally fragile, and unable to easily bear strain.[66] Yet if Charles Dilke attributes his childhood escape from rigidly masculinizing education to his own sensitive and impressionable nature rather than familial pedagogy, Dilke's texts also invert Nicholls's ascription of adult misfortunes to family inadequacies in engendering by representing the Sloane Street household as a site of "progressive" attitudes toward gender.

Dilke's texts, published and unpublished, present his family culture as one in which men like his grandfather were acutely concerned with the education of children and in which both grandfather and father participated in the construction of new, heterosocial public institutions. His grandfather supported the educational, literary, and artistic ambitions of women in the *Athenaeum*, and Charles grew up in circles that included many notable women. By a nice turn of fate, the earliest surviving picture of Charles Dilke is an undated miniature by a noted woman artist, Fanny Corbaux. Corbaux fit no stereotypes of saccharine lady-amateurs; her "Victim Bride" was inspired by Caroline Norton and she was a respected contributor to the *Athenaeum* for "researches in sacred literature and attainments in learned languages."[67] Among other contributors to the *Athenaeum* identified by Leslie Marchand are Lady Duff Gordon, Sarah Austin, Fanny Trollope, Anna Jameson, Hannah Laurence, Maria Jewsbury, Agnes Strickland, Louisa Costello, and Mrs. Percy Sinnett, and another *Athenaeum* author, Sidney Morgan, Lady Owenson, was a close friend of Old Mr. Dilke. Charles as an adult represented himself as taking great pride in possessing a miniature of the painter Elizabeth Vigée-LeBrun, given to him by Lady Morgan, and the pen "of bog-oak and gold" given to her "by the Irish people."[68] Charles Dilke's texts position his respect for women's abilities as an outcome of a liberal household education; the "almost patriarchal" household in Sloane Street produced a male liberal feminism.

In addition, Charles Dilke's memoirs and letters figure 76 Sloane Street as a space of absurdity and spontaneity, joking nicknames and affectionate baby talk. A note from Charles's mother on his ninth birthday revels in mock royal appellations, and Charles and Ashton called their grandmother "Dragon." To Mrs. Chatfield, Charles was "the Tsar," "His Highness," and "the Mogul."[69] As Nicholls notes, those who knew Charles Dilke as a distinguished public figure in adulthood were often struck by his "boyish" qualities, prankishness, and "childlike fondness for cats and other animals," and Charles's adult texts present him as physically playful—boasting, for instance, of a visit to the Chamberlains at Highbury in which he engaged "in the intellectually trivial but physically exhilirating sport of tobogganing down snow hills on tea trays" with the Chamberlain children.[70] If Dilke family culture produced an adult masculinity that was not relentlessly restrained, Dilke's texts make this a source of pleasure; emotional expressivity and silliness, as well as intellectual rigor and political ideas, are available to Sloane Street men. This is not to say that the Sloane Street household was not strongly structured by gender. Emilia Dilke claimed Charles was devoted to his mother and kept "locked & sacred to his best thoughts & associations the room in wh he was born his mother's bedroom & now mine," but Mary Chatfield Dilke is a very shadowy figure in Charles's autobiographical writings and letters; the other women of the household—grandmother, great-grandmother, and cousin—are phantoms, mostly caretakers and subjects of comic stories.[71]

Although the Dilke family culture can be represented as metropolitan and cosmopolitan against an implicit backdrop of more provincial or stodgy households, Leonore Davidoff and Catherine Hall's study of middle-class Evangelical family cultures is useful here. Hall and Davidoff have amply shown that the presence of highly developed forms of male domesticity, especially in relation to the teaching of children, did not mean men were as fully defined by or responsible for the maintenance of domesticity as women. The Dilke household valorized men's familial roles and emotional depth as well as self-control and engagement in political and cultural reform, but it was a site of prestigious modern and fluid modes of masculinity, not of gender equality. Neither Old Mr. Dilke's, nor Wentworth's nor Charles's interest in women's education and intellectuality interfered with their ability to be recognized as manly actors in the public sphere.[72] Rather, granting the possibility and attractiveness of female talent and intellectuality enlarged the range and pleasures of heterosociality for men.

Wentworth Dilke's overshadowing in the texts of his son and others can lead to an underestimation of his public career, but Charles's father actively participated in bourgeois political and cultural life, especially institution-building in art. Emilia Dilke later tartly worried that the involvement of "opulent millionaires and busy amateurs," "men of fashion" with "pretensions to birth," could adulterate standards in art institutions, but the institutions in which Charles and Francis Strong would meet were, in fact, the product of such mixings.[73] Wentworth too had been carefully educated in international affairs, culture, and politics by Old Mr. Dilke—"brought up differently from others"—and Wentworth became an active proprietor of his journals and an avid supporter of public provisions for art, although he became politically more conservative than either his father or his son. If Wentworth's notable public career as an owner of magazines, servant of his government, and friend of Prince Albert was in Roy Jenkins's words "marred only by his unimportance within his own family," he was nevertheless vigorously engaged in metropolitan and cosmopolitan modernity, including service as British Commissioner at numerous international exhibitions.[74] Undoubtedly Wentworth's greatest public role, in close contact with Prince Albert, was his work in organizing the Great Exhibition. He was also a member of the Society of Arts, organizing with Henry Cole—later head of the Government Design Schools at South Kensington—an "exhibition of art manufactures." He took an active role in securing the funding to build the South Kensington complex in which his son and Francis Strong studied. Charles Dilke implied that his attendance at the South Kensington school was an accidental result of its convenient location and his own childhood fragility, but physical proximity was probably only one of the reasons he was enrolled there: Charles Dilke's family culture of support for public institutions and the cultivation of multiple talents made the South Kensington school more than a convenience.[75] The South Kensington schools Charles Dilke attended provided an art education in a social framework that matched his grandfather's and father's public programs for cultural revitalization. Moreover, the schools were heterosocial sites in national discourses and debates that explicitly worried over the relations between gender and class, culture, money, and the state.

South Kensington: Gender and Public Art Education

In her formal experiences of art education, Francis Strong participated in an extraordinary upsurge in women's art education from the late 1830s through the early 1860s, precursor in some respects to the better-known later generation of ambitious, independent, and unconventional young women associated with the Slade School of Art.[76]

As with the later "Slade" generation, the women who studied and practiced art in the early to mid-Victorian era included a notable contingent of feminists, the most well known of whom was Barbara Leigh Smith Bodichon. The educational and professional experience of young women in art was a site of feminist thinking about women's access to economic autonomy and vocation.[77] The increasing number of unmarried middle-class women in need of paid employment—and the overpopulation of governessing—encouraged consideration of improving the standards of women's education to fit some women for respectable forms of paid work.[78] In 1848 Harriet Taylor wrote to the Radical editor W. J. Fox that art work was an exception to the general run of "poorly paid and hardly worked occupations" open to respectable young women, since "all the professions, mercantile clerical legal & medical, as well as all government posts [were] monopolized by men." Taylor linked the creation of such opportunities to "the emancipation of women from their present degraded slavery," and the Society of Female Artists, founded in 1857 by Harriet Grote, also defined itself largely in terms of the economic needs of women; its members sought to "open a new field for the emulation of the female student, and also a wider channel of industrial occupation, thereby relieving some of the strain now bearing heavily on the few other profitable avocations open to educated women."[79]

I have argued, however, that the possibility and shape of a woman's art education was not entirely determined by the need of some respectable women to earn independent livings. Middle-class women's art education was imbricated in wider discourses and was a crucial terrain for programs for infusing art into material life. Ruskin's *Sesame and Lilies* had implied that women might be objects of public art education not only because they were destined to act as makers and consumers of aesthetic objects in the domestic sphere but because they might participate in discussions about public space and the state's role in supporting art in the form of monuments, galleries, museums, and schools.[80] But discourses that justified women's art education by joined aesthetic values and gendered moral claims trapped as well as enabled. Women's art education was never principally about the development of women's talents or the insertion of female figures into Romantic discourses of autonomous artistic genius. If discourses of domesticity authorized, even mandated, women's aesthetic education, they also reiterated women's professional marginality.

Women were artistically educated in unprecedented numbers in the mid-Victorian period, art "could be a profitable and socially acceptable mode of employment," and becoming an art professional—teacher, designer, illustrator, critic, even a painter or sculptor—was imaginable. But it remained highly unlikely, and those who succeeded remained marginal in important respects.[81] Among the hundreds or thousands of young women educated in high art, barely a handful achieved recognition and economic independence, and some have even wondered if the encouragement given to women working in design and crafts was a diversionary response to the increasing clamor of women demanding training and recognition as creators of "fine art."[82] The most successful women were still excluded from the more golden realms of prestige and patronage and the highest institutional positions, whether membership in the Royal Academy or employment as professors of art in national institutions.

Two women who recalled Francis Strong from shared student days at South Kensington, Maria Theresa Villiers Earle and Frances Rosser Hullah, wrote texts that point to the possibilities and stresses of women's artistic ambitions. Earle's memoir's master trope is the extent of changes in social life since her youth, and she recalls being daunted by the social difficulty of "breaking away from the home life" and mustering "sufficient courage and perseverance to give up my life to art." Earle's text itself oscillates between representing her young self, Theresa Villiers, as working seriously at drawing and trivializing her youthful desires for an art career. She was encouraged by Louisa Waterford; many of her friends were also studying art; and she won a medal for drawing at South Kensington in 1863, but her text "confesses" she had also been ambitious "to be smart and in the fashion." Earle retrospectively deplores the artistic atmosphere of Little Holland House as too headily bohemian, and when she praises her friend Anne Dundas's talent in art, she positions that talent as "a great consolation for all [Dundas] had to give up": marriage and home life. Earle represents Francis Strong's marriage upon leaving South Kensington as natural and sees Emilia Dilke's professional art scholarship as laudable but less important than Dilke's more other-directed social reform activities.[83] Frances Rosser Hullah, who was probably enrolled in the "modelling" course at South Kensington in the 1850s and 1860s and who exhibited a sculpture titled "Italia" at the 1865 Royal Academy, presented her art studies with greater dignity.[84] Frances Rosser was the young woman with whom Francis Strong shared a "small room high up in a house under the control of a lady who had the confidence of the families of both" in order to pacify parental concerns about safety and respectability (they lived near the schools, too, to soothe Emily Weedon Strong's worry that Francis should not "walk home unaccompanied") and Rosser recalled to Charles Dilke that neither woman liked the arrangement. It compromised their "strong. . . . love of personal independence," and they "made it 'tolerable by drawing a chalk line' across the room by way of boundary, and compiling a code of minute rules 'to maintain our rights.' "[85]

All three of these young women—Strong, Villiers, and Rosser—were supported, however ambivalently, by their families in their art educations. All three married. Earle and Hullah remained friends with Francis Strong at least through her first marriage; Earle lauded Emilia Dilke as "the most clever, the most industrious, and the most courageous woman I have ever known."[86] All were later involved in overlapping realms of public life—Hullah in women's suffrage activities and as a supporter of women's education and Earle as a writer of advice and proponent of some modes of moral reform—and all three devoted later attention to the education of young women.[87] Together, these women represent not only the expansion of women's art education in the mid-Victorian period, but the continued centrality of marriage, the difficulty or unimaginability of sustaining art careers after marriage, and the possibility of recasting intellectual energies and ambitions into writing or social reform.

Victorian bourgeois interest in art and design both enabled and contained women's ambition, and the very structures of official art education embodied concerns about gender, which meshed with issues, contradictory and complex, of class. Art education in government-sponsored and other schools was overtly differentiated by class, and claims about art education's value included both concerns for bourgeois cultural capital and arguments for public sponsorship of art education for artisanal and working-class people. Questions about the investment of the state in art education raised arguments about art as economically useful—even crucial to national economic development—and spiritually valuable, simultaneously productive of superior industrial development and enriched subjectivities, maintaining *and* reshaping categories of class and gender. In the national network of twenty-three government schools of design, including the South Kensington School, the dependence of the very definitions of work, education, design, and art on fluctuating definitions of gender and class was spotlighted by institutional arrangements and public debates. Initially, both the male and female schools in the new schools (the London Head School was established in 1837) were rigorously defined as industrially oriented, in language that differentiated by gender between threats to the desired model of utility. Male students were forbidden to pursue careers in "Fine Art," while women were forbidden to enroll in order to acquire "accomplishments."[88]

The Government Female School of Design's first report (1843–1844) stressed that its mission was to encourage "commercial Art with reference to its use in industry," *not* "accomplishments."[89] Traditions that positioned female aesthetic education and achievements as "accomplishments"—furbelows of talent meant to attract sexual attention and success in "Society"—and associated women's art with amateurish aristocrats diminished the talent of aristocratic women artists and cast suspicion on all women artists, but they also threatened public support for female art education.[90] Arguing for women's art education at Queen's College, F. D. Maurice carefully stressed that art should be taught not as an accomplishment but as a way of "cultivat[ing] a power of looking beneath the surface of things for the meaning which they express"; art study should be a "handmaid of religion," homologous with other morally edifying modes of female education.[91] In 1863 Sir Richard Westmacott, a supporter of the Royal Female School of Art, grounded the value of female aesthetic education in a national culture of domesticity: "the English [do not] desire to see women over-demonstrative; the quieter qualities are what are admired, and instead of having them declaiming on the rights of women, we prefer believing that they can influence society more beneficially by their gentler virtues. . . . The arts are eminently calculated to assist in doing this."[92] Nonetheless, the use of government monies for "ladies' " art education—"contrivances, over which young ladies are made to lose time"—was periodically denounced.[93]

Class and gender were snared in discourses about art and the good of the nation. Government funding, it was sometimes suggested, would be better directed only to those women who might work as governesses or designers, or, as Earl Granville argued in 1856, such art education for working-class girls as would teach them the "precision and neatness" that made good domestic servants.[94] The classes at most of the Government Schools of Design were divided into sex-segregated courses for "gentlemen [amateurs]" and "male artisans" and those for "ladies" and "females" (in some cases, with the further category of "governesses").[95] Women art workers and students were sorted into "ladies or cheap labour"; working-class and lower-middle-class women were assumed to be learning mechanical skills to suit them for jobs as pattern cutters or china painters, "paid work" which was neither "lady-like" nor "Art."[96] Middle-class women's art education was similarly assumed to have limited goals and to occupy the consumption end of the economic spectrum, albeit consumption with spiritual benefits. Middle-class women's art education would allow them to act as responsible consumers and to " 'elevate' public taste . . . as gallery visitors [and] purchasers of pictures and engravings."[97] Demonstrating that the scale and ambition of women's art work should be limited, when the Female School was summarily relocated in 1848 to unsuitable—even unsafe—quarters, it no longer had rooms in which students could do (prestigious) large-scale works.[98] A brief widening of women's opportunities was portentous. Henry Cole, contributor as "Felix Summerly" to the *Athenaeum* and co-worker with Wentworth Dilke, became head of the "Department of Practical Art" in 1852. Cole encouraged middle-class women to attend courses, albeit at a higher rate of tuition, but this innovation led to the withdrawal of all government subsidies to the Female School (renamed "The Metropolitan School of Ornament for Females") in 1859.[99] The reasons given for the Female School's de-nationalization included that "for all the requirements of female students . . . the various district schools do, or may, afford ample and cheap opportunities of study"; an elementary training was sufficient for women. Charlotte Yeldham succinctly states, "the State [was not] willing to assist women whose aim was to become professional artists as opposed to artisans."[100] Cruelly, the existence of the Female School was nonetheless used as an argument against the admission of women to the Royal Academy School until 1860, on the grounds that women could already obtain all instruction proper to them.[101]

Despite these reinscriptions of the marginality of middle-class women's art education, during Cole's headship the central school thrived. Again renamed in 1857, the National Art Training School was consolidated at South Kensington, largely funded by surplus revenue from the Great Exhibition. There was no longer a separate government-sponsored Female School but the National School opened numerous courses to women as "general fee-paying students." Training programs for schoolmistresses were established, although the course for art-school masters was restricted to men, and a few women were even employed as instructors, although apparently always in tandem with male teachers.[102] Thus, despite and *because* of its class and sex-segregated classes, the South Kensington School was a public institution where training in art, design, and industrial applications coexisted and the relationships between art, government, and the public sphere were foregrounded. This very inclusiveness on unequal terms may have depressed the South Kensington School's reputation. When Edward Poynter was inaugurated as first principal of the Slade School of Art of the University of London in 1871, he emphasized that the new institution would provide an official setting for the study of "high art," as distinguished from "ornamental design" as fostered by the government schools. The Slade, while open to middle-class women, thus offered a refuge from contact with working-class and lower-middle-class students.[103] If South Kensington's reputation suffered by its association with industry, design, and workers, it educated students well beyond the formal curriculum, in the contested relations between artistic, political, and economic institutions, and between "artisans," "females," "ladies" and "gentlemen."[104]

Francis Strong's art education thus placed her in an institution in which questions of art and gender were fused with other debates about economics, the state, industry, and gender. Rosa Tuckwell and Charles Dilke claim that Ruskin's was the deciding voice in choosing South Kensington for Francis Strong, emphasizing its strength in teaching anatomy, its combination of scientific and artistic studies, and the continuity between Francis's Oxford and London experiences. Francis Strong's attendance at South Kensington from 1858 to 1861 was certainly a choice against alternatives;

although the Royal Academy School only began accepting women students in 1860, she could have attended one of several private academies, the Ladies' College in Bedford Square, the Lambeth School of Art, the school of the Society of British Artists, or the women-only Crystal Palace School of Art.[105] Emilia Dilke arranged that after her death her collection of art books (many of very high value) be given to the National Art Library at South Kensington, and Gilbert Redgrave eulogized that "in selecting a final home for her treasures, Lady Dilke was not unmindful of the days when she was herself a student at Kensington . . . where she, no doubt, was first impressed with the love of those phases of art, to which she was throughout life so devotedly attached, and to which she rendered such important services."[106]

Charles Dilke's account implies that South Kensington curriculum's mixture of "fine" and "applied" arts and its public status shaped Emilia Dilke's adult scholarly concerns: "it was . . . towards architecture and sculpture, and . . . towards ornament, and the application of the arts in industry, that her mind first turned; and . . . [t]o the end of her life it was . . . the history of art and its connection with the history of organized and civilized states . . . that roused her most."[107] Emilia Dilke's own 1890 essay on "Art-Teaching and Technical School" also refers directly to South Kensington as a site of arguments about art and the nation. Pointedly noting that the French had always understood "the right relations between art and industry," Emilia Dilke emphasizes the compatibility of developing the "individual force and excellence" of students and the "utmost advantage of the nation." The state should recognize and support comprehensive art education when private interests fail; ideally, "the State might co-operate with private effort," but in the past the Royal Academy "decided not to do its duty" in educating artisans even while "lavish ridicule was heaped on" the initial proposals for the South Kensington schools. The result is that England lags behind France in the "beautiful and artistic fashioning of objects of everyday use."[108]

Emilia Dilke quickly retracts her initial proffering of France—"[it is] pretty certain to be alien to our own genius"—and instead offers Austrian art education as a model but retains a rhetoric of art education as leavening the nation's economic and cultural development. The government schools are not adequately meeting their goal of fostering national industrial excellence because of continuing elitism and because they fail to attract and support sufficient numbers of "workmen" and to think clearly about working students' needs. The problem is not simply numbers but educational culture: art education can become only another form of industrial production, turning out "teachers and pupils alike . . . 'branded with the departmental stamp,' " its routinization exacerbated by the system of "payment by results" of art teachers who organize their teaching around their own economic needs. This particularly betrays students who rely on public provision for their education, that is, working-class students: "the soldiers of industry have a right to be furnished with the best equipment wealth can supply or wisdom can select." Proper instruction should "arouse and inspire new interest in [daily work], and render [a worker] sufficiently master of it to be capable at least of some variation of detail"; otherwise, students will have been taught "less than nothing." "It is the plain duty of the State to see that they have every means, not only of technical instruction, but . . . insight into all beauty . . . By making them more interested in their work it will make them happier men." Art is a democratically accessible form of spiritual pleasure in Dilke's text: "the soul of him to whom beauty has revealed herself, even in her humblest forms, is touched . . . by the finger of God.''[109]

In this essay, art education in public institutions is a source of pleasure, an education in desire, an entitlement for workers, a source of national economic strength, and a counterbalance to the pursuit of private economic interests. It will not substitute for material needs—workers still need to pursue other means, such as trade unions, to raise their wages—but neither is it a luxury for an "amateur" elite. Emilia Dilke's 1890 essay is of a piece with late-Victorian and Edwardian "progressive" appeals to art and education. Enobling influences will empower working-class actors to move into a democratic future with a proper sense of responsibility, moral seriousness, and commitment to preserving and extending a national culture identified with aesthetic pleasure as well as economic and imperial power. Chris Waters's analysis of the reach and limitations of this discourse in Labour and socialist cultural programs in the late nineteenth century and early twentieth century allows us to see, by implication, how typical Emilia Dilke's arguments are of 1890s Radical Liberalism and middle-class socialism.[110] But Dilke's essay's blend of economic, political, moral, and social arguments about public provision of art education, and its support of institutions with inclusive student bodies and expansive training in all branches of art and design, are also homologous with the language of South Kensington thirty or more years earlier.

Yet although E. F. S. Pattison/Emilia Dilke's art histories carry on some of the arguments about gender that animated the institutional history of South Kensington—for example, by including artists and craftspeople of both sexes—"Art-Teaching and Technical Schools" discusses the costs of class-differentiated educations without explicit address to gender. The essay may leave all the doors open for women by refusing to discuss gender as a term that might matter in discussions of access and curriculum in goverment schools, but it also erases women students with its masculine pronouns, "workmen" and "soldiers of industry." If South Kensington taught the inextricability of class and gender, those lessons did not always endure.

Life-Drawing

Visible Women: Francesca, Delilah, Dorothea

Maria Theresa Earle vividly remembered Francis Strong at South Kensington: "A more brilliant, fascinating, enthusiastic *Goldkind*, as the Germans say, could not be imagined." Earle reprinted and ratified a quotation from Frances Rosser Hullah, which Charles Dilke included in his "Memoir": "It is no exaggeration, but a true description, to say 'she was good to look at in the freshness of her youth, expressing, as every movement did, a boundless delight in mere existence.' ''[111] Hullah's letters too were enlisted by Charles Dilke as a knowledgeable source about Francis Strong in Dilke's memoir. Like Earle, Hullah remembered Francis Strong both for her "immense power and unremitting practice of work" and for being a striking figure. Hullah describes Francis Strong's ability to draw the attention of prestigious masters and gain their attention for her work while at South Kensington; Francis was a "pet" not only because of the quality of her drawing, which Hullah carefully notes, but because of her own status as an artistic object. Hullah emphasizes Francis's petiteness, youth, energy, attractiveness to older men, and dramatic use of dress, and recalls Francis Strong's drawing master, William Mulready, lighting up when his pupil entered: "I seem to see the old man's handsome but satirical face ripple all over with a welcoming smile as he saw the little figure come trotting in with a portfolio of drawings on her arm, attired in extremely unconventional, but often very picturesque, garments floating behind her."[112] These depictions of Francis Strong at art school as a vivid figure lead us to the significatory powers of aestheticized bodies, especially women's bodies, in artistic subcultures and institutions. Francis Pattison/Emilia Dilke's figures generated an array of texts that call attention to the imbrication of gendered bodies with narratives, practices, institutions, and powers of art, but in this section I read texts that represent Francis Strong as someone who studied and drew figures and was also an aesthetic figure. I continue by looking at Charles Dilke's depiction of Francis Strong as a religious figure, a woman whose body participated in contemporary theological discourses; finally, I return to the issue of exceptionality and the ephemerality of figuration.

According to Charles Dilke, a principal attraction of South Kensington for Francis Strong was the possibility of continuing "anatomical study." The set exercises in figure drawing and anatomy, using the Elgin Marbles, the Discobolus, and other Greek sculptures, would have been familiar exercises to one already practiced in copying the Ashmolean Museum's casts, but because Charles Dilke's texts are more concerned to endow Francis Strong with an unchanging essence than to impart detailed information, they give little precise information about her or his own studies at South Kensington.[113] Charles and Francis were clearly good students; both won "Queen's Prizes" in 1859, Charles "passed" a geometry course and won a "South Kensington Prize" in 1859, and Francis was examined and won two medals in 1860. Both were probably enrolled in the "Drawing Course," a ten-stage program progressing from "linear drawing with instruments" through "shading from the round" onto "human or animal figure" drawing both "from the flat" and "from the round or nature." The final stage of the South Kensington drawing course was drawing "flowers, foliage, landscape details and objects of natural beauty from nature . . . in outline and shaded," the culmination of art education resting in the ability to carefully attend to and represent natural objects.[114] Francis seems to have got through the set curriculum in 1858 and early 1859, and she was engaged in "studies in anatomy and dissection" by 1859. Moreover, in 1859 and 1860, Miss Strong pushed further, taking special courses with William Mulready without the imprimatur of the South Kensington authorities.[115]

Hullah's memory of Francis Strong's tutelage in drawing under the Irish-born Royal Academician William Mulready (1786–1863) highlights the necessity for even exceptional young women to gain access to knowledge through relationships with powerful men, relationships in which young women's personal charms, as well as talent or intellect, might play crucial roles. Charles Dilke says Francis had been introduced to Mulready by Pauline Trevelyan; "common affection and admiration for Lady Trevelyan . . . made [them] friends."[116] Although Mulready had many private students on whom he depended for much of his income, he had the power to accept or reject Francis Strong as a student; Elizabeth Eastlake found him in 1851 "most gentlemanly, animated, and prepossessing," but Frances Hullah and Samuel Carter Hall both remarked on Mulready's ability to inspire terror.[117] But Mulready was not merely one, rather frightening, drawing master among many: he was the one willing to give Francis Strong lessons in drawing from the nude.

Mulready joked about the differences between his views on art and the official program at South Kensington, but his transgression of the limits of Victorian art education for women was located most precisely in his teaching of life-drawing.[118] Francis Strong's drawings in the Ashmolean and her studies of anatomical theory were intellectually authorized by history-painting's emphasis on "expression" and the composition of human forms and by the Ruskinian emphasis on nature and scientific understanding, but at South Kensington the institutional limits of proper female art education were displayed. "Life-drawing," even from the draped human figure, was usually denied women students; drawing from nude casts was often prohibited; drawing the living naked human body of either sex was beyond the pale.[119] Paula Gillett cites an 1885 controversy in the *Times* over life-drawing that included the "scandalous" claim that "at the Government School of Art at Kensington, there are classes of young men and young women (*in separate rooms*) drawing from *almost* naked models— men and women." Gillett links the fear of women drawing the female nude to "fear of contamination by association with artists' models" and cites J. A. Jackson's contention that life-study is associated with "professional mysteries" and "socially sanctioned violation[s] of taboo . . . [like] the cutting up of cadavers by medical students . . . the probing of inner secrets by the psychiatrist, the examination of the body by the doctor."[120] What was at stake in debates over women's life-drawing was not just propriety but knowledge and power.

Women were excluded despite—or perhaps because—drawing from the nude was the pinnacle of art education, setting the aspiring artist in the Great Tradition and critical to the most prestigious genres of painting.[121] The very year Francis Strong began her studies at South Kensington, Dinah Mulock suggested that while "many lower and yet honourable positions are open to female handlers of the brush, art . . . in its highest form," might be "almost impossible to women" because of "the not unnatural repugnance that is felt to women drawing 'from the life', attending anatomical dissections, and so on—all of which studies are indispensable to those who would plumb the depths and scale the heights of the most arduous of the liberal arts."[122] Access to the nude was a consistent rallying point for women artists; an 1858 open letter to the Royal Academy was signed by Barbara Bodichon, Laura Herford, Caroline Hullah, Anna Jameson, Emma Novello, Bella Leigh Smith, Henrietta Ward, and many others.[123] But when the Royal Academy admitted women students, it barred them from life studios. Women RA students were not granted a separate class for life-drawing until 1903, and even the progressive Slade School only began allowing women to draw the "half-draped" model in 1897.[124]

The long contest over issues of access to life-drawing through the nineteenth century is displayed in texts written under Francis Strong's later names. E. F. S. Pattison's art-writing made intense interest in anatomical study characteristic of the Renaissance, the era she privileged as an epoch of passionate and pleasurable omnivoracity for knowledge and experience. Emilia Dilke's art-writings are even more specific: *French Painters of the Eighteenth Century* (1899) introduces life-drawing, specifically in the contexts of institutions, economics, and the exclusion of women, on its third page. Dilke's text lauds the French Academy's "fulfillment . . . of its often deferred promise . . . to open their Life School without charge," but notes in the same sentence the Academy's "vigourous decision . . . not to receive women, in future, as 'academiciennes.' " Dilke's account quickly adds that some exceptional women broke this barrier; Rosalba Carriera "made good her claims" and "exceptions continued to be made." Other women's names (Mlle Reboul, "the terrible Mme Therbouche," Anne Vallayer, Mlle Roslin, Madame Guyard, and Elizabeth Vigée Lebrun) are carefully included, in some cases with details of their arguments with authorities over admission, although without specifying whether or not they used the Life School. In any case, in Dilke's account the history of women's institutional exclusions is laid alongside assertions that the the Life School was "the chief boast" of the Academy and life-drawing a lively issue.[125] Dilke's "Art-Teaching and Technical Schools" also foregrounds life-drawing; it begins with a quotation from "one of the directors of a school for the living model" and argues that life classes should be introduced at South Kensington. The essay marshals French sources to attest that "the life-school [should be] regarded as the necessary complement" of more specific training in design and "study of the living model [should be] part of the training of those intended to lead the ranks of industrial artists." Life-drawing produces economic value and respects the dignity of working-class students: "The highest possible forms of artistic instruction are not too high for [the] needs" of "industrial artists," who deserve "a general and complete, rather than a special training."[126] Drawing the whole body benefits the whole nation; restricting the movement of prestigious knowledge is incompatible with the public interest.

Charles Dilke's "Memoir" alludes to Francis Strong's earlier "fearless advocacy of the necessity of drawing from the nude," drawing attention to these ongoing debates. Dilke's text also makes life-drawing an element of its stories of continuity and exceptionality, tying Emilia Dilke's later insistence on life-drawing for all art students to her student experiences. But although Charles speculates that Mulready ratified her views, he emphasizes that Francis Strong's abilities made her a welcome student: "I [have] a study from the nude by her which Mulready pronounced 'excellent.' "[127] Special pleading aside, Francis Strong's ability to enlist Mulready as teacher was a considerable coup; he was and is highly praised for his drawings of naked figures. His nudes were much admired by Queen Victoria but drew worries from Thackeray about propriety and denunciations from Ruskin as " 'degraded,' 'bestial,' 'vulgar,' and 'abominable.' "[128] (Emilia Dilke bristled, "Ruskin never erred more deeply than about Mulready."[129])

Mulready's private tuition of a young unmarried woman in life-drawing was potentially scandalous by definition, but his sexual and domestic history displayed and compounded risky conjunctions of men, women, vision, sexuality, and stories. Mulready had married the artist Elizabeth Varley in 1804; the sister of artist John Varley, Elizabeth also exhibited extensively.[130] The marriage broke up by 1810, amid accusations from Elizabeth that William had subjected her to blows and curses and had "taken 'a low boy' " into his bed. Professional rivalry too was a point of tension; "she is alleged to have sneaked into his studio and altered paintings . . . paint[ing] out the eyes if she was angry."[131] It was rumored that Mulready had, at the age of seventy, seduced and impregnated a young model, although he represented himself as a patron and protector of women models, cautioning them about the dangers of naïveté in a world of "smiling faces, flattering manner . . . painting and gilding," and exhorting them not to trust male artists. The majority of his private pupils were women, including Florence Nightingale's sister Frances Parthenope, and Mulready's ward (perhaps daughter) Mary Mulready Leckie Stone was an artist.[132] Emilia Dilke wrote, "No one felt more strongly than Mr. Mulready the difficulties and disabilities under which women laboured who wished to gain any serious knowledge of his art," and an 1890 Dilke essay on women's trade unionism invokes his teachings: "My dear old master, Mr. Mulready, used to say that 'the first step towards making women good artists would be the existence of teachers of their own sex capable of training them.' "[133] Mulready's private and professional life, combining sexual scandal and feminist attitudes, is a panoply of the opportunities and dangers for women artists negotiating access to cultural expertise through relationships—variously or simultaneously pedagogical, filial, romantic, or economic—with men.

To Pauline Trevelyan, Francis Pattison represented her relationship with Mulready as one of friendship and personal affection and periodically renewed "old familiar intercourse" even after her marriage. After Mulready's death in 1863, she wrote, "I can hardly say how grieved I was to hear of Mr. Mulready's death it was really the loss of a dear, true, friend . . . To me as to so many he had always been so good (there is no other word for it) & so sympathetic his vitality was so great that [when?] the thought of decay never did arise in connection with him."[134] Emilia Dilke later paid homage to her teacher and marked her own achievement of professional prestige in a more public text. In 1892, Dilke wrote a warm remembrance for the Fortnightly Review that figures her as an exceptional possessor of knowledge about her dead drawing master. Dilke's essay begins by recounting an incident in which Victor Pollet, "peintre et gravure," accosts her at the 1878 International Exhibition and is surprised by her knowledge of Mulready's work. "But I had known Mr. Mulready . . ." Dilke goes on to display her personal knowledge: Mulready soon ceased to treat Francis Strong with formality or distance he might have shown other students, they became "friends . . . in spite of all differences," and he showed "extraordinary kindness, patience and generosity" in "devot[ing] hours to the teaching of an ignorant schoolgirl." Dilke stresses that he behaved toward her with "fatherly goodness . . . exquisite tact and simplicity . . . a natural habit of extreme prudence and reserve," while noting that Mulready expressed confidence that her discretion and ethical standards would prevent her gossiping to other South Kensingtonians about his work or ideas, alluding to the risk of scandal even while banishing it. Dilke represents herself as having received his "Apologia" during a visit to his studio after she had left South Kensington; "he talked out to himself, rather than to me" his ideas. If Dilke's text represents her as invisible, it also makes her a recipient of trust, exceptional in her capacity to hear and comprehend exceptional men. The essay includes brief but knowing references to Mulready's difficult past and presents him telling Francis Strong stories of his impoverished childhood and domestic responsibilities in caring for younger children, and Dilke writes movingly about his illnesses and failing sight.[135] Dilke's essay thus covertly claims Francis Strong was not exceptionally talented—her artistic shortcomings under Mulready's tutelage are comically stressed—but exceptionally gifted at appreciating talent and commiserating with pain.

Dilke's Mulready is a powerful and witty teacher about the value of facts; Dilke quotes, "The work of those who wish to give life, to give real existence to the 'ideal' must be based on facts—no matter how selected—which have been observed in living organisms . . . You can't put imaginary trees in the Garden of Eden." The real and the physical are objects of passion, and human bodies are especially and subtly communicative. Emilia Dilke's essay presents Mulready as powerfully interested in bodies as palimpsests: "He would dwell fondly on any traces left on the body by special habits; he would trace out the signs of previous occupations and so amuse himself by drawing up a biography of his model. Hands invariably furnished matter for a lecture . . . Each tiny item was worked into its place so as to make up a human history." She repeatedly emphasizes Mulready's attention to detail and concern to capture bodies in motion; his "Apologia" stressed the meaningfulness, to educated eyes, of "little indications of character and . . . what were to some, perhaps, mere trivialities." Mulready trained Francis Strong to look carefully at every figure in a composition, to perceive truth in surfaces (to "represent everything exactly as [one] saw it"), and to educe narratives from physical attitudes. "If anyone guessed the motive of the work, or caught the suggestion he wished to convey in any of the figures . . . he was enchanted." Dilke gives an example like a nest of Russian dolls, her words presenting his words presenting a picture that tells a story about words and vision. Emilia Dilke remembers Mulready telling Francis Strong to look at a picture, "The Sonnet," which depicts a young man "try[ing] to read the effect of his verses" on his girlfriend's face "whilst she, as instinctively . . . endeavour[s] to prevent his doing so."[136] Words elucidate and re-present pictures, pictures tell stories, eyes search for signs, and bodies speak, ratifying or refusing stories told by words or silences.

Emilia Dilke's final image of Mulready is a bravura performance, a verbal figuration of a pictorialized body laden with meaning. On her last visit to him, after her marriage, Mulready is ill and sad but still friendly and interested in Francis Pattison's opinions. She cares for his physical needs—holds his hand, brings him water—but her essay concludes with a display of her command of visual codes, in a description of a scene as of a painting, in which every detail speaks and spells:

> On the threshold of the room I turned round for one more look, and I saw what I had never before realised, and I knew the thought that had been in his mind when he made his sketch in illustration of Tennyson's poem, "Life and Thought are gone away"; that sketch, in which one sees the painter lying dead in his studio, was actually before me. The familiar tools were standing idle in the spacious room; to the right, his favourite group of Cupid and Psyche, and beneath the open window, where the leaves fluttered against the sky, the straight, hard couch on which lay the motionless body of my dear old friend. I never saw him again.[137]

This scene of Mulready's body is a verbal image of a visual scene which had told of the thought behind a picture that had been based on a text. Emilia Dilke's words tell a story of a young woman who sees in life an accidental but eloquent "composition" in the sight of a dying artist who had expounded a passionate belief in the narrativity of pictures, and her words invoke one of the pictures that artist had made of a poem. Genre and time are destabilized: the older writer's young female protagonist-self can retroactively read the thought that Mulready once had by looking at his body as it now lies, but she can also recognize in this *tableau vivant* an approaching *tableau mort* that will echo the drawing Mulready made to illustrate a poem about a dead artist. Emilia Dilke's text dizzyingly displaces and displays her as a reader and writer of poems, paintings, and bodies.

Francis Strong's relationship with William Mulready allowed instruction beyond the formal curriculum of South Kensington and was a site for the enactment of exceptional qualities. But Mulready was not the only powerful, or dangerous, man whom others represented as charmed by Francis Strong. Frances Hullah recalled that G. F. Watts "took a more than ordinary interest in [Francis Strong] and her work, of which he had a high opinion."[138] Watts's interest admitted Miss Strong to the "Bohemian" circle at Little Holland House, a "highly coloured, idiosyncratic, energetically creative, comfortably-off milieu . . . of Anglo-Indian colonials, Pre-Raphaelite artists, and beautiful girls."[139] Like Thoby and Sarah Prinsep's other guests in this Melbury Road "elysium," Francis Strong addressed Watts as "Signor" and "breathed an atmosphere of Italy."[140] Yet as Lee's phrasing suggests, Francis Strong's status at Little Holland House would not have rested solely on her talent as a maker of art. Frances Hullah is explicit: Francis Strong made herself into a work of art, presenting herself as the young, gifted, pretty, and charmingly Italianate "Francesca."[141] Francis Strong's figure did not just appeal to men—George Eliot later addressed Francis Strong Pattison as "Figliuolina" [daughter] and signed a few of her letters "Madre"—and Frances Hullah and Theresa Earle depict themselves, as well as men, admiring Miss Strong, but Ellen Terry signalled the gendered dangers of the Watts circle's aestheticized play-acting.[142] Briefly married to and much painted by Watts, Terry found "Little Holland House . . . a paradise where only beautiful things were allowed to come, all the women were beautiful and all the men were gifted," where Terry "sat in a corner . . . the girl wife of a famous painter."[143] That marriage ended within a year, but Signor remained the center of a coterie of women, eventually marrying another much younger woman. The title given to the work of a woman artist in this circle by her twentieth-century editors preserves the disparity Terry registered; a selection of Julia Margaret Cameron's works was published by Leonard and Virginia Woolf's Hogarth Press in 1924 as *Victorian Photographs of Famous Men and Fair Women.*[144] Emilia Dilke's art-historical writing could gesture to similar histories. Her book on French engraving and drawing includes a citation of Hyacinthe Rigaud's self-portrait of himself painting his wife. Dilke's text not only depicts a scene in which male artistic self-regard and regard of a woman as model or muse are fused but offers a material history. Dilke recounts that Rigaud hired another artist to produce a marketable engraving of the image of his wife, inserting "her" into wider economic and visual circulation. In Dilke's art history, beauty is entangled with money and desire.[145]

The inextricability of Francis Strong's schoolings—in art and the aesthetic presentation of the self—is condensed in one of the few details Charles Dilke provides about Francis's actual art-work. G. F. Watts was sufficiently impressed by "a series of designs for 'Elaine' " to show them to Tennyson. A section of *The Idylls of the King*, "Lancelot and Elaine" was published in 1859.[146] Charles Dilke's "Memoir" says Francis Strong was and remained interested in Arthurian tales: in Oxford, Dr. Ince, later Regius Professor of Divinity, had encouraged Francis's art studies by presenting her with a copy of the *Idylls* as a "reward" for her efforts and a "favourite book" was

"Wright's 'History of King Arthur' " given to her in 1859. She went on to purchase many other versions. Charles Dilke aligns Arthurianism with Emilia Dilke's allegiances to causes of justice: she preferred Tennyson's Idylls to Malory's Morte d'Arthur because Tennyson had more of "the spirit of Spanish romance . . . [in which] valour and generosity were called forth for some object undeservedly troubled or wrongfully oppressed, while [Mallory displayed] a simple delight in fighting for its own sake, no matter which side was wrong or right."[147] More recently and critically, Alan Sinfield suggests the Idylls appealed to the Victorian bourgeoisie in part because of their "aristocratic display," costumery and production of history as spectacle.[148] Certainly the legends' popularity derived partly from their movement between pictures and words. The tales were, if anything, more popular in art than in literature, and Debra Mancoff has surveyed the huge number of post-Tennysonian Victorian paintings of the tales.[149] The legends' most celebrated Victorian rehearsal was highly pictorial and often pictorialized; like Emilia Dilke's depiction of the dying Mulready, the Idylls constantly and productively oscillate between texts and images, between genres, and between ideologically charged constructions of history and aesthetic pleasure.

As Ellen Terry discerned, moreover, aestheticized pseudohistorical objects and pleasures were deeply structured by gender. In painting Elaine, as well as in enacting Francesca, Francis Strong was participating in a wider project. Elaine was the most popular Tennysonian subject for painters, including many by women artists. In Mancoff's view, Victorian "Elaines" tend to be images of ideal but tragic maidenhood—chaste, devoted, beautiful, and doomed. Tennyson's "Elaine" can only be "the chaste, devoted lover, condemned to die with her love unrequited" or "the foolish girl who becomes a victim of her own dreams." She "lives and dies in isolation, defeated by the naive belief that she can achieve a world beyond her fate," destroyed by the conflict between her desires and her enclosed life.[150] While it would be difficult to argue that other major female figures in the Idylls—Guinevere, Vivien, and Enid—present more "positive images," Francis Strong's choice of subject—an image of female enmeshment in fictionalizing desires—is evocative. Two elements of Tennyson's "Elaine" and its history in images especially intrigue: the dangers for women of either looking or being the object of vision, and the theme of refused or chosen marriages.

Elaine is a double or mirror image of the Lady of Shalott.[151] The most famous depictions of the Lady of Shalott were, of course, by William Holman Hunt. His great painting of the Lady was not done until 1889–1892 but Hunt drew the Lady in 1850 and contributed the illustration for the 1857 Moxon edition of Tennyson's poem.[152] But beyond irony and beyond the overlapping iconographies of the Lady and Elaine—both were often depicted being ritualistically conveyed to their resting places on decorated barges—both stories depict sexual love as fatal to women and both deal with the perils of vision for women. Elaine misreads the meaning of signs while the Lady looks too directly at the world, but both are doomed by stories in which eroticism, knowledge, vision, and naïveté alike can kill.[153] The Lady and Elaine achieve their greatest aesthetic value as objects of vision at the point at which they can no longer look—at their deaths. But they cannot be reduced, any more than can Ellen Terry or Francis Strong, to figures of victimization. Elaine and, even more, the Lady are artistic makers: Elaine's needlework is principally an expression of longing for

Lancelot but the Lady has been more strongly read by Victorians and others as "an independent artist . . . self-sufficient, absorbed in creative activity."[154] Dorothy Mermin contends that the Lady of Shalott is an unusable figure for creative women because she "could only write her own name," but if Mermin's Lady is singular in meaning and nomination, Deborah Cherry points out that Elizabeth Siddall, "admired by men and women . . . for her beauty and codified in their drawings of her to-be-looked-at-ness," placed her Lady in a workroom filled "with evidence of past labour." Siddall's painting emphasizes the Lady's gaze, and the title of Cherry's work—Painting Women—slyly argues that "women looking and the look of women" are as enmeshed as the Lady in her tapestry.[155] Neither a story of women as simply commodified objects of subjugating male cultural practices nor a revisionary narrative of unfettered female creativity is adequate. Like women in life classes and in the worlds of art, Elaine and the Lady are at vague and mortal risk when they look or are looked at, but their relentless and varied reiterations in art and literature make clear that their stories cannot be reduced to their endings.

Recent scholars offer other tales of indirect female artistic agency. Dianne Sachko Macleod traces the careers of Eleanor Tong Coltart: like Francis Strong, Coltart was "in and out of the studios of pre-Raphaelite painters in her young days, she was one of them, and absorbed in their beautiful and poetic interpretations in art," and she remained close to the world of art by patronizing Pre-Raphaelite and Aesthetic artists.[156] Despite the asymmetry between male accomplishment and female spectacle in the title given her work, Carol Mavor sees Julia Margaret Cameron's photographs as collaborations in which the women before, as well as behind, the camera make meaning.[157] Emilia Dilke's texts too bring together female objectification and female agency, sometimes in cataclysmic narratives. The third page of French Engravers and Draughtsmen of the Eighteenth Century sardonically draws attention to images produced by self-serving men of culturally active women, including a plate of Mademoiselle Clairon sitting (clothed) to a life-drawing class of young men, while French Painters of the Eighteenth Century notes the vulnerability of successful women artists to the circulation of their names in "libellous" stories.[158] But these works also carefully and repeatedly include women's activities as patrons and employers (French Painters specifies that the Queen's intervention in support of women artists' claims could be decisive), contributors and conduits of money, property, and skills, and as amateur and professional artists. The status of (male and female) models is a surprisingly fraught topos: French Painters makes the regulation of models an example of the authoritarianism of the Academy, one of the "vexatious" and "exceptional exactions" that eventuated in the French Revolution, whose "rag[e and] violence" led to the Academy's closure.[159]

Emilia Dilke twice told scary stories that bring together female vision, sexuality, and power. She told her nieces a "Provençal story" in which an "unfortunate nobleman" married an "enchanting lady" who never slept. Her "gleaming eyes followed him wherever he moved, until the happy day when . . . a great writer and conversationalist came to see them. So good was his conversation that for a moment she took her eyes from her husband, who, springing through the window, plunged to his death in the neighbouring lake."[160] In Dilke's published "The Secret," male and female gazes meet and the female gaze is the more powerful. A little boy is haunted by a question of origins, "Whence does the river come?" When he matures, he leaves his home to find the Snow-maiden to ask her the secret, "hers alone." On his journey, he sees her in dreams, "radiant" and gloriously beautiful, "yet one thing was strange to him, though she smiled on him she saw him not, for her eyes were always closed"; he feels that if he cannot see her eyes, he will die. He finally reaches her cavern and enters to finds her; he is silent and in a "trance" as she "wooe[s] him with lovely sayings and signs." He lies in her arms but "still he spoke not and his eyes were as the eyes of one who sees not." Finally, he looks up to see her eyes are still closed and cries out in "agony" and "longing" for her gaze: "If I do not see thy eyes what good shall my life do me." She opens her eyes and "he knew all the ecstasy of love, and his soul fainted within him." His body is carried by the river back to his mother: the Snow-maiden "had taken his life, but . . . the light of her eyes was in his."[161] "The Secret" can obviously be read as a fantasy about male psychosexual fears and wishes, but if that is Dilke's tale's "secret," its images—like the story of Elizabeth Varley Mulready's obliteration of painted eyes that Dilke's tale evokes and alters, and like Dilke's Provençal tale—remain unsettling. Vision is both flooding ecstasy and annihilation for the man who seeks female beauty. His open eyes cannot see when they find the woman whose refused eyes have haunted his mind's eye, and the pre-ternatural ice woman is origin and end of the same quest. An object of desiring vision who chooses when to look, unlike the Lady of Shalott or Elaine, the Snow-maiden is not killed but kills and fulfills when sight and eros are joined.[162]

One more specific feature of Tennyson's Elaine can be read in narrower relation to Francis Strong's life. The "idyll" is a depiction of the (tragic and useless) love of a young and confined woman who "lives in fantasy" for a dangerous, prestigious and powerful man: Elaine loves Lancelot, a man with "marred . . . face" and "mood often like a fiend . . . of more than twice her years."[163] While I have suggested that Francis Strong's art education included schooling in the seductiveness of powerful, and sometimes "difficult" men, my point is not simply to prefigure Francis Strong's marriage to Mark Pattison. Rather, Francis Strong's choice of Elaine as a subject draws attention to a theme developed in the next chapter: the proliferation of stories about young women attracted to older men who offer access to cultural resources. Francis Strong's relationships with Mulready and Watts—men with complex personal histories in command of glamorous knowledges—brought teaching, affection, paternal spon-sorship, and sexualized aesthetic appreciation, and gave real if conditional resources to young women in formal and informal institutions of cultural creativity.

This story was rehearsed in Francis Strong's earlier relationships in Oxford, espe-cially her relationship to John Ruskin, and I want to briefly return to that relationship's narratives. Charles Dilke portrays Francis Pattison's "mature" relationship with Ruskin as one in which "before 1862," he was "the main influence in her life," but em-phasizes that she grew to "differ at every point" from his views.[164] In Charles Dilke's story, Francis Strong was a serious but feisty and argumentative student, and these qualities drew attention and tuition to her: she gained cultural resources—and aes-thetic and erotic interest—not because she was a good girl or dutiful daughter to a surrogate father but because she was a character. Ruskin ratifies this story in more threatened terms. Replying to an 1886 letter in which Emilia Dilke professed her enduring respect, he transformed young Francis Strong into a sexy, unsubordinated, dangerous and enticing figure, obstreperous and "beguiling": "I'm entirely delighted but more astonished than ever I was in my life—by your pretty letter and profession of discipleship—Why—I thought you always one of my terriblest—unconquera-blest—antagonisticest—Philistine—Delilah powers! I thought you at Kensington the sauciest of girls."[165] Not surprisingly, Ruskin wrote approvingly that this character's art studies would end when she married an eminent, older, charismatic, intellectually powerful, and publicly prestigious man.[166] The older Emilia Dilke defended herself by presenting her social reform work as compliant with Ruskin's teachings—showing herself as a good student after all—but still saucily insisted, " 'not doing as one is bid' is often the highest form of obedience in things spiritual . . . even if it is not done quite in your way."[167]

This invocation of the high call of "things spiritual" draws attention to another set of images of Francis Strong, in which she is represented as making herself into a religious figure and making her body into a meaningful form. As a student, Francis displayed a "rare combination of intense vitality, high spirits, and delight in life, with rigid devotion to a spiritual ideal, accompanied by constant self-discipline." Her South Kensington friends had to struggle to reconcile their perceptions of Francis as uncon-ventional and rebellious, nude-drawing, dissecting, and defiant of decorum to the point of "horrifying" some friends, with her devotion to an aestheticized, rigorous, self-denying, and hierarchical Christianity. Dilke and other friends were particularly disturbed by the fun-loving Miss Strong's "habit of doing penance for the smallest fault, imaginary or real, by lying for hours on the bare floor or on the stones, with her arms in the attitude of the cross.[168]

These images are carefully framed in Charles Dilke's "Memoir" but put pressure on Charles's ability to produce a wholly positive account of exceptionality. Dilke's account of Francis Strong as a visible and visionary figure at South Kensington is haunted by possible negative readings that it attempts to banish, and it recalls his treatment of Francis Strong's experiences of hallucinations and visions discussed in chapter one; his text worries, on both occasions, that it will give damning evidence. As with Dilke's framing of Francis's hallucinations, I cannot "read through" *accounts* of Francis Strong's religious practices to diagnose or interpret her actions or experiences as "hysteria," youthful rebellion, or simply posing, but only draw attention to per-sistent structures and analyze the work these representations do in their texts.

Charles Dilke's text had positioned its revelations of visions as evidence of Emilia Dilke's brave and truthful character; she "noted down, with her habitual minute care, all the apparitions of her life," and "she used to say, and even, with her invariable straightforwardness, often 'brutality' of intellect, to write, though most people do not write these things, that she had always been from time to time subject to hallucina-tions." Charles Dilke links Emilia Dilke's adult hallucinations to her imaginative writ-ing to reiterate her control and will: "She may have (a little wilfully, I think) allowed her mind to stray off in fantastic directions while composing her short stories." Dilke's memoir carefully surrounds the visions with explanations and assertions of Francis Strong's fundamental normality, and it fends off pathologization by allying the reader with Francis Strong: "With the exception of an early belief—*not infrequent in childhood*—in angel visits, the hallucinations were, *as with most of us*, invariably the result of over-work, and always *within the control of will*," and Dilke repeats that stress-induced hallu-cinations occur "with most of us."[169] Charles Dilke's memoir also placed the accounts of visions in the midst of a portrayal of the young Francis Strong as strongly religious and inclined to mysticism while asserting that these qualities were evidence of young Francis's strength, not weakness.

Charles Dilke had marked Francis's girlhood piety as so autonomous as to be misguided—she "scandalized her family" by praying for a Russian victory in the Crimean War "partly because she believed that the Russians were a more devoutly Christian people than were their British, French, and Italian, not to mention Turkish, foes"—and silently downplayed the friendship of individuals like Pauline Trevelyan and the Combes or Oxford's and even Iffley's status as a theological hotbed as influences on Francis's spiritual thought.[170] Dilke's accounts of Francis Strong at South Kensington reiterate these attributions of piety combined with intellectual independence. Representations of Francis Strong as a student could be read as giving evidence of the influence of her mother's religiosity as well as her father's art interests, but Charles Dilke detaches Francis's piety from family ties or peer pressure. She "developed for herself, when she came to London . . . an ultra-Puseyism concealed from those at home," and "there was no trace whatever . . . of any personal influence by any one of the family, of the clergy, or of friends, having led her in this direction." Dilke's account occludes Oxford's status as a center of Tractarian religiosity and theological debate and refuses to elaborate on Francis's daily attendance of "early Communion at Brompton Church," which might have suggested participation in a spiritual community in London, noting only that she attended "by herself."[171]

Dilke's memoir moves between figuring Francis Strong's moral self as praiseworthily exceptional and defusing any suggestion that she was not perfectly healthy and psychologically normal. Dilke's text cunningly positions his young self as a possible point of identification, both by letting readers see Francis's youthful extremism as interesting and impressive to young Charles's eyes and by emphasizing the peculiarity of Miss Strong's ultra–High Church zeal to his bewildered earlier self: Charles, as a young man, had considered Francis's views " 'bigotry.' " Yet Dilke defends against claims that Francis's "extreme" practices were signs of mental weakness: "there was not the faintest trace of the hysterical [in her actions]. Sanity of mind and judgement accompanied the daily practice of forms which in most people and to most people would seem to imply the contrary." Francis Strong's intense religiosity was a sign of sensitivity and seriousness, not "morbidity" or pathology, and Dilke emphasizes Francis's intellectual, as well as physical, self-discipline, detailing her theological studies in "the works of Augustine and of the Fathers"; "to the practices of confession and of penance she came, not by imitation—in defiance rather of all about her and of every influence—but by a strictly logical process, by calm thought, and by historical study."[172] Dilke's unpublished account stresses Francis Strong's intellectual rigor; "[she was] trained as few women are trained not only in the Puseyite practices [rasura: afterwards known as ritualism] but in the Ultra-High Church theories of the time, and possessed of, nay I might say equipped with a panoply of Tractarian philosophy."[173] Dilke's memoir insists that Francis Strong's religiosity at South Kensington was a temporary phase of youthful extremism but that it gave evidence of enduring character and aspirations that would later find more adequate expressions.

Dilke's account is at pains to stress Francis Strong's healthy "vitality," her vigorous unmorbidness as displayed in her "heterodox social views," "love of personal independence," and charm. He limns Francis's healthy humor and the "gaiety" central to her character; her games of trap bat and her moves beyond the set curriculum also show her "high" and "unconquerable" spirits. Moreover, Dilke gives a comic representation of Francis Strong's witty and honest defiance of authority on behalf of women's right to respect. When "a lieutenant of engineers" attached to the Government Schools lost his dog and posted a notice demanding that "the young lady who had taken away" his pet return it instantly, the women students were enraged by his presumption of their guilt. "All" the students felt "indignation," but Francis "alone had the courage, rebelliously, to express" it by erecting her own notice, referring to the lieutenant himself as a "sandy-haired puppy." Hauled before a "tribunal," she admitted authorship and looked with wordless scorn on the member of the committee who noted, "To do her justice, Miss Strong has not disguised her hand."[174] Francis's speechless figure displays her moral qualities, healthy self-respect and courage, balancing the image of a fanatic prostrate on a stone floor.

Charles Dilke's memoir ratifies his account of Francis Strong by quotations from other private texts like Frances Hullah's letters, but its most notable and strategic salvation of Francis Strong's religious views and practices as signs of her exceptional merit is its invocation of a highly public text. Dilke argues that, however misguided her particular theology might be, Francis's seriousness and ardor were endorsed by George Eliot and give evidence of Francis's status as a model for Dorothea Brooke. "It was of Emilia Strong that George Eliot was thinking when she wrote, 'Dorothea knew many passages of Pascal's "Pensées" and of Jeremy Taylor by heart,' and of her, too, as she was at 'the schools' in 1859, praying as 'fervidly as if she thought herself living in the time of the Apostles,' with 'strange whims of fasting like a Papist, and of sitting up at night to read old theological books.' " Charles Dilke enlists many stories to guarantee Francis Strong's honesty, high spirits, sense of justice, and sincere and original spiritual sensibility, but this is his trump card: Francis Strong's "rigid devotion to a spiritual ideal" marked her out to a prestigious novelist of moral life as a bearer of special qualities and destiny.[175]

E. F. S. Pattison/Emilia Dilke's own later writings could be sharply critical of female spiritual enactments. In E. F. S. Pattison's 1879 The Renaissance of Art in France, Valentina Balbiani's faults include "the easy anodyne of an enervating mysticism," and Emilia Dilke's late essay "Of Love and Sorrow" damns modes of spiritual self-aestheticization to which women appear especially prone. Dilke's essay suggests that Thomas à Kempis's The Imitation of Christ—which Charles Dilke's "Memoir" includes in Francis Strong's reading and to which I will return—may seduce the weak, with "an alluring charm," into theatrical displays of masochism and narcissism. "Its constant cry of 'Come. Come and talk of thyself with God!' [offers] . . . infinite possibilities of present satisfaction in the perpetual contemplation of [one]self illumined by the vision of eternal bliss." The Imitation's danger is illustrated by a contemptuous invocation of "Madame Desbordes-Valmore," whose "delicate and sincere" soul is continually proffering its anguish in an "incessant refrain" of "tears"; Desbordes-Valmore's picturesque tableaux of piety exempify morally dangerous feminine religious enactments.[176] The texts of Charles Dilke and others about Francis Strong's religious performances, as well as other accounts of her figure, mark South Kensington as a space in which the significatory possibilities of aestheticized bodies, especially women's bodies, were central. The possibilities and dangers of women's aestheticization reappear in later texts by and about Francis Strong's later incarnations. South Kensington is a microcosm of long-running arguments in the nineteenth century and a premonition of themes that appear and reappear in the texts of this life, including this one.

Invisible Women: Ishmael and Katie

When she ended her art training and returned to Oxford, Francis returned to her family home in Iffley and soon after became engaged to Mark Pattison. One of the few surviving texts written by Francis Strong casts a different light on figures of her youthful self as confidently exceptional and unconventional. The family-defying Puseyite art student, writing to her sister Rosa soon after her engagement, offered another way of naming her soon-to-be-discarded self, neither Francesca, *Goldkind*, Elaine, or Delilah. She told Rosa, "I feel now as if I loved and knew you more than I ever thought possible to me. I don't know how it was but what an Ishmaelitish position I always held at home & amongst my nearest relations during my vacations from London."[177] Becoming engaged was an escape from the marginality of exceptionality. Francis Strong entered the ranks of "ordinary" women, women who married, even if she found many ways of being an art worker after her marriage as an amateur, patron, cicerone, critic, and historian. A much later 1884 letter by Mrs. Mark Pattison more painfully evokes her student days in South Kensington. "Full of pity" as her husband was dying, Mrs. Pattison's letter wistfully recalls her "young days under the horse chestnuts at South Kensington, when I loved and trusted life and every living soul, and all seemed to have some good gift for me." But Mrs. Pattison's text swiftly subordinates her to the exceptional man to whom she was married: "If one life is to give way to the other, I feel sure it should be mine; his is worth much more—it represents much more, of much greater value to the world than mine."[178]

This letter records Francis Strong Pattison's fluency in the language of female renunciation and recalls an education in pleasure; she displays herself as a poignant object in a pictorialized setting and remembers an ability to imagine futures. But if Francis Strong returned to Oxford and marriage, her plot did not, in fact, end on this dying fall of youth, loveliness, and high spirits chastised or lost. Francis Strong Pattison did not die in 1884; Mark Pattison did. Francis Pattison was writing Francis Strong's story while already looking forward to becoming Emilia Dilke. Once widowed, moreover, Mrs. Pattison offered some of her late husband's money to the Royal Academy art school to found a scholarship for women art students, and she withdrew her offer when the authorities would not agree to her demand that the women be given exactly the same course of instruction as that provided to men, including life-drawing.[179] Francis Strong's first marriage may have brought her to a sad recollection of her art studies, but it ended with an unchastened claim for women's access to prestigious cultural resources.

Another marriage story, laid next to Francis Strong's, also illustrates how dominant was marriage—even if punctuated by temporary rejection and enlivened by the eventual embrace of exceptional men—as a plot outcome for young women, despite local differences and despite the "modernization" of some gender cultures and women's educations. It also shows how gender made very different narratives for men and women and how insufficient are stories of personal exceptionality, and it tells a sadder story of the mutability of names than Francis Strong's movement through even such dangerous nominations as Francesca, Delilah, and Ishmael.

Charles Dilke's texts represented his family as a site of metropolitan liberal culture, art, emotional nurturance, and intellectual heterosociality presided over by male heads of household. This story culminates in Dilke's accounts of his first marriage, as Dilke's texts present his marriage to Katherine Sheil as an extension of family and neighborhood relationships and construct an emotional history of unconventional romance and intellectual-political comradeship between men and women. "Katie" Sheil was the orphaned daughter of an army captain and his Devonshire wife; she lived near the Dilkes in Sloane Street with an older woman friend, Louisa Courtenay.[180] According to Charles, he had known Katie for some time but their friendship had foundered in 1869; "we had quarrelled, as she generally managed to quarrel with her friends from her violent temper and unwillingness, in spite of the possession of strong opinions on many points, to brook contradiction." Charles does not flatter Katie in conventional terms; she was "exquisitely lovely [although] she had features which would ruin most reputations for beauty . . . her voice was perfect." She had extraordinary powers of conversation and a "wonderful power of mimicry," and many "people were afraid of her . . . and she was known to have a violent temper. She was accused by her many enemies of laziness . . . of pride, of violence, and of mercilessness in ridicule . . . She was extravagant, and spent her capital as income—chiefly on horses and dress." A gifted singer, she was "extreme[ly] attractive" with a "perfect taste in dress," "a marked figure in every room." Katie also had a past:

> [Her fragile health was] largely owing to a disappointment in love of which I knew. Her great talent and extraordinary powers of sarcasm made her the terror of the ordinary 'dancing idiot,' and her love affair had been with a man old enough to be her father, a handsome man of great distinction, who was either married or believed to be by some; a fact which caused others to interfere and stop a half-engagement.[181]

Katie's strong-mindedness swung round in Charles's favor when he came under attack for expressing republican views on a speaking tour in the North and in the House of Commons. English republicanism had been at its high tide in 1871. Monarchical sentiment was revived by the Prince of Wales's recovery from typhoid fever in early 1872 and Dilke encountered both established opposition and a new groundswell of antirepublicanism. This temporary position as an embattled progressive brought emotional rewards: "The attacks on me in November, 1871 . . . led to an expression of sympathy on [Miss Sheil's] part," forgiveness for his earlier transgressions, and a marriage in January 1872.[182]

Charles and Katie, in Charles's account, understood their marriage as an act of progressive modernity; "we both of us had a horror of the ordinary forms of wedding ceremonies," and he wrote self-mockingly to a friend, "A real marriage, in a real church, with a real parson, and the whole thing! Is it not dreadful?" Most of Katie's family opposed her marrying "the republican." Charles's account places the marriage outside the conventional categories of romance; he quotes Laura Courtenay, "who knew us both extremely well": " 'A very suitable marriage. You are neither of you in love with one another, but you will get on admirably together.' [She] was, perhaps, at this time not far wrong." Charles felt "a profound respect of Miss Sheil's talent and a high admiration of her charm and beauty" and thought "she had more liking than love for me."[183] While Charles's texts construct his marriage as first an intellectual and political partnership, a microcosm of the pleasures of heterosocial culture, they quickly move to establish his and Katie's capacity for passionate emotion. The partners were soon behaving well within the roles of husband and wife in love; a surviving note from Katie Dilke addresses Charles as "my love Bird . . . the little one" from his "kittie," in the Dilke family tradition of joking, frequently infantilizing, personifications.[184]

Marriage also brought independence and social position and established Charles as an adult in a household that still included his grandfather and father. It gained Katie freedom from chaperonage; she became the female head of household since Charles moved his grandmother out of 76 Sloane Street into a nearby house. Charles later claimed "we were so wrapped up in ourselves that I have no doubt we were spoken of as selfish," but Katie was also an active political and cultural hostess. Charles's file of nonpolitical correspondence during his first marriage is filled with records of invitations, seating arrangements, and thank-you notes from parliamentary colleagues, writers, artists, and social reformers, including Robert Browning, Eliza Lynn Linton, Millicent Garrett Fawcett, the American journalist Kate Field, George Eliot, the ballerina Marie Taglioni and the actress Ristori.[185] Katie accompanied Charles in his travels to Paris—they made a pilgrimage to meet George Sand—and shared his Francophilia: "a novel feature at some of Lady Dilke's evenings was the production of French comedies . . . [the] house was a great meeting-place for those who loved and knew France and the French tongue," and they employed a refugee Communard as a cook. The Dilkes' social triumph was completed when Charles published *The Fall of Prince Florestan of Monaco*, a self-mocking satire on English Radical idealism and French secular republicanism.[186]

In short, Charles's texts, public and private, construct his first marriage as continuous with the cultures in which he had been educated: modernity, aesthetic culture, Francophilia, performative pleasures, liberalism, and heterosociality mingle, to the delight of men and women, fostering happy domesticity and public improvement. Never aggressively bohemian, the Dilkes' social worlds were politically radical and culturally heterogeneous within the boundaries of bourgeois reformism and respectability; the "communist cook with a carving knife," Katie's irreverence, or Charles's increasingly discreet republicanism added piquant notes to a privileged realm of solid wealth, taken-for-granted access to public realms of politics and art, and educated responsibility for social leadership.[187] Within these worlds, women could be clever, artistic, and charmingly unconventional, and men could be emotional, aesthetically sensitive, and playful. But Charles Dilke's ongoing public life displays gender differences within this heterosocial world. After leaving South Kensington Art School, he had attended Cambridge, where he played a prominent role in the Union and University politics, studied with Henry Fawcett, and rowed for the University. He then traveled around the world, wrote his first book—*Greater Britain*—and returned to London to embark upon a career in Parliament.[188] Obviously, youthful exceptionality's fulfillment in public accomplishment is always highly contingent, and equally obviously, Dilke was by no means typical even of young Englishmen of his class. But his career moved through institutions that systematically and explicitly excluded women. If all three of these young people—Charles Dilke, Katie Sheil, and Francis Strong—were exceptionally privileged, exceptionality for women culminated in the making of marriages through which access to public life was gained. The making of an exceptional marriage did not always preclude continuing intellectual or cultural work—Katie and Charles Dilke's guest lists include women with public careers as writers, actresses, performers, apart from or in addition to marriage—but marriage was the principal institutional form in which young and gifted bourgeois women could achieve and enhance their cultural capital. Other institutions—higher education, professions, and formal political life—remained the preserves of men.

The labors of heterosexual domesticity between women and men were also unevenly distributed, and not only in the daily assumption that it was women's fundamental responsibility. Domesticity included physical reproduction, and even in enlightened, Radical Chelsea, women's reproductive roles often killed them. Katie had a stillborn son in September 1873; "with a presentiment of death" she became pregnant again in 1874. Her son, Charles Wentworth Dilke, the fifth of that name, was born and she died on 20 September; she was 32.[189] Katie Dilke was not unmourned—Charles broke down with grief and he represented her vividly in his texts, and the Dilke papers include many letters of commiseration—but like most people and certainly most women, Katie Dilke would soon become a ghost, enduring in some memories but not preserved in public achievements.[190] More unusually, Katie's name would become strangely ghostly. Known and memorialized as Lady Dilke, in 1885 she was succeeded in that name by a woman who became a well-known public figure and who periodically returns to notice in history and fiction. When "Lady Dilke" appears in print in the twentieth century, Katie Dilke is virtually never signified. Exceptional in resources, Katie Sheil and Francis Strong were represented as exceptional in talent, intellect, attractiveness, desires, and willingness to be unconventional. They shared the choice of marriage to public men over careers as single women; eventually they shared a name. But Katie Dilke wrote no books, led no organizations, spoke on few platforms, and performed in no courtrooms—not because she was not talented or politically skilled or committed to public life but because she died young. Eclipsed by the name of her husband in her lifetime, after her death she was eclipsed again by a woman with whom she had much in common but who, fundamentally, had better luck.

3

MAKING A MARRIAGE

Scene: Dr. and Mrs. Edwin Hatch's drawing-room, Oxford, 1861

Enter Mark Pattison "with his somewhat hawklike nose pointing even more than usual towards the earth": Mrs. Hatch, I am a fool.

MRS. HATCH: Oh, Mr. Rector, that is impossible.

PATTISON: Yes, I am, and what is more, I am an old fool; I have just proposed to Miss Strong and she has accepted me.

—A. H. Sayce, *Reminiscences*

The engagement of forty-eight year-old Mark Pattison to twenty-one-year-old Francis Strong took place soon after Francis returned from London on completing her art studies.[1] The marriage ceremony was performed in Iffley Church on September 10, 1861, by William Tuckwell, the bride's brother-in-law.[2] No account by Mark or Francis of their courtship, engagement, and wedding survives, but the marriage entered the folklore of Oxford, and contemporaries made sense of it in conversation and letters.[3] The palpable shock with which the engagement was greeted in Oxford may entice us into trusting the normalizing explanations that circulated during and after the Pattisons' lives, although the marriage's semipublic status as a failure meant that stories of its making tended to take sides, especially after the circulation of novels purportedly based on the Pattison ménage. *Middlemarch*, after all, was published in 1872, well before Mark Pattison's 1884 death. The scandal that coincided with Emilia Strong Pattison's second marriage also inflected accounts of the marriage.

Yet even the most cursory eyewitness story, retrospectively recounted, was shaped by narrative convention. The historical marriage before and apart from its later novelistic and anecdotal representations was made by stories and the playing of parts. Before marrying, Mark Pattison and Francis Strong had to imagine plots that might culminate in a wedding; these plots were not the same. Marriage stories presume difference—the difference of gender. As Marcia Pointon remarks, any "representation of a marriage" must contend with the rigidity of certain norms: marriage "requires the partners to be of the opposite sex and, unlike commercial contracts, the parties are limited in the terms they can introduce into the agreement . . . this 'coming together' in the sight of the Church and State serves to underline and reinforce gender distinctions. Marriage involves very different social and legal requirements, rights and expectation for a man than for a woman [and] is the dominant state for a woman but not, necessarily, for a man."[4] Nor is it only the tight constraints of the legal discourses of marriage as a contract that limits available stories of marriage: modern marriage stories must also define themselves within or against the conventions of romantic narrative—that is, they must speak of love, whether to affirm or exclude the role of passionate emotion in determining marital unions.

Both partners in the Pattison marriage narrated their choices and confinements. Each contended with conventions that authorized and contained their ability to depict themselves as victims and agents, fools and fooled, lovers and betrayed, bodies and souls. In the scene recounted above, Mark Pattison inserts himself in and, by his sardonic awareness, distances himself from the mocking tradition of ill-fated May–December romances. Mark was neither old nor a fool, nor was the age difference between the partners unusual per se, although even one scholarly account renders the forty-eight-year-old Mark "elderly."[5] What stood out in the Pattison nuptials was the contrast between Mark's persona of age and bitterness and the romantic story he was enacting. The fit between Mark's self-narration and literary convention is affirmed not only by the skill with which Rhoda Broughton parodied Mark Pattison by skillful working of the trope of wizened age married to blooming youth—with a hint of male impotence—in her vengeful Oxford roman-à-clef, Belinda, but by the fact that Pattison, calling at Broughton's house soon after the novel's publication, had himself announced as "Professor Forth," the name of "his" character.[6]

Such narratives of the Pattison marriage—overtly fictional and purportedly scholarly—gesture toward but fail to examine fully the specificities within which the marriage was contracted and endured. In this chapter, I attempt to expand the stories of this marriage and to examine these marriage stories as stories, produced, reproduced, and revised. I examine three sets of stories: Pattison stories, Oxford stories, and Dilke stories. In all, knowledge is imbricated with desire; sexuality, books, and status circulate. Violence and silence compete in the Pattison family stories, which include horror stories of Gothic family life in which men and women love each other to the death, bitterly contend to punish themselves and each other, and suffer in mind, body, and spirit. I reconnect these Pattison stories of childhood, family, and education to structures of class and gender, and then tell the engagement of Mark Pattison and Francis Strong as a Pattison family story. I argue that the Pattison family's gendered division of education and prestige were ratified by the local stories of Oxford during a time in which Oxford was busily constructing stories of heterosexual domesticity as a right for male intellectuals, in which educated men were entitled to the love and subordination of exceptional women whose exceptionality would enhance the institutions they entered. Yet although Oxford women's stories have no secure institutional place, Oxford's stories of marriage included not only the legitimation of male access to the resources of private life but covert female access to the resources of intellectual life. This theme is carried into an analysis of the Dilkes' stories of marriage. In some such stories, as in the Pattison family stories, violence, hatred, and self-hatred erupt, and marriage is a potentially murderous strategy by which women reach for knowledge and resources. Through these retellings and rereadings, a historical account will emerge of how marriage stories may move across the conventions of Victorian fiction and the institutions—physical, legal, and cultural—of Victorian society.

Pattison Stories

Mark Pattison did not write a story of his marriage. His Memoirs ignore it, his diary for 1861 is missing, probably destroyed by him, and his surviving letters are discontinuous.[7] Others' accounts of the marriage have tended to represent Mark Pattison's interest in Francis Strong as natural, both as an emotional and erotic attraction and as a desire for power. Vivian Green assumes that Mark Pattison's desires were triggered by Francis's return to Iffley, presenting Mark as "wish[ing] to be loved . . . [t]here can be no doubt that he was momentarily delighted with this elegant and intelligent young woman," so different from "the sedate and dull daughters of the Oxford bourgeoisie" with her "élan . . . distaste for convention, a capacity for being educated, even moulded to ideal companionship." Green also suggests that Mark's matrimonial ambitions were only waiting for his accession to the Rectorship of Lincoln in January 1861, when he became eligible to marry without forfeiting his place in Oxford; James Glucker presents a similar theory and uses Middlemarch to underwrite his interpretation.[8] Betty Askwith too argues that Pattison "presumably chose [Francis Strong] because he thought she could be moulded to his requirements," and cites fiction as proof, noting the relevant passages of Middlemarch, Robert Elsmere, Belinda, and Vices Français.[9] Green and Askwith echo most of the letters of congratulation written to Mark Pattison by friends and colleagues upon his marriage. Frederick Shaw, a vicar and former student of Pattison's, applauds Mark's having "availed [himself] of that ordinance of God whereby He provides a help meet for a man," and quotes scripture on the husband's position as head of the house; others tactfully note that Mark must be preening himself on having won such a young and lovely wife.[10] Mark Pattison's interest in Francis Strong has thus been naturalized within models in which male desires for love and power are entwined. I want, however, to defer an account of Mark Pattison's marriage to consider other Pattison stories.

Mark Pattison's life before his marriage has been written by him and others as a story of three tragedies: his loss of happy family life, his loss of faith, and his loss of the 1851 Rectorial election in Lincoln College. In the twentieth century, John Sparrow, Green, and Jo Manton have variously told Mark Pattison's story as one in which childhood and youthful suffering, as well as adult disappointments, produce a tragic figure, a man rent and torn by internal pain, albeit also a man able to dominate, control, and injure others.[11] But the sympathy the reader ought to feel for Mark Pattison is not simply that for a pain-wracked child and young man. Rather, understanding Mark Pattison as a scarred survivor of family life, spiritual anguish, and professional betrayal has been joined to a larger project: defending Mark Pattison against the charge of Casaubonism. That is, while Mark Pattison's fame finally rested as much on his proclaimed dedication to learning alone and the book he did not finish as it did on the essays and books, including Isaac Casaubon, 1559–1614 (1875), that he did publish, Pattison's life-writers still struggle to extricate his reputation from the scandal of Middlemarch and especially any suggestion that Pattison was flawed by scholarly or other impotence.[12] Such writers thus inscribe Mark's childhood in a larger story which, paradoxically, elicits empathy for the familial pains of childhood and youth but contains the implications of adult domestic entanglements.

The Pattison family story has been told as a family "horror story" and compared to the Brontes and Barretts.[13] Mark Pattison's version in the posthumously published *Memoirs* (edited by his widow) was considered appallingly frank in 1885, but it is tame by comparison with historians' versions.[14] The Gothic childhood of Mark Pattison and his sisters—where horror resides within the domestic and familial sphere, and madness and violence emerge from corrupt power—seems to expose both monstrous deviations from, and the normative prison of, family life.[15] Within this central narrative, other stories clamor emotional demands: *Bildungsromane* of self-discovery; escapes from patriarchal authority and from the claims of women; spiritual and material re-creations of self; frightening secret narratives of madness and martyrdom. In my accounts of Strong and Dilke childhoods, I emphasized the construction of family stories, especially stories of exceptionality, and I challenge the adequacy of a rhetoric of exceptionality for the Pattison family as well. Writing the Pattison stories as horror maintains their status as extreme and confines them to extremity. The Pattison story becomes a case study of gruesome psychopathology—"Madness on the Moors." In this tale, the marriage of Mark Pattison and Francis Strong takes a place as evidence of a repetition-compulsion in Mark Pattison's relationships. But rather than simply linking Mark Pattison's familial, professional, and marital dramas, I read texts of his life for social and cultural meanings. Family stories are *social and historical*—shaped, legitimated, and contested in discourse and material relations. The Strongs' and the Dilkes' family stories may be read as accounts of privilege and cosmopolitan movement while the Pattison stories tell of violent imprisonment in a grim Yorkshire vicarage, but all these accounts of childhood speak of the determinative power of local communities and family narratives.

As in the Strong stories, the relations between siblings are illuminating. As Leonore Davidoff notes, sibling relations are a site for learning gender in all its seductions and violences; "the sexual division of labour, from tasks to emotions, can be rehearsed by brothers and sisters," and in large families, siblings may enact or refuse pseudo-parental roles in highly gendered ways. Yet these relations are not reducible to the "displacement of a deeper oedipal pattern" or "pale reflections of the central parental drama"; sibling relations are structurally ambiguous, since "siblings occupy the boundaries between familial and the non-familial, possible strangers."[16] Reading stories of sisters and brothers, as well as fathers and mothers, highlights the pervasiveness and differentiation of peril in the familial and the mentorial, the spiritual and the domestic; family rhetorics of status, selfhood, desire, and sacrifice; class, gender, and God.

The Pattisons' proliferation, within narrow spaces, of narratives—in letters, diaries, and other documents—offers a fragmented but compelling archive of representations of imagined and repudiated subjectivities. But I also want to draw attention to Pattison stories I cannot tell, silences that also destabilize the genre of accounts of exceptionally awful family life. Pattison stories offer multiple pleasures: the thrill of horror; self-congratulation at our own ability to bear the horrors we read about; the pleasure of "knowledge"; and the pleasure of believing we can decode stories for their "true" content. Reading terrible tales may be perversely easier than recognizing the irrecoverability of horrors that have not circulated in stories we can claim as hard—difficult, solid, negotiable—knowledge. Gothic offers thrills (tellingly, a film based on Jo Manton's account of the Pattisons, *Sister Dora*, is described in one movie guide as "adapted from a popular romance novel") and it may be easier to think about lurid eruptions of emotion and physicality than about day-to-day pain and mute not-knowing-differently. As Thomas Hardy's great novel of education, desire, and Oxford recognized, anguish is not always or even often interrupted by rescuers or by encounters of witness that mark out a moving plot. When Jude Fawley is alone and aching, "someone might have come along . . . But nobody did come, because nobody does."[17] Like the Strongs and Dilkes, the Pattisons produced publicly renowned individuals, Mark Pattison and "Sister Dora." Other Pattison stories have barely been preserved. The career of Frank Pattison, the "other" neglected Pattison son, as customs officer-cum-newspaperman seems as straightforwardly untouched by horror as an entry in *Who's Who*; he married an Oxford woman named Margaret Lever, became a loyal friend to Mark Pattison's wife, and left no public writings. He made no claim on history. I cannot tell his story. Frank Pattison's life as a *bourgeois gentilhomme*, like the defiant escape from familial domesticity into domestic service of Elizabeth Pattison and the immurement of Jane Pattison caring for her younger, "mad" sister, would be unknown but for their famous siblings. We can barely see, we might not have seen at all, the cruelty and loss locked in seemingly unexceptional lives.

Hauxwell Rectory: Class and Madness

The Pattison family did not move to Hauxwell Rectory until 1825, when Mark Pattison was twelve years old, but this country vicarage dominates Pattison stories.[18] Hauxwell's overriding characteristic of isolation especially formed the experience of the younger Pattison children. In the North Riding of Yorkshire, Hauxwell was a parish of perhaps three hundred people in the 1830s; insofar as it is near anyplace, it is near Catterick Camp; the nearest town is Richmond, about eight miles away, and it is still small and relatively remote. No railway approached until decades after Mark Pattison's birth; the journey to London by coach took three days.[19] But Hauxwell Rectory's isolation was not simply a function of geography; the paterfamilias, the Reverend Mark James Pattison, believed his family ought to be increasingly socially isolated from all around them except in relationships in which Pattison superiority was unquestioned. Mark Pattison's *Memoirs* naturalized his father's desires as "the instinct of good society" but scorned them, mockingly recalling that Mark James "liked to live with gentlemen, and to know what was going on the in upper world. His acquaintance with the peerage was accurate; he must have read *Debrett* . . . more than the Bible."[20] In his later years Mark James passed his time in reading and rereading obituaries in the *Gentleman's Magazine*.[21] Yet simply saying that the elder Pattison was a snob is to reduce to personal moral failing a complex and multigenerational social context of local, regional, and national status, property, and privilege that produced confidence in merit and bitterness at exclusion.

Mark James Pattison was born in 1788 in Plymouth, the son of a naval officer who had risen to the rank of Captain by merit but owed his original entry into the Royal Military Academy and subsequent commission to patronage. Mark James's grandfather had been a respectable but struggling farmer who gave up the struggle against debts and floods to join the navy. Both father and grandfather died before Mark James was ten; nothing is known of his early education nor of his family life with his mother (whose name is never given although she lived until 1843) and his two sisters. His family's recent rise to settled middle-class status was consolidated and extended by Mark James's arrival at Oxford in 1806. A member of Brasenose College, he was ordained deacon and priest in 1811 and 1812, and with the status of gentleman, clergyman, and scholar, his future career promised to continue and better his family's status. The rest of his life was spent in Yorkshire: after his ordination in 1812, he was appointed curate of Hornby, near Bedale in the North Riding, where he lived with his mother, his widowed sister, Mary Meadows, and Mary's daughter Philippa. Also in 1812, Mark James married Jane Winn of Prior House, Richmond; she was nineteen and he was twenty-four. Jane's father, a jeweller, had been Mayor of the Borough and she was an heiress by local standards, with a small dowry secured as her personal property.[22] She was relatively well educated at a boarding school near Doncaster; her family was probably one of upright Evangelical burghers. Certainly the newlywed couple were a respectable match, and Mark James was soon awarded the post of Chaplain to the Duke of Leeds. The Reverend and Mrs. Pattison were granted a parsonage house in the grounds of Hornby Castle where Mark Pattison was born in October 1813. Five sisters followed: Jane (1816), Eleanor (1817), Mary (1819), Frances (1821), and Grace (1822).[23] Mark Pattison's texts imply that his father's tenure as the Duke's chaplain, when Mark James was treated with familiarity and respect only slightly tinged by condescension, was responsible for his father's later bitterness and snobbish contempt for his surroundings. In Mark's account, Mark James's years as chaplain united with his years at Oxford to form his ideas of his own personal dignity and rising social status.[24] But in 1825 Mark James accepted the living of Hauxwell, perhaps having decided that he had no hope of succeeding to the regular living of Hornby. At Hauxwell, Jane Pattison bore Anna (1824), Elizabeth (1825), Sarah (1827), Rachel (1829), Dorothy Wyndlow [Dora] (1834), and Francis Winn [Frank] Pattison (1832). The Pattison family was thus composed of twelve surviving children, the first and last of whom were boys. Jane Winn Pattison was forty-one and Mark James was forty-six or forty-seven at the time of Frank's birth; Mark James then wrote his son Mark, "your Mother . . . does not regain her strength with the rapidity of former times."[25]

The Pattison ascent was typical of respectable families assisted by the luck of fortuitous gifts and patronage at crucial moments in the late eighteenth century, but the twists that the family tale later took expose the importance of continued good fortune, the fragility of such newly constructed identities, and the tenacious, even cruel, strength of the desire for higher class status. Despite his strong religious views, no account suggests that Mark James took much satisfaction in the performance of his clerical duties; the Church was a career. While still hoping for further advancement himself, Mark James projected a family narrative into the future in which his elder son would carry forward his own dreams. According to Mark Pattison, he was marked out from the moment of his birth to repeat, redeem, and surpass his father's triumphs; no destiny but Oxford and ordination was considered, and to this end his father lavished affection and tuition on him.[26] The Reverend Pattison was happy educating his son, telling stories of his own gentlemanly life at Oxford, and in 1830 making a grand expedition with his wife and son to settle the details of Mark's entry into Oxford, where Mark was dispatched in 1832, to Oriel—a choice made for its "gentlemanly" as well as its intellectual merits.[27]

Stories about the Pattison years at Hornby and the early years at Hauxwell are not all darkly unhappy, although the social isolation of the family increased during the 1820s and 1830s, as a strong Methodist presence shrank Mark James's congregations. Mark James's hopes for preferment diminished too, as rich livings went to the sons of the local squirarchy, an intermarried fox-hunting gentry to which Mark James had no entry. The geographical isolation of Hauxwell precluded frequent participation in bourgeois town life, which might have assuaged injuries to pride caused by the condescension of the gentry and involved the family in more far-reaching Evangelical intellectual and social life. Mark James's views about his children's class superiority to their surroundings intensified the enclosed quality of their family life; they were not allowed to play with the village children and were dependent on each other's company and that of their nearby cousin Philippa.[28]

This isolation would become more extreme in the mid-1830s, when Mark James famously opposed any of his daughters marrying, but the edict was continuous with earlier figurations of the Pattisons as better than their surroundings. Mark James's objection to marriage seems to have rested not on religious grounds but on his contempt for the men in the neighborhood whom his daughters might have wed, respectable, but not genteel, farmers. Rage and class-consciousness were a cycle: the only nearby family of modest gentility through whom Mark James's daughters might have met men he considered suitable had been estranged by being attacked from the pulpit in his sermons. When Eleanor defied her father in 1853 at the age of 36 and became engaged to Frederick Mann, a local parson, Mark James attempted to convince Mann and his father to break the engagement on the grounds that the Pattison family was marked by hereditary insanity but also sneered to Eleanor that the marriage was an abandonment of her class status: "He ordered her to fetch a bucket and scrubbing brush from the back kitchen . . . pointed and said, 'There is your dowry; there is your future.' "[29]

The exact progress of Mark James Pattison's emotional states are unclear—in Mark Pattison's rendition, the deterioration began after his own departure for Oxford—but he seems to have gradually become frighteningly prone to violent temper and depression. On 7 April 1833 Jane Winn Pattison wrote Mark, "How to convey to you a correct idea of your father's mind, I know not." Anger and irritability dominated Mark James's moods and particularly "toward yr aunt, Mr Seward, Philippa, and yourself it is constant."[30] In June of 1834 Mark James was considered to have "gone mad" and to require medical attention. Jane Winn Pattison turned to the family doctor, Richard Bowes, and to other Evangelical friends and relations for advice, and eventually consulted Dr. Thomas Simpson, a "mad-doctor" in York associated with the County Asylum. Dr. Simpson recommended the removal of Mark James Pattison to Acomb House, a private madhouse run by H. B. Hodgson in York. Jo Manton has noted the irony of the Reverend Pattison's placement at Acomb House, rather than to the Quaker York Retreat, pioneer of more gentle treatment.[31] The Retreat, however, would not have been considered for an Anglican clergyman; instead, Mark James was placed in a cell he later described as "the most noisome den to which a clergyman of the Church of England and that clergyman a gentleman could have been consigned."[32] Madness denied Mark James those respectable statuses to which he most desperately clung.

Acomb House probably resembled other madhouses of the time—at worst, with inmates cuffed and chained in bare cells, floors covered with urine-saturated straw, and "treatment" consisting primarily of violent physical shocks, and at best a regime of squalid and barren confinement.[33] But Mark James blamed his family not only for having confined him but for the conditions to which he was subjected; they had not adequately sought alternatives of "kind and soothing measures [which] would have saved me much pain" and spared him "the filth, meanness, noise and cant to which I was so long and so unnecessarily exposed." His lack of deserved status continued to torment him, and he developed a theory that the family's actions in confining him had doomed a career that had still held hope; "by this *fatal, fatal* step I have been deprived of every prospect in life however glittering that prospect was." He vented his rage and humiliation in threats against Jane Winn Pattison, whom he never forgave for committing him. When his threats led doctors to advise against her visiting him, he charged "that she had been 'too dainty to enter his 'loathsome dungeon.' "[34]

Mark James Pattison remained in Acomb House from June until 19 November 1834. Despite his release, however, he was judged still too violent and angry to be allowed to return to Hauxwell. Instead, Mark Pattison was summoned from Oxford. Father and son stayed in rented rooms in York until April of 1835; discussion of this period in Mark's published *Memoirs* is mutilated by ellipses. Mark James's undoubted suffering in the madhouse exacerbated Jane Winn Pattison's guilt. In an anguished letter to her son, while he was with his father in York, she wondered if she was responsible for his madness and if she had had any right to confine him, but confessed that she dreaded her husband's homecoming, especially in winter's isolation of Hauxwell. This pain and guilt may have been a heavy burden on Mark, pulled to respond to his mother while overwhelmed by his father's alternations between pathetic dependence and furious outbursts at the perfidy of the rest of his family.[35]

Mark James returned to Hauxwell in April of 1835, "cured." He continued to believe that his wife and daughters were in some way conspiring against him and he sank into dark moods of bitter recrimination with periodic outbursts of violence. Jane Winn Pattison never committed him again; she bore her husband's rages for twenty-five more years. The younger children had little memory of their father before his madness; Frank Pattison was less than six months old when his father was confined, and Dora's first memories of her father were of his silent scowling for hours and his pacing up and down the avenue of trees outside the house, "shouting abuse at anyone who came near him."[36] Mark James's wife continued to construe her Christian duty as obedience to his wishes. Jane Winn Pattison's behavior in relation to her husband was, within an Evangelical framework, heroic. She recommended to her children "two lines from my favourite poet, 'Improve the kind occasion, understand/ A Father's frown, & kiss his chastening hand.' "[37]

Gender and Education

In Mark Pattison's version of the Hauxwell story, the years of his own presence form a golden age of family life. Hauxwell Rectory had been a hothouse of love, attention, and assurance of his own importance, albeit one dominated by his father's ideal plan for his future. His texts often decry the intellectual impoverishment of local society, but Mark nonetheless lamented the loss of "a cosy and patriarchal life . . . where I never saw any one but my father and sisters . . . more pleasant to me than the society of my equals."[38] The elegiac note predominates especially in writings after his parents' deaths and the dispersal of his sisters; he wrote in his diary, "This dale with its reminiscences, is the shell in which home love once was, and is no longer."[39] In Mark Pattison's writings, homes are places where one is both loved and intellectually superior. They are also places love may abandon.

An egregious 1934 article by F. C. Montague normalized Mark's position of privilege in relation to his "sisters over whom he tyrannized and by whom he was spoilt as is usual with lads who have many sisters." Montague presented the Pattison girls as living a life "for the most part quiet and leisurely," free of the "strenuous amusements of to-day, tennis and motoring, conferences and congresses," enjoying instead a life in which "it was still possible for women to read long books and to reflect upon their contents."[40] Indeed, the Pattison sisters had leisure for reading, although the older sisters increasingly ran the household as Jane Winn Pattison's health declined, but their access to books and knowledge was limited by the local geography of gender. Their father's attention was focused almost entirely on Mark and later, to a lesser extent, on Frank; even after Mark's departure for Oriel, Mark James wrote long, affectionate, and controlling letters that sought still to direct his son's education, rather than redirecting his energy to his daughters. If all the children were educated at home, none of the girls received any education beyond that tutoring; unlike some Evangelical daughters, especially in more urban settings, the girls received little deliberate education. While Mark Pattison at Hauxwell was the recipient of a constant encouragement to learning in which theological learning was assumed to be the route to participation in a wider world of public prestige and remuneration, the girls' religious education was to fit them for the domestic sphere and the afterlife.[41]

Mark's position of intellectual superiority in his family was strengthened by his departure for Oxford; in his letters home and during his vacations he supplanted his father as the bearer of knowledge from the outside world, becoming his sisters' and his cousin Philippa's educator in languages, philosophy, and theology. Leonore Davidoff quotes Harriet Martineau: "brothers are to sisters what sisters can never be to brothers, objects of engrossing and devoted affection." Davidoff argues that this asymmetry of emotion—Harriet Martineau's relationship with her brother James was "the strongest passion of her life"—cannot be severed from asymmetries in access to resources in highly gendered societies: "all brothers, including the younger, start with power and privilege over all sisters," and a "brother acting as instructor, guide, or 'window on the world' for sisters was also being initiated into the wider sphere outside the family, an opportunity often denied many girls." Davidoff sees Harriet Martineau's passion as including envy and obsession. Certainly the Pattison sisters' love for their elder brother was enmeshed in a structural relationship of dependence.[42]

The girls and young women were dependent on Mark's gifts of books, journals, and letters of correction and information and on his kindness for encouragement and tutoring, which the older daughters then passed on to the younger girls by acting as their teachers. Mark sometimes perceived this inequality, writing to Eleanor from Oxford that he recognized that she sometimes saw him "as a schoolmaster or posture master, to whom all you say or do is a matter of remark and criticism . . ." and that this was "a position so disagreeable to [him] that [he was] trying to get quite out of it, and to regard her as [he did] other people, as fullgrown and no longer needing pupillage."[43]

Mark could not simply forfeit the privileges of his position nor prevent familial relations from freighting the inequalities of gender with intense emotional charges. He deplored the lack of educational provisions for women and was to be an advocate for girls' and women's education, but the female students—in and out of his family—he mentored could only ever be unofficial. Unlike male students, they could never achieve the status of colleague or equal in formal structural terms. Mark Pattison would achieve a position of national respect for his insistence on the importance of intellectual work as possessing an inherent dignity, unrelated to any practical or political consideration, but Mark Pattison's sisters could rarely have entertained other views. Eleanor Pattison never had the option of viewing her accomplishments in German, Latin, and Greek as preparation for a public career. The Pattison women's mental cultivation was forcibly disinterested—achieved without social approval and supporting institutions. Yet unlike Mark's, it was also vulnerable to charges of frivolity, inappropriateness, and transgression. Evangelical religious education stressed responsibility for the welfare of one's own soul but women's intellectual development was also susceptible to being read as a manifestation of "pride" and a temptation to neglect more womanly duties.[44]

Education, gender, and familial emotion are imbricated in the texts of Mark's education in Oxford as well as the stories of his Hauxwell-bound sisters. The *Memoirs* narrate his movement from Hauxwell as the discovery of ways in which his father's education had failed him. In Mark's account, his father's education had failed him by its isolation, rendering him vulnerable to feelings of extreme loneliness and inferiority. The *Memoirs* depict the student Mark as excruciatingly shy and almost totally lacking in knowledge of social behavior, including the ettiquette of gender; "I don't think I knew that I ought to take off my hat in the street to a lady."[45] The *Memoirs* display young Mark as deeply vulnerable and at the mercy of inferior others. His peers were "lazy, selfish, greedy, and rapacious," yet Mark is appallingly susceptible to their impress. This vulnerability derives from immaturity ("Surely no boy ever reached eighteen so unformed and characterless as I was!") and terror at his own feelings of alienation ("My unlikeness to others alarmed me; I wanted to be rid of it"), but also from a lack of adequate gendering. Mark gave way to each new person "with a surrender of the conscience and convictions to his mode of thinking, as being better than my own, *more like men*, more like the world."[46]

Mark Pattison's text depicts his young self as feeling less than a man in Oxford, lacking shape, form, and worldliness, as the result of his upbringing. The *Memoirs* imply that Mark was ungendered at Hauxwell; the position of masculinity was fully occupied by his father while femininity was embodied by his sisters and mother.

Configuring the household as consisting of a single patriarch, a mass of adoring women, and his unformed self allows Mark to stand as innocent in the world of his family, denying his own privilege and his sharing of his father's power. The innocence is doubled when Mark left the "cosy patriarchal world" of Hauxwell for Oxford, where he is an innocent abroad, a sensitive and vulnerable observer. His father's house was both desirable and blameworthy for its failure to prepare Mark for the worldly manliness of Oxford. The *Memoirs* further suggest that this Oxonian manliness is sexually charged.[47] *Some* men, the "greedy" and "rapacious," those who were "before [Mark] in manliness of character," could strongly affect those who were not really men and who had no "character" to pose against either the "selfishness" or the "conscience and convictions" of others; like women, some "surrendered." Mark Pattison's text retrospectively depicted Oxford as eliciting in him a willingness to "succumb to or imitate any type . . . with which [he] was brought in contact," to be "cowed by" and to "yield" to "any rough, rude, self-confident fellow." Mark responded by "mutability and chameleon-like readiness to take any colour," feeling himself "humiliated and buffeted" by others, their "sport and football."[48] Mark Pattison later presented his life at Oriel as that of someone both superior and inadequate—constantly gauche, yet intellectually capable of discriminating between the greater and lesser minds of Oxford, and grounded in morals and theology but unable to act on knowledge or resist "influences."

The *Memoirs* tell not only a story of mimicry and seduction but one of multiple splitting and division. Self-protectively Mark developed "a self-consciousness so sensitive and watchful, that it came between me and everything I said or did." This self-consciousness fell between the self and the world. He had "come up to Oxford a mere child of nature" but acquired an interior, observing self that hampered every physical act. This monitorial self directed the actions of a newly acquired social self, which "affected [the] phrases" of others and tried to "put on the new man . . . assimilating." This process of assimilation was "not wholly bad"; it created a public actor, "more like others," aware of social strictures "necessary for . . . common conduct." But it also destroyed spontaneity and authenticity. The *Memoirs* describe a "chameleon," able to absorb appropriate social behavior and to critically note his own inadequacies, alongside an inner self, "natural" but tormented by doubt and contempt for the other self's shape-shifting changefulness. These passages fluctuate between a rhetoric of natural selfhood—a "real self . . . [was] all the while dormant within"— and a rhetoric of character, in which an interior and exterior selfhood are built through processes of imitation and rejection. The inner natural self is not overtly gendered, but it is femininely vulnerable when plunged into an alien environment. Although a more manly outer social self can be generated through modelling on other men, developing such a public self involves processes associated with femininity: artifice, imitation, pretense, and constantly strained attention to social decorum.[49]

This story about Mark's vulnerabilities created by his father continues to a covert claim that his father's education and its (gendered) inadequacies constructed the conditions for Mark to betray Mark James. During his years at Oriel, especially after 1836, Mark Pattison famously became involved in the Tractarian movement of "High Church" Anglican theological and liturgical debate.[50] Historians have noted the attractions of Tractarianism: aesthetic emotionality; combined "intellectual and emotional appeal[s]"; "a crusading call," common purpose and inside knowledge; "the personal attraction of its leaders"; claims to historical depth and continuity.[51] Pattison's *Memoirs* summarize Mark's childhood religious beliefs as "fear of God's wrath and faith in the doctrine of atonement," but the *Memoirs* do not simply construct a contrast between childhood's austere, punishing faith and the intellectuality and vibrant sociability of the 1830s Oxford Movement.[52] Pattison's text insists that his Evangelical childhood laid the foundations for his seduction. His enmeshment in Tractarianism is tied to the "profound, I may say abject, piety" instilled in him by his family; this familial "*piétisme*" left him vulnerable to "depressing fits of conscientious superstition." Mark Pattison's turn to the Oxford movement was caused by his father's religious upbringing; his father is the agent of Mark's revolt against Mark James's authority. Even when Mark began to acquire a "healthy secular tone" in 1838—through distance from Hauxwell—his dark mood was renewed by the receipt of "one of [his father's] disagreeable letters, overflowing with pious resignation and moroseness."[53]

Mark Pattison's *Memoirs'* oblique linkage of his spiritual progress to career issues doubles the perverse linkage between his conversion and his father's influence. Mark's conversion to Tractarianism is bracketed in the *Memoirs* by long accounts of being cheated of fellowships by the patronage networks of Oxford.[54] A theological turn offered possible solutions to professional dilemmas, since the social networks of Tractarianism might offer routes to employment and, in any case, uncertain prospects were glamorized and enobled if the result of spiritual integrity. By 1839, the work of undertaking and disseminating Tractarian scholarship was absorbing Mark Pattison, and he lived for some time in a house rented by Edward Pusey for the young men of the movement. Even after returning to private lodgings, he remained in "the whirlpool" of the movement, engaged in intellectually challenging and spiritually valorized work.[55] Pattison's text thus signals a theme scholars of the Oxford Movement have noted; James Eli Adams suggests that Newman and other Tractarians both recognized and worried that the Movement's allure included its offer of styles and careers.[56] Just as its account of Mark's early days in Oxford tells a story about how his family made him ignorant, permeable, vulnerable to the performances of others, and wracked by anxieties about the relations between selves, souls, and social status, the *Memoirs* make his Tractarian involvement simultaneously a result of his family's failures, a move away from his father's authority, and a tribute to his father's training in spirituality as a route to class mobility.

Mark Pattison left the Oxford Movement by 1849. Ever afterward, his writings depicted that allegiance with bitterness, self-contempt, and contempt for others who had been similarly seduced. Mark Pattison developed a complex narrative of his deconversion, used it as a source of intellectual work, and wrote from it a rich and enduring autobiography, in which Pattison's disillusionment—his seduction and betrayal by Oxford's charismatic men—stresses not only Newman's conversion to Roman Catholicism, the famous "crash of 1845," but his own intellectual processes.[57] Pattison's *Memoirs* claim his attraction to the Oxford Movement was not simply a case of "the infection of party spirit," but nonetheless narrate Mark's turn to Tractarianism as a result of temporary but deep emotional forces—he was "gradually warped round" and "drawn into a whirlpool"—and his emergence is a victory of rationality. His diary is enlisted as evidence of the overcoming by rationalism of his "abject prostration of mind before some unseen power," his emergence from "degrading superstition" and "wasting and mind-drowning" devotions. Pattison's Memoirs summarize: "as I had been drawn into Tractarianism . . . by the inner force of an inherited pietism of an evangelical type; so I was gradually drawn out of it, not by any arguments . . . but by the slow process of innutrition of the religious brain and development of the rational faculties." This quasi-biological battle, fought between the self made by his parents and the self of his own original, not inherited, "rational" mind, ended with his recognition of the inferiority of Tractarian arguments and Tractarian minds alike, those "not intellectually equal companions" still beguiled by the movement.[58] Yet deconversion meant the loss of an emotional and physical community, and the story Mark told of his departure from Tractarianism was simultaneously one of the triumph of intellect and a spiritual tragedy, intellectual battle and angry mourning.

I hinted that Mark Pattison's Memoirs covertly assign him agency in bringing about his father's madness, depicting peace and family happiness at Hauxwell as ending only after his departure. Mark's spiritual narrative certainly gave him agency at Hauxwell, both demonstrating again his role as conduit of intellectual life to his sisters and renewing his father's violence. By the time it became clear to Mark James, in the winter of 1841, that his beloved son, his extension of self as gentleman, clergyman, and scholar, was an agent of the Pope and quite possibly of Satan, Mark had converted those of his sisters who were old enough to hold theological views. The eldest five Pattison girls were immersed in Tractarian practices under Mark's tuition. When Mark James recognized his son's "betrayal" and his daughters' apostasy in 1841, his rages and violence appear in family accounts very little short of those that led to his confinement in 1834. He threw objects, shouted that his elder daughters were infidels but otherwise refused to speak to them, and made their apostasy the text of his sermons before the village. He forbade the elder girls, those "above Sarah," to see the younger, and shut down the village school they had founded.[59] Even Mark was not entirely safe in Oxford; his father paid a surreptitious visit in 1846 to spread rumors about him to his College superiors.[60] Jane Winn Pattison kept silent, although subject to physical attacks and threats. Philippa Meadows told Mark his mother "seem[ed] to view any interference with [Mark James's] will as a breach of duty by her children." (Philippa thought Mark James needed "not a physician but an exorcist.")[61] When Philippa's mother offered to take in one or more nieces for their own safety, their mother forbade it.[62] Fanny and Eleanor wrote Mark in 1852 that their mother "licked [Father's] hand whenever it was raised to strike her."[63] In 1844, the fourth daughter, Grace, died of tuberculosis at twenty-two in a house ringing with her father's curses.[64] Jane Winn Pattison wrote "Let me bless the God who had sent [this death] . . . for we sorely need chastisement."[65] The same year, Anna, earlier described as a brilliant classicist, became ill with depression and physical paralysis.[66]

The Pattison sisters were encouraged by their cousin Philippa Meadows, who urged them to defy their father at least in conscience; Philippa was a fierce theological thinker who told her cousins that "the exaltation of family is contrary to the genius of true religion."[67] Piety was refigured as a ground of resistance to paternal authority. Tractarianism did not necessarily license active female rebellion, but it recast the relations between faithfulness and rebellion. Stripping their father of his ability to speak for

God, the Pattison daughters found a domain outside their father's authority and separate from but faithful to their mother's piety. Moreover, when the Pattison sisters
turned to Tractarianism, they were following the teachings of their brother, who
replaced their father as the source of intellectual and spiritual teaching. All the sisters
had been imbued, in Eleanor's words, with "a keen sense of their own inferiority in
mind, education, and sex."[68] Mark's male intellectual authority had been crucial to
their construction of their own spiritual agency. But when Mark Pattison left the
Oxford Movement, the Pattison sisters balked, remained committed to Tractarian ideas
and practices, and failed to follow Mark's intellectual and spiritual lead, remaining in
what he termed the "deadly grip" of "fanaticism."[69] They became subject to the
lasting anger and disgust not only of their father but of their brother; the language
with which Mark derided his earlier beliefs was turned on his sisters.[70] His sisters
became, in Mark's texts, the true children of his parents, a fate he had transcended
by the power of mind.

In their pious stubbornness, the sisters paradoxically rejoined their mother, figuring
suffering as spiritually valuable, and, in turn, Jane Winn Pattison rejoined her daughters in a final act combining resistance, fidelity, and pain. Mrs. Pattison had been
immobilized by arthritis and was so thin that she developed many bedsores; she died
of infection in 1860, after a long last illness in which she was barely able to speak
and unable to eat. Mark James demanded that she alter her will on her deathbed,
disinheriting those children who had displeased him—Mark and the daughters,
Eleanor and Rachel, who had defied him by marrying. Jane Winn Pattison refused
and bequeathed the property that had been secured to her on her marriage equally
to all her children. Mark James then denied her two last requests—to see all of her
children and to receive Holy Communion.[71] He refused to allow any other clergyman
to see her.

Selves and Submission

While the Church of England does not place the same weight on last rites as Roman
Catholicism, in the eyes of her Tractarian daughters their father had betrayed his status
as husband, father, and ordained priest, and their mother had died in spiritual anguish
in defense of her children. Yet in Mark's narrative of his transcendence of his family,
his sisters remain true children of his father. The overall trajectory of Mark Pattison's
text is the emergence and legimation of the inner natural self, but such a tale of
selfhood risks inscription as *selfishness*. This tension generates a persistent pattern in
Mark Pattison's text: the story of Mark's attainment of a true self is punctuated by
castigations of the alleged duplicity of other members of his family. Passages in the
Memoirs that describe Mark suffering from the "tyranny" of worrying about the inadequacies of his public self and his assimilation of others' views are followed by
allusions to Mark James Pattison. As noted, the *Memoirs* mock Mark James Pattison's
social snobberies and covertly associate Mark's fall into Tractarianism with his father's
education of his son in social ambition. The *Memoirs*'s Mark worries that the processes
of socialization into Oxford are fraught with moral risks, but subjection to the rules
of social behavior not only courted "dishonesty" but learning to "pass [himself] off
for something [he] was not . . . could slide into an endeavour to seem something

better than what [he] was," would be giving into tendencies that were "partly an inherited failing." His father committed the déclassé sin of "dressing the window for the customers" and "not adher[ing] to fact." In the Memoirs, Mark's inner self must triumph over "insincerity and affectation," spiritual and social climbing, family weaknesses.[72]

It was not only his father who occupies the place of unseemly self-interest in Mark Pattison's text.[73] The Pattison sisters are repeatedly charged with being self-dramatizing, acting insincere roles. The Memoirs are especially scathing about Dora; although they were very close for a time and Mark supported her departure from Hauxwell in 1861 for a teaching post, his support ended when, long after his own deconversion, Dora converted to High Church beliefs in 1862 and entered the Christ Church Order, an Anglican Sisterhood.[74] She found a public role for her spiritual passion in an active and ultimately heroic vocation of work in the world as a nurse, but Mark Pattison's diaries and Memoirs, mixing rage and contempt, sneer that she was a do-gooding and dishonest dupe of the Church. After her death of cancer in Walsall in 1878, Mark did not attend her funeral, writing in his diary, "I should be sadly out of place among those 'sisters' and long coated hypocrites.' "[75] Unlike Mark's mental independence from family, Dora's work is the performing of a part, not the revelation of a true self; her public career is not an escape from family weaknesses but an enactment of them. She "took after [Mark James]" as a fictionalist; like him, she was a falsifier who had "powers of self-glorification" but with even greater dishonesty and "a faculty of invention which would have placed her in the first rank as a novelist." An early hagiographic biography of Dora by Margaret Lonsdale is a "romance," in implied contrast to the Memoirs' truthful account that is free of the familial tendency to self-dramatization.[76] An "intimate friend" re-presented Pattison's version of Dora after his death, implying that Mark saw Dora as not only bad—"a habitual liar, driven by the dramatic instinct to impress her company"—but mad, "a brilliant hysteric," tainted by her father's disease. Mark Pattison was the only honest member of his family: "[Dora's 'self-dramatizations' were] so odious to the Rector that he never changed his estimate of her. The family did change, when they found she had a following."[77]

Yet despite Mark Pattison's texts' separation of him from his family, the charges of self-dramatization he flung at Dora and his father constituted a shared language of criticism within the family. Whatever their doctrinal differences, the Pattisons shared a language of intense concern about selves and a rhetoric that punitively blended valorization of authenticity with demands that selves be suppressed. When Dora broke away, several of her elder sisters exchanged letters with each other and Mark deploring her actions as a manifestation of self-regarding pride and self-dramatization.[78] The suspicion of "stories" and the sisters' policing of each other could mingle with status-consciousness and demands for feminine loyalty, as in the tortured history of Fanny Pattison. When Rachel Pattison became secretly engaged in 1856 to a local farmer, Robert Stirke, she confided in her sisters but swore them to secrecy. Fanny kept her vow to Rachel during a holiday spent with Mark. When Mark learned of the engagement he was angry with Rachel for marrying one beneath his family's dignity but he raged against Fanny as a traitor to him, writing in his diary that he "felt cruelly hurt at this deception—truly they deserve all they have to suffer."[79] Mark and Rachel reconciled and he performed her wedding ceremony, but Mark permanently withdrew from Fanny for her "treachery"; he wrote of her piety with contempt for the rest of his life, despite letters in which she pled for forgiveness. When Fanny broke down in late 1862 into "madness"—her first "symptom" a refusal to receive Communion because she was "unclean," followed by suicide threats and insistences that she had had incestuous relations with her much younger brother, Frank—the siblings' responses tangle blame with suspicion, excoriating "selfishness" and alleged dishonesty.[80] Mark's letters blame Sarah for not having realized Fanny's state sooner and his diary denounces Fanny for "stubbornly persisting in repeating her make-believe . . . she now fairly believes it—& the case is hopeless"; Fanny's sisters' letters mix concern over her state with assertions that her illness is at least partly a sinful manifestation of self-concern and self-dramatization.[81] Fanny "recovered" after treatment in a sanitorium outside London and joined Dora as a nursing sister in the Christ Church Sisterhood in 1863. After Rachel's death in 1874, Mark attempted to persuade Fanny to give up her work to live with Rachel's widower and care for her daughters, writing that their father was insufficiently well-bred to act as his nieces' sole parent.[82]

The Pattison children still at Hauxwell—Jane, Frances, Mary, "mad" Anna, Sarah, Elizabeth, and Dora—wrote more desperately of escape after their mother's death, but although Mark James Pattison occasionally threatened to cast them out, he refused to financially assist his daughters in leaving. Mary married in 1860, but routes of escape other than defiant marriages seem to have been almost inconceivable to the elder daughters, who also worried at leaving the younger children behind.[83] Mark wrote that such employment options as existed were beneath his sisters. Elizabeth, described as quiet and shy, was the first to leave, regardless, going to work in August 1861 as a nursery maid; her father threatened to send letters to her employers detailing her sins but never succeeded in locating her.[84] He later supported Dora's initial departure, but in 1857 Mark preached a sermon at Hauxwell to a congregation including his sisters on the text "The Kingdom of God is within you." Those who "have felt or still feel at times uncomfortable and discontented in the place where [they] are" ought to "correct [their] thoughts" and enter "into the Kingdom of God . . . without moving from [their] places."[85]

In November of 1861, Sarah, Frances, Jane, and Mary appealed for Mark's opinion of a plan they had formed of leaving with Anna, whom they were afraid of leaving to their father's "tender mercies"; although they "did not mean to assert that [their father had] brought himself under the penalty of being restrained . . . there has been a week this autumn when he was very nearly gone and we were in fear of our lives . . . anything were better than living on as we are doing here." Fears for their economic, physical, and mental futures entwine: "The net is to be drawn much more tightly around us and then it will be a struggle between he and us who can last the longer—he would I feel sure—our health could not stand it—and with ill-health what could we do for a livelihood were we then compelled to earn for ourselves— before it comes to that who can blame if we escape from this prison of both mind and body."[86] Mark replied that, having no legal way of compelling their father to provide any support, they had better stick it out. In 1863 Sarah left by marrying Richard Bowes, the doctor who had attended her father's madness, her mother's deathbed, and Fanny's breakdown. Mark James Pattison did not die until 1865, at the age of eighty, of cancer of the stomach. Mark and Dora refused to visit his deathbed.[87] As he had promised, Mark James disinherited his married daughters and left little to his sons. Mark wrote that his father's will cheated his own "just expectations"; the apparent refusal of some of his sisters to make over part of their inheritance to him was an indication of their "selfish heartlessness."[88]

"An opposite of her new sisters"?: Francis Pattison

Although he had completed his degree with a disappointing second class and his career prospects were threatened by his spiritual perambulations, the luck of geography had allowed Mark to remain in Oxford. A fellowship marked for a Yorkshireman fell vacant at Lincoln College; he won it by examination and took it up in November, 1839. This sent him "quite off [his] head" and "the joy at Hauxwell equalled [his] own."[89] Professional embitterment followed when Mark failed to achieve the Rectorship of Lincoln in 1851, but, soon after his mother's death in October 1860, his life changed.[90] The death of his mother may have already stirred his imagination; in late November of 1860, the diary cryptically refers to a regrettable indulgence in "a dream in which I have been pleasing myself" before moving on to resignation—"O God grant I may never again be betrayed into leaning on an arm of flesh"—and grandiose pain ("No help, no hope, which way I turn . . . [only] a miserable future. My God, my God, why hast thou forsaken me!")[91] But the death of Rector Thompson brought Mark Pattison a sudden fulfilment of ambition and the loss of a long-cherished bitterness: he was elected to the Rectorship of Lincoln in January 1861.

Mark moved into the Rector's Lodgings in April 1861 amid a general outpouring of good wishes and congratulations.[92] Becoming Rector meant that Mark Pattison became entitled as a Head of House to marry without forfeiting his academic rank. He at first intended that a woman cousin should "keep house" for him, but in the short term, Mary Pattison Roberts assisted him in getting settled and stayed at Lincoln through his absence during the Easter vacation. Mary wrote Mark a series of letters.[93] These letters and the letters of Mark's sisters on Mark's engagement form a set of texts that make sense of Mark's marriage within the longer story of the Pattison family.

Mary's letters to Mark matchmake. The Strong family appear in Mary's letters as members of the Oxford society into which the Rector's sister was introduced; she accompanied them to a boat race and dined with them a few days later, remarking with some acerbity on another of the Strong daughters—probably Marian—having a tendency to "flirt."[94] The warmth between the Rector's Lodgings and The Elms, Iffley, extended to a stay by Francis at Lincoln with Mary during Mark's absence.[95] Through the fortuitous accident of Francis's becoming ill, her visit was prolonged and gave Mary opportunities to observe and expound the virtues of her "little patient." Mary depicts Francis's moral qualities: her conversation "when she is in her serious moods" impresses one with her "beautiful nature," but "her goodness and innocence is not that of one who has never been tried for she has been through much for one of her age." Francis was charmingly innocent despite her bohemian studenthood ("quite interesting . . . her naive revelations of her London life"), unlike her "flirtatious" sister. Mary's letters repeatedly emphasize Francis Strong's exceptionality: "She is an uncommonly superior girl"; to Rachel Stirke, Mary represented Francis as "greatly superior" and with "the tact to conceal her superiority." Francis combines freshness and youth with intellect and "seriousness"; she was not flighty or interested in young men. During an expedition in the country, "Fr was too simple and youthful not to extract some pleasure . . . [but] neither her head or her heart could find any gratification from intercourse with" the young men in the party, who are "indolent" and "indifferent," a callow schoolboy and a successful flirt. Francis has "immense spirits," but she cares for "deeper things" and "feels weary of the banter and nothings that young men so often make the staples of their conversation with girls."[96] Francis is too good for ordinary (young) men and remarkably well-suited for the attentions of Mark Pattison. Unlike those sisters who "betrayed" Mark by engaging their affections elsewhere, she has no interest in lesser men. Mary's letters repeatedly cast Francis Strong as worthy of her brother's attention and susceptible to his wooings; her letters offer Mark a young woman who offers a sister's virtues of youth, educability, and hero-worship *and* romantic interest and high spirits.

Whether Mary was taking the initiative in calling her brother's attention to Francis Strong or responding to an interest Mark had already expressed by her paeans on Francis's virtues, an engagement resulted. The Pattison sisters dispatched letters of ostensible delight when Mary broke the news. Dora's and Rachel's letters claim an awareness of Mark Pattison's desires in a wife. Dora expressed her intense curiosity to "see *your choice!!!!*" who "*must be* clever and observant . . . loving and affectionate, lively and witty, pretty and young." Just as Mary had depicted Francis as particularly suited to Mark's needs, Dora wrote that she could imagine Francis Strong because Mark had "often [said] . . . *what* [he] would like." Francis must be pretty and *young*. Rachel "amused [herself] in picturing [Francis] . . . She must be intelligent . . . but very affectionate & loving & a warm heart"; she would not be the sort to "go to sleep over the Prelude." Francis's youth promises unfolding pleasures; "Tho the fact of her being so young may come [startlingly?] before you it becomes nothing with such a person & . . . it may in *some things* be a gain"; she has "bloom and freshness" but with such "maturity of character" in youth "what may she not become."[97]

Rachel's and Dora's letters of congratulations ambivalently place Mark's engagement in the history of his relations with his sisters. Dora daringly ventured to hope that marriage might improve Mark: "Many of your best qualities have not yet been called out yet all these years they have been lying dormant. You have had a most cruel desolate life, and how your lonely heart will be brightened and you will be a different man." Rachel's letter imagining Francis Strong's virtues invoked the "Prelude" of Wordsworth—the axiomatic poet of relations between (exceptional) brothers and (loving) sisters—while implying that the Pattison sisters had insufficiently emulated the Wordsworthian ideal. Rachel teased, "If your sisters plagued you what will a wife do?" but her letters more sadly muse, "I know I shall never have seen her equal— she will be an opposite of her new sisters." While assuring Mark that Francis must truly want him (Francis's very "*worth[iness]* to be your Lady companion & *friend*" must mean that she "would not . . . have consented had she not loved you"), Rachel represented herself as likely to lose Mark; "there is a strange gap between me & such a character & so I must inevitably lose you. . . ." Rachel's letters voice the possibility that homes can be places of confinement—warning Mark, "there is an independence a freedom in [your life] which cannot be yrs again after this step"—and she refused to applaud marriage as an institution, depicting her own marriage as self-diminishing, but she hoped that Mark would at last feel "loved and cared for & have always some one near you who appreciates you—that now you have a home."[98] Rachel casts Mark as in need of continuous appreciation and as orphaned by their father's actions; his lack of access to a domesticity serviced by mother, sisters, or wife constituted home-lessness. Rachel wrote Mark's engagement as a deserved compensation for the pains of family life and as a chance for him to achieve a new, better relationship of love and pedagogy with a deserving and wholeheartedly devoted woman.

Mary earnestly hoped that Mark's "little bright hearted happy loving companion" would make him happy, and the Pattison sisters generally made the marriage a happy ending for one who had previously been disappointed and hurt.[99] Francis could enter into a legal tie more binding and patriarchal than that between brother and sisters. When she became Francis Pattison, Francis Strong preserved the initial of her patro-nymic—the "S." at the middle of her signature—but nonetheless occupied a peculiar nominative place in the Pattison family.[100] Her name was not that of Frances (Fanny) Pattison, Mark's now-despised sister. Her name was legally almost identical to that of Mark's brother, Francis (Frank) Pattison. Neither brother nor sister, she became a wife.

Oxford Stories

The story of the Pattison marriage as a happy ending to Pattison family life reiterates other stories of marriage that do not depend on particular histories of family suffering, spiritual and professional struggles. The story of the Pattison marriage is not simply a Victorian story but an Oxford story. Francis Strong became not just a wife, but an Oxford wife. Oxford and the local discourses and practices that framed the marriages of dons and the status of college wives need fuller consideration. The next two chap-ters say more about the Pattison marriage as written by its participants in letters and published stories, and about the public stories about Francis Pattison as an exceptional Oxford wife, but I want to briefly explore the specificity of Oxford marriage in order to illuminate the institutions Francis Strong entered in 1861.

Oxford was made up of stories as much as it was of libraries and gardens, mythic spires and raging cholera, great men and hidden women. Like London and Manches-ter, Victorian Oxford was inseparable from its stories and images; the site of ferocious political and religious conflict for centuries, it remained contested territory, the town both consumed and spurned by the university. As Robert Bernard Martin notes, the town in the 1860s was literally cut off on three sides by rivers which could only be crossed by toll bridges; the railway was admitted into the sacred precincts only in 1852 against the will of the University.[101] Even as Victorian Oxford grudgingly lurched to modernity, it reshaped and polished elaborate constructions of its past constituting both "modernity" and "tradition" through rhetorics of class, gender, faith, nation, and empire.[102]

As John Sutherland notes, "one can be in Oxford and at the same time feel excluded . . . The place makes Jude Fawleys of us all."[103] Oxford University constantly positions one as insider or outsider, member or "guest," bearer of rights or intruder, whether suffered or expelled. But Susan Hitch draws attention to the paradoxical presence and absence of women in the University.[104] A central element of the story of Oxford is the representation of the university as a place of universal maleness, whether deplored or recounted with open nostalgia. Oxford was for so long monastic in its organization and purpose that even wives and daughters of College men are latecomers; the status of college wife that Francis Strong assumed was in important respects relatively new. Women's own college walls are more recent yet, and women's admission as students to previously male colleges are only a few decades old.[105] But if Victorian Oxford was certainly patriarchal and its power was founded on riches and "material things" denied "most uneducated Englishwomen [who] like reading," Hitch suggests that feminist critique is better served by the exposure of Oxford's fragility and the dubiety of its claims of male self-sufficiency than by reproducing Oxford's image as an impenetrable and beautiful bastion of patriarchy.[106] Restoring women to Oxford's history reassigns the terms of historical significance. Hitch juxtaposes the assumed maleness of the status of Oxford student or scholar "for just about a thousand years before the rest of us arrived," with the unofficial and usually unacknowledged presence of women "for almost as long" as college servants. The majority of such women were confined, given the male monopoly of porters' positions and, in the nineteenth century, the predominance of male "scouts" and even private valets, to the less visible and more menial jobs of laundry, scullery work, and heavy cleaning; when the wives of porters and scouts worked for the university, they did not necessarily command separate wages. A few such women's names are preserved in the Colleges; "in the cloisters of Corpus Christi there are memorials to dons on the walls; below, in the paving stones with other servants there are women's names: Alice Parson's with her husband Isaac, Sarah Gee. There is nothing to explain why they deserved this succinct recognition. Most never had it."[107] Virginia Woolf's satirical "A Society" (1921) foreshadows Hitch's insight. A fictional conspiracy of women infiltrates male institutions in order to take the measure of men's "civilization," and the agent assigned to "Oxbridge" goes undercover, and undetected, as a charwoman.[108] Hitch might have added to her roster of invisible women the women of the town of Oxford who provided services to students and dons; in the nineteenth century, these included three hundred to five hundred women who worked as prostitutes.[109]

The women who married into Oxford University were not wholly different from the servants they employed. Both inhabited a context in which women were exceptional, subordinate, and possibly scandalous. Sometimes, like Sarah Gee's, their names reach the chapel stones—Sarah Acland is eulogized as a Christian lady and wife in Christ Church Cathedral, the plaque simultaneously inducing wonder at its presence and acceptance of its oddity—but most have no memorial in the walls in which they lived. Even after the foundation of the women's colleges, women remained marginal in Oxford, their official status one of sufferance. In public, as late as 1884, Dean John Burgon of New College could wishfully exhort his female congregants: "Inferior to us God made you, and inferior to the end of time you will remain."[110] Women's official tangentiality to the grand sweep of Oxford's history shows in the disposition of the women's colleges founded from 1879 onward; although not so distantly quarantined as Girton and Newnham at Cambridge, the Oxford women's colleges are on the edges, "spaced round the outskirts of the city centre, divided . . . by a cordon of river, parks, housing, shopping streets," strikingly excluded from the densely built-up center of town, where the historically male colleges are within five minutes of each other and where the streets long functioned as an extension of the colleges' public space. The women's colleges themselves—"domestic . . . and sensible of the proprieties"—fail to look like Oxford ought. When the BBC in 1986 filmed Dorothy Sayers's *Gaudy Night*, they filmed not in Sayers's Somerville but in Corpus Christi; "they wanted the *real* Oxford, the Oxford of the myth, the Oxford of the imagination. The *real* Oxford has towers and pinnacles and lots of gargoyles, it is vaguely and generally old and there aren't many women in it."[111] Women's fundamental antipathy to the "real" Oxford is stated with relish by Paul E. More, who deplored "the encroachment of the feminine into a society so archaically masculine."[112] Moreover, as Susan Leonardi has argued, women's presence in Oxford as scholars, students, teachers, and principals in the new colleges did not grant them self-confident access to dominant discourses, and women's subcultural discourses were often crosscut by violent self-doubt and terror. Even college-educated women worried that college-educated women would "get out of hand," "reject and even attack men," "threaten family life, destroy 'womanly women,' refuse marriage, and seize power." Whether as heroine or monster, the figure of the educated woman was unassimilable to established narratives.[113]

If the college-educated woman is a disruptive figure in narratives of femininity and Oxford alike, her status is nonetheless more official than that of her predecessors, Oxford women before the foundation of women's colleges. Like the women servants whose badly paid labor was both necessary and discursively invisible (and whom Mrs. Pattison would attempt to organize into trades unions), the middle-class women of Victorian Oxford were active and vivid figures in subgenres of University history, in footnotes and anecdotes. Some are heroines and "eccentric" legends: Annie M. A. H. Rogers for her brilliant intellect and witty, tireless campaign for women's admission to full status in the University, and Clara Pater, sometime tutor to Virginia Woolf, unflappable, luminescently aesthetic in "peacock-blue serge ornamented with crewel sunflowers."[114] Tellingly, however, a high proportion of the names by which they survive are those of the men to whom they owed their own access to Oxford: Mrs. Arthur Johnson, Mrs. T. H. Green, Mrs. Humphry Ward, Mrs. Mandell Creighton, and, of course, Mrs. Mark Pattison.[115] Excluded from college education, they built the cultural spaces for younger women, however poor Somerville, Lady Margaret Hall, and the other women's colleges were compared to male institutions. E. F. S. Pattison took care to show modern women that they did have forerunners, including women in her published art-historical work and donating the work of a woman artist, Claudine Bouzonet Stella, to Somerville College, and Somerville's very name attests to histories of female intellectuality that preceded institution-building.[116] But in building the women's colleges, the Victorian ladies of Oxford inserted their own names and those of other women into the history of institutions to which, again, they did not properly belong, and which framed the stories about marriage Oxford told.

It was impossible for mid-Victorian women to belong to Oxford, to be members of college or university. The women's colleges' students had at least competed for entrance, taken exams, and been judged, but wives, daughters, and sisters of dons gained access to library, hall, or quad entirely through the grace of men. Some were recognized as intelligent and gifted—Sarah Acland did, after all, translate Dante and read Greek and political economy—but female achievement had no official place. A lady might shine in her drawing room, and Rachel Burton, daughter of a Canon of Christchurch, might submit a winning poem for the Newdigate prize, but that lady would never hold a university position and the Newdigate would be bestowed on the second-best, male-authored poem.[117] M. Jeanne Peterson proffers Sarah Angelina Acland's work as a photographer in Oxford as an example of the ability of some "gentlewomen" to "find ways of expressing their talents, commitments, and desire to do meaningful and enjoyable work," but Peterson elides the limits of private and local acknowledgement by male luminaries. Peterson presents "Angie" Acland's exclusion from the official public realm in terms of happy escape—she "had no need to earn a living," but instead "served as hostess for her widowed father." But despite her interest in and significant contributions to photographic chemistry, Angie Acland utterly lacked access to a scientific career like her father's; only after her death was her work exhibited.[118] In such achievements as they nonetheless reached, college wives or daughters were always somehow indebted to men, forced to use their influence with men to assert or create, and aware that their place in Oxford did not include a place in its representations, history, and myths. Oxford's subculture of homoeroticism, too, could also be experienced as marginalizing women; Josephine Butler, who left Oxford in 1857, castigated the nominally celibate male society of the University for its temptations to "hellenistic" male bonding as well as its crude sexualization of women.[119]

Even in the 1880s, with a growing number of faculty wives and the growth of heterosocial circles of friendship amongst younger fellows' wives like Mary Arnold Ward, Bertha Johnson, and Louisa Creighton, female intellectuality remained marginal to Oxford—literally located outside the colleges in the new suburban houses of North Oxford.[120] As A. J. Engel notes, the heterosexualization of Oxford, with the gradual abolition of prohibitions on married men holding or retaining fellowships in the 1870s, did not diminish so much as expose the "radically dichotomous conceptions of the roles of men and women" that affected every aspect of thought about education at Oxford, "from the value of personal supervision to ideals of education and appropriate careers." The growing number of faculty wives marked the professionalization of male dons; the right to establish heterosexual and reproductive households "was seen as essential for men." That is, male dons were increasingly figured as having the right to *unpaid* female support in their public roles, as opposed to the use of servants and prostitutes for domestic and heterosexual services; hearing of the Pattison-Strong engagement, Ruskin asked, "Why shouldn't heads of college marry whom they like?"[121] But "marriage and a professional career were considered incompatible for women" and women dons in the new colleges could not marry.[122] Sexual relations, not monastic celibacy, were the modern male academic's birthright, but a woman who was intellectual was institutionally positioned as an asexual spinster. The aspirations of college wives to the status of intellectual were nonsensical in Oxford's institutions, insofar as such aspirations brought together incompatible statuses of sexuality and intellectuality, domesticity and scholarship. Simultaneous contempt for overmasculine bluestockings and condemnations of the display of female sexuality came from women as well as men. George Eliot sneered that women writers' works "are usually an absurd exaggeration of the masculine style, like the swaggering gait of a bad actress in male attire," while Margaret Jeune scorned a visiting Frenchwoman who, despite her cleverness, wore an "exceedingly small quantity of sleeve."[123] It might be an Oxford "joke" that Henry Smith, Savile Professor of Geometry at Balliol and a noted classicist, was "with one exception, the most brilliant man in Oxford and that exception was his sister," but the joke condenses the incompatibility of femininity and intellectuality in Oxonian discourses.[124]

Francis Strong, in marrying Mark Pattison, thus married into a status in which she would always also be outside, tangential, unofficial in Oxford. Moreover, Francis Pattison's marriage preceded the formation of a new generation of younger dons' wives. She became a member of a smaller group consisting only of the women married to college heads, many of whom were much older than she was. Marriage to a head of house meant living in college in a fundamentally public marriage. The more prestigious the husband, the more difficult it was for wives to claim separate time and space. Frederick Shaw had ponderously hoped Francis Strong would not give herself airs as the "Rector's Lady" but be "Mark Pattison's wife," but the wives of rectors, principals, and presidents, like the wives of headmasters and vicars, were expected to preside over domestic arrangements that extended beyond their own families and included serving tea, with or without sympathy, to undergraduates and dons, as well as husband and children.[125] Peculiarly public households must be gracefully managed by women who, in formal terms, had no membership in these institutions.[126]

Margaret Jeune, wife of a Master of Pembroke, never protested the assumption that college wives—like other Victorian wives—would be "helpmates in [their husbands'] careers." She wrote of pleasure in her position as an exceptional woman at Oxford events, and found that as her husband rose to become Vice Chancellor, she gained access to a varied life vicariously. But her diary also presents a story in which "subordination and docility," and willingness to place "her feelings and desires . . . second" cost her a sense of "hollowness in her life." She wrote with telling ambiguity, "Our life is so monotonous that I am often induced to give it up (keeping a journal I mean)."[127] Margaret Woods (d. 1945), novelist and poet, daughter of a Master of University College and wife of a President of Trinity, emphasized the sheer amount of time these expanded womanly duties required. A long poem on "Oxford Bells" evokes the incessant ringing, the constant institutional sound of the University.[128] More privately, Woods lamented that it had been impossible for her to be a "University wife" and to do her own work, to fulfill her desires:

> When I go to Oxford & see women . . . who started far stronger physically & have no career of their own to think of, worn out by the same work, I only marvel that I have ever written a word since 1887. Yet if I only had left my dear freedom I could have faced the frustration of lifelong hopes and aims with courage . . . though I have things in life which would have made many women happy I have never had what would have made me happy—but on the contrary the shoes that would have fitted them so well, have pinched my feet all over. And now it seems to me I can walk no further.[129]

Oxford and marriage had real walls, of stone and convention: seductive, confining, labyrinthian and unyielding. In marrying, Francis Strong entered new institutions legally and literally. Ten years after her marriage, a French admirer made a picture with his words to describe her standing, startling against Oxford's old stone walls, her

expression "near mutiny."[130] In chapter 5, I look at how Francis Pattison was represented as refusing her role as the Rector of Lincoln's wife through acts of stagy self-
removal, in Oxford but not really. But a woman's simultaneous presence and absence
in Oxford was never just a choice. Moreover, the double status of women in Oxford,
visible and invisible, institutionally encompassed yet unofficial, was not unique to the
local institutions of Oxford wifehood: it was homologous with other Victorian discourses about women—including the legal contract of marriage, in which two persons
became one and that one was the man. Oxford's discourses about the incompatibility
of femininity and intellectuality were overt and institutional, but they were not local
peculiarities. Mrs. Mark Pattison customarily signed her art writings "E. F. S. Pattison"
(the "S." to recall, according to Charles Dilke, her resistance to coverture). In 1871,
the Pattisons fell into conversation with the Keeper of the French Collection of the
Imperial Art Gallery in Vienna and he recommended to their attention "the best
authority on his subject . . . an Englishman, 'Mr.' Pattison."[131]

Dilke Stories

Charles Dilke's Memoir of Emilia Dilke deploys Middlemarch to construct a story of marriage as the result of an exceptional young woman's natural desire for a wider intellectual world. Rather than providing a narrative of the Pattison courtship, Charles Dilke
refers to Middlemarch in a complex passage located between his discussions of Francis
Strong's early hallucinations (i.e., her vulnerability to suggestion) and her marriage.
I argued in chapter 2 that Dilke uses Middlemarch to certify the fundamental nobility,
praiseworthiness, and intellectual depth of Francis Strong's girlhood religiosity, and I
pointed out that Dilke claims that specific acts of reading "prove" a relationship
between Dorothea Brooke and Francis Strong. Dilke's text also claims textual access
unavailable to other readers: "it is impossible to compare the Prelude and several
passages in the first book of "Middlemarch" with passages still existing in the diaries
and manuscripts of Miss Strong, penned before 1862, and not see whence came
George Eliot's knowledge of the religious ideal of her Dorothea Brooke." Dilke's use
of Middlemarch as an intertextual guarantor of his text continues in innuendos about
Francis Strong's first marriage: "Dorothea's defence of her marriage with Casaubon,
and Casaubon's account of his marriage to Dorothea in the first book of 'Middlemarch,' are as a fact given by the novelist almost in Mark Pattison's words. Here the
matter ends."[132]

"The matter" is by no means clear. An unpublished draft of Charles's memoirs
amplifies his story of the relationship between Middlemarch and the Pattison marriage,
but even the unpublished account hedges and turns away from naked assertion, its
elisions extended by the erasure of several words and lines. Dilke confesses, "I had
on the appearance of Middlemarch been one of those who saw how [rasura] George
Eliot had drawn from Emilia Strong the opinions [?] of Dorothea Brooke and how
she had tried to draw [rasura] a [rasura] view of the Revd Mark Pattison's character
in that of the Revd Mr Casaubon to whom she indeed gave a name which could only
show that she both meant Pattison & meant to be known to mean him." Dilke's text
moves back and forth, acknowledging and denying similarities between Casaubon and

Pattison but argues that, minimally there was a textual relationship between the two courtships: Dilke claims that George Eliot's fictional letter of proposal from Edward Casuabon to Dorothea Brooke is a close paraphrasing or actual quotation of a letter by Mark Pattison. "George Eliot must have worked hard . . . to get at every fact which had a bearing upon his character. For example, Casaubon's letter to Dorothea at the beginning of the 5th chapter of *Middlemarch*, from what George Eliot herself told me in 1875, must have been very near the letter that Pattison actually wrote and the reply very much the same."[133]

The staggeringly pretentious letter of Edward Casaubon which Charles Dilke enlists depicts an older man, convinced that he is not of "the commoner order of minds" and his own "work [is] too special to be abdicated," wooing a young, idealistic woman. She is the object of his desire because she possesses "an elevation of thought and a capability of devotedness" not often found in those with "the early bloom of youth or with those graces of sex . . . [which] win and . . . confer distinction when combined . . . with the mental qualities above indicated." This "rare combination of elements both solid and attractive" allures Casaubon, whose own contribution to the marriage will be "affection" and his previous chastity. Dilke implies that Francis Strong accepted Mark Pattison in the same spirit as Dorothea Brooke accepted Casaubon—with a rapturous sense that "a fuller life was opening before her: she was a neophyte about to enter on a higher grade of initiation," moving beyond "her own ignorance and the petty peremptoriness of the world's habits" by "devoting herself to [Casaubon/Pattison], and . . . learning how she might best share and further all his great ends." But when Dorothea accepts him, Casaubon betrays his allegiance to a theory of gender which makes Dorothea's vision of marriage as access to intellectual activity impossible from the outset. He tells her, "the great charm of your sex is its capability of an ardent self-sacrificing affection . . . [and] its fitness to round and complete the existence of our own." Dilke's text silently invites the reader to imagine Mark Pattison sharing Edward Casaubon's narcissism: "Mr Casaubon was touched with an unknown delight (what man would not have been?) [but] he was not surprised . . . that he should be the object of it."[134]

Charles Dilke refuses to tell the tale outright but George Eliot's mordant account of the engagement of Casaubon and Dorothea Brooke lurks behind his half-stories. The cumulative effect is to harness readers' knowledge of George Eliot's novel. But Dilke's representation of himself as a reader of *Middlemarch* and an asker of questions raises an edgier possibility—that his own understanding of his second wife's first marriage was shaped by *Middlemarch*. Rather than seeing Charles Dilke as a master of narrative, self-consciously deploying Eliot's novel to bolster or conceal other, truer, tales of the Pattison marriage, we can retain the possibility that *Middlemarch* formed Charles Dilke's believed, as well as written, stories. Margaret Oliphant, after all, thought she perceived Francis Pattison appropriating *Middlemarch* to organize her self-understanding, remarking after a visit to Oxford that Mark Pattison's wife "considers herself the model of Dorothea."[135]

Moreover, Charles Dilke's use of *Middlemarch* meshes with the complex of stories both Dilkes told about the marriages of young women and old men. The convergence of stories told by Charles Dilke, Emilia Dilke, and various novelists does not mean such stories are "true," but highlights how plausible stories that collectively participate in a wider nineteenth-century narrative project might be. Like Charlotte Bronte, in *The Professor* (and, in some respects, *Villette* and *Shirley*), Mrs. Alfred Sidgwick in *The Professor's Legacy*, Louisa May Alcott across the Atlantic in *Little Women*, and even Chekhov in *Uncle Vanya*, the Dilkes engaged in a genre of stories of young women who marry professors.[136] This set of stories of intellectual seduction, which the Dilkes retrospectively enlisted and contributed to, had a life beyond any single text and, as Barbara Hardy notes in her discussion of novels of "loveless marriage," including *Middlemarch*, need not be thought of in terms of "sources and influences" but of "affinities."[137] In some tales, the professor is literally a teacher, while in others he is simply the possessor of knowledge. The tutelary quality of such marriages is stressed by considerable age differences between the partners. Despite enormous differences, what is common to these stories is the lucky or unlucky turn by ardent young women to marriage for knowledge.

Such novels may not simply have been consumed and reiterated. Stories of marriage as a route to the getting of wisdom have material and historical referents. Marriage into Oxford did provide access—on highly unequal terms—to contemporary intellectual life, making possible the continuation of Francis Strong's childhood access to Oxford society, but now as a social leader. Further, marriage to one of the notorious contributors to *Essays and Reviews* and the theological and philosophical editor of the *Westminster Review* was a path to the most "advanced" thought.[138] Mark Pattison's absorption in learning, bitterness about his familial and professional past, and biting contempt for most other people might even be alluring to young women intent on proving their special sensitivity and capacity for selflessness, condensing in the same act exceptionality and socially lauded feminine virtue.[139] Ruskin, tacitly invoking Milton, flippantly scripted Francis Strong's marital choice as an act of feminine devotion to a great man, writing "Frances [sic] Strong will write Greek beautifully. But I'm glad she's done with her drawing."[140] Richard Jebb portrayed the Pattison marriage as an act of kindness and homage to a great man's suffering: "[Mrs Pattison] knows the gloom that rests on her husband, and she has resolved to be the sunshine of his life; she knows, too, that a man of such large & quick perception can only be amused by what is socially original."[141] Jebb portrayed Francis Strong Pattison as deliberately placing her exceptionality—her "originality"—in the service of Mark Pattison. Charles Dilke's citations of *Middlemarch* too imply that, like Dorothea Brooke, Francis Strong intended "devoting herself to [Casaubon/Pattison], and . . . learning how she might best share and further all his great ends."[142] Francis Strong herself had written her sister Rosa Tuckwell in terms that positioned her giving up her "Ishmaeliteish position" to behave like a proper woman.[143] Francis wrote a mutual friend a letter passed on to Pauline Trevelyan: "Do you remember saying one day how passionately you thought I should love if I ever did [get married]? Well you were quite right in your conjecture. I am really becoming a little mad I think by our happiness."[144] To female intimates, Francis's letters present her unusual choice of fiancés as conformity to a feminine script.

Robert Elsmere, a fiction linked to the Pattison ménage, satirically develops this story of the seductiveness of great but tragic men to younger women, mocking young women's beliefs that these courtships mark their exceptionality.[145] Mrs. Humphry Ward (a sometime Oxford wife), dissects an intellectual seduction. Mr. Langham, a depressed don, begins by attempting to disillusion Rose Leyburn about Oxford's "clever people" but ends by confiding in her with "a sudden breach in [his] melancholy reserve." That is, Langham both offers Rose insight beneath the surfaces of a prestigious community and emotionally appeals to her. Rose, "a girl hardly out of the schoolroom," is flattered by Langham's attention and finds in it material for perceiving herself as an adult: "After all, she said to herself angrily, with a terrified sense of importance, she was a child no longer, though her mother and sisters would treat her as one." Rose berates herself for "never behav[ing] like other girls" but also desires distinction; she is "vain, ambitious, dangerously responsive." Rose is indicted by the narrator for her "ambition" and the desires that render young women collusive in their seduction by intellect and theatricality.[146] Tellingly, Rose wishes for "a little life! . . . a little *wickedness!*" and self-mockingly describes herself as "a bundle of wants." She is filled with a "strange girlish pride" by Langham's confidences and a "crude intoxicating sense" of her own power," mingled with a desperate anxiety to *play her part well.*" But if Rose is foolish and morally immature, Langham "wantonly play[s]" on her faults. He performs the role of tortured genius, confiding his "cramped childhood and youth," clerical father and Evangelical mother; although he depicts himself as flawed and anguished, he does so in "words with an extraordinary magic and delicacy of phrase" and with "a kind of pleasure in the long analysis, which took pains that it should be infinitely well done." Langham's self-depiction as gripped by a love of learning and tormented by "something cold, impotent, and baffling in himself"—as a character of exceptional depth—combines glamorous asceticism and extraordinary need. Langham is somewhat conscious of his self-dramatization: "What had all this scene, this tragedy been about? . . . He—the man of thirty-five—confessing himself, making a tragic scene, playing Manfred or Cain to this adorable halffledged creature . . . the critic in him [made] the most remorseless mock of all these heroics and despairs the other self had been indulging in." Ward depicts both characters as half-selfconsciously theatrical, but Rose is the more vulnerable: "if [Rose] had known more of literature" she could have placed Langham's analysis within its genre; "but she was not literary."[147]

The genre Ward satirized was never merely a matter of literary history. Marriage to men whose attractions were primarily intellectual for the sake of prestigious knowledge and covert or vicarious access to cultural capital was not a path in which Francis Strong was alone. Francis Strong's own sister Rosa—earlier an example of female selfdevelopment and artistic accomplishment—may have set her a specific example of a suitable marriage as well. Rosa's marriage to William Tuckwell, a forward-thinking scholarly cleric and supporter of women's education with whom "it was sometimes an effort to keep pace" in intellectual matters, may have represented a scenario to which Francis Strong might aspire and simultaneously exceed by marrying a man more prestigious and more scandalous.[148] Virginia Woolf's description of the Carlyles' courtship catches the allure and hints at danger: "It was his intellect that she admired, and it was her intellect that she would have him admire . . . [And he] did his best to draw up a programme for the cultivation of it."[149] If the Carlyle marriage became a byword for the Victorian wastage of women's talents in marriages to difficult men, other "exceptional" and feminist women like Josephine Butler and Millicent Garrett Fawcett also chose men whose commitment to learning led them to foster their wives' educations and activities. In the case of the Butlers, the urban and suburban subcultures of the Evangelical middle class provided narratives of marriage as a partnership of spiritual development in which women as well as men were expected to read and think seriously about theology, politics, and the moral condition of society.[150] Mark Pattison, like George Butler and Henry Fawcett, was avowedly liberal and supported women's education; as Chief Commissioner on the Schools Enquiry Commission of 1864, he scoffed at arguments against rigorous education for girls and women: "An average man of the middle classes prefers a woman who is less educated to one who is more. The preference of a man for a less cultivated woman arises from his own want of culture."[151] A man capable of voicing such views must surely take a woman's intellectual aspirations seriously. Such marriages sometimes blended a rhetoric of heterosexual partnership with a covert rhetoric of parent/child relations; Francis Strong's London roommate, Frances Rosser, married the much older musician John Hullah, whom she met through her friendship with his daughter, her own contemporary. Rosser noted that part of Hullah's attraction was that he was "peculiarly fitted" to educate young women; she seems to simultaneously take up the positions of daughter, student, and wife.[152]

Later young "New Women" like Beatrice Webb continued to be allured by the hope of a marriage of minds, and the phenomenon of young women marrying men who might educate them and rescue them from familial parochialism is by no means exclusively Victorian.[153] In the mid-Victorian period, not marrying at all had higher costs, and alternative routes to knowledge and worldly pleasures were elusive. However privileged and "exceptional" a young woman, social roles as a woman artist or intellectual were difficult to achieve. Continuing as a young woman alone in London and Oxford is not presented as an option in Charles Dilke's memoirs; a limit to Francis's family's tolerance may also have been reached. If marriage was an accepted inevitable goal, most marriageable men outside of the Oxford elite were depressing prospects: members of the "squirearchy" and men of her father's class—middle-level professionals, army officers, or the provincial clergy. Virginia Woolf could sardonically note, considering middle-class Victorian women's aspirations, "It is difficult to be sure, after all, that a college don is the highest type of humanity known to us," but few other men could compete with Oxford's material resources or its glamor as the site of intellectual purposes allegedly transcending mere personal ambition.[154] Marriage to a male artist had its own perils. As a protégée of several University families, moreover, Francis Strong was positioned to know that marriage into Oxford provided covert and vicarious but real access to contemporary intellectual life for women.[155] Moreover, Oxford's culture included a highly developed tradition of relationships in which tuition, desire, and status were enmeshed; Oxford male homoeroticisms joined pedagogy and eros in unequal but sometimes deeply felt personal relationships.[156]

Charles Dilke's account of the Pattison marriage represents not the privileges but the perils of marriage for the young and idealistic woman. Dilke represents the early years of the Pattison marriage as marked by continuous work and the absence of any "personal resistance [on Mrs Pattison's part] to the influence over her of her husband" because of Francis Pattison's "reverence for scholarship." Charles Dilke's texts struggle not to depict the youthful bride as passive; he stresses in his published discussion of *Middlemarch* that "the grotesque attempt to find a likeness between . . . the somewhat babelike Dorothea and the powerful personality of the supposed prototype [beyond certain specified limits], was never made by any one who knew . . . Mrs Pattison." But while Charles Dilke stresses the essential innocence of Francis Strong's motives, the rebelliousness of youth of Francis Strong's school days is mastered by marriage: "[Mark Pattison's] mind and learning deserved the surrender of the educational direction of a young girl, however gifted, to his mental and philosophical control; and he obtained it. Although full of love of personal liberty, she had an unusually disciplined reverence for Authority as represented by those she thought really competent in ability and learning." Mark Pattison's motives are left vague, but Dilke implies that the inequalities of the marital relationships derived not only from unequal mental resources but from the man's desire for control. Dilke complicates this tale by contending that Francis "resist[ed] any too absorbing influence of [Mark's] actual opinions . . . [keeping] an imaginative side and part of life, in which [he] was hardly allowed to share: to this she alluded as 'off hours on my own time,' " but the mitigation of Mark's power emanates from Francis's resistance rather than his scruples.[157] In Dilke's story, Francis Strong's marriage was not an entry into resources, prestige, and public space; a special young woman was diminished, not enriched.

E. F. S. Pattison's *The Renaissance of Art in France* offers one possible marriage story in a reading of a painting. Clouet's wedding portrait of Elisabeth of Austria shows an "animated" young woman whose vitality, "charm," and most of all, innocence and "girlish eagerness" acquire a "pathetic appeal" through the viewer's knowledge of the "miserable marriage" and "premature death" to come; her ornaments and privilege recede before that knowlege. Elisabeth, "frank and simple" and trusting, like Francis Strong under the horse chestnuts in South Kensington, needs no special qualities to appeal to sympathy in Pattison's acount; her youth and sad fate are enough, overshadowing her material wealth and status.[158] But Pattison's innocent, even average, Elisabeth is not the only or most characteristic figure of youthful vulnerability in Pattison/Dilke's texts. Rather, Emilia Dilke repeatedly wrote stories about young people whose vulnerability to intellectual seductions is evidence of their exceptionality.

Emilia Dilke's 1897 essay, "The Idealist Movement and Positive Science," develops an overtly ungendered theory of the seduction of the sensitive, intellectually serious young by knowledge and power, as well offering a passage of disguised autobiography in the story of a young male friend's spiritual struggle. The change of gender in the friend's tale along with the general framing, moves the essay outside the "Woman Question" and keeps it from telling a marriage story. Instead, "The Idealist Movement" is a nest of narratives about youthful choices and mature misgivings in which the young are drawn not into marriage but into bad philosophy. Positivism is an intellectual attitude of "petrified negation" and the "crippling" of the "free play of the intellect," whose embrace disallows imaginative and emotional perception. Those who embrace positivism "reject all testimony, save that which they can lay bare with the knife"; antimetaphysical and self-deprived of imagination, the positivist believes only in the surface of things. But positivism appeals to the clever and sensitive young person because it meshes with a natural tendency to refuse accepted wisdom and seek knowledge. "Like children who carry everything to their mouths in order to be sure that their eyes do not deceive them," they are unwilling to trust any emotion or perception not grounded in "sense-experience." The young have moved beyond "the lovely peace of early implicit belief" and submission to authority but lack sufficient education to form a more nuanced faith. "There is a critical moment, when the mind gains consciousness of its own independence, and the growing activity of the reasoning powers begins to cause a not unnatural distrust of the emotional impulses, so that their leading is questioned and rejected."[159]

Spiritual questioning and desire for independence are normal demonstrations of a genderless tendency of youth to revolt; young people are naturally drawn to the claims of "science" against orthodox "religion." If young people make bad choices, in Dilke's account this tragedy results from the misguidance of qualities that are, in themselves, signs of merit. The young have been ill educated and their desires imperil them, but those desires are not wrong. At worst, the laudable rebelliousness of the sensitive and intelligent may be contaminated in those "in whom a very real desire to learn truth, and be true to it, coexists with the weakness of wishing to be thought advanced"; some, especially if inclined toward fanaticism, imagine discarding convention "g[ives] proof of . . . worthiness to share" in enlightenment and modernity and cannot disentangle fads from the march of progress. Despite these chidings, Emilia Dilke's essay is shot through with flashes of more vivid and disturbing imagery when it suggests a story of seduction. Authoritative philosophers draw to themselves young persons of the best type, abetted by the innocent but hungry desires of the young for access to knowledge and truth. The sensitive soul is drawn away from belief in angels into the "prison-house" of a barren philosophy that has destructively "stripped from knowledge those sacred garments of beauty and truth, whereby her nakedness was, aforetime, veiled in the eyes of men." "Childish" ignorance and "crippled" and sterile age are disastrously conjoined. In the essay's supplementary account of Dilke's young male "friend," his self-subjugation is exacerbated by those who exploit his moral seriousness for selfish ends.[160]

Emilia Dilke's short stories also offer stories of young minds, bodies, and souls led by intellectual aspiration into confinement, but these are specifically accounts of marriage and vastly unequal resources. Dilke wrote bleak stories of young girls seduced by older, wiser men, Death, and demons—stories of misguided hope and spiritually, even physically, murderous betrayal. Unlike the ungendered or male seekers of "The Idealist Movement," the characters in her stories who marry for learning are female, and their desire for knowledge betrays them to sexuality. Marriage for knowledge is a female variant of the Faustian compact.[161] Such marriages are not happy endings but the beginning of grimmer stories. The young protagonists' desires for exceptionality, whether youthful idealism or a more culpable desire "to be thought advanced," sets their stories in motion, but seduced young women rue the relationships—to knowledge, devils, Death, and men—into which they enter and become imprisoned. In these unequal marriages of minds, husbands are explicitly motivated by a desire for control, and young women are misled by a desire for knowledge. Repentance crosscuts and undercuts the protagonists' anger, but none of Dilke's protagonists fully deserve their ends.

"The Physician's Wife" is a furious story of marriage as murder. A naive young girl marries a much older man, a doctor-scientist. The doctor is, like the positivist philosopher, a wielder of a knife.

At first she was not ill-pleased to watch the wonders of his laboratory, and . . . to do his errands; but gradually her gaiety forsook her, and her life grew irksome to her . . . Now, in the sight of this man, Science, pursued for her own sake, was the one absolute good, and dwelling much with his own thought he had come to be uplifted with zeal, believing that in truth science had yielded to him the deepest secrets of nature, and that he was thus marked out from all other men. . . . So it came to pass, that whilst he himself worshipped Science as the true principle and lamp of life, he demanded of all those who approached him the recognition in him of that deity which, so to speak, should be revealed to them in his person.

Dilke's male physician conflates "Science" and his self; he "deem[ed] that he saw all men truly and all things truly, since his passions [were] wholly drawn into the service of Science." The young wife at first accepts his authority to determine the meaning of her own acts, even her motives, since that authority is not merely legal but intellectual and "scientific." The doctor's "wonderful tongue . . . so charmed her ears that she . . . [strove] to put the passion of her balked desires into the daily services demanded of her." Science has all the authority of religion and rebellion is both stupid and sinful, but the subjection of the female protagonist is also a subjugation to domesticity and "daily service." Dilke's story not only reiterates "The Idealist Movement" 's narrative of disastrous seduction by, and anguished confinement in, inadequate forms of knowledge but it culminates in madness and death. The protagonist eventually kills the "malicious" physician. She then (unconvincingly) repents and belatedly understands him ("his very cruelty arose out of devotion to ends beyond the common aims of men"). The male figure is recuperated into the status of victim but the protagonist dies alone and unmourned.[162]

In "The Silver Cage," the nameless protagonist draws the attention of the devil by the beautiful song of her soul; the devil then schemes to gain possession of the soul's voice. Seducing her with false knowledge, the devil "entered the garden and took possession of the woman, and all that was hers." In Dilke's Faustian tale, the woman gains nothing from her bargain; whatever desires had led her to "open the gate" to him did not involve her soul. A woman who has "chosen" to allow a man access to her self and her possessions and later regrets that choice is allowed no second thoughts; Dilke's fiction again ends in the woman's death.[163] In another chilling tale, "The Shrine of Death," a young girl "from infancy before all things, desire[s] to know the secrets of life," a longing which, joined with courage and compassion, sets her apart. She queries a witch, "Tell me, what are the secrets of life"; the witch replies, "Marry Death, fair child, and you will know." The risk of enslavement in the quest for knowledge is spelled out: Death's image in his shrine is surrounded by four "discrowned but majestic" statues of "women whose heads were bowed and whose hands were in chains" and the book of knowledge that Death opens for her is incomprehensible to her. Marriage for knowledge is the mark of a noble nature; it is also fatal. "What shall the secrets of life profit me, if I must make my bed with Death?"[164] As if in a mordant commentary on the line from Ruskin's Sesame and Lilies that Charles Dilke placed as an epigraph to his "Memoir" of Emilia Dilke, published with her Book of the Spiritual Life—"the path of a good woman is indeed strewn with flowers; but they rise behind her steps"—roses fall from the young woman as she descends into the crypt to marry Death.[165] In "The Outcast Spirit," another young woman seeks Death to "put her hand in his"; as in "The Shrine of Death," the young woman is refused by Death but nonetheless dies; flowers cover and fall from her body, like those of the Lady of Shalott and Elaine, as she is entombed.[166]

Whether or not Francis Strong was seduced by Oxford as by Mark Pattison, Emilia Dilke repeatedly wrote stories of young women who marry for tuition and knowledge and of marriage as a set of walls into which women enter and within which they may die. Detached from the Pattison marriage and Oxford, set in strange and uncanny places of death and demons, Emilia Dilke's stories embody the unexceptional institutions of marriage and gender in demonic male figures. Female desire is both meritorious and violently punished, and there are no happy endings. If Emilia Dilke's texts do not directly address the specificities of her status as an Oxford wife, Oxford's gendered allocation of domestic and public power, status, and freedom is not reducible to Oxford's specificity, any more than the Pattison family stories of madness, status, education, and escape are adequately understood as a single family's psychopathology. Dilke's allegoricizations heighten our ability to see these stories as not just about Oxford marriages. Like the Pattison stories, the Dilke stories condense local imprisonments into memorable tales. Yet in all these stories, real goods are on offer: brothers offer resources to their loving sisters; spiritual passion endows suffering and submission with value; marriage is a route to knowledge and resources for women. The tensions in each of these stories—brothers offered their sisters access to knowledges they would not otherwise have had; spiritual passion endowed suffering and submission with depth and significance; marriage in and to Oxford was a route to real material resources and cultural prestige for women—do not mitigate but expose the binding powers of the structures of domesticity, family, and the violences of gender.

Woolf's essay on the Carlyles concludes, "How shall we, when 'ink-words' are all that we have, attempt to make them explain the relationship between two such people?"[167] I end with more ink words. Another text by E. F. S./Mrs. Mark Pattison, which predates Emilia Dilke's short stories and "The Idealist Movement," also suggests the legitimacy of passionate female desire for knowledge, inscribes that desire in history, and gives it intense, uncanny power. Emilia Dilke's "The Idealist Movement" would argue that positivism and other scholarly discourses are not that which the young seek but what they must struggle past to get to the true wisdom, Sophia, and her short stories would suggest that half-ignorant young women were seduced Eves whose pursuit of knowledge betrays them to sexuality and death. E. F. S. Pattison's scholarly *The Renaissance of Art in France* (1879) also presents a desiring Eve, in a painting by Jean Cousin (the Elder) titled "Eva Prima Pandora." But Pattison's text erases the canonical ending to the narrative it invokes and resists an ending, happy or unhappy; it offers instead a positive, enrapturing, and evasive picture.

E. F. S. Pattison's Cousin's Eve is strongly female, "the fertile mother of nations, the source of all life . . . [in whom] the manifold forces of Nature herself are embodied," the condensation of "all desirable charm of beauty," "passion," and "bodily strength." More: "this woman rules not the dominion of sense alone"—positivism cannot contain her—but "holds the keys which open the house of wisdom" because of her *controlled, intellectual, and clear desire.* "The fruit of the tree of knowledge was plucked in deliberate choice, not in lustful passion . . . [and] in her right hand, the sceptre which speaks her sovereign and author of life, is the broken branch from which the golden apples hang." As in Dilke's short stories, entry into sexuality as a condition of knowledge is suggested, but this is not a story of female subjugation to male sexual privilege: if the snake is phallic, he does not subject this female figure. In Pattison's text's reading of Cousin's picture, the serpent was *Eve's* tool, her "instrument" which *she* had "summoned," no devil but a servant, and she does not "shrink" from contact with his body. Here is "no sickly revulsion from the necessary means by which complete experience has been sought; no instinct of feeble disgust," but only clear eyes, without "melancholy regret."[168]

The Renaissance of Art in France places its story on Cousin's painting as if its presentation of this Eve is simply the obvious meaning of the picture, but Pattison's text participates in a series of feminist revisions of the biblical story. Some earlier learned women defended Eve against the charge of responsibility for the Fall by pleading her weakness, but Pattison's text more closely resembles some feminist Eves it predates. Elizabeth Cady Stanton recast Eve's act as the result of a laudable thirst for knowledge, and Honnor Morten would thank Eve that "we know the good and evil and are not lapt in ignorance"; Adam would have stayed ignorant but the braver Eve "was given the strength to grasp the apple, to proclaim that woman at least prefers wisdom." In 1925, Virginia Woolf merged Eve with a Victorian woman and the female figures in that woman's fictions. Woolf's essay on George Eliot claims that, for Eliot and Eliot's heroines, "the burden and complexity of womanhood were not enough; she must reach beyond the sanctuary and pluck for herself the strange bright fruits of art and knowledge . . . we behold her, a memorable figure . . . reaching out with 'a fastidious yet hungry ambition' for all that life could offer the free and inquiring mind and confronting her feminine aspirations with the real world of men."[169]

In the introduction, I too associated apples, vision, and knowledge, imagining in words the multiple and inexhaustible possibilities of vision in cutting, slicing, and turning a sensual object. Although I have just inscribed E. F. S. Pattison's Cousin's Eve into a feminist tradition in the making, two of the next three chapters of this book offer more possibilities and other frames into which Pattison's Eve can be placed. Chapter 4 examines the stories told by some texts of the Pattison marriage as a struggle over bodies and women's sexual subjection in marriage. We may read *The Renaissance*'s Eve against these other stories as a form of whistling in the dark or as a defiant rewriting by Mrs. Pattison of the relations of sex and knowledge. Pattison's Cousin's Eve has already grasped the apple of knowledge and sexual sin and is motionless, "body and mind alike poised in calm," but she is "dignified and indifferent," un-diminished by her choices, unafraid, seeing "all things" with "equal eyes."[170] Or we might suspect that Emilia Dilke's short stories and "The Idealist Movement," like Charles Dilke's "Memoir," are the resumption of the battle for stories about the Pattison marriage. After all, many readers of Emilia Dilke's allegories and essay could comfortably be assumed to know that she had been Mrs. Mark Pattison, and they might well know of scandalous linkages of the Pattisons to novels of disastrous con-jugality. Dark and violent stories of bad marriages written and published by Emilia Dilke could be both as a private working-through and a gloatingly public blow in a final round of conjugal conflict after Mark Pattison was safely dead. Chapter 6, how-ever, offers some accounts of the public politics of sex in the 1880s and 1890s and allows us to speculate that the differences between the 1879 *Renaissance of Art in France,* the 1886 and 1891 volumes of short stories, and the 1897 "The Idealist Movement" index a larger history of contestation over feminist representations of women as sexual actors. Did heterosexual activity in a male-dominated society in general and "instrumental" heterosexual activity in particular come to be represented as more dangerous, more unsurvivable, for women in late-century feminist texts? Did stories about the costs of sexual barters, which represent marriage for knowledge and resources as a fatal bargain, become more tellable once other, nonconjugal routes to learning came to exist—for example, in the founding and expansion of women's colleges? Women's walls were built in Oxford in the very year of *The Renaissance of Art in France*'s publication with the foundation of Somerville and Lady Margaret Hall. More narrowly, an implied status of victimization in Emilia Dilke's first marriage, hinted through stories published after her second marriage, might covertly bolster her status as a noble victim of the Crawford-Dilke divorce case. In between, chapter 5 returns to some themes of chapter 2 and emphasizes that representations of women in/as pictures may be exhilarating and politically ambiguous.

I offer possible frames for E. F. S. Pattison's Eve without resolution. Pattison's text reads a picture of a story. Emilia Dilke's stories and essays suggest that bonds can be self-imposed and bad choices can be made—souls can be sold to devils and girls can marry death—but *The Renaissance of Art in France* stops the story, freezing it midway, Eve still unpunished and unrepentant. Instead, *The Renaissance* provides a teasing reminder of the profuse meanings in the absent image—"Every detail helps the complete expression of that deliberate revolt of the human intelligence against self-imposed bonds."[171] But Pattison also tells a story about the absence of a picture. The owners of *Eva Prima Pandora,* according to Pattison, maintain a tradition of refusing to allow it to be reproduced. The present owner says, "Look as much as you like; when you have left my house you may see how your memory will serve you. Write if you like, but draw a line you shall not."[172] Looking and writing, we cannot draw a line that ends these stories.

4

BODIES

Marriage, Adultery, and Death

This chapter, like the last, ranges through three sets of stories: stories that depict marriage as a site of mortal conflict over bodies and minds; stories of extramarital relationships that invite and elude scandalously sexual interpretations; and stories about dying. In each section, I show stories embedded in the texts of relationships and stories that circulated more widely; the story of sex told by Francis Pattison's letters and the stories Emilia Dilke published about women's bodies; the story constructed by Mark Pattison and Meta Bradley about their innocence and the novel Rhoda Broughton published in revenge for Mark Pattison's involving her in his stories; the story of Mark Pattison's death his wife/widow told and that death's ironic relation to novels. In these tales, bodies—conjugal and celibate, wedded and unlicensed, expressive and paralyzed, healthy and suffering, living and dead—form the stakes in and gesture to urgent struggles over minds, souls, families, and writing.

I begin by examining Emilia Dilke's stories of marriage as a battle over bodies. Francis Pattison's epistolary struggles with Mark Pattison and her relationships of confidence with other women oscillate between fury and guilt, as sexuality forms both a crucial site of struggle and anguish in the Pattison marriage and a language through which other struggles are waged. Francis Pattison/Emilia Dilke presented bodies as sites of suffering and grounds of resistance, but these stories are not reducible to sexual meanings, and Pattison/Dilke's stories—published and private—about marriage as a violent contest reveals the usability, as well as the importance, of the language of bodies in other angry narratives of refusal. This theme is continued in the second section. While the program notes for Tom Stoppard's Oxford play, The Invention of Love, easily categorize Mark Pattison as "a cuckolded married celibate," I refuse the question of who did what with whom in the relationships between Francis Pattison and Charles Dilke and between Mark Pattison and Meta Bradley and instead look at how usable stories were made by sustaining ambiguity about bodies. I do not read the texts of these possibly adulterous pairs as if the goal were the decisive breaking of a code or the unmasking of texts' "secret" sexual truths, not only because the presence or absence of specific acts can never be settled by texts, but because, I argue, "resolution" would strip away precisely those elements that constructed these relationships—their movement among discourses, subject positions, and rhetorics. In chapter 3, I argued that rhetorics of family romance and gendered pedagogy sometimes fused in stories of seduction and marriage.[1] These letters' shifts between erotic and comradely affections; partnership and mentoring; political strategy and romantic poetry; spirituality and worldly sophistication; fatherhood, daughterhood, brotherhood and sisterhood; mirroring and difference; communion, dependence, and power also give evidence of the multiplicity of desires and men's and women's unequal access to economic and cultural resources.

Despite ambiguities, vigorous denials and erasures of "evidence," these writers could not contain their relationships in safe categories or keep sexualized gossip from permanently imbuing them with the whiff of scandal. Had Francis Pattison or Meta Bradley been characters in a Victorian novel, the behaviors in which they engaged would have ensured their deaths by the final page. The punitive economy of the novel punished even the appearance of female sexual impropriety, let alone the secret engagement of a married woman anticipating widowhood or an unmarried "girl" snogging with an older man in a taxi.[2] These relationships were guilty whether or not they were adulterous. But that these participants could refuse to narrate their relationships as doomed and sinful reveals the presence and strength of other discourses through which eros might circulate, even if no terrain could be permanently marked out as innocent.[3] Of course, the fact that in life thunderbolts do not strike with the same punctuality and precision as in novels cannot have been lost even on the most unquestionably guilty Victorians, but Emilia and Charles were aware of dangers nonetheless. According to Marie Belloc Lowndes, when Constance Flower, Lady Battersea, told a friend a story about Charles and Emilia meeting by private arrangement at her house—including "a funny little incident of a dropped and picked-up geranium"—Charles reacted with panic. He called on her for "fourteen consecutive days" before finding her in; after exchanging social pleasantries, "suddenly he said, 'You don't look like a cruel woman!' . . . you have been very cruel without meaning it to a noble, beautiful, and innocent lady. You told a friend of yours that I had met Mrs. Mark Pattison at your house.' Then he burst into tears!"[4] In Lowndes's tale, Charles Dilke was both fully in command of the language of innocence and intensely worried about the costs of appearances.

Relationships between marriage, adultery, and death recur in the third set of stories I tell. Emilia Dilke wrote and published stories easily read as angry, guilty allegories of her first marriage, but the death that ended the marriage was not hers. Mark Pattison's death allowed her to enact and write stories of virtuous attendance and loving care; to tell stories about his family, his scholarship, and his soul; and to write an Oxford story in which patriarchal institutions kill men. But in a final turn to the absurd, the history of the Pattison Papers as a long-running headache for the Bodleian

Library's staff offers a comic story about death and the contestation of narratives long after bodies had lost any chance to enact murderous, tender, or transgressive desires.

Marital Bodies

Mrs Pattison's Parrot

The cruelest story Francis Strong Pattison told about her marriage to Mark Pattison was not in a published short story. It was a parable she told in letters and in company, which George Meredith abbreviated as the story of "Mrs Pattison's parrot."[5] The fullest rendition is in a letter Mrs. Pattison wrote from France to her confidante Eleanor Smith in 1881, when Francis and Mark's relations were at their nadir. First recalling that Thomas Carlyle had described Mark Pattison as looking like "Joost a human birrrd of prey," Francis Pattison's text claims:

> I feel sometimes as if my life cld never hold out against the incessant peck, peck, peck of the cruel beak. The weakness of nerve wh the life at L[incoln College] created disappears only to be fretted into being again by these incessant worries. For nineteen years I have been struggling to keep down the longing for deliverance—I cannot, it is always there—I can stifle it by working but it springs up stronger than ever. No one can know, not even you, all that I've had to bear—it seems very weak to complain but its safe with you & you know that I soon ma[y?] fight again as hard as ever.

Francis Pattison's body is a site of oppression; Mark Pattison's demands have "fretted" her nerves to weakness, even collapse, and his demands impede her ability to carry out sustaining work. Hinting at unspeakable pains but representing herself as valiantly fighting on, Francis Pattison continues the bird motif and reminds her friend of a "joke."

> Do you remember the American parrot who was shut up with a monkey—They found her without a single feather even in her tail, she remarked as the door opened "Oh! I've had a Hell of a time" & then proceeded beak & claw undaunted to go it again. When I feel bad, I try to reflect on that parrot! I don't know whether she got the better of the monkey, but I think she deserved to. May I deserve it![6]

This "joking" story has an edge of extraordinary brutality, both as a depiction of the Pattison marriage and as a story Francis Pattison told about Mark Pattison; Gertrude Tuckwell sought to have this letter suppressed or destroyed.[7] The language is not only "intemperate" but sexual; the "parrot" is female and is "stripped" by the malicious monkey. The monkey's pulling away of feathers parodies a common Victorian trope of men's pursuit of knowledge as dissecting and dismembering, including Emilia Dilke's essays' and allegories' figures of female knowledge's veils rent by knives. The sexual connotations are heightened by the detail that the monkey left "her" not even a feather in her tail.[8] But Mrs. Pattison's parrot is not passive. She refuses decorous feminine language, cries out with blasphemous vigor, and returns to the fray, combining moral right (she "deserved to" win) with physical resistance. Like Francis Strong/Emilia Dilke's family in Dilke accounts, she is American in ancestry and in "unconquerable physical and moral courage."[9]

Emilia Dilke's allegorical fictions often tell highly physical stories of girls and women's bodily confinements and sufferings, and in private texts, Francis Pattison portrayed a warfare with Mark Pattison over his legal and "moral" claims over her body. Even in their incessant epistolary arguments over money, Francis reads Mark's letters as implying that her physical well-being was unimportant to him and that she was physically undisciplined, eating and dressing above his means.[10] In other letters, Mrs. Pattison's ill health appears as the result of Mark Pattison's demands, and even her life is at stake. A chronology of Francis Pattison's medical history is not easily reconstructed, even within the diagnostic terms of her time. Charles Dilke placed her first "great illness"—which dulled her "bright gold" hair—in the winter of 1867/1868 and claimed she collapsed again the following winter.[11] Francis Pattison wrote to Rosa Tuckwell in 1868 that her health was precarious and she was only just on the mend from a great collapse. Illness and the return of her girlhood "delicacy" thus seem to coincide with the breakdown of her marriage.[12]

A few letters reinforce the implications of sexualized struggle and suffering in the parrot joke and in Emilia Dilke's fictions by suggesting that gynecological complaints coincided with emotional distress and inability to tolerate Oxford and Lincoln College. She wrote from France of a painful abscess on her vulva which appeared just before Mark Pattison was due to visit her.[13] But letters to Mark Pattison, Charles Dilke, and Eleanor Smith also associate her menstrual periods with illness; they weakened her and "brought out" latent ailments.[14] Again, we cannot know very much. We do not know what knowledge or expectations about sexual relations Francis Strong possessed before marriage. However anatomically informed Francis may have been by virtue of her art studies, there is no way to know she knew about heterosexual intercourse or how she envisioned her marriage, nor can we know whether Francis and Mark Pattison had sexual intercourse very often. There are no surviving traces that Francis was ever pregnant, but that need not denote a lack of penile-vaginal intercourse since Mark certainly possessed the financial resources to command methods of contraception.[15] Despite the bride's youth, scarcely any comments on the Pattison nuptials suggest the possibility of little Pattisons: none of Mark's sisters expressed such an expectation.[16] Gertrude Tuckwell and Charles Dilke represent Emilia Dilke as fond of children, but this is no evidence that Francis desired them.[17] Mark and Francis may have jointly decided children would interfere with scholarly work and household tranquility.

Mark Pattison easily named his wife's physical and emotional status and claimed the right to say whether or not her doctors were correct, whether or not her pain was real, whether or not she was in a fit state to attend to conjugal duties. Francis Pattison's letters to Eleanor Smith relay Mark Pattison's "mad" accusations that she "made [her]self ill on purpose to get away from him, & be in town" in a larger account of their marriage as a struggle for interpretive control.

I do think the more blame one takes to oneself (wh is what I've always been doing for the sake of peace) the worse he gets. I think it is better for him that I had never gone on that line but I was too young [to] not feel somehow guilty whenever a person so much my superior in every way chose to think so . . . If he is convinced, & the thing once gets into swing of talk nothing will satisfy him short of my saying that it was so.[18]

Francis Pattison suggests that Mark's assumption of the power to name reality and to treat her subjectivity as an object to which he had access superior to her own was at the core of her marital distress. As in "The Idealist Movement," the young are vulnerable to powerful stories told by older, more intellectually sophisticated persons.

I resist naming Francis Pattison's illnesses as only a weapon in her marital war. Our inability to know the physiological status of Francis Pattison's body, in sex or otherwise, need not align us with Mark Pattison or with Lord Acton's caustic summary: "Mrs Mark Pattison . . . seems to live in these parts [France] because her husband is in England."[19] There is a rich literature on the Victorian uses of female invalidism, but recognizing that illness was highly scripted and that it may be read— sympathetically or condescendingly—as strategy or self-expression does not require us to dematerialize suffering or translate bodily ailments into psychiatric or social discourses.[20] That a body is represented in highly mediated texts and that Francis Pattison experienced her body within discourse, does not mean that a body of nerves and bone and blood did not feel pain or pleasure. Francis Pattison's own texts specify that mental suffering can bear physical effects: the 1868 letter to Rosa Tuckwell foregrounds the entangling of bodily and mental.

> At present (wh is just what dearest mother fails to comprehend) I am still a "nervous invalid," & this they [doctors] say wld have been just the same, even had there been no *local* derangement. I used to tremble for half an hour if I heard a bell ring, & now I still cannot suffer much external distraction. A stranger or acquaintance is torture to me & if I force myself to meet the terror the reaction is serious in its results on sleeeping, & on my heart wh will be the last thing to right . . . *little* things wh I cld meet bravely at any other time are often a heavy trouble.[21]

Francis's reported symptoms can be placed in typologies of organic or psychosomatic illness: heart palpitations and weakness were the result of "nervous" stress ("I have been in a state of collapse & the mere thought of encountering anyone I *know* is horrible to me"), but she also reports, in straightforwardly physiological terms, weakness and even paralysis in the left hand and both arms and difficulties with her eyes.[22] The portions of Francis's body most affected by illness—hands, eyes, and genital/reproductive system—were those Mark Pattison commanded for sex, writing his letters and business correspondence, and reading to him, but these debilities also interfered with her own studies and her vision remained fragile and her heart weak in later life; she probably died of a heart attack. The possibility of complex relations between physiology and psychology does not mean physiology can never be causal: Francis Pattison may have "really" suffered from gout, arthritis, and other illnesses exacerbated by the foul standing water and poor drainage of Oxford.

Charles Dilke told a heroic story in which Francis Pattison fought to prevent her illnesses from interfering with her attendance on Mark Pattison, but her health was most precarious at Lincoln and necessitated spending more and more time away.[23] In 1868, she recuperated from illness in Iffley and visited other friends; in 1875, she stayed with the Charles Newtons in the presumably more healthful environs of Bloomsbury.[24] Finally, after 1874, she required lasting escape from Oxford. By July of 1875, she had been sent by her physicians to the Continent, first to Wildbad in Germany and then to the south of France.[25] Mrs. Pattison settled in Draguignan, an inland village eighteen or twenty miles west of Grasse; the capital of Provence, Draguignan was somewhat off the most heavily beaten track of ailing English folk abroad, who were concentrated in Nice and Cannes.[26] At Draguignan, she eventually took a house, Île des Rosiers, named for the "miraculous" thornless "roses of St. Francis" growing there. The house was owned by her Burgundian housekeeper, Madame Moreau, who recalled Mrs. Pattison "revell[ing] in the sunshine and look[ing] out over the garden with its orange trees to the distant hills"; a surviving drawing of the garden by Francis Pattison is peaceful and serene.[27] It obviously compared very well indeed with the living quarters of most people in England or France at the time, but Francis, Charles Dilke, and Gertrude Tuckwell all saw Île des Rosiers as offering a "simple life" in keeping with Francis's purportedly Spartan tastes.[28]

Francis's letters, from the moment she arrived at Wildbad, represent Mark Pattison as having resisted her leaving and as hurling blame at her. A letter to Eleanor Smith quotes a letter of Mark's claiming, with her departure, that his "home is broken up & all [his] dream of happiness . . . vanished." By Francis's account, Mark claimed her illness was an act of volition; she quotes him, "I . . . hope that you may be . . . given back again to life, *such as you have now arranged that your life shall be.*" Francis's letter continues,

His letters almost drive me out of my mind & I feel so helpless to combat—& yet so irresponsible for the state in wh he is . . . what is one to say, how is one to deal with this? I'm at the end of my resources. I've tried affectionately comforting, I've tried reasoning, & I've tried taking no notice. All is vain. And if you could only know that I've never said a word abt any arrangement nor expressed any wish except for such as might give me most opportunity of looking after him.[29]

Francis's letter claimed Mark had even accused her of conspiring with her doctor. Francis Pattison asserted that her own state of body and mind were not the only causes of the deterioration of her marriage; "it is *not* I who am weaker but . . . he is getting worse with years."[30]

Francis's letters to Mark Pattison mitigate rage with guilt and attempts to placate. Francis had casually depicted herself, during a brief separation from Mark in 1866, as "thoroughly weary of idling" in her visits to friends and "longing to see my little den & get a scold from you," hitting notes of devotion to duty and love of scholarship and addressing Mark less as a wife than as a child or student.[31] These tones, which both diminish Francis's adulthood and remove her from wifehood, are also present in her 1875 letters. One letter reassures the "unreasonably gloomy" Mark that she wanted to reestablish as far as possible their past; they "must look forward" to being together again, "hard at work . . . you in your room & I in mine, when we shall encounter each other in Bodley . . . & end up with a long lesson, & reading in the evening." An overt language of parent/child relationship—"Your sick child is getting very anxious to have a line from you"—sometimes appears.[32] Another "confess[es]": "I always feel myself responsible for the state of mind you are in," while representing her as dependent on him ("you must pluck up your courage & give me a little. I want it"), covertly emphasizing the reality of her physical illness and positioning her as a good girl, wishing to please. "I cannot prevent myself from making an effort to cheer you when I see you depressed, & that exhausts me too much when I am so weak." Self-deprecation and self-justification, pleading and irritated claims of moral integrity, anger, guilt, and self-righteousness mingle: "Do trust me a little. I'm not perhaps the sort of person you quite approve but I have got *some* feelings & *some* sense of duty."[33]

Confidantes and Imitations

Francis Pattison's letters to Mark from July 1875 through the spring of 1876 repeatedly stress her devotion and desire to be with him although they include notes of frustration and bitterness. Letters to her Oxford confidante Eleanor Elizabeth Smith use a more intense rhetoric of desperation, fury, and guilt. Before examining the letters to Mark that most overtly assert her body can no longer be available to him, I want to examine Francis Pattison's letters to her female confidante and to place them in a set of suggestions about women's roles in sustaining each other's rebellions and submissions.

Francis Pattison's letters to Eleanor Smith represent her as impatient with or enraged by concessions to Mark and yet constantly undercut this rage with guilty self-doubt and fear of disapproval.[34] A letter imagining return to Oxford refers to a letter to Mark and to Smith's approval of a moderate tone: "I'm glad you thought I wrote 'wisely on the whole' to the Rector. By the 'coaxing' I suppose you mean the bit in wh I tried to make him look forward to my coming back well enough to go into harness again. Bodley—croquet—& ten lines of Greek in the evg. But I really am at a loss as to how to deal with him . . ." [35] Another letter claimed Mark's requirements of a woman were that she should be a "kind of contented machine" at his disposal and confessed "the only things I miss downright are you & the Bodleian." But this letter then attempts to excuse its tone of frustration ("Don't think I'm complaining") and to recast anger and impatience in more acceptable terms while emphasizing Mark's unreasonableness, the high costs of submission to him, and her own attention to legitimate duties.[36] Elsewhere, Francis argued, "I invariably do & have considered all that is due to him *before* I . . . do what I th[ink] best for myself . . . before deciding to absent myself in the winter—all medical opinion concurring . . . that I must gradually become a helpless cripple if I do not—I spent hours weighing the question whether my duty enjoined me to sacrifice my whole future at the age of 33."[37] Expressing willingness to sacrifice her health for Mark if that should be the "right" thing to do, Francis Pattison's texts present her as tempted to martyrdom; "I should like to know what it wld be *right* for me to do abt the winter [i.e., whether she should return to Oxford against doctors' advice]. I don't wish to be a cripple, but if crutches wld buy peace I must consider whether I'll pay for it. I'm in a good deal of pain, & of course this perpetual worry is extra-trying . . ."[38] These emphases on the high stakes in her marriage—her health, her future, her pain—earn their anger by repeatedy underlining the outrageousness of Mark's demands.

These tensions between guilt and fury, self-abnegation and self-assertion, astonishing frankness and clichéd convention reflect the complex roles "Ellen" or "Nell" Smith played in Francis Pattison's life. They probably met before Francis's marriage through Henry and Sarah Acland and their friendship lasted until Smith's death in 1896.[39] The friendship between the two women can be read as a relationship in which

Francis Strong Pattison was a surrogate daughter to a caring, somewhat unconventional, loving and listening older woman, parallelling Francis's relationship to George Eliot. To both women, Francis seems to have poured out "all affairs of the heart." Rosemarie Bodenheimer has analysed Eliot's letters to several younger women—Elma Stuart Fraser, Georgiana Burne-Jones, and Edith Simcox as well as Francis Pattison—and noted Eliot's construction of a role as "motherly mentor" to "spiritual daughters."[40] Eliot's letters to Francis Pattison use an overtly maternal rhetoric, addressing Francis as "Figuolina" [daughter], "Goddaughter," and "daughter," and signing herself "Madre."[41] Such care and supportiveness implicitly compare favorably with Francis's representations of her mother, whom she represented as unsympathetic and failing to recognize her daughter's distress. Moreover, Eleanor Smith and George Eliot positioned Francis Pattison as a shared object of care and concern; Eliot was pleased that "at last the precious Miss Smith came to [Francis] with loving guardianship."[42] (Other older women could also enact this role of comfort, advice, and encouragement; according to Charles Dilke, Madame Moreau, whom Mrs. Pattison's guest Randolph Caldecott drew as a nurse in his Babes in the Woods, also offered Mrs. Pattison close physical care and sympathy along with toughmindedness and worldly experience.[43]) Smith's and Eliot's letters emphasise Francis's fragility and employ diminitives in addressing or referring to her: Eliot's letters consistently stress Mrs. Pattison's smallness of stature and appearance of youth and Smith calls her "our poor little friend."[44] George Eliot's letters are also acutely and commiseratingly concerned with Francis's physical state: "your long, wearisome endurance of pain which eats itself into every cranny of mind & body [and] may sometimes [have] seemed to you to deserve the name of agony." Eliot expressed horror that Francis requires chloral to sleep and writes of being "haunted" by the sight of Francis's "white face & lips" and her "acute & disabling pain." Eliot urged Francis Pattison to continue her "virtuous industry," encouraging her to ground her sense of self in the triumph of her "vivacious" "mental energy" over her "bodily suffering," but she ratifies Francis's pain as important.[45] Like Eliot, Ellen Smith affirmed Francis's strength; Smith advised a despairing Charles Dilke in 1885 to rely on Francis's vitality: "You must remember what a different temperment hers is to yours—much more elastic. So long as she is not touched in her deepest confidence and affection, she rises, like an indiarubber ball, in the face of trouble."[46]

But Smith offered more than quasi-maternal nurturance and support. Eleanor Smith had a career as a highly intellectual, philanthropic, devout, and feminist woman. She was the daughter of an Irish barrister who died when she was six; her mother, Mary Murphy Smith, moved the family to Oxford to better educate her four children, although only two, Eleanor and Henry, survived to adulthood. Henry Smith became Savile Professor of Geometry and later Curator of the University Museum, and the brother and sister lived together until his early death. Eleanor Smith was widely depicted in Oxford as learned, pious, and fiercely dedicated to work; an emblematic story claims that when as a child she was told to keep a younger sister quiet during an uncle's mortal illness, Eleanor found "a Hebrew Grammar & a Dictionary & taught her small charge Hebrew." As an adult, she was renowned for organizing practical measures for alleviating distress. On the Management Committee of the Radcliffe Infirmary and the Committee of the Sarah Acland [Convalescent] Homes, she was an early proponent of state measures to alleviate social distress and paid out of her own pocket for a District Nurse for the poor in the Jericho section of Oxford for many years while also lobbying to have the city take responsibility for public health.[47]

Smith played an active role in expanding education in Oxford. In 1871 she ran a hard-headed independent campaign for the Oxford School Board, stressing women's superior knowledge of the needs of children in general and of girls in particular and her own status as someone the poor of Oxford knew "as a good friend." In a very acrimonious election, she was attacked as antireligious for her support for nonsectarian schools and as overstepping the proper bounds of womanhood; "excellent as ladies are in their own sphere, we take leave to doubt whether public government is the place for them. Mere acquaintance with the poor, and interest in girls, however estimable, can scarcely constitute a claim which can overbalance the unseemliness of the spectacle [of women public officials]." Smith won and as a Board member was largely responsible for establishing a local "industrial" day school which ended the removal of children from their families.[48] Francis Pattison positioned Smith as an influence on her belief in the historical inexorability of spreading working-class education and enfranchisement; Smith taught her to want to learn how to "deal with the 'public' . . . [and] work with them," so when the "great Leviathan of Democracy" came "they" should be fitted to "use as well as to possess power."[49]

Eleanor Smith supported Somerville College and the Oxford High School for Girls, an important institution in increasingly heterosocial and familial Oxford, and she was deeply involved in a metropolitan venture in women's education as a trustee of Bedford College.[50] Elizabeth Jesser Reid founded Bedford—then encompassing a college and a girls' school—in a spirit of intensely visionary and practical feminism to "elevat[e] the moral and intellectual character of Women," counter the "enemy" of antifeminism, and fulfill a "dream" she had had "since childhood." In a powerful metaphor, Reid hoped the college would be "as an Underground Railway, differing in this from the American U.R. nobody shall ever know of its existence." Like the better-known Langham Place group, Reid and her first two trustees, Eliza Bostock and Jane Martineau, shared with Smith a language of morally serious but ecumenical feminism that stressed the value of women's work, commitment, and self-development through education and social responsibility. Bostock wrote in 1848, "I would like women to enjoy the right to work, to labour, to earn independence, and then they would be in a condition to make themselves heard . . . self-reliance I would rather give to women than anything else because it is just what they want and they have it not . . . there has been no room for its existence . . . a good education . . . placed within reach of a young woman by her own exertions . . . would be a stimulus to her whole nature and give her power over herself." Bostock and Martineau, proposing Smith as a trustee, represented her as a woman who did not want the post "from love of power and patronage" and, while pious, was not motivated by "religious zeal" or a wish to "throw [the students] into the hands of a priest."[51] Smith took up a leading role in Reid's "Great and Good Cause" as an institution builder with an eye for political strategy. She became "a power in the College . . . which made itself felt for more than a quarter of a century." She brought Oxford allies to London, helping integrate Oxbridge and London intellectual life—Mark Pattison, Albert Dicey, Ingram Bywater, and Nevil Story-Maskelyne served on the College Council—but staunchly fought demands by male teachers and supporters to adulterate Elizabeth Reid's vision. (She organized a "coup d'état" to prevent the conversion of the college into a girls' day school and to retain power in the hands of the women trustees rather than the male-dominated Council.) In 1881, on "the day when the Graces allowing women to take the Tripos examinations at Cambridge were passed—she burst into the dining-room at Bedford College, where [the students] sat at dinner, crying excitedly, 'We have won! We have won!' "[52]

Mary Arnold-Forster (daughter of Nevil Story-Maskelyne) found a "deep-seated tenderness and understanding which drew young people to her and inspired their enthusiastic devotion," but some students found Eleanor Smith frankly "alarming." She was known for "caustic humour," "directness of speech," "distinction of mind, enthusiasm, and sincerity of purpose," lack of self-consciousness and "indifference to externals."[53] Francis Pattison referred to Smith's "usual witch-of-Endor costume" and Charles Dilke joked of her tendency to indiscretion; a Bedford student recalled her as "a stout, active figure, clad in an ill-fitting brown holland dress buttoned up the front—carrying triumphantly down the Edgware Road long rolls of French bread for her brother's breakfast."[54] A photograph in the Bedford College history presents Smith plump and pensive in a full dark skirt, quietly reading in a typical Victorian parlor pose.[55] A photograph by Angie Acland of a stout woman in dark brocade whose lacy cap contrasts sharply with her raked-back grey hair, protruding lower lip, and steel-rimmed spectacles nonetheless has an indefinable element of pretense, as if Smith were purposefully looking "severe"; a second Acland photo has Smith pointing a lecturing finger at Henry Acland.[56] Willingly eccentric, Eleanor Smith appears uncompromising, self-mocking, and slightly theatrical in the service of ideals.

These strains run through Smith's few surviving letters. Like Felicia Skene, an Oxford contemporary who also influenced younger Oxford women, Smith tempered injunctions with comfort, was a warm friend to unorthodox women, and supported women's entry into public life from a foundation of piety and frank moral rigor.[57] Smith even acted as a private banker for Francis. The wages of Francis Pattison's intellectual work were Mark Pattison's by right until the 1875 Married Women's Property Act, and Mark had tried to claim Francis's inheritance from her mother as his by "moral right," so Francis sent her earnings to Smith for safe-keeping.[58] As well as offering such feminist services, Smith may have found covert pleasure in Francis Pattison's knack for denouncing Oxford. But by the 1880s, Eleanor Smith was represented by some younger Oxford residents as a figure of convention, censorious of youthful pleasures, and despite her enthusiasm for young people, her advice often emphasized controlling one's desires.[59] Smith expressed concern to Ingram Bywater when Francis Pattison's letters betrayed "a strain of exasperation" and applauded when Angie Acland seemed to be gaining in "character & comfort to others."[60] Albert Venn Dicey cast her as his unofficial undergraduate tutor; she had "rare ability and force of character . . . laboured more for the town than any other woman [and] . . . I owe more than I can say to Ellen for stirring up energy within me . . . [and teaching] the absolute moral need of working in some way or another. This belief in work was really ground into me by Ellen . . . it is an immense defence, though not a complete one, against temptations."[61]

Smith counseled Francis Pattison in the ways of righteousness and Francis's letters suggest a belief that her words and actions would be scrutinized for adherence to high standards of duty and right conduct.[62] Francis's letters oscillate between expressions of anger and attempts to convince her correspondent of her sense of guilt and good intentions, struggling to extricate refusal of wifely duties from tainted expressions of selfishness. She insisted she could hardly bear to "take any step without [Smith's] approval," and her 1876 letters to Smith work almost as hard to convince Smith of the moral legitimacy of her separation from Mark as those to Mark himself.

> The attitude of mind [Mark's "moroseness"] implies can only be quieted by the ruthless sacrifice of the peace of everyone abt him . . . he is incapable of recognising as lawful any other wants than those he himself can & does feel . . . I fear that open war, or be ground under his heel is the only choice. You know I do & have tried, & will for what may lie between but I cannot *die* & *I was dying* . . . Don't think me even if I seem so, hard or unfeeling for "the other" I am not, & I do know that I went to the very edge, & I doubt that any compromise such as you always preached was possible there is a tyranny of instinct.[63]

Francis Pattison's syntax breaks down as she attempts to write freely of strong feelings but fears "Nell" will judge her or advise compromise. Pattison's text reaches frantically to justify her refusal of Mark Pattison as a matter of life and death and of nature's laws beyond preachments, warding off imputations of "hard, unfeeling" unnaturalness. Francis's letters periodically reiterate that her ability to exert desirable self-control over her emotions is increasing, but remind Smith that this was an achievement against great odds; an 1882 letter claims she was beginning to be able to tolerate Mark Pattison's "monstrous" irrationalities without breaking into that "passionate resentment" that had "poisoned so many years of [her] young life and drove [her] to desperation & the verge of the utmost folly." She owed this attainment to her dear "Nell": "I feel as if I never could be sufficiently grateful to you for having divined the terrible struggles wh were behind the restlessness & levity & for having believed that I shld work through."[64]

Francis Pattison thanks Eleanor Smith not for having encouraged her in revolt but for strengthening her fortitude within her marriage while reminding Smith that any revolt would have been strongly provoked. Again, in 1884, as Mark descended into his final illness, Francis insisted to Smith that her moral fiber was strong and she was a good wife *despite the odds*: "Encouraged by you & hoping agst hope I have gone on striving for years for the relations wh you always prophesied might be possible . . . [Recently] though I have given way to fits of impatience . . . I was at heart beginning to see things as you wished me to see them . . . [and] to feel the most real desire to give him sympathy & comfort."[65] Eleanor Smith's love and feminism did not license Francis Pattison to behave in ways susceptible to interpretation as selfishness, indiscipline, or the overriding of sense by emotion.

Francis Pattison also shared a moral discourse of work, discipline, and service with the artistic, politically sophisticated, and personally unconventional Pauline Trevelyan, whose picture Emilia Dilke wore in a locket until her death. As in Francis's narratives of shared political engagements with Smith, letters to Trevelyan depict writer and recipient as engaged in ongoing public art careers. Francis takes up etching and lace design, assists Trevelyan in efforts to market women's craftwork, boasts of continuing to draw and paint "averag[ing] 6 hours a day steady drawing" when on holiday, enters a commissioned drawing in a "Ladies" exhibition (perhaps the Society of Female Artists annual show), sends a picture to the Dudley Gallery where she hoped it would sell for twenty-five pounds, and recounts plans for "decidedly modern" works that "pay best."[66] Throughout these letters, Francis Pattison represents herself at work, attempting to master the representation of "action." One letter even evokes Trevelyan as an ally in complex relationships with male art authorities, pointedly asking her to tell Ruskin "not to give [her] up yet," and assuring her: "I am working hard [and] . . . my old master thinks well of my progress . . . & thinks me fairly in the way." As in letters to Smith, Francis emphasizes the odds against her—"Sometimes I get hopeless & ask to what?" but quickly asserts her morality and natural sense of obligation, adding "not often however in spite of what Mr Mulready calls my ascetism of tone the 'on & be doing' call always has a response."[67] But if Pauline Trevelyan was, like Eleanor Smith, a supporter in independent, public activities, Betty Askwith and Raleigh Trevelyan surmise Pauline Trevelyan also played another role, setting an example, in her own unhappy marriage, of duty, self-abnegation, and quiet.[68]

The exaltation of feminine moral power need not lead to feminism: Albert Venn Dicey, who testified so strongly of Eleanor Smith's influence on him, was a leading opponent of women's suffrage.[69] More complexly, although Eleanor Smith and Pauline Trevelyan each fostered women's participation in public spheres, neither necessarily encouraged active rebellion rather than morally laudable acceptance of women's lot in the private sphere. Rebellion against customary gender arrangements could be formulated as a form of solidarity with other women and an adherence to duty; Victorian feminists later in the century developed a powerful language legitimizing refusal of male sexual access, even in marriage, as obedience to higher laws. But the letters of Francis Pattison remind us that the "female world of love and ritual" could include the development and elaboration of discourses in which loving women, offering each other the consolations of sisterhood and high-minded inspirations to spiritual attainment and public responsibilities, also teach each other and themselves to submit to male authority.[70] As in the family languages of gendered submission in Hauxwell Rectory, high standards of personal ethics that took women seriously as moral agents could glamorize duty and self-restraint.

Emilia Dilke's "The Physician's Wife" concludes with an unsettling inscription of the protagonist's penitent death as an example to other women, an uncanny but powerful lesson in suppressing female rage. The protagonist, having killed her "malicious" husband, repented and atoned, dies and is "buried in a nameless grave" by her own wish. "But not long ago another, whose life was also torture," came to the place. "And the tempest in the air spoke to the fury in her soul, so that in wrath and anger she took her way . . . 'Has any,' she cried, 'ever borne the like!' and, as she said this, the gusty wind made answer," revealing beyond a tree "a tall white cross of wood, bearing neither name nor date but . . . [only] the words, 'Dites-moi un Pater,' and above and below she saw drops of agony or tears." The agony is not only Christ's but the dead woman's, who is nameless in death, life, and Dilke's text. Speech and silence contend: the physician's wife's "anguish liv[es] beyond the grave" but the grave's words dare not address God but implore passersby to ask for mercy from a divine patriarch on her behalf. The passing woman falls to her knees, eschews her angry words, then goes "silently away."[71]

These texts suggest how difficult and fracturing for Victorian women it could be to repudiate ideals of self-constraint and domestic subordination without self-hatred and a sense of failure to meet deeply felt standards. The paradigmatic literary treatment of this theme is Henry James's *Portrait of a Lady* but it is also central to Dorothea's dilemmas in *Middlemarch*.[72] But if "The Physician's Wife" extracts not one but two female penances for transgression, Francis Pattison/Emilia Dilke elsewhere engaged in a long-running argument with another text about these issues. Eleanor Smith gave Francis Pattison a Latin copy of the *Imitation of Christ*; Smith herself read the book every day.[73] The *Imitation* famously figures in one of the great nineteenth-century novels of tragic female desire, George Eliot's *The Mill on the Floss*. Carla Peterson argues that the *Imitation* endangers Maggie Tulliver by seducing her toward selflessness, contrasting it to John Bunyan's *Pilgrim's Progress*, so important to Alcott's "Little Women" and other Victorians. Peterson contends that Bunyan's story hallows movement and comradeship, but Kempis's offers "passivity and interiority . . . [and] in social terms . . . submission . . . to society's strictures."[74] Charles Dilke places the "Imitation" as one of "the two books which alone [Emilia Dilke] carried about and read throughout her life," and quotes her "constant declar[ation] that the 'Imitation' offered to her, of all single books, the 'richest nourishment.' "[75] But if the *Imitation* was a precious possession, Emilia Dilke's texts criticize it as a potential encouragement to feminine masochism, moral irresponsibility, and immobility. In "The Idealist Movement," the *Imitation* occupies a special place in Dilke's friend's reading; his "constant companion," it is inadequate to his needs. It "demanded . . . a self-abnegation . . . complete"; "the Imitation fails . . . us as soon as the sense of duty to oneself comes to form a part of one's conception of duty to others." Charles Dilke's "Memoir" repeats: Emilia Dilke came to see "so far as a sense of duty to one's self should form part of one's general conception of duty, the 'Imitation' failed."[76]

The *Imitation* is not just unhelpful; it is dangerous. Emilia Dilke's texts argue that Kempis's call to selflessness can be perversely morally corrupting. In "The Idealist Movement," Kempis's volume is implicated in the young man's struggle to accept confinement; he hopes "by self-discipline, all cravings would be stilled." The young man's attempts to render despair a form of resignation, and to translate "deadness" into "withdrawal from the world" and "monotony" into "aspiration to the higher life," are a kind of self-murderous dishonesty, the production of spiritual false currency.[77] "Of Love and Sorrow," in Dilke's posthumous *The Book of the Spiritual Life*, again insists the *Imitation* "fails us as soon as the sense of duty to oneself comes to form a part of one's conception of duty to others" and indicts it as fostering a covert form of greed for spiritual suffering. As noted in chapter two, "Of Love and Sorrow" warns of gendered seductions to histrionic piety, and "The Idealist Movement" also surreptitiously hints: the *Imitation* "must always be a source of strength and nourishment to those under the impression of the paramount moral obligation of self-sacrifice."[78] Dilke does not add: "for example, women," and the transgendering of the protagonist blocks such a muttered addendum, but the point remains: beloved spiritual discourses may ennoble silence, suppression, and lies.

The Common Life

Francis Pattison's struggle with her husband over control of her body was not simply about her health, her need to spend winters in France, or her provision of domestic service and scholarly assistance when in Oxford. Also at issue was Mark's right of sexual access. Until 1884 (thus for all practical purposes, for the duration of the Pattison marriage), a woman could be imprisoned for denying her husband's "conjugal rights." This right of command over a woman's body had provoked feminist ire by midcentury; Harriet Taylor criticized it on the grounds that women's pre-marital sexual ignorance and lack of economic autonomy negated their ability to make an informed and free decision. Marriage was therefore a contract in which "one of the parties, the necessarily virginal woman, could have no idea of what she was committing herself to."[79] This contract was, however, irrevocable; an 1880 decision held that "a husband cannot be guilty of a rape committed by himself upon his lawful wife . . . for by their mutual matrimonial consent and contract the wife hath given up herself in this kind unto her husband, which she cannot retract."[80] Despite reforms granting married women control of their earnings and some other rights of self-possession enacted in the third quarter of the century, a married woman was still her husband's property as a sexual outlet.[81] Dr. William Acton made the connection between feminist criticisms of marriage law and the possibility that women might refuse husbands' sexual access, claiming John Stuart Mill encouraged "women . . . [to] regard themselves as martyrs when called upon to fulfill the duties of wives."[82] By the 1870s and 1880s there was a pattern of public denunciation of verdicts upholding the rights of obviously brutal husbands, especially in cases involving other violence or in which the spouses were separated, but the legitimacy of marriage as a contract by which a woman ceded sexual control of her body to her husband remained law and "common sense."

Although feminist resistance to marital rape in the late century sometimes included a critique of sexuality tout court and a rhetoric, in social purity circles, of the desirability of marriages nearly or wholly sexless, in most feminist discussions of the theme the issue of "conjugal rights" is explored through discussions of marital rape, violence, venereal disease, and pregnancy.[83] Because there is no suggestion that Mark Pattison enforced his "rights" against his wife's consent after 1876, however, the Pattison case offers a struggle over "conjugal rights" free of these other issues. Rape, venereal infection, and unwanted pregnancy were certainly the most serious effects, and in practice the law of conjugal rights has not been gender-neutral but has granted men property in women, but the doctrine of conjugal rights can be seen as pernicious in itself, granting married persons property—in the form of usufruct—in each other's bodies. Thomas Hardy's Jude the Obscure implied that the notion of conjugal rights made a mockery of the romantic language of love and exposed the cruelty of a legal contract from which escape was difficult or impossible; the letter, as Hardy saw it, killeth.[84]

Francis Pattison's letters of sexual refusal to Mark Pattison contain the same taut confusion of anger, apology, guilt, and self-defense as her letters to Eleanor Smith; they also evoke her fictional accounts of young women married to sadistic men and devils. I quote these letters at length because the structure of each letter displays the difficulty Francis Pattison faced in writing sexual refusal and locating that refusal in legitimating discourses. The crucial letter of 21 January 1876 was written from France; it approaches the subject of Pattison marital relations by a circuitous route.[85] Francis Pattison's letter depicts herself as still devoted to Mark but reminds him their future is contingent on considerations of health and geography, implying that Mark needs to limit his expectations. Opening with assertions of her continued intellectual admiration for Mark and requests for his assistance on a number of points of Latin grammar, Francis's letter protests her appreciation of Mark's Oxonian virtues and proffers her own intellectual activity as evidence of her commitment to him and his ideals. Although she had "been getting rather fagged, excited & depressed" lately, she reassures Mark she is stable physically and her life is one of economic moderation, although she hastens to add that she shall need to winter in France "every year" since "the least cold affects me seriously, & damp even more so." "Nice . . . is not so great a punishment as [she] thought it wld be" and she has quiet for her art-writing, but she reassures Mark she will return to Oxford; she looks forward to "finishing & perfecting [The Renaissance of Art in France] in Bodley . . . & seeing all my friends in town with renewed zest in the hot weather."

Francis's text then conflates Mark with Oxford and, assuring him of her continuing respect for both, marks the limits of their compatibility: Oxford is "deficien[t in] the interests wh really stimulate my 'intellectual life,'" but offers "a type of life (of wh you seem to me the most perfect & complete expression) with wh I deeply sympathize." That sympathy and desire are not the same thing soon becomes clear.

> So deeply indeed [do I sympathize with Oxford's appeal] that there is but one side of the life with you into wh I do not enter—& that is so distasteful to me that the fear of its renewal has often preoccupied me to the exclusion of all other considerations. It is a physical aversion wh always existed, though I strove hard to overcome it, & wh is now wholly beyond control. But into your "intellectual life" it has, & always will be a pleasure, & a pride to enter, to be allowed in any degree to share . . . I am constantly thinking of you, thinking of whether you have all that you can desire for your comfort. . . .

Francis's letter then scurries to insist that her expenses in Nice are really lower than he thinks, imparts news of impending social engagements, and invites Mark and Ingram Bywater to help themselves to her imported French "cigars." She concludes with concern for Mark's lumbago. In short, this letter gave notice that sexual relations with Mark should cease while reiterating intellectual kinship and devoted pupillage. It affirms the importance of Mark's physical comfort by expressing a warm concern for his health and the proper management of his domestic arrangements—even offering the compensatory pleasure of exotic smoking materials—but ultimately this letter says Francis is willing to give everything he might want except one thing.

That one thing is doubly positioned. On the one hand, sex is minimized; merely "one side of the common life," its withdrawal will not affect Francis's willingness to care for Mark in other ways. This downplaying of sex trivializes in advance any objections Mark might make; his texts will need to reestablish the legitimacy and importance of the body against Francis's relegation of physical relations to a lesser plane than allegedly enduring intellectual bonds. (Ironically, Mark would dismiss concern about the presence or absence of corporeal pleasure as the mark of smutty little minds in defending his relationship with Meta Bradley.) This line of argument—sex's unimportance by comparison to mental and spiritual ties—was not only a generic deployment of a gendered binarism in which women's love is a matter of emotion and spirit so that gross physicality is beneath refined and proper women, if natural to men. In the Pattison marriage, the binarism of sex and spirit had particular resonance because it was undergirded by the discourse of intellectuality. Mark Pattison, as an Oxford cleric and don and in his specific persona, was a man who claimed to live only for the mind and advocated defining the university as a site of pure knowledge. If, therefore, the mind was what truly mattered, how could Mark object to Francis's withholding her body? On the other hand, however, Francis's letter asserts that sexual relations are not a trivial matter to her but have life-threatening consequences. Mark's expectations of sexual access have nearly driven her mad, filled her mind and inspired wild distress. Francis's text thus announces that her decision is final and nonnegotiable ("it is wholly beyond control") and the price of any insistence on Mark's part may be his wife's descent into despair. In such a state, her mind will be too full of fear of sexual intercourse for "other considerations"; the threat is not that Francis will die but that she will become useless, ruined for intellectual life or domestic management.

Francis Pattison's later letters elaborate these themes—the emotional and intellectual continuation of her marriage to Mark and the impossibility of a continuing sexual consummation. We do not have Mark's letters of reply, although it seems clear from Francis's texts that he reacted with considerable distress.[86] An undated letter from Francis seems to reply to Mark's immediate response with desperate reassurances of her devotion in the face of accusations that she neither loved him nor valued his love. Addressing "My dear dear Mark," Francis's reply insists "I am in no wise really changed to you . . . my first & constant thoughts are devoted to you . . . I value to the full all the goodness, & care you shew for me." Francis seems to ward off an accusation that her decision had, in effect, dissolved their marriage, reiterating that she is still bound to Mark and his wishes are hers. "You say I am 'free as to my movements' The only wish & intention I have is to return to you to Oxford as soon as the weather & my health permits . . . I do believe that when you have seen that you have all my thought, & anxiety to be your companion, & comfort the disappointment you feel at the state wh I have now confessed will be softened."[87]

Francis counters Mark's apparent definition of the marital tie as fundamentally constituted by sexual relations with an emotional counterdefinition. But while this letter asserts the superiority of emotion and common intellectual milieux to mere bodily relations, it also aims to convince Mark that her body *does* matter and its distress has a history and a claim to be respected:

> I will not attempt to defend myself agst the accusations either stated or implied wh you bring agst me. But you cannot forget that from the first I expressed the strongest aversion to that side of the common life, during 73–74 this became almost insufferable—but I tried to conceal it hoping that it might settle itself—you had told me constantly all along that it wld soon ease & when I thought it had by Acland's directions I rejoiced because I felt saved from any chance of wounding or distressing you. For believe me I wld suffer a great deal rather than give you a slight pain—much less a pain wh I feel not a slight one.[88]

Francis's history of the Pattisons' sexual relations—including the detail that they had consulted Dr. Acland (John Ruskin's confidant in the sexual debacle of his marriage)— positions Francis's suffering in sexual relations as both mental and physical. Her text implies that sexual intercourse with Mark Pattison hurt her and that she had become increasingly unable to bear that pain.

While we cannot know what happened to Francis Pattison's body in sex, she did have a body, and pain is no less "real" if expressive of a variety of meanings. Even in modern clinical terms, vaginismus resulting in painful intercourse is characterized as a syndrome in which priority of causation cannot be assigned solely to either physical or mental factors, as pain, fear, and memory may converge in muscle as well as mind. Francis Pattison's letter fuses physical and "tempermental" explanations. After a half-hearted attempt to placate Mark by telling him she was currently so sick and weak that sexual relations "must be impossible for a long time to come," her letter continues:

> All I meant when I said "the fear preoccupied me" was that when you were with me I have often refrained from shewing you the affection I feel on that account. I cannot but think I am differently constituted to most, & that the excessive nervous irritatility wh is always engendered by the malady under wh I suffer [i.e., her gout?] is the reason for the distress I laboured under throughout 74. You know you were greatly annoyed with me at le Locle, at Geneva, & in Paris, & I was trying hard for self-control.

Francis's letter concludes with a despairing cry, "Oh forgive me," a large and noticeable tear stain, and a reiteration of her love for Mark and her desire to fulfill his needs in every other way. But yet again, she asserts the unalterable physicality of her refusal of Mark while repeatedly striking the note of admiration for his intellect and commitment to his comfort. This repetition again conflates the discourse of married love with the admiration of a student for a teacher or a disciple for a master: "I never vary or have varied from feeling for you the deepest respect & regard, & . . . I shall never cease to wish dedicate my best energies to you & . . . I am suffering in saying what I have but when I see how deeply I have wounded you I hardly dare entreat your pardon or accept your generous forbearance."[89] This concluding supplication for pardon or forebearance constructs Mark and Francis's relationship as tutorial rather than explicitly erotic.

The final letter from Francis overtly addressing the issue of sexual relations was probably written only a few days later, again in reply to a missive from Mark. It begins with a more argumentative and less petitionary tone, correcting with brio Mark's "misinterpretation" of some comments she had made about money, and continues with a refusal to back down on her decision to cease sexual relations, despite another reassurance that Mark still has her affection. Mark seems to have claimed a sexless marriage would be unnatural, "a false groove," but Francis's letter moves to recuperate "nature" as a ground for her own claims, returning in mounting panic to the phrase, "fighting agst nature." Just as she wrote to Eleanor Smith that there was "a tyranny of instinct" she could not overrule, Francis wrote Mark that her body could not be controlled:

> I have honestly, & steadily endeavoured to take a shape of mind, & habit wh is essentially foreign to me, & have suffered greatly [in? by?] affronts agst nature—[from?] the year

before last (74) I was fighting agst nature recognizing this, & the conviction was daily becoming clearer to me. The key to my life lies in very excessive sensitiveness to a class of impressions wh find you wholly insensible, & I cannot wonder that you distrust their action. In July 74 it became evident to me that I was fighting agst nature & wasting my strength in a fruitless endeavour to become that for wh I was not fitted. I had gone on longer in this course, & was slow, & unwilling to believe in my mistake, because of the horrible pain it gave me to think of paining you as I knew any apparent change in me [certainly?] wld

Francis Pattison is presented to her husband as a failed student, offering an account of her shortcomings complete with dates. Her handwriting disintegrates along with her syntax. The letter ends in a nearly unreadable scrawl while displaying the respectful language of the pedagogical relationship with inappropriate precision: "I have no time for more, but do believe me always yr grateful pupil & yr faithfully affectionate EFS Pattison."[90]

Enforced Courses

The Pattisons did not continue to exchange letters on this topic, although later letters from Mark to Meta Bradley strongly suggest that their sexual relationship did indeed end in 1876. But on close examination of Francis Pattison's letters, it becomes less and less clear *exactly* what Francis can no longer bear. Is it only sexual relations, the ostensible site of conflict? The fragmented rhetoric of her letters to Mark suggests not only that Francis has been unable to rise to the challenge of accepting his sexual desires and "tuition," but that the body is a location of a more multidimensional rejection of Mark Pattison. Drawing upon liberal discourses of self-possession as well as medical languages of "nature" and objective physiological states, Francis Pattison's letters represent her body as the site of natural laws. Her assertion of special sensitivity to "a certain class of impressions" not only echos her letters' references to her health more generally, as in her claims to Rosa Tuckwell about the realness of the physical effects of ringing bells on her heart—realness her mother failed to understand—but recalls her account of her childhood hallucinations, misunderstood or denied by household members. As with Emilia Dilke's account of her childhood visions, her letters include assertions of intellectual difference from Mark but also claim an exceptional physiology.[91] Francis Pattison's bodily responses make her different from Mark and from other women, and no one can alter this body-based difference. As with the hallucinations, aesthetic sensitivity and physiology together produce psychic and physical experiences, but it is the body's double presence—as cause and effect—that makes suffering real and intractable to the claims of others and attempts to override it by volition. This doubling of the body is compounded by the claim that Francis must not sacrifice the health of her body or mind: the body is not only exceptional but an object within a normative ethics and rationality.

In E. F. S. Pattison's art-historical texts, the body may be a ground of pain or fear and implacably resistant; moreover, it is expressive. An essay on the artist Carstens evocatively describes a "clay-sketch" of a female figure: Carsten's roughly sculpted form expresses "a real sense of the beauty of flesh . . . instinct with original vigour and power," but it is also a *figure*, "the embodiment of a passionate outcry against fate, the expression of a wounded but untameable soul, to be subdued only by death."[92] Conversely, the joyous is physical, psychological, aesthetic, and spiritual all at once in an essay on Nicolas Poussin. Poussin is most "individual . . . in . . . his intense sense of the sympathetic union of humanity and nature," especially in fusions like fauns and satyrs in which the sexual is unmistakably present; bodies, emotions, and narratives, are mixed, as in Bacchic processions in which "children, instinct . . . fearless joviality . . . dogs, goats, and flowers," are "inextricably tangled in a wild wreath."[93] These oscillations of bodies, stories, emotions, and aesthetics suggest that stabilizing Francis Pattison's argument with Mark Pattison into a struggle over marital sex may be inadequate. I want to preserve ambiguity by reading Pattison/Dilke's texts "in both directions," continuing to read overtly ungendered texts by Pattison/Dilke as evoking sexual conflict but also reading stories of struggles over sex as accounts of other combats.

Emilia Dilke's short stories, I have argued, often developed plots of female figures seduced into marriage who come to regret their choices; like the story of Mrs. Pattison's parrot, they display fury; like Francis Pattison's letters, they narrate guilt. "The Silver Cage" and "The Physician's Wife" are especially readable as accounts of sexual subjection. In "The Silver Cage," Dilke's nameless protagonist draws the attention of the devil by the beautiful song of her soul. Her soul is not indissolubly bound to her body but is kept in a silver cage while the woman does domestic work, sewing a wedding garment she no longer believes she will need. The woman accepts the devil's contention that "Love does not dwell in the hearts of men," silences her soul by covering its cage with her abandoned wedding-dress, and "open[s] the gate and bid[s] him . . . welcome." The woman's loss of faith in her female destiny of romance and her splitting of mind and body from soul make possible her sexual capitulation to the devil. Her soul, like women's sexual bodies in marriage, becomes the property of another and vulnerable to violence. After the devil "entered the garden and took possession of the woman, and all that was hers," he demands more: "Shall not thy soul sing for me, since it is mine?"[94]

Robert Browning's *The Ring and the Book* also depicts a man's demand for not just compliance but desire in images of purchase, singing bird-souls, and devilish husbands. Count Guido Francheschini reasons:

> Purchase and sale being thus so plain a point,
> How of *a certain soul bound up, may-be,*
> I' *the barter with the body and money-bags?*
> From *the bride's soul what is it you expect?*'
> Why, loyalty and obedience,—wish and will
> To settle and suit her fresh and plastic mind
> To the novel, nor disadvantageous mould!
> . . .
> There is the law: what sets this law aside
> In my particular case? . . .
> . . . the law's the law:
> With a wife I look to find all wifeliness,
> As when I buy, timber and twig, a tree—
> I buy the song of the nightingale inside.

> Such was the pact: Pompilia from the first
> Broke it, refused from the beginning day
> Either in body or soul to cleave to mine . . .
> Before we had cohabited a month
> She found I was a devil and no man . . .[95]

In both Dilke's and Browning's texts, the devil-husband desires more than access to the woman's body; the soul is a desirous and true inner self. In Dilke's tale, the woman is bitterly punished for desire's absence:

> Yet though in all ways she strove to do the devil service and in all things she obeyed him, he would not be satisfied since in the one thing she failed and her soul was always silent . . . She asked counsel of many, and some mocked and some would have found their own advantage in her straits, and others cried "Shame," and bid her keep silence . . . the voices outside grew every day louder in rebuke, crying, "Ah, the shameless one, whose soul sings not for him to whom she hath opened the gate."

Dilke's protagonist has chosen to allow a man access to her self and possessions and later regrets that choice but is judged "guilty" if she refuses to live up to the terms of the marital contract. She seeks relief in work, "toiling without hope." Real "Love" eventually comes and calls at the gate, and hearing him, the silent soul again begins to sing. The enraged devil wrenches open the cage and attempts to strangle it. The woman's soul will be reunited with "Love . . . in the gardens of Paradise," but she falls dead.[96]

The meaning of the soul in "The Silver Cage"—sexuality, spirituality, selfhood—cannot be stabilized. "The Physician's Wife" also mingles multiple sufferings and subjections. The naive young girl married to a much older husband is at first seduced and silenced by his command of language; the doctor overcomes his wife's misgivings in the early days of their marriage by being "merciful"; "by his wonderful tongue, he so charmed her ears that she, believing the melancholy which arose in her to be sinful, fought with herself, striving to put the passion of her balked desires into the daily services demanded of her." But "gradually her gaiety forsook her, and her life grew irksome to her." As in Francis Pattison's letters, the language of unmasterable nature gives legitimacy to the young wife's growing unhappiness: "Her nature was . . . too strong for her will, and her life became very bitter to her." She tries to conceal her pain from the frankly sadistic eyes of her husband; "there was now bred in her the cowardice of the slave, so she gave no outward sign, though her rage and her anguish became greater with each day." As in "The Silver Cage," the young woman's awakening to her own desires comes through heterosexual love with the arrival of a new, younger, more attractive lover. This turn of the plot inscribes the story in the genre of romance; it also foregrounds the imbrication of mental and physical suffering. But again, the discovery of true love is useless. When her love is discovered by her viciously mocking husband, her lover abandons her. She kills her husband but Dilke condemns and punishes her protagonist's murderous anger, offering her grave as an example for other women who feel their lives are "torture."[97] These fatal dé-nouements both suggest that it was extremely difficult for a woman to find a language to lay claim to bodily autonomy and freedom from sexual possession, and that such a language—wrested into a ramshackle discourse with great difficulty—could para-doxically signify more than a refusal of sex.

Emilia Dilke's "The Idealist Movement" hints at overlaps between bodily refusal in sex and the refusal of possession more generally in its tale of a young man's spiritual crisis, embedded in the essay's broader themes. The young man's story resonates with the stories told in Francis Pattison's letters and Emilia Dilke's fictions of confined women, but Dilke's shift of genders universalizes the story into an account of generic spiritual struggle. The life of Dilke's male "friend," like that of the physician's wife, was initially undertaken voluntarily but became one of toil without satisfaction or meaning, against the grain of his nature. He "regarded the protest of [his] own nature as immoral, and strove yet more earnestly to suppress it," but despite his efforts, "the falsity of [his] life" amounted to "a cheat which destroyed [his] soul." "I appeared to myself to have been robbed, to have robbed myself, of life." He is bound by "horror" at the "narrowness and pressure of [his] immediate surroundings" but still feels his desires to be "truly sinful"; wracked by guilt, he falls into self-murderous despair. For a time, he seeks "to cheat [him]self by forcing the very passion with which [he] desired other things into the one outlet that [he] believed to be authorized, carrying this so far as to feign pleasure in these enforced courses." Pointedly, Dilke's essay explains that the young man's suffering was unjustly overshadowed by the more audible complaints of others: "this was a period of much distress and suffering to him and to those about him . . . [although] it might have been thought—though falsely—that it was they rather than him who endured the chiefest pain."[98]

Emilia Dilke's young man finds ecstatic revolt in a language of liberal selfhood that locates grounds in human "nature" for the rejection of self-denial in favor of self-ownership: "It was something so new to one such as I, to recognise that the individual had rights, had a right to live in the development of his own nature, to satisfy his own aspirations, to possess himself." Like Francis Pattison's letters, "The Idealist Movement" invokes nature as a guarantor of selfhood, but now inherent desires for liberty, not inherent incapacities for meeting others' demands, have natural bases. If, in the nineteenth century the emancipatory potential of "natural" rights was undercut by the confining regularities of "natural" differences, Pattison/Dilke's texts display the continued usability of the language of nature. The discovery of the legitimacy of the claims of nature and self does not resolve her young man's mental anguish; he must still fight off the temptation: "in the desperation of the struggle, which seemed like one for life—I was . . . ready to thrust aside all claims that others might have on me, lest my own should be eternally foregone." Emilia Dilke's "friend," like Francis Pattison in her letters, negotiates between his rights and his self-conception as virtuous.[99]

"The Idealist Movement" 's submission and feigned pleasures are obviously read-able as metaphors for unwanted sexual intercourse, but the essay's change of gender deters reading it as a critique of gendered social organization or of an individual bad marriage. The young man in "The Idealist Movement" rails against subjugation to duties he hates but feels have a rightful claim upon him. Dilke's protagonist's fury is directed at those who control his mental life and with whom he lives: " 'Why should I renounce my own interests and convictions because they were alien to those with whom I dwelt? . . . Why . . . should I never take my will of anything? Why should my days be all duty and those of others all demand?' " Although the young man's soul, truth, and life are at stake, he is not subjected to another individual but to a "system" whose "wheels [were] grinding all around" him. "The Idealist Movement" locates the power of discourse not in gender ideology but in philosophy: Comtist positivism allured the young man for a time but reiterated his earlier Christianity's emphasis on obligation and self-renunciation. Comtism offered an "admirabl[y] logic[al]" exposition of moral conduct; a test by reference to which [one] might judge [one]self" with "uncompromising rigor." Tellingly, "the fulfilment of the obligations of [Comtism] demanded . . . a self-abnegation as complete as that exacted by the 'Imitatio Christi.' "[100] This story's shift of gender is deeply undermining: calling people to eschew self-abnegation for a demanding life of self-realizing work through a young man's story was hardly radical. Even though the young man's enslavement to ideals of selflessness are compounded by the selfishness of intimate others who exploit his moral seriousness, the particularities of his domesticity are left unspecified. A female narrative would have risked more clearly drawing attention to the ideological links between femininity, self-abnegation, possession by others, and household relations. Other, dominant, and diffuse discourses beyond particular religious or philosophical commitments might be indicted.

Another reading of "enforced courses" is suggested, not without subtexts, by Charles Dilke's "Memoir" of Emilia Dilke. I have shown how Charles Dilke's account of the Pattison's marriage stressed its tutelary quality, and Dilke's evocation of Middlemarch may remind readers of stories of male scholars who demand to be their wives' principal concern to the point of expecting the wives to continue their work after their own deaths, a plot element shared by Middlemarch, Belinda, and The Almond Tree. If Emilia Dilke's "friend" had one "authorized outlet" for "passion," Charles Dilke's "Memoir" emphasizes the channelling of Francis Pattison's intellectual and spiritual life. Dilke's "Memoir" doubly produces a story of enforced courses, not only carefully noting that "immediately on her marriage, Mrs. Pattison began to work for and with her husband," but also recounting that Mark Pattison had strongly advised Francis to choose a subject in which to become an authority. If Mark Pattison's direction is readable as an attempt to encourage Francis Pattison to become powerful in her own field, in Dilke's "Memoir" it is a direction away from her own desires. The "Memoir" ambiguously claims, "before she took up her work upon the Renaissance, and . . . 'specialized,' much against her will, on the arts, of France, she had intended to publish a work on classical art." Greek studies had been Francis Pattison's first love and "she never intended to give up her hold upon classical art, and except when actually absorbed in writing for publication upon the arts of France, she never did so." Charles Dilke's text implies another, economic, struggle between the Pattisons: Francis Pattison's "desire to embrace, by hard study, a complete view of the whole field of art and art-history" was mitigated by her "natural wish to find by publication additional income, especially for the sake of personal independence," and her "subsequent specialization for a time in French art was probably caused by the fact that for work in that field there seemed a sufficiently large interested public."[101] (Dilke's texts do not speculate on why studies in Hellenic art—a booming field in Victorian Britain—could not be similarly remunerative.[102]) Dilke's story renders the shape of Pattison/Dilke's intellectual career a result of Mark Pattison's sometimes contested guidance, while implying Emilia Dilke was moving away from her specialization on French art in her later life with him. He tells us that, before her death, she intended to construct a master narrative to trace art's social relations from the Greeks through the Renaissance to the present, making Mark Pattison's advice of specialization a detour in a longer intellectual history.[103] Charles's account occludes the degree to which Emilia Dilke's unfinished book echoes Mark Pattison's work on the history of scholarship; in Charles's story, the Pattisons' participation in overlapping intellectual projects is over-shadowed by dark hints about Mark's control.[104]

Charles Dilke's "Memoirs" 's version of Francis Pattison's religious direction by Mark Pattison is notably different than "The Idealist Movement" 's spiritual narrative. Mark Pattison "encouraged" Francis to study philosophy, "at the expense of her earlier theology," in which Francis Strong was a debater and theorist to a degree "rare among women"; that is, Mark Pattison took from Francis both a set of beliefs and a realm of power. Dilke's "Memoir" repeatedly situates Francis Pattison's spiritual history as a process of pain, loss, and binding. Mark Pattison "unsettled [her] foundations" and "threw her" into Comtean positivism as a refuge against "shock" and "anarchy," which gave Francis Pattison "a code sufficient to preserve her previously existing standard of duty," grounded in "scientific" rather than purely moral arguments. In sharp contrast to Charles Dilke's account of Mark Pattison's influence on Emilia Dilke's spiritual history, "The Idealist Movement" 's story of its protagonist's spiritual history omits such external influences, dwelling on the young man's thorough reading through which his views "slowly materialised" and "gradually assumed less and less of an emotional character."[105]

Although Charles Dilke's "Memoir" 's and Emilia Dilke's "The Idealist Movement" grant powerful ideas and systems of thought greater weight than the deliberate in-tentions of one individual to control another, neither text overtly offers spaces for—and Emilia Dilke's essay explicitly excludes—an overt analysis of gender as an ideo-logical system including far more than conjugal sexual subjection. "The Idealist Move-ment" 's happy ending, with no deaths and the young man's self-transformation or attainment of a new synthesis of social responsibility and personal integrity, may depend on the absence of any legal or material bars to his liberation; it is not a story of marriage. "The Silver Cage" and "The Physician's Wife" hint that gender is relevant to the female protagonists' plights and in their hopes of escape, but neither tale disentangles gender from hetero-romantic plots; real or better Love and lovers arrive as moments of hope but both stories culminate in punitive deaths of women. In "The Physician's Wife," even female self-sacrifice to male endeavor fails. When the wife who has murdered her husband repents and comes to respect his devotion to science, she attempts to complete his work but "her brain was now weakened and refused its service"; after years of struggle, she dies "crying out in a voice of anguish, 'It will not come right.' "[106] Charles Dilke's story, despite its concluding death, has a happy ending in the submerged romantic narrative of the Dilke marriage and Emilia Dilke's second life. Thus, none of these stories are simply stories of the Pattison marriage; their excesses and multiple agendas should remind us that the Pattison marriage in its most intimate, as well as most public, texts and acts was never just a story about the Pattison marriage either.

The Adulteries of True Minds

Francis Strong Pattison and Charles Wentworth Dilke, Mark Pattison and Meta Bradley would not have accepted the term "adultery" as applying to them. Past sexual relationships are notoriously difficult to appraise for an obvious reason—a general absence of unimpeachable witnesses—but many historians have also come to recognize that answering the crude question, "did they or didn't they?" necessarily involves knowing exactly what would have constituted sexual relations in the eyes of the historical actors, and that late-twentieth-century "common sense" is utterly irrelevant in framing such questions and answers. Was it "adultery" if they kissed? Did pretending to be wild animals and wrestling in nightclothes constitute "sexual" behavior?[107] We lack the "evidence" that would allow us either to state decisively that "adultery," the physical consummation of erotic entanglement outside of marriage, occurred or to rule it out; nor can we decisively state that Mark and Meta, and Emilia and Charles, experienced their relationships as sources of "guilt" or as utterly "innocent," or within that pair of opposed choices at all. The relationship between Emilia Pattison and Charles Dilke is certainly amenable to a conventional romantic reading, emphasising the trials and tribulations of (extramarital) love long thwarted, nobly enduring, culminating in a marriage. Despite the temporary culmination of their story in a moment of romantic fulfillment—a wedding and a public, legal and aboveboard marriage of true minds after long unsanctioned intercourses—and, soon after, the envelopment of their marriage by dangerously public narratives about erotic relations, during the long prehistory of their marriage, discourses of politics, God, and family were not just averting or disguising adultery. The texts Charles and Emilia wrote made a relationship across a variety of registers of desire—intellectual, professional, and political, as well as tender and erotic. Similarly, Mark Pattison's and Meta Bradley's texts authorize a range of readings besides the overtly erotic; their vocabularies of love constituted as well as expressed relationships by exceeding and evading the boundaries of a scandalous sexuality.

Charles and Emilia

The letters of Charles Dilke and Francis/Emilia Pattison are heavily mutilated; the two correspondents and Gertrude Tuckwell wielded scissors freely. Ironically, the emergence of a rhetoric of romantic or erotic intimacy between Charles Dilke and Francis/Emilia Pattison is obscured and spotlighted by the presence of names. From late 1875 on, the salutations of many of Charles's and Emilia's letters have been carefully snipped away, presumably because the terms by which the correspondents addressed each other would imply something about their relationship they preferred posterity should not know.[108] Despite this beheading, surviving letters from Charles's grandmother, Caroline Chatfield, position Emilia as being on sufficiently intimate terms to be inducted into the Dilke family culture of joking nicknames, addressed as "My dear Mrs. Bunnie" and regaled with news of the household affairs of 76 Sloane Street.[109] By May of 1878, Charles's letters to Emilia referred to him in the third person as "the Tsar," or "Zz," and Emilia was, minimally, his "Dear Lady."[110] After Mark Pattison's death although before their own marriage, the mutilations become much less severe and Charles and Emilia address each other almost exclusively in endearments; Charles was "dear," "Darling," "Zz," or "Tz" and "B.P." (an abbreviation of the name of one of his cats, in whose *persona* he sometimes wrote), while Emilia was "Hoya," "Tots," "Totsian," "little one," "my child," "dear Puss," "L.P." (another cat), and always "dear." A typical letter from Charles foregrounds the pleasure of names: "My Hoya—I call Tots now Emilia in writing & speaking to *others* [their engagement having been announced]: that is right I suppose. Bless & keep Tots for Zz, and Zz for Tots. Please. B.P."[111] In all these endearments, Charles's letters were the more exuberant, often constructing a childish persona, full of references to "Zz's" dependence on and adoration of his "Hoya." In encouraging or drawing Emilia into these rhetorics of affection, Charles drew her into his own family culture and echoed her own family's penchant for nicknames, in warm contrast to the chill formalities of Oxford.

Francis Pattison became Emilia in her relationship with Charles Dilke.[112] No clear date can be assigned to the transformation; Francis and Emilia existed simultaneously. Charles Dilke himself foundered on the issue; a note appended to his correspondence with Francis/Emilia labels it "My letters to Mrs Mark Pattison afterwards Emilia Lady Dilke." He attempted to explain, "I called her 'Francis' until 1859 to 1877 or 1877 [sic] after which she dropped her 'Francis' a good deal, except in the childish form of 'Fussie.' Ellen Smith continued to call her 'Francis' & Mrs Hullah 'Francesca' (till death)."[113] His own letters use a wide variety of names. This proliferation of names— private and public, joking and intimate, familial, formal, and literary—across romantic, political, and spiritual texts, mirrors the multitude of rhetorics of relationship through which the relationship between Charles Dilke and Emilia Pattison was constituted. Mrs. Pattison's entire public name, not just her surname, changed by her choice upon her marriage to Charles Dilke, but despite inconsistencies and obfuscations, it seems clear that Francis Strong Pattison privately reshaped her baptismal "Emily" much earlier in her relationship with Charles Dilke.

E. F. S. Pattison's *The Renaissance of Art in France* snippily describes the visual display of names in Diane de Poitiers's chateau of Anet—"on all sides the decorations recall the story of the goddess whose name the Duchess ostentatiously bore"—but if Diane's invocation of narratives through names reveals her "half-checked arrogance," Diane de Poiters was not unique in being a woman whose relation to public political power was entangled with her sexuality.[114] If Diane's proclamations of her affinity with the chaste Diana was in bad taste, as E. F. S. Pattison's text implies, what are the implications of "Emilia"? Despite Charles Dilke's and others' emphases on the continuity of Emilia Dilke's character, Francis Pattison's self-renaming as Emilia marked a separation and set a new character in motion through various narratives. The new name's Latin root, *aemilius*, is provocative—to *emulate* suggests the formation or re-formation of some object by following a model, as in the copying of an image, with implications of improvement and making better. What kind of character might an Emilia be?

The name summons up several echoes beyond the etymological. Four literary and one geographic Emilias suggest themselves, all associated with rebellious women and powerful institutions. Emilia, or Emelye, in Chaucer's "The Knight's Tale" also appears in Fletcher and Shakespeare's *The Two Noble Kinsmen* (1634). In both stories, Emilia/Emelye is beloved by two men who are forced to compete for her hand; because of a fatal accident to the victor, Emelye marries the other after long mourning. In the background of these romantic plots is Emelye/Emilia's identity as a defeated *Amazon*, the sister of Queen Hippolyta.[115] Shakespeare's Emilia, the wife of Iago in *Othello*, may also have come to mind, tactlessly and appositely. In the first folio, although not the quarto, text of the play, Emilia delivers a worldly and pointed speech to Desdemona, counselling Desdemona against decorous female passivity and arguing that adulterous or angry wives are often well justified:

> But I do think it is their husbands' faults
> If wives do fall. Say that they slack their duties
> And pour our treasures into foreign laps,
> Or else break out in peevish jealousies,
> Throwing restraint upon us; or say they strike us,
> Or scant our former having in despite—
> Why, we have galls, and though we have some grace
> Yet have we some revenge.

Othello's Emilia argues for women's anger and right to renegotiate or withdraw from the marriage contract when husbands are adulterous and when they diminish or insult women.[116] However minor a figure in the play as a whole, and however ineffective her speech in saving Desdemona, this Emilia has sharp and strong words to say about adultery.

The original 1864 title of George Meredith's *Sandra Belloni* was *Emilia in England*.[117] Mrs. Mark Pattison certainly knew and handled this novel: she donated three copies to Somerville College in 1884 with other contents of Mark Pattison's library![118] Emilia Sandra Belloni is an "ardent and natural girl" of great singing ability, not above a bit of scheming for a good cause. At the novel's end, she has seen through the indecisiveness of a weak suitor and his Dickensian family, prevailed on a Greek impresario's motivated kindness for help, offered another suitor hope, and gone off to Milan to study music. Her story is continued in Meredith's *Vittoria* (1867) in which Emilia, now Sandra but with the professional name "Vittoria," is swept up in the Italian revolutions of 1848 and sings out the signal for revolt in Milan.[119] Meredith's Emilia/ Sandra/ Vittoria's indebtedness to Germaine de Staël's *Corinne* is obvious; her change-ability as a performing self, gift for self-transformation, political commitments and artistic talents, and palpable impatience with the plot of standard romance are intriguingly extreme. Corinne and Sandra/Vittoria, of course, also choose their names. France was the place to which Francis Pattison fled from her marriage and, as the next chapters detail, the imaginative ground on which she often performed, and precisely because Mrs. Pattison could have become Francesca, we notice that she did not take on an Italianized version of her middle name. Nonetheless, one of her texts links Italy, women's intellects, and rage at confinement:

> Yes I know that it is good for me to have been at Rome again, good in every way. I get an amount of stimulus intellectual & moral from that kind of visit wh is just want I want & wh I can't quite find the like of anywhere else certainly not in London *in the summer* [double underlining], & Oxford is too middle-class—in addition to wh the *warm* sympathy of so many active minded liberal intelligent *women* creates an atmosphere wh is all the pleasanter for its rarity. Do you know I got terribly *cowed* all those years in Oxfd,- they were a variation of Corinne's experiences in Northumberland poor Corinne![120]

In England, women of complex and divided affinities suffer and are misunderstood, but Rome is a the place of intellectually and politically engaged women. Mrs. Pattison cites and participates in a tradition of texts following *Corinne*—including Elizabeth Barrett Browning's *Aurora Leigh*—which invoke Rome as a setting for freedom-seeking women.[121] In *Middlemarch*, Rome's "stupendous fragmentariness" first makes Dorothea Brooke aware that "her husband's mind" contained not "large vistas and wide fresh air" but "anterooms and winding passages which seemed to lead nowhere." Francis Pattison apparently wrote George Eliot that Rome gave her too a "shock" and overwhelmed on her first visit; Eliot replied with advice about achieving perspective and remembering the mutability of human institutions.[122] Rome is the central city of the province of Emilia Romagna.

One last Emilia: Emilia Viviani in Shelley's *Epipsychidion* (1821), "Verses Addressed to the Noble and Unfortunate Lady, Emilia V—. Now Imprisoned in the Convent of _____." *Epipsychidion* was certainly known to Charles Dilke, grandson and best student of Charles Wentworth Dilke, the friend and protector of Keats; William Tuckwell reported that Charles's copy of Shelley was "heavily and with wise selections scored."[123] A character/symbol in an extremely complex poem, Emilia Viviani was a beautiful young woman whose father confined her in a place of sterile monasticism; the poem narrates the blockage of spiritual union with a beautiful, brilliant, and morally superior woman by a multitude of social barriers. Despite rapid tangles of allusions and Neoplatonist allegory, Emilia Viviani is clearly figured as a "poor captive bird," which "beat[s] . . . unfeeling bars with vain endeavour,/Till those bright plumes of thought, in which array/It over-soared this low and worldly shade,/Lie shattered. . . ." Shelley's speaker calls his Emilia, his "Spouse! Sister! Angel!" to sail away with him, to a "simple life" where they might " by each other . . . love and live/Be one . . ." It is here too that Shelley famously assaulted marriage as a "code of modern morals" which dictates that "poor slaves with weary footsteps tread" to the grave with "one chained friend, perhaps a jealous foe,/The dreariest and longest journey go."[124]

Charles Dilke narrated his second marriage in both his "Memoir" of Emilia and his own unpublished memoirs. In these accounts, Charles Dilke positioned the re-emergence of his relationship with Francis Strong Pattison and the birth of their adult intimacy in the aftermath of a spiritual crisis caused by the death of Katie Sheil Dilke. Charles narrated the effect of Katie's death as catastrophic, producing not only grief but insanity. When Katie died, Charles collapsed and "fled the scene of his suffering"; "[I] walked down the street quietly to my grandmother's, and there told her what had happened, and asked her to lie down by my side on her bed for a few hours, and we lay there side by side holding hands. I then asked her to do everything . . . and I went to Victoria Station, and, having shaved off my beard to prevent myself from being recognized and spoken to by any friend, went to Paris and there took careful steps not to be found . . ." Hiding, incommunicado and incognito, Charles immersed himself in "historical work" which he claimed he could not later recall; "for all practical purposes I was mad." Eventually reemerging through the friendships of Leon Gambetta and William Harcourt, Charles remained emotionally fragile through 1875 at least. "For many months I was completely changed and out of my proper self and not really responsible for what I wrote or said or did . . . my hand still shook, and I had contracted a bad habit of counting the beating of my heart, and I was so weak of mind that the slightest act of kindness made me cry."[125]

In his retrospective account, Charles's state of psychological anguish and physical weakness led him to reconsider his religious convictions. He had given up regular Christian observances at Cambridge in 1863, after a "somewhat devout" youth; in doing so he aligned himself with his "in their way religious" but nonobservant father and grandfather rather than the mother who had worried on her deathbed about Charles's religious education.[126] At Cambridge he had been greatly influenced by Henry Fawcett and Leslie Stephen and fallen "into a sceptical frame of mind which lasted for several years." This skepticism remained sufficiently strong that his response to most letters offering consolations on Katie's death was to write back arguing against their writers' religious views.[127] "At this time I was what most people would call very mad on these subjects [of faith and doubt]; that is very logical and disagreeable to argue with. I worried those with whom I corresponded in a manner which had been unknown to me before, and happily did not last, with perplexing doubts which did not affect people in good health." His reminiscences recall a more helpful correspondence with Frances Power Cobbe on religious questions.[128] By late 1874, during a tour of North Africa, Charles turned to reading Balzac and de Staël and to writing Mrs. Mark Pattison.[129]

According to Charles, in February 1875 he "revived an acquaintance . . . destined not again to drop." This friendship was more than pleasant, it was therapeutic; "the effect on me of much conversation with Mrs. Pattison . . . was wholly beneficial" and inspiring. "Mrs. Pattison's higher standard in all things greatly affected my way of looking at many matters and brought me back to where I had been before recent inferior days," a barely-coded allusion to recent *sexual* conduct, a fateful liaison in 1874–1875 during "the winter in wh I was mad."[130] Charles placed their reacquaintance not just in the context of his own need but also Mrs. Pattison's. She was "convalescen[t] after a frightful attack of gout" and his visits to her began at the London home of Sir Charles Newton, Keeper of Antiquities at the British Museum, Mrs. Pattison's friendly instructor in ancient art who also, in Charles's accounts, offered her a haven from Oxford and a "safety-valve" from "too absorbing an influence of [Mark Pattison's] opinions."[131]

Charles's text hints at divisions between Mark and Francis Pattison by asserting Mrs. Pattison's own state of spiritual uncertainty. He recalled, "when first I knew her," Francis Strong had been "a devoted High Churchwoman . . . equipped with a panoply of Tractarian philosophy"; he was thus "astonished" at the transformation wrought by an "Oxford training." She "had ceased to go to Church [and] ceased to believe the ordinary doctrines of the faith" and "yet used to satirize unmercifully those who held the ordinary negative philosophy." Her witty attacks on the "crude commonplaces of materialism" were so rapidly convincing, however, that Charles soon "went beyond [his] teachers"; "while neither Pattison, although he was in Holy Orders, nor his wife seemed to me in 1875 to 'believe' much, I learned enough from them to set me [going?] in a very different line of thought . . . [and] I gradually found in the words of Christ recorded in the Gospels, as contrasted with the Pauline doctrine of the epistles, a satisfaction . . . in a faith in which I think Mrs. Pattison afterwards followed."[132] Roy Jenkins, falling prey to stereotypes of Victorian spirituality as a feminine purview, thus gets it exactly wrong in glossing Charles's story as one of Francis Pattison "influenc[ing] Dilke" in the direction of Christian pietism.[133]

Charles did, in one later letter, refer to Emilia as his "spiritual grandmother," but that was in relation to a wholly worldly matter: Italian politics.[134] In Charles Dilke's story of their relationship in the 1870s, religious concerns were not gender-specific and Charles offered spiritual and emotional resources as well as political and social cosmopolitanism to Francis Pattison. Charles wrote his re-engagement with Francis Strong Pattison in terms that associate emotional spirituality with his male self and ironical intellectual rigor with Francis Pattison, a tale continuous with his larger self-narration as an exceptional man and his stories of his marriages as egalitarian meetings of intellectual and emotional passions. Elsewhere, Charles's memoirs emphasize his pleasure in the company of vital and lively women ("one of the most agreeable parties of clever people to which I ever went was a luncheon . . . at which I was the only man, the party chiefly consisting of old ladies"), and he drew up a list of "clever women" he knew, including "Lady Morgan who was my dear kind friend," Eliza Lynn Linton, George Eliot "whose books I worship [but who] never says anything in conversation," Mrs. Fawcett, who "has no feelings at all and no comprehension of other people's feelings," Adelaide Anne Proctor, Lady Waldegrave, Mrs. Mark Pattison "a woman not to be forgotten," and "of the Women's Suffrage Party" Clementina Taylor and Emilie Venturi.[135]

Charles Dilke's interests and entrées are reflected in letters to Emilia from March 1875 on. Dilke shared Mrs. Pattison's interests in art and France while offering access to close knowledge of parliamentary politics, political ambitions, and a fierce commitment to Radical Liberalism.[136] By mid-1875, Charles was writing Emilia at least every few weeks, even considering only surviving letters; the frequency increased to virtually daily. Charles's letters rapidly took Emilia into his confidence and welcome her interest in politics to the point of indiscretion. Jenkins summarizes, "Dilke poured out all his political information to Mrs. Pattison and asked her advice about every difficult decision which he had to take," frequently requesting her opinion on his speeches and her responses to particular issues and even sharing with her the contents of secret despatches and filling letters with mocking and gossipping references to other politicians. Charles's letters positioned Francis Pattison as a clever and trusted confidante, and they were openly aware of the roles ambitious women might play in politics through networks of influence despite and because of their exclusion from formal political participation.[137]

Mrs. Pattison's letters as well assume her ability to think politically with an eye for strategy, an understanding of ambition, and an awareness of personalities and compromises. An 1880 letter to Eleanor Smith depicts her as bearing an "uncomfortable sense of responsibility [when she] formed any [opinion]" on political questions, a depiction which by no means excludes her expressing pleasure at sharing in Charles's political career and at impressing him with her knowledge and acumen.[138] Emilia and Charles's common political engagements were not restricted to letters; both were members of the Radical Club, a group of twenty Radical M.P.s and various other politically engaged figures to which Mrs. Pattison was elected in 1878; the five women members included Helen Taylor. Charles notes Emilia did not attend all meetings, but she did present at least two papers, one on "the conditions which should determine the wages of female labour" and another on technical education.[139] Emilia's opinions did not always accord with Charles's; she regarded herself as highly qualified to speak on reform of the Royal Academy and they engaged in a long debate.[140]

A consistent note in Emilia's letters is her assumption that Charles's political fate concerned her for reasons beyond personal affection; they were members of a single party with a great historical task before them. She writes of the "transition from Whiggism to Liberalism" in confident "we's," as an historical campaign in which she is a "soldier," even if she deplored the scarcity of real "men to officer our ranks."[141] Charles's letters accepted Emilia's assumptions of their common project and sometimes suggest her commitment to the political life exceeds his own. In 1878 he joked, "I always feel when you order me to stick to politics that it is really because I'm not fit for anything else"; after 1885 he would complain he could not both be an active politician and write books ("All creative energy has been driven out of me by the overwork, & that I think will not come back . . .").[142] He laments that he must be "the hardest worked member of a great governing [party?] . . ." but nonetheless insists Emilia's "influence in [his] politics" meshes with his own ambitions. "[I was] not taught . . . to look upon [politics] as apart from life's religion," and when they agreed to marry, "all my life [became] one . . . & there are not things to pick among, & things to be cast aside, but duties only which are pleasures in the doing of them well . . ." They both believed political power "can be used for good that it is a duty so to use it, & [he] would not continue in political life for a day if [he] did not think so."[143] Moreover, Charles and Emilia's letters treated feminist politics—suffrage, trade-unionism, and education—as a shared terrain. Indeed, the first surviving letter from Charles tells her of Randolph Churchill "damning your soul to me . . . without knowing I know you . . . for sending a woman to lecture at Woodstock [on woman suffrage]," and later remarks, "the House [of Commons] never makes such an ass of itself as it does on this question [woman suffrage] once a year."[144]

Emilia and Charles may have been unique in the particularities of their situation—her marriage to Mark Pattison and the exact nature of her intellectual and feminist commitments, the specific shape of his parliamentary career, the emotional rhetoric of his family life, and his status as an eligible widower. Other widely publicized relationships that combined unconventionality with high morality—like that of George Eliot and G. H. Lewes—were within their social world, but two specific stories of passionate friendships-cum-romantic-marriages between intellectuals were close at hand. Without claiming either of these relationships was a model for Emilia and Charles, I draw attention to the stories of John Stuart Mill and Harriet Taylor, and Robert Browning and Elizabeth Barrett Browning—widely circulated tales of exceptional relations that illuminate the availability, as well as the difficulty, of narratives of heterosexual feminist romance.[145]

These parallels are compounded by the relative smallness of the social world in which these characters moved; biographical coincidences, political affinities, and personal relations overlay narrative similarities. Charles venerated John Stuart Mill; Roy Jenkins claims "the acquaintance [from 1869 onward] rapidly developed into a close friendship, with Dilke happily accepting the role of disciple," and Dilke's official biographers represent Mill as "complet[ing] the work of old Mr. Dilke" in educating Charles. Mill substantially assisted Charles's career, introducing him into the Political

Economy Club, and Dilke became an ally in Mill's move to "lead the club away from
. . . rigidly individualist doctrine[s] . . . towards his own, recently developed, semi-
socialist views." After Mill's death in 1873, Charles continued "[to] use Mill's name
with a respect that was little short of reverence," commissioned G. F. Watts's portrait
of Mill, and wrote, "I loved him greatly."[146] In the case of the Brownings as well,
the male partner moved in the same social worlds as Francis Pattison and Charles
Dilke; Francis participated in a somewhat flirtatious correspondence with Robert, and
he and Charles attended the same dinner parties.

Readings of Mill's and Browning's texts until recently attempted to contain these
relationships in far less fluid, let alone feminist, narratives even when this required
rejecting the authority of the male partners' texts.[147] But the texts of Mill and Browning, like those of Charles Dilke, mark their authors' status as exceptional men in
limning their relationships with more-than-exceptional women. Mill met Harriet
Hardy Taylor after she had married John Taylor, a Radical republican druggist whose
political and religious contacts enlarged her world; she became discontented in her
marriage despite her appreciation of the intellectual worlds he had opened to her,
both because of her husband's intellectual inferiority to her and because she resented
his "conjugal rights."[148] John Stuart Mill attributed Harriet Taylor's first interest in
him to his feminism; in an intensely textual relationship, they exchanged essays on
marriage soon after first meeting. Although Mill's *Autobiography* insists Harriet was a
full partner in his work, stresses her logical rigor and keen judgement, and presents
her as a Diotima for her time, her mind "a perfect instrument" and her philosophical
genius superhuman, Mill's feminism is not presented as Harriet Taylor's creation.[149]
As Susan Groag Bell notes, Mill's *Autobiography* struggles to depart from the "Victorian
Romantic" script of heterosexual relations by assigning Harriet Taylor an important
role as an independent thinker and refusing her a position as muse.[150] Similarly, Robert
Browning's emphasis on Elizabeth Barrett's position as a writer of considerable fame
long before she met him and his insistence on her superiority as a poet retained a
space of difference between them in order to avert attempts to cast either poet as
derivative or to limit Elizabeth to the position of muse.[151] Mill's and Browning's
assertions of their own exceptionality, like Charles Dilke's, guarantee the exceptionality
of their wives, since a shortage of exceptionality in their consorts would reduce the
women themselves to clever women whose intellects are nonetheless subordinate to
their sentimental or sexual passions.[152] The specific emphases in Charles Dilke's texts
on Emilia's independent achievements—her art-historical career and feminist and
trade-unionist careers—mark larger historical changes in the possible lives of women.
Emilia became, at least in law, far more independent than Harriet Taylor and other
earlier Radical women, and Charles and Emilia profited from their ability to draw
upon earlier heterosocial discourses of feminism and Radical Liberalism.

The histories of their loves by these three "exceptional men" struggle to portray
their relationships as inhabiting and transcending categories while wrestling with the
potential for scandal. Mill's and Dilke's texts especially need to depict their marriages
as fully romantic and sexual—affirming their partners' femininity and securing their
own masculine positions—but averting implications of *illicit* sexuality and adulterous
prehistories to their marriages. After all, Harriet Taylor and John Stuart Mill were
deeply involved from the spring of 1833 but John Taylor did not die until 1849. Like

Francis Pattison, Harriet Taylor lived apart from her first husband during the major part of the last ten years of her marriage. Taylor and Mill were in some respects even more heedless of convention than Emilia and Charles—they travelled abroad together and Mill sang Harriet Taylor's praises to his friends—but Mill erupted after he and Harriet finally married if, after "twenty years of friendship . . . hiding their meetings, misleading people about their travel plans, enduring malicious gossip," anyone dared suggest their premarital relationship had been anything but platonic.[153] If Harriet and John were troubled by the conventions of marriage, they were more troubled by the possibility that anyone might read their earlier intimacies as sexually guilty, not least because of the philosophical commitment to the supremacy of reason over physicality crucial to their liberal feminism. John Stuart Mill wrote, "we disdained, as every person not a slave of his animal appetites must do, the abject notion that the strongest and tenderest friendship cannot exist between a man and a woman without a sensual relation."[154] The Dilkes had their reasons, as we will see, to be somewhat less troubled by the philosophical point to be made and concerned with more immediate dangers of sexual scandal.

Bodies and Figures

Pet names and endearments, political and spiritual confidences, and even plans to eventually marry, however intimately exchanged, do not of course constitute adultery. My focus thus far on the discourses in which Charles and Emilia constructed their relationship should not mean that we ignore the question of eroticism. Without deciding whether or not they "had sex" before their marriage, we can consider how the erotic might be constituted by discourses of political intimacy, playfulness, and spiritual aspiration. But readers may reasonably wonder about the relationship between these writings of intimacy and Francis Pattison's letters to Mark Pattison, in which she represented herself as naturally incapable of sexual intercourse. Rather than taking her letters to Mark Pattison as representing either the truth of her body—evidence that she was "frigid"—or simply as instrumental lies exposed by other texts evincing sexual passion for Charles Dilke, I read both sets of letters among other texts in which Emilia Dilke authorized or repudiated sexual desire. Two nexes of texts especially discuss sexuality as a problem of representation: Emilia Dilke's accounts of sexuality and theatricality in her two erstwhile nemeses, Meta Bradley and Virginia Crawford, and E. F. S. Pattison's art-critical and art-historical discussion of passionate bodies.

Emilia Pattison Dilke had little difficulty labelling Mark Pattison's friend, Meta Bradley, and Virginia Crawford, the woman who would "confess" to committing adultery with Charles Dilke, as motivated by illicit though natural erotic passions, and she linked their eroticism to suppressed ambition. Emilia's letters emphasize Meta Bradley's and Virginia Crawford's alleged strong sexual desires, "perverted" into dramatic enactments, and come very close to locating both women in the precincts of "hysteria." After accidentally seeing some of Meta's letters to Mark, Francis Pattison diagnosed them as betraying "a perhaps *unconscious* condition the cravings of wh are *cheated* by relations such as those in wh she placed herself with the Rr . . . [Meta's] 'cold-heartedness' in family relations alluded to by [Meta's stepmother] confirms it because I have once or twice observed its presence in similar physiological states."[155]

Her letters to Ellen Smith and Emily Thursfield claim to have heard that Meta had made "repeated & violent sets at men of all sorts & sizes," and her texts label Meta an erotic exhibitionist: Meta's letters displayed the "marks of a wish to *accaparer* [Fr.: to hoard or monopolize] exclusively & to be *known* to do so," and Meta had told scandalous and unfounded stories about Mary Stirke.[156] Although she thought Meta an "imposter," a potential exploiter of Mark and a bad influence on other young women ("the flattering of a man near seventy by suggestions that he is not in old age & by assuring him that he [had] shown her that she had a heart is something worse than outrageous bad taste"), Francis Pattison still implied Meta's imputed sexual desires were natural.[157] They deserved a more legitimate fulfillment and Mark was culpable in encouraging her. (Francis seems not to have imagined "fulfillment" in Meta's relationship with Mark; she hints at open adultery only after Mark's death when she was enraged by his will.[158]) A later letter about Virginia Crawford invokes the same trope of sexual exhibitionism; Emilia Dilke compares Virginia Crawford to a female student of whom she had heard, "one especially remarkably handsome & winning in manner of 'strong sexual instincts' [who] was in the habit of pouring forth the foulest inventions as confessions . . . this girl wld say anything—do anything for *notoriety* [triple underlining]."[159] By implication, Mrs. Crawford's sexuality was too strong and had been perverted into shameless public theatrics.

Emilia Pattison/Dilke's texts authorize female sexual desire—constituting it as natural—but stigmatize its displaced expression; if women cannot gain "legitimate" fulfilment, their repression of eros should be paradoxically readable and complete—visible not through hysterical enactments but by spectacular sublimation into other, self-sacrificing passions. Mark's sister Dora had "differed from them all [the Pattison family] in having latent possibility of physical & moral passion wh if it had been worthily aroused wld have put her at the point of the grandest self-sacrifice," but Dora's "physical passion" is a source of positive social energy because expressed through "self-sacrifice."[160] In E. F. S. Pattison's art-historical writings, too, unrepressed female desire is deplorable, as in the contrast between Marguerite de Valois, a "luxurious sensual animal . . . unworthy to be the wife even of Henri IV," her "debaucheries" and "midnight excursions" worthy of contempt, and Marguerite de Navarre's laudable direction of her "mystical devotion and sentimental passion" into visionary religiosity and "spiritual life."[161]

John Kucich has conceptualized "repression" in some Victorian novels as not purely or even primarily a phenomenon of negation or destruction but as creating a rich and mobile internal economy of desire; E. F. S. Pattison's writings also argue for the productivities of channeled energies.[162] *The Renaissance of Art in France* lauds not the absence of desire but its sublimation: if human passion has "its coarser side, and sometimes . . . burn[s] . . . an impurer flame," the direction of this passion in aesthetic and "morally ideal" pursuits is utterly praiseworthy.[163] In Pattison's description of a statue of Diana the Huntress by Jean Goujon, desire is beautiful because it is visibly restrained. Pattison's Goujon's *Diane* gives evidence of a "struggle of the voluptuous element against a self-imposed restraint, a struggle which seems to be reflected in the very outlines as well as in the general sentiment of the figure." Passion has been molded and confined within an aesthetically pleasing form; "Venus herself has lost her air of frank expansion," and Diana "sits reflecting," an artwork in which "[t]he most voluptuous moments are so full of sadness that they never reach direct sensual expression," and the "desire which questions in the eyes and mouth . . . [are] contradicted by the conscious dignity of the attitude and the general severity of form and line."[164] In E. F. S. Pattison's art-critical writing, female sexual potential is most highly praised when suggested but powerfully restrained by aesthetic skill and spiritual discipline.

Pattison's *Renaissance* does not just mark sublimation as an ideal for women but tells a tale of controlled desire as productive for men and, through them, good for women. Pattison contends that medieval culture, suppressing and hating desire, produced art that celebrated only "saintly virgins whose meagre forms had been blanched and attentuated by the shade of cloistered discipline," while male Renaissance artists, sublimating rather than suppressing, produced female figures beautiful, strong, and full of spiritual and mental power. Renaissance female nudes prove that the "French artists of the Renaissance stand the severest test to which the artists of any epoch can be put."[165] Pattison placed the positive value of physicality at the center of a progressive narrative: "delight in the nude" is a "sign" of liberatory energies, the "progress of art" was "its passage from the representation of spirit to the representation of body."[166] But gender works across these texts: strong female sexuality properly sublimated enobles women like Dora Pattison into doing passionate good for others; the alternative to female sublimation is hysterical license, while for men proper sublimation produces noble, respectful, but desirable images of women and men's repression risks body-hating asceticism that damages both women and culture. In E. F. S. Pattison's texts, male sublimation need not be total; her Renaissance men can retain passionate physical and sexual being short of license. E. F. S. Pattison's texts do not defend corporeal realism in art, let alone in the world of practical transgression, without ambivalence, and I will discuss pleasure's ambiguous place in Pattison/Dilke's histories and politics further in chapter 7. But these ambivalences are not adequately read as simply convoluted versions of personal squeamishness about sex or "Victorian prudery."

If the sexualized female body could be a site of degradation by others or by a pathologically performative self in many of Pattison/Dilke's texts, in other texts a proper marriage combines minds and bodies. A letter to Charles written after their marriage stressed the intimate proximity of bodies: "It seems very sad to lie down & know the door is shut between us [because of a temporary illness], but that is only for a while and . . . I shall be with you one more always at your side bodily as well as in spirit . . ."[167] In Emilia Dilke's discourse of moral tuition of younger women, too, sexual passion—within legitimate bounds—is a site of desirable moral self-expression. A letter to Gertrude Tuckwell repudiates the views of "Tennyson's . . . 'curate Edward Bull [who said]/ I say God made the woman for the man/ To keep him tight & warm & snug o' nights' " and emphasizes that the purpose of marriage was not to provide men with sexual access to women. While Gertrude should reject understandings of marriage as a contract—including a sexual contract—in which there could be "all claim one side all duty on the other," the letter also forcefully stresses erotic desire as a necessary (though not sufficient) element of a proper marriage:

If [a woman] can marry in such a way as to satisfy the requirements of her own nature, if she & the man whom she marries are drawn together not only by that strong physical attraction wh is commonly called love [written above line] & wh is indispensable but can also strive together after the same moral and intellectual ideal—then marriage is the greatest bliss that life can offer.

In the absence of such combined attractions, especially when women marry primarily for economic support, they neglect their "moral responsibility" to self-development "in mind & soul & body" and are reduced to the same position as "the wretched Protestant ladies who were expelled from La Rochelle, & sold themselves to the soldiers for a morsel of bread."[168] The legitimate pleasures of the flesh are also endorsed in Emilia Dilke's late—and tragic—allegory, "The Mirror of the Soul": the people of a far country "honour the blossoming of the pomegranate . . . for it is the flower of passion, and from its heart springs that liking that the man, in his manhood, hath towards the woman." Those who "honour this flower with a whole heart" possess "great virtue" and "neither can any shame or fear overtake them that worship this flower rightly." While in this passage Dilke represents sexual desire as a male force, in the same story she also represents it, albeit obliquely, as mutual: "she made him great cheer . . . and when he had put off his armour, she showed him all the treasures of her hours: there was not anything that she kept back from him, and she brought him to her secret chamber, and she unveiled her mirror before him . . . and they two had great joy of each other."[169] Thus, while some of Emilia Pattison/Dilke's texts represent sexuality as a point of vulnerability, aesthetic embarrassment, scandal, and potential degradation, others make it a site of morally valuable pleasure when cultivated between true spouses. The absence of sexual desire is damaging, too. After her death, Charles Dilke claimed he once dared to ask Francis Pattison about the taboo topic of *Middlemarch*. Although her reply is thoroughly mutilated by scissors, what survives are words of pity for Mark: "To give all to a woman who can only feel intense compassion, be patient and forbear . . . [rasura, with the following in margin:] I would give my life to free him from the mistake that was made;—that I made."[170] If her regret that she could not "free" Mark from "her" mistake draws attention away from the ways Francis Pattison did extricate her mind and body and is silent about the possibility of intense rage rather than "intense compassion," it nonetheless positions sexual desire as legitimate.

A letter after Mark Pattison's death, detailing while dismissing some light flirtations by Emilia, positions Charles as having been sexually jealous of Mark in the past: "I know all that you have been used to feel in that way on my account."[171] But as for "acts" before their marriage, who knows? In some texts, Emilia capably appraises the risks of open scandal with a practiced political eye in terms owing little to specifically moral concerns but acknowledging the importance of appearances and the inadvisability of shocking onlookers. Emilia wrote Ellen Smith in 1880, "looking at the situation from a worldly point of view, I know I have everything to gain by keeping on outwardly decent terms with [Mark Pattison], but if no other interests than my own were involved I shld be inclined to take a far more decided line," implying that her principal concern is to preserve appearances for the sake of Charles Dilke and a future marriage.[172] Pattison/Dilke's art-historical writings can be extremely soignée in proffering their sexual sophistication; *The Renaissance of Art in France* smoothly displays familiarity with French erotic paintings of orgies and asserts "little doubt" about the sexual nature of male-male relations in the court of Henri III.[173] More privately, Charles and Emilia could write scathingly and knowingly of other women to whom sexual adventures were attributed (Madame de Noailles "used to have 4 lovers, one for each season . . . M. de Noailles was only the summer one"), while capably dismissing censure for their own breaches of decorum.[174]

Opportunity for sexual relations was certainly available, with as much chance for secrecy as people who lived always with servants might hope. Careful contrivances could have allowed trysts in England or in in France, where Charles kept a cottage near Toulon. The widowed Mrs. Pattison seems to have stayed at Charles's river cottage, Dockett Eddy, before their marriage, and a highly intriguing letter by Emilia depicts her "longing . . . to be lying in port at Dockett . . ." and associates the swans at Dockett with those in Elizabeth Barrett Browning's "The Romance of the Swan's Nest." In the poem, the swan's nest is a figure for female sexuality, and Emilia half-remembers to Charles a few lines: " 'I will have a lover gallant gay, of glorious deeds/ And to him I will discover'/'The swan's nest among the reeds.' "

> He will kiss me on the mouth
> Then, and lead me as a lover
> Through the crowds that praise his deeds:
> And, when soul-tied by one troth,
> Unto him I will discover
> That swan's nest among the reeds.

Like the mirror of the soul, the swan's nest will be revealed to the true lover. Although, as Dorothy Mermin notes, Barrett Browning's poem is a tragedy in which Ellie's imaginative desire for the future prevents her noticing "the wild swan had deserted,/ And a rat had gnawed the reeds!" and Ellie's "fantasy of displaced power and . . . ambition" and "dreams of annexing male power" lead to a punitive ruination of the erotic self, in Emilia Pattison's half-memory, this story is not told.[175] Emilia Pattison's selective quotation does not continue to the end of the poem, and erotic fulfillment and a share in the man's public glories remain attainable. Emilia Dilke's account, in her study of French engravers and draughtsmen, of the relationship of Claude-Henri Watelet and Marguerite LeComte, the wife of another man, also entices with its evocation of waterside romance: Dilke's text explicitly quarrels with an account by George Sand that claimed Watelet and Madame LeComte suffered when she left her husband. Dilke's account debunks Sand's "two poor old people" and instead offers "a rare conformity of tastes and pleasures" that not only forged an "indissolubl[e] attach[ment]" but was accepted by sophisticated friends like Elizabeth Vigée-Lebrun, and even by Monsieur LeComte, and was enjoyed in a charming and luxurious retreat—an "enchanted isle" of unsanctioned but utterly unpunished intimacy.[176]

Whatever happened among the reeds of the Thames, Emilia Pattison was courting scandal in her oblique invocations of a sexual harboring, and Emilia and Charles, in their more general conspirings of meetings, skirted the rules of maintaining appearances.[177] Yet E. F. S. Pattison's representation of Goujon's *Diane chasseresse*, chaste goddess of wild things, again offers a warning about attempts to read past appearances, to presume we've found secret nests of meaning in texts that settle questions of desire and behavior. Colin Eisler cleverly notes that in Pattison's drawing of the *Diane* in her text, the head bears more than a passing resemblance to photographs of Mrs. Pattison. He suggests we read the *Renaissance*, with its language of a "struggle of the voluptuous element against a self-imposed restraint," as a coded narrative of a history of sexual passion contained.[178] But Pattison's text unsettles claims to knowledgeable reading. Goujon and his contemporaries bore "peculiarities of a frame of mind and temper" difficult for later interpreters to understand except through "intimate" study. Their works are riveting in their "mystic worship of life," "melancholy and mad horror," "death" and "pleasures," entangled and tightly disciplined by Christianity and by skill, but they are nonetheless "foreign." It is not "easy to enter into [their] passionate enthusiasm," and learning more facts is not enough. Indeed, understanding eludes those who know too much since modern interpreters, puzzled by the strangeness of past minds, will be unable to set aside the frameworks of their own mental day. Too much, as well as too little, reading renders understanding impossible. If, in Pattison's text, passion skilfully controlled is readable in the *Diane*, the *Renaissance* immediately rebukes claims to read through time and representation to "knowledge."[179]

One measure of the undecidability of the exact nature of Charles's and Emilia's relationship is the response of Mark Pattison. Mark's diary and letters present him as both sneering at Charles and receiving him at Lincoln College with deliberate, even mannered, courtesy (which Charles found distinctly unnerving). Mark's letters to Francis blandly assume she and Charles are in continual communication, while to others he cuttingly referred to Charles as Francis's "fancy-man." He lamented to Meta Bradley in 1881, "she is now wholly unsympathetic [to me], reserving all her interest for the other man and his affairs," and asserted unequivocally, "she hates me and wishes me dead, is quite impatient at me dying so slowly," but he insisted he trusted his wife's propriety and believed she had not sexually betrayed him.[180] Mark's most savagely anguished writing about Francis's "betrayal" of him was expressed not in the language of adultery but of her dereliction of duty as the keeper of his house and provider of sympathy. And Mark may have had reasons of his own for maintaining the possibility of intense yet "innocent" extramarital friendships between men and women and for resisting language that too tightly restricted the meanings of heterosocial intimacy.

Mark and Meta

> It's a miserable life for the girls who cannot play
> The game of love, or wash their cares away
> With comforting wine, a miserable life for nieces
> Flayed by an uncle's tongue till their nerves are in pieces.
>
> —Horace, *Odes*, book 3, ode 2 (trans. James Michie)

Vivian Green has tried to rescue Mark and Meta from the genre of comedy into which they slid in the twentieth century; as he suggests, their relationship has long lost the dignity of serious scandal and become just another example of Victorian repression's toll on male-female relationships. But Green erases too much as he inscribes Meta and Mark as true lovers: "Normally the passion of love seems romantic when it concerns only the handsome and beautiful of both sexes, young in mind, body and spirit. But love's frontiers are never closed nor exclusive, in terms of either gender or appearance, or age or looks. Mark and Meta came tentatively within its territory."[181] In trying to place Mark and Meta within the precincts of "romance," Green implicitly argues for a transhistorical understanding of emotion. The category of romantic love is both fixed and freely available. In expanding the ground of "romantic love" beyond presumed contempory associations with the young and beautiful, Green not only enshrines that emotion as "natural" but also neglects the ways romantic love itself has been figured precisely as a transcendent union between persons in highly differentiated positions—for example, between older, educated, legally autonomous, powerful, propertied, enfranchised men and younger, badly educated, legally dependent, propertyless, voteless, *femes coverts* for whom sentiment should substitute for legal rights and material self-determination. Mark loved Meta and Meta loved Mark; both said so. But the rhetorics of affection between them are more diverse, sometimes more naive and sometimes more calculated, sometimes more affecting and sometimes more disturbing, and their excess is marked by the power relations of gender.

Mark's and Meta's texts cannot be reduced to suppressed eroticism badly disguised, but reading Mark's relationship with Meta through a psychological theory that aligns the liaison with Mark's relationships with his wife, sisters, and (hidden) mother is also dangerous. Mark's seduction of and by Meta can be read as reenacting earlier scenes, but the ambiguity in Mark Pattison's relationship with Meta Bradley troubles readings of this relationship as simply a repetition of an established plot. Seeing the letters of Mark and Meta as simply the legible evidence of psychic compulsions misses the historical point: these texts' oscillations between eros, paternity, siblinghood, nurturance, demand, romance, and pedagogy signal how these categories collided, colluded, and shaped each other in Victorian discourse. The figuration of heterosexual romance as the reproduction of earlier family life—marrying a girl just like the girl who married dear old dad—always risked the scandalous conflation of "adult" and infantile desires. Further, if romances were often constructed in terms of pedagogical relationships—as in stories about professors who marry young girls—pedagogical relationships too could be eroticized and rendered familial.[182] That is, the ambiguity of this relationship illuminates the erotic ambiguities produced by historically specific material and cultural conditions. Further, just as letters between Francis Pattison and Ellen Smith suggest that women's loving intimacies could include coaching each other in submission, Mark's and Meta's letters show that relationships which move across registers, in which partners inhabit multiple rhetorical positions, are not necessarily egalitarian. Fluidity and power can coexist.

Mark's and Meta's relationship has been thoroughly chronicled by V. H. H. Green, John Sparrow, and Betty Askwith.[183] Although impossible to fully demonstrate without reproducing the entirety of their correspondence, the most striking feature of their correspondence, especially during the first year, is the complex saraband of expectations and desires the writers enact. Carefully withholding labels for their relationship, Mark Pattison's letters draw Meta into a web of expectations and promises whose exact nature remains ambiguous to the last. For once, we have both sides of a correspondence and can therefore examine the ways expectations and desires were not voiced but suspended between ambiguous words and sentences; the tentativeness and incompleteness of our reading of these letters echo the complex and hazardous exercises in de-crypting undertaken by their original recipients and by those who gained surreptitious access to them. But these textual dramatics were not performed by two players alone on a bare stage with equal discursive resources. Meta was a talented amateur to Mark's experienced professionalism in textual seductions and emotional escalations.

Mark offers Meta friendship and attention, figured as selflessly paternal; Meta replies with intense gratitude and warm affection; Mark is textually delighted and surprised by Meta's warmth and "reads" in it an offer of "sympathy" to which his letters reply with confidences and gratitude. Meta, honored by Mark's trust, replies with assurances that it will not be betrayed (and confidences of her own); Mark accepts her assurances with delighted surprise, and his letters wonder whether it can really be true that she is "offering" what it seems; Meta replies that of course she loves him; Mark writes that he can scarcely believe that Meta is "offering" to replace all that is missing from his (marital) life; Meta is incredulous but thrilled that Mark should see her as a replacement for his absent wife; Mark is incredulous but thrilled that Meta is "in love" with him . . . and Meta is awed that he should be "in love" with her. . . .

This script's dramatic unfolding hinges upon Mark's letters construing each offer of sympathy and affection as a raising of the stakes. Meta's letters depict her as honored at being so wanted and as struck slightly off balance by his readings. (Did I really offer that? Is that what my words really meant? Is that the never-quite-named nature of my feelings? Am I that name?) Mark's letters's praise of Meta's kindness and dutifulness—and their frequent self-dramatizations of his own forlorn state—allow and encourage her replies to occupy the position he has named for her, as his loving and sympathetic and faithful admirer. Meta may well have felt pleasure at being emplotted in a drama naming her as exceptional and marking her as admirable for her intelligence in admiring Mark. Moreover, reticence in applying exact names to feelings allowed their relationship to escalate without culminating in overt sexuality.

Mark Pattison first met Meta Bradley in March of 1878 when, during a visit to Oxford, her cousin, Margaret "Daisy" Bradley brought her to tea at Lincoln College. Mark summarized his early impressions: "she is interesting, & I endeavoured to say what I thought would be useful [to her]."[184] Mark's diary thus placed him in relation to Meta as an advisor and positioned her among the serried ranks of young Oxford-connected women in whom he took an interest. Meta's cousin Daisy, Mark's several nieces (his sister Rachel's daughters Jeannie and Mary Stirke, and Gertrude Tuckwell), Grace Toynbee (sister of Arnold), Nancy Paul (daughter of Kegan), Mabel Bradley, and Fanny Kensington, as well of course as Mark's sisters and perhaps Francis Strong, had been recipients of Mark's attentions and nothing in his texts initially marked his friendship with Meta Bradley as distinctive; she was simply another young woman to be given tea, taken for walks, lent books, perhaps admitted to evenings at Lincoln for readings aloud of Shakespeare, poetry, and even Mark's early diaries, and carefully scrutinized for signs of flaws, the most important of which was failure of "sympathy."[185]

If Meta Bradley stood out among the other young women in this brigade, it may have been through her overt and unhappy occupation of the position of "superfluous woman," unmarried and dependent. The daughter of the Reverend Charles Bradley and Anne George Bradley, Meta was born in 1853; she was twenty-six when she and

Mark met. Charles Bradley's father, also Charles, had been a prominent Evangelical preacher and member of the Clapham Sect; solidly middle-class, the elder Charles Bradley married twice and had twenty-one children; one of Meta's uncles was Granville Bradley, Master of University College, Oxford, and later Dean of Westminster. Meta's father is vividly depicted by Augustus Hare, whose murderously Evangelical childhood was enlivened by a stint at a school Bradley kept near London. Hare described Charles Bradley as "very eccentric" but with "a natural enthusiasm for knowledge" and gift for teaching, although Hare's account includes Bradley's penchant for humiliating punishments.[186] Charles Bradley's bizarre pedagogy was not restricted to his students. In a terrifying tale, Hare claims Bradley would "teach" his children through family stories, telling his daughters tales of his "poor dead first wife" and his son stories of a dead son of Mrs. Bradley "by her first husband." The reminiscences of lost saints, whose perfections were detailed as examples for the children, reduced teller and audience to tears. *Neither the first wife nor her son ever existed.*[187] Charles Bradley invented the dead half-brother, whom little Charlie Bradley could only palely imitate, and a lost angel of the house his daughters should regard as their proper model rather than their own mother. The children's existence was narrated to them as the contingent result of previous and regretted losses, in stories in which love, virtue, and death were intertwined by a father who enacted his own suffering to elicit passionate responses. This tale reminds us: stories can make, rather than reveal, psychic experience.

Against Hare's Charles Bradley—clever, charismatic, cruel, and intolerant of challenges to his authority—Anne George Bradley appears faintly: "sensitive and somewhat reserved," kind to students, vulnerable to her husband's eccentricities, loving to her children, and deeply religious. She died in 1866 when Meta was twelve, a loss Meta wrote as the great agony of her life. Meta wrote Mark (what "[she had] never said to anyone else"), "when I lost my mother I lost the one person whom I almost worshipped—& tho I was only 12 I don't think I feel much less wretched about it than I did at first," adding that she believed her father "fe[lt] just the same" but they never spoke of it. She felt "dread of getting to care about anyone else very much."[188] Meta's anguish resembles Virginia Woolf's conflict at the memory of her mother; both women could simultaneously idealize and express angry ambivalence at their own difference from such angels, perhaps exacerbated in Meta's case by her father's fiction-making. The cultural links between mothers' love and religious faith did not create exclusively feminine patterns of loss—Mark and Meta may have shared suppressed guilt for their failure to sustain their mothers' Evangelical faith as well as rage at their fathers' religiosity and power—but gender mattered in how children might extricate themselves: Meta wrote that she cared little for her father and his second wife, Anne Hathaway Bradley, but was economically dependent on them (if she were to maintain her class position).[189] Meta's letters position her as tormented, too, by implications that she failed to properly transform economic dependence into feminine emotionality. She was "a girl who cd not care very much for her nearest relations, & was always being told by them that she had no heart."[190]

Mark Pattison offered close and flattering attention to this lonely young woman. Mark's diary had presented him as particularly bitter, isolated, persecuted, and inclined to seek a new warm friendship during the winter of 1879–1880.[191] He soon began to address his "Dearest Meta!" in letters of considerable ardor. Mark's letters assured

Meta how little and how much the difference in their ages mattered and intimated that his marriage was a dead letter; "There is nothing left to me in life, out of which I can get such nutriment for heart and interest, as out of this kind of paternal relation—it is the only comfort for growing old! I long so to be of use of any stray or struggling heart!" Positioning himself as a loving father/friend, grateful to the point of pathos for her attention ("I can't expect you to give more than a fleeting moment [to my letters]. Of you I often think in my solitary wanderings . . ."), open to and actively soliciting her every confidence (why did she not confide in him? "Do I not answer? Do I not shew an interest in what you are saying? Do I not try to interest you in some of the things in which I am interested?"), Mark's letters repeatedly drew attention to his own loneliness and seduce through performances of self-disclosure.[192] He reveals himself as, behind the outer surfaces of institutional and intellectual power, a man gripped by pain and loss—a great man with a great wound only a very exceptional woman might nurse.

The issue is neither the accuracy nor the self-consciousness of Mark's self-construction but its deployment in particular social contexts. The fact is that Mark's solutions to his dilemma of loneliness consistently involved the love of young women who could both demonstrate their exceptionality and obliterate it by devoting themselves to the most quotidian female task, the tending of men. Mark impressed upon Meta her own nobility and generosity. When she wrote that she resented being "compelled" to spend the summer cruising on her father's yacht, Mark replied, "I can estimate the amount of the sacrifice you are making to your sense of duty, and . . . it has greatly enhanced my esteem for you." By not telling her father her real feelings, Meta showed "a pitch of virtue beyond the limits of martyrdom and which even the most stoical moralist could not exact." One might suspect irony but Mark's letters seem quite serious as they commiserate with Meta for "the discomforts and trials which inevitably await[ed]" Meta, while commending her obedience to her father and insisting her "sense of duty" would prove an "ideal support."[193] The necessity of daughterly duty is reinforced by an implicit contrast between the nobly obedient Meta and his niece Mary Stirke. Mary, previously "the most amiable and lovable girl in the world" had proven herself not "the girl she ought to be" in refusing to come at Mark's call to Lincoln to nurse him. She was soon after cast out from Mark's good graces for ignoring his desire by spending time with Frank and Margaret Pattison in London, sampling metropolitan pleasures and running the risk of having her "childish nature" ruined by "flattery" instead of returning promptly to her father's Yorkshire farm when Mark no longer needed her.[194] Just as he had sermonized his sisters from Hauxwell's pulpit, Mark's letters to Meta draw a line between sympathy for suffering daughters and encouragement to active revolt, and he suggests that Meta should not only comply but express pleasure at her father's will.

Unlike Mark's sisters and his wife, who had in various ways described themselves as longing for worlds beyond family life, Meta's self-writing depicted her as discontented with her public life and longing for a true home. Her friendship with Mark is a recuperation of a lost past of family pleasures: she wrote that she had not been so happy since she was a child, implicitly aligning Mark with her lost mother. In these texts, Mark could occupy the position of both Meta's parents and compensate her for her present family life—which Meta's letters depicted as a prison of near-hatred—by offering an object for the emotionality blocked in her relations with father and step-mother.[195] A long letter narrates their relationship in the third person to construct Mark's role in Meta's life as a relationship in which she reexperienced *familial* emotion. Her story was that of a young woman who had been "obliged to confess to herself that she didn't love any living being *very* much" but had resigned herself to "being useful to a few people in a mild way" (especially through public work like distributing information on "sanitary reform" in the Paddington district) and leading "a rather dreary, because loveless life—(with no certainty as to any better future existence)." But then she met a man of whom "she ha[d] always heard as a mine of learning etc, & to her gt surprise he actually takes a friendly interest in her." Her emotions moved from fearful gratitude to recognition that "her kind friend feels as lonely & wretched as she does"; she found "by degrees" that she felt for him "what she feared she never sd feel for anyone—what other people say they feel for *several* of their relations. . . ." Mark was the one "who ha[d] shown me that I still have a heart." As her engagement had transformed Francis Strong from an "Ishmael" in her family, by Meta's account Mark gave her a sense of her own ability to express a whole range of "normal" emotions. More, too: Meta felt for Mark "a unique mixture of what people feel for their God, their husband, & their child," all combined in a single object, loving whom was not at all like caring for an "ordinary man."[196]

Mark's letters respond to and reinforce these representations of Meta's emotion as intense, unique, familial, and selfless. An early letter compares Meta with Jeannie Stirke, who is "a very dear girl—but a child . . . who cannot give what you can give, so I read your letters over & over, to suck all the honey I can out of them." Meta is the one who gives unstinting love, who is not "cold" like his sisters and wife, not disobedient and ungrateful like Mary Stirke or too worldly like Gertrude Tuckwell; Meta is "unspoiled," sustains him, and her affection is irresistible.[197] Mark's texts place Meta in the "respectable" roles of niece, student, young friend, and handmaiden but link Mark's desire to bestow tender love with Meta's subordination and his gender. When Meta sprained an ankle, Mark wrote: "I shall enjoy petting you so and nursing you upon the sofa . . ."; when her ankle improved, he wrote of regret: "the idea of you rather helpless, and dependent on my charitable attentions, had begun to be gratifying to my man's sense of superiority . . ."[198]

Mark's letters also link the pleasures he drew from Meta's affection to those he "ought" to have found in marriage. He metaphorized Meta as an "anchor" to replace the one "on which [he] had placed all [his] trust" and lost.

> Oh! that your good will towards me may only last my life, that is all my prayer now, what a consolation it will be to me in my time of decay! And, indeed, I have much need of consolation. Do you know the 10 September [his wedding anniversary] is an anniversary which depresses me to the lowest depths of misery. The heart-pain which it brings with it lasts for days, and is still vivid [rasura] . . . responding with quickest sympathy to every mood and phase of thought or fancy. Now that [rasura] and has not [rasura] . . . 4 years . . .

Recalling a time when Francis had been a good wife to him, and lamenting the period since 1876, Mark's letter aligns Meta's good will and consolation with lost erotic relations. In Mark's account, romance and eros merge with the provision of that perfect "sympathy" his wife had withdrawn; in being sympathetic and loving, Meta provides not merely sisterly or daughterly devotion but something in the realm of romance.[199]

Meta's letters endorse Mark's account of his marriage and join in lamenting the "wall of ice" between him and Francis ("separation by death would have been far less agonizing") and wondered that "such love as [his] should be rejected." Meta's texts insist on her own inferiority to Francis Pattison in intellect and in Mark's affections, but she nonetheless ventures that her greater affection gives her value, wishing she "had some right to be with [him] whenever [he] felt extra lonely and wretched." In Mark's letters, Meta saw offered a role "more than [she] ever dared hope [for]," and understood her position as the replacement of Francis Pattison in Mark's heart, if not his bed. Mark's letters also read Meta's devotion as repetition: he had "again found someone to care for me!"[200] Both Mark's and Meta's letters contrasted their intimacy to the frigidity of their customary domestic lives; in both, Meta's long visit of 1880–1881 is a blessed moment of domestic counterpoint, marked by cuddles, Meta's warming Mark's coat before the fire for him, reading aloud to him, writing his letters for him, and generally attending to his comfort.

At no point do these letters stabilize a single category of intimate relationship. In one letter, Meta masculinizes her feelings for Mark, associating her daydreaming about him with the feelings of an intellectual man "deeply in love," writing their relationship in terms nearer those of Oxford homoerotic pedagogy than those of conventional hetero-romance.[201] Similarly, near the end of the long visit, Mark seems to have briefly contemplated the possibility of making "some arrangement for the future of a more permanent kind . . . to which [Meta's] father may be a party," regularizing their relationship by adopting Meta as his daughter. Near the same time, he bought Meta a ring, an act with obvious significance within romance plots, only to soon after write a letter explicitly erasing the possibility of divorce and remarriage by vetoing even the notion of a legal separation from Francis.[202] This intermingling of roles—familial, pedagogical, and romantic—formed, rather than disguised, the letters' language of intimacy. Their excessiveness to any one pairing—teacher/student, elder/younger, parent/child, uncle/niece, mentor/acolyte, man/woman—made that relationship possible, at least for a while.

Mark's idea of adopting Meta may have been, in part, a fantasy that such a step would remove the hint of scandal provoked by their living together in Lincoln College, but their ambiguous idyll of domesticity ultimately provoked active attempts to end their relationship. The initial stirrings of scandal emanated from Meta's family; the villains of the piece were Meta's rigid father and her aunt Marian, Mrs. Granville Bradley, who was concerned by the blotting of the Bradley eschutcheon in general and by the specifically Oxonian ramifications of any scandal unleashed by Meta's three-month encampment at Lincoln College in 1880–1881.[203] It became difficult, and finally impossible, for Mark and Meta to convince the wider world that their relationship was not sexually compromising, was not (at the least) quasi-adulterous, when Meta had lived with Mark (albeit with servants and visitors) and filled the role of homemaker Francis Strong Pattison had deserted.[204] Even before Meta's stay at Lincoln, Mark had worried about placating "Mrs. Grundy, who is a very important personage" in Oxford, and Meta's continued insistence that only people with wicked minds could construe their relationship as anything but "perfectly innocent" was optimistic in light of references in letters and diary to "loving hugs," snuggles on the sofa "with infinite possibilities of kissing," and bedtime tuckings-in.[205] Not surprisingly, the relationship became an open scandal because of letters and a debate about authorship, culminating in a novel.

Francis Pattison's written responses to Mark and Meta's relationship do not provide a key to the relationship, nor do her texts explicitly draw parallels between Mark's liaison with Meta and his courtship of her twenty years earlier. The dominant note of her letters is pique, but that very pique kept at a safe distance any closer inspection of the nets that had enmeshed both women in relationships with Mark Pattison. Francis's letters place much of the responsibility of the relationship on Meta, whom she represented as slightly vulgar, unconsciously guided by thwarted sexuality, and opportunistic for the prestige and (after Mark's death) the money accrued by the Rector of an Oxford college.[206] If Francis's texts about Meta raise questions about the purity of her own motives for marrying Mark, they also display anger. Francis had, for long years, played by the rules of marriage—first by serving Mark, then by maintaining a careful discretion about her relations with Charles Dilke, honoring Mark's mental authority, tolerating his satirical cracks about her friends, and at times acquiescing to his sense of decorum. And yet, while Mark went on denouncing her in private and public for shattering his home, suddenly *he* should apparently kick over the traces of conventionality! Francis's letters are deeply irritated by the scandalous fallout, even if she claimed never to have suspected Mark of fullscale adultery.

If Francis Pattison refused to go on record with the most scandalous interpretation of Mark and Meta's relationship, such interpretations circulated. Mark and Meta's letters may have been concerned about possibly scandalous interpretations of their relationship from early on, but the setting of the cat among the pigeons only occurred when letters from Oxford made it difficult for Francis Pattison to allude to Meta as just another, if unworthy, young woman in Mark's entourage.[207] In March, 1881, someone wrote Francis at least one anonymous letter about Meta. Francis refused to rise to the bait openly, but her letters to Mark raised the issue and he badly bungled his attempts to find the culprit. Mark suspected the novelist Rhoda Broughton, a friend of both Pattisons with whom he often read German; Broughton lived in Holywell Street with her sister, Mrs. Newcome, and was a satiric observer of Oxford society as well as a slightly scandalous figure as the author of "racy" novels.[208] Mark recruited his friend May Laffan, an outspoken Irish writer with whom he conducted a semi-flirtatious correspondence, to find out if he was right. Laffan asked Broughton outright and Broughton was furious at being suspected.[209] The consequent brouhaha introduced the anonymous letters into open discussion and consolidated the Bradleys' fears that the relationship was a scandal in Oxford.

Whatever Rhoda Broughton's private views, she produced a public text Mark and others read as her revenge: her novel, *Belinda* was widely considered to be a satire on Mark Pattison.[210] *Belinda* depicts a misalliance between a young, beautiful girl and the much older, much uglier, dessicated Professor Forth; its title redoubles the point, as "Belinda" is the name of the heroine in the Italian version of the tale of Beauty and the Beast. Professor Forth woos the young Belinda by offering her the chance to assist his work, and his seduction techniques—which include reading Robert Browning's

"A Grammarian's Funeral" aloud—along with his emotional impoverishment and domestic tyranny, are mocked by the narrator.[211] The fairness of Broughton's alleged portrait was immediately contested but Broughton's intention of aligning the Forths with the Pattisons was assumed; after Mark Pattison's death, Andrew Lang published a satirical series of letters passed between Professor Forth and the Reverend Edward Casaubon, Belinda Forth and Dorothea Brooke, which not only read *Belinda* as a roman-à-clef but reminded readers of the Pattisons' other purported fictional counterparts.[212] The circulation of stories through anonymous letters had incited more public narrations of the secrets of Oxford married life, and Lang wittily and aptly brings together the epistolary and the novelistic. Unlike Mark's, Meta's, and Francis's letters, the anonymous letters and Broughton's and Lang's fictions banish ambiguity: the anonymous letters insist on a scandalously eroticized reading of Mark and Meta, and Lang's and Broughton's fictions inscribe the Pattison marriage as a comically failed romance. Less comically, the wrath of the Bradleys and their allies made it nearly impossible for Meta and Mark to meet openly; they resorted to trysts at the British Museum or National Gallery followed by long cab rides, but neither Mark's nor Meta's letters broached the possibility of defying the forces of family and scandal. Mark's letters to Meta had always depicted him as unlikely to brave Oxford condemnation or embark on a new life elsewhere; Vivian Green reads Mark's capitulation to Mrs. Grundy as the result of his parsimony and attachment to the position, if not the labor, of Rector.[213]

Anonymous letters, family stories, local scandal, and comic novels blocked Mark and Meta's field of action and narrowed the terrain on which they could linguistically depict their relationship. In the last two years of their relationship, until Mark's death in 1884, the texts of their relationship become a series of complex intrigues to arrange brief and rare meetings. As the possibility of enacting, rather than imagining or recalling, domestic intimacy receded, Mark's letters lost some of their ambiguous eroticism. Meta's position in Mark's texts became less romantic than familial, his tone mentorial and avuncular in less nurturing ways as he subjected her to caustic criticisms for her social-reform activities and alleged mental stagnation. Several letters seem to repudiate earlier desires that their relationship could replace and repair the coldness of his marriage by preaching the virtues of *mariages de convenances* and mocking her assertions that marriages should be based on love.[214] Meta was in no position to demand a less textually safe relationship, and her letters too shift their emphases. Her letters continued to figure their relationship as the great event of her life, but she wrote in elegiac tones of the relationship as a powerful friendship rather than a blocked romance: "Nothing can ever rob one of the past. Not even death can alter the fact that you & I were friends for years—which fact I still ponder with perplext pride." Mark was her greatest mental influence and the touchstone of her self-image as one who could love and be loved, and that was enough: "You mustn't think for a moment that I wish our friendship had been other than it has . . . Whatever anyone may say or think, I am absolutely content I cdnt alter it in any way and wd sooner have been the little comfort I have been to you than the whole world to anyone else." Meta's letter continues, however, with a reminder, disavowed but expressed, that their relationship could be interpreted within the genre of romance: "And you mustn't, dearest Rector, moan that you have spoilt my life. I don't believe I should ever have loved anyone well enough to marry him. *I've never had the faintest sparks of feeling of that sort for anyone* . . . But friendship isn't marriage . . ."[215] Meta's letters thus maintain ambiguity by reminding the reader of the possibility of erotic interpretation even while valorizing the more innocent category of friendship. Her letters maintain this openness to the end: she sent the dying Mark a copy of an ode, almost certainly Horace's *Te maris et terrae numeroque carentis harenae*, with a note: "[it] just expresses my feelings & wish . . . & as it was written by a man to a man, I don't see why any one sd think it 'sentimental,' or 'improper' when copied for a woman by a man!"[216] Repudiating the "improper" reader, she acknowledged his/her reading even while refusing it.

Meta Bradley and Francis Pattison never met. But they would be bound together over Mark Pattison by Horace's words, just as they had been by stories and letters. On his deathbed, Mark asked Francis Pattison to read him "Te mensorem"; she "cld not for a moment guess why this was" but "fortunately a sudden memory gave [her]" the broken reference. She fetched a volume of Horace and read aloud the words Meta Bradley had silently traced onto another page. Mark, two days from death, followed along but Francis wrote, sadly or smugly, "I had to guide him all through—a strange reversal" of their usual pedagogic relations. Francis's letter concludes "since this I have heard" but breaks off abruptly, so we can never know if she later knew anything of the poem's passage between Meta and Mark. What is left is the scene she wrote about herself, a mistress of tongues, speaking another's words over a dying body. Horace's poem, too, is the ventriloquized speech of a ghost.[217]

Death Stories

The Grammarian's Funeral

> Here's the top-peak; the multitude below
> Live, for they can, there:
> This man decided not to Live but Know—
> Bury this man there?
>
> —Robert Browning,
> "A Grammarian's Funeral"

Mark Pattison rehearsed his death for many years before it came; his diary confidently expected his imminent demise for a full twenty years. In 1873 he transcribed a pathetic verse beginning "One little space prolong my mournful day!/One little lapse suspend thy last decree! . . . Ere I with death shake hands . . ."[218] Mark's doctors generally diagnosed him as suffering from complaints of the intestine; he was susceptible by his own account to "cold and fever . . . gout [and], rheumatism, [had] no teeth and inactive liver!" He complained frequently of failing eyesight and a lack of energy and vitality to support his mental ambitions; these complaints gained frequency in the 1870s, after the collapse of his wife's health in 1868–1869 and again after Francis began to spend winters away from him in 1874.[219] During these years, Mark's diary increasingly denounced his wife's entertaining at Lincoln College as a conspiracy to sap him of time and strength, but the diary also records that Mark played lawn tennis and croquet virtually daily and the majority of his vacations were spent fishing in Scotland and Dartmoor. If Mark's health was never precisely "good" and was continually misdiagnosed by his doctors, it was not markedly worse than that of most inhabitants of mid-Victorian Oxford, whose letters and diaries reveal nearly unending major and minor illnesses.[220]

Francis Pattison's letters took a jaundiced view of Mark's reports of his failing health, especially after he accused her of "contriving" her illnesses in order to be away from him. Resentful of his demands that she act as his nurse despite the state of her own health, she suspected him of deliberate or unconscious malingering in letters to Ellen Smith: "The 'fainting' is exaggerated like everything else wh can excite commiseration. I have seen him throw himself down on the landing in similar attacks. . . ." Diagnosing his ills as "ordinary diarrhoea" and gout, Francis tartly added, "He never does anything that can try him in any way." But although Mark's illness during the fall of 1883 was in many respects virtually indiscernible from the digestive difficulties he had complained of for thirty years, his forebodings of death were this time more accurate. Mark's diary and letters voiced little doubt that the end was near and he was sufficiently ill by late 1883 to overcome Francis's suspicions ("I have seen the whole thing too often, & it is quite clear . . . that *for the present* there is no cause for 'alarm' ").[221] Despite Mark's long practice in being at death's door, his actual decline into final illness was unresigned. Through his last six months, Mark's illness waxed and waned, at times causing "such pain [he] would fain have got ease by dying" but at other times allowing him enough energy to read and dictate his memoirs, letters, and diary entries. Mark's last letters to Meta Bradley and final diary entries represent him as frustrated by his inability to accept illness, "impelled by an invisible force" to go on reading "promiscuously" and storing up knowledge (the last words in his diary list his reading, ending with "Goethe's 'Iphigenie' ") and repeatedly strike an elegiac note. Mark's last writings each end as if the writer were constantly aware that each page might be his last and wished to end on a poignant note. "Our Parks [in Oxford] have been a blaze of pink May such as I never remember—May & laburnum are now faded, & with them the glory of summer!" Again, a week later, he sent Meta "a few lines of farewell" with exhortations to "be [her]self! and go bravely on—."[222] But he wrote once more.

Mark's deathbed also gave Francis a last chance to perform and recount a scene of reconciliation, enacting both her sense of duty and her desire to begin a new stage in her own life. When she began considering a return to Oxford during the winter of 1883–1884, Francis hoped in letters to Eleanor Smith that meeting the depressing demands of nursing Mark might allow them a final reconciliation.[223] Francis wrote a story in which Mark really, if inconsistently, wanted her there. Although he could still write the kind of "letter wh made me almost sick—an *evil* letter, in his worst mood, forbidding &c homecoming with a wonderfully clever & cunning mixture of truth & lies," other letters were "full of that tender sentiment he makes so captivating," which led her to think she "shld not have been in the house 24 hours before he would declare there was 'no one like [her].' " Despite the ambiguity of Mark's expressed desires, Francis insisted on returning; Mark would "after the first movement of irritation . . . rejoice and be pleased." Pain and anger flared in her letters when

Ellen Smith criticized her decision to return, apparently for hypocrisy; Francis claimed her desire to give Mark "tenderness & sympathy" was "honest," penitent, and reflected a process of self-examination and stock-taking of her life with Mark.[224] These two claims, of male difficulty and female self-criticism, are echoed in Emilia Dilke's "The Physician's Wife": the cruel husband deliberately tries to drive his suffering young wife away by "harshness and sarcasm and insult" when she is no longer compliant with his wishes, but after she murders him, the wife comes to "see him in a light different to that in which she had conceived of him in her youth," regretting her violence and her earlier anger and wilfulness.[225] Smith's reaction to Francis's letters seems to have suggested that Francis was able to take a generous line only when an end to self-sacrifice was in sight—Francis's letters present her as in little doubt that Mark was dying—but "The Physician's Wife" makes even more obvious the necessity of male death to female penitence.

Francis attended Mark from 4 Feburary 1884 until his death on 31 July 1884. Mark tactlessly lauded her nursing and organizational skills to the despondent Meta Bradley.[226] Assisted by professional nurses, her nieces, and Frances Pattison, Francis cared for Mark, removing him in June 1884, from Oxford to lodgings in Harrogate for the "iron water."[227] The narrative of Mark's last days continues in her letters to Eleanor Smith, with a thread of lingering bitterness over Smith's questioning of her motives. She wrote repeatedly of her compassion for Mark ("he is so piteous") and of his moving gratitude to her; "He can hardly bear me out of his sight . . . he is all gentleness to me." Francis's account is self-satisfied, despite protestations that she was constantly on the verge of emotional collapse; she tells of Mark's rejection of her offer to bring "*anyone* whose presence wld be a pleasure" to him and recounts Mark's insistence that Francis was "*all*-sufficing . . . [his] comfort and consolation."[228]

In Francis's account, Mark told her that her " 'independence was too much if one was well, but ill it was the one perfect thing.' "[229] She narrates an incident of her and Mark gently disputing the stories their marriage might have enacted:

MARK: How good you are to me if you had always been like this what a reminiscence

FRANCIS: My dear soul no one cld be for anyone *like this* for long . . . it takes all my intelligence & all my strength fixed in the one thought of you to be like this.

According to Francis, when Mark lay dying, both of them recognized the marriage story Mark had sought to live out, but Francis did not offer to enact it at the end. She reminded Mark of "all the calls & objects of a life like [hers]" and of her own ill health. Portraying herself as the wrong character for his plot, she presented herself instead as an exceptional resource in exceptional circumstances, "constant help in [his] direst need," to "sensibly lessen the misery of dying."[230]

Emilia Dilke's later art history included a painful story. The sculptor Etienne Falconnet had an "original" character of austerity sharpened by early hardship; he had "rebelled against the injustice of men," and (like the doctor in "The Physician's Wife") "acquiring early a sense of his own power, took a pleasure in letting people feel that he knew himself to be their superior." "In all things Falconnet selfishly followed his humour, and that humour, if sometimes generous, was always awkward and often offensive." Dilke ladles out evocative adjectives over six pages—"severe," "harsh," sometimes angry, "dogmatic," producing "dry and often futile dissertations," "aggressive," "irascible," continually complaining, "intolerable," and "self-absorbed"—and develops a story in which Falconnet causes himself pain and anger by being difficult. Yet Falconnet's story is prelude to a briefer story: after he had a stroke, "for eight long years [Falconnet] kept his room, tyrannically insisting on the close attentions of his daughter-in-law, Anna Collot, who had been one of his few pupils . . . Death delivered her and him on the 24th January 1791, but Anna Collot never again touched the chisel which she had been forced to abandon. Eight years of nursing had left her without the courage to take up again the art in which she had displayed no inconsiderable talent." Dilke notes the high quality—"keen and strong perception of character," "virility and delicacy," "life" and expressivity—of Collot's earlier work and offers a photograph of her head of Diderot, but the moral is clear: exceptional women recruited into domestic attendance on difficult men have their exceptionality destroyed.[231]

The assumption in 1884 that Mark Pattison's life was ending allowed Francis Pattison's letters to muse on Mark's life as a failed story and to represent it as one of unmet and unmeetable desires. She wondered what comfort she could offer him, being unable "to conceive of [his] life as a whole or with any touch of great or true humanity in it—it seems an *unspent* life, neither enjoyed nor used. . . . this makes one feel embarrassed." She could offer "pity & sympathy for the suffering and weakness" but could not imagine how to comfort one who had neither "faith in hereafter" nor the consciousness of having "done what they would with their lives."[232] A mutilated letter (probably to Charles Dilke), even situates her care for Mark within *Middlemarch* :"I am all [Mark] has to look to . . . I purposefully never read [*Middlemarch*], but to judge by what you tell me, and what I have heard from all, *Mr. Casaubon was much more to be pitied than Dorothea.*"[233] Dorothea survives her first marriage.

Mark's last letter to Meta Bradley located him in Hauxwell at the end; he wrote of "poignant, bitter regret" for his lost childhood among the Yorkshire dales.[234] Francis Pattison's account of her husband's death also invoked his family history. Providing a pathetic contrast to Mark's reconciliation with herself, she portrayed his sister Frances. "She distressed him so I had to keep her away . . . & this seemed cruel for she is passionately devoted to him, but *wholly* incapable of showing it . . . She crawled all about the house a shapeless speechless black body of anguish eaten up with heartache at her own inability to be anything to him . . ." Francis wrote that Mark spent some of his scant remaining energy in dictating "a letter calculated to wound most deeply his sister Eleanor," one of "out of daily similar occurences" of Mark railing against those "who have loved him best."[235] (In 1902, Emilia Dilke's history carefully included a cruel quotation from a letter by the engraver Wille sneeringly dismissing his sister; in Dilke's account, Wille's self-interest during the French Revolution and lack of compassion for the death of Marie Antoinette could hardly surprise one in a man capable of such an act.[236]) Her account of Mark's physical state is harrowing—"his despairing cries ringing out" through the house; "the terrible *smell* [and] retchings"—but the greatest emphasis is on Mark's mental torment: "the every uncontrollable will, the rage the pathos, the abject fits of terror—we are all half killed by it." Francis gives Mark's niece, Mary Stirke, the most damning words: "Poor Mary said 'It is as he has been all his life only we think it so dreadful now *because* he is dying.' "[237]

It was only ascertained after Mark's death, on 30 July 1884, that, like his father, he had died of advanced stomach cancer. Francis quickly made arrangements for his funeral, burying Mark near Harrogate, "in a country graveyard where the hills he loved will look forever on his grave," and barring everyone but Mark's family from the funeral. She met criticism with "it is a horrible thing to think that you must be a Prince before you can be buried without . . . intrusion." In these arrangements, as in her editing of Mark's Memoirs, she insisted she was following Mark's directions or, at most, capitulating to the wishes of his family. She positioned herself as righteously acting for her dead husband, writing Ellen Smith that in all things she felt a "knowledge of obligations fulfilled to what [she] conceive[d] to be the uttermost." Smith thought it "a cruel mistake to try to prevent people from coming [since] Francis has made some mortal enemies by her action & she has not too many friends just now," but Francis stood her ground in scorn for Oxford.[238]

Emilia Pattison, Charles Dilke, and their confidantes knew the end of the Pattison marriage would not put an end to its stories: Eleanor Smith claimed that on the day of Mark Pattison's death, "there was betting in London on who she would marry & how soon!"[239] E. F. S. Pattison's account of the French Renaissance had sardonically described other women's displays of their widowhood: Diane de Poitiers is represented on an enamel dish in a "black and white cap, emblem and relic of widowhood, [which] renders the absense of all other clothing the more conspicuous," while for Catherine de Medici, the "tragedy which ended her husband's days brought to his wife the first possibility of independent life and power, but she took upon herself all the signs of seemly affliction."[240] Betty Askwith presents an account by one who recalled Mrs. Pattison enacting widowhood with impeccable costuming and a palpable merriness: Bessie and Edwin Hatch, to whom Mark Pattison described himself as an "old fool" when he became engaged to marry Francis Strong, had a daughter, and "as a schoolgirl of fourteen or so Miss Hatch remembers Mrs Pattison [in 1884] . . . She was swathed in widow's weeds from top to toe, never . . . had so much crepe swirled and eddied around the human form; but what struck the sharp-eyed young girl was the contrast between the all-enveloping blackness and the charm, not to say the radiance of Mrs Pattison herself."[241]

In Middlemarch, Edward Casaubon attempts to dictate his wife's life from beyond the grave by a will that will disinherit her if she should marry Will Ladislaw; Casaubon's will both threatens Dorothea's economic future and attempts to dictate the meaning of Dorothea's past, since a marriage with Ladislaw would be taken as the continuation of a past adultery. Mark Pattison's will did not give him the last word in their marriage story. Mark's will was a powerful performative text, bestowing and refusing material resources, but it made Emilia Pattison a rich woman and gave her means for speaking about the ends of women's education.[242] Rapidly dispersing the Rector's household from the safe remove of a rented house in Headington, Emilia Pattison ignored Mark's frugal directions that she should sell his books and furniture, instead giving many of them to the library at Somerville College.[243] When Francis Pattison discovered Mark had subtracted a thousand pounds each from previous legacies to Jeannie and Mary Stirke in order to leave Meta Bradley a total of five thousand pounds, Francis's letters rage that he had lied to her on his deathbed about his will, had told one story and performed another, as well as that Mark had cheated his nieces.[244] Mark's bequest to Meta could not be denied—Meta promptly claimed it and refused all coercions from her family to give it back, seizing the means to independence Mark had given her—but Emilia "made good" Mark's neglect of Mary and Jeannie Stirke, giving each two thousand pounds from her own inheritance. She also sought to set in motion several women's educations, sending Mary to Bishop Otter College, a teacher-training school where Gertrude Tuckwell was already studying, and attempting to send Jeannie to Somerville. As earlier noted, Mrs. Pattison tried to use some of her inheritance to found a scholarship for women art students at the Royal Academy school and withdrew her offer when the authorities would not agree to her demand that the women's education include drawing from the nude.[245] At the end of Mark Pattison's life, Emilia Pattison's completed and attempted bequests recall her premarital life, make claims about women's need for bodily knowledge, set choices before other young women, and affirm her ability to reject powerful institutions.

Emilia Pattison could now afford to display open contempt for Oxford, "that hole." In "The Last Hour," published posthumously by Charles Dilke, Emilia Dilke punished scholars cruelly; "they seemed to the woman as they had been possessed of madness, and it was as the madness of a House of Fools." In that story, "those by whom Wisdom had been beloved beyond measure and who had sacrificed to her possession all the joys of life" (including, perhaps, the joys of others) were destined to "go down into the pit"; Dilke's narrator sends scholars and such to hell.[246] Emilia Dilke published another story in her own lifetime, a countermyth of Oxford full of furious compassion. In "A Vision of Learning" (as in "The Idealist Movement"), Dilke's hero is not a bitterly angry woman but a nameless young man. "Born to all the joys of the South," he is exiled by his desire for knowledge to a beautiful but cold and fog-shrouded northern city. Cold and darkness are stressed: the city is shrouded by "ghostly wreaths of fog," "there was no heat in the summer," and rain falls in "torrents" from an "inky grey" sky; surrounded by floodwaters, the city is a cage, the "perpetual dripping" of rain maddening by its "dull metallic echo." The student longs to see "Learning" for himself, but his wishes are met by injunctions to humility from those who claim to "bear rule over [the] city in [Learning's] name." But lured by a black bird of "evil omen," he becomes obsessed with finding a hidden courtyard of the city, beyond the chapel. Night after night, he searches in the snow for the secret sanctuary but finally finds it is a graveyard, where "men clothed in robes of black or of scarlet" sit in open graves, "holding with each other in high dispute" in the snow. The student begs them to tell him where Learning is or if the members of the city have seen her; with shrieking laughter, the ghosts cry out, "Neither to them, nor to us, not to any that have ever abided in this city hath Learning revealed herself." The student lies down in an open grave. Found by the city authorities in the morning, he calls them liars, bereft of knowledge: "the dead have spoken, and have put you to shame." His accusations of betrayal, of promises broken, cause him to be declared mad; he is confined in chains, where he raves and threatens violence. After many years, a "woman who felt great compassion and sorrow for those in suffering and in bonds" visits him. When he asks if she is Learning, she ignores the counsel of the authorities and declares, "I am but Love." Her gifts to him—of kindness, honesty, and a rose that reminds him of the South—reduce him to silence. His chains are removed, but returning three days later, the woman is told he is dead and buried in a secret place.[247]

"A Vision of Learning" is readable as a story of women's exclusions, exiles, and humiliations in Oxford, but the figure's maleness not only (as in "The Idealist Movement") makes the story a "universal" allegory of the desire for knowledge and consolidate associations with Oxbridge, but makes the story readable as a compassionate and cruel narrative of Mark Pattison. Gender matters in this reading as well. Unlike Jude Fawley, Dilke's protagonist is not undone by sexuality, nor, like the doctor-scientist in "The Physician's Wife," killed by transgressive femininity. He is betrayed by the frigidity of the male guardians of knowledge. The hidden Learning is not the discourse of the university but the feminine Sophia, who evades the shrill chatter of the masters; in this male city of learning, the absence of "even the skirts" of female knowledge is the sign and guarantee of the city's sterility and empty prestige. "A Vision of Learning" respects and repudiates Mark Pattison's claim to be one who lived only for learning, evoking the seductive promise of the city and exposing its cruel failures. Walls and lies lure the student to pursue a lost cause and imprison him in a bleak history. In this story, romantic emotionality is admirable but helpless: the woman who names herself Love is mortal and powerless against the authorities. Like Francis Pattison in her letters, she can feel "pity" but cannot redeem the protagonist who, like Mark James Pattison, is enchained when he raves with desire and hate, and, like Mark Pattison, ends a story by dying.

The Librarian's Revenge

Emilia Dilke let a death put an end to her story of the city of learning, but the history of "the Pattison papers" in Oxford did not end with Mark Pattison's death and Emilia Pattison's remarriage. Struggles over the survival, custody, accessibility, and interpretation of the "documents" lasted well into the next century. These struggles over words were always struggles over meaning and the custody and use of the past. Yet the continuing history of dispute over the making of Pattison stories need not be inscribed in the genres of portentous tragedy, replete with bad marriages, dark cities, and mad deaths. The history of the textual traces of the Pattison marriage shifts to more comic terrain, in stories of ludicrously embattled but cunning librarians.

The Pattison Papers in the Bodleian Libray run to more than 160 volumes of materials, including Mark Pattison's diary, family letters, letters from scholars, intellectuals, and cultural figures, manuscripts of published works, address books, date-books, and travel notes. Most of the letters were not written by Mark or Francis Pattison but to them: their figures are constituted by those who address them, often as objects of power, desire, anger, or loss. These texts are far from pristine and whole even as pieces of paper: they have complicated material histories as artifacts and property. Many pages were unequivocally edited by the scissors, eraser, or ink wielded by Emilia Pattison Dilke, who marched through Mark's diaries, doing her best to obliterate the traces of Meta Bradley and even removing most mentions of her own name. Gertrude Tuckwell also did her part in the process of "laceration" to which many Dilke papers were subjected.[248] But one group of papers remained relatively unscathed. Mark Pattison entrusted a small trunk of papers to the Principal Librarian of the Bodleian in 1884, less than two months before his death. Pattison's locked deposit included manuscripts of scholarly work and a group of letters, "selected and arranged as of special

interest;" the latter includes Francis Pattison's letters from France. Mark Pattison proposed this box be sealed until 1920 but was persuaded to change the date to 1910,
when Emilia Pattison Dilke might well have still been alive.[249]

In a thickening plot, Francis Pattison's letters to Eleanor Smith were also placed in
the Bodleian, albeit after sojourns in other hands. Emilia Dilke arranged with Smith
that the letters be deposited with their friend James Thursfield after Smith's death.
Thursfield would act as a repository in order to prevent any accusations that Emilia
Dilke had tampered with them, should they need to be produced. Thursfield spelled
out that such a need might arise if Mark Pattison's locked box contained "slanders"
on Francis; Francis's letters would give evidence of Mark's own failings. Although
there is some evidence that Smith mutilated a few letters, Emilia Dilke thus took pains
to avoid any appearance that she herself had edited these letters, but her plan was
twice vitiated. First, Albert Venn Dicey, Smith's executor, who found the letters in an
envelope with directions to send them to Thursfield, sent them to Emilia Dilke instead.
Although Dilke sent them on to Thursfield, allegedly unaltered, Thursfield later granted
Gertrude Tuckwell access to the papers after Charles Dilke's death in 1911. Tuckwell
and May Abraham Tennant briskly wielded scissors and erasers.[250] Not only was the
exculpating "evidence" thus tainted, but each transit of the letters motivated a secondary flurry of correspondence about who had, or should have, access to and power
over such intimate pages.

The custody of these Pattison papers devolved on the unfortunate heads of the
library staff in stages. The opening of Mark's box provoked concern first, especially
the letters about Mark James's and Fanny Pattison's mental breakdowns. At one point,
Bodley's librarian entertained the happy thought of returning such papers to Pattison
family hands. Henry Craster tried in 1913 to unload the most problematic materials
onto Mark Pattison's surviving executors, Frank Pattison and Ingram Bywater, although
he expressed a commitment to preserving many private letters so that "persons should
be enabled to form a just estimate of the character of the donor."[251] But Bywater took
a worldly tone, invoked the law, placed himself above the Pattison "family dissen-
tions," and dodged the attempt to ensnare him.[252] Without his collusion, although
the library staff could and did withhold sensitive materials from the public, they were
stuck with the papers. The addition of the Pattison/Dilke-Smith correspondence multiplied the librarians' nightmares. Those papers too were placed under very tight
controls; only Gertrude Tuckwell was allowed unrestricted access until the death "of
any person mentioned in [the letters] and for one year after the death of the last
survivor of any such persons," although she tried to introduce a proviso that the
letters be made available should "an attack on [her] aunt's memory" occur.[253] Despite
these extraordinary restrictions, the interminable correspondence between interested
parties and the staff of the Bodleian provoked a tired moan in 1926: "Every now and
then I touch the fringe of the wearisome Mark Pattison-Dilke business . . . I agree with
Lady T[hursfield] that it is a pity that everything relating to Mark Pattison's domestic
troubles wasn't burnt long ago!"[254]

Alas, the Bodleian librarians' troubles were not over. The following year, 1927,
T. F. Althaus approached the library. A favorite student of Mark Pattison who had
become a friend of Meta Bradley, Althaus was Meta's posthumous ambassador. Meta
had bequeathed Althaus "a tin box, containing a voluminous correspondence with

the Rector,'' a photograph of Mark, a drawing of his grave, and various oddments she wanted preserved, both for Mark's future biographer and to salvage a place in history for her relationship with Mark. Althaus donated the papers to the Bodley and provocatively refrained from placing restrictions on the letters' use.[255] It took some time for word of the deposit to reach Gertrude Tuckwell; she reacted with tactful distress and an instant desire to read the letters.[256]

Tuckwell also enlisted several descendants of the Pattison family in an attempt to suppress the Bradley letters, but this tactic led to a more complex struggle, in which women battled over the control of the past while the staff of the Bodleian looked on. Tuckwell placed her own correspondence with Mark Pattison in the British and Bodleian Libraries but nonetheless subordinated his historical respectability to Charles and Emilia Dilke's.[257] Mark Pattison's niece, Jeannie Stirke, now Jane Newton-Robinson, however, represented Mark's next of kin and differentiated her family's interests from Tuckwell's. Newton-Robinson's letters rehearse old grievances and construct her uncle as a great man whose warts must be hidden if not erased. The erstwhile Mrs. Pattison had not only gone through Mark's diaries "carefully with a scissors & a blue pencil,'' and generally failed to honor her first husband's memory properly but, worse, gone on to be associated with the scandalous Charles Dilke. The connection with Charles Dilke meant that a primed and prurient public would not wish to understand that Mark's relationship with Meta Bradley had been an aberration "wh took place in the last years of his life as an old man suffering from an incurable and harrassing disease.'' Worse, Newton-Robinson worries that Emilia Dilke's posthumous interests may conflict with her first husband and imagines a scenario in which Emilia Dilke's allies will someday need to defend her relationship with Dilke and may do so by smearing Mark's good name, using the Bradley letters to justify Mrs. Pattison's extramarital interests by exposing the Rector's.[258] Outright destruction was not an option for Mark's nieces in 1936, but locking up the Bradley papers was. On this, Tuckwell and Newton-Robinson could agree.

But neither Gertrude nor Jane, nor Mark, Meta, or Francis, had the last word—no one will. A librarian, however, had the most ironic. Robert Liddell, a scion of the noted Oxford family that included Lewis Carroll's Alice, was on the staff of the Bodleian in the 1920s and 1930s. Even while the Pattison Papers were off limits to the public, Liddell took advantage of his access to the "sealed" deposit, and converted privileged, if not quite licit, access to hidden texts into a ground for storytelling. In The Almond Tree (1938), Liddell brilliantly republicized the Pattison marriage in a novel structured by three alternating narrations: the headmaster Paul Ramus's, his estranged invalid writer-wife Mildred's, and that of his young devotée, Vera Bunbury. The transparency to Oxford eyes of Liddell's roman-à-clef flaunts the longer history of story-making about the Pattison marriage. Liddell's story, like Emilia Dilke's fictions, ends in a death: Paul's. Liddell gives Mildred the last words of his book. Those words might be ventriloquized onto the figure of Emilia Pattison—exhausted, vengeful, exuberant, leaving. They also mark the place of Liddell and every writer who has battened on the mutilated, contested, surviving texts of the Pattisons: "After so many deaths I live and write.''[259]

5

THE RESOURCES OF STYLE

None of her early friends . . . can ever think of the 'Frances Pattison' of
Oxford days without a strange stirring of heart.

—Mrs. Humphry Ward, *A Writer's Recollections*

Francis Pattison was famously associated with novels and domestic stories, but she
was also written as a performer and a spectacle, a woman who enacted theatrical
roles, proffered herself to vision, and made herself aesthetic and public, while eluding
easy interpretation. This chapter uses the language of theater, performance, and painting to read some memoirs, letters, and nonfictional texts about Mrs. Pattison in Oxford, then places these stories of performances and pictures in relation to varied texts
by E. F. S. Pattison/Emilia Dilke. I ultimately range across genres, from art history to
newspaper reports of speeches, but because different media and genres construct
somewhat different relations to knowledge, clarifying without rigidifying some differences between novels, plays, and pictures may illuminate my choice of initial vocabulary.[1]

The Victorian novel provides readers with a multitude of subject positions and
detailed exploration of interior states, but in many cases a confident narratorial voice
directs, highlights, emphasizes, and explains. The narrator claims access to and elaborates the subjectivity of characters—meanings, motives, intentions, and emotions—
even while those subjectivities are, overtly at least, harnessed to the requirements of
the plot and movement toward closure. Inner movement and fluidity coexist with
authority and structure. But in theater, the interior, subjective, and secret are subordinated to the visible and audible, spoken words and actions; audience members are
able to see only what is shown and hear only what is said, usually without time for
prolonged analysis, repeated viewing, or voice-over narration. Drama consumption
thus heightens self-consciousness about the making of sense from spectacle and
speech. Accounts of Francis Pattison in Oxford similarly attempt to surmise meanings
and motives, to read the private from the public, but are unsettled by the awareness

that much happened offstage. Enactments are presented in texts that oscillate between reading surfaces as pure artifice and as legible signs of inner meanings. Like figured women in art, women on stages were both highly visible and unknowable; Ellen Terry in *Macbeth* and Queen Victoria in her Jubilee parades were simultaneously objects of vision and sites of interiority that could not be directly grasped but only imagined from surfaces and speech.[2] Every text that tries to hold Francis Pattison worries that she is escaping it.

The possibility of reading Francis Pattison's images in Oxford still allures, especially since her figures can be read as making claims. Francis Pattison is described by contemporaries as *acting* in ways that marked her as different from and not bound by Oxford, especially through extravagant performances of femininity, aristocracy, and Frenchness. Her Oxford contemporary, Oscar Wilde, famously wrote, "in all important matters, style not sincerity is the vital thing," and style can be read as a way of criticizing the local and expressing a wish to get to other places.[3] Carolyn Steedman has argued that style, fashion, and knowledge of one's "betters" have been modes by which working-class women have remade themselves and refused their "destinies," crossed the river, gotten out of where they were.[4] Francis Pattison's style can be read as an expression of desire and a form of cultural critique, especially because her theatrical performances beckon us to the specific genre of melodrama. Among nineteenth-century narrative forms, melodrama is particularly associated with narratives of gender, sex, class, and danger, an association that will recur in the next chapter.[5] Some scholars also stress melodrama's moments of silent but vivid and highly gendered bodily display in which the central figure is separated from the world she inhabits. The melodramatic actress, like the diva, "overrides the constraints of the narrative" and seems "remote" from the story in which she is emplotted; her extravagance of "gesture, posture, and facial expression" mutely "carr[ies] the excess and contradictions surrounding the character's struggles with a world which is unyielding."[6] Melodrama thus offers pictures as well as stories, moments in which narrative is challenged by stillness, and a composed female figure is the locus of meanings, beyond or instead of words, about her own exceptionality and the inadequacy of existing and licensed discourses. As we will see, Francis Pattison was represented as a performer of *tableaux vivantes*, briefly frozen living pictures abstracted from longer stories that will not be fully narrated. Like the melodramatic star, she is depicted as a subject who is also an object, a maker of herself into pictures that set her apart. We could perhaps read contemporary descriptions of Francis Pattison as telling us about a woman crafting and exercising control over a critique of her surroundings. We could read Francis Pattison as a self who makes meaning by evoking stories and striking poses.

Such readings could be supported not only by Francis Pattison's letters from the period of her first marriage and Emilia Dilke's published allegories, with their tales of frustration, confinement, and rage, but by E. F. S. Pattison/Emilia Dilke's historical and critical writings. Pattison/Dilke's art history repeatedly makes claims about the pleasures of artistic intentionalities in complex relations with powerful institutions. Emilia Dilke wrote that, in the Renaissance, one found the intensely liberating idea that one could "mak[e] one's life into a work of art," and her *Art in the Modern State* is a sustained argument about the uses of aesthetic display by oppressive institutions.[7] E. F. S. Pattison's *The Renaissance of Art in France* conjoins the control of exteriors with rebellion. Pattison's Renaissance, an epoch of surging individuality, is an epoch of surfaces. "Monotonous" and "oppressive uniformity" is feared, and surfaces are "subtly varied" or bear "wild and daring conceits"; details constantly move—"enrich," "wind," "fall," "rise," "ascend," and "curve." "Exuberant ornament . . . tangles" the eye but "fantastic devices" are brought under "controlling force." Artistry subtly draws attention to agency, as the trace of effort "leaves the edge on [the] touch" and "impart[s] a vivacious accent" of shadow to surfaces.[8] Emilia Dilke's *French Architects and Sculptors of the Eighteenth Century* even licenses the language of performance; Dilke's study discusses "staging" and "theatricality" and argues that spectacles can be meaningfully read into the great narrative of French history.[9] Pattison/Dilke's own aesthetic histories instruct us to read intentionality and inner force in aesthetic displays and to pose questions about the political contexts and resistant or hegemonic meanings of visual culture. Her books entice as enlistable evidence of a theory carried across practical performance and scholarly writing.

But Pattison's history also underlines the limits of reconstructions. Spectral histories hang in the engraver Jean Duvet's works, and the gazes of figures carry and withhold meanings; in "the wide-opened eyes of the Mother of Harlots, in the averted gaze of Avenging Angels, in the brooding and mysterious regard of the Most Holy, we read the burden of a long past . . . a double existence . . . It is this consciousness which lends a marvellous strange haunting power to these faces . . . appealing to our imagination with a ghostly insistence, with the half-formed expression of their untold secrets ever hovering . . . part past in fact, and part conceived in thought . . ."[10] Thus, although I will return to Pattison/Dilke's art historical writings about display, gender, and power, and the cultural projects in which those texts participate, I will not do so in order to ratify an account of Francis Pattison's intentions or to break the code of her reported visual spectacles. An eschewal of claims about intentionality shapes this book as a whole but is especially important in this chapter.

I engage in a performance of my own here. In the first half of this chapter, I make Francis Pattison's figures in Oxford texts a figure for an argument about the usefulness to historical analyses of some poststructuralist, feminist and queer theoretical writings. I especially make use of a mode of feminist analysis that descends from Joan Rivière's 1929 psychoanalytic essay, "Womanliness as a Masquerade," and from Judith Butler's theory of performativity.[11] Butler argues that gender is performative, contingent, enacted, rather than expressive of a stable essence; drag and other flagrantly antinatural forms of gendered show therefore tell a truth about all gender. Francis Pattison was represented by contemporaries as exhibiting a highly aestheticized femininity, and retrospectively she may appear to offer an exemplary performance of a "histrionic conception of gender," her extravagantly artificial images enactments of Butler's theory.[12] But although contemporary theories of performativity free us from attempts to find the "real" woman beyond the textual images and suggest provocative affiliations between Victorian discourses and ongoing cultural debates, I am insistently *not* claiming that Francis Pattison preternaturally possessed a postmodern theory of gender as performance. Such an imputation would be unjustifiable historically and would foreclose a richer understanding of Victorian theatricalities. Moreover, arguing that Pattison was deliberately debunking naturalizing discourses of gender covertly reinscribes a "true" knowing subject at the middle of her performances, a self in control of and separate from the selves performed, a self we can identify as real and intention-laden.[13]

Rather than detecting a self, I am interested in how Francis Pattison was read and written in others' texts. If Francis Pattison's enactments can be read by late-twentieth-century audiences as performed critiques of constructed social identities—gender, nation, and class—my concern is with how Francis Pattison was figured in the texts of her contemporaries as engaged in critique. I refuse to separate the "real" Francis Pattison from her enactments or to attribute to her a settled quantity of intentionality, even a clear-eyed desire to annoy male Oxonians. Circulating in texts and pictures, she stirred, troubled, and excited contemporaries and her behavior and body were read and written as posing a threat to some local and national hegemonies, whatever she meant or didn't mean to say, within specific geographies and histories. Thomas Elsaesser suggests that some filmic melodramas can be productively read through an analogy with the speech of the analysand, in which intentionality is of limited interest but excess is "a sympton of something elsewhere."[14] Francis Pattison's circulations allow us to explore and map how gender and class structured specific local intellectual cultures and institutions and longer-lived cultural discourses that extend well beyond Oxford. However, in and beyond Oxford, hegemonies could be tenacious. In the second half of this chapter, I offer an oddly assorted set of stories by and about Emilia Dilke—about statues, pictures, trade unions, Indians, and actresses—which range far from Oxford. These texts and tales disallow easy inscriptions of Francis Pattison's performing figure into a narrative of resistance to tyrannies and hierarchies.

"That Woman": The Scandal of Heterosociality

First in France, where the style originated . . . and then in the rest of Europe, rooms were created which were lighter and more elegant and charming than those of any previous period. They were also audacious, often astonishingly so, in their treatment of space and their denial of solidity or stability. It is easy to forget this because these rooms are more easily reconciled with modern ideas of luxury and comfort . . . [and seem] to epitomise an ideal of polite but informal and mixed society which is still current . . . [but] originally it seemed novel and fantastic. . . . [Such rooms are] often vertiginously enticing as well as diverting . . .

—Nicholas Penny, "Vertiginous"

Residents of Oxford in the 1860s, 1870s, and early 1880s, recalling the Pattison marriage as mésalliance, also remembered Lincoln College as the setting of a heterogeneous social life and sharply etched scenes. Those impressions became part of the story of the Pattison household. Francis Pattison's contemporaries described her as vivacious, defiant, dedicated to work and play, and, above all, embodying a personal style. Mrs. Pattison's status as the wife of the Rector of Lincoln gave her the resources for a public life, but Mary Arnold Ward represented "Mrs. Pat" as deliberately subverting the institution she inhabited by "her gaiety, her picturesqueness, her impatience of the Oxford solemnities and decorums, her sharp restless wit, her determination not to be academic, to hold on to the greater world of affairs outside."[15] In Ward's account, Mrs. Pattison enacted otherness and difference from Oxford.

Ward's account stresses the sheer visual unexpectedness of Francis Pattison: "in '68 or '69 . . . I remember my first sight [in] a college garden lying cool and shaded between grey college walls . . . a figure that held me fascinated—a lady in a green brocade dress, with a belt and chatelaine of Russian silver, who was playing croquet [and] seemed to me . . . a perfect model of grace and vivacity . . . a handful of undergraduates made an amused and admiring court." Mrs. Pattison made the Rector's Lodgings a very un-Oxonian place in the heart of Oxford:

> Her drawing-room was French, sparely furnished with a few old girandoles and mirrors on its white panelled walls, and a Persian carpet with a black centre, on which both the French furniture and the living inhabitants of the room looked their best. And upstairs, in 'Mrs Pat's' own working-room, there were innumerable things that stirred my curiosity—old French drawings and engravings, masses of foreign books . . .[16]

Other visitors' remarks share Ward's sharp memory of furniture and furnishings; "Mrs Pattison's black carpet," on which "both the French furniture and the living inmates . . . looked their best," became a sign of its owner's unusual displays.[17] Much later, Emilia Dilke's *French Furniture and Decoration in the Eighteenth Century* and *French Architects and Sculptors of the Eighteenth Century* attend to the creation of spaces and domestic interiors which, in Nicholas Penny's words, exhibit a "playful spirit [and] . . . determination to tease the mind as well as delight the eye."[18]

Emilia Dilke's books on French furniture and engravings would not appear until long after Mrs. Pattison's black carpet, girandoles, and engraving tools had departed Oxford, but her spectacles of anachronistic and foreign femininity drew attention to her intellectual work. She was an active writer on French art in her Oxford years, and, however unofficial, a scholar; a later *Who's Who* entry dated her earliest publications as in the *Saturday Review* in 1864. Hippolyte Taine depicted Madame Pattison during his 1871 visit to Oxford as a public figure of intellectual activity; "le 'leading mind' de la société féminin d'Oxford dans la domaine de la littérature et des arts," she was "très versée dans la peinture, connait particulièrement la peinture française moderne." Although she was "érudite sur les beaux-arts de notre Renaissance" and worked "huit ou dix heures par jour," Madame Pattison was a distinct contrast to Taine's representation of Oxford's scholarly masculinity. Oxford men, including Mark Pattison, were "érudits et solides" but lacked "le fin sentiment littéraire, le don de comprendre les âmes et les passions éteintes."[19] Her growing career as an intellectual in her own right, rather than an ardent helpmeet to a man of genius, disrupted expectations of college wives. Worse, Charles Dilke's "Memoir" claims Mrs. Pattison's publications had feminist as well as scholarly motives: her writing of reviews and essays was partly motivated by the desire "to increase her personal income" since she was "naturally" desirous of independence and economic autonomy from her husband.[20]

However Mary Pattison Roberts insisted exposure to metropolitan bohemia had not "spoiled" Francis Strong, art education and independent life in London had given Francis a more worldly education than most daughters of Oxford. But Mrs. Pattison's parties and her embodied style also emphasized changes in Oxford. Oxford's old guard could be very clear about a sense of threat: when Maurice Bowra, later Warden of

Wadham College, was shown Lincoln College by an elderly Fellow in 1916 or 1917, the Rector's Lodgings were pointed out with the comment, "This was where *That Woman* used to have her parties."[21] Oxford's enclosed separation was eroding and Mrs. Pattison fostered and reflected Oxford's increasing integration with metropolitan culture.[22] Her social receptions included novelists and artists as well as scholars, gesturing beyond the private spaces of family life or Oxford's local hierarchies to the "greater world" of other publics of politics, intellectual life, London, and France. Mrs. Pattison maintained contact with art friends and was known to enjoy a public life and entrées beyond Oxford, especially in London. Her salon could be seen as an adaptation and importation of the Prinseps' Little Holland House; Little Holland House, too, combined an aesthetic drawn from the past ("Venetian" colors in draperies, walls, and dresses), intellectual modernity, and the erotic pleasures of feminine display and heterosocial conversation.[23] Francis Pattison moved in prestigious metropolitan circles, especially by serving as intermediary between artists and potential patrons; she interceded between the painter Le Gros and Prince Leopold, Duke of Albany, and her friendship with Robert Browning arose partly from her position as someone who might help his son Pen become an artist.[24] Charles Dilke's "Memoir" unsubtly positions her activities in London as a form of resistance to Mark Pattison, stressing that Charles Newton, Keeper of Antiquities at the British Museum, both aided her studies of classic art and gave her a bolt-hole away from Oxford in 1874.[25] More scandalously, Mrs. Pattison's wider circulations made it easier to organize meetings with Charles Dilke in London and authorized time away from Mark Pattison.

Oxford was also gradually repudiating clericalism. Ward recalled her pleasure at the "gay, unceremonious" meals to which she was invited on Sundays but also her discomfort and sense that Mrs. Pattison's fashionability and light-heartedness on the Sabbath were transgressive.[26] Mrs. Pattison's friendship with George Eliot and her inclusion of Mary Arnold in a party to meet "Mrs." Lewes must have shocked some traditionalists.[27] But more than outraging the most rigidly moralist, Mrs. Pattison marked the increased heterosociality of Oxford.[28] The fluctuating scandal of her marriage and her self-display as an object of beauty and potential eroticism marked Francis Pattison as unmistakably feminine—her fashionability, unconventionality, her mobile, studied, and fascinating surfaces making it impossible to erase her sex—but her femininity was not bound by heterosexual reproductivity. Neither desexualized bluestocking nor matronly academic wife, she was not containable in established local categories of womanliness. Ward's Francis Pattison is an earlier, more respectable version of Max Beerbohm's Zuleika Dobson whose seductive femininity wreaks comic chaos in masculine Oxford.[29] Her youth set her apart from most other wives of college heads, but Francis Strong Pattison was a harbinger of the influx of young wives of college fellows in the 1870s and 1880s, when restrictions on fellows' marrying were relaxed. Tellingly, the later generation of intellectual women, especially the cohort that included Mary Ward, Bertha Johnson, Louisa Creighton, were also recalled in texts that emphasized style (especially distinctive dress) and heterosociality. Their subculture of arts-and-crafts medievalism—with "aesthetic" dresses of Liberty cotton or serge with crewelled sunflowers—paradoxically made their modernity all the more visible, drawing attention to women as possessors of ideas and ambitions and as participants in cultural creation and social reform.[30] Francis Pattison's independent and professional and political life, including her ominous activities for women's suffrage and university education, not to mention her attempts to promote trade unions among Oxford's working-class women, also foreshadowed and signalled the expansion of middle-class women's public activities and aspirations, which these later college wives would share.[31]

E. F. S. Pattison's first book, *The Renaissance of Art in France* (1879) not only celebrated and enacted feminine intellectuality—it thematized the development of heterosocial institutions. Its first chapter lauds the transformation of daily life by the artistic elaboration of domestic interiors, praises a shift from "grim reserve" and the increased "importance" of "social life," and links these changes to the increased "presence of women at the Court." In an argument that recalls Josephine Butler's linkage of Oxford's male homosociality to demeaning representations of women, Pattison's Renaissance heterosociality not only increased "pleasures" and "refinements" but increased respect for women. The heterosocial culture of Pattison's Renaissance court fostered representations of female figures as active, "free," healthily sexual, moral, beautiful, direct, and dignified. Heterosociality improved cultural images of women on both aesthetic and moral grounds; *The Renaissance* repeatedly emphasizes that the shift produced great art and, while Pattison "admits" and deplores that the increased presence of women purportedly heightened the power of "priests" at court—the reverse of Oxford, where heterosociality marked the decline of clericalism—her study makes a woman, Marguerite de Navarre, an "exceptional" but admirable figure of the Renaissance's "spiritual passion" at its most profound.[32]

George Eliot's "Woman in France" defined and praised French salons as "reunions of both sexes," and despite ascriptions of responsibility to "That Woman," the Rector's Lodgings' status as a site of heterosocial intellectual and political modernity was not the creation of Francis Pattison alone.[33] Mark's diary is ambivalent about Francis's social activity; he sometimes snarled about her "bohemian friends," frequently bewailed the time entertainments took from his studies ("a dinner-party [and houseguests] . . . upsets the house, strains and exhausts the service, and makes a demand on my nervous powers . . . this can hardly be required"), and worried about age and work left undone. But although he suggested that the trouble of entertaining "might be given over exclusively to the persons who can do nothing else, who have no inner life," and developed his own Greek code name for disturbances to his household peace, *ta egkuklia*, signifying (unwanted) mixing and the social round, Mark also wrote of pride in Francis's beauty, social skills and wit.[34] Bertha Johnson recalled that Mark Pattison "declared [Francis] was the cleverest woman he had ever met." Johnson—a participant in founding women's colleges at Oxford—represented Mark as pleased by his wife's combination of intellect and femininity; Francis "had the talent for dressing becomingly which the Rector thought was much wanted . . . I remember his entreating me later to do all I could to induce our students to dress carefully and have gentle manners."[35]

Mark Pattison's persona and style were as much a part of the household's public image as Francis's beauty and intelligence. Like Little Holland House's resident lion, G. F. Watts, Mark was on exhibit at Lincoln, and his figure too was paradoxical. A voice of modernity and change in Oxford, he participated in national and international intellectual culture, fostered and shared his wife's views on women's public activities, supported women's suffrage and working women's benefit societies, and was an intermittent but important figure in the movement to establish women's colleges.[36] But although he had enjoyed a reputation as a superb, intellectually demanding but inspiring tutor in earlier years, after the rectorial debacle of 1851 his relations with students deteriorated, and he was notoriously unpleasant to most undergraduates. Vivian Green provides a fair compendium of Pattison's comments on undergraduates, which range from condescending ("These schoolboys are washed out before they come up to Oxford") to abusive ("dismally ignorant," an "utter dolt," "detestable," and "weak, slippery-minded"). John Hullah, who admired Mark, commented in 1868, "I pity the poor shy undergraduate . . . who tries to eat [breakfast] in the presence of the rector . . . Each morsel must stick in the gullet when the rector's severe eye is upon him. Why does a man who possesses such limitless power of giving pleasure without the smallest trouble make himself now and then so disagreeable?" R. W. Church of Oriel remarked that Mark "seemed to take a perverse delight in establishing" himself as a misanthropic "character." Fittingly, Tom Stoppard's The Invention of Love makes a character of Mark, mordantly advising the young A. E. Housman that "a genuine love of learning" can only lead to blindness and ruin. Oxford folklore offers a walk with an undergraduate from Oxford to Iffley: "Pattison was silent. The freshman felt that he must say something of a literary character to draw the Rector out. Accordingly he observed, 'The irony of Sophocles is greater than the irony of Euripides.' Pattison gave him a sour look but said nothing. On they went till they reached Iffley, and there they turned. Then Pattison broke the silence. 'Quote,' he snarled."[37] The undergraduates returned Mark's contempt in rhyme:

> And now the Rector goes
> With a dewdrop at his nose,
> And his skinny hands in loose black gloves enrolled;
> Irresistably, I fear,
> Suggesting the idea
> Of a discontented lizard with a cold.[38]

Despite his support for modern causes, Mark had become a figure of tradition.[39] Ward Fowler, Pattison's subrector, wrote, "to the ordinary undergraduate [Pattison] remained the very embodiment of Donnishness, and they came to the college and left it without knowing more about 'Pat' than what could be gained from such a view . . . or from a single ceremonial breakfast with him and Mrs. Pattison."[40]

Yet despite and because of his role as an irascible and embittered tragic man of genius, Mark could resemble Mary Arnold Ward's "the Master of Beaumont" in Lady Connie (1888). "Under . . . a harsh pedantic exterior . . . [was] a very soft heart and an invincible liking for the society of young women," and the Master's "stately and old-fashioned" courting of young women was "quite different from anything ever bestowed upon the men students of his college."[41] Francis Pattison's heterosocial salon gave Mark access to young women with whom he could be a generous, interested, curious, and warm Pygmalion free of institutional obligation. Mark depicted himself taking pleasure in "mix[ing] with the young and eager souls, full as they are of fresh aspirations, set off with grace and refinement," as well as taking for granted the usefulness of such young women to read aloud and write his letters for him.[42] He could be playful as well as mentorial; Walter Pater caustically recalled "the Rector . . . romping with great girls among the gooseberry bushes." and Edmund Gosse found the Rector's conversation irritatingly full of "croquet and petticoats" instead of books.[43] We have seen intelligent young women, admiring Mark and gratefully conscious of the condescension implicit in his attention, drawn into intense relationships of love and tutelage with an older, powerful, and charismatically tortured member of the Oxford elite. Such young women could find Mark seductive as he quizzed them on their interests and implored them to develop their minds. Gertrude Tuckwell was perhaps the best-placed of Mark Pattison's "pets" to criticize him, but she wrote that Mark's attention was addictive and correspondence with him exhilirating. He condescended ("Don't dissipate yourself upon so many books"), lectured her on duty, counselled utter obedience to her parents, predicted dire consequences should she attempt an independent career in nursing ("you will . . . take on the colour of the creatures with whom you live, i.e. vulgar, common-place stupidity"); demanded her services as his secretary; preached drearily sexist theories ("violence and brutality . . . belong to the male character") and confirmed her self-doubts (he agreed that women must be inferior since "the whole intellectual sphere has been open to them . . . [and] they do not show an aptitude for such pursuits, and when they do, the pursuit unsexes them, and turns them into disagreeable half-men"), yet she recalled him with gratitude. His letters apostrophized her as "speculative, intense, intellectual, hard," a "girl of feeling [who] . . . desires to improve herself," and he was willing to respond to her religious doubts and to demand "hard work."[44]

The contrast between Mark Pattison's performance as a glowering and potentially nasty Oxford intellectual and Francis's French stylishness and sociability—Lord Rosebery recalled him looking "wizened and wintry by the side of his blooming wife"—gained clarity from its setting.[45] Francis, "one of the most perfectly lovely women in the world," was very close in age to the undergraduate men over whom she presided as the Rector's wife.[46] Her salon allowed respectable contact with young men of similar interests while testing the boundaries of decorum; several visitors noted her habit of drawing young men apart to smoke French cigarettes in cosy starlight tête-à-têtes in the College gardens.[47] Henry James, after a lunch at Lincoln, noted the "spectacle [of] the dark rich, scholastic old dining room in the college court—the languid old rector and his pretty little wife in a riding-habit, talking slang."[48] A wonderful, if hard to attribute, tale relayed via John Sparrow presents Mark Pattison as self-consciously playing his part in dramatizing the destabilizations a woman's presence in Oxford might unleash: Francis Pattison and one of her sisters—unnamed but "rather giddy"—were making a parlor game of putting male undergraduates' hair up in curl papers during an "impromptu party" when the Rector came in unexpectedly. Mark "punished them effectively by going around the room, and very slowly and ceremoniously shaking hands with all present, while they wished that the floor would swallow them all."[49] Another possibly apocryphal story brilliantly threatens: an undergraduate of Lincoln arrived late at College breakfast but proffered the excuse, "Sorry I'm late . . . but I've been to the gym, watching Mrs. P learn fencing to polish off her husband."[50]

Youthful high spirits, athleticism, disregard of decorum and (imputed) hostility to her husband could make Mrs. Pattison intriguing and dangerous. Hippolyte Taine was struck by her youth—although he thought her five years younger than she was—and recalled how she stood "*charmante, gracieuse, à visage frais et presque mutin*" among the college's "*vielle architecture avec lierre et grands arbres*" and how she told him that Oxford turned people into mummies.[51] James suspiciously construed her as an example of all he feared in "modern" women. "The Rector is a dessicated old scholar, torpid even to incivility with too much learning; but his wife is quite another fashion—very young (about 28) very pretty, very clever, very charming and very conscious of it all. She is I believe highly emancipated and I defy an English-woman to be emancipated except coldly and wantonly . . ."[52] Mrs. Pattison certainly ignored some of the rules that separated respectable women from the "wanton." Margaret Oliphant and the artist William Bell Scott voiced anxiety and hostility about such a self-possessed young woman; Bell Scott initially saw "a beauty . . . tremendous in anecdote and conversation," an Oxford "pet," but decided she was "a kind of monster" to be hated "like brimstone" for her "artificiality" and "heartlessness."[53] Rosebery suspected Mrs. Pattison's "blooming" had *caused* her husband's "wizening"; "the secret of his character . . . I presume that . . . his relations with Mrs. Pattison give the key?"[54] More temperately, Bertha Johnson found Francis Pattison intimidating (there was "more learning in [Mrs. Pattison's] little finger than in my whole body!") but consoled herself that she was more comfortable company. Mrs. Pattison was uncapturable; "there was a sense of strain in her talk at one time and a provoking frivolity at another, often when you specially wanted her to be serious and helpful."[55] Francis Pattison is artificial, unconfined, undependable, a character, a wanton, a monster—not a proper woman.[56]

With interested and less judgmental eyes, Richard Claverhouse Jebb (1841–1905) portrayed Francis Pattison as simultaneous blurring and exploiting expectations of femininity to produce a scandalous charm. "Dick" Jebb came from a family of remarkable women: his sister Eglantyne Louisa, like Francis Strong, attended art school and later founded an organization to spread arts and crafts ideas and encourage rural production; another sister, Louisa, had "masculine" tastes for carpentry, outdoor games, and metal work, and wrote pamphlets on Darwinian evolution and "Votes for Women"; and his nieces included Eglantyne Jebb, cofounder of the Save the Children Fund; Eglantyne Mary Jebb, lecturer at Birmingham University and Principal of the Froebel Educational Institute; and G. E. M. Jebb, lecturer in economics at the University of Newcastle-on-Tyne and later Principal of Bedford College. Although later a Unionist MP, Jebb was a Liberal regarding women, writing to his American fiancée Carrie of his belief that "the future of the world depends, in every large question, on the higher education of women," and insisting that "the commonplaces repeated in society . . . by the men with complacent contempt, by the women with devout resignation . . . about women's 'sphere' (which seems to mean vacancy) sicken my very soul."[57]

Dick Jebb sketches Mrs. Pattison's exceptionality and the possibilities Oxford offered her:

> [Mrs Pattison] is difficult to describe . . . She is very clever: she has tenderness; great courage; and an exquisite sense of humour. In manner she is inclined to be brusque, though, by that instinct which women of a fine strain never lose under any vagary, she never fails in perfect taste; she is joyous, and affects a certain specially Oxford type of feminine fastness, which it would take too long to define, except by saying it is based upon the jocose ease of cultivated youths;—she talks of art and books and philosophies,—

yet rather about them than of them;—but to any one who can clearly see her whole nature in one view, she is most captivating . . . We have just been sitting in the open air in the court, under the starlight, and Mrs Pattison and I have been smoking her particular cigarettes—made for her in Paris by somebody. She is a connoisseur . . . [58]

Jebb's Francis Pattison is a woman combining masculine and feminine qualities in a setting that allows her to draw upon quite particular models of manliness and womanhood in feats of self-multiplication. She is "captivating" but not seductive in the sense feared by James; a woman "of a fine strain" she is yet like a young gentleman. Her "fastness" is Oxonian but she is also a Parisian presence. Left unsaid yet implicit in Jebb's description is a greater conundrum: Francis Pattison, in Jebb's sketch, is a lady who does not observe the rules of being a woman.

Tableaux Vivants

If we . . . take a figure from its place and isolate it from the lines in unison with which it was conceived, we at once destroy those relations which constituted its peculiar charm, and are left undefended to the painful impressions of incorrect design, loose drawing, superabundant draperies, and elegantly awkward action . . .

—E. F. S. Pattison, "Jean Goujon"

Mary Arnold Ward tells of helping Mrs. Pattison make pictures in the "mysterious process" of etching; the lady's fashionability and composure fall by the wayside when splashes of acid burn fingers or clothing and lead to "dire misfortune"; Ward evokes both the artist's skill and her iridescent dissolution into "helpless laughter."[59] Francis Pattison also appears in Ward's and others' texts as a maker of herself into pictures, containing herself in frames yet alive and mobile, only temporarily composed, every stylized moment liable to break open.[60] Ward displaces her most intensely pictorial impression onto *another* woman: Ward's text claims to reproduce George Eliot's perception of Francis Pattison. During a visit of "Mr and Mrs George Lewes" to Lincoln:

Suddenly at one of the upper windows appeared the head and shoulders of Mrs Pattison, as she looked out and beckoned smiling to Mrs Lewes. It was a brilliant apparition as though a French painting by Greuze or Perroneau had suddenly slipped into a vacant space in the old college wall. The pale pretty head *blonde cendrée*; the delicate smiling features and white throat, a touch of black, a touch of blue, a general 18th century impression as though of powder and patches. Mrs Lewes perceived it instantly . . . [61]

Ward's 1918 *Writer's Recollections* implicitly allude to the circulation of images beyond, as well as their production within, Oxford. Evoking the possibility that Eliot had in 1872 depicted Mrs. Pattison as Dorothea Casaubon, Ward shows herself seeing Eliot see Mrs. Pattison as an aesthetic vision, created by Francis Pattison, of Frenchness, femininity, and aristocracy. In Ward's description, Francis Pattison's appearance proclaims her differences of language, culture, class, and history from the Oxford walls that frame her; she transcends time and place even as she exhibits her scholarly expertise.

Charles Camino's 1882 miniature on ivory gives a memorable image of Francis Pattison as an anachronistic French lady. But Mrs. Pattison's style is also visible in an

1864 collaboration, a picture drawn by Pauline Trevelyan and painted by Laura Capel Lofft. (As with Emilia and Katherine Dilke, the artists eventually shared a name, "Lady Trevelyan"; Laura married Pauline's widower.) Mrs. Pattison is seated, painting a panel of sunflowers for the circular atrium of the Trevelyan house at Wallington. The sunflowers themselves were never completed; the painting is a picture of an incomplete creation.[62] The gold of the flowers matches her hair, in an intricate braid around her face and loose down her back. She is wearing a vaguely Renaissance dress of green brocade, theatrically half-framed by a curtain on the right that is drawn to reveal her; dress and curtain are strewn with gold fleurs-de-lys, emblematizing her studies in French art. Someone who has made herself into something to be represented, she is depicted in the act of making representations; the painting and painted Mrs. Pattison is art object and artist twice over. Compounding these tanglings, Charles Dilke claimed the painting was a good likeness of the young Mrs. Pattison by noting its resemblance to other paintings of her from the 1860s, while nonetheless arguing that Trevelyan had reshaped Mrs. Pattison's image to accord with aesthetic convention: her "decided chin and heavy brow" were "fined away" to Pre-Raphaelite standards of beauty.[63] Charles Dilke deposited a photograph of Francis Pattison in the same dress in the British Library, but it cannot stand as an unretouched image; it is, in fact, half of a photograph. Mrs. Pattison is holding the hand of someone no longer present, probably Mark Pattison, who has been cut out of the history to be preserved.[64]

Chapter 2 argued that women's aestheticized representation and self-representation were central to the histories of Victorian art culture and institutions. More Victorian examples of texts that place women in complicated relation to pictures will appear in this and the next chapter, but quite recent feminist scholars have also imagined the making of women into paintings in order to theorize the construction of femininity. Ideas about the relations between performance and prescription in women's aesthetic self-fashioning have diverged. One influential set of arguments represents women's enactment of images of valorized femininity as directly or indirectly coerced; an idiosyncratic but memorable formulation is Hélène Cixous's ventriloquization of patriarchy addressing "woman": "we're painting your portrait so you can begin looking like it right away."[65] Janet Todd, in The Sign of Angellica, develops a more ambiguous relationship between "real women" and painted femininity. Todd's title refers to a painting in Aphra Behn's The Rover, which Angellica, a courtezan, "hangs out the window of her house" as an advertisement; "as men gather below to comment on the picture's beauties and lament Angellica's high charges, the lady herself stands above with her maid, discussing [the men] in derisory terms." Todd points out that Angellica chooses to "draw attention to [her portrait's] construction" rather than "wearing it close to her face as a mask," and that "it may indeed have borne a great likeness to the lady—or she may have crept out to look at it in the night, so as to recreate herself more fully in its image." There was a woman before there was a painting and that woman could make choices about how closely to conform to a constructed image of femininity. Todd argues that Behn's play deals with "the social construction of woman," the "travelling" of characters between stories, and the "constructed nature of female consciousness, formed . . . to an extraordinary extent through fiction." Yet by emphasizing that "Angellica . . . did not hang herself, but a sexual, social, historical and artistic artefact," and creating a distance between the real and the recreated Angellicas, Todd implies that Angellica "herself" is separate from the "social, historical and artistic." But all these Angellicas—Behn's and Todd's—are signs and figures in texts; Todd's Angellica is her figure for the woman writer.[66]

Another mode of feminist analysis, following Rivière's "Womanliness as a Masquerade," sidesteps the distinction between real and prescribed femininities to propose that all gender is enacted.[67] In this view, although the framed head of Mrs. Pattison in Mary Ward's representation of George Eliot's view, and the other living icons into which Francis Strong Pattison made herself were, flagrantly, pictures, inhabiting sometimes harsh rules of genre and gender order, the body and mind that Mrs. Pattison fancily dressed never existed "outside" masquerade. Or, as Wilde's Lord Henry Wotton laughed, "Being natural is simply a pose and the most irritating pose I know."[68]

As citing Lord Henry hints, theories that emphasize gender as performance have strong affiliations with theories of camp; Judith Butler, as noted, gives drag a special place in her work.[69] Camp is generally associated with gay men's performances of "effeminacy," but some contemporary feminists find in it intriguing possibilities for women. Camp can be not "bad" taste but the flagrant, stylized, over-the-top exhibition of "good" taste—complying with the rules while refusing to respect them. The contemporary literary critic Jane Gallop explicitly associates her exaggerated performances of femininity with camp, arguing that camp means imagining "feminine style not as some restrictive role but as something one could put on and take off as a kind of performance . . . [gender is] made theatrical, put into quotation marks."[70] Performing a highly stylized gender role demonstrates that gender is art and artifice, convention, aesthetic, and perception. A woman's performance of femininity can reveal the theatricality of gender, shown on but not determined by the body; campy femininity can be "a form of theatrical excess which both celebrates and undermines what it mimics."[71] Gallop and others suggest that extravagantly feminine self-costuming is especially subversive when performed by femme lesbians, whose visible femininity is explicitly not directed toward nor at the service of men, or in institutional contexts scandalized by female eroticism.[72] Gallop argues that "adopt[ing] ultra-femme wear . . . in the academic world" destabilizes assumed patterns of authority "because femininity is so deeply excluded—from the lectern, from the position of knowledge."[73]

Jane Gallop is an employed, if controversial, professional with an official status in the academic world, and her enactments of hyperfemininity occur in very different contexts than Francis Pattison's and are enunciated in a language of intentionality and contemporary politics and theory.[74] Gill Frith usefully argues that in Victorian women's fiction, scenes of ritualized hyperfeminine dressing-up—often involving a foreign female friend who temporarily initiates an English heroine into the artifices of attire—are "fantas[ies] of agency," which "magic away" rather than confronting "significant questions of power."[75] Emilia Dilke's writings sometimes more desperately signal the power of dress. The stripping away of women's garments is linked with nightmarish marriages in many of Emilia Dilke's short stories, and she told Gertrude Tuckwell a "Provençal" story, which Gertrude could "never track down" in other sources, about a "fascinating lady." As she was bending to sign the register on her wedding day, the blue ribbon of her costume was pulled away and the lady turned into "a little heap of ashes" on the floor, evaporating at the moment her name and identity are legally changed.[76] E. F. S. Pattison's art history also signalled the complexity of the boundary between body and attire: a review of the 1876 French Salon claims the power of clothes over obscured but real bodies, praising a painting by Laurens for "the definiteness with which the pressure of every band is made to tell against the body yet solid beneath."[77] Pattison preserves both the "actual" and the power of changeable surfaces in her essay on Poussin; for Pattison's Poussin, "the past was no mere wardrobe, from which he might supply himself with a various succession of the costumes best fitted for representation," but "a veil through which the actual became visible. A veil whose thin folds did not obscure the eternal sameness of human life, but rendered its features more strangely beautiful."[78]

Nonetheless, Gallop's suggestion that self-presentation as a highly sexualized but obvious artificial object of vision can have charged meanings in specific institutional settings need not be true only in circumstances in which we can point to explicitly claimed intentions and theories. Moreover, there are specific historical and geographical reasons that theories of camp produce resonant readings of Francis Pattison's performances in Oxford. As a writer of art history and criticism in Oxford, Francis Pattison participated in Victorian discourses about the making of the self as an aesthetic as well as a moral project in which bourgeois homosexual men were formulating stylistic and intellectual discourses of identity, difference, and performativity. Oxford, Cambridge, and art history, especially of the Renaissance, were terrains on which male homoerotic discourses and styles were elaborated.[79] However slippery notions of generations must be, Pattison/Dilke (1840–1904) was a close contemporary of John Addington Symonds (1840–1893), author of a four-volume study of the Renaissance and two crucial, if privately circulated, arguments on behalf of accepting male homoeroticism that circulated among homosexual men; Walter Pater (1839–1894), whose *Studies in the History of the Renaissance* (1873) has a foundational status amid writings of male homoerotic aestheticism, was her contemporary in Oxford; Oscar Wilde (1854–1900), although much younger, was a striking presence during his student days.[80] Richard Dellamora has shown how Pater and Symonds were threatened with controversy over the relationships between sexuality and scholarly enquiry in Oxford in the 1870s, but they were the most well-known and influential figures in a wider subcultural group.[81]

Mrs. Pattison's Oxford contemporaries sometimes radically travestied femininity, claiming artificiality, performance, excess, and difference from (prescribed) bourgeois masculinity, constructing what became camp in their texts and sometimes in performances. Similarly, Francis Pattison's art-historical writing on the Renaissance, as well as her figure in the texts of contemporaries, thematizes femininity, display, unnaturalness, and undecidability. Ekphrasis—the verbal depiction of visual objects, especially works of art—has been understood as often working to produce artworks as feminized objects of a male gaze, but Pattison's *The Renaissance of Art in France* offers doubled stories about aesthetic figures of femininity.[82] Pattison's text portrays some female figures as depictions by artists of *already* posed bodies—that is, as artistic images of artificial femininities.[83] Pattison's discussion of Goujon's *Diane chasseresse* closely follows an account of his *Fons Nympium*; both passages describe motionless female figures that escape and attract interpretation because they expose their own construction. The *Fons* "neither fad[es] into flat insignificance nor approach[es] the directness of obvious appeal";

its "sensuous curves of lines . . . fascinate [and] check." The nymphs are "weird sisters . . . [who] have maintained their value in men's eyes as things specially precious and apart" because they display control; their "beauty has a strange ascetic calm."[84] The *Diane* is a work of "skill . . . at its height," full of "ease and spirit" which "give value and variety to the surface," but it also exhibits its own construction. "Elegant and severe at the same time . . . its elegance has an air of fashion, and the severity something of constraint." The artist has not depicted nature but "accentuate[d] features selected by the caprice of taste"; the result is "a beauty which has an artificial cast, a nobility which has a slight touch of effort." Pattison's text refuses to commit itself as to whether the *Diane* is a portrait of Diane de Poitiers but depicts both statue and lady as figures of control and passion: "the desire which questions in the eyes and mouth . . . contradicted by the conscious dignity of the attitude [and the composition of] form and line" may be what "we should expect to find enshrining the narrow energy which at once animated and controlled the wishes and conduct" of Diane.[85] Like Francis Pattison in Oxford, Goujon's goddess evades containment in life stories; sculpted forms cannot be read through but only read.

Artificiality, interiority, and evasion also combine in the *faïence Henri II*. The *faïence* is an "artificial creation" but also "stamped with the signs of personal character . . . [and] highly-wrought individuality." It evades history; a "mystery . . . hangs over its origins" and it has "no beginning, no culmination, and no decay." It may have originated in a woman's activities—the sponsorship of Hélène Hangest de Genlis— but that story remains "tantalising and provoking."[86] Thus, *The Renaissance of Art in France* marks the circulation of figures in economies of value "in men's eyes," evokes sexualized relations to power, and suggests stories of female art-making agency, but insists that figures cannot be made into sure knowledge. The ekphrastic moments in *The Renaissance* are not, any more than the texts of Mrs. Pattison's performances in Oxford, pieces of evidence "through" which Francis Pattison can be known; these accounts of objects cannot be contained in biographical readings. Instead, Francis Pattison's texts and Francis Pattison's performances in the texts of others are haunted by possible but ungraspable stories of passion while participating in a wider history of writing and acting stories of gender, art, and display. Peter Wollen, describing Aubrey Beardsley as "quintessentially Decadent" in his "excessive stylisation, combined with his tantalising eroticism," perceptively insists that the entwinement of camp, aesthetic theorizing, flamboyant costuming, and gender/sexual transgression is not reducible to specifically homosexual histories.[87] Francis Pattison's figures hint that this ramified intellectual and cultural history of transgressive travestizing and aestheticizing may not be an exclusively male history either.

Theaters of Class: Aristocracy in Oxford

Francis Pattison in the texts of her contemporaries is described not only as artificially feminine but as French and aristocratic; the woman Francis Pattison "plays" is puzzingly separate from the woman she "is" by class and birth. In the next section, I consider Francis Pattison's "Frenchness," but claims that she enacted aristocracy also bear examination in relation to the gendered histories of knowledge and prestige in Oxford.

Francis Pattison's texts are ungenerous to Oxford. The city was "that hole" whose very "atmosphere" invoked in her an "intense repulsion . . . morbid & even absurd"; after her physical breakdown, she wrote of imagining a future life, "realising . . . all (according to my strength) that I desire to do & be for myself & other brings a consciousness of power, wh can be patient & healthy . . . at any rate . . . as long as its out of Oxford."[88] Sympathetically, Walburga Paget narrated Francis Pattison's life as one in which she was "chained so many years" in an Oxford "extreme[ly] stiffish and narrow in outward things, irksome as well in the want of facility, grace, and elevation in the forms of daily life." Oxford, in Paget's text, is not only provincial, but, in a coded language of class, it is bourgeois.[89] In Paget's description of Oxford, Francis Pattison and Paget herself are women of fluidity and breadth, naturally at ease, graceful, and elevated in their every movement, who deserve better places. Francis Pattison's own texts repeatedly denigrate bourgeois life as stultifying and imprisoning. The Renaissance of Art in France remarks that "bourgeois" culture "efface[s]" more aristocratic "refinements."[90] More pointed private texts by Mrs. Pattison make Oxford the epitome of a tedious middle class; Oxford is ridiculed for its domination by a heavy-handed middle-class morality. "The worst . . . [of Oxford life] is the sense of personal degradation which accompanies the exercise of what people call 'tact.' " "Morally lowering" compliance with the rules of this society caused her more shame than should a crime, although "once out of it [Oxford] . . . it shakes off like dirt." She instructed herself, "surely one ought to find a way to keep an even freedom of soul under any conditions," but it sometimes "seems as if one sank into the mire past hope."[91] Francis Pattison wrote that in Oxford she learned "on peut dominer ce qu'on ne peut pas franchir."[92] One means of achieving a dominating height, and a view beyond walls, is by constructing a superior class persona.

Constructing a superior class persona can reframe the norms of gender; class can offer a usable language of difference. John Kucich claims that contests for status, prestige, and authority within the middle class were sometimes waged through representations of selves as "moral sophisticates"; constructing a position of aristocratic "exceptionality" marked by "flexibility and freedom" from the constraints of sincerity was not outside middle-class culture but a strategy pursued by some middle-class élites against other sectors of the middle class.[93] Cora Kaplan has pointed more specifically to the resources aristocracy offered women's imaginations. Kaplan views Virginia Woolf's Orlando as "at one level at least a celebration of, and fantasy about, an androgynously unified class subjectivity—aristocratic rather than bourgeois." In Kaplan's view, "Woolf suggest[s] that a historically plausible middle-class androgyny is an impossible fantasy," since sexual difference was integral to middle-class identity and made bourgeois women's stories "nasty, brutish, and short." Imagining one's way out of gender roles required imagining one's way out of the bourgeoisie, since "for women [of the middle class] there can be neither exciting Bildungsroman nor picaresque."[94] "Cultivation," political interest, ironic wit, and disregard of "bourgeois" morality were imputed to aristocratic women like Anthony Trollope's Lady Glencora Palliser—cultured and cosmopolitan, high-spirited, able to risk unconventionality, and ultrafeminine even when "unwomanly."[95] In Wilde's plays, aristocratic women can be "dandies," adept at the composition of surfaces, their "frivolity" critiquing the self-sanctifying seriousness of bourgeois morality.[96]

In different ways, Kucich and Kaplan hint that writing oneself as a character superior to one's assigned and proper class assignment may express a wish not merely for riches and status but difference and escape more broadly.[97] Nancy K. Miller hypothesizes that implausibility in some novels by women—stories that "fail" at verisimilitude and depend on contrived and unrealistic turns of the plot—may "manifest the extravagant wish for the story that would turn out differently" and rebellion against the constraints of respectable plots for women.[98] E. F. S. Pattison defends extremity, praising the "*poses affectées*" of some of Goujon's figures for their "challenge," "energy," and "grandeur," and vociferously lauding a figure by Jean Cousin against those who have "frequently censured" its "fantastic intermixture of figures and ornament" which "forcibly challenge attention." "Combinations of art and nature" that might seem "preposterous" or tasteless attain beauty in exceptional hands, and the death of the Renaissance is the triumph of "correct[ness]" and "good taste."[99] Pattison's and Miller's arguments thus agree with Kaplan's: excessive figures can express desire. But although in *The Renaissance of Art in France* a sensitive and cultivated aristocracy are a precondition for the "independent" artists who will "seize the liberties of the whole subject world of sense," so that Pattison's aristocrats create freedom for others, Kaplan argues that historically, middle-class women writers' imaginary upward transcendences of class have been purchased through degrading and bigoted representations of working-class women. Margaret Maynard similarly contends that anachronistic images of female aristocracy in the 1890s were explicitly antidemocratic.[100] Parodic performances of aristocracy may mock bourgeois norms but glamorize class hierarchy. Imagining aristocracy as a true elite of cosmopolitans not bound by local rules can evade wider politics.

Francis Pattison's aristocratic performances in Oxford may be symptomatic of the continued power of aristocratic culture as a "residual" and frequently reinvigorated discourse, struggles for power within the middle class, and women's desires for transcendence of bourgeois norms, as well as being continuous with narratives of Strong family life in combining intellectual and artistic interests with politics.[101] Francis Pattison's performances can also again be productively read in relationship to emergent forms of homoerotic camp. Alan Sinfield and Joseph Bristow have convincingly shown that "effeminacy," as an available, if stigmatized or dangerous, masculinity has depended since the eighteenth century on an association with aristocracy; effeminacy is a transvestism of class as well as gender.[102] Sinfield especially insists that the language of effeminacy cannot simply be read as a code that was always already hiding the figure of the "homosexual." The conventions imputed to a leisured aristocracy—of aesthetic "refinement," self-representation as an artificial and crafted object of vision, embrace of the trivial, mockery of the serious, and contempt for the alleged vulgarity and utilitarianism of middle-class domesticity—were a privileged discourse for the elaboration of the image of the "queer" in the late nineteenth century; Jack Babuscio's definition of camp as "irony, aestheticism . . . theatricality, and humour" strongly suggests a stylish appropriation of the "aristocratic" highly usable by gay men as a rhetorical counter to norms of sincerity, usefulness, authenticity, and seriousness.[103] But the discourse of effeminacy was volatile and sexually multiform. The affected, artificial, and "profoundly unnatural" effeminate male aesthete deployed signifiers of class to modify gender, repudiating middle-class conventions by performing in accordance with another set of more glamorous, if morally ambiguous, rules and conventions, but this repudiation could encompass implications of transgressive heterosexual activities.[104] Camp is not, therefore, an unambiguous language of "resistance"; texts and contexts determine whether performing leisure-class effeminacy and dandyism was subversive or reactionary, a "radical disturbance or an instrument of containment" in relation to hegemonies of gender, class, and sexuality.[105] When effeminacy became queer, it became a clearer threat to heteronormative domesticity, but even then, campy aestheticism retained a distinctly classy allure; mocking and claiming exemption from the rules of respectability through an appeal to socially and economically as well as aesthetically "higher" standards offered career paths out of bourgeois orthodoxies.

Campily aristocratic styles thus carry politically ambiguous but charged gender and sexual meaning. Francis Pattison's performances of cosmopolitanism, cultivation, and aesthetic savoir faire shared a vocabulary of aristocratic superiority to local gender conventionalities with some sexually dissident men, and also, like some of these contemporaries, operated within Oxford. The flamboyance of Francis Pattison's costuming and framing in the texts that describe her exposes another open secret: official Oxford's pervasive theatricality and self-display. Francis Pattison wrote that Oxford added to general dull middle-classness "a dash of pretension wh always accompanies officialism however small."[106] In Oxford's spaces of theatricality—lecture-halls, the Sheldonian Theatre, the public domesticities of the colleges, and the streets themselves— the university constituted its own prestige and corporate identity through costumes, regalia, and ceremonies.[107] Francis Pattison's aristocratic self-costumings were scandalously continuous with the relentless local enactments of artifice, hierarchy, and self-aggrandizing pageantry. Oxford's figure, not just Mrs. Pattison's, knowingly pretends a "natural" superiority, costumes itself elaborately, and asserts identity.

E. F. S. Pattison's Goujon's *Diane* of Anet "crowned the fountain" in a setting in which "every figure, every ornament . . . fulfilled some designed office of subtle service to the eye."[108] Pattison/Dilke's art-historical writing insists on the inextricability of display from power, contending that aestheticized public shows by institutions are not innocent. *The Renaissance of Art in France* and Dilke's *Art in the Modern State* offer a history of French art in which vital aesthetic energies are released by political and social change then corrupted and reharnessed by powerful and self-aggrandizing institutions. Pattison's textual trajectory is a descent from intoxicating and pleasurable shows and elaborations of surfaces, selves, and spaces to a seventeenth century of "formal stage[s]," "stilted eloquence," "pompous palaces," and "grandiose art," in which the arts are enlisted, directed, appropriated, and damaged by an expansionist and authoritarian state.[109] Colin Eisler has called *Art in the Modern State* a "brilliant" study of "what lurks beneath the surface of art, a study of the use by power of seduction and display."[110] The *grand siècle* shrinks art to local and trivial uses; "we have stepped from the great stage to the puppet show." However "brilliant" were "many of these men" and however seductive the displays they created ("all too fascinating the idylls of their theatrical Arcadia"), their works are unsatisfying and small; "nothing but little pictures, mean thoughts, frivolous compositions . . . charming littlenesses, prettinesses, emptinesses . . . glorified upholstery. . . ." Perverting art's potential to give pleasure and to foster rebellion, the pageantry of institutions enmeshes art in "tyranny" and "destroy[s] all life and liberty" that does not undergird its hierarchy, violence, and exclusion.[111]

If Pattison/Dilke's historical texts license a critique of Oxonian pageantry, the figure of Mrs. Pattison in Oxford texts—its extravagance and obvious contrivances—suggests a critique in the form of a parody. Francis Pattison's self-costuming as an aristocratic lady invited comment not only because the story her tableaux told was not "true" but because her artificial figure can appear a mocking condensation of the artifices of Oxford. Moreover, if any campy enactment in Oxford could be read as exposing Oxford's own artificiality and performativity, Francis Pattison's position was different from Pater's or Wilde's: Oxford's theaters were gendered. Francis Pattison posing as an aristocrat performed a class persona severed from her actual economic position as the daughter of a middle-class professional and wife of a don, and she was represented as magically different from the institutions, sites, and statuses that held her, but *women in Oxford already and continuously inhabited a double position.* Women's class status in general, mediated through relationships to men, was everywhere ambiguous. Further, women's place in the institutions of Oxford social hierarchy was especially unstable. The wives of college heads in particular lived in complex relations to public status, constantly present and on display, yet never "members," in but not of Oxford. E. F. S. Pattison's study of the French Renaissance assigned aristocrats an awareness of "the disposition of the composition . . . the movement of the personages . . . the ordered arrangement of their splendid habits . . . the touch of forethought which composes their bearing" which marks "those accustomed to appear in public state." Mrs. Mark Pattison, and the other personages of the university, official and unofficial, also lived much in the public eye.[112] As Francis Pattison's enactments of difference converted exclusion into otherness, they also displayed Oxford's gendered paradoxes.

Imaginary Expatriation: France in Oxford

In the texts of her contemporaries, Francis Pattison is a Frenchwoman manquée, an image of counterfeit, displayed and displaced, French femininity; attributions of an uncanny foreignness underline other tropes of difference. In Emilia Dilke's account of architecture, Frenchness is aesthetic choice: sensibility "to the effect produced by . . . design . . . is the essential mark of the French genius" and artistic decision is a "distinguishing" sign of French art.[113] But Francis Pattison and Charles Dilke also produced texts which inscribe Pattison/Dilke's "Frenchness" as a selfhood that, owing nothing to natality or legal nationality, is nonetheless natural.

Charles Dilke wrote of Emilia Dilke's "Frenchness" as a hidden, truer self and claimed that her worth was appreciated in France, where "she held her own and shone in those circles of the Parisian world in which conversation is still practised as a fine art." Charles also laid claim to Emilia's Frenchness as evidence of her second marriage's success. "The distinguishing feature of Lady Dilke in the opinion of all who saw her [was] her constant gaiety of spirit," and when French, she was happy.

She "invariably made, at all events in Paris" an "impression of brilliant gaiety," and her French friends "would be amazed at the attribution to her of gloominess of mind" and "supposed sadness of her spirit" held by English people who read her short stories. Frenchness is an inner essence contiguous with joy: "In Paris she was French, with sufficient difference to give distinction . . . [but] on this side of the Channel, a reserve taken for sadness by those who didn't understand her." Dilke cites a claim that only the young and the French could see Emilia Dilke in her full magnetic power, "her capacity for absolute abandonment to pure animal spirits and childish gaiety." By being French, in short, Emilia Dilke could be young, physical, and happy. Charles Dilke sets these descriptions of Emilia Dilke's French gaiety next to a quotation in which she asserts that their marriage had been one "of 'unbroken happiness,' " implying that, in making her happy and sharing her Francophilia, he knew and his text presents her "real" self. (As we will see, however, Charles Dilke's Francophilia could be enlisted in more lurid stories.[114])

Being English is a confinement of Emilia Dilke's real being; only when she was other could she really be seen; "to translate bright French conversation into English is impossible."[115] Francis Pattison too confided to Ellen Smith that her true home was not that to which she legally belonged. Rhapsodizing from Draguignan of her "joy in the full glory of the sun the blaze & the barrenness of the south . . . like a cordial bath to one's weariness of men & books . . . [which] at once sobers & stimulates," she could scarcely communicate the "intense enjoyment wh the south is to me so that I can sit down by the burning wayside & bathe in the golden heat & renew the ravishing sense of being one with the earth & sky wh never comes to me till I am past Marseilles." The daughter of empire shamefacedly added, "yet I love England I love my people, though English landscape is strange and foreign to me, & here I feel at once at home."[116]

Pattison's art history also plangently thematizes displacement. A gap between a figure and its surroundings may convey wrenching emotional, physical, and spiritual significations: in Duvet's print of the Crucifixion, the "calculated dissonance" between the central dramatic figures—frozen in silent "anguish stretched to the utmost"—and the "surrounding circumstance" that "enframes" them, creates a "shock," and a "keener pathos as of a cry in sharp distress . . . [a] more acute impression of pain."[117] French figures suffer from being moved from their places. Enamels "lose incalculably" when removed from "the frame they were destined to fill"; they "urgently need" these frames or they may be judged "defect[ive]." Goujon's fountain nymphs and his *Diane* are given histories of aesthetic isolation and loss; the houses surrounding the *Fons*'s female tableaux were demolished and "in its isolated position it looked unfinished"; a subsequent relocation had only "ill-success" since "to displace work of this class is to destroy it." The *Diane* of Anet is "rescued from destruction" but its resiting can at best only "recall" its lost origin. "Diane lying on a clumsy pedestal in the gallery cannot be to us the Diane who, at a very different elevation, crowned . . . the *cour d'honneur*."[118] Proper places are lost; figures sadly recall irretrievable histories.

A great mental liberation can also be conferred by belief in one's own exile; if one is really from "someplace else not here," one is not truly bound by local regulations. Twentieth-century British and American expatriate women in France could find lives impossible to lead at home.[119] "Frenchness" was only one of several modes by which to make visually apparent difference and detachment from one's immediate social world; other women displayed Italian or Greek or otherwise exoticizing styles. Gill Frith argues that Germaine de Staël's *Corinne* is the foundational text for stories "nineteenth-century women told themselves . . . about the relationship between gender and national identity," and we have seen Francis Pattison compare herself in a letter to Charles Dilke to *Corinne's* transnational (French, Swiss, exiled) heroine, out of place in Oxford.[120] Naomi Schor points out that *Corinne* contrasts nations as spaces of performance: England is a "land of the living dead," a "cemetery where a brilliant public woman . . . can only be buried alive" (like the protagonist of "A Vision of Learning") but Rome's "ruins and crumbling tombstones" offers history-laden stages.[121]

Pattison/Dilke's "Frenchness" thus participates in wider discourses about gender, hybridity and foreignness. But "Frenchness" also had specific, if contradictory, meanings. The subtexts of "Frenchness" in Victorian England included a rich tradition of hostility, mapped by Linda Colley, Stella Cottrell and others.[122] "Franco-phobia" constituted oppositions between Britain and France to imagine a natural community of Britons. France's alterity was not described simply in terms drawn from the national past or France's recent history of un-English revolution and Terror, but in multiple forms of unnaturalness: the French were "slave-like," tyrant-loving, monkeyish, effete, frivolous, dishonest, cunning, immoral, atheistic, wanton, brutal, mad, savage, restless, and lecherous; they "threatened to unleash all that was contained, incarcerated, suppressed, or made subordinate in English society, and to challenge or subvert all that seemed secure and natural."[123] The more feverish pitches of Francophobia coincided with overt political threats, but hostile figurations of France remained in the discourses of Englishness. The bishop's wife in George Eliot's *Daniel Deronda* was "a woman of taste and also of strict principle, and objects to having a French person in the house." The French novel was, by definition, pornographic.[124]

English horror for all things French was always undercut by licit and illicit fascinations and desires. France was the nation of bloody and unchristian Revolution; it was also the site of liberty, Enlightenment and seemingly continual political change. If, to some eyes, this was evidence of the paradoxical French character, half monkey and half tiger, it was to others a scene of perpetual interest, hopes, fears, and engagement.[125] France was not merely the beautiful land of "Gothic cathedrals and picturesque countryside known to Ruskin or to bourgeois dons during vacation tours," but of "sophisticated beliefs in the arts for their own sake . . . there exuded a sense of unbridled passion which was at once exciting and evil."[126] French culture produced horrifying confusions of gender—effeminate men and oversexual, overintellectual women; suspected perversions and dangerous theories—and alluring transgressions.[127] France was the place of George Sand, who defied gender norms in every direction; she smoked cigars and wore trousers but lived a life of passionate romance and maternal devotion that made it impossible to name her as wholly unfeminine.[128] Even in more conventional realms of sexuality, the air of France was supercharged with romance and matters adulterous were handled with, depending on one's perspective, either a gross lack of decency or a charming sophistication.[129]

E. F. S. Pattison's art-writing typifies the malleability of "French" as a term applied with great definitiveness to almost any quality. There is Frenchness in Nicolas Poussin's "selection of forms," color, "sentiment," "treatment of subject"; in the "clear, defined, spare, and supple shapes of his nymphs" and an "instinctive preference for modulations in the highest key"; in "strange white, and fitful gleaming yellow, and weird magic threadings of black" that "cry to us," and in the absence of "suggestive mysticism" or "sombre deeps." Frenchness is harmonious but full of "dramatic energy"; it offers "an infinite variety of pleasure" within small compasses; combines "vivacity of impulse" with "purity of tone"; it is "dignified, yet not dull; licentious, yet not coarse"; it transforms "common vulgar incident" and "transmutes" the "sordid and mean." French painting is most French in its "uncompromising realism" and "unflinching truth" combined with "wonderful breadth," "grace," and "opalescence" even in the face of horror.[130]

Francis Pattison was not explicitly associated with the most disreputably exciting possibilities of French womanhood. Some of her Francophilic performances were playful: in taking up fencing, she practiced a sport associated with men, aristocracy, and France, and, like Katie Dilke in London, she organized amateur theatricals at Lincoln College (including a piece titled *Ici on parle français*) and made a point of going to London to see any French plays.[131] Texts like Ward's made Francis Pattison's Frenchness continuous with her dislocations of class and time, but the trope of a Frenchness at odds with Oxford middle-class convention was not always associated with anachronism or aristocracy. She could be a figure of the modern Paris of the Second Empire and Third Republic as well as of the ancien régime. Walburga Paget thought Francis Pattison's "idealism" and "extremely advanced and impracticable views" most un-French but saw her as "a very charming and pretty little Radical lady . . . [who] looked like a dapper little Frenchwoman."[132] Stephen Gwynn describes her as a *femme moderne* alongside the dying Mark Pattison:

> [Mark Pattison was] drawn in a bath-chair by a shambling menial, lying more like a corpse than any living thing I have ever seen . . . Beside him walked his wife, small, erect, and ultra Parisian, all in black with a black parasol—I did not know then how often Frenchwomen thus enhanced the brilliance of a personality: still less did I know how few but Frenchwomen could do it. But there . . . was the gift of style . . . her presence conveyed detachment from her convoy with an emphasis that absence alone could never have given.[132]

Frenchness is something the reader will recognize, and it marks Francis Pattison as other than the milieu she inhabits.[134]

France's associations also included a historical trope combining femininity with power and knowledge. If Mark Pattison could sneer in a review that a volume of Pascal's letters was "a truly French production, having more of style than of philosophy, and more of wit than of learning" and Margaret Jeune scorned a "clever" Frenchwoman for her immodest dress, George Eliot represents the French past as a place quite unlike Oxford. Femininity, intellectuality, and worldliness were not only compatible but valorized: "in France alone woman has had a vital influence on the development of literature . . . The women whose tact, wit, and personal radiance created the atmosphere of the Salon, where literature, philosophy, and science, emancipated from the trammels of pedantry and technicality, entered on a brighter stage of existence."[135] Eliot exclaimed "Heaven forbid that we should enter on a defense of French morals!" but nonetheless claimed that, in seventeenth-century France, an elite female life script of a "*mariage de convenance*" followed by "a career of gallantry," produced "good results," giving women a "vivid interest in affairs," a "quicken[ed] intellect," and a "life of passion [which] deepened . . . nature by the questioning of self and destiny."[136] The French past also offered a place unlike Oxford in that femininity and sexual availability to men could be separated. French *salonières* had claimed exemption from the bodily requirements of more ordinary women, desiring " 'the respect that is the woman's due' . . . [and] the emotions love inspired but not the pregnancies" or other physicalities to which it led.[137] Eliot's essay valorizes heterosociality over heterosexuality: such women provided an expanded range of pleasures to fitting men. Madame de Sablé "was not a genius, not a heroine, but a woman whom men could more than love; whom they could make their friend, confidante, and counsellor,—the sharer, not of their joys and sorrows only, but of their ideas and aims."[138] Undoubtedly few of her contemporaries were aware of the details of Francis Pattison's refusal of "conjugal duties" and the intimate battles of her marriage, but whatever her own uses of the discourse of *les précieuses*, Francis Pattison's absences from the conjugal household were widely known and associated with a bodily delicacy some represented as a matter of convenience.

Francis Pattison's ill health increasingly authorized spending most of every year out of Oxford, usually in the south of France, but her scholarly needs to do research united with the demands of her body. In her intellectual activity, France was physically as well as figuratively the "wider sphere" in which Francis Pattison moved beyond Oxford; as with Symonds and Pater's Renaissances, the Renaissance of E. F. S. Pattison's study was not English.[139] In some accounts, Francis Pattison's professional identity as historian and critic merge with her style and disrespect for convention. W. J. Humble-Crofts, recalling the Pattisons in France in 1873, remembered a library at Tours where "she was so excited at finding [a particular medieval text] that she would not wait for a chair and table, but sat down on the floor. and became absorbed in it" and that "Mrs. Pattison [was] the first lady I had ever seen smoke a cigarette, and read the *Figaro pari passu*" in a cafe.[140] Francis Pattison's Frenchness confounds the boundaries between artistic creator, art object, and scholar of art.

Renaturalizations and Containments

There are perils in embodying otherness. Images of the self as outside of, unbound by, and excessive to the social hierarchies and institutions one inhabits may be mystifying but ineffective. Throughout Victorian culture, powerful discourses of authenticity competed with discourses of the self as mobile and labile, and, as in marriage, legal definitions could trump less official performances. Francis Pattison was never "really" French nor "really" aristocratic; aristocracy was a matter of blood and lineage she did not have and nationality was defined increasingly rigidly. Whatever her inner "Frenchness," in France Francis Pattison was liable to exclusion from local communities and vulnerable to stereotyping as just another English lady in the south of France.[141] More cruelly, an anonymous essay in the *Quarterly Review* published after Emilia Dilke's death virtually demanded authentic Frenchness as a qualification for the work she had attempted. The author extravagantly praised Dilke's art history and her mind (she was "probably the equal in intellect" to Jane Austen, Macaulay, and Charlotte Bronte) and asserted her uniqueness among British women of genius: unlike Austen, Bronte, George Eliot, and Elizabeth Barrett Browning, who "won their fame in the realm of imagination," Emilia Dilke's place in history "will rest on her mastery of the positive facts and tendencies of history" and her "technical knowledge of the fine arts." Dismissing Dilke's fiction as well as other British women art and historical writers, the author locates Dilke's true peers in France—Madame de Staël and Madame de Sévigné—but proclaims the latter "the only woman whose learning, breadth of view, and powers of critical observation" would have been fully adequate to Dilke's task. The implication is harsh: if only Sévigné could have truly succeeded, Dilke had not been quite adequate to the task she chose, perhaps debarred by birth.[142]

The *Quarterly Review* article may have been written by J. E. C. Bodley, a member of Oscar Wilde's circle during undergraduate days in Oxford who became, through Francis Pattison's recommendation, Charles Dilke's private secretary in the 1880s.[143] Bodley was extremely ambivalent about both Dilkes' liberalism and feminism; he also went on to have his own career as an interpreter of French culture to British readers. Attributed texts by Bodley on Emilia Dilke demonstrate the ambiguity of Francis Pattison's performances. If Pattison's stagy femininity could be read as undermining masculine scholarly monopolies, it could also be reappropriated. Bodley nostalgically recalled an Oxford before "the ever-multiplying progeny of college dons and its corollary, the invasion of Oxford by the higher education of women," when only a few women like Mrs. Pattison had the "rare privilege" of "dwell[ing] within the sanctuary of the University" as "cultivated" sisters, wives, and daughters of heads of house who would not disturb "the calm tradition of ancient Oxford." Bodley's text uses Pattison to mourn a lost era in which women properly decorated the institutions of men and ties her value to her exceptionality.[144]

Bodley praised Emilia Dilke because her "exterior aspect was not that which is popularly associated with the bluestocking, still less with the feminine orator . . . she seemed to impart a reminiscence of the canvases of Boucher and Van Loo, which she celebrated as the types of the *Grand siècle* when the highest forms of feminine intelligence were not yet divorced from exterior signs of feminine grace."[145] In *Art in the Modern State*, Emilia Dilke made Boucher an example of talented but constrained and trivial artists corrupted by the institutions they served and specifically criticized the female figures in such work: "the powdered charms of their voluptous nymphs" are contrasted to more powerful Renaissance female figures.[146] Read against Emilia Dilke's text, Bodley's praise of Emilia Dilke as a Boucherian figure ensconses her performances on the "puppet stage" she denounced and makes her a fascinating powdered nymph whose principal interest is sexual exhibition. Moreover, Bodley's texts valorize feminine intellectuality only insofar as it is combined with utter fidelity to the performance of femininity. Even if her labor organizing was "virile," she was "the exemplar of womanly amenity in her hours of social recreation."[147] Francis Pattison/Emilia Dilke could be applauded as unlike those "bluestockings" who were still available for ridicule, but intellectual women will not be considered masculine only so long as they are relentlessly feminine. Eliot's "Women in France" lauded French *salonières* because their writings, however intellectual, were "but a charming accident of their more charming lives, like the petals which the wind shakes from the rose in its bloom";

Bodley's praise similarly uses Emilia Dilke's French femininity, drawing invidious comparisons to police less perfectly feminine women intellectuals.[148] Femininity and intellect not only can be reconciled but *must* be equally displayed for a woman to earn respect. An account by Frank Harris that uncharacteristically calls Emilia Dilke a "blue-stocking" combines sneers that she was short and stout and that she claimed too much floor time to propound her own intellectual views rather than listening to men's, especially his. Harris's report inverts Bodley's praise of Emilia Dilke but shares Bodley's logic.[149]

Her class and national travesties also doomed Francis Pattison to being read as pretentious. Emilia Dilke scorned the foreign pretensions of the "soi-disant Italian" architect Servandoni; "those who knew all about him" knew he was the son of a Lyonnais carriage maker, but Francophilia can draw specific attacks.[150] The pseudonymous "Ouida" (Maria Louise Ramé, 1839–1908), a wildly popular Victorian novelist, could be mocked by Malcolm Elwin for having "cultivated Gallicisms . . . signed her surname 'de la Ramée' . . . professed an intimate interest in French politics . . . [and] affected an odd style of dress"; sharing the "extravagent eccentricity" of George Sand, "she was an instinctive *poseuse*, for ever acting a part." Elwin enlists her success in his own large claims; she gives evidence of the "worthlessness and artificiality" of modernity.[151] Those who had at least public confidence in their own taste and qualifications, and worried about the solidity of social boundaries, could find Mrs. Pattison as *fausse française* laughable or threatening. Nancy Mitford, no mean Francophile herself, heaped satire on her fictional Mrs. O'Donovan: of "the category of English person, not rare among the cultivated classes, and not the least respectable of their race, who can find almost literally nothing to criticize where the French are concerned . . . in London she was considered the great authority on everything French, to all intents and purposes a Frenchwoman, and . . . had . . . come to have a proprietary interest with regard to France."[152] Pattison/Dilke's aristocratic airs could be described through insinuations about social climbing; achieving a position from which "on peut dominer" can be seen as getting above oneself. Beatrice Webb stops only just short of calling Emilia Dilke common; a mix of "the *grande dame* and the adventuress," Dilke was a "brilliant woman with strong sense, great industry and capacity for manipulating" but ambitious and "coarse—coarse to the backbone: a born intriguer with an unswerving faith in 'cleverness'; an utter cynic as to 'righteousness.' "[153] Other, more recent commenters have been troubled by an advocate of working women who studied elite French art and wore fancy dress.[154] Finally, Francis Pattison's exaggerated femininity can be read not as camping up a storm but as a betrayal of other women who more bravely defied bourgeois norms by presenting themselves as "masculine" bluestockings or "natural" women. The long histories of misogynist and homophobic contempt for bluestockings and punitive uses of "femininity" amply warrant suspicion of hyperfemininity as a *model* for feminists, although as Martha Vicinus shows in the case of the suffragettes, other women have found feminist uses for feminine stylishness.[155]

Annette Kuhn reminds us, "[d]isputing the givenness of social categories like class, race, gender identity, and sexual preference confers no exemption from the necessity of negotiating their social meanings in daily life"; even women "fully aware that femininity is a fabrication" must "as far as the world is concerned—and indeed, as far as [they themselves are] concerned" live with "the very real consequences of a particular gender label."[156] But too glibly criticizing Francis Pattison as mannered or pretentious or getting above herself may rest on assumptions that she had a true self—middle-class, womanly but not overfeminine, and English—to betray. These critiques can renaturalize class, gender, and nation, rather than exploring how persons simultaneously inhabit multiple subject positions and how lives exhibit fierce tensions between material circumstances, subjectivities, and singularizing legal and institutional statuses. Ann Snitow contends that feminism has always contained a tension between accepting and rejecting the category of "woman," between asserting a solidarity based on sexual difference and dissolving the binaristic logic of "sex" by exposing not only its injustice but its inadequacy and falsity.[157] This tension structured Victorian feminism, although the main current of Victorian middle-class feminism, especially from the 1870s forward, embraced the category of "women" with great historical efficacy. By the late nineteenth century, naturalist theories of gender that emphasized difference were used to argue for women's rights on the basis of their difference—and hence distinct capacity to contribute to public life—and their unrepresentability by men.[158] Francis Pattison/Emilia Dilke's highly contrived performances of an artificial, emphatic, French aristocratic femininity, and her art-historical and art-critical writings' emphasis on the relations of art and social life, the motivation and mutilation of aesthetic activities by politics, were homologous with liberal feminism's emphasis on the social construction of existing femininities, but she also took part in feminist activities advocating the establishment of new institutions for women "as women" and she contributed to "essentializing" discourses about women.

"Nature" 's status in Pattison/Dilke's texts fluctuates. As in Francis Pattison's letters about her first marriage, she could write of selves as real and immutable.[159] Pattison/Dilke could also denounce artificiality as a particularly feminine vice, especially when dangerously coupled to power.[160] E. F. S. Pattison's account of the works of Germain Pilon both lauds and excoriates him with gendered insinuations. His effigy of Valentina Balbiani reveals Balbiani's "frivolous pleasure and the companionship of lapdogs," "pride," "egotism," "empty habits" and "undeserved ease," "passion and vanity," all overlaid with "exquisite exterior finish . . . of dress, of attitude, of movement." Valentina is a "complete type of artificial elegance." Pilon's work possesses "never failing charm" and "the most exquisite grace," but his female figures, "praised by French critics as types of perfect womanhood . . . are the highly artificial rendering of a highly artificial product. Attitude and expression are cultivated, polished, finished, but without truth, without simplicity, without honesty . . . overflow[ing with] dainty affectations and over-refined elegancies." By contrast to Goujon's figures, which Emilia Dilke commends for their "virile feeling for style," Pilon's skill both exposes his own limitations and damns the women he depicts.[161] Pattison implies that Valentina was murdered by her husband for political reasons, but the greatness of Pilon's sculpture resides not in its pathos but in its revelation of its subject's probable destination in hell.[162] More generally, Pilon's female figures embody the "taste and tone" of Catherine de Medici's court: "meretricious," and "incapable of giving adequate expression to any male virtue."[163] Emilia Dilke's French Painters of the Eighteenth Century similarly connects male artistic inferiority, female performativity, and illegitimate and eroticized female power. Dilke's text respects "the remarkable force of character" of Madame de Pompadour and praises two of Boucher's portraits of her, but asserts that it was Boucher's defects, his *"vulgarité élégante,"* which won him Pompadour's unremitting patronage as he provided the "scenes and costumes," furniture and fans, for the marquise to act her parts. Damningly quoting Diderot (Boucher "loved everything but truth" and his late works show "degradation" of taste, colors, composition, characters, expression, design, and even morals), Dilke concludes, "the influence of Mme. de Pompadour had survived her death." Boucher and Pompadour together embody their inferior epoch's "artificial tone and temper," facile decorativity and corrupting performance.[164]

In a less misogynistic passage, E. F. S. Pattison contrasts the "wide-winged angels" with the female form they enclose on the title page of a fifteenth-century French *Metamorphoses* to assert that while the angels offer "empty grace devoid of . . . character . . . [and] mannered prettiness," the central figure gives evidence of the designer's real ability because that female body exceeds decorativity. Rather, it is full of "distinct individuality . . . and the keen flavour of actual existence."[165] Similarly, when Emilia Dilke scorns the female images in an illustrated *Émile* for their "enticing airs . . . mincing manners and wanton fluttering ways," the figures' trite charms are proof of the artists' (and perhaps Rousseau's) inferiority.[166] Nonetheless, stereotypical femininity remains contemptible. As noted earlier, Emilia Dilke's late essay, "Of Love and Sorrow," castigates spiritual self-aestheticization, especially that of women. Dilke contrasts theatricalized masochism to true sainthood, contemptuously dismissing "the perpetual contemplation of [one]self illumined by the vision of eternal bliss."[167] "Of Love and Sorrow" briefly offers Chateaubriand as an example of a "magnificent attitude" unable to "mask . . . [the] tawdry poverty of . . . self-pity" and the "weakness of a nature unable to trust in its own power," but the essay's lengthier condemnation of Madame Desbordes-Valmore's histrionic tableaux of sensibility implies that women are more prone to such forms of pious enactment and surreptitiously marks such displays even by men as feminine.[168]

But Dilke's essay need not be read simply as hypocritical in light of Francis Strong's own earlier performances, or simply as misogynist; its themes are not idiosyncratic. Josephine Butler allegedly invited young men whom she wished to morally inspire to view her in a mirror while she prayed, so that others might find in her framed example, poised and rapt, an image to inspire their own piety; at least one of her viewers, J. A. Symonds, was unsettled by the narcissistic undertones.[169] George Rae, a banker who collected his twenty-one Rossetti paintings in a separate shrine in his house, recalled his wife Julia posed motionless before Rossetti's "The Beloved," "as certain devout Catholic ladies . . . before their favourite shrines"; Julia displayed her own worship of art and, kneeling before an ideal feminine image, is an ideal feminine image herself.[170] These overt Victorian linkages of spirituality and feminine bodily spectacle suggest that Dilke's essay registers patterns of feminine self-display whose dangers were not illusory, even if her texts oscillate between blaming women, those who portray them, and wider histories, for the moral and intellectual deficiencies of female figures.

The ambiguities of Pattison/Dilke's art-historical and spiritual texts about femininity, artifice, and nature, and the tense relationships between identity and materiality, are also visible in her political texts and practices. An essay by Emilia Dilke on the history and present need for women's trade-unionism subtly thematizes style, femininity, class, and exclusion to produce an origin story for the Women's Trade Union League.[171] This is Dilke's story: Mrs. Mark Pattison met Emma Smith through her work for "the Society for the Promotion of Women's Suffrage." Smith, born in 1848, was a Londoner who had been involved with the Victoria Press, founded by Emily Faithfull, as well as with the suffrage society. When Mrs. Pattison called on her one day in 1873, Smith explained that she was being sacked from her organizing position: " 'The ladies have complimented me on my zeal,' she said, 'but they say my bodily presence is weak, and my speech contemptible; so I must make room for someone who can represent them better.' " But all would be well because, Smith went on, "I've saved a little money, and I'm going to America to see for myself how the women's friendly societies work there. You know I don't think the vote the only panacea for all the sufferings of the weaker sex. I am a working woman myself . . . and I hope to induce Englishwomen to try whether they cannot help themselves, as men have done, by combination."[172] Smith married Thomas Paterson, who was involved in organizations for working-class men, soon after and they went to the United States to study American trade unions on a working honeymoon. On returning to Britain in 1874, Emma Paterson founded the Women's Protective and Provident League, which later became the Women's Trade Union League (the words "trade union" were thought too incendiary at first).[173] Paterson led the League until her death in 1886, when Emilia Dilke became its president.

Emilia Dilke's account clearly implies that Smith was sacked by the Suffrage Association for class reasons, for being insufficiently a lady. Dilke thus places the origins of her own activities as a middle-class trade unionist in a scene that signals the inadequacy of "ladies' " suffrage organizations. Dilke's Emma Smith specifically voices a critique: suffrage organizations are limited, see the vote as a "panacea," and do not encompass working-class women's material needs.[174] They are also exclusionary, barring those whose words and bodies are "contemptible." The women's suffrage society in Dilke's tale neither sees working-class women as the same—women who might "represent" them as middle-class women—nor does the society recognize working-class women's differences as legitimate and meaningful variations their organization was obliged to serve. Emma Smith was displaced for someone who could represent the ladies better while Smith's representation of working women was not part of the society's program. But Dilke's Emma Smith embarks on the foundation of an organization in which well-intentioned middle-class people will join working-class women to assist working women to represent themselves.

Gertrude Tuckwell claimed Emilia Dilke had worked up her account of Emma Smith Paterson's creation of the League as an inspirational story. Several details in Emilia Dilke's account are slightly "off"; Smith was not a printer, as Dilke has her call herself, but a bookbinder (Tuckwell further transforms her into a "tailoress," evoking Thomas Hood's "The Song of the Shirt"); Thomas Paterson was a cabinet-maker, not a printer.[175] More importantly, Tuckwell's Emilia Dilke describes Paterson as a martyr who "died before our eyes of her work for working women," and an obituary of Paterson which Emilia Dilke almost certainly wrote compares Paterson to another modern saint, Dora Pattison.[176] Like her story of Kitty Davis and Francis Strong, Dilke's essay recounts the mutative influence of another woman's enunciation of class identity, and, just as Dilke's account of Davis was shaped by the narrative needs of the 1890s, her account of Emma Smith Paterson operates within larger discourses. In both stories, too, Emilia Dilke claims to re-present the spoken words of another woman, but although, unlike Mrs. Davis's, Smith Paterson's historical existence is indubitable, the accuracy of Emilia Dilke's quotation is not. Dilke places in Emma Smith's mouth words she may never have spoken, but the words Dilke's Emma Smith speaks are not just Dilke's version of Smith's words. They are an unattributed quotation from a character in a novel by another woman. The phrase "my bodily presence is weak, and my speech contemptible" is a direct quotation from Charlotte Bronte's *Villette*.[177] If Emma Smith quoted *Villette* so exactly, it is unlikely that Emilia Dilke re-presented those words fifteen years later with equal precision; Dilke's use of Bronte invites consideration.

The silent embedding of Bronte's text in Dilke's "memory" of Emma Smith conjoins class and style in the birth of a working women's organization. The line from *Villette* Dilke attributes to Smith are placed by Bronte in the mouth and mind of Lucy Snowe in a passage in which a self is split and tortured over a woman's access to representation. Lucy's words are said/thought in an internal argument with a personified female voice of "Reason" which attempts to convince her that she must not hope for or attempt any future correspondence with Dr. John Graham. "Reason" argues against Lucy's openly representing her desire by informing her of her inadequacies as a speaking subject. Lucy's words reveal her impoverishment to the world: "You converse imperfectly. While you speak, there can be no oblivion of inferiority— no encouragement to delusion: pain, privation, penury stamp your language . . ." Lucy's protests that "[w]here the bodily presence is weak and the speech contemptible, surely there cannot be error in making written language the medium of better utterance than faltering lips can achieve?" and then she pleads, "But if I feel, may I *never* express?" But Reason repeats: "*Never!*" In short, the passage Emilia Dilke covertly quotes occurs at a textual moment of bitter reflection on a woman's lack of rightful access to desiring speech and textuality. Further, the voice of debarring "Reason" is *female*; "[t]his hag, this Reason" is a "step-mother" who beats and starves her charge. This cruel and punitive female authority, the false mother who will not empower Lucy's language, is counterposed to "her bright soft foe," Imagination.[178] In the story Emilia Dilke secretly invokes, as in the story she tells, class marks female bodily displays, and limiting and enabling feminizations contend.

Emilia Dilke's origin story of the Women's Trade Union League (WTUL), like her tale of Kitty Davis, is a story of hope. Some middle-class women (like her) can recognize the legitimacy of differences among women and move from an irresponsible form of femininity to a progressive position of gendered solidarity. Emilia Dilke and her Emma Smith attempt a feminist combination of imaginative identification with analytic awareness of separation and difference; feminist trade-unionism will bring working-class and middle-class women together to address class-variable needs. Emilia Dilke can work for other women's well-being; differences between women can circulate productively. Yet debates about women's self-representation, differences, speech and bodily presences run through Emilia Dilke's feminist career. Her texts, like the Women's Trade Union League as an organization, wrestle with dilemmas of difference and commonality, and tensions recur.

The League's goals depended on working-class women recognizing their interests where they were and on middle-class women moving outside their immediate class positions and the less desirable aspects of their feminine socialization to take up a cause of reform. This doubleness is visible from the beginning. The League's texts both emphasize that working-class women feel a natural solidarity with one another and desire class solidarity with working-class men, but they also sometimes speak as if middle-class people are more lightly bound by class. Paterson herself wrote in an early call for support that the League could be "an independent body composed of persons who are neither employers nor employed" who might "moderate" "cases of dispute."[179] While Paterson and Dilke both sometimes implied a more complex if unsatisfactory argument—that middle-class women's attentuation of or ability to eschew class loyalties derives from their lack of full rights to property and citizenship—the simultaneity of the WTUL's appeals for class-based solidarity within the working class and claims about the possibility of cross-class solidarity between women created cruxes also visible in Emilia Dilke's texts. Cross-class unity between women could sometimes descend to a trite rhetoric of imaginary kinship. In an 1889 speech, Dilke claimed that while "[the audience] might feel that she had no right to speak to a meeting of working women . . . she had had so much sympathy and friendship from working women in her life that she felt as if she belonged to them," erasing the significance of material and experiential differences between her and working-class women while tacitly assigning working-class women the job of appreciating her willingness to care about them.[180] But I want to focus on a more complicated issue than this strain of sentimentality: the different access of working-class and middle-class women to self-transformation in Dilke's texts.

In Emilia Dilke's recruitments of middle-class women, the rhetoric of potential transcendence of class is marked. Unlike some other middle-class reformers, Emilia Dilke never masqueraded as working class, but Dilke grants middle-class women the ability to remove themselves from existing social identifications through effort and ethical purpose.[181] Dilke stresses that the process of self-transformation to which she is calling bourgeois women is demanding and makes the League different from other philanthropic arenas for women's activity:

> The League . . . requires a different order of instruction and a higher class of mental effort than is demanded by the social work in which women are more ready to engage. In the study and advocacy of the important principles of trade combination there is nothing sensational—nothing that appeals to the emotions or gives play to that spirit of patronage, the exercise of which attracts ladies very largely to undertakings of the 'friendly' order.[182]

Throughout such texts, Dilke echoes her critique of unproductive forms of feminine spirituality. Engagement in this cause is different from idler forms of feminine charity; "not by mere talking, not by mere gifts of money, but by taking trouble; by taking trouble to master the grave problems of industry; by taking trouble to learn and know first, and then by the devotion of whole-hearted personal service to the work," privileged women can join in a great cause.[183] "It has always seemed to me that to sit quietly watching the operation of the laws of social and political economy in an attitude of respectful fatalism is an absolutely untenable position."[184] One must be up and doing! "It is far more pleasant, it is certainly easier to give individual alms and to receive thanks with a gratified sense of patronage," but "we want none of such charity." Images of aristocratic women nobly dispensing gifts are rebuked: "the intelligent and devoted service of heart and hand" is "righteous [and] womanly"; in the "labour and heat of the day," privileged women will not gain the degraded and degrading "pleasures of charity"; they will forward the cause of justice rather than dispensing mercy. "No queenship sh[ould] be more royal."[185] After Emilia Dilke's death, the former "Lancashire mill lass" and leading women's union organizer, Annie Marland-Brodie, claimed pictorial language to argue that Dilke had offered an image of what she espoused: "I saw how very earnest she was" and how she "took the trouble to know so much," unlike most of "her class." In "little miserable East-end halls" surrounded by "poor, ill-clad and ill-fed women," Marland-Brodie had "often wished that I was an artist and could put it on canvas for the benefit of our common enemies."[186]

Emilia Dilke's emphasis in her advice to the younger women she mentored reiterates these lessons: study and analyze social conditions, ground analyses in historical and economic knowledge, perceive oneself as a worker rather than a lady bountiful, make "wide culture a spur to, not a brake on, an intense and unremitting devotion to the cause of the less fortunate," and in doing so, achieve true nobility.[187] Emilia Dilke employed, usually as secretaries, May Abraham, Clementina Black, Emilia Monck, Mona Wilson, Emily Holyoake, Gertrude Tuckwell, Mary Macarthur, and Constance Smith.[188] In the stories these young women told, Emilia Dilke is an inspiriting teacher and encourager; Beatrice Potter envied Dilke's circle of young women, and one secretary, Margarete Boileau, wrote of "my beloved Lady" whose very presence was joy and for whom she felt "love and reverence."[189] Emilia and Charles Dilke encouraged and assisted young middle-class women's careers across varied interests; Newnham-educated Mona Wilson was interested in art, Constance Smith a gifted linguist, Florence Routledge an economist, and Gertrude Tuckwell and May Abraham involved in labor issues and—in Gertrude's case, the welfare of children.[190] Tuckwell stressed that the Dilkes gave young women educations in the labor and pleasures of self-transformations that prepared them for responsible entry into public life; the "daughters" of this household were encouraged to be independent and mobile.[191] Wide worlds were open to women who could make themselves public figures, and stasis was a sin. The Dilkes modelled public engagement and hard work rather than ladylike philanthropy and accomplishments, but "Lady Fussie" and Charles Dilke also stressed "the bond between oneself and the world and beauty and knowledge," athleticism, relaxation, talk, and movement across registers. "[L]ife at 76 Sloane Street was a lesson in the art of living," and pleasures were not demeaning frivolities but self-expanding connections.[192]

Emilia Dilke's preachments to other women reiterate the stories of moral action and public responsibility she and Albert Venn Dicey claimed to have learned from Eleanor Smith and belong not to the longer history of bourgeois women's discourses of social housekeeping but to that of cross-gendered middle-class rhetorics of reform. But, as many historians have noted, the late-century movement of middle-class women into education, public activitity, and the emergent professions of social work and welfare was enabled by their construction as authorities on working-class women in particular.[193] The young women Emilia Dilke gave access to public life through the

WTUL are figures in this story, and Dilke's texts and those about her remind us of two central dangers in this longer history. Dilke's story of Emma Smith's encounter with the Women's Suffrage Society shows how working-class women's own speech could be occluded in middle-class organizations, and Dilke's political sermons calling bourgeois women to overcome their socialization and achieve objective knowledge of working-class needs tend to elide the possibility that even well-intentioned and progressive privileged women reformers were implicated in class hierarchy. A microcosm of the emergence of social reform activity as a field of middle-class female employment can be seen in Emilia Dilke's history as an employer. The women Dilke employed as secretaries for herself and the WTUL were overwhelmingly middle-class, although the League did also recruit and sustain working-class women as organizers, and Margaret Bondfield, a former shop assistant, and Annie Marland-Brodie were members of the Dilkes' London circle as well as respected trade-unionists.[194] When looking for a new League secretary in 1903, Dilke said she wanted not a proper lady but someone with the ability to "rouse" a crowd, but Mary Macarthur, who got the job and could rouse with the best, was a petit-bourgeois draper's daughter who was converted to passionate trade-unionism and socialism by the men attempting to organize her father's employees.[195]

Emilia Dilke's trade-union texts and practices also exhibit more complicated dangers. The story of the women factory inspectors disturbingly replays Dilke's story of Emma Smith and the suffrage society. In 1885 the Trades Union Congress capitulated to the League's repeated demands and began including calls for women inspectors in its agitation for increased factory inspection; the first were May Abraham and Mary Paterson of Glasgow in 1893. Emilia Dilke pressed H. H. Asquith to appoint ever more women inspectors, and when Lucy Deane was appointed in 1894, the Dilkes held a celebration at 76 Sloane Street.[196] But Mary Drake McFeely has found that when Emilia Dilke considered the possibility of pushing working-class women as the first inspectors and had "one or two to stay with her" at Sloane Street to appraise them, she found the candidates lacking in preparation, especially in "tact," "initiative," experience in "office work," and report writing. Dilke ended by pushing for the appointment of highly trained middle-class women. Emilia Dilke may have insisted that young middle-class women work very hard, preparing themselves throroughly in all the fields their work would require, including "Applied Mechanics," but she implicitly denied working-class women's capacity to learn the job.[197] Middle-class women should use their class privileges—education and social confidence—in strenuously useful ways, but Dilke simply, if sadly, sent working-class women back whence they came. Whatever the strengths or weaknesses of the particular candidates, this story exhibits the creation of new and satisfying jobs for middle-class women on behalf of and in place of working-class women, jobs that demanded "style" and cultural capital in which working-class women were found lacking.

I earlier suggested a second tension in Emilia Dilke's trade-unionist texts. Dilke's speeches and writings tend to assert the desirability for working-class women of class loyalties and affiliations—which are often contrasted to irresponsible or misguided individualism. This emphasis, right or wrong, is quite different from the arguments about self-development she offers middle-class women. In Dilke's rhetoric, while trade unions offer material and social benefits for women and are a morally laudable form of self-preservation, working women are also consistently implored to join unions as an advancement of a greater good and as a specifically feminine familial responsibility. In Dilke's speeches to working-class audiences, women's trade-unionism is often explicitly cast as a form of solidarity with working men and a realization of family ties. "Loyal support to your union . . . constant support" would "protect . . . [your]selves [and] the future of your children," and not joining a union betrays working-class men by allowing employers to pay lower wages.[198] An 1891 essay asks, "How can we blame the mother who . . . sells her labour cheap? Yet that is what we must do, for we have to tell her that in accepting less than a fair day's wage for a fair day's work she is betraying her own interests, the interests of her husband, and the interests and future of her children . . . 'Women,' we say, 'unite, combine, help your men to protect themselves and you. You will make things a little better for yourselves and . . . a great deal better for the children who shall rise up to call you blessed.' "[199] A late speech summoned men and women alike to enter on a "new crusade" in trade-unionism, to "preserve to the nation all that is noble in human life" and to "deliver the sacred city of the spirit from captivity to the heathenish conditions of modern industry" by creating a future in which "men [can] be men . . . [and] women women. . . ."[200]

Pattison/Dilke's position on the vexed issue of protective legislation was far from stable, but even when opposing legal limits on women's employment her arguments often depend on the family. Although other feminists opposed legislation by making claims about women as economic individuals, one Dilke text opposes one proposal because it will "inflict evils far deadlier to the woman *and the family* than it can possibly cure." Another text is Ruskinian, invoking women's natural "place at the hearth" and wishing for a world of women's "entire relegation to her natural and sacred sphere of home, to the fulfilment in blessed leisure of her natural and sacred functions of mother and wife," even as it opposes legislation that forcibly excludes women from the marketplace.[201] In addition, although Dilke's texts and the policies of the League also and often stressed the necessity of working-class women's access to public speech, the WTUL's policy under Dilke of emphasizing bonds between women trade-unionists and their male counterparts, however strategic and beneficial, tended to silence discussions about whether working-class women's interests might sometimes conflict with men's.[202]

Dilke's implied theory of social reform is thus bifurcated: voluntaristic for middle-class women and naturalizing for working-class women.[203] This division is visible in an 1890 appeal for support for the women matchbox makers of Shoreditch by Emilia Dilke. A letter to *The Speaker* recounts a meeting held by the WTUL at Holy Trinity Church. Dilke stresses the long hours and low wages of the women workers and the traces of labor on their bodies, and depicts a Christian inversion of social hierarchy as the Church members "moved from table to table waiting on these slaves of labour . . . our guests," but she also carefully notes that, although many were illiterate, "some . . . were women of considerable intelligence and ability."[204] Dilke's appeal for middle-class people to help the WTUL organize a union emphasizes that volunteers must bring skills as well as virtue to the job: "patience," "time," "attention," "punctual and orderly habits," an understanding of "the details of carrying on a small business," and "a clear head and a clear tongue," in order to teach working-class women "so that in due time they may themselves conduct their own affairs." The capacity of working-class women and the inadequacy of middle-class kindliness alone is stressed, but nonetheless, middle-class and working-class women are positioned differently in relation to the claims of others. Working-class women should form unions—in which they will be "educated" and gain an "interest in life" as well as material benefit—not only for themselves but for their "pinched and white-faced children." Middle-class women are instructed by Dilke that their ability to cloyingly and demeaningly appeal to working-class women's loyalty to their families is the test of their own moral capacity: "do you feel that you can, without flinching, lay your arm about the shoulders of one of these soiled waifs of our civilization and say, as a friend might, 'Well, dear, and what does your man do?' " Trade-unionism and social reform rest on middle-class women's ability to imagine themselves outside their or-dinary responses, to "forget the rags, the dirt, the possible degradations of mind and body," so that they can successfully appeal to working-class women to respect and maintain their responsibilities to children and husbands. Middle-class women require "experience and training," and working-class women will gain the ability to "conduct their own affairs" in time, but the achievement of a "brighter future" depends on a class-differentiated allocation of transcendence or fulfillment of assigned identities.[205]

Emilia Dilke's 1889 essay on missionary activity in India also divides women into two categories: those who can, through strenuous efforts, place themselves outside inherited prejudices and loyalties, and those inextricably and properly bound to ex-isting social solidarities. Dilke's text narrates her movement from a position of dislike for missionaries founded in her family's imperial culture—a "prejudiced" view pro-duced by "the accidents of early association, the chances of relationship"—to an appreciation of the value and selflessness of missionary efforts, especially those of women medical missionaries. This text too tells a story of an individual's self-detachment from culturally constructed beliefs to a chosen and educated revision. Like her trade-union texts, it self-congratulatorily emphasizes that people like the mission-aries and herself had engaged in difficult learning, relentless study, humility, and "painful and weary labours." Reformers are shaped by conscious and unconscious prejudices but can overcome them. However, Dilke praises her missionary informants for refusing to allow Hindu women to convert to Christianity against family oppo-sition: "dangerous revolt against sacred family laws" is discouraged and Indian women are counselled to submit and stay put in the relationships they inherit.[206] Indian women are not only made by their cultures but are morally obligated to remain in obedience to them; transcendence of one's given position through imaginative intellectual and ethical engagement with difference is the privilege of white men and women.[207] Bourgeois white people are capable of and obligated to undertake self-transformations which in working-class women and colonial subjects would constitute breaches of powerful and natural ethical ties.

In chapter 1, I argued that in Emilia Dilke's "The Outcast Spirit" and her tale of Kitty Davis, class and mothers were knotted together, and that the apparent inextri-cability in these texts of stories about mothers and stories about class conveys a history. Class, gender, and family relationships *were* indisseverably bound in the nineteenth century. Resolving those texts into a single claim—that Dilke's class politics shaped her view of mothers or that her views of Emily Weedon Strong affected her class politics—would obscure that larger history. Similarly, in considering these texts about trade unions and missionaries, my goal is not to show that Emilia Dilke was, as an individual, myopic about working-class women or colonial subjects and that these myopias mar her politics. A larger history is visible here, too: Dilke's language of familial and moral responsibility for working-class women overlapped with powerful and ethically complex working-class political discourses; trade-unionist agitations also appealed to men's family responsibilities and stressed the labor movement's moral bases in families, communities, and localities. But the pattern of bifurcation in Emilia Dilke's texts does complicate conclusions about the political valencies of Francis Pattison's enactments of self-transformation.

The limited availability of self-transformation in Dilke's texts reminds us that, while Francis Pattison's apparent "self-fashioning" may display and have been glamorously energized by powerful currents of theatricality in Victorian culture, and Pattison/ Dilke's intellectual works can be read as gesturing toward the emergence of intellectual projects and subcultural styles laden with transgressive theories and politics, neither Mrs. Pattison's enactments nor Pattison/Dilke's art history were politically unambiguous. However legible to radical readings, Mrs. Pattison's figures did not constitute a theory and a politics. Performing femininity, nationality, and class in transparently artificial ways may imply that identity is a system of arbitrary, and mockable, significations, but the history of middle-class women's movement into professional social reform, as well as Emilia Dilke's dismissal of some women's capacity for or right to self-transformation, reminds us that unequal access to resources, material and historical differences of position, privilege and experience, and powerful structures of prestige and exclusion, are not magicked away by masquerade. If Francis Pattison's performances in Oxford can be read as denaturalizing class, gender, and nation, naturalizations and fixities return in other texts she wrote and spoke, especially when speaking of others. Retrieving the texts that represent Francis Pattison's activities and embodiments in Oxford as a critique of structures of class and gender would be wishfully misguided if, in attempting to locate temporary resistances, we neglect overarching institutional and discursive powers.

Another Dilke text about a picture condenses this chapter. Charles Dilke recounts, "Once when we were in Paris and had seen Sarah Bernhardt in a male part, Lady Dilke could not sleep until she had disposed of her impression and dispelled nightmare by a sketch."[208] The collapse of stable systems of oppositions generates outright anxiety. The "nightmare" is of a woman playing a man who was yet always known as a woman and whose performative self transcended any single role—a woman famous for dramas on and off stage and who was inscribed in a multitude of sexual stories. The Divine Sarah, also French/not French, in a trouser part through whose masquerade one was meant to see and yet in which one was meant to believe, worked the same terrain as Francis Pattison had done in the texts of her Oxford contemporaries— playing herself and other, enacting, embodying, and escaping identity—and, in Charles Dilke's account, produced a necessity to project an internal vision of fear outward. In this anecdote, the fearful is both produced and contained. The limits of Emilia Dilke's individualism when discussing working-class and colonial subjects shows another containment of the implications of style. Francis Pattison may, in the texts of observers, appear as a woman acting as if birth and body were not self, as if one need not stay where one was put, as if choices are revocable and one might change and change again, but her own texts do not consistently offer these discourses as available and desirable. Another containment is also evoked in Charles Dilke's story of Emilia Dilke's caricature. Whether displaying the transgressive possibilities of Victorian femininities or producing anxious renaturalizations, the texts that describe Francis Pattison in Oxford shift visual spectacle into memorializing words about an irrecuperable past and make her into anecdotes about an exceptional individual, eccentric to official Oxford history. Gertrude Tuckwell tells us that Charles Dilke claimed "whenever any difficulty occurred to [Emilia Dilke] . . . she wove it into a story and so cleared . . . anxiety away."[209] The sometimes snarling, sometimes tempted, but mostly unread texts that retain traces of "That Woman" preserve images of an exceptional individual, but they may be the equivalent of Emilia Dilke's fictions and her Bernhardt—vivid sketches that dispel "nightmare."

In E. F. S. Pattison's history, images tell only partial tales of lost or misplaced works: "We are . . . obliged to summon to our aid such drawings as were executed while [Goujon's] work was still in place, and taking them in conjunction with detached fragments, reconstitute a shattered moment, in idea for ourselves."[210] Francis Pattison's performances vanished when she left Oxford to become Emilia Dilke, a legally constituted rather than simply performed Lady. Mrs. Pattison's "famous" salon, parties and scholarship, like her French cigarette smoke, disappeared from official Oxford history, just as other women in Oxford evaporated from the official histories and public exhibitions of heritage in the institutions in and against which they lived. I have not offered these pictures and stories of Francis Pattison in Oxford to stabilize and retrieve a lost heroine of feminism, let alone a queerly theoretical postmodernist *avant la lettre*. But how these stories and images haunt Oxford, and how they are contradicted or complicated by other stories about other people in other places, relays historical meanings. We can borrow an image from one of Francis Pattison's Oxford contemporaries. The Reverend Charles Dodgson observed that Francis Pattison "acted very fairly" in her French amateur theatricals. Her images hang in the texts of her erstwhile audiences like the Chesire cat's smile: unframed, brief, ambiguous.[211]

6

FRENCH VICES

In January 1895, Oscar Wilde's Mrs. Cheveley, in his newly opened play, *An Ideal Husband*, told a politician, "Nowadays . . . everyone has to pose as a paragon of purity, incorruptibility, and all the other seven deadly virtues—and what is the result? You all go over like nine pins—one after the other. Not a year passes in England without somebody disappearing. Scandals used to lend charm, or at least interest to a man—now they crush him." Mrs. Cheveley was retrospective as well as prescient. Through the late nineteenth century, a series of highly mediated but detailed scandals, causes célèbres, and exposés permitted diverse constituencies to struggle over the construction of meaningful stories about bodies and danger.[1] The 1885–1886 divorce case of *Crawford v. Crawford and Dilke* shares with other scandals a great mixing and competition of narratives in court, press, and street, which revealed and contributed to class and gender tensions. The divorce court, like the courtroom in murder trials, was a space of sociosexual spectacle, promising access to the secrets of sex and marriage.[2] In retrospect, Charles Dilke's fate appears a rehearsal for Charles Parnell's, especially since their two cases were heard by the same judge, but each of the famous cases of the 1880s displayed tensions and possibilities differently. The Colin Campbell case of 1886 produced a vivid spectacle of upper-class male degeneracy, the "Maiden Tribute" exposé incited anxieties about childhood and class, and the Cleveland Street scandal combined male homoeroticism with the secrets of aristocracy. In the Parnell case, gender and sexual ideology were most overtly harnessed to national and international politics, but all these cases show the imbrication of gender and sexual ideologies with other politics, and all drew on the versatile generic language of melodrama, of guilt and innocence, villainy and victimization.[3] In and beyond the truth-seeking theatricality of the courtroom, stories multiplied.

Judith Walkowitz has characterized the 1880s as marked by "middle-class women's forceful entry into the world of publicity and politics, where they claimed themselves as part of a public that made sense of itself through public discourse," especially in campaigns of opposition to varied forms of sexual danger.[4] Women were at the center of plots detailed in the cases of the 1880s—in public and on view, but women were not only actors in suddenly public domestic dramas. They were also active audience members. Although, at first glance, Emilia Dilke inhabits the margins of this chapter and the sidelines of the "Dilke case"—centerstage was famously occupied by Virginia Crawford—in becoming "Lady Dilke," Emilia Pattison entered upon a second career as a "character" in novels, theatre, newspapers, gossip, and law, and her figure performed in a proliferation of dramas, variously staged as tragedy, comedy, melodrama, morality play, and farce. As in Oxford, audiences engaged in interpretive labor, off-stage action was retold in different voices, and the private was made public—this time on a grander scale, as claims and stories told in the courtroom were retold by a press whose members were also actors and whose accounts were redeployed in further enactings, reviews, and interpretations.

The struggle over narratives of the Crawford divorce case has not ceased in the twentieth century; it tends to devour the histories in which it is embedded. Charles Dilke's authorized biography by Gertrude Tuckwell and Stephen Gwynn carefully avoids direct mention of the scandal, but Roy Jenkins gave it titular status in both editions of his modern biography: *Sir Charles Dilke. A Victorian Tragedy* and *Victorian Scandal: A Biography of the Right Honourable Gentleman Sir Charles Dilke*. (The post-Profumo paperback of *Victorian Scandal* featured a "bodice-ripper" cover illustration). Betty Askwith devotes five of twenty-one chapters of her biography of Emilia Dilke to the case.[5] The political uses of recounting the case are demonstrated by Jenkins, who made the case the occasion of a threnody on the lost possibilities of Liberalism, and by Conservative M.P.s Enoch Powell and Robert Rhodes James in their biographies of Joseph Chamberlain and Lord Rosebery, respectively, and the case has been mentioned as a precedent in conjunction with more recent sexual revelations about highly visible politicians like Alan Clarke.[6] Charles Dilke makes an unbilled guest appearance as the very type of the male seducer endowed with Svengalian powers of suggestion in a 1922 account of the "brides in the bath" murderer.[7] In its own time, the case occupied hundreds of newspaper accounts, was the subject of popular ballads and jokes as well as more formal political and moral invocations, and is recalled in memoirs by descendents and friends of the principals.[8]

Marie Belloc Lowndes wrote in 1928, "I feel certain that some day if a great novelist of the stature of Thackeray got hold of the [case's] story, a very wonderful novel might be made of it, or a play."[9] While the stature of the writers may not have attained Lowndes's standards, several writers had already contemplated or carried out overt fictionalizations by the time of her writing and more have followed. The first fictionalization, Hector Malot's sensational pro-Dilke roman-à-clef, *Vices Français*, barely bothers to dissemble about its relation to the case; the novel's pirated English version, *Josey*, shows Virginia Crawford, in riding togs and holding a crop, in its frontispiece.[10] In the twentieth century, Betty Askwith's 1960 novel of the case, *The Tangled Web*, preceded her life of Emilia Dilke. The case has inhabited real as well as metaphorical theaters. A French producer provoked Emilia Dilke to worry about a proposed stage version of *Vices Français*, and William Archer also considered the case's dramatic possibilities.[11] Michael Dyne-Bradley's *The Right Honourable Gentleman* had a successful run in the mid-1960s; the case has twice been made into television films; in these productions, the "characters" appear under their "real" names.[12] The case also has its place in the canon of Victorian scandals organized around the predictable (and often pornographic) binarism of "Victorian prudery" versus "secret lives," in compendia of examples with titles like *Society Sensations*; a recent witty and enjoyable fiction in this genre, John Duigan's 1994 film *Sirens*, contains a Charles Dilke joke.[13] But the logic of repression versus license does little to illuminate the case's gendered stories and their historical efficacies, especially because, in modern recastings, the feminist and class politics of the trials are largely absent; Dyne-Bradley's play, for example, vaguely alludes to Lady Dilke's "noble" concern for working-class women.[14] More complex and ambitious class and gender politics were central to the original enactment of the case and the contests over its meaning, but the theatrical history of the case, like the histories of debate about *Middlemarch* and the Pattisons, contains the case in the category of puzzles and unsolved mysteries.

The "truth" never clearly emerged in court and has not emerged since, despite some highly motivated efforts. I will not solve the mystery here either. Just as the stories of possible adultery I told in chapter 4 are inadequately understood if reading is undertaken as code-breaking for sexual secrets, approaching the Crawford case as a sexual mystery to be solved is inadequate for a historical narrative that aspires to be more than soap opera. Moving the case out of the history of prurient tales and unsolved mysteries, I focus on the competition and indisseverability of gender and class in the politics of Radical virtue. Refusing to find a hero, heroine, or villain, a heroic or tragic story, I emphasize how narrative plots and conspiratorial plots entwined in competing social discourses and political movements.[15] I begin, however, after sketching the story whose telling set events in motion, by showing how the case produced an invigorating new marriage story for Emilia Pattison. I then recount the legal proceedings and examine the stories of sexual danger and sexual agency produced by "anti-Dilkeites" and "pro-Dilkeites." I then read some other late-Victorian stories that both repudiate and reinscribe the case as a story of sex, class, and gender, stories in which Emilia Dilke's figure is surprisingly vital. Roy Jenkins's subtitle situated the case as a "Victorian tragedy"; I end by offering some comic endings instead.

Marriage Stories

No story of the case can be separated from a mesh of competing narratives. No official transcript of the full court proceedings survives, and the published records that purport to be verbatim accounts conflict with each other and declare their allegiances openly.[16] Competing stories laid claim to different audiences, and the "facts" sometimes seem very well scripted.[17] On the evening of 17 July 1885, Virginia Mary Smith Crawford was confronted by her husband, Donald Crawford, M.P., who had just received another in a series of anonymous letters; this one read "Fool, looking for the cuckoo when he has flown, having defiled your nest. You have been vilely deceived but you dare not touch the real traitor."[18] Crawford testified in court that after reading this letter, he went to his wife's bedroom, where she was waiting for him. He said he read her the letter and asked, "Virginia, is it true that you have defiled my bed? I have been a faithful husband to you." He said that Mrs. Crawford said it was true, but he had previously suspected innocent men; he "had never suspected the person who was guilty ." Crawford replied that he had suspected only "Captain Forster"; Virginia Crawford responded, "It is not Captain Forster. The man who ruined me was Charles Dilke."[19]

All the principal middle-class characters of the unfolding drama inhabited a dense world of bourgeois familial and political ties in which sexual secrets circulated well before their airing in open court. At the time of Mrs. Crawford's confession, which was followed in Donald Crawford's account by many more details, the couple had been married for five years; Donald was twenty-two years Virginia's senior. The Crawford and Dilke families were bound by a thick web of familial, political, and social ties. Charles Dilke and Donald Crawford were both Liberal M.P.'s, as was Virginia's father, Thomas Eustace Smith, an immensely wealthy Newcastle shipbuilder. Virginia Smith Crawford was one of nine surviving children, including six daughters; Virginia was the fourth daughter, and Charles Dilke's brother, Ashton, had been married to Maye Smith, Virginia's elder sister. Ashton Dilke died in 1883, but Charles remained in contact with his widowed sister-in-law, her young children, and the Smith clan. Maye Dilke was also active in Liberal feminist and suffage political circles.[20]

Virginia Crawford's and Maye Dilke's mother, Mary Dalrymple Smith, was also linked to Charles Dilke and Emilia Pattison by shared social and intellectual milieux and mirrorings. The daughter of a Scottish officer, Mrs. Eustace Smith was rich in her own right because her father made her co-heir to his fortune. She was granted a character as an extremely worldly woman by her descendants, who depicted her as ambitious for her family's social and political connections in London and anxious for her daughters' marriages. According to her granddaughter, Marion Rawson, Mary Dalrymple Smith presented her daughters on the marriage market one at a time and "they were expected to accept the first proposal of marriage made to them." Virginia had refused two men, and her mother "shut her up in her bedroom on bread and water" when she initially refused Donald Crawford. Rawson claimed Mrs. Eustace Smith "was determined that Virginia should marry a middle-aged man who would ride her on a tight rein."[21] Mrs. Eustace Smith was also, in several senses, a figure in London art circles. She chose to be known as "Eustacia" instead of Mary and took up a role as patroness and aesthetician in London, decorating the Smiths' Prince's Gate home in "the apotheosis of Aesthetic style," with dramatic black-and-gold drawing room walls painted by Frederic Leighton (of whom E. F. S. Pattison wrote a brief biography); her boudoir's walls were red with a frieze of cockatoos by Walter Crane. She favored meaning-laden Pre-Raphaelite images of women on her walls, including a Rossetti "Pandora" and G. F. Watts's "The Wife of Pygmalion." Like Francis Pattison in Oxford, she was depicted, verbally and visually, as presenting herself as an eroticized artistic object. Leighton painted a portrait of her in high aesthetic costume, but Nathaniel Hawthorne's evocation is the more striking and overtly sexual: "She was dressed this evening in dark blue silk, open in front, but caught together at the throat by an insolent diamond: one thought, Were that clasp to come undone, what an expanse of white loveliness would be revealed! But it held." Leighton and Hawthorne converge on another image: according to Hawthorne, Eustacia had posed for Leighton's nude, "Venus Disrobing," which hung in her drawing room; although she had only offered her naked *feet* as models for the artist, Hawthorne describes the painting as an image of tantalizing and narcissistic femininity. Charles Dilke had frequented Mrs. Eustace Smith's London artistic and social gatherings.[22]

Emilia Pattison probably knew Maye Dilke and perhaps Eustacia Smith; she definitely knew Donald Crawford and his family. Donald had been an undergraduate at Lincoln College, and he, his young wife, and her mother remained friendly with Mark Pattison. If the Crawfords may also have known of the Oxonian scandal surrounding the Pattison marriage (Mark openly deplored his marriage and characterized Charles Dilke as his wife's "fancy-man" in conversation) and Mark's relationship with Meta Bradley, Donald and Virginia Crawford were, in turn, the subject of gossipy speculation between Mark and Meta.[23] Meta characterized Virginia as one who was "very young and ha[d] never felt very much" but "liked her"; Mark replied he too thought Virginia "a child." Both remarked that the Crawfords had little in common, Meta with slight acerbity regarding Donald ("Is Donald at all improved?"), which Mark countered with a homily on the trials of marriage: "from her eagerness to contradict him [Donald], one might infer that there existed . . . a secret antipathy but this she will no doubt get over when she finds that her interests are identified with her husband's, and how necessary it is for a pair to make common cause against the world."[24] This exposition of the doctrine of *feme covert* was a bad prediction on Mark Pattison's part; legal and social changes had created other opportunities for Virginia Crawford. Meta Bradley's account is more interesting: in 1883, she depicted Mrs. Crawford as "a curious mixture of worldliness by education, and straightforwardness by nature. She flirts by night and is most energetic at the east end by day" and regards her mother's censures of her activities as "no business of hers!" Meta concluded, "I shouldn't think Donald saw much of her."[25] However significant their differences, both of these young women depicted themselves as alienated from their families and longing for socially useful work; both were swept into vortices of scandal and fiction. In these similarities, they recall the woman who wrote with fury about both of them.

The news of Mrs. Crawford's accusations, and Donald Crawford's intention of suing for divorce and naming Dilke as corespondent, was brought to Dilke by a mutual friend, Christina Stewart Rogerson, on 19 July 1885. Although the divorce petition was not actually filed until 5 August, rumors were soon heard in London. Dilke, long in the ascendant in the Liberal Party, had recently triumphed in drafting legislation for the redistribution of parliamentary seats and remained in the spotlight through his position as chair of the Royal Commission on the Housing of the Working Classes; he was seen by some as Gladstone's likely successor, an outcome predicted by Disraeli and Gladstone.[26] And of course, at the time of Mrs. Crawford's confession, Dilke's "secret" engagement—far less secret than the principals thought—to Emilia Pattison was nearing consummation at last; Mark Pattison's death had intensified gossip in Oxford and London.

Emilia Pattison's texts of this time include anxieties about the shape of the story a new marriage would bring. When Virginia Crawford confessed, Mrs. Pattison was spending a discreet year of mourning in India with friends, drafting *Art in the Modern State* and revising the stories of marriage, imprisonment, and death that became *The*

Shrine of Death and Other Stories.[27] *The Shrine of Death* and *Art in the Modern State* deal with confinement and the struggles of creative and sensitive minds; both are readable as a psychological working-through of Francis Pattison's first marriage. This reading is apparently ratified by a letter to Charles Dilke, replying to an expression of concern about the pain in her stories; he need not worry; "all these were made long ago but to have written them out then wld have made me too miserable I can afford to write them out *now!*"[28] But there are less-finished narratives in Emilia Pattison's letters to Charles Dilke from this period, narratives that consider the risks of reentering marriage and the status of marriage in relation to institutions of public prestige and social and political power. The eruption of the Crawford divorce scandal interrupted and recontextualized these Dilke marriage plots.

Emilia Pattison's letters to Charles Dilke at first took considerable pains to reassure him of her "courage" and returning strength after the strain of Mark Pattison's final illness and the disposition of his property. She insists from the Red Sea that the southern heat has worked its usual magic on her; "in this bright sun as my strength returns my courage comes back & smiles spring up . . . instead of sad yearnings & the sense of heartbreak."[29] She worried about her inability to assimilate her experiences ("It is so strange, I can't feel that this is part of my life") and echoed her assertions to Mark Pattison that she is simply too sensitive, her nerves too exposed ("I suppose everything impresses me very keenly that impresses me at all"). But she reassures Charles that he is her link to life ("Sometimes I feel as if, were it not for you, I shld have been carried off by fairies & even here its so unreal"). She has been a sleeping beauty, but Charles offers a life in a new story: "its like dreamland & it seems as if you had to come to wake me."[30] Emilia cautions Charles against thinking her an invalid—"I feared you had made me too nervous by being nervous for me that I shld have lost my pluck"—and asserts her physical vitality: a good horse ride had put in her "tremendous spirits," she looks forward to fencing with him, is "constantly stimulated & excited by the very newness of scenes & people & . . . [with an] hourly increasing buoyancy of spirits." Invoking their shared youth, a letter assures Charles and herself that despite "these many long years," he is not marrying a "jaded" or "tired" woman; "my old high spirits come back & make a child of me."[31]

Emilia Pattison's letters also develop a story about fear. At first blaming some of her depression on domestic tensions between her hosts, the Governor of Madras, Mountstuart Grant-Duff and his wife Julia (known as "Venetia" to her friends) Emilia's letters nonetheless broach the subject of her "terror of ties and [rasura: of] obligations wh the past has left upon [her]." These fears "fall on [her] sometimes like a black cloud," although she quickly asserts her confidence that they will disappear once they are married. Although she immediately backpedalled ("it seems wicked even to feel for an instant what I wrote . . . you will know that it is not cannot be felt as 'a tie' with you"), she reiterates that her first marriage has left scars on her. "I did not know how dreadful my life was till now when the re-action has made itself fully felt," she reveals, "there come moments of passionate horror & loathing & a frantic fear of chains wh at the instant leaves no room for any other feeling." Emilia Pattison's letters return to confinement and emotional extremity; another letter figures her as a suffering animal, "a creature at bay."[32]

Emilia Pattison's letters also depict her as strained by misgivings about her future status. She will be married to a man whom the world considered her superior; she worries about being Sir Charles Dilke's socially inferior mate in the glittering political *monde* of London.³³ Charles casts her fears as partly due to the relative haste of their engagement, the long-standing gossip about them, and the inevitable publicity that will attend their wedding.³⁴ Emilia alludes to Charles's reputation as a high flyer and "a man 'eaten up' . . . 'by political ambition,' " and frets that malicious gossip will make their marriage a political mistake for Charles; others will deride her as "a woman who don't bring great connection or great fortune . . . an impossibly bad match." As if disavowing earlier masquerades of aristocracy, her text moves to self-reassurance that their true friends will recognize their marriage as "decreed in heaven," but still, "outside . . . people see the great [Zz] & the little person of no importance in their world!" Grateful though she is that "[Charles] give[s her] . . . all the world prizes most," and no matter how much more important their love is than the "world's" opinion, she wishes more people would see that "even from the world's point of view" she was not an insignificant person.³⁵ In one letter, her returning "child-like" high spirits are transformed from evidence of her health into a worry that she will seem underbred:

> Dear, there is one thing I am really a little afraid of that is that you will think my manners, now I am happy, too gay. When I have knocked off two or three hours work & go out of my rooms to the others I am as lighthearted as a child—all the house feels it . . . yet I check myself sometimes with the sense that if you were here the laughter & the play wld not quite please you.

The letter goes on to defend Emilia Pattison's right to express her "true" and inherent self ("but it is *me* & its *natural*") and to claim that her unconventionality has its rewards; "it is what gives me (coupled with tact) *social success*."³⁶

If Emilia Pattison's letters worried about her ability to transform her romance with Charles Dilke into a marriage of partnership, Virginia Crawford's allegations rapidly shifted the plot to one in which she could be a heroine. Instead of the recipient of a superior man's favor, Emilia Pattison became the embodiment of strength and giver of resources to a man in need. The melodramatic circumstance in which she heard of the catastrophe fostered this plot; she was recovering from a bout of typhoid fever that followed closely upon nervous prostration caused by the accidental death of an officer she knew.³⁷ Details of the allegations were telegraphed to India by Joseph Chamberlain at Charles's bequest; Charles himself wrote offering her freedom and despairing of any good outcome. "You may be ill when you get my telegrams,—and they may kill you! I don't think ever man was so unhappy as Zz . . ." Charles Dilke represented himself as "broken down" by the letter and by Emilia's illness and lacking the strength to fight the charges; he also attributed his prostration at Mrs. Crawford's allegations in part to his having for several years received other anonymous letters threatening his career with vague intimations of sexual scandal; he implied a longer story of persecution in which the adultery charge could take its place.³⁸ Charles Dilke's first letter to Emilia Pattison also oscillates between despair for himself and for Mrs. Pattison—"they will have dragged yr name in some foul way & that wd have killed me." But Charles Dilke's figurations of Emilia Pattison in his letter, despite his textual horror at the besmirching of her reputation and his offers to release her, return to assertions of her nobility and his trust in her love. Indeed, his attestations of trust in Mrs. Pattison's loyalty would have been difficult for her to betray; he represents his life as dependent on her. "The only thing I can do in future is to dedicate my life entirely to you . . . I fancy you will have the courage to believe in me, whatever is by madness and malevolence brought against me, & to live a life-long exile with me, wh *if you can do at all* will be a dream of happiness."[39]

In reply, Emilia Pattison wired her faith in him and sent a telegram to the *Times* announcing their engagement; this was published on 18 August.[40] Charles Dilke continued to shower letters upon her in India and at every stage of her return voyage, and laud her "pure faith" in him, like that of "one of our Ruskin heroines or Shakespeare." His letters express fear for her health, despair for the future—"tho I am in despair about you & feel as thos I were killing you, I can't kill myself because of you"—and faith in her love and courage.[41] Dilke found in early August the perfect indirect language for their relationship: the French of Madame de Staël. "These Mme de Staël things . . . are my consolation at this moment, because the pictures & these & *your Ruskin* together . . . are all I have till I hear from you or see you . . ." Page upon page of transcriptions follow, ending "Please Hoya read this: . . . *tout est sacrifié tout est oublié de soi dans le dévouement exalté de l'amour, tout est bonté tout est pitié dans l'être qui sait aimer.*"[42] Emilia's letters to Charles, Joseph Chamberlain, and Ellen Smith respond to Charles's need and faith, depicting her as overcoming physical weakness nearly instantly. Indeed, the Dilkes later claimed typhoid "cured" her of the "arthritic gout" which had necessitated her absences from Oxford.[43] Her letters written from the ship on her return voyage are full of energy and create an image of Mrs. Pattison standing at the ship's prow, pushing against the railing to impel it to go faster. Charles Dilke met Emilia Pattison in Paris in September; they were married on 3 October in Chelsea.

If Emilia Dilke moved out of *Middlemarch* with her second marriage, the air of sexual scandal that clung to Charles Dilke invites the suggestion that she had moved from the Reverend Doctor Edward Casaubon to Mr. Rochester. The Dilkes and several of their allies during and after the Crawford case were therefore careful to replot the Dilke marriage as an act of courageous generosity on Emilia Pattison's part rather than the consummation of a long-secret affair. This marriage story would not only deflect older rumors about their relationship but ward off potentially costly implications that Charles Dilke was sexually guilty with anyone. Shortly before his marriage, Charles wrote Maye Ashton Dilke, positioning the timing of his planned marriage as at least partly political: "Chamberlain . . . thinks that if Mrs. Pattison & I believe that there is any chance at all of future happiness . . . it shd be marriage soon rather than . . . later." Depicting the marriage as the result of "27 years of friendship," Charles then simply lies: "we have not been, till this happened, writing very fully of late."[44] Gertrude Tuckwell reiterated this version of the Dilke marriage; Emilia married Charles when the divorce scandal broke, "with the idea that she could throw the protective shield of her love and loyalty round a man whom she had known as a boy," surely a selfless act.[45] J. E. C. Bodley also cast "Sir Charles" and "Mrs. Mark Pattison" as longtime friends whose marriage was precipated by Emilia's "hop[e] that by marrying Dilke she could clear his name."[46] The possibility of sexual love and a preexisting relationship during Mark Pattison's life is carefully avoided.

The Case in Court

The case of *Crawford v. Crawford and Dilke* opened in the Divorce Court on 12 February 1886; the evidence occupied only a single morning. Mrs. Crawford did not appear in court and the case was undefended on her part. On the advice of his counsel, Dilke did not enter the box; the judge concurred with this decision on the grounds that Mrs. Crawford's unsworn statement of having committed adultery with him was un-supported and "not entitled to be received or even considered in a Court of Justice," that is, an unsworn statement admitting to adultery without any further evidence meant there was no case for Charles Dilke to answer.[47] The judge therefore dismissed Dilke from the case and ordered Crawford to pay his costs. However, he granted Crawford a divorce. The fact that the judge granted Crawford a divorce on the grounds that his wife had committed adultery, but that he found no evidence Dilke had com-mitted adultery with her (and Donald Crawford had cited no other corespondents) made possible the agitation that followed. Moreover, despite the brevity of the trial, the details of Mrs. Crawford's adultery in Donald Crawford's retelling contributed to the continued life of the case.

Donald Crawford testified that Virginia Crawford had claimed Dilke had approached her with seduction in mind during her honeymoon, consummating the liaison some months later in a house off the Tottenham Court Road. Donald Crawford said Virginia alleged that she and Dilke met for sexual relations in several houses, including his own, until July 1884, the month of Mark Pattison's death. Virginia Crawford, in Donald Crawford's testimony, also alleged that Dilke had asked her on several occa-sions to take part in a ménage à trois with him and one of the maids, Fanny Grey; this, she said, she finally did. Donald said Virginia said Dilke told her Fanny Grey was also his mistress and used to spend most nights with him. Donald's account of Vir-ginia's story added that Charles Dilke urged her to become friends with Mrs. Rogerson and relayed an implication that Rogerson too had been Dilke's mistress. Before the case reached the court, the Dilkes heard that Virginia Crawford alleged Dilke had also had "unnatural relations" with her brother, but this charge was never made in court.[48]

The lack of clear-cut evidence and of any *positive* verdict in the Crawford-Dilke "case" have assured its long-term survival as a site for fiction and guesswork, but even in the narrowest sense, the legal case was from the beginning a complex of stories. Mrs. Crawford's confession was a highly staged event, played out by theatrical conventions and using stereotypical language, in the anonymous letters and in her confession. In the first trial, Donald Crawford, a lawyer, re-presented her language to the court. He told a complex story of suspicion and denial, but omitted from the narrative any evidence that might blur his own role as wounded husband or link his wife with other men than Dilke.[49] Crawford told the tale as the seduction of an innocent young married woman whose subsequent depravity demonstrated the work-ings of the rather dated "slippery slope" theory of fallen womanhood, in which primary sexual agency was placed in the hands of men and men only, but in which women, once fallen, could only continue to fall. Virginia Crawford, in her husband's testimony, was depicted as helplessly passive under Charles Dilke's influence. Donald Crawford claimed she had admitted that, even while she was making her confession, she should still have to do whatever Dilke wished were he in the room. Of the alleged threesomes, he said she said, "I did not like it at first, but I did it because he wished it. . . . I should have stood on my head in the street if he had told me to do it." In the most memorable line of the trial, Donald Crawford quoted Virginia Crawford presenting herself as Dilke's sexual student: "He taught me every French vice . . . He used to say that I knew more than most women of thirty."[50]

An intriguing and deeply ironic possibility regarding this statement—and an answer to the logical question What does a woman of thirty know? intersects with themes that developed in the case's continued life: Frenchness and the acting of parts. The doubly ventriloquized phrase may be an allusion to Balzac's *La Femme de Trente Ans* (c. 1832), a volume of the *Comédie Humaine*.[51] Balzac's loosely constructed novel concerns a young woman who makes "an early mistake" by marrying a man who causes her intense sexual revulsion and pain; she learns to use illness and her greater intelligence to shield herself from her husband and take part in a wider world of politics. Her first lover's death plunges her into grief and "something of the mortification of the actress cheated of her part," but by the age of thirty, she has become a "beautiful picture . . . a kind of artistic success." Balzac explains: "a woman of thirty has irresistable attractions . . . a woman of thirty knows all that is involved. . . . [she is] armed with experience, forewarned by knowledge . . . she satisfies every demand . . ." Wise, ambitious, clever, she can "play all parts." She understands and manipulates the limits on women's erotic liberties in patriarchal society.[52] But if, in Mrs. Crawford's account, Dilke positioned her as a sexually knowing, mature, and active subject, the narratives she directly told stressed her initial naïveté, ignorance, and continued sexual passivity, and she claimed that, in the courtroom at least, she was not "playing a part."

Another detail in Donald Crawford's retelling of Virginia's "confession" which reiterates Dilke's unnatural lust was her explanation of why Dilke broke off the affair: " 'Oh! I suppose he had had all he wanted of me . . . besides he had made himself ill,' and then she said, 'I dare say he would like to give me a baby,' and then after a pause she added, 'but he always used French letters.' "[53] Combined are the implication that Dilke became ill through sexual overindulgence—invoking a medical discourse that emphasised the dangers of overspending one's vital energies—and a double-edged contraceptive motif. Dilke was guilty either of having allegedly wanted to father a child on another man's wife or of having indulged in nonprocreative sex through the use of a foreign artificiality.[54] In the stories of the case, France did not signify transgressive, stylized, and alluring feminities, as in the texts of Francis Pattison in Oxford, but that feminity's opposite and dangerous double: rapacious, destructive, foreign, and degenerate male sexuality, purportedly embodied in that notorious Francophile, Charles Dilke.

These details, and the apparent lack of resolution in the case, were seized upon by W. T. Stead, editor of the *Pall Mall Gazette*, fresh out of prison from his conviction for the "purchase" of a young girl in his journalistic exposé of child prostitution, "The Maiden Tribute of a Modern Babylon."[55] Presenting himself as interested only in the truth of the case and assuring the Dilkes that he would champion their cause as soon as he was convinced of Charles's innocence, Stead published numerous stories arguing that Dilke's name had not been cleared and he ought not be allowed to act in public life. Stead's publications played up the more sensational details of the case but also argued that Dilke's failure to testify must mean he had something *even worse* than Mrs.

Crawford's allegations to hide. By the end of February 1886, both Dilkes were being denied platforms, even for speaking on matters unconnected with the case.[56]

The second case opened on 16 July 1886 but was not structurally another divorce trial. Instead, the proceedings involved the Queen's Proctor, an officer of the court, reopening the case in order to determine whether or not the first verdict had been wrongly given. According to Gail Savage, the proctorial system was prompted by fears that spouses could collude to obtain divorces by inventing tales of adultery or cruelty or that one partner might obtain a divorce through the presentation of evidence of adultery when he or she was also guilty.[57] In other words, the proctorial system was embroiled in complicated negotiations between its needs to license the telling of multiple, partial stories, and its need to produce "truth" and to secure at least one position of "innocence." The entire court system depended on the telling of stories, and the divorce court relied especially on the elicitation of sexual stories. Yet while the presentation of the most powerfully detailed individual story might assure "victory," narratives that were too smooth, too precisely conjoined with each other, were suspect. Stories should conflict. "Truth" could best emerge through the determination that someone was lying.[58] Further, Savage suggests that the proctorial system was established in reaction to concern at the large number of women filing for divorce. By scrutinizing the evidence in divorce cases more closely, the King's or Queen's Proctor should reduce the sheer number of divorces, which had scandalously exposed the dire state of marital relations, as well as freeing disaffected spouses who were "desirous of forming new engagements."[59] The number of officially credited narratives of bad marriages must be limited by a secondary level of controls in the very system which elicited them, and that control could only be exercised through retelling and rescrutinizing stories.

There were crucial structural differences between the first and second trials. In the second trial, Dilke had no official standing; the official parties to the case were Donald Crawford and the Queen's Proctor, and Dilke's counsel could neither intervene nor cross-examine nor call witnesses.[60] Finally, the burden on the Queen's Proctor was a negative one, to prove Dilke and Virginia Crawford had not committed adultery.[61] (Emilia Dilke furiously wrote Eleanor Smith, "How can anyone prove that he did not [triple underlining] do or say such things—he can only challenge his accuser to prove he did."[62]) Virginia Crawford, put on the stand, proved to be an excellent witness, sticking to and embellishing her earlier story. Although she admitted she had another adulterous relationship—with Henry Forster—this admission tended to confirm her status as truthful on the stand. Dilke, on the other hand, was hesitant and stammering. He, in turn, admitted that he had upon two occasions, in 1868 and 1874—before and after his first marriage—had an adulterous relationship with Mary Eustace Smith, that is, with Virginia Crawford's mother. (In her testimony, Virginia Crawford claimed Dilke had said he was attracted to her because of her resemblance to her mother.[63]) Emilia Dilke was briefly called to testify as to Charles Dilke's whereabouts on a day when Virginia Crawford claimed Dilke was with her having a tryst; Henry Matthews, acting for Crawford, implied in his final speech that Emilia Dilke's evidence was worthless, while in W. T. Stead's printed version of the judge's summing-up, Hannen implied that the degree of familiarity between her and Charles Dilke during Mark Pattison's life was itself a matter of impropriety.[64] Fanny Grey, the maid, was not produced by either side to either confirm or deny her participation in the *ménages à trois*.

In sum, the second trial adduced no new evidence. New statements were made but little corroboration offered by either side. Instead, the issue became one of credibility. The issue that the judge put to the jury drew directly upon sexual ideology; "Which is the more probable," he asked, "that a man should do these things or that a woman should invent them?"[65] The details of Mrs. Crawford's confession, especially what Henry Matthews referred to as the "Frenchified orgie" involving Fanny Grey, were such, he argued, that (English middle-class) female invention was unlikely.[66] In the end, the jury concurred in Donald Crawford's divorce; but as in the first case, the legal form was not that Dilke was found guilty but that he had failed to prove his innocence. The legal waters were also muddied by the possibility that Charles Dilke could now be prosecuted for perjury in his testimony; a conviction would have brought a prison sentence, but the government did not move to such action.[67] The Crown's failure to proceed left the meaning of the first two verdicts available for continued debate.

The Conscience of England Addresses Lawless Lying Lust

The case's stories continued long after the official court proceedings. In their continued struggles over the proper outcome of the Crawford divorce case, Stead and the Dilkes, and their diverse friends and allies, were never simply divided on their versions of the "truth." To a considerable extent, both sides shared a moral and juridical language of guilt and innocence, of evidence and proof, and of sexuality as predation. But circulating uneasily and occasionally surfacing violently throughout these narrations and interpretations of the "case" was a disquieting set of disagreements about the relationship of the politics of sex and gender to other politics.

Stead was particularly concerned to prevent Charles Dilke's return to active politics, while the Dilkes and their allies were vehement that the Crawford case should not prevent his standing for and serving in Parliament. (While Charles Dilke lost his long-held parliamentary seat for Chelsea in the 1886 general election, his loss was probably only slightly attributable to the "Crawford case"; the Liberals lost heavily in London and Dilke lost through a relatively small swing of marginal voters.[68]) Much of the struggle over the meaning and salience of the Crawford divorce case thereafter centered around Dilke's real and perceived desire to reenter national politics. Having rashly stated in 1887 that he would not return to public life until his name had been cleared, Charles Dilke faced the difficulty of explaining to potential supporters and, eventually, voters the meaning of his promise. The Dilkes claimed the publication by an "impartial" investigatory committee of "additional evidence" collected by private detectives and others, which cast doubt on Virginia Crawford's veracity and the verdict, meant Dilke's name was cleared by 1891.[69] This interpretation of the meaning of vindication was not shared by all: numerous late Victorian social reformers, especially women involved in the social purity and suffrage movements, understood the outcome of the trials as having been the conviction of Charles Dilke as guilty and the establishment of Virginia Crawford as his victim.

Virginia Crawford emerged from the divorce case with a surprising new status as a feminist heroine. Her career demonstrates the extent to which sweeping attacks by feminists and others on the sexual double standard created new narrative possibilities for "fallen women," not only as reformed sinners but as victims of male lust. In 1886, Virginia Crawford was notorious for her sexual adventures or victimage, but she became a New Woman saint by converting to Roman Catholicism by 1889 and embarking upon a public career of religion, feminism, and social reform.[70] In Stead's overwrought terms, she was a latter-day incarnation of Elizabeth Gaskell's Ruth, a rescued magdalen, fallen because of a bad upbringing and the predation of an evil man, her repentance demonstrated by her full confession of her sin, and now reborn through her suffering and the kindness and good example of her sisters:

> [H]ere and there among good women she found sympathy and help, and, after a time, she bravely set herself to the almost impossible task of rearing a new and nobler life on the smouldering ruins of her shameful past. Step by step, she toiled onward, out of the darkness into the light, out of the gloom and cynical despair of the atheism in which she had been reared, into the radiance of Christian hope.[71]

Mrs. Crawford's subsequent career also illustrates the increased employment opportunities of the late century. Supporting herself by journalism, first in the *Pall Mall Gazette* but then in the feminist and Catholic presses, Virginia Crawford became deeply involved in Catholic feminist and suffrage organizations and European left-liberal Catholic social reform, wrote on art and literature, edited an anti-fascist newspaper called *People and Freedom* in the late 1920s and early 1930s, and served as a Labour member of Marylebone Borough Council. She did not remarry.[72] The Eustace Smiths and their younger children left England after the scandal to live in Algiers for some years.[73]

Although Virginia Crawford refused to speak publicly of the case in later life, the story she told in court, in which she frankly portrayed herself as fallen, was endorsed and embellished in continuing narratives of the case.[74] Mrs. Crawford's fall resulted neither from direct coercion nor any active desire on her part but from the hypnotic power of male desire itself. This narrative of female sexual victimization did not depend on male violence but on the magical power of male desire. In the second trial, she admitted to a guilty relationship with Henry Forster but remained firm that Dilke was the man who had "ruined her" and set in motion her subsequent conduct. As Henry Matthews orated in court, the first seduction was what counted; "if after that she fell again and again, and forgot her duty to her husband, who is responsible? Why, the man who has destroyed everything that can constitute womanly feeling and womanly chivalry."[75] In discussions of Dilke's purported adulteries he was, although unmarried, more guilty than the women with whom he was implicated; in her own and others' narratives, Virginia Crawford was the object but never the subject of outré sexual desire. She had learned Dilke's lessons and fulfilled his wishes, but her own sexual subjectivity, let alone pleasure, was not only not present—its very absence was invisible.

Henry Matthews had taken care to adduce, in his cross-examination of Charles Dilke, that Dilke had "spent a good deal of time in France" and was "familiar with French habits and ways."[76] Stead suggested Charles Dilke was "one of those men whose vice was not ordinary but abnormal," a man who frequented a specialized house of ill repute run by a "Madame Mourez," and, Stead ritually intoned the magical phrase "French vice" to emphasize the horrors of "unnatural" male desire.[77] This emphasis on the alien quality of Dilke's depravity drew upon the long and rich tradition of British Francophobia, but if "France" and "Frenchness" could operate as protean signifiers for sexuality and otherness in which horror and fascination were entwined, in Stead's obsessive reiteration of charges of Dilke's Franco-eroticism only horror could be avowed.[78] Dilke's crime in subjecting a young woman "to the last outrages of depraved and unnatural vice" was far worse than, for example, Charles Parnell's commonplace adultery since "Mr. Parnell did not initiate Mrs. O'Shea in all the mysteries of 'French Vice'."[79] The "subjection" of Virginia Crawford to Dilke's depraved, Frenchified taste for lesbian eroticism violated the boundaries of class as well; Mr. Parnell had not "force[d] Mrs. O'Shea to endure the humiliation of passing the night with an Irish Fanny."[80] Stead also emphasized Dilke's violations of class lines in a different register; if part of the horror of Mrs. Crawford's seduction was that it brought her to sexual servitude alongside a maid, Stead also melodramatically cast Charles Dilke, a member of the Victorian urban professional gentry, as an aristocratic rake preying upon an innocent girl. Dilke's seduction of Mrs. Crawford was both a violation of her class status and a demonstration of his own illegitimate class power.[81]

Justifications of the sexual double standard had consistently figured men as naturally lustful agents and women as the objects of their predations, but by the 1880s and the 1890s, feminists strongly argued that men could learn to attain women's higher standard of sexual self-control. Feminist and social purity discourses around the Dilke case made Charles Dilke an emblem of unreformed male lust. The proliferation of Charles Dilke's possible victims emphasized his inscription as embodiment of depravity. Accusations and intimations that Dilke had been involved with other servants besides Fanny Grey, including a former housekeeper, floated through the press.[82] Rumors that Dilke had been involved with Christina Rogerson were circulated by the novelist Henry James, among others; in the first trial Donald Crawford had relayed Virginia's implication that Rogerson was an accomplice in her seduction, in a plot resembling Victorian pornography.[83] Charles Dilke's relationship with Mrs. Pattison before her husband's death was vulnerable to suggestions that it constituted another adultery, or that, at the least, the pair had been involved before Mark Pattison's death and had waited impatiently for Mark to die. Even without such supplemental charges, in seducing Virginia Crawford Dilke not only "infinitely degrade[d]" Mrs. Crawford but "cruelly wronged" all women.[84] Stead insisted Charles Dilke was "no longer a mere individual evildoer. He has come to be regarded as the incarnate challenge which a lawless and lying lust addresses to the conscience of England."[85] Dilke's admitted liaison with Mrs. Eustace Smith added horrifying incestuous undertones. The American feminist Woman's Journal (Boston), displaying a fine, free, careless disregard for arithmetic, went so far as to suggest "there was only too much reason to fear" that Virginia Crawford was Dilke's daughter by that liaison, underlining her status as a victim of corrupt patriarchy.[86]

Women's party political organizations, as well as other feminist groups, had become increasingly aggressive in attempting to enforce higher sexual standards on the men whose political careers they supported, emphasizing the indissolubility of public and private life.[87] Not only should men and women be held to the same high standard of chastity, but the violation of such a standard indicated an insufficient dedication to the cause of women's betterment that no other feminist credentials could rectify. The Editor of the *Women's Herald* put it bluntly: Dilke had "grossly insulted all womanhood" and "despite his adherence to the cause of Woman Suffrage" could expect nothing from the feminist women for whom she spoke.[88] Numerous Liberal women's organizations passed resolutions in 1891 affirming their implacable opposition to any candidate whose "private character rests under grave public imputations" and their conviction of the intense danger represented by a man whose election would "not only be gravely injurious to the cause of Liberalism but dangerous to the moral and social interests of the whole nation."[89] A petition circulated by Stead and others was headed "Private Morals and Public Life"; a more specialized "Women's Petition Against Sir Charles Dilke," signed by, inter alia, Millicent Garrett Fawcett, Annie Besant, and Ellice Hopkins, dwelt on the necessity of Dilke's clearing himself of all sexual charges.[90] "Sir C. Dilke and Mr Parnell had forced on the nation the vital question of whether character shall tell in politics or not" and character was measured by adherence to standards of sexual propriety: "All honour . . . to those noble outspoken women who protest against their Liberal cause being represented by either Dilke or Parnell, however great the political abilities of both." [91] The U.S. *Woman's Journal* rhetorically set Dilke the rake against Lady Henry Somerset, the social purity activist; Dilke's attempt at a renewed political career was a bitter illustration of the irony of women's lack of the parliamentary franchise, Dilke's debauchery an ugly contrast to Lady Henry's "ability, philanthropy, and 'large stake in the community.' "[92] Even allies of Dilke found it necessary at times to distance themselves in order to maintain feminist authority; Eliza Orme, editor of the *Women's Gazette and Weekly News*, had to deny rumors that her paper was secretly financed by Dilke.[93]

In 1889, when rumours surfaced that Dilke might stand for Parliament, the Women's Liberal Federation promptly asserted such a candidature could not rely on their support, but in doing so, the WLF displayed the entanglement of gender and class politics in ways their discourse of cross-class social reform could not wholly contain.

> The WLF consists very largely of ladies whose social position renders it impossible for them to recognize, or even in a distant way countenance, a man in Sir Charles Dilke's position. It also consists very largely of those working women who form the backbone and mainstay of England's purity, and who speak with English frankness on questions which are of Public Morality. French vices do not find favour with the women of England.[94]

Liberal "ladies" invoke their own respectability *and* claim to speak for stalwartly moral working women, in a combative rhetoric of feminine or feminist revulsion against un-English male vice. The WLF's statement implies that any working-class woman who does not agree with them is no part of the "backbone of English purity," even as they simultaneously deed the "English frankness" necessary in speaking of "French vice" over to working-class women.[95] As much as in Stead's texts, therefore, the cross-class moral and gender solidarity is both affirmed and undermined. The usefulness of the case as a site for plotting the entanglement of class and gender politics recurred through the following years. Sylvia Pankhurst's history of the suffrage movement

claims that when Charles Dilke introduced a Bill into Parliament for adult suffrage in
1901, not only did some "Suffragists and Suffragettes [treat] the measure as an interloper," a decoy away from a women's suffrage bill (they thought a measure granting women the vote on the same basis as men, i.e.,with a property qualification, stood
a better chance of victory and would be a more direct blow at "the sex barrier"),
but they claimed Dilke "had done it in spite, because some of the suffrage ladies had
reviled him for the divorce case which wrecked his Parliamentary career."[96] Complex
issues of strategy and principle are deflected onto a theory of male perfidy.

Emilia Dilke became the subject of feminist debate because of her association with
the man Beatrice Webb called "that beast."[97] The Women's Liberal Federation's executive committee was split on the issue of allowing her to participate in WLF activities, and as late as 1895 she was denied the right to speak on French art at Toynbee
Hall because of her association with Charles Dilke.[98] Emilia Dilke was thus sometimes
excluded from spaces of feminist comradeship that could sustain activist women, and
her position in feminist circles affected more intimate ties.[99] The case of Constance
Flower, later Lady Battersea, most vividly displays how the feminist politics of the
Dilke case could be played out in personal relations.[100] Constance Flower, Lady Battersea (1843–1931), became a friend of Emilia's during the latter part of her marriage
to Mark Pattison, probably through their shared Continental art affinities and their
mutual friends Theresa Earle and Rhoda Broughton; she and her husband, Cyril, were
among the three or four friends to whom Charles and Emilia confided news of their
engagement before Emilia's trip to India.[101] A daughter of Anthony de Rothschild and
Louise Montefiore and a cousin of Lady Rosebery, Constance de Rothschild was a
member of the rich but still socially insecure English Jewish elite. Although accepted
in high society, especially in Liberal circles and the "Marlborough House set" around
the Prince of Wales to an increasing degree, members of this elite continued to face
not only frequent casual anti-Semitism but, Anthony Wohl argues, rising levels of
vitriolic racialization later in the nineteenth century.[102] Cyril Flower was reportedly a
man of limited political distinction but considerable personal charm, a parliamentary
colleague of Charles who shared artistic interests with Emilia Dilke, and he was noted
for his intense friendships with men and strong personal loyalties.[103] Constance
Flower's loyalty was, however, disseminated across a network of relationships, and
she moved from a position as a staunch supporter (she met Emilia in Paris on her
return from India and accompanied her to her wedding) to a complete break with
the Dilkes.

Constance Flower engaged in public good works and efforts to educate the British
bourgeoisie about the commonalities between Judaism and respectable middle-class
Christianity. She was also active in women's liberal reform activities, such as the
Association of Working Girls' Clubs, the Union of London School Teachers, and visits
to women prisoners. She was involved for some time in the Women's Trade Union
League, contributing fiction to its journal, and in the National Union of Women
Workers, both founded in 1874.[104] E. F. Benson thought Lady Battersea "had a boundless fund of vague goodwill for the world in general" and placed her as a woman of
rather conventional if heartfelt charitable impulses; certainly, her writings on less
fortunate women and her diary are infused with pious philanthropy and admiration
for the social purity branch of the women's movement, especially that of Ellice Hop-

kins.[105] In those feminist and sex-reform circles, Charles and Emilia Dilke were outcasts.[106] Flower's diary for 1885 and 1886, written very selectively and often retrospectively and later "edited," depicts her friendship with the Dilkes as a site of a
struggle with her husband over their differing moral standards. Soon after the news
of Donald Crawford's divorce case broke, Constance fretted that Cyril, loyal to Charles,
was not concerned with "whether he has done right or wrong. Oh the misery of
sin . . ." After the first verdict in January 1886, Constance Flower described a visit by
the Dilkes ("he . . . very uncomfortable, she excited & tearful"), and then announced,
apparently on the basis of these appearances, "I believe him to be guilty [quadruple
underlining]." Constance takes the moral high ground: "Cyril of course takes his part
violently, he seems to me to lose his proper judgement in such cases—makes it all
the harder—more unpleasant for me, as I must stick to what I think right and I will
[triple underlining]."[107] Constance Flower's volte-face demonstrates how anti-Dilke
views might mobilize tropes associating women with upstanding morality against
men's presumed easy acceptance of each other's sexual conduct.

Emilia Dilke figured in W. T. Stead's texts not simply as a loyal if misguided wife
but as a complex and untrustworthy performer of parts. In his 1892 pamphlet *Deliverance or Doom?*, aimed at preventing Charles's reentry into Parliament, Stead produced
an account of an 1886 interview with Emilia Dilke after the first case, when he met
with both Dilkes at their behest. Asserting that he was a seeker of truth hoping to
find Dilke innocent, Stead's text first relays Charles Dilke's purported account of his
relation to Mrs. Mark Pattison. In Stead's story, Charles depicts Emilia as "the guardian
angel of his tempted virtue . . . an inspiration calling him to loftier things than the
low pursuit of pleasure and of adulterous intrigue." Stead's Charles narrates his spiritual history as one of salvation by Mrs Pattison; she had been a "martyr missionary
of Social Purity" in Oxford, a "second Mrs. Josephine Butler." Stead thus makes
Charles Dilke's encomia on Emilia's virtue ("he spoke of her as devout Catholics speak
of the Madonna") a form of self-indictment. Stead's account renders his meeting with
Emilia Dilke too as highly charged. Emilia Dilke speaks "with much emotion" of her
"agony," shows "evident distress" which Stead seeks to "comfort," and is "gloomy."
But in Stead's story, while open-minded he is never fooled. The Dilkes "overplayed
their assumed parts," their speeches contain "a good deal of humbug," and Emilia
Dilke is no Josephine Butler. Although he is not yet convinced after this first meeting,
Stead is able to consider the possibility that "Ananias and Sapphira were saints compared with Sir Charles and Lady Dilke."[108] Ananias and Sapphira were early Christians
who covertly denied their community's ethic of shared property, retaining some of
the profit from a piece of land they had sold; Ananias lied to St. Peter when challenged
and was struck dead on the spot, a fate Sapphira shared three hours later. Like Stead's
Dilkes, these sinners were not only liars but pretended to spiritual standards they did
not truly uphold. Ananias and Sapphira are, moreover, figures of the dishonest rich,
reiterating Stead's suggestions of upper-class corruption.[109]

Stead's *Deliverance or Doom?* goes on to tell of a further meeting with Emilia Dilke
that consolidates his suspicions. Again, she is intensely emotional, telling him that the
"thrill" of their last meeting moved her and they should always "be one in sympathy," but Stead is able to see through the "theatricality of the scene." He "was sorry
for the lady whose ambitious projects had been thwarted," but could not sustain "the

idea [he] had tried to form of her." He sees through her attempts to recount her "autobiography" to him as a woman of moral passion who had suffered "odium and obloquy" for righteousness's sake, although he is moved by her "tears" and "plaintive" pleas. In subsequent meetings she "implores," "is much affected and cr[ies] a good deal," and forms a "pitiable sight . . . sobbing there before [him]." Stead's text places confessions of Charles Dilke's guilt in Emilia's tear-drenched words; she tells him with "eyes filling with tears" that "the cruel thing . . . is that I often think if [Charles] had gone on living his old life that this trouble would never have befallen him." Stead's Lady Dilke felt "she had brought all this trouble upon Dilke by trying to wean him from his worldly life; that if she had only let him go on with his intrigues and life of pleasure, none of this trouble would have come on him; and it made her doubt whether it was not better to let men go on in their vice . . ."[110] In *Deliverance or Doom?* Emilia Dilke oscillates between emotionality, manipulativeness, pathos, falsity, and confession; she is a sometimes attractive but untrustable woman, verging on hysteria, constructing life stories she hopes will further her "ambitions" but betraying the truth about her husband's nature nonetheless. A tellingly unbalanced sentence evokes and occludes her: Charles Dilke's reentry into public life "would amount to a practical canonisation of Ananias and Sapphira."[111] Emilia Dilke must be punished by the destruction of Charles's career; her own status in public life is unnamed.

Feminists, Misogynists, and Other Middle-Class Pro-Dilkeites

Edmund Gosse wrote in 1886, "London is horrible, simply horrible, heavy dead air everywhere. The political world has gone mad. Sir Charles Dilke has been discovered in an intrigue with his sister-in-law, and all the social purity people are screaming that he must retire from public life . . . The fact is infinitely discouraging. It is hardly doubted that, but for this, Dilke would have been the next Liberal Prime Minister. The P.M.G. triumphs at this . . . and the world has, in fact, gone vulgar mad."[112] Gosse's response to the case displays a number of tropes: confusion about the familial relationship between Charles Dilke and Virginia Crawford; an assumption that Dilke had been "discovered" rather than accused; an assessment of Dilke's political prospects had the case not occurred; an appraisal of the role of the *Pall Mall Gazette*; and a linkage between a screaming mass of (hysterical) social purity advocates, a popular newspaper, and "vulgarity." Gosse's view of the case does not concern itself with Charles Dilke's guilt or innocence but rather with the parameters of acceptable political debate, in terms of issues and personnel.[113] Gosse represents one possible response, less "pro-Dilkeite" than anti-social purity and antidemocratic, but two other male writers with enduring and committed relations to feminism and progressive reform sought to undermine the association between presumed sexual guilt and political life. Richard Pankhurst "refused to judge, or even to consider the charges against Sir Charles Dilke, insisting that the man's public work should not be prejudiced by the case," and George Jacob Holyoake argued that Dilke had been "a powerful friend of liberty and social improvement" who should be welcomed by "Radical and co-operative voters in a constituency." Like Pankhurst, Holyoake suggested that even if Dilke had been "rightly accused" (which he did not believe), "he had made ample amends . . . to the public loss." Holyoake believed the "conspiracy of fanaticism," and even the protests of social purity advocates whom he respected, were politically dangerous (it "len[t] countenance to political party malevolence") and ultimately betrayed social purity's own goals by "creat[ing] a distrust of morality itself which the public discern to be pitiless and vindictive. . . . Relentless virtue is a form of vice."[114]

Olive Schreiner, too, worried privately but eloquently about the conflation of feminism and social purity agendas, and the case became a point of conflict between her and W. T. Stead. Like Pankhurst and Holyoake, Schreiner opposed collapsing politics and sexual behavior. She wrote, "Dilke can be of great use to the world as a politician . . . and therefore I dare pass no judgment on his personal relations, which are entirely his own affair and those of the men and women concerned," but with refreshing evenhandedness she resisted reallocating oppobrium onto Virginia Crawford. "When the Dilke case occurred some people cut me because I said I would still regard Mrs. Crawford as a woman if on meeting her we had tastes in common, not because I think it right to deceive one's husband, but because we are here in the world to love and help each other under all circumstances." To Schreiner, "all departure" from the "pure and beautiful ideal" of "absolute love and friendship of one man and one woman . . . whether in marriage or not," was "evil," but she did not "feel called upon to crush those who depart from the ideal." Such people might still have "other great and beautiful qualities"; it would be "heaven" to have "great all-loving, all-tender, all-true, all-wise men for our politicians and writers and editors . . . [but] in the meantime we must prize any humanity or goodness or intellect in our fellows, and seek to develop it."[115] Schreiner's letter to Stead strongly implied that his pursuit of Dilke could end their friendship.

Despite such powerfully articulated exceptions, most feminists perceived arguments for a distinction between public life and private conduct as illegitimate and a betrayal of women's interests. When Elizabeth Cady Stanton offered an "apology for Mr Parnell," she was seen as offering a "defence of the 'Watertight Compartment' theory of public men" and analogized to "Mrs. Jacob Holyoake, Mrs Byles, and Miss Orme" in relation to Charles Dilke; the *Women's Herald* offered the comparison as adequate indictment of Stanton's position.[116] Progressive reformers had long deployed a political language that grounded claims for rights and freedoms in moral virtue, and arguments like Holyoake's and Pankhurst's challenged both the "Gladstonian synthesis" of Liberalism and Evangelicalism and this wider moral-political vision.[117] Thus, rather than engaging in debates on the relationships of the public and the private, social and sexual moralities, and the diverse constituencies of social reform directly, Charles and Emilia Dilke and the majority of their middle-class supporters rested their arguments for the legitimacy of Dilke's return to Parliament on assertions of his innocence of the sexual crimes with which he was charged. A significant subset of Dilke's defenders were legal thinkers who argued that flaws in the formal conduct of the court and the standards of proof—of storytelling—that the Divorce Court evoked had created an injustice, but most of the Dilkes' allies offered alternative plots. These plots did not directly question the relationship of sex and politics or the equation of sexual initiative with "guilt," and they often used motifs of misogyny in redistributing innocence and guilt, victimization and desire, natural and unnatural behavior.[118]

To some liberal defenders, Dilke was the victim of a woman explicitly branded "hysterical", in a story that drew upon the medical language of female sexual madness—Mrs. Crawford believed her own stories but was no sort of reliable witness. Emilia Dilke wrote a version of this story. As noted, Emilia Dilke's emplotment of Virginia Crawford resembled her account of Meta Bradley; both hunger for stories to enact in their lives and displace sexual passion into dramas that place them on center stage.[119] (Emilia Dilke wrote a more spiritually ambitious role for herself: a letter to Ellen Smith describes her feelings upon beholding Charles Dilke in the box during the second trial as like those of the Virgin Mary at the foot of the Cross.[120]) Her texts overtly cast Virginia Crawford as ravenously sexual; her "chief motive was less to ruin my husband than to get free from hers without exposing the really guilty persons . . . [Earlier anonymous letters] suggested to Mrs Crawford the opportunity to gain her freedom while protecting her lovers." Emilia Dilke participated in the construction of stories of female plots—darkly insisting "it cannot be held to be a case of *pure* hysteria, but rather . . . it is mixed up with a scheme carefully prepared, prepared over a long period of time, & with much skill fixed onto difficulties connected with other people." Emilia Dilke's letters also wonder about the motives of men, asking why Donald Crawford focused his attention on Charles Dilke when he had "evidence" of Virginia's involvement with other men, and produce a story about W. T. Stead. Stead is a would-be fixer who initially presented himself to her as a potential ally interested only in the truth but eventually revealed that his motive was to use the case to drive a wedge between Charles Dilke and Joseph Chamberlain.[121]

Other defenders utilized even more misogynist stories of female sexual predation, figuring Mrs. Crawford as a voraciously sexual woman with no moral sense. The converse of Virginia Crawford's self-depiction as sexually inert, these stories depict female lust as a destructive force. The Dilkes' investigatory committee uncovered new "witnesses" who implied that Virginia Crawford's sexual education, including her knowledge of *ménages à trois*, came from a career of sexual adventuring with her sister Helen; in these tales, the dénouement unmasks women as carnal and in need of containment.[122] Such stories proved especially attractive to Dilke's most conservative defenders since they allowed for the mockery of social reformers as hopelessly out-of-touch with the reality of female nature while also permitting defense of the sexual double standard, as they relegated desire to "bad" women. For example, *The Dwarf*, a deeply conservative "humorous" paper written and published by Hugo Ames, depicted Charles Dilke and Charles Parnell alike as the victims of "self-seeking-notoriety purists," who were, when male, far inferior in masculinity to the injured politicians. Ames devoted many pages to attacking social reformers of both sexes as "notoriety seekers," "bloodhounds," "would-be public inquisitors," "Puritan-Socialists," and "self-appointed censores morum of the nation," but his stories ultimately depend upon female agency for their effect. Not only in the Crawford case but in his accounts of the Tranby Croft scandal and the Russell divorce case, Ames conjures fast, immoral, petulant bad women telling lies and laying traps for stalwart, hearty men.[123]

D. F. Steavenson, a long-time friend of Charles Dilke, also favored tales of wicked women. Steavenson grants Christina Rogerson pride of place; she "wanted to marry him and revenged herself when she found she could not" and his Mrs. Crawford is "a foolish woman . . . tired of her useless husband" who served as "putty in the hands of the other. The worst details were the invention of two shockingly immoral women.''[124] In these stories, the "woman scorned" plot floats freely from figure to figure, so that any one or more of these women can be credited with the acting out of sexual jealousy and rage. In an even nastier vein, an unsigned 1887 article in the obscure Land and Water implied that behind the anti-Dilke plot was a Jewish conspiracy concocted by Lady Rosebery, née Hannah Rothschild, who was motivated by a lethal combination of "feminine hatred" and "racial prejudice."[125]

Another complicated misogynist story was purveyed by J. E. C. Bodley, Charles Dilke's secretary.[126] Bodley later wrote the Dilke case as his own tragedy (the case "cruelly compromised" him and robbed him of "irrecoverable years of my ruined youth") and he sought to compete with Gertrude Tuckwell for custody of Charles Dilke's legacy, insisting he was Dilke's rightful biographer.[127] In Bodley's account, Virginia Crawford was the hysterical tool of other "old women . . . bent on ruining" Dilke.[128] Bodley was among the first, though by no means the last, to finger Joseph Chamberlain as the archvillain conspiring with Dilke's enemies while pretending to be his closest friend; Shane Leslie presents Bodley as a rival with Chamberlain for Dilke's affections in a story whose homoerotic subplot is left just short of explicit.[129] But Bodley's tale depends on women. Naming Chamberlain as the hand pulling the strings left ultimate agency in a male hand but women acted crucially in this plot, whether as malicious agents or innocent dupes. Bodley cast Emilia Dilke as a naive and unworldly lady whose action in standing by Charles was in fact his downfall.[130] In Bodley's tale, had Dilke remained single the "great political ladies of London" would have united their presumably considerable forces to save their friend Charles. Bodley's stories make him an arbiter of reputations and possessor of true knowledge. As we have seen, Bodley claimed a special understanding of Emilia Dilke and emphasized her proper ladyhood, but his account of the case removes her heroic role as steadfast defender of a wronged man. Bodley insisted he knew better than she the truth of the case—"poor" Lady Dilke "cherished [an] illusion" about her husband. Bodley's story does not include Emilia Dilke's knowledge of Charles's liaisons with Mrs. Eustace Smith nor allow anything but innocence in the Dilkes' premarital relationship.[131]

The playwright and critic William Archer in 1895 suggested to his friend Elizabeth Robins that "the Dilke subject" might make a good play. In his scenario as well, Emilia Dilke is primarily a deceived innocent. A woman "hears by telegraph" of a "dreadful scandal" that has "overtaken" a man she knows (Archer offers the possibility that she "had refused him" earlier) and "instantly to proclaim her faith in him telegraphs home announcing her engagement." Later, the trial "conclusively proves his guilt."[132] Archer offers two alternatives for the woman's part, damning or tragic, but neither endows her with any desire of her own. She may have "kn[own] very well that [he] was guilty," and hence was a sort of accomplice, or she had not known and thus was deceived and then caught in a marriage she had contracted on betrayed trust. Again, Emilia Dilke is deprived of heroism and desire. If she is not Stead's "Sapphira," conniving at her husband's vices, she must be a good and ignorant victim, albeit subsequently enlightened in Archer's version. Like Virginia Crawford in other stories, she had no sexuality of her own, and the possibility of an adultery in which Virginia Crawford and her mother had no part is erased.

The stories told by Dilke defenders, like those of anti-Dilkeites, refuse any association between positive femininity and sexual desire. Pro-Dilkeites like Hugo Ames and J. E. C. Bodley divide women into the scheming and sexually perverse bad and the passive, asexual good; doing so locates sexual and political guilt in women while covertly dismissing male sexual activity as trivial; the range of female roles is restricted to manipulators for evil (Lady Rosebery), lying hysterics (Virginia Crawford), or well-intentioned fools (Emilia Dilke).[133] These stories leave little room in politics for even "good" women, and the dangers of "bad" women to the proper conduct of public political life is stressed. Similarly emphasizing female agency, Roy Jenkins lamented in 1958, "no one, other than Dilke, has got within striking distance of 10 Downing Street and then been politically annihilated by a woman's . . . accusations."[134]

In Another Part of the Forest:
Reconsidering "A Victorian Tragedy"

The diverse stories I have re-presented seem, paradoxically, to return us to familiar ground. The late-Victorian period appears as an era of polarization, in which attention to female sexual danger is bought at the price of the ability to articulate female sexual desire, which can only appear as aberrant and dangerous. The stories of the Dilke-Crawford case seem dominated by a rigid sexual ideology of opposed terms: guilt and innocence, predation and promiscuity, seduction and hypnosis, marriage and adultery, the perversity of all things French and the sanctity of English womanhood. We can find a positive transformation of existing melodramatic scripts in Virginia Crawford's ability to escape the traditional tragic ending of the fallen woman; in the theatre of the divorce court, Virginia Crawford portrayed a helpless victim of male lust, but after that curtain fell, she became the magdalen as New Woman, able to rise again, self-supporting and able to go forth not only to sin no more but to do good in public and political spheres as a feminist. Shane Leslie cast Mrs. Crawford's later life as "accept[ance of] the role of the penitent Magdalen," but if her postcase career might be read as a repudiation of sexuality for penitential service, it was also a choice of independence and public activity (a brief entry into a convent lasted only a few months) and she became a Catholic feminist and democrat.[135] We might find in this new ending the materials for a new heroic tale: the case appears to provide an example of feminist power, of the strength of late-Victorian bourgeois feminism to create new endings to old narratives. The downfall of Charles Dilke would seem to offer an example of a highly specific kind of feminist hegemony in the apparent ability of middle-class feminists and social purity advocates—despite a rhetoric in which they positioned themselves as brave and gallant outsiders daring to speak boldly against opposition and public indifference—to occupy center stage, denounce loudly and clearly the sexual double standard, and make male sexual behavior a political issue. Understanding the case in this way risks reiterating the marginalization of pro-Dilke feminists as not-really-feminists-at-all, but one might celebrate the flexing of feminist public muscle. Dianne Sachko Macleod has recently attempted another, less optimistic, feminist twist on the tale, presenting Eustacia Smith as a protofeminist rebel who "embrac[ed] both the artistic and sexual principles of Bohemia" in her aesthetico-erotic self-display and her liaison with Charles Dilke; Macleod laments Mrs. Eustace

Smith's "far greater" punishment than Dilke, her temporary exile from England the price exacted for her daughter's alleged adultery as well as her own.[136]

Such understandings of the feminist politics of the case are considerably more illuminating than the traditional positioning of Dilke's downfall as yet another instance of "Victorian prudery" to be deplored or mocked, and they avoid plotting the Dilke case as a detective story. Yet even recognizing these possible feminist readings, the Dilke-Crawford case can remain a tragedy on a larger stage. Roy Jenkins and, more recently, David Nicholls have written Charles Dilke's life as a story of lost hopes; Jenkins's first edition of his biography was subtitled "A Victorian Tragedy" and Nicholls titles his *The Lost Prime Minister*. Jenkins's story, perhaps inflected by his own complicated history in party politics, is that had Dilke not fallen the Liberal Party might not have fractured so severely, the Tories might not have enjoyed "twenty years of hegemony" after 1886, the Irish question might have been settled much earlier, and "a more radical Liberal party might have turned, in the 'nineties, to a massive programme of social reform . . . and consequent effects on the history of the Labour Party."[137] Both Jenkins and Nicholls write Dilke's story as one in which the new politics of sex and gender deprived Britain of a needed Liberal leader.[138] But the loss of a Dilke premiership can also be mourned in relation to lost feminist possibilities. Dilke had, as president of the Local Government Board, appointed several women to public offices, attempted to appoint women factory inspectors and to place Maude Stanley on the Royal Commission on the Housing of the Working Classes in 1884. He was, after the death of Jacob Bright, the most consistent introducer of parliamentary bills calling for women's suffrage, a sharp contrast to the intransigent antisuffragism of Asquith.[139] Against other stories that emphasize the personal costs for the Dilkes and endow them with exaggerated pathos—Enid Huws Jones claims Emilia Dilke's second marriage brought her "fearful ostracism" and Marie Belloc Lowndes says they only kept one or two friends—these tragic narratives can dwell upon the costs to a wider public life of the removal of Charles Dilke's feminist and Radical commitments from high office and perhaps the impairment of Emilia Dilke's feminist career.[140]

But two salutory reminders are in order: far worse things might happen to one in late-Victorian Britain than that one failed to fulfill one's hopes to become Prime Minister, and Charles Dilke might have fallen to another unforeseen circumstance, whether another scandal or being hit by a bus. More importantly, it is simply not adequate historical argument to contend, but that "Mrs. Crawford Intervene[d]," not only would Charles Dilke have remained at the highest levels of the Liberal Party and eventually succeeded as Leader but also Dilke's placement at the head of his party would have allowed the Liberals to return to and hold power longer than the Gladstone/Rosebery ministries of 1892–1895.[141] This story, in which a Dilke leadership alters the Tory dominance of turn-of-the-century politics from 1886 until 1906, places far too little weight on the formidable political and social forces challenging Liberal politics in the late century and reduces politics to the presence or absence of individual gifted leaders.[142]

Charles Dilke placed a line from Ibsen's *John Gabriel Borkman* as an epigraph to his unpublished memoirs: "We are all of us run over, sometime or other in life. The thing is to jump up again, and let no one see you are hurt."[143] Dilke's choice of text not only signals a calm awareness of the vicissitudes of political careers but also marks a larger point: the continuation of life after nonfatal collisions. Some skepticism is in order about the degree to which the Dilkes' public political lives were actually impaired by the effects of the Crawford divorce case.[144] Charles Dilke's 1886 loss of his Chelsea seat can only dubiously be attributed to the effect of the "case," and Dilke was being courted by new constituencies as early as 1889.[145] In 1891 he accepted the invitation of the Forest of Dean Liberal Association to stand as their next candidate for Parliament, was elected in the general election of 1892, and held that seat by enormous majorities until his death in 1911.[146] Charles Dilke's "exile" from formal political life was therefore relatively short and thereafter consisted of his exclusion from the Cabinet rather than from Parliament per se. Moreover, even during the period of "exile" (1886–1892), both Dilkes prosecuted active public political lives in extra-Parliamentary realms which were arguably as significant in late-Victorian political life as the formal legislative domain. These extra-Parliamentary careers included continued participation in some forms of feminist social reform and, besides their continued participation in the public world of the "Woman Question," both Dilkes participated in the public political world of the labor/Labour movement. In that domain, their status as sexually scandalous "outcasts," as Stead's "Ananias and Sapphira," was only a partial impairment. The Dilkes' political careers after 1886 pose some questions and cast doubts on the degree to which middle-class feminist and social purity campaigners' reliance on the continued existence of a coalition of social reform and moral certainty was justified.

The radicalism and ambition in the late nineteenth century of middle-class social reform, including feminism, the metropolitan press, and the discourses of sexual normalization, matter enormously, and the Dilke case demonstrates the power of melodramatic sociosexual scripts. But while the Dilkes' working-class and Radical supporters rarely simply rejected the general terms of sexual scandal—the stories explicitly told by pro-Dilke forces tended to share with anti-Dilke stories a rhetoric of guilt and innocence and a commitment to chastity and heterosexual monogamy—the terms of liberty, class, morality, conscience, sex, and loyalty could be used in many different stories within late-Victorian Radicalism. Feminists, Liberals, social purity activists, newspaper writers, miners, Foresters, and others sought to display and construct a virtuous public realm through conflicting narratives of the Dilke case. The limited ability of any story to silence class in favor of gender, gender in favor of class, and the crosscutting of these categories by other hierarchies and bigotries signals the complex contestations of virtue in the late nineteenth century. Feminist and social purity discourses entailed heavy costs when they erased the possibility of female sexual desire while raising complex questions about speaking for others and democratic processes, while assertions of female agency, sexual and otherwise, were often wholly contained within misogynist demonizations or contempt for women, or subordinated to forms of class politics that excluded intraclass gendered conflicts. Hyperboles, absurdities, and elisions, as much as narrative fluency, produced powerful stories, and these stories—generated in the courtroom, the press, and the hustings—were enacted as well as told, offered roles as well as explanations.

W. T. Stead presented himself during his pursuit of the Dilke case as the stalwart voice of social purity, of women, and of a progressive, Evangelical, moral middle class, but his ventriloquization of even middle-class urban Radicals can be questioned: the Cobden Club held a special meeting "to enable the Executive to express its heartiest congratulations upon the prospect of Sir Charles Dilke's return to public life," and in their campaigning tours the Dilkes received support from "advanced" middle-class Radicals, local and imported, and were accompanied by Non-Conformist clerical friends, Radical M.P.s, and political hopefuls like Reginald McKenna and William Macarthur. Even a few Women's Liberal Associations, like that of Fulham, endorsed Dilke.[147] Stead also claimed a vast working-class constituency that shared deeply rooted "family values"; this constituency was morally revolted by Charles Dilke and would not countenance his return to public life. In order to construct this army of working-class allies, pro-Dilke working-class people, Evangelicals, and leaders of the labour movement who, like Henry Broadhurst, defended Dilke had to be ignored, branded as fools, or actively opposed.[148] Some organized working-class political groups remained willing and able to construct alternative narratives in which the melodrama of sexual scandal competed with the melodrama of class relations. These alternative narratives were not stories in which gender ceased to matter, but it mattered differently; the tensions between the politics of class and the politics of gender I examined in the Women's Liberal Federation's statement were differently harnessed, and they produced the other stories about the case elsewhere in late-Victorian Britain. Social actors' constructed and reiterated narratives of class competed with narratives organized around solidarities like "the women of England" or Stead's moral majority, and in some of these stories, Emilia Dilke was used to develop a story that both recognized and contained women's political agency.

It was possible to refuse Stead's Charles Dilke, the aristocratic libertine, in favor of George Holyoake's Dilke, the "powerful friend of liberty." Charles Dilke clearly enjoyed a welcome from some working-class political constituencies even before his return to Parliament, especially among miners; his public political life was neither confined to nor dependent on the status of his Parliamentary career.[149] In 1891, he was an invited speaker at meetings held by miners' organizations in the Rhondda Valley, Somersetshire, Bristol, and North Wales. In Festiniog, he was greeted "with great applause" from the quarrymen and other labor organizations despite some local Methodist opposition. The Aberdeen United Trades Council invited him north, while the South Wales Federation of Labour Unions invited him to speak in Cardiff.[150] Moreover, from almost the moment he lost his Chelsea seat, rumors circulated that Dilke was being courted as a candidate by some of the most Radical Liberal constituencies in Britain, including several Scottish and Welsh constituencies, before he accepted the invitation of the Forest of Dean in 1891.[151] Within days of his election in 1892, hailed by "Mabon" (William Abraham, the Welsh "Lib.-Lab." M.P.) as "not only a political leader, but a real Labour leader," Dilke was addressing a meeting of 30,000 miners in Derbyshire.[152] In subsequent weeks, he spoke at mass working-class gatherings in St. Helens, Dowlais, Liverpool, Swansea, and elsewhere, and continued to do so throughout the 1890s and early 1900s. Once he was back in Parliament, Dilke's exclusion from the Cabinet, although a real loss of direct political power, may have fostered his close affiliations to the emergent Labour Party and his ability to influence younger M.P.s across party lines. By 1897, "Marxian" could write in the *Labour Leader* that Dilke was kept from being "the statesman of socialism" only by his "intense individuality."[153] Charles Dilke's political "downfall" was not only strictly relative but by no means constituted a complete rejection by a hegemonic social formation that cut across classes and political loyalties.

W. T. Stead may have cast pro-Dilkeites in the Forest of Dean as "only ignorant miners," but a more complicated political geography of the Forest can be constructed. Charles Dilke called the Forest "a microcosm of England, industrial and agricultural."[154] Between the Severn and the Wye, the Forest was a deeply radical mining and quarrying consituency in which the local Liberal Party was "a Radical body Gladstonian in the extreme . . . and 99% of the electors are so too," and had deselected their previous Liberal MP, G. B. Samuelson, despite being generally satisfied with his Radical performance, because of his opposition to the Miners' Eight-Hours Act. The Forest was home to a burgeoning Labour association of miners and quarrymen, boasting four thousand members and employing G. H. Rowlinson, a member of the national Executive Board of the Miners' Federation, as their agent.[155] Charles Dilke's reentry into Parliamentary life by standing for the Forest produced a flurry of narratives about the Dilke-Crawford case, especially through the Forest's Radical newspaper, the Dean Forest Mercury. The Mercury expressed unswerving support for Dilke and mourned his absence from party politics from at least 1888 onward, and a close reading suggests that its editor, J. Cooksey, was involved in orchestrating a close affiliation between Dilke and the Forest Liberals over the course of several years. Dilke became honorary President of the Cinderford Liberal Association and delivered a series of speeches throughout the district in 1890, and the 1891–1892 canvassing that led to Dilke's election was very well organized.[156] Moreover, the Mercury systematically contested anti-Dilke arguments not simply by repudiating but by recasting the relationship of social purity, Evangelicalism, and feminism in a discourse of Tory plots, a metropolitan press, outside agitators, and meddling do-gooders. The Mercury's stories cast Charles and Emilia Dilke and the Foresters themselves as heroes.

John R. Cook has described the Forest of Dennis Potter's childhood in the 1930s as "its own little enclosed world of villages scattered amongst woods and fields which were reachable only by steep and narrow country roads," stressing the Foresters' remoteness and "tight-knit community," which combined "a fierce, almost evangelical devotion to religion," passionate "English patriotism," and "a staunch commitment . . . to socialism and the Labour Movement."[157] The Forest Radical story of the Dilke case in the 1890s was inflected with a strong aversion to what was perceived as metropolitan domination of the discourse of social purity and a suspicion of the class implications of social purity campaigns. The Mercury developed a long-running counternarrative that merged the Foresters' claims to difference and moral worth while awarding them a special role in the nation's destiny. In this story, the gallant Foresters were not only the defenders of a wronged man but were the defenders of British liberty itself. The Mercury enthused in 1891, "O Dean Forest, with all thy faults, I love thee still . . . most of all for thy liberty of thought and speech, uncontrolled by parson, squire, Primrose Dames, Tory showmen, and would-be despots of the the Press in London and elswhere."[158] This story, recounted in every issue of the Mercury and rehearsed at the dozens of pro-Dilke meetings through the spring and summer of 1891, not only offered clearly identified heroic roles but easily discerned villains: dictatorial metropolitan interferers with workingmen's political liberties. Anti-London sentiment was vehement: "It is notorious that London is far behind the country in healthy Liberalism, and greatly overestimates its importance in the guidance of public affairs."[159] Quite apart from explicit defenses of Dilke's "innocence," the Forest of Dean Radicals cast the issue as one involving the defense of the rights of working-class and Radical voters. This was a struggle with vast implications for all those who were righteously committed to political modernity:

> The Forest of Dean Election is conceded to be the most notable and important of all in the United Kingdom, for it is fraught with momentous issues of a personal and general character . . . The actions of Sir Charles Dilke's enemies is an attempt to lay down the principle that a constituency has not the right to choose whom it will to represent it; but the attempt can be no more than an attempt because it is too late in the day to foist an arrogant and obsolete principle upon any constituency.[160]

Voters must especially protect their right to determine for themselves the relevance of the Crawford case and Dilke's fitness for the job against illegitimate encroachments by religious authorities. Cannily asserting the supremacy of freedom of conscience over the views of Nonconformist religious leaders, the *Mercury*'s anonymous "Q." mocked the Methodist minister Hugh Price Hughes. "Without intending any irreverence we may remind the Rev. Hughes that Sir Charles's return to public life does not depend upon the divine commission the reverend gentleman has the presumption to claim, but upon the votes of the electors of the Forest of Dean."[161] While tactfully insisting that the Nonconformists of the Forest itself were "men of honour and integrity," and defending them against "a Liverpool paper [which] bracket[ed] the Non-Conformists of the Forest of Dean with Atheists," the *Mercury*'s writers implicitly recalled the historical linkage between nonconformity and liberty of conscience.[162] The *Mercury* also repeatedly and ironically drew upon old traditions of anti-Catholicism to stigmatize social purity. Stead and Hughes were scorned as would-be "Popes," who demanded confessions and undermined democratic government; Stead was a "Torquemada," persecuting innocents "without malice" and in the name of God.[163] Against these interlopers on freedom of conscience, the Forest Radicals and the *Mercury* foregrounded the Miners' Eight-Hours Act as far and away the most important issue.[164] A correspondent who signed himself "Watchman" further pointedly suggested that anti-Dilke forces with overactive "Non-Conformist Conscience[s]" concentrate on their own business practices, on unemployment, and on the plight of badly paid workers.[165] But even as the Forest of Dean pro-Dilkeites and others disputed the right to determine the salience of sexual scandal in the prosecution of politics, they demonstrated the usability of sex scandals in their own politics.

The *Mercury* consistently attacked W. T. Stead and expressed a deep suspicion of "professional purity people" in general, but it relocated rather than simply erased the politics of gender.[166] Defenses of Dilke through attacks on social purity shared elements of the conservative or misogynist arguments of people like Hugo Ames. The *Mercury* compared Hugh Price Hughes to "a gossiping old woman", and the editor attributed Stead's influence to his ability "to work on the feelings of maiden and other ladies"; Thomas Blake, a Forest Liberal, accused Stead of "attempt[ing] to frighten the women of England out of their wits by Bogies," dismissing women's fears of sexual danger as the result of a press full of "filthy insinuation and recitals of vices previously unknown."[167] The Mercury's stories of suspicions of illegitimate attempts to control the Foresters' political freedom were also directed at "outsider" middle-class feminist reformers. The resolutions of Women's Liberal Associations and the "Women's Petition Against Sir Charles Dilke" were evidence of the skewed priorities and improper desires of middle-class women to override working-class and Radical voters' freedom. Such women were at best dupes of the Tories.[168] Lady Henry Somerset was not only a "fanatic" but betrayed her temperance principles by her support for Dilke's Tory opponent, a man involved in "the liquor trade"; she had "lent herself as a tool [to Stead] in trying to damn one man in preference to serving many."[169] The Mercury carefully noted that the views of "Mrs. McIlquham" that "the return of Dilke proves that men are not fit for the franchise which should be exercised by women" appeared in a Tory newspaper, the Birmingham Daily Gazette.[170] The Mercury combined the misogynist motifs of other pro-Dilkeites with a form of feminism linked and subordinated to a politics of class. To politically suspect outsider women, the Forest Radicals counterposed the Liberal good sense of Forest women and the affection of both men and women for Emilia Dilke.[171]

The Second Member

The Dean Forest Mercury's Emilia Dilke is a good woman who sends donations and a representative to Church bazaars, acknowledges the Foresters' Nonconformist piety by giving an admiring lecture on Wesley as a spiritual leader, and displays womanly virtues by coming immediately to console the widows and children of men killed in a "terrible mine accident" and hold weeping women in her arms. Her own letters too cast her as bound to the Forest by ties of affection and diverse friendships with "a Congregationalist minister . . . a baker head of our Salvation Army, a Socialist tobacconist & an Inspector on [the] G.[reat] W.[estern R.[ailway]."[172] Emilia Dilke properly plays the role of a political wife—campaigning for her husband, denouncing the Primrose League's perfidy, and accepting flowers, all with an extra fillip of "courage and devotion" because of her standing by Charles through the Crawford divorce scandal. But the emplotment of Emilia Dilke went beyond that of a "good" woman—a woman perhaps inaccurately purified of any taint of sexual scandal—standing by her man and serving his constituency. Emilia Dilke's own long-standing relationship to working-class politics as a L/labour sympathizer and organizer of women's trade unions and her own status as a national figure in the politics of gender and class mattered to the Mercury's stories.

It is impossible to date the start of Francis Pattison's involvement with the Women's Trade Union League; she did not serve on the League's committee in the 1870s but was on its Council by 1881. In 1881, in response to bad working conditions at "Hyde's Clothing Factory" in Oxford, she held a meeting in her Lincoln College drawing-room of "over 100 women working at various trades in Oxford" and their supporters (middle-class people of both sexes and working-class men) at which Emma Paterson spoke. According to her WTUL co-member Mrs. Nettleship, Francis Pattison's "unflagging energy & great personal influence among the women" were central to the Oxford Protective and Provident League's survival.[173] Emilia Dilke later recounted how ridiculous she thought it when a "university professor" (surely in Oxford) who attended a meeting called by the League denounced its goals and withdrew his support; "He was quite ready to give money in charity,—that is, as a voluntary rate in aid of insufficient wages,—but he regarded as criminal any attempt to enable . . . suffering women to obtain by combination better remuneration."[174] Dilke succeeded to the presidency of the League in 1886 and her activities were widely reported in the labor press. Her regular attendance of the annual Trades Union Congress meeting, where she gave at least one, usually several, speeches in meetings sponsored by the WTUL and supported by prominent male trade-unionists and Labour leaders like Ben Tillett and Tom Mann, and her speeches and organizing activities were reported in considerable detail. In 1889—even before Charles Dilke's return to Parliament—the *People's Journal of Dundee* printed four long articles on Emilia Dilke, from verbatim accounts of speeches to an interview.[175]

Emilia Dilke was admirable and usable for the *Dean Forest Mercury* not only for her wifely loyalty to Charles Dilke but because of her own position as a figure in class politics. She was set apart from other, stigmatized, middle-class political women by her understanding of specifically working-class concerns. "[T]here was [no] person in Gloucestershire who took as much interest in the working classes as Lady Dilke", and her labor on behalf of working-class people ("the work she was doing for the organization of women engaged in the factories") and her commitment to and respect for working-class self-organization were lauded (she "exhorted the women whose claims she eloquently enforced to be up and doing themselves" and urged "combination . . . and . . . loyalty to the Union").[176] Besides undertaking numerous speaking tours, presiding over meetings, giving considerable amounts of money, and writing on trade-unionism in the League's papers and the general press, Emilia Dilke attempted to forge more positive relationships between the League's women's trade unions and the TUC and its male-dominated membership, using honey as well as vinegar.[177] The League, under Emma Paterson, had established regular evening receptions during the TUC's annual Congress week, beginning in 1877 at Leicester, and these "social" or "women's conferences" grew under Dilke's presidency, bringing together working-class men and women involved in trade-unionism, middle-class supporters and reformers, and (through Charles's connections) such M.P.s as were available.[178] Beatrice Webb recorded that the Dilkes "were the genii of the scene [at the 1892 TUC in Glasgow], entertaining the Congress wholesale to lunch, tea, and dinner."[179] In 1890, the League targeted the TUC delegates from Ireland and Emilia Dilke promised to come and personally work to organize Irish women workers, a promise she kept.[180] One of her most inspired measures was the establishment of a scheme by which predominantly male or "mixed" trade unions could "affiliate" with the League for the payment of a half-pence per woman member; in exchange, the League sent organizers at its own expense (usually experienced working-class women like Sarah Reddish, Ada Nield Chew, and Annie Marland) to help recruit women members into the existing union and to support the union's activities more generally. Emilia Dilke forged an alliance in 1892 with the Manchester Trades Council, and the League provided an organizer who worked for several months leafletting local women workers.[181]

Emilia Dilke's speeches frequently combine expressions of desire for cooperation with male trade-unionists and the TUC with criticism of male intransigence.[182] Norbert

Soldon has claimed that Emilia Dilke and the League seemed, on the whole, "content to allow men to be the leaders" in mixed organizations, and Dilke's texts sometimes emphasize working-class women's need for help; "to add two and two together would have been for them an effort too great . . . [and] it was absolutely no use telling them how they could better their condition [through a union] because bodies and minds had been so starved. . . . [that] they had no heart and no energy."[183] Dilke also wrote that generally women did not yet know how to run unions properly because of past exclusions: she called for male trade-unionists to help women develop their "business powers," to "give them adequate representation in management," and to keep in mind that "women had been for so long treated as a class apart, and as an inferior class, that they naturally distrusted the good intentions of men, who they had been led to regard only as rivals."[184] Dilke thus stressed that male-female working-class cooperation depended on men's actions as well as women's, and she emphasized male self-interest: failure to involve women into unions—and of women to stay in those unions—allowed employers to undercut male wages and even the best paid men were exploited in relation to "the earnings of capital."[185]

The most controversial—and still bedevilled—aspect of the League's early political philosophy, its opposition to protective legislation, is related to this theme of the relations between men and women within trade-unionism.[186] Emma Paterson was unalterably opposed to protective legislation; her experiences in bookbinding and printing gave her direct encounters with the tendency of the male trade-union movement in the 1860s and early 1870s to attempt to exclude women workers, while her commitment to suffrage and awareness of women's exclusion from the political process fostered opposition to state restrictions on women's work and hours. Francis Pattison in 1877 spoke against a bill that proposed limiting women's work hours not only by total hours but by time of day:

> Women of full age under the Bill are subject to the same regulations as boys under eighteen. Should they wish to work at other hours than those permitted by this Bill, it is illegal for them to do so . . . Now I do not intend to discuss whether it is or is not desirable for women to work on Sundays, or at hours not specified in this Bill, or during meal times; all that I wish to maintain is that these points are best left to the discretion of the women themselves, to be decided by their convenience, and that of the trades in which they are engaged, and by the action of the Unions by which their interests should be protected.

The bill to which Francis Pattison was opposed was supported by male trade unionists; strikingly, it sought to order women's wage-work around notions of their domestic obligations and attempted to legislate women's work into enforced divisions of waged and domestic labor without women's direct participation in the legislative process. Francis Pattison's speech emphasized women's rights to be treated as autonomous adults and depicted women workers as members of collectivities—their trades and unions.[187] But although the League's opposition to protective or exclusionary legislation was a matter of internal debate and considerable subtlety, the balance of opinion shifted away from "pure oppositionism" before Paterson's death in 1886. Under Emilia Dilke's leadership, a rapid rapprochement with state agencies took place, as Dilke was committed to the introduction of Trade Boards and women factory inspectors.[188] Moreover, in the strongly protectionist Gertrude Tuckwell's account, Emilia Dilke rejected the "purely 'feminist' " policy of opposition to protective legislation in favor of cross-gender working-class alliances.[189]

In Tuckwell's tale, Emilia Dilke "early realized that [the League] was put at a disadvantage by a purely self-protective legislation, and in the 70's as in the 90's she taught the necessity for women workers to ally themselves with the men organized in Unions, and favoured stringent Factory legislation and the shortening of hours for both causes."[190] But Dilke's movement was from an oppositionist position to one of support for specific protective measures. Like most protectionists, she argued that ideally such measures should apply to all workers, not just women, but she was willing to endorse separate regulation of women's working conditions, especially in circumstances in which women were badly underpaid and physically injured. Although sometimes attributed to the alleged influence of Charles Dilke, the shift in Emilia Dilke's views and in the League's policy mirrored larger changes in the labor movement, especially the emergence, with the Miners' Eight Hours agitation, of willingness to regulate adult men's hours by legislation.[191] (In the Forest of Dean, as we have seen in the Forest Radicals' deselection of G. B. Samuelson, these larger shifts were exceptionally visible.) Moreover, Dilke was flexible in her appraisal of tactics—even in 1890 she could trenchantly note, "I am perfectly ready to accept State aid whenever it can do something for me which I can't do for myself, but I am unwilling to appeal to State Legislation except as a last resource."[192] Dilke's texts can also place opposition to some forms of protective legislation in relation to the cost to society and the family, rather than employing liberal-individualist rhetoric. Invoking the spectre of prostitution, Dilke reasoned:

> When we see . . . the hideous results of unchecked competition between women and men, it is only natural that our first impulse should be to fly to prohibitive legislation; that we should fancy that the only course open to us is the prohibition of women's labour, and her entire relegation to her natural and sacred sphere of home, to the fulfilment in blessed leisure of her natural and sacred functions of mother and wife. But on reflection we see that . . . [t]he choice for these girls . . . does not lie between home and the market-place; it lies between the market-place and the streets. . . . Any attempt to legislate against the employment of women's labour . . . is likely to inflict evils far deadlier to the woman and the family than it can possibly cure.[193]

The tensions in Dilke's views were continuous with the League's strength, originated by Emma Paterson, of seeing working-class women as inhabiting multiple subject positions that structured their political needs and desires and were not easily assimilated into middle-class feminist programs. But these aspects of Dilke's rhetoric also allowed working-class and Radical Liberal male voters to distinguish Emilia Dilke from other feminists who were cast as insensitive to issues of class. Not only did her moral language of utopian Christian socialism envision a bright future when "all class differences [would] fall away," but Emilia Dilke's feminist trade-unionism also sought to stress the solidarity of working-class people and downplayed conflict between working-class men and women.[194] Emilia Dilke's 1891 article, "Trade Unions for Women," cast its theme in high language of family values (inflected as well by the fear of dysgenic degeneration): "the homes of England are at stake; we are fighting for the manhood of her men, for the health of her women, for the future of her little children. It is the home and the true welfare of the family which are menaced by . . . unregulated competition."[195]

Further, Emilia Dilke's commitment to women's suffrage was by the late 1890s encompassed within support for adult suffrage; both Dilkes, and Gertrude Tuckwell, argued that the franchise should be extended not only to middle-class women but to working-class persons of both sexes.[196] Adult suffrage was seen by some women's suffragists and, later, suffragettes, as less likely to succeed than a more limited women's suffrage measure and as less radically feminist than a direct assault on the sex barrier; it also relied more on liberal theories of universal self-representation than on arguments about middle-class women's potential contributions as "social house-keepers" caring for others' interests. Some women's suffragists, like Millicent Garrett Fawcett, were directly opposed to working-class men's enfranchisement; Fawcett wrote in the *Women's Herald* in 1891, "I have never been in favour of either Manhood or Womanhood Suffrage. The lowering of the franchise has gone more than far enough already; and one chief recommendation of women's suffrage, to my mind, is that it would tend somewhat to raise the average of intelligence, education, and character among the electorate."[197] Emilia Dilke was not hostile to women's suffrage campaigns per se and she had been involved in explicitly women's suffrage organizations in Oxford. Both Dilkes, along with Richard Pankhurst, opposed an effort in 1890 to mount a campaign for a bill that would grant a limited franchise to unmarried women (with a property qualification), but she nonetheless attempted to vote in a County Council election on the basis on her ownership of the property of Pyrford Rough.[198] But the Dilkes' shift to adult suffrage was compatible with growing Labour politics, and, like Dilkes' trade-unionism, was enunciated in a language of respect of working-class self-representation: Gertrude Tuckwell claimed Emilia Dilke saw herself as supporting movements of "the people themselves" and regarded her role as "help[ing] them to help themselves" by aiding them in achieving votes and trade unions.[199] Shortly before her death in 1904, she proclaimed in a speech at the People's Trade Hall in Leeds that she was no longer a member of any Liberal women's organizations but "belonged entirely to the Labour Party and the Labour cause."[200]

Emilia Dilke was available as a figure of a middle-class woman both radical and properly unselfish in her commitment to wider democracy, an active figure in the public realm and a useful figure in the texts of Forest of Dean Radical politics, a suitable heroine in a Radical/Labour discourse that admitted the value and necessity of women's political engagement but swerved away from direct engagement with sex-antagonism. The Dilkes' annual visits to the Forest once Charles had won the seat kept Emilia Dilke's political connections and activities in the Foresters' eyes; they generally brought with them several of the young women—Gertrude Tuckwell, May Abraham, Emilia Monck, and Constance Smith—who were employed in various capacities by Emilia Dilke, the League, or other feminist social reform organizations, to assist with the largely ceremonial election campaigns. The Forest Radicals often referred to Emilia Dilke as a kind of auxiliary representative, their "Second Member," and Gertrude Tuckwell claimed that even in Charles's first campaign in the Forest, "more than one [voting paper] had been spoilt by too enthusiastic votaries [sic] who wrote across their papers, 'For Lady Dilke.' "[201] These public appreciations of Emilia

Dilke capture the Foresters' use of her as a political figure *and* their inscription of women's political activities as properly folded into partnership with men.

Nor were the Foresters alone in stressing that Emilia Dilke's virtues were a combination of Radicalism and proper wifely loyalty to men; Ben Turner's obituary of Emilia Dilke in the *Cotton Factory Times* would later emphasize both her devotion to trade-unionism and her "love, trust, and faith" in Charles Dilke, to whom "this brave little woman" had been a "good wife and a grand helpmate . . . a domestic helpmate and consoler also."[202] In the heat of political battle, even a Conservative newspaper could share the *Dean Forest Mercury*'s construction of Emilia Dilke's political activities as important to the voters. In 1891, the *Yorkshire Post* produced a story of the Foresters' rumored plans to adopt Charles Dilke as their candidate as the outcome of Emilia Dilke's work. While the *Yorkshire Post*'s Emilia Dilke is similar to W. T. Stead's ambitious woman who has taken her husband's derailment from the road to power as a challenge to be overcome—"we fancy . . . that Lady Dilke, who from the first has shown a touching and profound confidence in her husband's moral integrity, has set her heart upon his restoration to public life. . . . Lady Dilke has been unremitting in her efforts to secure a turn in the tide of popular feeling"—the *Post* goes further. Emilia Dilke's trade union activity is a strategy, born of "shrewd womanly instinct" of philanthropic wooing of the working classes:

> . . . [S]he has concentrated her attentions upon the needs of the industrial poor, and especially those female operatives, whose lack of organisation and general helplessness has furnished a wide field for sympathetic and effective service. Lady Dilke has visited most of the industrial centres in which the lot of women workers called for such alleviation as a woman was specially fitted to attempt. She has visited factories and workshops, addressed meetings, promoted entertainments, and organised unions for the special advantage of her sex. These labours have earned her the gratitude of working men and women alike, and nowhere have they been more appreciated than in the mining districts of the Forest of Dean. It is no matter for surprise that this gratitude should find expression in the form which it was known would be most pleasing to Lady Dilke . . .

The *Yorkshire Post* condescendingly adds, to "those who analyse such things with a nicer appreciation of the canons of public morality, the practical sympathy which this rough mining district is showing towards [Charles Dilke] appears ill-considered and premature," but "it is at least to be treated as a weakness that springs from no discreditable sentiment . . ." The nicer elements of society know better than either helpless working women or rough grateful Forest men, but "[t]he miners absolutely control the seat."[203]

Charles Dilke's politics, including his relations to the Miners' Federation, are virtually erased from this narrative in favor of a remarkable story that places women's cross-class gender politics at the center of political agency. The *Birmingham Daily Post*, however, restores Charles Dilke to a position as plotter in his own right. The Birmingham paper contends that it is not simply as a Radical that Sir Charles comes forward; he expounds "a social programme beyond that which most of the older school of Radicals would care to adopt [and] has captured the miners by this programme." The *Post* demotes Emilia Dilke's status as a strategist but it too grants weight to working-class women as counters in high political struggles and makes Emilia Dilke a figure on the gameboard. "With a keen eye to the future, [Charles Dilke] is placing a second string to his bow by endeavouring to secure the growing strength of the women trade union-ists; and . . . Lady Dilke has been at the [TUC] where the woman question was more than usually at the front."[204] Even much later, one observer sought to make Emilia Dilke's moral credentials a matter of political profit for Charles Dilke. J. E. C. Bodley thought Charles's "Memoir" of Emilia might redound to Charles's own political good, and "she would have been glad to think that . . . the public mind would be full of the idea, at the coming political crisis, that you had been the husband & companion of this admirable woman & almost perfect character," a suggestion both remarkably tasteless and revelatory of a wider and persistent wish to recast women's work as most important in enabling men's public lives.[205] Even Charles Dilke's "Memoir" struggles to stress that Emilia Dilke was both an autonomous figure and a perfect wife and does so by quoting Marie-Thérèse Ollivier, wife of former French prime minister Émile Ollivier. Madame Ollivier makes Emilia Dilke exceptional among the wives of politi-cians: "We other women have enough need for forces sufficient for our double bur-den, that of our task and that of our husbands. You have spent yourself in this mission more than any other."[206]

Emilia Dilke's own texts vigorously participated in constructing her as a figure in the class history of the case. Emilia Dilke is a recipient of working-class loyalty and a sympathetic and emotionally moved reteller of working-class people's stories about the case in these tales.[207] Emilia Dilke offers stories of working-class appreciation of her and Charles in letters to Eleanor Smith—poor people attended their wedding and wished them blessings, a "poor 'shop-girl' " wrote to Charles with congratulations on their marriage; an "elderly woman in a red plaid," looking "rough and unfriendly," forced her way through a crowd and "folded [Emilia] in her arms" and called down blessings upon her and Charles. Like the *Mercury*'s later stories about Emilia Dilke as a beloved good woman, Emilia Dilke's letters position her and Charles as objects of working-class affection. "[T]he way in wh the poor women show their sympathy—& the children! . . . The sense of all this is of course a help." Another letter tells of re-ceiving a demonstration of seven or eight hundred working-class local women who presented her with flowers and "an album with solid mounts of pure gold," bought by donations of pennies: "We were all very much upset. A working woman who had got up at 4 all summer to mend & wash in order to spend her day collecting told us the feeling abt Charles was so strong when in some of the poorest houses they offered their penny & wished it £5 they added 'She has our hearts if we cld take our heart out of our bodies to give them her we wld.' "[208]

Emilia Dilke's authority to speak about working-class views on the Dilke case trumps Stead's. Contra Stead, she has plentiful personal evidence of working-class pro-Dilke sentiments even in London, and she proudly relays Alice Westlake's report that "the London workmen say the howling is 'set up by the rich to deprive them of the services of their Charley.' " Emilia Dilke insisted "the 'masses' don't believe [Mrs. Crawford] & are with us. it is the 'classes' who are taking a revenge prompted . . . [by] the sentimentalism wh was roused by Stead."[209] In Emilia Dilke's account, the skilled working class of Chelsea was solidly pro-Dilke *because* of their own sophistication about stories; she claims some "small tradespeople" argued " 'we never heard a whis-per of anything of the kind [e.g., Mrs. Crawford's claims] all these years we must have known something of it if there had been any truth in it.' "[210] If "commonsense" awareness of the efficacy of local gossip networks overrides Stead's claims in this tale, more generally Emilia Dilke's stories claim superior knowledge of working-class sentiment while positioning herself as repeating without amendment views shared by working-class men and women. Emilia Dilke's letters relay every sign of popular support for Charles and herself against that "dirty dishonourable criminal" Stead. A letter to Charles Pearson chortles that Stead once "had his ignominious existence secured" only by Charles's intercession against an angry crowd of miners in the Forest of Dean and narrates in relishing detail the burning of an effigy of Stead "in a funeral pyre greatly composed of Stead's own ravings pamphlets in great stacks &c &c."[211]

Emilia Dilke was relatively dissociated from the middle-class social-purity feminism that dominated Liberal women's organizations in the 1890s because of her husband, but working-class politics offered an alternative set of narratives into which she could inscribe herself as a virtuous and committed political actor, roles perhaps more satisfying than the position of wife to a very powerful man about which she wrote with trepidation in 1884. Her later texts suggest that unexpected plots produced political good: "There are times when it has seemed best for me, perhaps ultimately it may appear best for him too:—only I think I could have helped more people, done more work, and of course I feel that about him, but it may not be so with me, it may be that I have all I can do or that this will help us by and by to do better than we should ever have done otherwise."[212]

Happy Endings?

> He
> If Fate, like an unfaithful gale,
>   Which having vow'd to th' ship a faire event
> O' th' sudden rends her hopeful sail,
>   Blow ruine; will Castara then repent?
> She
> Love shall in that tempestuous shoure
>   Her brightest blossome like the blackthorne show:
> Weake friendship prospers by the poure
>   Of Fortune's sunne: I'le in her winter grow.
>
> —author unknown, transcribed
> in Emilia Dilke's private letters

Emilia Dilke sometimes came near admitting that the case may have produced private good as well. She wrote Eleanor Smith the morning after her wedding of overflowing happiness and a sense of strength.[213] Letters to Smith about the case stand in sharp contrast to the ambivalence and guilt circulating through Francis Pattison's letters to Smith, depicting anger as vitalizing and moral. Emilia Dilke was provoked to "rage" at the "wanton & ghastly cruelty" Mrs. Crawford had inflicted on Charles, but this anger was "not on my own account." If she felt sometimes "mad with anger," the Dilkes' "love & trust" remained "perfect."[214] Emilia Dilke's letters repeatedly emphasized, "the sense of being innocent is [double-underlined] an immense support

. . . One cannot be humiliated when one is in the right," a sharp contrast to the guilt in letters written during her first marriage. The letters project a future narrative of vindication; in time, "the world" would recognize the right. But vindication was not necessary to happiness: "We are so blessed and serene in our home . . . that I tremble with fear lest if our name were cleared some of these rarest gifts we *have* should be taken from us."[215]

The mission of resuscitating Charles Dilke's reputation and political career was, like Emilia Dilke's feminist trade-unionism, an arena in which she could fight for justice from a public stage. Her letters repeatedly figure her as deriving pleasure in combat and gleefully narrate every move and countermove in the battle to vindicate Charles. Long-honed gifts for anger and contempt, on the edge of self-righteousness, buoy Emilia Dilke's letters as they had Francis Pattison's, but this time they demonstrate what a *good* wife she was, how noble and deserving was the man to whom she was bound, how true to him she was.[216] During the two trials, she rallied herself to fortitude by linking these current difficulties to a longer autobiographical narrative of allegiance to moral standards, reflecting, "To love duty & to love the ideal in life those have been my guides from a child & now when the two combine instead of being at war duty shld be easier than ever & I unworthy to 'lighten this great dark' if I turn weak."[217] Later letters claim, despite anger, that her position as defender of a wronged man is unmarred by vindictiveness because superior morality will have its fruition in God's time beyond any human court, although she hoped the "truth" about Virginia Crawford was "filtering gradually into common knowledge." In Pattison/Dilke's art-writing, bad people can create good art; in these letters, good may come from the "evil" of Mrs. Crawford's accusations: " [I do not] share [Stead's] view that if [other people's faults] are as we know [Mrs. Crawford's to be] it is our duty to hunt them down and expose them, for I feel 'Let the wheat and the tares grow together till the harvest!' And, after all, it is impossible to say what good we may not have been brought by their hands . . ."[218] Her faith in Charles allowed her alignment with divine authority: "Nothing can cloud my unshaken confidence in the ultimate triumph of God's truth. I am not even bitter with these His fools in their foolishness. Somehow I feel as if I had my feet under me for the first time in my life. I have no fear of people or their opinion."[219]

Even in relation to damaged or lost friendships, Emilia Dilke positioned herself as sustained by righteousness, approvingly quoting her friend Mrs. Jeune that "no one whose opinion you value will even think for a moment of believing he is anything but innocent."[220] Constance Flower may have placed herself on the firm terrain of morality, but so did Emilia Dilke; according to Charles Dilke, writing after Emilia's death, Flower "made many tries to be taken back into favour" in later years, "but the door was inexorably shut."[221] In Charles's account, Emilia dropped "those . . . whom she had classed as 'cowards' & dishonest," including Ingram Bywater, Venetia Grant-Duff, and Theresa Earle, and was especially scathing about those former intimates whom she depicted as sacrificing their friendship with the Dilkes not from conviction but to preserve their own reputations and ambitions from taint.[222] Retrospectively, Charles claimed Emilia had been right in her "universal rule," but his letters are gracious to those who wrote him with condolences and regrets for lost friendships after her death. His memoirs depict him as sadly realistic about "inevitable" desertions. Emilia's absoluteness had not been feasible for him since "in politics it is not easy."[223]

Despite Charles's summary, the case's many plots had demonstrated the multitudinous entanglements of moral principles and political programs. Moreover, I have argued that, although not often at center stage, Emilia Dilke's figure circulated in the intimate and public, gossipy and official, and always political stories of the case. Apparently an onlooker to the central conflict, she could be cast as "a Ruskin heroine" for Charles Dilke, a helplessly noble and tragically mistaken dupe for J. E. C. Bodley and William Archer, "that beast" 's wife for Beatrice Webb, a Virgin Mary or occupier of privileged access to working-class affection and knowledge in her own various texts, a "Sapphira" for W. T. Stead, a scandalous and disinvited presence for the Warden of Toynbee Hall, a "Second Member" for the Forest of Dean, a properly political woman for the *Dean Forest Mercury*, and an upstanding embodiment of and incitement to fidelity to principle in her own texts. The mobility of her figure condenses the larger lesson of the case: the productivity of stories—their political effects and their continued pleasurable complexities—is far more significant and compelling than any resolved story of what two, or perhaps three, bodies might have done in a bed could do, and that productivity depends not on resolution but on unsolved mysteries. But I want to end by offering other figures of Emilia Dilke and the Dilkes together in their postcase lives.

Emilia Dilke's stories of the case as bringing about good, both in public life and in her heart, are similar in some respects to the story of the Dilke marriage in Gertrude Tuckwell's unpublished "Reminiscences" and the official biography of Charles Dilke that Stephen Gwynn wrote under Tuckwell's direction. Tuckwell's accounts shy away from direct discussion of the Crawford case, and do not draw a direct line between Charles Dilke's compromised political fortunes and the joys of the Dilkes' later lives, but her texts endow both Dilkes with a happy ending. That ending resembles not only the one Emilia Dilke proffered but the ending I have offered in this chapter. Tuckwell's account, like mine, refuses to accept that the Crawford case ended the Dilkes' political activities and instead emphasizes Charles and Emilia Dilke's continued participation—not just hapless figuration—in the politics of class and gender. I do not, of course, take Tuckwell's account as proof of mine, or vice versa, nor am I committed to happy endings. But I want to explicate Tuckwell's accounts because they are political texts, in which the Dilkes' figures perform work. Charles and Emilia Dilke underwrite a form of progressive politics; as in the *Dean Forest Mercury*, in Tuckwell's tales politics can be forged by cooperation across class and gender lines. Moreover, Tuckwell's texts about the Dilkes ground her adult political career in the Sloane Street household. The Crawford-Dilke case was astoundingly productive of conspiracies and villains—"outsiders," from Frenchified aristocrats to Jewish women to interloping "Torquemadas," whose dangers exceed the boundaries of class or gender transgression—but it also produced virtuous political personae for feminists, victims, crusaders, voters, and defenders of wronged women—whether Virginia Crawford, Emilia Dilke, or Britannia herself. But in Gertrude Tuckwell's accounts of Emilia and Charles Dilke's later lives, the Dilkes are lovable and rigorous enablers of women's careers. Tuckwell tells stories in which love produces labor and Labour, and hints at a plot that confounds transgression and virtue: class politics and a perfect heterosexual marriage empowers love between women.

Tuckwell's accounts of the Dilkes' postcase lives cast the Dilkes' romantic union as unshifting, profound, and permanent. Charles and Emilia were "so absorbed in intense sympathy . . . that one felt an interloper in the marriage of true minds, the entire and serene accord of two beings' spiritual lives."[224] Beyond this bedrock of bliss, Tuckwell presents images of movement in varied company. The Dilkes roamed the world, visiting India, Turkey, and Greece, as well as going to Paris every year; these trips combined political fact-gathering, art-historical research, care for their health, visits to friends, and the collecting of awards. (Charles was a particular favorite in Greece, while Emilia accepted an honorary order from the Sultan of the Ottoman Empire.[225]) Tuckwell was by no means inventing the Dilkes' far-flung political engagements: Charles, a leading Liberal Imperialist, was involved in organizations dealing with the rights of colonial subjects in the British Empire, while Emilia wrote essays on missionary activity in China, supported women's medical colleges in India, and summarized contemporary French politics for British readers.[226] Within Britain, the Dilkes' annual round included the Trades Union Congress meeting, solo speaking engagements on trade-unionism in Scotland and Ireland as well as England, and visits to the Forest of Dean.

In Tuckwell's accounts, all the Dilkes' domesticities, in London and on the Thames, are full of happy activity and centers of brilliant society offering affection, fun, politics, and culture, but "the happiest period of [my] life [was] when my aunt and Sir Charles were in London and . . . [76 Sloane Street was] a second home for me."[227] The "Reminiscences" contrast Sloane Street to her own family and to the drudgery of a training to be a schoolteacher.[228] Tuckwell highlights the Dilkes' care, education, inspiration and excitement, and the resources—people and knowledge—to which she gained access through Uncle Charles and "Lady Fussie." Tuckwell remembered trade-unionist Will Crooks but "admitted" that when she was "young," it was the "personal beauty" of many guests that struck her most, especially when she met literary luminaries and "exotic" figures like the Ranee of Sarawak. French friends of Emilia Dilke's, including "old painter friends," various ambassadors, a millionaire, Cornelie Renan, Marie-Thérèse Ollivier, and Auguste Rodin are noted, as are daily fencing on the terrace with a French master. Although 76 Sloane Street felt "more like a country house than a house in London," lined with pictures of ancestors of whom Charles was very vain and about whom Tuckwell quickly learned as if they were her own, it was also intensely urban, humming with activity, as M.P.s, organizers, lobbyists, secretaries, and delegations came and went. "Tea on Sundays . . . was a gathering for all sorts of people," but Tuckwell emphasized her introduction to Labour society, especially that of activists who impressed her by their "kindness and generous acceptance."[229] "Gee" gained knowledge that helped her create a public career and she learned that class and political lines could be crossed.

I have noted the dangers of such lessons. Emilia Dilke's writings sometimes produced boundary-crossing as the privilege only of those already privileged, and, like the Forest of Dean Radicals, ignored or scorned forms of feminism that suggested that men's and women's interests might not be identical; feminist historians have examined the construction of female professionalism in social and political work as potentially resting on the silencing or disciplining of working-class subjects; and other historians have examined assumptions that elite culture was or should be unproblematically desirable to working-class subjects. Moreover, although Tuckwell wrote that Emilia Dilke's "presence dominated all," in many respects, Tuckwell's account of Sloane Street during her youth reiterates Charles Dilke's account of metropolitan childhood.[230] As Tuckwell tells it, Dilke household culture forged and expressed Radical convictions and enshrined public life—the motto of the house was "nothing must ever come before the work"—while simultaneously offering an ethos of cultivated leisure and intellectual self-development. Social obligation and self-development were saved from deteriorating into noblesse oblige by the Dilkes' political convictions and the moral force of their characters. Tuckwell's 76 Sloane Street is a site of nonantagonistic, polite, and career-forwarding progressive politics, and the stories Tuckwell tells enmesh politics in a language of service and culture. These stories not only echo earlier Dilke stories, but the whole oeuvre of Dilke family stories condenses wider liberal middle-class self-narrations whose strengths, blindspots, assumptions of adequacy, and hidden tensions with class politics were identified by Raymond Williams.[231]

Tuckwell's account also echoes earlier accounts of 76 Sloane Street in its emphasis on heterosociality and women's intellectual activity. Tuckwell's Charles and Emilia "*concentrated on their own*" work and Emilia Dilke is not identical to her husband; "the interests of the two were divergent," although they "read and thought together" and the "intellectual sympathy between them" was "complete."[232] Tuckwell quotes Constance Smith that "Lady Dilke's charm and gaiety appealed to her, but . . . she was chiefly won by a sense of the mental discipline to which both my aunt and my uncle had subjected themselves"; femininity and gaiety were less impressive or seductive to some observers than an undertone of ruthless focus. Tuckwell claimed that Emilia, because of her dedication to labor and lack of interest in luxury (apart, of course, from travel, paintings, books, and picturesque dress), created an impression of Spartan simplicity, but Tuckwell includes a provocative remark by Maud Pember Reeves: "It is a pity she should always have a footman and a maid in attendance. She ought to be on a desert island, where she would adapt anything to her service."[233] Tuckwell's account of Charles stresses his purported selflessness, lengthily lauding his reputation among younger men as " 'wiser than most and more generous than any' in placing his vast ordered knowledge at the service of young beginners." Tuckwell cites Reginald McKenna: "Exact knowledge, unremitting industry, lucid expression, he might have learned for himself, but it was at the house in Sloane Street that he had received his introduction to Liberal society" and "had been taught to prefer logic and hard facts to rhetoric and emotion." Although "constantly accused of omniscience," especially about "industrial conditions in other countries . . . French history from 1848 onwards, or English politics," so encyclopedic was his knowledge, Tuckwell's Charles is self-effacing, replying to those who urged him to "take more credit," "What does it matter who did it so long as the thing is done."[234]

Tuckwell's texts make the Dilkes' river houses on the Thames, Pyrford Rough and

Dockett Eddy, auxiliary synecdoches of activity, cosmpolitan company, and comedy. Pyrford, the smaller house, was more private and nominally a retreat for the Dilkes alone; it was a four-room cottage on fifteen acres near Woking which Charles had given Emilia as a wedding present, largely furnished with the belongings Emilia kept from her life at Lincoln College, combining "Empire furniture and family relics."[235] Pyrford is evidence of the Dilkes' natural and warm qualities. They deliberately planted "no formal garden" but allowed "Nature [to] ha[ve] her way" in the plantation of pines, and Charles prided himself on his natural historical observations of the local owls, beetles, and "large, black, and horrific" spiders.[236] Charles and Emilia took pride in their "cattery," where they bred "Persian tailless cats" in great numbers, giving them silly and mostly French names—"Babettes, Papillons, Pierrots, and Pierrettes, Mistigrises and Beelzebubs"—before presenting them to unwary friends.[237] Tuckwell describes Charles's enslavement to his own cats—Zulu, Calino, and others—in endearing detail.[238] Even in this informal retreat, the Dilkes entertained friends, including Charlotte and Bernard Shaw, Mary Arnold-Forster and May Abraham Tennant; after Emilia's death, Charles established William and Rosa Tuckwell as permanent residents.[239] Dockett Eddy was a larger house near Shepperton, to which the Dilkes brought substantial parties for long weekends, lodging them in a separate house.[240] At Dockett, the natural interests were water voles and birds, especially the swans of which Emilia had written before their marriage. Gwynn and Tuckwell recount pitched battles between rival groups of swans for Charles's lavish daily feedings; Dilke and his friends stoutly defended the "local" swans against interlopers, and "even in the night, when sound of warfare rose, the master of Dockett was known to scull out in a dinghy, in his nightgear, carrying a bedroom candlestick to guide his blows in the fray".[241]

Dockett life placed demands on visitors: in addition to riding, Charles was a passionate oarsman, and Emilia had a dinghy, the "Bumble Bee." The expectation that guests should be equally devoted to exercise led one to remark that Dockett was "less a country house than a camp of exercise. You did as you pleased, but under Sir Charles's guidance you were pleased to be strenuous" and to swim at seven a.m.[242] Here the Dilkes brought Reginald McKenna and Sir Ian and Lady Hamilton; Rhoda Broughton and the French actors Guitry and Coquelin; the painter DaCosta and the head of Mansfield College; Maud Pember Reeves and Annie Marland; Will Crooks, Lloyd George, and others. A tale of Emilia Dilke's friendly relations with a community of "gipsies" near Dockett is offered as more evidence that her aunt, despite her title and the possibility of a life of ease, transcended class.[243] In her accounts of "country life," Tuckwell reiterates the themes that dominate her stories of the Dilke marriage, the crossing of boundaries and the mixing of intellectual, political, and social life. Her depictions of Charles Dilke condense her theme of mobility across registers: readers might think him "always serious," a political workhorse, but Tuckwell quotes Anna de Rothschild on his rapid transitions; full of "joyousness and boyish laughter . . . his face became grave immediately" if the subject changed to political work.[244]

These emphases on joy and work run throughout Tuckwell's images of the Dilkes together; her texts speak of loving them for their combination of pleasure and purpose. Happiness also circulates through the texts framing Emilia Dilke's death. According to

Charles Dilke, Emilia Dilke's penultimate visit to Paris was a time of "gaiety . . . un-restrained," and in her last visit to the Forest of Dean, her companions found Emilia Dilke "never so bright, so gay." Just before her death, Charles Dilke wrote, Emilia insisted to him that she had "never been so happy," and, Tuckwell relays, told Mary Arnold-Forster she had had "nineteen years of unclouded happiness" with Charles.[245] In Tuckwell's account, not only is romantic happiness politically productive, but Tuckwell ascribed to both Dilkes theories that happiness was possible even in sorrow if one could continue to work. After Emilia's death in 1904, Charles told Gertrude "he meant to continue finding [life] interesting." When, in 1911, Tuckwell lost the second of "these two great figures who had inspired us," she found comfort recalling her aunt's reply to a question about how she had felt in Draguignan. In work, even alone, one could be "content."[246]

Tuckwell's tale of her aunt's happy ending also provides her with some plots of her own about politics, work, and romance. Tuckwell repeatedly suggests that the Dilke household of married partnership empowered unmarried women. Certainly, she gained means to economic independence there, not only because Emilia Dilke bequeathed her an annuity which gave her a guaranteed income but because she, like other young women working with Emilia Dilke in trade-unionist activities, gained employment, training, encouragement, introductions, goading, and excitement that enabled a career in politics and social reform.[247] In Tuckwell's account, loving respect for Emilia Dilke, as well as shared moral seriousness, united these younger women with each other; Beatrice Potter envied Emilia Dilke because "her pretty secretary is devoted to her, so are all the women with whom she is connected in the trade union propaganda—she has distinctly the milk of human kindness," and one secretary wrote love poems to her Lady.[248] But affection and eros was not only directed from the younger to the older woman in Tuckwell's tale. The young women introduced new members into the circle—Eliza Orme brought May Abraham, Gertrude introduced Constance Smith, and Margaret Bondfield "found" Mary Macarthur.[249]

Virginia Crawford and W. T. Stead had mapped 76 Sloane Street as a site of lesbian perversities under the direction of degenerate men. In Tuckwell's accounts, however, the Dilkes' heterosexual households were sites of comedy and labor and 76 Sloane Street was the setting for the formation of loving and working bonds between independent women. It was also a seedbed for the establishment of new homes. Tuckwell's romantic friendship with May Abraham brought "fun" into her life, and they lived together until Abraham married H. J. Tennant in 1896. The Crawfords and Stead twice told stories of depraved triangulation. The story that Charles Dilke had affairs with both Virginia Crawford and Eustacia Smith offered the scandal of incestuous sameness, while the allegations of threesomes with Fanny Grey offered scandalous breeches of the lines of class difference. But Gertrude Tuckwell's texts hint at triangles in which family ties and class politics create respectable female romances. Gertrude Tuckwell and Constance Smith became close as members of the Sloane Street circle. Smith strikingly resembles Emilia Dilke in Tuckwell's texts: she is multilingual, combines fiction writing with social reform, a passion for detail and "intervals of lovely play," is Rhoda Broughton's friend, and takes joy in work and "all knowledge for her province." Smith travelled with Gertrude and Charles after Emilia's death and was with Gertrude at Charles's deathbed. Gertrude and Constance then lived together, at least for a few years, in Mecklenburgh Square. After Smith's 1931 death, Tuckwell wrote her life story. In Tuckwell's unpublished reminiscences and her elegiac *Constance Smith*, Tuckwell inscribes Smith, the Dilkes, and herself in a large and unended narrative of morally valorized historical change, but the politics of social reform also enable romantic happy endings for women. Smith appears as one of Tuckwell's great loves.[250]

7

RENAISSANCES

E F. S. Pattison's two-volume *The Renaissance of Art in France* (1879) was followed by a biocritical study in French, *Claude Lorrain, Sa Vie et Ses Oeuvres* in 1884; Pattison published at least a hundred *signed* articles and reviews between 1869 and 1884. Emilia Dilke wrote *Art in the Modern State*—on French art and the state under Louis XIV—and her four volumes on French art in the eighteenth century, covering painting, sculpture, engraving, drawing, architecture, furniture, and decoration, as well as essays, reviews, and contributions to the *Encyclopaedia Britannica*.[1] Pattison/Dilke's works on French art extend from the fifteenth century through and beyond the *Salon des Réfusés*; Colin Eisler claimed, "To this day, no other scholar can be said to have been so profoundly cognizant of five hundred years of French art as this Englishwoman, who was largely self-educated in the fields of her professional activity."[2] Pattison/Dilke's range is unnerving. Her work drew on source texts and scholarly works in many languages and historical knowledge of Italy, Germany, early Christianity, and ancient Greece. She routinely reviewed works in German and French, and according to Charles Dilke, read French, Latin, German, Greek, Italian, Spanish, Portugese, Dutch, and Provençal and was learning Swedish and Welsh before she died.[3] Her texts give little help to less knowledgeable readers; she rarely translated quotations from French or German. Eisler aptly describes *The Renaissance of Art in France* as written "utterly without compromise . . . for the reader without a mastery of the French language and considerable familiarity with the period and with art history in general."[4] In 1868, E. F. S. Pattison claimed or admitted, " 'an author cannot be lively and amusing' when treating of the object of his life's labours; 'he is overburdened by the very fulness of his knowledge,' " and publishers and other critics must understand that "sound works [especially on engraving, sculpture, and architecture] . . . could not . . . be rendered fit for the general reader"; Pattison foresaw that erudition alone might not secure a wide readership.[5]

Emilia Dilke wrote of the eighteenth century, "the subject is so vast that to attempt to treat it . . . may be likened to the child's effort to 'put the sea in yonder hole.' " Similarly, this chapter cannot examine all of Pattison/Dilke's art-historical and critical writing, but even if it could, I do not want to pull her writings into a single object to be read for a theory of art and history. Pattison/Dilke's texts confidently make assessments of aesthetic and intellectual value, but I shall not judge them by standards of consistency or originality or against current scholarly or political thinking. Moreover, although Emilia Dilke once suggested that another scholar's work was displaced self-portraiture—in Pater's *Imaginary Portraits*, "the very incompleteness of these portraits . . . adds to the reality of their characterization as pictures of states of [the author's] own mind"—her contorted phrasing (incompleteness produces the effect of reality? portraits offer characterizations of pictures of states?) gives a warning about reading texts for access to her "own mind."[6] This chapter, rather, reads very selectively to consider the lability and power of some stories, the mobility and usefulness of some themes, and homologies of figuration and argument across diverse texts.

This chapter has an evocative name and inhabits an awkward genre. It is not a conclusion, nor, although Emilia Dilke's death appeared in the last chapter, an epitaph by way of epilogue. In chapter five, I noted Francis Pattison's participation in wider constructions of the Renaissance as an object of study and fantasy and a site for theorizing subjectivity, sometimes infused with gendered and sexual meanings. In Pattison/Dilke's writings, the Renaissance can be a privileged moment, a touchstone, an object of desire and love, loss and futurity; a field of knowledge and expertise; an analogy; a plot element in stories of liberation.[7] In this chapter, I read some Pattison/Dilke texts of "the Renaissance" to revisit some themes that move across her texts and mine—violence, pleasure, bodiliness, knowledge, nature, and history. Some of the texts I consider will be familiar; "Renaissances" is a repetition and a microcosm of some themes of *Names and Stories* as a whole. But this chapter's title also recalls issues raised in the introduction. The word "Renaissance" is a metaphor based on a woman's body, carrying within it a narrative of a life creating another life. The Renaissance is thus the name given a particular history and a figuration of history; rebirth is both repetition and newness, and in Pattison/Dilke's texts, the Renaissance is a future as well as a skein of stories about pasts. My history ends with a story about a future as well.

Renaissance Stories

> Periods of question, of doubt, of examination; periods in which improper methods are employed to ascertain their value—such periods in the world's history have their little image in the life of the individual.
>
> —Emilia Dilke, "The Idealist Movement
> and Positive Science"

The first Renaissance story I present is not in Pattison/Dilke's scholarly works. Emilia Dilke's "The Idealist Movement and Positive Science" flagrantly tempts us to read it as an autobiographical text; we even have permission. Charles Dilke's "Memoir" of Emilia Dilke tells us that the story of her male "friend" was her own story, and several passages from the "friend's" narrative appear in essays in Emilia Dilke's *The Book of the Spiritual Life*.[8] I have read "The Idealist Movement" in relation to religiosity and aesthetization and to stories of seduction, marriage, and sex, noting overlapping languages between the essay, Emilia Dilke's short stories of bad marriages, and Francis Pattison's letters. If the transgendering of the narrative of Emilia Dilke's "friend" obscures or delegitimizes some meanings, another text authorizes reading stories of pain across gender lines: *The Renaissance of Art in France* describes portraits of Henri II as having "a touch of silent suspicion and distress, as in the face of a woman long oppressed . . . sometimes softened by inquiry, or entreaty rather, sometimes crossed by a shade of dull regret."[9] "The Idealist Movement" is legible as an emotional history, and its narrative of revolt and exultant dénouement is appealing. But without blocking readings of "The Idealist Movement" as autobiography or cancelling the other uses to which I have put it, I want to read its story about the Renaissance.

The essay does not begin with the Renaissance. Quoting St. Augustine, it grandly announces its purpose: to define "the whole duty of the spiritual life." According to Gertrude Tuckwell, Emilia Dilke always carried Augustine's *Confessions* in her pocket but Dilke's constant access to the text does not mean she stops at transcription.[10] The first lines quote Augustine's admonition, "O amare, O ire, O sibi perire, O ad Deum pervenire," then offer a "translation" and elaborate on Augustine's ideal of selflessness. "To love, that is to learn the Divine charity; to press forward beyond all earthly barriers . . . to die to the world, so that we may live to God."[11] The translation signals the essay's direction: it tells a story of education, barriers, and achievement in which selflessness and self-attainment are entwined, oscillating between admonitions to achieve and to eschew selfhood. The Renaissance authorizes this story.

"The Idealist Movement" thematizes, as discussed in chapter 3, the generalized struggles of the ardent young, but then diffidently offers an individual story explicitly marked as unfinished. "[T]he experience even of what St. François de Sales might call 'an incomplete soul' may have some interest for, or be of some use to, those who share its aspirations and desires." The "fragment of self-history" is that of "one well known to me," a young man.[12] This soul's story doubly resists closure, not only because, like the Renaissance, it is uncontained by an ending but also because it is disavowed by the authorial voice. Yet it is a "true" story ("he" is well known to the author) and meaningful because this young man shares his predicaments with others. The young man, brought up in the High Church, "took to heart the moral code of Anglo-Catholicism with intense fervour," especially in his dedication to "self-abnegation and self-sacrifice." The importance of reading and the dangers of misreading are prominent; the "friend" found his early spiritual bearings through a rigorous course of reading and he is reshaped by other books. His reading, although "directed solely by the desire to find confirmation and support of the principles in which he had been instructed," leads him away from "emotional" practices like confession and penance, although he retains the ethical system of Christianity; he was not spiritually fickle but one of those "to whom it seems . . . that in cutting themselves adrift from their most cherished associations they are obeying a higher call."[13] But the young man's philosophical and theological peregrinations did not move him toward greater freedom; when he subscribes to positivism, "the fulfilment of the obligations of [Comtism] demanded too a self-abnegation as complete as that exacted by the 'Imitatio Christi,' " and the friend's "determination . . . to work out the Comtist system in daily life brought no change into [his] . . . conception of the standard of duty."[14]

The protagonist is increasingly unhappy as he grows:

> I began to be aware, as my powers and character matured, that my whole nature fought against the self-imposed yoke. I became aware of an intense desire for the enjoyment of life—not in any limited or common sense, but a desire for knowledge and experience in every direction, utterly incompatible with the ideal of entire self-renunciation. . . . But I regarded the protest of my own nature as immoral, and strove yet more earnestly to suppress it.[15]

He feels "horror" at the "narrowness and pressure of [his] immediate surroundings" but believes his desires are "truly sinful." Confinement and guilt lead to despair. "Then it would seem to me as if all the capacity for pleasure, all the energy which prompted me to ask for the widest possibilities of life, were tied and bound as with chains." He hopes that "by self-discipline, all cravings would be stilled" and attempts to translate his experience into spiritually valorizing terms, to define his sense of "deadness" as "withdrawal from the world" and "monotony" as "aspiration to the higher life." He is isolated and misunderstood, but seeks to "cheat [him]self by forcing the very passion with which I desired other things into the one outlet that I believed to be authorized, carrying this so far as to feign pleasure in these enforced courses."[16]

I earlier suggested some possible readings of "enforced courses," but here I want to focus on another issue: the young man's hope that "constant acting would become second nature." This may be read against Francis Pattison's legitimizing her sexual refusal in marriage by referring to her bodily "nature," but in "The Idealist Movement" concerns with "nature" are varied. The young man hopes a nature can be made and that the line between acting and being may be porous. Paradoxically, manufacturing "self-sacrifice" and enacting self-abnegation may produce a new selfhood.[17] If this element of Dilke's essay implies a commonality with nineteenth-century discourses of self-construction or contemporary theories of narrative and performativity, Dilke goes on to complicate the young man's attempt to remake his self. In Dilke's account, studies of selflessness lead to revolution. Through studies in religious history, the young man reaches the Renaissance.[18] Studying the Renaissance and classical sources via the Renaissance, Emilia Dilke's friend embraces "the Aristotelian conception of the satisfaction of all the energies as offering a complete and splendid theory of life." This discovery combines anger and ecstasy:

> To conceive of such a theory . . . was to conceive of a justification of revolt. It was light in the darkness . . . a true man should demand, as of right, all pleasure, all knowledge, life at full stretch between morn and night . . . The system of which I felt the wheels grinding all around me . . . added to my intolerance. I appeared to myself to have been

robbed, to have robbed myself, of life . . . It was more than a reaction against Christian and Comtist ideals, it was a revolt. It was something so new to one such as I, to recognise that the individual had rights, had a right to live in the development of his own nature, to satisfy his own aspirations, to possess himself . . .

Philosophical study allows critique of daily life: he rebels against the "falsity of [his] life," and poses questions: " 'Why,' I asked, 'should I never take my will of anything? Why should my days be all duty . . . ?' 'Why should I renounce my own interests and convictions . . . ?' "[19]

The acquisition of anger and desire is painful; self-assertion brought "no joy" but "terrible catastrophe," "so painful a divorce" was it from previous "principles of action" and convictions. This pain guarantees the morality of the young man's re-volt—the demand for "all pleasure" may be a revolt against "feigned pleasures" but is not itself pleasurable—but Dilke's essay confirms that her young man is at moral risk. "The self, which I had so long held at bay, now avenged the subjection to which it had been condemned, and—in the desperation of the struggle, which seemed like one for life—I was . . . ready to thrust aside all claims that others might have on me, lest my own should be eternally foregone."[20] Reassuringly, the friend's rebellion against authority and rigidity does not continue at the high pitch of exhilaration and fury with which it began; he swings back to more considered views, coming to recognize, after the initial violence of his "divorce," that some parts of his earlier mental framework were still valuable. Like Eliot's Dorothea, Dilke's young man learns that "permanent rebellion, the disorder of a life without some loving reverent resolve was not possible for [him]."[21] Dilke underscores that revolt leads not to self-absorption but to empowered ethical engagement with worldly life; he has renewed energy and "we all observed in him an ever-deepening absorption in the problems of modern life." His ability to act meaningfully in the world, by comparison with his earlier paralyzing despair, rests on his experience of passion and individualism. Respecting the claims of self leads to socially worthy ends and even, in "absorbtion," a new and more legitimate form of self-forgetfulness.[22]

On the surface, Dilke's tale is about religion and "science," metaphysics and pos-itivism, conversion, deconversion, and reconversion. The young man moves from faith to doubt, which is then exposed as another form of faith, to doubt again, and on to new, more complex faith, reconciling "the wide views of the Humanists" with "the narrow lines of Positivist theories," to finally conclude that "metaphysics really give scientific form to the very truths which religion offers to our apprehension through the emotions." The resolution of the young man's crisis may be the rather banal conviction that science and religion are complementary branches of human knowledge, whose truths are in fundamental accord, and hackneyed assertions of "the impossibility of arriving at a correct estimate of any fact of human life by reason alone." But Dilke's young man also develops a historical theory. He envisions a "model society," a new "ideal, perhaps less romantic but as imposing as that of the feudal times with which Church history had brought him into early familiarity." Dilke's protagonist connects his historical theory and his political/social ideas to the ideal of an expansive Renaissance self, in a vague and brief invocation of evolution. He "became . . . deeply impressed by the fertility of the Darwinian idea of the 'per-petual increase of facts in the universe' in its application to questions of a political and social nature, and began to conceive of the modern revolution and of the irre-sistible development of democracy from a new point of view . . . it appeared to [him] that the ideal of the world, and that of every form of human energy, must necessarily transform itself with the new wants and new discoveries of each generation." These proliferations—of facts, political subjects, and desires—have an analogue in his mind: developing an evolutionary scheme of "the whole hierarchy of human knowledge," his story ends with the recognition of the impossibility of ending.[23]

"The Idealist Movement" swings between endings and unendedness, nature and history, to its last page. Dilke's essay quotes Goethe to maintain this tension, again invoking nature: Dilke lauds those who "wander astray on a path of [their] own . . . If [they] ever find the right path . . . the path that suits their nature, they will never leave it." The ending is a future, but, through Goethe, Dilke also asserts that the past is meaningful, that every turn of the young man's tale was expressive and valuable. Past wisdoms, collective and individual, are recuperable for the future—the Renais-sance and the classic past are rediscoverable and powerful—but the peroration to "The Idealist Movement" emphasizes again the endlessness of the future and the natural unboundedness of the self, by urging an ideal "habit of never resting satisfied with the forms of knowledge." Dilke's essay envisions selves that are expansive and unlim-ited; the self is both a natural ground of rights and the site of continuing and laborious transformation, always "pushing on" with an awareness of constant change.[24] Nature and history offer permanence without the price of foreclosing the future.

"The Idealist Movement" 's rhetoric of recursion, social and individual suppres-sion, necessary and earned revolt, also organizes Pattison/Dilke's art-writing. The terms of history, nature, pleasure, violence, morality, social engagement, endings, recuperations, losses, and returns circulate unstably throughout her art-historical and critical texts. In Emilia Dilke's "friend" 's tale in "The Idealist Movement," the Re-naissance eloquently reveals and legitimates the demands of "nature"; in Pattison/ Dilke's art history, the Renaissance is an eruption of natural, vibrant energy, "Nature . . . reassert[ing] herself."[25] But Pattison/Dilke's somewhat hydraulic accounts are his-torical as well as natural; her art-historical texts emphasize suppression as strongly as explosion, the perversion as well as the power of natural forces, and produce a history of art that is social, economic, and political as well as aesthetic. In her 1873 review of Walter Pater's *Studies in the History of the Renaissance*, E. F. S. Pattison argued that Pater underemphasizes the necessity of fostering social conditions for the historical pro-duction of art objects. His Renaissance was "an air-plant, independent of the ordinary senses of nourishment," "a sentimental revolution having no relation to the condi-tions of the actual world." In Pater's account, "we miss the sense of the connection between art and literature and the other forms of life of which they are the outward expression, and feel as if we were wandering in a world of unsubstantial dreams."[26] But if Pater's Renaissance was too ethereal, E. F. S. Pattison's *The Renaissance of Art in France* is material twice over, locating historical agency in nature and in politics, in the human body and in worldly events and institutions, and these themes move across other Pattison/Dilke texts.

The doubling of materiality is displayed, and compounded, by an emphasis on violence. Pattison's French Renaissance is violent: "imprisoned instincts burst their bonds," "life" which had "languished under an enforced repression . . . foreign to

[its] temperment" erupts, and this "contagion" spreads. Pattison's Renaissance is also *produced through* violence, not only by natural forces surging powerfully but through acts of human force. Pattison's history begins with a specific and detailed political history of war, "men sinning in full knowledge" and French armies committing "treachery," "plunder," "rape and rapine," against the "ancient spirit of independence" in Italy. In Pattison's tale, French art profits from Italy's ruin and good things come of bad.[27] Pattison's narrative alternates emphases on the French Renaissance's dependence on the contingent violence of historical events and on the violence of inevitable, recurring human passion. Yet Pattison's Renaissance is also a repudiation of violence. Most narrowly, Pattison's Renaissance ends with the murder of Bernard Palissy and the assassination of Henri III in 1589; more broadly, the loss of the Renaissance is a violent suppression.

Several aspects of this history of force are especially notable. First, Pattison's story of the Renaissance is defiantly antimedieval. Pattison's narrative of the Middle Ages recalls "The Idealist Movement," in which the young man is oppressed by outer circumstances and tormented by interiorized ideals; Dilke depicts his ruthless self-repression under the influence of a powerful belief system as a form of violence.[28] In Pattison/Dilke's histories, the Middle Ages too oppress both outwardly and inwardly. Pattison's medieval artist is suppressed and subjected in an "inexorable order" that cruelly contains, and her Middle Ages are marked by the violence of ideals against selves. "A Gothic Cathedral oppresses the mind as heavily as the Pyramids with the sense of the subjection of the individual."[29] Elsewhere, Pattison finds danger in too little social amity; her essay on Poussin present him as endangered not only by repression but by a crisis of social cohesion, since in his time, "Frenchmen . . . held no faith, no hope, no interest in common." Poussin can only achieve his great work after he experiences a sustaining social community in Rome, where he "began to trust in others, and to have confidence in himself"; thereafter he can be "alone, but free," but creative genius first requires the teaching and nurturance of others.[30] But in Pattison's Middle Ages, this developmental narrative is impossible and moral ideals only oppress.

Moreover, in Pattison/Dilke's histories, the Middle Ages are a period of damage to bodies. In *The Renaissance of Art in France*, during the Middle Ages the "senses and their appetites had been debased and degraded in the estimation of men."[31] The culture of asceticism resulted in representational violence against bodies: an early essay on "Art and Morality" by E. F. S. Pattison claims medieval Italian painting could only "stammer . . . under the burden" of religious injunctions; however "intended to express majesty and religious awe," these images offer "staring eyes, shapeless hands, and crude colouring," and only gradually did artists struggle free of "the trammels of asceticism."[32] Elsewhere Pattison repeats this claim that "the sentiment of the devout ascetic is foreign to the sympathy of the artist," and can only produce "emaciated forms."[33] Moreover, as mentioned earlier, Pattison contended that because medieval culture denied and hated sexuality, its images of women in particular were tortured— "saintly virgins whose meagre forms had been blanched and attentuated by the shade of cloistered discipline." Emilia Dilke reiterates: in the Middle Ages the arts were "devoted to a virgin image . . . [of] beauty born of . . . self-imposed conditions of moral and physical suffering," while the Renaissance brings a "queenly Venus."[34]

Pattison's Renaissance is both liberation from and the containment of violence and desire. In "Art and Morality," Renaissance artists struggle free of medieval constraints and produce bodies of "grace," "majesty," "meaning," and "supple . . . limbs," in a microcosm of a grander history: "That which is depicted by mature art is not 'man as a moral being' . . . so much as man as a physical being—man in possession of bodily perfection . . . The progress of art . . . consists of its passage from the representation of spirit to the representation of body . . ."[35] In Pattison's *The Renaissance of Art in France*, as in Dilke's "The Idealist Movement," there is a temporary plot twist: the medieval hatred of the senses produced a period that precedes the Renaissance in which the result of long asceticism is license. In Pattison's history, medieval moralism produced sinfulness in this far from precisely defined but dangerous intermediate period. People became "as vile as they had been accounted," with "utter foulness of manners and habits of indiscriminate excess."[36] Pattison proffers François Villon as an example of the transitional period, a figure of talent and vitality consumed by understandable but inadequate revolt. "Villon is a voice of the reaction. The cry which he utters is simply, 'Let us live!' . . . only by no means die without having tasted the pleasures of life." In an analogue of "The Idealist Movement" 's young man's period of repudiation of all obligations, Villon's embrace of "passion" is comprehensible, but while Dilke's young man's story then moves on a further stage of self-development, Pattison's Villon is a sad manifestation of history's power. Born late enough to revolt against self-suppression, he is too soon to achieve a nobler form of freedom.

Pattison's tale of the Middle Ages—of violence and bodies—and her construction of an intermediate stage sketches a larger historical trajectory which, absolving her Renaissance, abuts a complicated terrain of arguments about politics, especially class politics, and cultural histories. Pattison's text is strongly and obviously anti-Ruskinian. If it is a simplification to say that, for Ruskin the medieval period occupied pride of place and the Renaissance was an unmitigated disaster, it is a simplification Ruskin himself was willing to make; he wrote Emilia Dilke, recalling her in youth: "when you sate studying Renaissance with me in the Bodleian I supposed you to intend contradicting everying I had ever said about Art-History—or Social Science. . . . To obey me is to love Turner—and hate Raphael—to love gothic—and hate Renaissance."[37] More generally, Pattison/Dilke's views were at odds with romantic medievalisms of all kinds, from Thomas Carlyle's reactionary nostalgias to William Morris's socialist visions of medievalized futures.[38] The political valencies of medievalism were obviously diverse. Pattison/Dilke's antimedievalism also reminds us that the emphasis on craftsmanship and the value, dignity, and beauty of labor which is central to the whole array of Victorian medievalisms and which can be associated, in the case of Morris, with radical politics, could also be detached from medievalism; Pattison/Dilke's works argue for the importance of studying and cherishing the skills of anonymous or forgotten laborers in the French courts of the seventeenth and eighteenth centuries.[39] Pattison's *Renaissance* implicitly denounces histories that forget the work and talents of artisans; such are complicitous and continuous with more overt violences. History has "embalmed the brutal freaks of Charles . . . the midnight excursions of Margaret of Navarre, the suppers and intrigues of Catherine de Medici," but not the lives of those who did the work that "made the court lustrous"; their lives and their "inspired labours," "delicate pencil[s]," "nobl[e] arts," and "coloured glass" have been "despised" and "trampled under foot." Pattison's Palissy, "man, artist, [and] martyr," is an emblem of this violence; he was doubly murdered, when, after he was killed by bigotry, his skills were degraded by successors who command only "clumsy correctness [and] slovenly facility."[40] Inadequate histories compound this violence. At the least, Pattison/Dilke's combination of an ardent embrace of the Renaissance and vehement repudiation of the Middle Ages with scholarly commitment to craft labor and active public engagement in reform politics including trade-unionism, offers a reminder of the multiplicity of possible combinations of aesthetic theories, histories, and political positions. In addition, Pattison/Dilke's antimedievalism directs us to attend to the theories of history at play in texts that ground social and political critiques of the present in stories of the past. Pattison/Dilke's Renaissance is a touchstone for the future as well as an expression of natural energies—therefore, in two senses, timeless—but her language of historical development commonly deploys images of progression rather than return and insists on irremediable historical losses as well as survivals.

Pattison's Renaissance history reinscribes the terrible power of violence in its accounts of endings: The Renaissance of Art in France ends with deaths. Both The Renaissance and other Pattison/Dilke texts argue that the Renaissance is followed by a period in which art, nature, and selves are violated. Pattison/Dilke's Renaissance "failed to obtain social and political expression" and was therefore followed by an epoch in which the individual was subjected to "arbitrary government."[41] This longer history, of the Renaissance's occlusion, is the trajectory of Pattison/Dilke's art-historical oeuvre as a whole, but this account is also repeatedly adumbrated in individual works. Pattison's essay on Poussin, for example, stresses the damage done to art and the artist by social and political power; the French Renaissance's movement towards worldly engagement was constricted by political institutions that harnessed art to the State. "It had come to be felt in France that the strivings of thought . . . brought nothing but ill to the State" and the "State police" sought to contain "the evil tendencies of unfettered thought."[42]

The weight of Pattison's liberal narrative in this essay and in Art in the Modern State is on the power of social and political institutions and milieux to damage, thwart, or retard individual development and to suppress nature. The repression of thought is not only through direct state action against dissenters; in the essay on Poussin as in "The Idealist Movement," mental isolation cripples the self when society fails to properly hold and sustain the individual. However, in Emilia Dilke's studies of the eighteenth century, especially her books on sculpture and architecture and on painting, the violence of false ideals is stressed. "Pseudo-classicism" is "dead" and deadening; "dry and futile"; "strict and cold"; ideas are subordinated to "artificial ideals" and "inexorable . . . logic and strict conformity" kill "fancy"; it produces "frigid" works, "pulseless effigies," and "mere archaeology" in art.[43] As in Pattison's Middle Ages, no license could be as bad as such suppression. Art done under the aegis of "correct[ness]" is marked by "vice" and "evils." If earlier artists had fallen victim to "the madness of the curve" and their exuberance had been "ridiculous, sometimes even grotesque," it had "often" been "entertaining and delightful"; "the madness of the straight line" was death itself, its abstraction free of "vitality."[44]

Individual genius and creativity are responsible for artistic greatness but cannot ensure it against social, political, and philosophical repression. But Pattison/Dilke's narratives of the Renaissance, like Oscar Wilde's, are hopeful.[45] The Renaissance is a past of possibilities tragically foreshortened, but its very name promises recurrence. As in the Middle Ages and "The Idealist Movement," energies corrupted and enfenced will reemerge. In *Art in the Modern State*, the process is inevitable and present: "Now for the last hundred years the protest against the suppression of the Renaissance has been gathering strength. To fight against it is as irrational as to become its fanatical apologist; it requires neither advocacy nor apology, it is an inevitable transformation— an historical evolution."[46] The eighteenth-century works offer a less smooth narrative, arguing, like "The Idealist Movement" and *The Renaissance of Art in France*, that violent suppressions create violent returns. Even in the early eighteenth century, "claims . . . ignored since the days of the Renaissance, made themselves felt with all the arrogance of recovered liberty," and Dilke's eighteenth-century works locate the origins of the French Revolution both in the betrayal of the Renaissance and in the return of its spirit.[47]

Pattison's essay on Poussin also stresses both violent loss and survival: the French Renaissance was a blossoming "plant . . . cut down, and in its place, well be-fenced and guarded, flourished the gaudy parasite of courts"; this "vain cultivation received the apples of Sodom." Poussin's genius "flourished as it might under the shadow of the stone which France had rolled to the mouth of her own grave" in a "sterile and exhausted . . . age." Despite this tragedy, however, Pattison's botanical metaphors reinscribe the Renaissance as a natural phenomenon and claim the possibility of another rebirth. Pattison's Poussin is himself a post-Renaissance figure, a repository of "the lost hopes of the Renaissance," a brief "reviv[al of] the dying embers of that quivering flame which the reactionary party had well-nigh succeeded in putting out on the soil of France."[48] That is, Poussin is both the sign of the Renaissance's defeat and the embodiment of its survival; "the great days were indeed gone; but some reflection of their brightness lingered yet."[49] Moreover, Pattison's Poussin may be "solitary," "the only fruit borne by a tree on which we early count a thousand blossoms," and a reminder of "uncertain beauty too soon extinct," but he nonetheless survives, works, and can be narrated by Pattison's text.[50] As in the essay on Palissy, Pattison simultaneously mourns history's depredations and, by re-presenting these figures, annuls the silences she names.[51] The Renaissance is therefore not forever lost. Pattison's "Nicolas Poussin" concludes with an ambiguous passage that may read an unnamed picture or may be a condensation of all Poussin's work: Poussin shows a scene in which "when the noon of revel is past . . . [comes] the hour of the elders, who . . . pass along the valleys holding solemn converse of that which has gone before, and shall follow after."[52] Pattison's text describes or invents a picture that is an image of a history without losses, extending backward and forward in time.[53]

Pleasure and Knowledge

Readers of Pattison/Dilke's art criticism and art history could reasonably conclude that few words appear more often than *pleasure*. Pattison's Poussin creates scenes of "perfect joy." An 1870 review by E. F. S. Pattison of Ruskin's *Lectures on Art* also announces this theme that runs through Pattison/Dilke's art writing and her political texts. Pattison's review derides Ruskin's utopian social vision as, unlike Poussin's golden images, an unattractive "Social Science Association Arcadia," and also baldly asserts: "art is only truly herself in giving pleasure." Times in which "violence and excess" "run riot" are the times when art "catches its most fervid glow of human beauty and naturally so . . . *because* it reflects [the] perfection of sensual pleasure."[54] *The Renaissance of Art in France* modified the history condensed in Pattison's review of Ruskin by deploying an intermediate phase of history as a cordon sanitaire, rendering Pattison's Renaissance distinct from the period of reactive license. In the *Renaissance*, the Renaissance is not a period of libertinage but what comes next. But the issue of pleasure is relocated rather than abandoned: the Renaissance "bridle[d]" the excesses of the antiascetic reaction by offering a new pleasure: the pleasure of aesthetic control, which "proclaim[ed] honour to every manifestation of human energy, [and] gave each a claim to be considered worthy of culture."[55] Pattison's 1879 *Renaissance* sublimates and shapes violent but valuable forces, but art and history nonetheless depend profoundly on individual, natural, erotic, and bodily, infinitely malleable, aesthetic, and emotional energies of enjoyment. "The most vigourous and highly endowed of human creatures," like the strongest "animal[s]," have the "keener senses," and "fullest energy means fullest possibility of pleasure." Human passion has "its coarser side, and sometimes . . . burn[s] . . . an impurer flame," but the direction of this passion in aesthetic and "morally ideal" pursuits is utterly laudable.[56] Pattison's text even suggests her own writing may derive from these forces: "woo[ing] the secrets of the past" and "kiss[ing] out . . . lives on the lips of . . . earthly loves" draws on "the same burning zeal."[57] Art and pleasure, individual pleasures and social life are repeatedly entwined. Even in the eighteenth century, the best of French architecture, in Emilia Dilke's judgment, was the result of pursuing individual pleasure and the worst sacrificed pleasure to false ideals.[58]

But pleasure also carries anxieties in Pattison/Dilke's texts. Some pleasures may come too easily and corrupt, not least because they erode or prevent the ability to fathom other pleasures. In her critical review of Ruskin, Pattison, ironically, worried about the pleasures of his texts: Ruskin's ability to write eloquently of color and line and to convey "forcibly and convincingly" the "impressions of beauty which he has himself received" are seductive; his ability to "give of his own joy to others" can "charm" or "infect" readers, leading them onto "unsafe and dangerous ground," that is, to accept his strictures on the limits of proper art.[59] I earlier noted E. F. S. Pattison's strictures on the smooth seductions of Pilon and Emilia Dilke's cool condemnation of the cheap pleasures of degraded art in the seventeenth and eighteenth centuries, from sculptors of the *genre érotique* to the paintings she compared to upholstery.[60] *The Renaissance of Art in France*'s account of Villon is paralleled in one of Emilia Dilke's overtly political texts, a more moderate story of understandable but regrettable license, with a distinct tone of condescension and preachiness mixed with its sympathy and historical theory. In 1889, Emilia Dilke told of walking in Dundee on a Saturday night and meeting "a great many tipsy mill-girls coming out of the wretched gin-palaces." Dilke was not "shocked," but "she just thought" that given their poverty, "miserable" and "horribly uncomfortable" homes, and the "cold East wind," that "it was a very natural thing" that the "lasses should turn in and get a drop of gin."[61] As with Pattison's Villon, "exulting in evanescent fits of drunken gaiety" is a "natural" response to repression. But in both texts, Pattison/Dilke goes on to contrast these befuddled figures with representatives of higher forms of pleasure. Pattison's Villon is contrasted to Ronsard, for whom "physical passion" is "always veiled by . . . exquisite refinement . . . and . . . presents itself also under its moral aspect." Ronsard is an emblem of human energy directed toward "an exalted ideal," in which physicality is not, as in Pattison's Middle Ages, hated but transformed. If not "foul" or "indiscriminate," Dilke's gin-drinking mill girls are nonetheless contrasted to women workers who belong to the trade union, with whose "conduct and appearances [they] were in marked contrast."[62] These latter women workers, like those born late enough to be a part of the Renaissance, have a different share in history; they are nobler because they belong to a great cause—they are made by the history in which they participate—but they also make history.

Emilia Dilke's trade-union texts and speeches value female figures in whom "stimulus" and "sacrifice" are united.[63] *Art in the Modern State* repeats this emphasis on service. Emilia Dilke theorized the Renaissance as "the bridge [art] needed to cross the gulf between faith in the unknown and service to the known," and the Renaissance shifted art from "the *service* of religion to that of . . . an idealized conception of man."[64] In "The Idealist Movement," too, the Renaissance fostered movement into service for Dilke's young man, leading him to "the problems of modern life" and culminated in renewed and enabled social labor. A story of understandable revolt moves across Dilke's semiautobiographical tale, Pattison's scholarly *Renaissance*, and Dilke's history and trade-unionist speeches; in all these texts urgent desires are legitimate and historically meaningful but must be reinvested in morally and socially responsible actions. Yet only the identifiably autobiographical figure—the young man in "The Idealist Movement"—moves from one epoch into the next, from immoderate rebellion to balanced liberation, rather than serving as an instance of a historical moment. Pattison/Dilke's historical narratives sacrifice some. Villon is succeeded by the nobler Ronsard; the mill lasses are not Dilke's audience but a contrast to them. Pattison/Dilke's narratives of repression, eruption, and redirection of vital energies are projected into an endless future, and she claims the return of the Renaissance in movements of modern democracy: "the Renaissance inaugurated a revolution of which we inherit . . . [the] third phase" in which "Art . . . is passing . . . to [the service] of the People."[65] But if Pattison/Dilke's art history and her trade-unionist texts alike enlist historical inevitability and nature's force, some are left behind and some are cast out. Emilia Dilke could appropriate the language of another band of social saviors to describe women's trade-unionism as "the Salvation Army," redeeming souls and moving society forward to a millenium Christian and democratic, but in the same essay Dilke savagely attacks the "loafer" or casual laborer unwilling to take part in the grand movement of uplift and she agrees with "John Law" [Margaret Harkness] that such should be exiled to the colonies.[66] There is violence in these histories, too.

In chapter 4, I argued that Pattison/Dilke's texts are divided about the value of erotic passion, permissible and degraded pleasures, and do not defend physicality without ambivalence. A similar tension stretches E. F. S. Pattison's art-writings. Charles Dilke claimed Emilia Dilke "insisted on the doctrine known as 'art for its own sake,' " but in "Art and Morality," E. F. S. Pattison took pains to differentiate her views from the "extreme" views of contemporary aesthetes, especially Gautier, Swinburne, and Baudelaire.[67] Pattison writes that what she objects to is not "immorality" but an allegedly inadequate and limited aesthetic theory; these other writers, she contends, rigidify the relations of art and morality into "a relation of mere oppugnancy." In doing so, they have a secret commonality with those who condemn them. In Pattison's argument, "decadent" Swinburne and the very academic Victor Laprade are both transgressors against art, since "the same arguments which prove that it is not the business of art to promote morality, prove also that its business is not to promote the want of morality."[68] The business of art is pleasure, and pleasure can set limits as well as lift them.

As an art-writer, E. F. S. Pattison, true to her education, admired physiological realism, and her texts' concern to keep open a space between "art" and "morality" may provoke an unanswerable question: were Pattison's strictures against moralizing influenced by the extent to which restrictions of knowledge on "moral" grounds was disproportionately directed at women? The review of The Renaissance of Art in France in the Academy displayed quite clearly the boundaries on proper feminine knowledge. Villon is "a writer whom we should have thought few ladies would care to acknowledge"; the reviewer implies that Pattison's claim to ladyhood is besmirched by her display of such knowledge.[69] Yet Pattison's position on bodily pleasures appears more confusingly in an epistolary debate with Charles Dilke in 1877. Emilia Pattison vigorously defended Zola's L'Assommoir against Charles Dilke, insisting he had missed the point by focussing on the unpleasantness to him of the subject matter. Charles's apparent wish for easy pleasure is swiftly dispatched, but Emilia's letters concede that one must "question the degree in which [Zola's subject] was susceptible of finished literary treatment," that is, could ever give aesthetic pleasure.[70] "Art and Morality" argues that art's power resides in its ability to evoke multiple subjective experiences and to erode ordinary bodily identifications: "The power of sympathy are indeed sufficient to . . . reconcile us . . . to things in the highest degree distasteful in experience," and "most of the pleasures of the lower senses, and all the intellectual and emotional pleasures, many things unpleasant and some even disastrous may become delightful when contemplated in the ideal."[71] Art should provoke fantasy, using the body's senses to entice us away from ordinary bodily wants. The power of art to pull viewers to extremes is vivid in The Renaissance of Art in France, but this text also displays near panic about such pleasures: Duvet's print of Babylon shows "a wickedly beautiful woman about whose eyes and lips flits an evil charm," her "powerful seduction" reducing the male figure in the print to "passionate[ly] gaz[ing]" subjection. The representation of "delight of luxury, the joy of unchecked indulgence in the pleasures of sense" are the artist's triumph, but Pattison's language is stirringly ambiguous: Duvet's work gives evidence that he himself "embraces" his subject "with the agonised fervour of hysteric passion," while the print shows us the consequences of "the hot pulse-throb of instant passion," as the angel of destruction sweeps downward on "the band of those who seek to live deliciously."[72]

In "Art and Morality," Pattison's argument for the ability of the viewer to maintain both pleasurable identification and aesthetic appreciation ultimately excludes some subjects from the pinnacle of artistic achievement by insisting on the unacceptability of representations of "extreme and exclusive bodily pains and pleasures." The depiction of sexual acts for their own sake—which Pattison attempts to separate as a category from permissible depictions of immoral sexual desires or Greek seductions and disreputable but edifying historical incidents—is not compatible with good art. Naked bodies are quite acceptable, but the "exhibition of animal paroxysms" is "indecent" and assaults a sense of "restraint" and disgust, "both inherited and acquired."[73] Explicitly sexual scenes are inherently unaesthetic, "ugly" in the same way as the gorier martyrdoms of saints, with their "highly-finished jets and spurts of blood." "Art and Morality" explicitly severs art from the dictates of contemporary morality but reintroduces decorum through a theory of nature. Explicit sexual passion and extreme physical sufferings are alike bodily extremes whose representations are assaults on the body's senses, causing distress "akin to the displeasure caused by bad colour in a picture or by harsh chords in music."[74] Pattison's essay on Poussin similarly ends with a quarrel with realism in the name of pleasure, in which, unlike the "apples of Sodom," apples of delight are offered. Poussin refigures commonplace and "vulgar" scenes of power and pleasure, with "more than moral grace and greediness . . . [so that] the orchard is a garden, and the crabbed apple-trees are trees from a child's dreamland, whose lithe boughs sway under the weight of heavy golden fruit. . . . everything sordid and mean is transmuted . . . even Death . . . His day is a day of paradise, south winds blow amidst eternal fruit and blossoms; the cruelty of the beast is but strength; the merriment of children a perfect joy . . . ." Pattison adds an image of erotic and hybrid animality ambiguously tamed by or perhaps embracing, even in amorous union, the human: "the satyr lurking in secret shades comes forth to make fast the link with man."[75]

E. F. S. Pattison's reviews of early Impressionist works attempt to ground their judgments in a theory of pleasure rather than propriety. Indeed, the Impressionists are mirror opposites of artists like Boucher and Pilon, whom Pattison/Dilke castigates because "Nature had endowed [them] with the power of pleasing easily."[76] As with the facile artists deplored in her art-historical texts, Pattison/Dilke does not deny the technical merit of the Impressionists, but they please strangely, if at all. They stir confusion. Pattison's review of an early Impressionist show acknowledges that "the critic must set . . . aside personal predilections" and respect the intentions and "terrible effectiveness" of Manet and Courbet, but art that "puts so forcibly to the eye the commonest, the most vulgar, the most salient facts . . . has from its very intelligibility a much to be dreaded seduction . . ."[77] These works attract, but their attractions are outside the boundaries of ordinary artistic pleasures: Sisley's works proffer "a voluntary renunciation of the usual sources of pleasure, a selection of nature which attracts neither by charm of colour nor by mystery of chiaroscuro nor by play of line." Courbet "*attacks* Rocks at Ornans" and his work "giv[es] . . . perfectly just relations of tone . . . but colour . . . is not sought for in the spirit of a colourist instinctively seeking for lovely harmonies, but rather in the spirit of an adventurer eager for the execution of tours de force, for the production of startling and unforeseen effects."[78] Pattison worries, "What is likely to be the effect on taste of the production in art of work which corresponds in style to the style of the sensation writers in literature?" Works too bold block access to the "true secrets of nature and art" by ruining the viewer's eye for "work of more subtle quality, which is less readily to be comprehended."[79] Pattison oddly assigns the Impressionists a position like that of Academic painters in her ancien regime: both have dangerous attractions, both seduce, and both contain possibilities of violence.

The ambiguities in Pattison's treatment of the Impressionists echo tensions in other texts. On the one hand, Pattison/Dilke's art writings sometimes struggle to disentangle a commitment to historicity from discussions about morality. Despite her emphasis on the *history* in art history, Pattison/Dilke objected vigorously to efforts to collapse aesthetic judgments into moral judgments about historical societies, especially taking issue with Ruskin. In a review of Ruskin's *The Queen of the Air*, Pattison defends the right to love the works of "bad" people: "A man may do a particular thing excellently well, and yet be in other respects nearly a worthless man."[80] This insistence recurs in Pattison's review of Ruskin's *Lectures on Art*:

> Art itself is neither religious nor irreligious; moral nor immoral; useful nor useless; if she is interpreted in any one of these senses by the beholder, is she to bear the blame? Not one of these qualities are essential to fine art, and as to perfecting the ethical state, that by means of art comes to pass, not by "direction of purpose", but by her constant presence indirectly refining our perceptions, and rendering them more delicate and susceptible.[81]

Pattison mocks Ruskin's alleged belief that "the poor must be well off and happy, sanitary laws carried out, and things generally well-ordered before the arts can become great." Pattison seems, therefore, to split art not only from moral injunctions but from history. Historically specific conventionalities are deplored. To "forc[e the artist] to dwell on the moral influence of his subject" would mean the end of real creation, since the true artist was less concerned with the "message" of his work than its aesthetic qualities.[82] Moreover, heavy-handed treatments of historical subjects—the bane of art in her own day—is as damaging to true art as medieval asceticism: "Work which is not done for its own sake, in which the chief place is claimed by the historical or the moral, in which attention is seized by the subject rather than the rendering of the subject . . . loses its aesthetic character, and cannot possess those poetic elements which fire the fancy and rouse the emotions."[83] In short, moral or historical weight not only stifles artists but limits pleasures: art should enlarge subjective experience, not confine it.

In Emilia Dilke's studies of the seventeenth and eighteenth centuries, highly critical appraisals of artists are tempered by claims that the defects of art works were at the least exacerbated by the defects of the age, but in Pattison's review of the Impressionists an important difference further disarms the critic: neither these artists nor their era can yet be fully historicized. The Impressionists, however unnerving their work, are modern, and Francis Pattison had earlier included herself as an artist in modernity: boasting that she was planning "decidedly modern" works because "the most real persons live in their own time & . . . this archaeology [in art] is not substantially true & real."[84] In Dilke's multivolume account of the eighteenth century, the cold asceticisms of neoclassicism, like those of the Middle Ages, even contribute to the violences of the Revolution. Thus, however uneasily, Pattison's review of the Impressionists finally fears the tyranny of the past more than the ambiguous pleasures of the future: "What will the next turn take—whether the movement has a living

principle of growth which will issue in crowning success; or whether a speedy reaction will set in which will place French art more completely than ever under the
yoke of tradition and authority—it seems at present impossible to predict."[85] The
present's terrible pleasures are necessary.

As well as enacting anxieties about easy pleasures, Pattison/ Dilke's texts insist on
the value of pleasures that are demanding and require hard work. E. F. S. Pattison's
texts are not notably troubled by artwork that is "difficult" or dark; a lack of obvious
pleasures does not dissuade admiration. Carstens is a hero in an 1870 essay—his work
is "inharmonious, violent, irregular" but powerful, and in some of his most painful
work, emotionally and morally moving.[86] Among modern artists, Whistler is lauded;
his treatments are "stiff, and harsh even to painfulness" and he "voluntary
ren[ounces] any attempt to rouse pleasurable sensations by line, or form, or colour,"
reminding Pattison of inward-looking Protestantism; his pictures become "more cruelly vivid" the more one looks and offer "the presentment to us of life with its sources
of joy sealed or exhausted." Yet Whistler nonetheless "takes a foremost place in virtue
of the intellectual power which he shown."[87] Pattison's texts thus claim the high
ground for work that does not overtly say too much but forces the knowledgeable
reader to decipher its charms. In Pattison/Dilke's histories of French art, such reading
is marked as temporary and historical ("one cannot expect . . . that enthusiasm should
be readily roused for forms, however beautiful, which embody . . . ideas wholly foreign to modern life," and Renaissance artists had "peculiarities of a frame of mind
and temper in itself difficult for us to realise") but there is value in these difficult
pleasures.[88]

E. F. S. Pattison defended her Renaissance as a whole as the site of difficult and
valuable pleasures. Pattison's Renaissance is not the Italian Renaissance but the French,
and, she says, her Renaissance is hard to understand, to like, to appreciate. Its art is
not for everyone, not because there are explicit boundaries as to who is fit to enjoy
it, but because of the difficulties and lack of immediate appeal of much of the work
her texts praise. Moreover, these works' challenging pleasures are the result of individual pleasures located in history. The Renaissance of Art in France opens with assertions
that this art is "the result of individual needs, individual taste, individual caprice,"
and yet "it requires perhaps more than the art of almost any other time a knowledge
of the conditions under which it was produced in order to arrive at an appreciation
of its excellence." Pattison's Renaissance contends that her chosen objects are worth the
time of study because they do offer pleasure. For those who take time and trouble,
Pattison's Renaissance is rewarding, proffering both highly individualized aesthetic
and historical pleasures: it is "rich in colour" and "strongly marked character," but
it also tells a story "for those who read in it the signs of the times in which it was
produced."[89]

The greatest pleasure in Pattison/Dilke's texts is the most demanding: the taking
on of enormous tasks of learning. Pattison/Dilke's oeuvre could be said to be defined
by encyclopedism: it not only considers many branches of art—painting, drawing,
sculpture, furniture, decoration, architecture, ceramics, glasswork, and tapestry—but
attends to social and historical contexts, especially the role of the state in encouraging,
suppressing, or influencing creativity and the economics of art. This ambitiousness
"placed her in the vanguard of scholarship" in some views, but it was occasionally

derided in reviews in which a hint of misogyny lurks behind sneers at the display of so much learning.[90] A rejoining note of bitterness may be detected in the preface of Dilke's *French Architects and Sculptors*, which claims that however much critics had praised *Art in the Modern State* as more accessible than her other works, it was the encyclopedic *The Renaissance of Art in France* that sold consistently and remained a standard reference, and therefore Dilke is again aiming for completeness.[91]

Charles Dilke insists on Emilia Dilke's encyclopedism. Francis Pattison had "desire[d] to embrace, by hard study, a complete view of the whole field of art and art history"; she " 'specialized,' much against her will," and "the praise which she most valued was that . . . for the completeness or 'universality' of her art-knowledge." Even her "specialization" in French art is only temporary in Charles Dilke's account; Emilia Dilke was moving, in her later life, back to everything. According to Charles, at the time of her death, Emilia Dilke was not only revising her *Art in the Modern State* and thinking about doing the same for *The Renaissance of Art in France* but contemplating a volume of reminiscences of "artists whom she had known" and a book on the nineteenth century that would "develop the philosophy of the future relations of democracy to art." In this last project, Emilia Dilke intended to construct a master narrative in which ancient Greece was a model now being surpassed; she would trace the development of art's social relationships from the Greeks through the Renaissance to the present, in terms of a widening conception of democracy and knowledge. "To the Greek, certain types only were worth the full honour of perfect expression. To the modern artist all forms of life are sacred."[92]

The ambition to be encyclopedic occurs with varying degrees of hopefulness. Pattison's review of Pater's *Renaissance* emphasized the enervating effects of too much knowledge: "the consciousness of the wider training and further outlook which fall to the lot of us, the heirs of all the ages . . . has engendered in [some] minds . . . a great hesitancy, due to the very vastness of their inherited possessions—a hesitancy which seems to paralyze the happy putting forth of their powers."[93] Pattison could write with impatience and despair of the desire for complete knowledge, not only of French art, but all human culture: "Quelque-fois je pense même que le plus bel usage que l'on puisse faire de sa propre vie serait de se vouer à tout savoir, à se rendre maître—au moins dans sa signification générale—de tout ce que l'ésprit humain a conquis sur tous les terrains:—mais, j'ai quarante ans, et c'est trop tard."[94] While composing *The Renaissance of Art in France*, Francis Pattison wrote of the difficulty of continually expanding her historical knowledge and keeping up with contemporary politics and culture:

> All depends on whether one can keep [contemporary political and economic questions] in relation to the whole of life. One cannot write these chapters of modern history without trying to form one's own opinion on the questions of the day, and that inspires one with the wish to at least try to find the bond which must exist somewhere between the fine arts themselves and the current of national life. So it seems to me that even the little bit of work one tries to do one's self must gain in value.[95]

Yet despite difficulty, Pattison asserts the value of the attempt to encompass.

Emilia Dilke's posthumously published essay "On the Spiritual Life," shares some of the language of "The Idealist Movement "and the theme of knowledge and pleasure. This essay contends that the goal of the spiritual life is neither just self-fulfillment nor just socially valuable right action in the world. Rather, as in "The Idealist Movement," intellectual and moral aspirations allow for the periodic transcendence of self, a transcendence untainted by enforced self-abnegation but produced by knowledge and linked, as in Pattison/Dilke's art-writing, to intensely aesthetic pleasures. The transcendence of mystical ecstasy is a moment of perfect knowledge of the Incarnation, and a moment in which the boundaries of the self are evaporated in an experience of self-loss indistinguishable from limitless self-expansion. "On the Spiritual Life" cites a "mediaeval legend of the Atonement"—that is, a human-authored story, located in history—which sees in "Christ crucified, the stolen apple of Life restored to the Tree of Knowledge." But the status of the purely religious is unclear; if Jesus is the perfect figure of knowledge to which a latter-day Eve may reach, Socrates is also a model. His life was "a pure ideal," since as a human being he was "and remains the figure of greatest originality in the history of the human spirit." His teachings offer "a confident vindication of the free exercise of reason . . . the right of the human soul to climb the heights and search the depths by which it is encompassed."[96] Jesus and Socrates are both fit objects of emulation and perfect figures of knowledge and intellect as well as morality; their doubling dissolves together religion and rationality, the sacrificed god and the godlike self; divine and human histories are equally terrains of powerful experience. Dilke adds another pair of inspirations: in "the splendid and tempered strength . . . [of] the fine Pagan stoicism of the greater figures of the eighteenth century" is an inspiration to "unfaltering courage" as admirable as the ecstatic self-abandonment of Saint Teresa.[97] "Clear-eyed" reason and passionate emotional and physical fervor, "pagan" fortitude and Christian mysticism, merge without competing. Moreover, Dilke's essay presents appreciation of these models as aesthetic, an experience of sensory and especially visual apprehension; her moral exemplars—Socrates and the philosphers—are figures upon which to look, while Christ is invoked in pictorial language as a man hung on the Cross and a metaphorical object of vision hung on the Tree of Knowledge. Despite Dilke's warnings elsewhere about the dangers of the aestheticized spectacles of (feminine) piety, her Saint Teresa, too, displays ecstasy, perhaps tacitly citing Bernini's statue. Beholding these objects, the self is enriched, eroded, and reconstituted.

As in other texts that emphasize the goodness of hard work, in "On the Spiritual Life" spiritual labor is historically productive and personally pleasurable. The free exercise of reason and devotion to perfect knowledge can challenge "the order of settled society"; it might bring "the pain of isolation" to the individual but there are compensations. First, it offers the pleasure of autonomy. "Of the Spiritual Life" praises "solitary perfection" of "aims and hopes" and counsels, "Live then apart and rely upon no man," but this self-sufficiency is also an experience of wishing. "The soul is . . . set free to listen to the voice of its desire." Second, there is pleasure in righteousness: one may achieve "that high courage and directness of thought, which, rooted in the profound conviction of personal duty, gives birth to an invincible constancy of spirit." Third, there is social utility even in apparent inaction: "the life of meditation . . . is the life out of which the law goes forth, by which the life of action is ultimately governed." Again, Dilke offers the pleasure of participation in history: her contemplative self is, like Shelley's poet, a maker of history, since "all the great changes that have taken place in the lives of men . . . have had their departure from the secret places of thought." However, the contemplative can also escape from history, at least for a moment: "shame, and insult, and injury . . . fall away . . . [and] the bitterness of life is overpast." Thus, Dilke promises not only the pleasures of futurity—in the experience of desire and in participation in making history—but escape from the pains of the past. Finally, service to ideals is evidence of a heroic self; only the soul that is a self, "whose source of strength is within itself," can "combine the perfection of self-realization and self-renunciation." Pleasure, history, social value, and spirituality depend on a self that is, as in "The Idealist Movement," both a source and a boundless space.[98]

"On the Spiritual Life" links knowledge, aesthetics, history, and ecstasy, but Pattison/Dilke's encyclopedic ambitions can also be inscribed in more mundane contexts. It is possible to suspect that the allures of scholarly encyclopedism were gendered. Despite the perceived openness of art history as a field to women, Dilke was anomalous in the scholarly standards to which her work aspired. But although her work is more clearly "academic" than that of most of her contemporaries, male or female, art history was, as a field, being masculinized during Pattison/Dilke's career. Art-writing remained accessible to women but as art history was established in educational and other institutions, prestigious and well-paid *professional* positions were overwhelmingly reserved for men. Pattison/Dilke's demanding standards and profusion of footnotes can be read as attempts to demonstrate scholarly worthiness in the context of her unofficial status in relation to museums and universities.[99] Such attempts may have backfired: a review of Pattison's study of Claude sneered at the work's full title, *Claude Lorrain Sa Vie et Ses Oeuvres, d'après des documents inédits*, "the phrase [*d'après des documents inédits*] implies . . . the undue parade of the virtues of research . . . or . . . the actual belief that some burrowing among forgotten archives is an achievement so valuable that it makes literature unnecessary and original thought of nothing worth."[100] Setting aside the contemptuous assessment of Pattison's prose and thought, Betty Askwith notes that Pattison's "burrowing" had unearthed Claude's will, surely some evidence of the "virtues of research."[101] Pattison/Dilke's books were, on the whole, well praised, but when contempary reviewers criticized, they tended to take issue with her abundance of facts. The suspicion that the implication that Pattison/Dilke was overfond of facts might have a gendered subtext is heightened not only by Walter Pater's smooth assertion that "the scholarly conscience" was male, but by the comments of some twentieth-century critics who have clustered around E. F. S. Pattison's 1873 review of Pater's *Studies in the History of the Renaissance*.[102]

Pattison's critique of Pater's historicity—as noted earlier, she asserted that his claims "are not history nor are they ever to be relied upon for accurate statements of simple matters of fact"—has been taken as a typically dense Victorian response to Pater's original genius. Validating Pater's exceptionality is surely unnecessary, but John J. Conlon makes Pattison an aunt Sally, a typical benighted Victorian, who did not understand that Pater's project was to "transform the presentation of history by writing his interpretation of it, what it means to him."[103] Drawing on stereotypes of Victorians and historians, both Conlon and Peter Allan Dale leap on Pattison's phrase that Pater's work lacks "the true scientific method"; Pattison then stands in for all the naively empiricist historians a literary critic might wish to revile (Dale aligns Pattison with Ranke, whom he misleadingly simplifies).[104] Moreover, both Conlon and Dale covertly appeal to stereotypes about women critics; both refer to "Mrs. Mark Pattison"— a practice definitely passé by the time they wrote—although her article is not only signed but listed in their own notes and bibliographies as by E. F. S. Pattison. Renaming her as her husband's wife and making certain that the reader is aware of her sex locates Pattison as an amateur, whatever her claims.[105]

More narrowly, Pattison/Dilke's encyclopedism can be placed in relation to Mark Pattison's. Mark Pattison's erudition and intellectual ambition were renowned (if suspected of Casaubonism), and Mark encouraged Francis Pattison and other young women to achieve total knowledge of a chosen field.[106] Charles Dilke later implied that Francis Pattison had regretted or resented Mark's injunctions to achieve completeness within a specific field—she " 'specialized,' much against her will, on the arts, of France"—but Emilia Dilke repeated Mark's advice to Gertrude Tuckwell, adding that one should restrain one's labors and "reject even well-paid things that would lead [one] off the track" of one's main studies."[107] E. F. S. Pattison's encyclopedism can be seen as participating in a household culture of ambitious knowledge not entirely unlike the Dilkes' Sloane Street household, where Charles Dilke was "suspected of omniscience" and young women were enjoined to endless intellectual labor.[108]

But Pattison/Dilke's encyclopedism can also be read as engaged in a more complicated argument with Mark Pattison, or, more precisely, with a theory of history and gender he once expounded. Mark Pattison claimed, in a letter to Gertrude Tuckwell, that women must be inferior in mental endowments as well as physical strength since, although "the whole intellectual sphere has been open to them . . . they do not show an aptitude for such pursuits."[109] Pattison/Dilke's art-historical writing can be read as a riposte to this charge in two respects. First, Pattison/Dilke's studies include women in the history of art as artists as well as subjects, patrons, and family members. Second, and more challengingly, Pattison/Dilke's encyclopedism, especially her emphases on the material, economic, political, and social, makes sense insofar as an art history in which institutional or material structures do not matter to artistic production fosters the naturalization of women's underrepresentation. Pattison/Dilke's histories of violence, academies and monarches, patrons and markets, emphasize the blockages, losses, and destruction of even natural genius and the contingency of art production. Her accounts of women's struggles for access to the French Academy tell of resistance and unfair exclusion as well as occasional triumph, but in any case, institutions matter. Pattison/Dilke's encyclopedism, which made the work of art (not only the object but the process of making it) the terrain of art history, can be read as feminist even when it is not explicitly focused on women or gender. In "The Idealist Movement," "even those who love things of the Spirit suffer from the unfavourable conditions amongst which they find themselves." Unfavorable conditions include intimate social arrangements; the domestic can oppress or enable. In Dilke's Art in the Modern State, the analogy between oppressions is explicit: "the life of the state, like the life of the family, is founded on much renouncement of personal liberty, on much self-restraint and self-abnegation. . . . [But] the teaching of the Renaissance was . . . the sacredness of liberty and of life." "The Idealist Movement" instances, besides Dilke's "young man," Andrea del Sarto, "knit to [his] soulless wife who did not understand, or care to understand, about his art," and Pattison's Palissy too suffers for his art, his science, and his faith both on the grand stage of history and at home; his wife lurks in Pattison's text as a betrayer of genius.[110] More sharply, in the case of Anna Collot, Emilia Dilke lamented the particular wastage and loss of women's energies in domestic labors.

Finally, Pattison/Dilke's double-encyclopedism—both the omnivoracity of her art-writing and her range of activities—can be read as a reply to Mark Pattison's insistence that social-reform work was fit only for the intellectually inferior and not worth a true scholar's time.[111] The two Pattisons' eruditions participated, in short, in larger Victorian arguments about divisions between and the values of professional, political, scholarly, and cultural domains. These arguments can still be discerned in the posthumous career of Mark Pattison's erudition. Mark Pattison's works no longer command a general audience, anymore than Pattison/Dilke's, but he continues to figure in debates about university education, for example through contrasts between Pattison and Benjamin Jowett.[112] Jowett's particular version of university-education-as-training-for-public-service was impoverished and imperialist, but it is criticized by Hugh Lloyd-Jones by a contrast to Pattisonian devotion to university-education-as-the-pursuit-of-pure-knowledge (-in-which-students-may-be-an-inconvenience).[113] At times, defending Mark Pattison against imputations of Casaubonism has been a form of debate about university reform. Noel Annan's review of John Sparrow's Mark Pattison and the Idea of a University showed an immediate grasp of the contemporary political stakes in rehearsals of Victorian history, discerning that Sparrow sought to create a geneaology of true scholarship to set against 1960s educational innovation, but Annan's perspicacity owed something to his own participation in those debates.[114] Unlike the aspersions cast on "Mrs. Mark Pattison," Mark's reputation as an exemplar of pure scholarship has been uncompromised until recently, but in 1983, Anthony Grafton offered a savage reassessment. Grafton's studies of Joseph Scaliger brought him in close contact with Mark Pattison's texts, and he concluded: "Repeated encounters with [Pattison's] inability to quote a document accurately, his ineptitude at establishing dates, and his incompetence at summarizing plain German accurately in English have led me to wonder whether he deserves the authority he still enjoys." For Grafton, Mark Pattison was as susceptible as Jowett to the lure of popular acclaim; "like other dons, [Pattison] wrote for money and applause rather than to win a chair or contribute to knowledge. . . . [H]e lacked the courage to practice the Spartan intellectual virtues that he loved to praise, when there was no English public to applaud or pay him for doing so." Grafton concludes that Mark Pattison misrepresented not only himself but his subject; Scaliger too "wanted fame and honour more than truth" and his career was shaped by "trifling and personal" factors rather than the pure pursuit of knowledge.[115] Grafton's own rhetoric, however, displays how contemporary academic politics as well as appraisals of Victorian erudition continue to deploy a comparative language of virtue.

In E. F. S. Pattison/Emilia Dilke's texts, too, the call for encyclopedism can be a stick with which to beat other scholars. A review of a history of aesthetics by Schasler criticizes its rigid chronological scheme—its structure is "a Procrustean bed," insufficiently nuanced and elastic for the history it recounts, and Schasler's inadequacies are implicitly contrasted to "the renaissance movement [when] the yoke was cast off, and art freed went on its ways [and ran] through the whole domain of nature," evoked in the same review.[116] More complexly, when Pattison criticized Pater's Renaissance, her review contended that Pater's attention to subjectivity was not improper in itself but was flawed by an inadequate understanding of the relationship of knowledge and subjectivity. Pater makes factual errors that a properly all-knowing scholarly account would not commit, and in doing so, "he loses a great deal of the meaning of the very objects he is regarding most intently."[117] Pater's account of the action of objects on the self is diminished because he does not include more knowledge, more objects, more history, that would allow more effects, more pleasures. Not only her imperial goals for an art history that includes everything but her theory of an endless, expansively pleasured self subtends Pattison's criticisms of Pater.

In Pattison/Dilke's own Renaissances, omnivoracity and pleasure are conjoined both for the scholar and for the Renaissance individuals about whom she writes. In Pattison's French Renaissance, "Learning, poetry, science, satire, speculation;—the altar of all knowledge, like that of all pleasure, was thronged."[118] The Renaissance "proclaim[ed] honour to every manifestation of human energy" and claimed "the senses" as well as the mind and spirit "should be served like princes." In "lieux de plaisances," "consecrated precincts of private pleasure," and "home[s] of every human exercise and pleasure," "infantile pleasure;" is taken in decoration; the "liberties of pleasure" are provided for; heterosocial pleasures proliferate; and "license" has admirable results. If Pattison's formulation that "all pleasures should be brought within the domain of Art" moralizingly contained desires, stressing the superiority of the "aesthetic direction" of desires over "indiscriminate excess," the expansion of art is also a promise of proliferating pleasures.[119] This Renaissance is emblematized by Pattison's choices of figures, especially, as I have suggested, in her choice of the multifaceted Palissy as her final subject, but The Renaissance of Art in France begins its Renaissance with a fiction.

Rabelais's Gargantua is E. F. S. Pattison's Renaissance man: his studies in one day "embrace" all, "classic literature and language, mathematics, botany, and astromony; . . . wrestling, swimming, riding, and all manly exercises . . . thought is taken for the pleasures of the table . . . company and converse . . . music . . . elaborate dress. . . . even to perfume." Gargantua is offered as "a fantastic picture," a comically "superhuman performance," an "extravagant fiction," but he is offered. Pattison's study concedes that "the passionate effort to get everything into this short day, to taste all pleasure, to know all knowledge, to see all beauty, defeated itself," but it is entranced, despite failures of "achievement," by the beckoning power of the "attempt." Such exuberance has its costs—Pattison admits that few of the greatest of her Renaissance men made an old age, since "consuming passion both in work and pleasure" shortened their lives—but the weight of tragedy in her account is not on the early deaths of individuals. The tragedy is the end of the Renaissance through the betrayal of pleasure, whether by violence—the St. Bartholomew's Day massacre destroys Delaulne's ability to depict pleasure—or by corruptingly lowered standards, as Palissy's "joyous pleasures" are eclipsed by expensive but tawdry substitutes.[120] Endings—in violence or degradation—foreclose the enjoyment of endless desires.

Tom Stoppard's dramatized A. E. Housman jokes, "When he died it was the first time [Mark] Pattison finished anything he started," and his continuation evokes E. F. S. Pattison as well, refusing endings and casting vision widely—"he was a spectator of all time and all existence."[121] But E. F. S. Pattison's gargantuan appetites are overtly tactile and pleasure-claiming, and they lead not to paralysis but action. In "The Idealist Movement," too, Emilia Dilke's young man's discovery of the Renaissance summons, against the "yoke" of self-inflicted selflessness, a "natural," expansive, voracious, exuberant appetite that would expand the boundaries of the self "in every direction," sweeping in "knowledge and experience," an "[i]ntense desire" to consume the world. It also licenses revolution and liberation from social strictures and constraints. The Renaissance brought the young man "to demand, as of right, all pleasure, all knowledge," against the "pressure," "chains," "horror" and "deadness" of his daily life. Pleasure and knowledge are inordinate and passionate rights, "life at full stretch between morn and night," "every form of human energy," "the whole hierarchy of human knowledge." The young man learns to "never rest satisfied," but to keep "pushing on always," using all his mental powers—"reason" and "the intuitive forces of emotion and imagination." The "goal" is "the essence or truth," but the Renaissance's lesson is boundlessness, a whole but infinite self in an unending process.[122]

Envoi

The ambivalent yet compelling reiterations of pleasure in relation to knowledge in Pattison/Dilke's texts may recall my earlier suggestion that Pattison/Dilke's writing of history could fall within the terms of her argument about the direction of powerful pleasurable drives; "woo[ing] the secrets of the past" is an enterprise of "burning zeal."[123] Pattison/Dilke's construction of knowledge as pleasure infuses learning with eros and delights in endlessness; epistemophilia edges toward epistemomania. In earlier chapters, I wrote of entanglements of eros and knowledge in Francis Strong's educations and in the Pattison and Dilke stories of gender, marriage, and learning; I also discussed, disapprovingly, attempts to produce claims of sexual knowledge from stories of adultery in and out of the courtroom. Pattison/Dilke's texts' suggestion of Gargantuan appetites—the wish to eat the world—also recalls images of apples of desire and knowledge I have invented and have found in her writings. The craving for consumable knowledge is not only a trope in the texts of the dead. But if, as I have argued, the desire for holdable, knowable lives can be a desire to deny time, loss, and the contingency, textuality, and fragmentation of the historical "record," in Pattison's *Renaissance* insatiability seems to be the true object of desire.[124]

I could continue by presenting more texts, especially from Pattison/Dilke's artwriting, which compound these stories of knowledge and pleasure. For example, I could add an argument that, in Pattison/Dilke's art-critical reviews and in her art-historical accounts, the language of description occasionally bursts with intense textual pleasure; her texts revel in detailed and exuberant descriptions of objects, especially glorying in the language of color, in making of stories from pictures, and in recounting lives of artists to be loved and mourned. By doing so, I could offer an ironic ending: exploring Pattison/Dilke's ekphrastic and narrative projects while emphasizing their construction, textuality, and historicity would draw attention again to the ways in which I too have sought vividness, told stories, offered images, and marked losses.

Even in suggesting such an ending is possible, of course, I draw attention to these themes and variations. But rather than rest with irony, I end with an invitation.

This chapter and the texts I cite in it have reiterated themes in my introduction: the desire for knowledge, the instability of selves, the productivity of self-figuration, and the poetics and politics of life-writing. By ending with an assurance that there are far more examples, more words, more tales, more texts, that could be presented, I hope to incite readings and perhaps pleasures beyond my *Names and Stories*. Throughout this book, I have foregrounded the partiality of readings. In this chapter, I especially mirror a feature of Emilia Dilke's later scholarly texts: in her works on the eighteenth century, the pronoun "I" is freely scattered across the pages, perhaps producing an effect of confident assertion but also continually reminding readers of particular eyes and a particular writing hand. This envoi's repetition of incompleteness, however, has a purpose beyond noting again the provisionality of readings. I hope that emphasizing the immensity of Pattison/Dilke's oeuvre—thousands of pages, banal, generic, arresting, clever, and troubling, including letters, essays, speechs, art history, and more—will encourage other readers and writers to discover and examine these texts by a famous but by no means canonical Victorian, and that some readers will expand, revise, overwrite and add to the relationships and divergences I discern. E. F. S. Pattison's *The Renaissance of Art in France* bears as epigraph, "On le peut, je l'essaie, un plus sçavant le fasse": "It can be done, I am attempting it, let someone more knowledgeable than I do it."[125] My wish is not, however, for further readings that "finish" my work and deliver a final comprehension. Rather, I have emulated Pattison/Dilke's texts as they speak of loss and incompleteness as well as histories, as they celebrate the impossibility of endings and long for continuation without completion.

NOTES

This book was enabled by the work of many scholars in history, literature, feminist studies, and cultural studies, but the notes can, for reasons of space, cite only works quoted, paraphrased, or with the most direct bearing on the topic or theme at hand.

Abbreviations

Initials for the name of Emily/Emilia Francis Strong Pattison Dilke are those which applied at the time of the cited text or incident.

EFS Emily Francis Strong
EFSP Emily/Emilia Francis Pattison
EFSD Emilia Francis Strong Dilke
CWD Charles Wentworth Dilke (2nd Baronet, 1843–1911, only)
ES Eleanor Elizabeth Smith
GMT Gertrude Marian Tuckwell
MB Meta Bradley
MP Mark Pattison
VMC Virginia Mary Crawford

CWD, "Mem." Charles W. Dilke, "Memoir" [of Emilia Dilke], in Emilia Dilke, *The Book of the Spiritual Life*, 1–267

MP, Mem.   Mark Pattison, *Memoirs*, 1885; all citations to 1969 Centaur Press edition unless noted.

EFSD, BSL   Emilia Dilke, *The Book of the Spiritual Life*.

Jenkins, Dilke   Roy Jenkins, *Sir Charles Dilke: A Victorian Tragedy* (London: Collins, 1958); references to the revised, 1965 edition, *Victorian Scandal: A Biography of the Right Honourable Gentleman, Sir Charles Dilke*, will be specified.

DFM   *Dean Forest Mercury* newspaper

UNPUBLISHED AND ARCHIVAL SOURCES:

AM   Additional Manuscripts, British Library, London

GMT, "Rem."   Gertrude Tuckwell, "Reminiscences," typescript, Trades Union Congress Library, London

PP   Pattison Papers, Mss. Pattison

Mss. Acland   Acland Papers

Mss. Bywater   Papers of Ingram Bywater

Mss. Max Muller   Max Muller Deposit

Mss. Don   All in Bodleian Library, Oxford

Mss. Eng. Hist.

Mss. Eng. lett.

Mss. Eng. misc.

BLR   Bodleian Library Records

REND   Roskill-Enthoven-Dilke Papers, Churchill College Archive Centre, Churchill College, Cambridge

Trevelyan Papers   University of Newcastle-upon-Tyne Library, Newcastle-upon-Tyne

INTRODUCTION

1. *Women's Trade Union Review*, Jan. 1905: 1; appreciations of EFSD, 1–19.

2. "The Art-Work of Lady Dilke" [unsigned], *Quarterly Review* 205 (1906): 439–67.

3. "Art-Work of Lady Dilke," 339–40, 442–443.

4. CWD, "Mem."; see also AM 43946, a somewhat different ms. annotated by J. R. Thursfield.

5. CWD, "Mem.," 126.

6. Marquise de Sassenay, qtd. in CWD, "Mem.," 127, my translation.

7. CWD, "Mem.," 116.

8. CWD, "Mem.," 127.

9. CWD, "Mem.," 116, 128.

10. AM 43919, fol. 55 (R. Salter Essex to CWD, 1 May 1906) and fol. 69 (Augustine Birrell to CWD, May 1906); AM 43918, fol. 65 (Theodore Watts-Dunton, 31 Jan. 1905); for "Greek statue," fol. 86 (S.W. [unknown] to CWD, 20 May 1905).

11. The DNB's conventions are not gender-neutral; entries usually include the occupation of the father but not mother of the subject's spouse; Angela John, personal communication, 1990; see also Biddy Martin, "Feminism, Criticism, and Foucault," *New German Critique* 27 (1982): 21–23.

12. DNB, s.v. "Dilke, Emilia"; Lee was a writer on art and friend of both Dilkes. See also Biddy Martin, *Woman and Modernity: The (Life)styles of Lou Andreas-Salome* (Ithaca: Cornell University Press, 1991), 1.

13. David Lodge, *The Art of Fiction: Illustrated from Classic and Modern Texts* (New York: Viking, 1993), 37.

14. CWD, "Mem.," 19.

15. For "nomination and narration," see Yopie Prins, *Victorian Sapphos* (Princeton: Princeton University Press, forthcoming 1998).

16. George Eliot, *Middlemarch*, ed. Bert G. Hornback (1872; New York: W.W. Norton, 1977); Rhoda Broughton, *Belinda* (1883; London: Virago, 1987); Andrew Lang, *Old Friends: Essays in Epistolary Parody* (London: Longmans Green, 1890), 123–134; W. H. Mallock, *The New Republic: Or Culture, Faith, and Philosophy in an English Country-house* (1877; London: Michael Joseph, 1937); Mrs. Humphry [Mary Arnold] Ward, *Robert Elsmere* (1888; Oxford: Oxford University Press, 1987) and *Lady Connie* (1888; London: Smith, Elder, 1916); Dorothy Mermin, "Some Sources of Browning's 'Bad Dreams'," *Studies in Browning and His Circle* 9 (1981): 81–86; Hector Malot, *Vices Francais* (Paris: G. Charpentier, 1887); and pirated English edition, *Josie* (c. 1886–87); Robert Liddell, *The Almond Tree* (London: Jonathan Cape, 1938); Betty Askwith, *The Tangled Web* (London: Victor Gollancz, 1960); and Michael Dyne Bradley, *The Right Honourable Gentleman* (London: Samuel French, 1966; first copyrighted in 1962 under title, "An Element of Truth"). On *Belinda*, see Tamie Watters's "Preface" to Virago edition; see also T[amie]W[atters] Cole, "An Oxford Provocation," *Encounter* 36 (April 1971): 34–42, and subsequent correspondence, and "Rhoda Broughton," D.Phil. thesis, St. Anne's College, University of Oxford, 1964. On Malot, see Betty Askwith, *Lady Dilke: A Biography* (London: Chatto and Windus, 1968), 172–74.

17. CWD, "Mem.," 17, 87, and 87n; EFSP was sufficiently familiar with *Middlemarch* to denounce an allusion to it by J. A. Symonds as "in the most senseless taste" (Mss. Pattison 57, fol. 40v. (EFSP to MP, n.d. [1875], on reverse of letter dated 26 Feb. 1875); emphasis in original but perhaps not EFSP's; Margaret Oliphant, *The Autobiography and Letters of Mrs. M.O.W. Oliphant*, ed. Mrs. Harry Coghill (New York: Dodd Mead, 1899), 277; see Askwith, *Lady Dilke*, 172–4, on EFSD's probable cooperation with Malot.

18. AM 43918, fol. 73f. (Bodley to CWD, 21 Mar. 1905).

19. Maria Theresa Earle, *Letters to Young and Old* (London: Smith, Elder, 1906), 90; AM 43918, fol. 91f. (M.T. Earle to CWD, 24 May 1905).

20. For an intriguing overlapping analysis, see Marcia Landy and Amy Villarejo, *Queen Christina* (London: British Film Institute, 1995), 18, 30, 70.

21. Toril Moi, *Simone de Beauvoir: The Making of an Intellectual Woman* (Oxford: Blackwell, 1994); Martin, *Woman and Modernity*; Jacqueline Rose, *The Haunting of Sylvia Plath* (London: Virago, 1990). These works appeared after this book was well under way, as did Joan Wallach Scott, *Only Paradoxes to Offer: French Feminists and the Rights of Man* (Cambridge, Mass.: Harvard University Press, 1996), with which my project also has affinities. See also Alison Booth, "Biographical Criticism and the 'Great' Woman of Letters: The Example of George Eliot and Virginia Woolf," and Sharon O'Brien, "Feminist Theory and Literary Biography," both in *Contesting the Subject: Essays in the Postmodern Theory and Practice of Biography and Biographical Criticism*, ed. William H. Epstein (West Lafayette, Indiana: Purdue University Press, 1991).

22. J. Rose, *Haunting*, xi, 5, 104; Martin, *Woman and Modernity*, 2, 22; Moi, *Simone de Beauvoir*, 3, 4, 5; see also Susan Horton, *Difficult Women, Artful Lives: Olive Schreiner and Isak Dineson In and Out of Africa* (Baltimore: Johns Hopkins University Press, 1995), 13.

23. Moi, *Simone de Beauvoir*, 3, and ch. 1; Martin, *Woman and Modernity*, 26; see also Judith Newton, *Starting Over: Feminism and the Politics of Cultural Critique* (Ann Arbor: University of Michigan Press, 1994), 28, 39.

24. See Nina Auerbach, *Ellen Terry: Player in Her Time* (New York: W.W. Norton, 1987); Dorothy Thompson, *Queen Victoria: Gender and Power* (London: Virago, 1990); Adrienne Munich, *Queen Victoria's Secrets* (New York: Columbia University Press, 1996); and Carole Mavor, *Pleasures Taken: Performances of Sexuality and Loss in Victorian Photographs* (Durham: Duke University Press, 1995);

see also Alison Booth, "From Miranda to Prospero: The Works of Fanny Kemble," *Victorian Studies* 38 (1995): 227–54.

25. See Carlo Ginzburg, "Microhistory: Two or Three Things that I Know about It," trans. Anne Tredeschi and John Tredeschi, *Critical Inquiry* 20 (1993), 21 and 33: "the more improbable sort of documentation . . . [is] potentially richer."

26. For important formulations of such projects, see Raymond Williams, "The Significance of 'Bloomsbury' as a Social and Cultural Group," in *Keynes and the Bloomsbury Group: The Fourth Keynes Seminar Held at the University of Kent at Canterbury 1978*, ed. Derek Crabtree and A. P. Thirlwall (London: Macmillan, 1980), and Peter Wollen, "Wild Hearts" [review of James King, *Virginia Woolf*], *London Review of Books*, 6 April 1995.

27. EFSP, *Renaissance*, 2: 247–48; see also EFSP, "Bernard Palissy."

28. For "life-writing" and other terms, see the excellent interdisciplinary collection edited by the Personal Narratives Group, *Interpreting Women's Lives: Feminist Theory and Personal Narratives* (Bloomington: Indiana University Press, 1989); see also Ginzburg, "Microhistory."

29. Elizabeth Robins, *Way Stations* (London: Hodder and Stoughton, 1913), 66, 68.

30. Catherine Hall, "The Economy of Intellectual Prestige: Thomas Carlyle, John Stuart Mill, and the Case of Governor Eyre," *Cultural Critique* 12 (1989): 167–96; see also J. Rose, *Haunting*, 10, 26–27.

31. See Scott, *Only Paradoxes*, xi.

32. This is an appropriate point to clarify this book's relation to Askwith's *Lady Dilke*. Although Askwith's book, written in 1968, unavoidably suffers from the lack of a larger historiography, I have used it for occasional guidance to sources and as a source for stories; her father, Sir George Askwith, was a friend of CWD and GMT, and Askwith was able to speak to persons who remembered EFSD and VMC. I have examined archival sources myself and transcriptions are my own unless noted.

33. "Multiplex" has nineteenth-century meanings, despite contemporary associations with suburban cinemas. Multiplex telegraph systems carried more than two messages simultaneously over a single wire (duplex systems carried two messages); the word also referred to what would now be called multiple personality; see Frederick W. H. Myers, "Multiplex Personality," *Proceedings of the Society for Psychical Research* 4 (1889): 500–522.

34. See also Ginzburg, "Microhistory," 28–29.

35. Liz Stanley, "Moments of Writing: Is There a Feminist Auto/Biography?" *Gender and History* 2 (1990), 62, 63–64; see also Stanley with Ann Morley, *The Life and Death of Emily Wilding Davison*, with Gertrude Colmore's *The Life of Emily Davison* (London: The Women's Press, 1988), 70–71; Ginzburg, "Microhistory," 23–24, 28, 32; O'Brien, "Feminist Theory," 129–30; Robert Padgug and Jon Wiener, "From the Abolitionists to Gay History: An Interview with Martin Bauml Duberman," *Radical History Review* 42 (1988), 78–79; Ann Lane, *To Herland and Beyond: Charlotte Perkins Gilman* (New York: Pantheon, 1990), xi, and Daniel Boyarin, *Unheroic Conduct: The Rise of Heterosexuality and the Invention of the Jewish Man* (Berkeley: University of California Press, 1997), xii.

36. Angela V. John quotes Elizabeth Robins on her diary as a consciously and unconsciously "cooked account," in "Through the Mental Looking Glass: Biographies, Diaries, and British Feminist History," paper delivered at Women's History conference organized by the Swedish Council for Research in the Humanities, Stockholm, 1990; see also Stanley and Morley, *Life and Death*, 69; but I do not share this goal of an endpoint of attained knowledge (ibid., xi, xiv)

37. Jenkins, *Dilke*, 278–80, and photograph facing 240; David Nicholls, *The Lost Prime Minister: A Life of Sir Charles Dilke* (Rio Grande, Ohio: Hambledon Press, 1995), 114.

38. EFSD edited the mss. of her books with scissors; see ms. for a revised edition of her *Art in the Modern State*, National Art Library, London, 86.EE.

39. Stanley and Morley, *Life and Death*, takes a similar approach to Colmore's 1913 biography of Davison.

40. Katherine Cummings, "Of Purebreds and Hybrids: The Politics of Teaching AIDS in the United States," *Journal of the History of Sexuality* 2 (1991), 70–71; see also Steven Cohan and Linda M. Shires, *Telling Stories: A Theoretical Analysis of Narrative Fiction* (London: Routledge, 1988), 1–3, 52.

41. Cummings, "Purebreds and Hybrids," 71; see also Peter Brooks, *Reading for the Plot: Design and Intention in Narrative* (New York: Knopf, 1984). For other disciplines' uses of narrative, see, for example, anthropologist Brinkley Messick, "The Trial of Writing: Murder Narratives from a Shari'a Court," paper presented to the Center for the Comparative Study of Social Transformations Colloquium, 4 December 1996; sociologist Ken Plummer, *Telling Sexual Stories: Power, Change, and Social Worlds* (New York: Routledge, 1995); and philospher Mark Johnson, *The Moral Imagination: Implications of Cognitive Science for Ethics* (Chicago: University of Chicago Press, 1993), 11.

42. Alan Sinfield, *Literature, Politics, and Culture in Post-War Britain* (Berkeley and Los Angeles: University of California Press, 1989), ch. 3.

43. On reading stories, see Martha Vicinus, "What Makes a Heroine? Nineteenth-Century Girls' Biographies," *Genre* 20 (1987): 171–88; Carla Peterson, *The Determined Reader: Gender and Culture in the Novel from Napoleon to Victoria* (New Brunswick: Rutgers University Press, 1986); Kate Flint, *The Woman Reader, 1837–1914* (Oxford: Oxford University Press, 1993); Pat Jalland, *Women, Marriage, and Politics, 1860–1914* (Oxford: Oxford University Press, 1988), 102–9; and Barbara Sicherman, "Sense and Sensibility: A Case Study of Women's Reading in Late-Victorian America," in *Reading in America: Literature and Social History*, ed. Cathy N. Davidson (Baltimore: The Johns Hopkins University Press, 1989). For the larger issue of print culture and identities, see Benedict Anderson, *Imagined Communities: Reflections on the Origins and Spread of Nationalism* (London: Verso, 1983).

44. EFSD, "Mulready," 349.

45. Anthony Trollope, *Autobiography*, qtd. in Jonathan Raban, *For Love and Money: A Writing Life* (New York: Harper Collins, 1987), 71. There is a vast critical literature on Victorian selfhood, especially on autobiography; see, e.g., Avrom Fleischman, *Figures of Autobiography: The Language of Self Writing in Victorian and Modern England* (Berkeley: University of California Press, 1980); and Jonathan Loesberg, *Fictions of Consciousness: Mill, Newman, and the Reading of Victorian Prose* (New Brunswick: Rutgers University Press, 1988); for works focused on gender, see Valerie Sanders, *The Private Lives of Victorian Women: Autobiography in the Nineteenth Century* (London: Harvester Wheatsheaf, 1989); Mary Jean Corbett, *Representing Femininity: Middle-Class Subjectivity in Victorian and Edwardian Women's Autobiographies* (New York: Oxford, 1992); Nina Auerbach, *Woman and the Demon: The Life of a Victorian Myth* (Cambridge: Harvard University Press, 1982), esp. 187–93, ch. 6, and epilogue; Auerbach, *Private Theatricals: The Lives of the Victorians* (Cambridge: Harvard University Press, 1990) and Regenia Gagnier, *Subjectivities: A History of Self-Representation in Britain, 1832–1920* (New York: Oxford University Press, 1991). See also Dina Copelman, "Victorian Subjects," [review essay], *Journal of British Studies* 34 (1995): 412–22, and James Kincaid, "Performance, Roles, the Self, and Our Own Charles Dickens," in his *Annoying the Victorians* (New York: Routledge, 1995), 77. On narrative and selfhood in Victorian politics and culture, see Patrick Joyce, *Democratic Subjects: The Self and the Social in Nineteenth Century England* (New York: Cambridge University Press, 1994); cf. Anne Humphreys, "Turn and Turn Again: a response to the narrative turn in Patrick Joyce's Democratic Subjects," *Journal of Victorian Culture* 1 (1996): 318–23.

46. Eliot, *Middlemarch*, xiii.

47. George Eliot, *Adam Bede* (1860; New York: Dutton, 1972), 287.

48. Virginia Woolf, *A Room of One's Own* (New York: Harcourt Brace Jovanovich, 1929), 3; see also Hermione Lee, *Virginia Woolf* (New York: Knopf, 1997), 3–20.

49. Raymond Williams, "Base and Superstructure in Marxist Cultural Theory," in Williams, *Problems in Materialism and Culture* (London: Verso, 1980), 31–49.

50. Cummings, "Purebreds and Hybrids," 79.

51. Michel Foucault, *Discipline and Punish: The Birth of the Prison*, trans. Alan Sheridan (1975; New York: Pantheon, 1978), 191–92; see also David Halperin, *Saint Foucault: Towards a Gay Hagiography* (New York: Oxford University Press, 1995), 127ff.; and Michel Foucault, *The History of Sexuality*, vol. 1, *An Introduction*; vol. 2, *The Uses of Pleasures*, both trans. Robert Hurley (New York: Pantheon, 1980, 1986), 29.

52. Qtd. in Richard Howard, *No Traveller* (New York: Alfred Knopf, 1989), 63. In some biographies, the individual in the title is granted only indefinite and contingent agency, but *everyone else* in the book is self-motivated and integrated, paradoxically reconstructing the subject's exceptionality.

53. Categories of analysis are also produced and reproduced through interpretation and narratives; see Michael Roth, *Knowing and History: Appropriations of Hegel in Twentieth-century France* (Ithaca: Cornell University Press, 1988), vi.

54. See Moi, *Simone de Beauvoir*, 3–4, 7, and Foucault, *History of Sexuality*, vol. 1, *An Introduction*, and *Power/Knowledge: Selected Interviews and Other Writings*, trans. and ed. Colin Gordon (New York: Pantheon, 1980).

55. Among the texts under implicit critique is my own; this book revises, if not repudiates my "Style and Strategy in the Life of Emilia Dilke," in *Constructions of the Self*, ed. George Levine (New Brunswick: Rutgers University Press, 1992). For other feminist critiques of the trope of self-making, see J. Rose, *Haunting*, 26, 74, and Martin, *Woman and Modernity*, 21. See also Adam Phillips, "Getting Ready to Exist." [Review of Lisboa, ed., *A Centenary Pessoa*, and Pessoa, *The Keeper of Sheep* and *The Book of Disquietude*] *London Review of Books*, 17 July 1997.

56. Phyllis Rose, "Fact and Fiction in Biography," in *Nineteenth-Century Lives: Essays presented to Jerome Hamilton Buckley*, ed. Laurence S. Lockridge, John Maynard, and Donald D. Stone (Cambridge: Cambridge University Press, 1989), 195–96; see also P. Rose, *Parallel Lives: Five Victorian Marriages* (New York: Knopf, 1984).

57. P. Rose's theory also conflates the subject's self-making and the biographer's construction of a persuasive narrative of self-making, especially since she contends that biography necessarily aspires to the novel ("Fact and Fiction," 188); cf. J. Rose, *Haunting*, 25, 38.

58. See also Carolyn Steedman, *Childhood, Culture, and Gender in Britain: Margaret Macmillan 1860–1931* (New Brunswick: Rutgers University Press, 1990), 251; Gagnier, *Subjectivities*; Naomi J. Miller, *Changing the Subject: Mary Wroth and Figurations of Gender in Early Modern England* (Lexington: University Press of Kentucky, 1996), 1; Donna Haraway, "The Virtual Speculum in the New World Order," *Feminist Review* 55 (1997), 29; and Prins, *Victorian Sappho*.

59. Gagnier, *Subjectivities*, and Mary Poovey, *Uneven Developments: The Ideological Work of Gender in Mid-Victorian England* (Chicago: University of Chicago Press, 1988); see also J. Rose, *Haunting*, 104.

60. Susan Groag Bell and Marilyn Yalom, eds., *Revealing Lives: Autobiography, Biography, and Gender* (Albany: State University of New York Press, 1990), 3. For accounts of psychological as well as intellectual engagements, see Carol Ascher, Louise DeSalvo, and Sara Ruddick, eds., *Between Women: Biographers, Novelists, Critics, Teachers, and Artists Write About Their Work On Women* (Boston: Beacon Press, 1984); Pamela Walker points out that some contributors seem to have interpreted their "relationship" to their (usually dead) subjects as remarkably interactive and judged their projects' success by the emotional rewards or disappointments of these imagined relationships; review of Ascher et al., *Between Women*, *Canadian Women's Studies* 6 (1985): 20–22; see also Dea Birkett and Julie Wheelwright. " 'How Could She?' Unpalatable Facts and Feminists' Heroines," *Gender and History* 2 (1990): 49–57; Booth, "Biographical Criticism," 89; Cheryl Walker, "Feminist Literary Criticism and the Author," *Critical Inquiry* 16 (1990): 551–70; and O'Brien, "Feminist Theory," 129. For the surge in personal writing, see *Confessions of the Critics*, ed. H.

Aram Veeser (New York: Routledge, 1996) and *Women's Review of Books*, special issue on "the memoir boom" (July 1996); see also Nancy K. Miller, *Getting Personal: Feminist Occasions and Other Autobiographical Acts* (New York: Routledge, 1991), ix–x, 2–3.

61. EFSP, review of Pater, *Renaissance*, in *Walter Pater: The Critical Heritage*, ed. R. M. Seiler (London: Routledge & Kegan Paul, 1980), 71–73; John J. Conlon, "Walter Pater and the Art of Misrepresentation," *Annals of Scholarship* 7 (1990), 168–69.

62. I do not cite specific biographies as examples because any work I might invoke may be an excellent and powerful study in many ways; placing it only as a negative example would be unfair. Moreover, my argument is that conceptualizing problems in terms of individuals is inadequate. On feminist romanticism and exceptional heroines, see Ellen Moers, *Literary Women: The Great Writers* (New York: Doubleday, 1977). Note that narratives of exceptionality can also be found in some collective biographies; works not biographical in the narrow sense may shift exceptionality from a single individual to, for example, "the woman writer."

63. See also O'Brien, "Feminist Theory," 128. I use "identication" loosely and colloquially; for a much more complex examination, see Diana Fuss, *Identification Papers* (New York: Routledge, 1995). My argument is not with an particular psychological theory; I am concerned with the political, ethical, and epistemological risks of texts organized by fantasies of sameness.

64. For such debates, see Joan Wallach Scott, *Gender and the Politics of History* (New York: Columbia University Press, 1988), esp. 1–50; but Scott rightly notes that life-writing can be theoretically engaged (44); see also Scott, *Only Paradoxes*, 15–16; O'Brien, "Feminist Theory," 123–32; and Ellen Rooney, "What's the Story? Feminist Theory, Narrative, Address," *Differences* 8 (1996), 11–16. For overlapping critiques of biography, see Steedman, *Childhood*, 243–50; and Stanley, "Moments of Writing," 58–67.

65. Kathryn Hughes, "The Voyage Renewed" [review of James King, *Virginia Woolf*], *New Statesman and Society*, 2 September 1994, 38; cf. Benjamin Disraeli's *Contarini Fleming*: "Read no history: nothing but biography, for that is life without theory"; qtd. in Mary Ann Smart, "The Lost Voice of Rosine Stoltz," in Corinne Blackmer and Patricia Juliana Smith, eds., *En Travesti: Women, Gender Subversion, and Opera* (New York: Columbia University Press, 1995), 169. See also Liz Stanley, *The Auto/Biographical I: The Theory and Practice of Feminist Auto/Biography* (Manchester: Manchester University Press, 1992), 250–53. I agree with Stanley's general points but am wary of her offering of Woolf's *Orlando* as an example; fictionalization reiterates biography's relationship to the novel and moves it further from history.

66. I echo Stephen Greenblatt, "I began with the desire to speak with the dead . . .''; *Shakespearean Negotiations* (Berkeley: University of California Press, 1988), 1, 20. But see also Eric Santner: "the work of mourning is an emphatically empirical procedure; mourning without historical knowledge is effectively and affectively empty"; qtd. in Constance Penley, *NASA/TREK: Popular Science and Sex in America* (New York: Verso, 1997), 59. This tension between a recognition of irrecuperability and a commitment to the work of creating partial but real historical knowledges animates my work. See also James E. Young, *Writing and Rewriting the Holocaust: Narrative and the Consequences of Interpretation* (Bloomington: Indiana University Press, 1988). On unadmitted knowledge, see Eve Kosofsky Sedgwick, *Tendencies* (Durham: Duke University Press, 1993), 23–51.

67. J. Rose, *Haunting*, xi.

68. Caroline Walker Bynum, *Fragmentation and Redemption: Essays on Gender and the Human Body in Medieval Religion* (New York: Zone Books, 1992), 14.

69. Bynum, *Fragmentation and Redemption*, 25, 23, 10.

70. EFSD, "Idealist Movement," 645; see also EFSD, "Physician's Wife," in EFSD, *Shrine of Death*, 40, 43.

71. But see introduction to Eve Kosofsky Sedgwick and Adam Frank, eds., *Shame and Its Sisters:*

A Silvan Tomkins Reader (Durham: Duke University Press, 1995), on the need for analyses that count past two but stop short of infinity.

72. See also Lawrence Grossberg, ed., "An Interview with Stuart Hall," in *Stuart Hall: Critical Dialogues in Cultural Studies*, ed. David Morley and Kuan-Hsing Chen (New York: Routledge, 1996), 137.

CHAPTER ONE

1. C. Peterson, *Determined Reader*, 28–31, 86; Eileen Simpson, *Orphans: Real and Imaginary* (New York: Plume/New American Library, 1987); Luisa Passerini, *Autobiography of a Generation: Italy, 1968* (Middletown: Wesleyan University Press, 1996), ch. 2.

2. See Stephen Mintz, *A Prison of Expectations: The Family in Victorian Culture* (New York: New York University Press, 1983); Leonore Davidoff and Catherine Hall, *Family Fortunes: Men and Women of the English Middle Class, 1780–1850* (London: Hutchinson, 1987); and Dianne Sadoff, *Monsters of Affection: Dickens, Eliot, and Bronte on Fatherhood* (Baltimore: Johns Hopkins University Press, 1982).

3. CWD, "Mem.," 3.

4. GMT submitted her text to her cousin Ward Boys and her brother, Henry Tuckwell; the ts. is annotated by another hand.

5. It is not clear whether Henry (and Emily) Strong lived wholly in Ilfracombe or sometimes in Oxford, or elsewhere, between Henry's retirement from the army, his marriage in 1825, and 1840 when EFS was born. On Ilfracombe, see F. B. May, "Victorian and Edwardian Ilfracombe," in *Leisure in Britain, 1780–1939*, ed. John K. Walton and James Walvin (Manchester: Manchester University Press, 1983), esp. 188–89; and Susan Chitty, *The Beast and the Monk: A Life of Charles Kingsley* (London: Hodder and Stoughton, 1974), 34. For EFSD's great-grandfather "Admiral Bowen," see AM 43938, fol. 354; the *London Times* of 29 Jan. 1876 gives a death-notice for Miss Teresa G. L. Bowen of Ilfracombe, aged 73, "last surviving daughter of Rear-Admiral Bowen." See also Jane Johnson, compiler, *Works Exhibited at the Royal Society of British Artists, 1824–1893* (Antiques Collectors' Club, 1975), q.v. "Strong, Henry." See also catalogue, *Exhibition of Oxford Amateur Art* (Oxford: I. Shrimpton, 1851) in Bodleian Library, G.A. Oxon* b. 113(62).

6. See also Davidoff and Hall, *Family Fortunes*, 207, 245–47.

7. On Iffley, see Edward Marshall, *An Account of the Township of Iffley, in the Deanery of Cuddeson, Oxfordshire: from the Earliest Notice*, second ed. (Oxford and London: James Parker, 1874), and Edward Cordrey, *Bygone Days at Iffley* (1956; Iffley: The Pica Press, 1981). The Elms was not the present Elm House Hotel, already a tavern and inn by 1836 (Cordrey, *Bygone Days*, 34–35). Askwith describes the Strong home as "a pleasant early Victorian house with bow windows . . . with a sloping garden running down to the Iffley-Oxford road," but it is unclear whence she derived this description (*Lady Dilke*, 5). The Strong house was probably substantial, holding a middle-class family of two adults and six children and at least one or two servants. GMT, "Rem.," A24, gives Emily Weedon an Oxford background; Henry may also have had family ties to Oxford; see Morton N. Cohen, ed. *Letters of Lewis Carroll*, vol. 1: *1837–1885* (London: Macmillan, 1979), 538n.

8. Marian was born in 1844 or 1845, Ethel between 1846 and 1848; Rosa and Owen Henry, at least, survived EFSD.

9. EFSD, "Samuel Strong," 23–28.

10. EFSD, "Samuel Strong," 23.

11. EFSD, "Samuel Strong," 24.

12. EFSD, "Samuel Strong," 24–26; see also CWD, "Mem.," 1, 117. CWD adds that Thomas was "naturally violent" in his later years as a consequence of his treatment in America; AM 43946, fol. 4. By an odd coincidence, EFS's great-uncle lived at 76 Lower Sloane Street and the Dilkes at 76 Sloane Street; CWD, "Mem.," 8.

13. EFSD, "Samuel Strong," 27, 26; AM 43946, fol. 4–5; CWD, "Mem.," 2.

14. AM 43946, fol. 4; see also Askwith, *Lady Dilke*, 5.

15. EFSD, "Samuel Strong," 27. Henry Strong's will bequeathed all his property and goods to his wife, appointing her sole executrix; Emily Weedon Strong's will, written in 1879, bequeaths properties "at Leeds and Hollingbourne and in Toville in Kent" to Owen Henry Strong and his heirs, and "all other Leasehold Estate and personal estate and effects" to the four surviving Strong daughters, "[to be] paid into their own hands for their sole and separate use . . . notwithstanding coverture"; wills in Somerset House, London. Some of the property Emily bequeathed may have been her own.

16. AM 43938, fol. 354. CWD's standard for distinguished persons appears to have been very high—one of those dashing sailors was an Admiral.

17. AM 43946, fols. 2, 5f.; EFSD carried some leaves "in a paper cover marked by her 'from the old home at Augusta, Georgia' "; see also EFSD, "Samuel Strong," 28.

18. AM 43946, fol. 4ff.

19. EFSD, "Samuel Strong," 27–28; CWD, "Mem.," 2.

20. Carolyn K. Steedman, *Landscape for a Good Woman* (New Brunswick: Rutgers University Press, 1987); Annette Kuhn, *Family Secrets: Acts of Memory and Imagination* (London: Verso, 1995).

21. Gayatri Chakravorty Spivak, *In Other Worlds: Essays in Cultural Politics* (New York: Methuen, 1987); Anita Levy, *Other Women: The Writing of Class, Race, and Gender, 1832–1898* (Princeton: Princeton University Press, 1991); Nupur Chaudhuri and Margaret Stroebel, eds., *Western Women and Imperialism: Complicity and Resistance* (Bloomington: Indiana University Press, 1992); and Chandra Talpade Mohanty, Ann Russo, and Lourdes Torres, eds., *Third World Women and the Politics of Feminism* (Bloomington: Indiana University Press, 1991). Antoinette Burton, *Burdens of History: British Feminists, Indian Women, and Imperial Culture, 1865–1915* (Chapel Hill: University of North Carolina Press, 1994), considers how white British feminists' views of colonial women shaped British feminism. On imperial children, see Elizabeth Buettner, dissertation-in-progress, Department of History, University of Michigan.

22. CWD, "Mem.," 9.

23. EFSD, "Great Missionary Success," 677.

24. EFSD, "Great Missionary Success," 677; CWD, "Mem.," 9; see also Burton, *Burdens of History*, 72–73.

25. AM 43906, fol. 66f. (EFSP to CWD, 30 Apr. 1885). The letter continues over several days; the passage cited is dated 2 May and reads "I get on so well with them & am" then breaks off because of a mutilation probably aimed at the other side of the page.

26. By 1905, when his "Mem." was written and published, CWD was deeply concerned with the European arms race and the escalation of imperial and Continental tensions; for his imperialism, see CWD, *Greater Britain: A Record of Travel in English-Speaking Countries during 1866 and 1867* (New York: Harper and Brothers, 1869); *Problems of Greater Britain* (London and New York: Macmillan, 1890); and CWD and Spencer Wilkinson, *Imperial Defense* (London and New York: Macmillan, 1891); see also Jenkins, *Dilke*, ch. 2 and 371–2, and Nicholls, *Lost Prime Minister*, ch. 2, and 93, 99, 117, 306–9.

27. AM 43946, fol. 4–5. MP refers to Major Strong (PP 130, fol. 127 [16–19 Feb. 1876]), but EFSD, CWD—generally a stickler for detail and very knowledgeable about Army matters—and Marian Strong Wilkinson's obituary refer to him as Captain, adding, in some cases, H.E.I.C.S. (Honorable East India Company's Service); CWD, "Mem.," 1; PP 130, fol. 57 (MP diary, 13 Feb. 1865).

28. Another relative, O. A. Strong, requested MP's assistance in obtaining a "Regimental Paymastership"; PP 56, fol. 297f. (O. A. Strong to MP, n.d. [1866]).

29. EFSD, "Samuel Strong," 27fn., says "Francis" is a family name, but CWD, "Mem.," 3, attributes EFS's name to Francis Whiting.

30. GMT, "Rem.," A11.

31. Marian married "F. Wilkinson, Esq., C.S.," and died on 13 Jan. 1865; see PP 130, fol. 57 (MP diary, 13 Feb. 1865).

32. PP 140, fol. 4, n.d. (EFS to to Rosa Strong [Tuckwell]); and fol. 10–11, n.d. (EFS to Rosa Tuckwell, summer 1861); but fol. 1, an envelope, is marked "from Poppie," another nickname.

33. CWD, "Mem.," 19.

34. William Walrond Jackson, *Ingram Bywater: The Memoir of an Oxford Scholar, 1840–1914* (Oxford: Clarendon, 1917), 20fn.

35. Marianne Hirsch, *The Mother/Daughter Plot: Narrative, Psychoanalysis, Feminism* (Bloomington: Indiana University Press, 1989); see also Passerini, *Autobiography,* 26–36; Pederson, "Rathbone and Daughter: Feminism and the Father at the Fin-de-siècle," *Journal of Victorian Culture* 1 (1996), esp. 111–12; cf. Beth Kowaleski-Wallace, "Milton's Daughters: The Education of Eighteenth-Century Women Writers," *Feminist Studies* 12 (1986), 290.

36. GMT, "Rem.," A24; Rosa Tuckwell, "A Visit to the Langdale Linen Industry," *Women's Gazette and Weekly News,* 6 July 1889, 571, alludes to an aunt "near Penrith" who may have been part of Emily Weedon's family, as may Albert Fleming of Ambleside, who addresses EFSD as "Dear Cousin" in AM 43907, fol. 278v [14 Oct. 1887]). See also Davidoff and Hall, *Family Fortunes,* 208–11, 219–22, 275–79.

37. The Elms was mortgaged, perhaps to support Emily; PP 130, fol. 128f. (MP's diary, 23 Feb. 1876).

38. Jalland, *Women, Marriage and Politics,* chs. 5 and 6; Pat Jalland and John Hooper, *Women from Birth to Death 1830–1914* (Brighton: Harvester, 1985).

39. Eileen Yeo, unpublished paper on Frances Power Cobbe, presented at Rutgers University, 1988.

40. CWD, "Mem.," 4, 8.

41. PP 140, fol. 6 (EFSP to Rosa Tuckwell, 19 Feb. 1868).

42. CWD, "Mem.," 9; see also AM 43946, fol. 13.

43. EFSD, "Idealist Movement," 650.

44. EFSD, "Physician's Wife," in EFSD, *Shrine of Death,* 48–50.

45. EFSD, "Parables of Life I: A Stainless Soul"; see also "The Crimson Scarf," in EFSD, *Shrine of Death,* 101: a vision of the protagonist's dead mother appears, seemingly to offer comfort after a girl abandoned by her male family members for sexual "dishonor" colludes with her brother's death, but the cloak she wraps around the girl is "wet with blood."

46. *People's Journal of Dundee,* 7 Sept. 1889 (account of speech of 2 Sept. 1889); Askwith, *Lady Dilke,* 6.

47. Thomas W. Laqueur, "Bodies, Details, and the Humanitarian Narrative," in *The New Cultural History,* ed. Lynn Hunt (Berkeley and Los Angeles: University of California Press, 1989), 177–80.

48. See Leonore Davidoff, "Class and Gender in Victorian England," and "Mastered for Life: Servant and Wife in Victorian London," both in Davidoff, *Worlds Between: Historical Perspectives on Gender and Class* (London: Routledge, 1995); Davidoff and Hall, *Family Fortunes,* 388–96; Bruce Robbins, *The Servant's Hand: English Fiction from Below* (New York: Columbia University Press, 1986); Pamela Horn, *The Rise and Fall of the Victorian Servant* (Gloucester: Allan Sutton, 1986); and especially Brian McCuskey, "Servants' Characters: Below Stairs in the Victorian Novel," Ph.D. dissertation, Department of English Language and Literature, University of Michigan, 1995.

49. EFSD, "Parables of Life," 535–36.

50. Elizabeth Barrett Browning, *Aurora Leigh,* ed. Gardner B. Taplin (Chicago: Academy Chicago, 1979), 110–11; Judith R. Walkowitz, *City of Dreadful Delight: Narratives of Sexual Danger in Late-Victorian London* (Chicago: University of Chicago Press, 1992), chs. 3 and 4, esp. 116–20.

51. EFSD, "Parables of Life," 540.

52. EFSD, "Parables of Life," 541.

53. AM 43907, fol. 278v. (Albert Fleming to EFSD, 14 Oct. 1887); Fleming referred to the Gray's Inn woman as "Aunt Sophy".

54. Davidoff and Hall, Family Fortunes, chs. 2 and 3; Kathryn Gleadle, The Early Feminists: Radical Unitarians and the Emergence of the Women's Rights Movements, 1831–51 (New York: St. Martin's, 1995); Hester Burton, Barbara Bodichon (London: Constable, 1949); Sheila R. Herstein, A Mid-Victorian Feminist: Barbara Leigh Smith Bodichon (New Haven: Yale University Press, 1985); Muriel Clara Bradbrook, Barbara Bodichon, George Eliot, and the Limits of Feminism (Oxford: Blackwell, 1975); and Candida Lacey, ed., Barbara Leigh Smith Bodichon and the Langham Place Group (London: Routledge Kegan Paul, 1987).

55. On sisters in families that encouraged art studies, see Deborah Cherry, Painting Women: Victorian Women Artists (London: Routledge, 1993), 46–47.

56. On girls' education, see Margaret Bryant, The Unexpected Revolution: A Study in the History of the Education of Women and Girls in the Nineteenth Century (London: University of London Institute of Education, 1979); Joan Burstyn, Victorian Education and the Ideal of Womanhood (London: Croom Helm, 1980); Felicity Hunt, ed., Lessons for Life: The Schooling of Girls and Women 1850–1950 (Oxford: Basil Blackwell, 1987); Martha Vicinus, Independent Women: Work and Community for Single Women, 1850–1920 (Chicago: University of Chicago Press, 1985), ch. 5; and Carol Dyhouse, Girls Growing Up in Late Victorian and Edwardian England (Boston: Broadway House, 1981).

57. William Tuckwell, Reminiscences of Oxford (London: Cassell, 1900), 6–10.

58. GMT, "Rem.," A15–16. GMT and her sisters were amused by Miss Bowdich's scripture lessons, having "heard of the Stone Age" from their scientific father.

59. GMT, "Rem.," A15.

60. AM 43946, fol. 6–7; CWD, "Mem.," 3.

61. GMT, "Rem.," A15–16.

62. AM 43946, fol. 6–7.

63. GMT, "Rem.," A16.

64. Leonore Davidoff, "Where the Stranger Begins: The Question of Siblings in Historical Analysis," in Davidoff, Worlds Between, 211; see also Helena Michie, Sororaphobia: Differences among Women in Literature and Culture (Oxford: Oxford University Press, 1992).

65. GMT, "Rem.," A230, 233.

66. GMT, "Rem.," A9ff, A133, and passim.

67. GMT, "Rem.," A20; W. Tuckwell, Reminiscences, ch. 6.

68. There has been little analysis of Victorian women and music, but see Mary Burgan, "Heroines at the Piano: Women and Music in Nineteenth-Century Fiction," Victorian Studies 30 (1986): 51–76.

69. GMT, "Rem.," A5, A133–34.

70. GMT, "Rem.," A20.

71. Rosa wrote for the Women's Gazette and Weekly News in the 1880s, and GMT cites her as educating her children about "Dizzy's 'Two Nations' "; GMT, "Rem.," A20f.

72. GMT, "Rem.," A138.

73. GMT., "Rem.," A273; GMT characterizes William Tuckwell's childhood as "brutal" and situates Rosa as healing him.

74. GMT, "Rem.," A5, A133–34, A272, A273.

75. GMT, "Rem.," A6, A59.

76. AM 43907, fol. 262 (Rosa Tuckwell to EFSD, 21 Apr. [1887?]).

77. GMT, "Rem.," A73; ch. 5 and 6 below.

78. GMT, "Rem.," A12, A62, A43.

79. CWD, "Mem.," 12–13, 14–15. EFSD recounts less frequent auditory "hallucinations,"

"'occasionally voices calling,—always voices I could recognize, but more often musical sounds.'"

80. CWD, "Mem.," 13–14.

81. CWD, "Mem.," 15, 14. EFSD's reference is probably to the late 1860s and early 1870s.

82. PP 140, fol. 2, probably written on Rosa's birthday or engagement: "Dear Rosa May your path be all flowers/May happy and joyful be your hours/May they pass by on a silver wing/And music and sunshine with them bring/May your joys be many your sorrows few/ And blessings ever shower on you." The handwriting is very young.

83. PP 140, fol. 3f. (EFS to Rosa Tuckwell, n.d.); EFS offers Rosa the choice of two penwipes she has made and apologizes, "I have not much money as you know or I would have bought something that was better worth your having."

CHAPTER TWO

1. D. S. Maccoll, "Rhoda Broughton and Emilia Pattison," *The Nineteenth Century and After* 137: 815 (January 1945), 30; the Holywell address may have been a relative's or a Strong house preceding the move to Iffley. For Maccoll (1859–1948), see his *Confessions of a Keeper and Other Papers* (London: Alexander Maclehose, 1931).

2. CWD, "Mem.," 3, 4.

3. CWD, "Mem.," 5.

4. PP 140, fol. 92ff.; the article, dated 1 Oct. 1893, is marked "D.C.," probably *Daily Chronicle*; see Askwith, *Lady Dilke*, 7, 214, n. 20. The clipping is heavily "corrected," probably by GMT. Cf. EFSP, *Renaissance*, 1: 174, 236, 290.

5. Frontispiece to EFSD, BSL; also in Askwith, *Lady Dilke*, facing 86.

6. Ms. Don. e. 64, fol. 78 (H. K. Hudson to F.G. Stephens, 28 Oct. 1904).

7. Ginzburg, "Microhistory," 34.

8. On Victorian pictures and little girls, see Mavor, *Pleasures Taken*; on artistic families and their daughters, see Jan Marsh and Pamela Gerrish Nunn, *Women Artists and the Pre-Raphaelite Movement* (London: Virago, 1989), 157, and Cherry, *Painting Women*, 19–31.

9. EFSD, *French Engravers*, 4.

10. CWD, "Mem.," 3.

11. On such bourgeois and genteel cultural contexts, see John Brewer, *The Pleasures of the Imagination: English Culture in the Eighteenth Century* (New York: Farrar Straus Giroux, 1997). EFSD, *French Engravers*, 15, marks the possibility of artistic talent being inherited from mothers, and EFS's mother could have been related to artists; see Johnson, comp., *Works Exhibited*, q.v. "Weedon, Augustus Walford" (1859–1892); Christopher Wood, *Victorian Panorama: Paintings of Victorian Life* (London: Faber and Faber, 1976), 156; and *Dictionary of Victorian Painters*, 2nd edition (Woodbridge, Suffolk: Antique Collectors' Club, 1978), q.v. "Weedon, Augustus Walford" and "Weedon, Edwin." Another possible family connection is suggested by EFS's sister's name, Ethel Rigaud Strong; Miss E. A. Rigaud showed a "Ruth and Boaz" at the 1800 Royal Academy; see Charlotte Yeldham, *Women Artists in Nineteenth-Century France and England: Their Art Education, Exhibition Opportunities, and Membership of Existing Society and Academies, with an Assessment of the Subject Matter of their Work and Summary Biographies*, 2 vols. (New York: Garland, 1984), 2:3; see also EFSD, *French Painters*, ch. 6, and *French Engravers*, 59, 63, for Hyacinthe Rigaud; but see also W. Tuckwell, *Reminiscences*, 171–72.

12. Wood, *Dictionary*, s.v. "Strong, H., f. 1840"; Johnson, *Works Exhibited*, s.v. "Strong, Henry."

13. Catalogue, *Exhibition of Oxford Amateur Art*.

14. W. Tuckwell, *Reminiscences*, 47.

15. Askwith, Lady Dilke, 5, no source; Maccoll, "Rhoda Broughton," 30. On genteel flautists in provincial cultural life, see Brewer, Pleasures, 557–58.

16. On early Victorian Oxford, see E. G. W. Bill, University Reform in Nineteenth-Century Oxford: A Study of Henry Halford Vaughn, 1811–1885 (Oxford: Oxford University Press, 1973); W. Tuckwell, Pre-Tractarian Oxford (London: Smith Elder, 1908); A. J. Engel, From Clergyman to Don: The Rise of the Academic Profession in Nineteenth-Century Oxford (Oxford: Clarendon Press, 1983); C. E. Mallet, A History of the University of Oxford, vol. 3: Modern Oxford (London: Methuen, 1927); and Lawrence Stone, ed. The University in Society, vol. 1: Oxford and Cambridge from the 14th to the early 19th Centuries (Princeton: Princeton University Press, 1974).

17. Earle, Letters, 89; cf. CWD, "Mem.," 4. Earle (1836–1925) was disingenuous in presenting herself as less well-connected than EFS; the granddaughter of Baron Ravensworth, daughter of Elizabeth Liddell and Edward Villiers, niece of Lord Clarendon, and cousin of Lady Harcourt, she moved in high aristocratic and political circles and spent her youth on the Continent, in the "Great Houses" of England, and at Little Holland House; see Earle, Memoirs and Memories (London: Smith, Elder, 1911), 242–44.

18. John Steegman, Victorian Taste: A Study of the Arts and Architecture from 1830–1870 (London: Century, in association with the National Trust, 1970), 264. W. Tuckwell adds "Monro the sculptor," Reminiscences, 49.

19. John Dixon Hunt, The Wider Sea: A Life of John Ruskin (New York: Viking, 1982), 245–46; see also Robert Hewison, Ruskin and Oxford: The Art of Education (Oxford: Oxford University Press, 1996); W. Tuckwell, Reminiscences; 47, 49; Steegman, Victorian Taste, 264, and Louise Creighton, Memoir of a Victorian Woman: Reflections of Louise Creighton, 1850–1936, ed. James Thayne Covert (Bloomington: Indiana University Press, 1994), 44, 56.

20. J. Hunt, Wider Sea, 89; see also Raleigh Trevelyan, A Pre-Raphaelite Circle (London: Chatto & Windus, 1978), 1–6; J. B. Atlay, Henry Acland, A Memorial (London: Smith, Elder, 1903).

21. Timothy Hilton, The Pre-Raphaelites (London: Thames & Hudson, 1970), 161; S. Gaselee, "The Aesthetic Side of the Oxford Movement," in Northern Catholicism: Centenary Studies in the Oxford and Parallel Movements, ed. N. P. Williams and Charles Harris (New York: Macmillan, 1933), 423. On Pre-Raphaelite medievalism, see Browning Institute Studies 8 (1980), special issue on Victorian medievalism, esp. Herbert Sussman ("The Pre-Raphaelites and the "Mood of the Cloister," 45–56), W. David Shaw ("Browning and Pre-Raphaelite Medievalism," 73–84), and Helene Roberts ("Victorian Medievalism: Revival or Masquerade?" 11–44).

22. See P. G. Hamerton qtd. in Marsh and Nunn, Women Artists, 18.

23. W. Tuckwell, Remininscences, 49.

24. See Paula Gillett, Worlds of Art: Painters in Victorian Society (New Brunswick: Rutgers University Press, 1990), 3–5; Dianne Sachko Macleod, Art and the Victorian Middle Class: Money and the Making of Cultural Identity (New York: Cambridge University Press, 1996); Janet Wolff and John Seed, eds., The Culture of Capital: Art, Power, and the Nineteenth-Century Middle Class (Manchester: Manchester University Press, 1988); Bernard Denvir, The Early Nineteenth-Century: Art, Design, and Society, 1789–1852 (London: Longman, 1984); Elizabeth Gilmore Holt, ed., The Triumph of Art for the Public, 1785–1848: The Emerging Role of Exhibitions and Critics (Princeton: Princeton University Press, 1983); David Robertson, Sir Charles Eastlake and the Victorian Art World (Princeton: Princeton University Press, 1978), chs. 4, 5, 10; Steegman, Victorian Taste; Francis Haskell, Rediscoveries in Art: Some Aspects of Taste, Fashion, and Collecting in England and France (Oxford: Phaidon Press, 1976); Debra N. Mancoff, "Samuel Carter Hall: Publisher as Promoter of the Fine Arts," Victorian Periodicals Review 24 (1991): 11–21, esp. 12–14; Nikolaus Pevsner, Academies of Art Past and Present (1940; New York: Da Capo Press, 1973), ch. 6; and Quentin Bell, The Schools of Design (London: Routledge Kegan Paul, 1963). Frances Borzello, Civilising Caliban: The Misuse of Art, 1875–1980 (London: Routlege Kegan Paul, 1987) is a trenchant critique of Victorian art culture; see also Kate Flint, "The English Critical Reaction to Contemporary Painting 1878–1910," Ph.D. thesis, Brasenose

College, University of Oxford, 1983, ch. 1; and A. L. Rees and F. Borzello, eds., *The New Art History* (London: Camden Press, 1986).

25. For science, see Robert H. Kargon, *Science in Victorian Manchester: Enterprise and Expertise* (Baltimore: Johns Hopkins University Press, 1977); Arnold Thackray, "Scientific Knowledge in Cultural Context: the Manchester Model," *American Historical Review* 79 (1974): 672–709; and Ian Inkster and Jack Morrell, eds., *Metropolis and Province: Science in British Culture 1780–1850* (Philadelphia: University of Pennsylvania Press, 1983); for social science, see Eileen Yeo, *The Contest for Social Science: Relations and Representations of Gender and Class* (London: Rivers Oram Press, 1996) and Mary Poovey, *Making a Social Body: British Cultural Formation 1830–1864* (Chicago: University of Chicago Press, 1995); for art, see J. M. Bourne, *Patronage and Society in Nineteenth-Century England* (London: Edward Arnold, 1986); Macleod, *Art and the Victorian Middle Class*, ch. 2; and Trevor Fawcett, *The Rise of English Provincial Art: Artists, Patrons, and Institutions outside London, 1800–30* (Oxford: Clarendon, 1974).

26. The story of the middle class as Philistines was a story generated by disaffected members of the bourgeoisie; see Jerrold Siegal, *Bohemian Paris: Culture, Politics, and the Boundaries of Bourgeois Life* (New York: Viking Penguin, 1986). On middle-class cultural claims, see Davidoff and Hall, *Family Fortunes*, chs. 1, 3, and 10; Dror Wahrman, *Imagining the Middle Class: The Political Representation of Class in Britain, c. 1780–1840* (Cambridge: Cambridge University Press, 1995); and Catherine Hall, *White, Male and Middle-Class: Essays in Feminism and History* (New York: Routledge, 1992), ch. 10. See also John Pemble, *The Mediterranean Passion: Victorians and Edwardians in the South* (Oxford: Oxford University Press, 1987), 75–77; and ch. 5 below.

27. Gillett, *Worlds of Art*, 156–57; see also Cherry, *Painting Women*, esp. ch. 4; Helene E. Roberts, "Exhibition and Review: the Periodical Press and the Victorian Art Exhibition System," in Joanne Shattock and Michael Wolff, eds., *The Victorian Periodical Press: Samplings and Soundings* (Leicester: Leicester University Press, 1982), 79–108; Flint, "English Critical Reaction," ch. 2; Borzello, *Civilising Caliban*, 4; Denvir, *The Early Nineteenth-Century*, ch. 3; and Kathy Alexis Psomiades, "Beauty's Body: Gender Ideology and British Aestheticism," *Victorian Studies* 36 (1992): 31–52. For cultural capital, see Pierre Bourdieu, "Cultural Reproduction and Social Reproduction," in *Knowledge, Education, and Cultural Change: Papers in the Sociology of Education*, ed. Richard Brown (London: Tavistock, 1973); and "Outline of a Sociological Theory of Art Perception," *International Social Science Journal* 20 (1968): 589–612. Macleod notes the importance of expanding economic capital at mid-century; *Art and the Victorian Middle Class*, 195.

28. Macleod, *Art and the Victorian Middle Class*, 152–55, 451.

29. Qtd. in Yeldham, *Women Artists*, 1:9.

30. Marsh and Nunn, *Women Artists*, 27–28.

31. Qtd. in Stuart Macdonald, *The History and Philosophy of Art Education* (New York: American Elsevier, 1970), 147.

32. Marsh and Nunn, *Women Artists*; Jan Marsh, *Pre-Raphaelite Women: Images of Femininity* (New York: Harmony Books, 1987) and *Pre-Raphaelite Sisterhood* (New York: Quartet, 1985); Lynda Nead, *Myths of Sexuality: Representations of Women in Victorian Britain* (Oxford: Basil Blackwell, 1988); Griselda Pollock and Deborah Cherry, "Women as Sign in Pre-Raphaelite Literature: the Representation of Elizabeth Siddall," *Art History* (June 1984): 206–77, and "Patriarchal Power and the Pre-Raphaelites," *Art History* 7 (1984): 485–86; Pollock, *Vision and Difference: Femininity, Feminism, and the Histories of Art* (London: Routledge, 1988); Lynne Pearce, *Woman/Image/Text: Readings in Pre-Raphaelite Art and Literature* (Toronto: University of Toronto Press, 1991); Marcia Pointon, ed., *The Pre-Raphaelites Re-viewed* (Manchester: Manchester University Press, 1989); Susan P. Casteras, *Images of Victorian Womanhood in English Art* (Rutherford, N.J.: Fairleigh Dickinson University Press, 1987) and *The Substance of the Shadow: Images of Victorian Womanhood* (New Haven: Yale Center for British Art, 1982). See also Christina Rossetti, "In an Artist's Studio" (1856/1896), in Angela Leighton

and Margaret Reynolds, *Victorian Women Poets: an Anthology* (Cambridge, Mass.: Blackwell, 1995), 365.

33. Marsh and Nunn, *Women Artists*, 31, 153.

34. See William Rossetti's definition of Pre-Raphaelitism and the *Magazine of Art* (1880), both qtd. in Marsh and Nunn, *Women Artists*, 14–15, 154; see also Herbert Sussman, *Victorian Masculinities: Manhood and Masculine Poetics in Early Victorian Literature and Art* (Cambridge: Cambridge University Press, 1995).

35. On PRB domestic interiors, see Pearce, *Woman/Image/Text*, 63–64, 125–26, and Kate Flint, "Reading *The Awakening Conscience* Rightly," in *The Pre-Raphaelites Re-viewed*, ed. Marcia Pointon (Manchester: Manchester University Press, 1989); David Masson, "Pre-Raphaelitism in Art and Literature" (1852); Jerome McGann, "Rossetti's Significant Details" (1969); and John Dixon Hunt, "A Moment's Monument: Reflections on Pre-Raphaelite Vision in Poetry and Painting" (1971), all in *Pre-Raphaelitism*, ed. James Stanbrook (Chicago: University of Chicago Press, 1974); see also D. G. Rossetti's "The Girlhood of Mary the Virgin" and Millais's "Christ in the House of His Parents." More broadly, see Henry Ladd, *The Victorian Morality of Art: An Analysis of Ruskin's Esthetic* (New York: Ray Long and Richard R. Smith, 1932), chs. 1, 3; Denvir, *Early Nineteenth Century*, ch. 6; and Charles Locke Eastlake, *Hints on Household Taste*, ed. John Gloag, 4th rev. ed. (1878; New York: Dover, 1969). Marcia Pointon, *Strategies for Showing: Women, Possession, and Representation in English Visual Culture, 1665–1800* (Oxford: Oxford University Press, 1997) suggests a pre–Pre-Raphaelite history of these issues; cf. Macleod, *Art and the Victorian Middle Class*, 279, which locates them later.

36. Nunn and Marsh, *Women Artists*, 153–55; see also Cherry, *Painting Women*, 117 and ch. 7; Psomiades, "Beauty's Body," 33, 44–45, 50; and Loeb, *Consuming Angels*; cf. Macleod, *Art and the Victorian Middle Class*, 289–90.

37. E. T. Cook and Alexander Wedderburn, eds., *The Works of John Ruskin* (London: George Allen, 1902–12), vol. 18, *Sesame and Lilies*, "Of Queens' Gardens," sections 80, 68 (I cite section rather than page for ease of reference to the many editions of this work); see also Casteras, *Images*, ch. 4; Jennifer Lloyd, "Raising Lilies: Ruskin and Women," *Journal of British Studies* 34 (1995): 325–50; and Malcolm Hardman, *Six Victorian Thinkers* (Manchester: Manchester University Press, 1991), 56–60, 64–69.

38. CWD, "Mem.," 3, 4 (citing Rosa Tuckwell).

39. R. Trevelyan, *Pre-Raphaelite Circle*, 12–15, 29, 30–31, 34–48, 75, 137; see also Virginia Surtees, ed., *Reflections of a Friendship: John Ruskin's Letters to Pauline Trevelyan, 1848–1866* (London: George Allen and Unwin, 1979), and Macleod, *Art and the Victorian Middle Class*, 170–71, 480–81.

40. For a late-century familial combat about the ends of women's education, see Susan Pederson, "Rathbone and Daughter: Feminism and the Father at the Fin-de-siècle," *Journal of Victorian Culture* 1:1 (Spring 1996), 105–8.

41. William Stebbing, ed., *Charles Henry Pearson, Fellow of Oriel and Education Minister in Victoria* (London: Longmans Green, 1900), 83–84; see also Sarah Angelina Acland, unpub. memoir, Mss. Acland.

42. Diana Holman-Hunt, "Introduction," to Anne Amor Clarke, *William Holman Hunt: The True Pre-Raphaelite* (London: Constable, 1989), 9; Macleod, *Art and the Victorian Middle Class*, 155–60, 402–3.

43. Hunt qtd. in A. C. Gissing, *William Holman Hunt: A Biography* (London: Duckworth, 1936), 68; see also Diana Holman-Hunt, *My Grandfather, His Wives and Loves* (London: Hamish Hamilton, 1969), 58, 73, 75, 87, 92–93; Clarke, *William Holman Hunt*, 70–71, 248; Hilton, *Pre-Raphaelites*, 29, 66, 68; W. Tuckwell, *Reminiscences*, 48; and Macleod, *Art and the Victorian Middle Class*, 156–60. Thomas Combe was the first purchaser of Hunt's midnight Christ, "The Light of the World" and the Combes owned the largest collection of Hunts.

44. Holman-Hunt, *My Grandfather*, 94, 73, 87–88, 95, 200–201; Clarke, *Holman Hunt*, 92,

104, 167, 240. On Annie Miller, see also Marsh, *Pre-Raphaelite Sisterhood*, 58–66, 102–9, 162–68. There is little doubt that "Miss Strong" was EFS; Rosa and Henrietta were already married and Marian and Ethel were younger.

45. Holman-Hunt, *My Grandfather*, 201 (qtg. letter by Hunt, 26 Feb. 1859), 202.

46. Holman-Hunt, *My Grandfather*, 201–2, 207; on *The Scapegoat* and Syria, see Hilton, *Pre-Raphaelites*, 110–11, and Clarke, *Holman Hunt*, 105, 167.

47. Holman-Hunt, *My Grandfather*, 94–95.

48. See also Cherry, *Painting Women*, 34–38.

49. Holman Hunt also proposed to and was refused by Julia Jackson (later Stephen), who, like EFS, went on to marry a "difficult" man; Lee, *Woolf*, 87. See also Barrett Browning, *Aurora Leigh*, 50–53, another deferral of a romance plot.

50. AM 43932, fol. 137f; CWD, "Mem.," 9.

51. CWD, "Mem.," 9.

52. AM 43932, fol. 137f.

53. James Glucker, "The Case for Edward Casaubon," *Pegasus* [University of Essex Classics Society magazine] (November 1967), 14, has CWD and EFS "in love" at South Kensington.

54. CWD, "Mem.," 7–8; AM 43932, fol. 137f.; trap-bat or trap-ball was played with a bat, ball, and a "pivoted wooden instrument" called a trap, on the end of which the ball can be set; the ball is both flung into the air and hit by the batter; *Oxford English Dictionary*.

55. Ben Weinreb and Christopher Hibbert, eds., *The London Encyclopedia* (Bethesda, Md.: Adler and Adler, 1986), s.v. "Gore House."

56. CWD, "Mem.," 8; Thackeray's daughters became Anne Ritchie and the first Mrs. Leslie Stephen; see Lee, *Woolf*, 35–36, 75–77.

57. For the Dilkes and class, see Nicholls, *Lost Prime Minister*, xxiii–xxv.

58. Gwynn and Tuckwell, *Life of Dilke*, 1: 6, 8, 9; see also GMT, "Rem.," A80.

59. William Garrett, *Charles Wentworth Dilke* (Boston: Twayne, 1982), preface, 12, and ch. 2; see also Leslie A. Marchand, *The Athenaeum: A Mirror of Victorian Culture* (Chapel Hill: University of North Carolina Press, 1941), esp. ch. 3.

60. Marchand, *Athenaeum*, 68, 175 (qtg. *Athenaeum*, 14 May 1831); John Charles Olmstead, *Victorian Painting: Essays and Reviews*, vol. 1: 1832–1848 (New York: Garland, 1980), reprints many *Athenaeum* articles.

61. Gwynn and Tuckwell, *Life of Dilke*, 1:10, 12–16; GMT, "Rem.," A80–81; Nicholls, *Lost Prime Minister*, 2.

62. Gwynn and Tuckwell, *Life of Dilke*, 1:14; Marchand, *Athenaeum*, 83, qtg. CWD to Old Mr. Dilke, 5 July 1864; Garrett, *Charles Wentworth Dilke*, 184–85, reads CWD's imperialism as a repudiation of his grandfather's ideas but underexplores links between imperialism and liberalism.

63. CWD qtd. in Gwynn and Tuckwell, *Life of Dilke*, 1: 9; for Mary Dilke's death, ibid., 1: 8–9; see also Jenkins, *Dilke*, 13–15; and Nicholls, *Lost Prime Minister*, 4.

64. Nicholls, *Lost Prime Minister*, 11.

65. Nicholls, *Lost Prime Minister*, 6; Gwynn and Tuckwell, *Life of Dilke*, 1:13, 15.

66. Gwynn and Tuckwell, *Life of Dilke*, 1:14, 1:16.

67. In Gwynn and Tuckwell, *Life of Dilke*, facing 1:10; on Corbaux (1812–1883) and her sister Louisa, see Pamela Gerrish Nunn, *Victorian Women Artists* (London: The Women's Press, 1987); 41, 44, 100, and Yeldham, *Women Artists*, 1: 281–83; 3: 8–11, 4: vii, and plate 116.

68. Marchand, *Athenaeum*, 47, 113n., 222–24; Gwynn and Tuckwell, *Life of Dilke*, 1:16, 2: 236; see also Clara Thomas, *Love and Work Enough: The Life of Anna Jameson* (Toronto: University of Toronto Press, 1967), 177–78. Sydney Owenson Morgan (1780–1859) wrote poetry, novels including *The Wild Irish Girl*, and prose, including the feminist satire, *Woman and Her Master* (1840); see Mary Campbell, *Lady Morgan: The Life and Times of Sydney Owenson* (London: Pandora, 1989); Clarissa Campbell Orr, "The Corinne Complex: Gender, Genius, and National Culture," in

Women in the Victorian Art World, ed. Orr (Manchester: Manchester University Press, 1995), 93–96; and Garrett, *Charles Wentworth Dilke*, 111–12.

69. For "Dragon," see, e.g. AM 43902, fol. 61 (Ashton Dilke to CWD, Nov. 1874); fol. 76 (CWD to Ashton, 21 Feb. 1877); Askwith claims "this was a family nickname derived from the Dragon of Wantley, because when she was on the rampage she got up on her hind legs" (*Lady Dilke*, 118n.). For CWD's other nicknames, see AM 43908, fol. 28 (Caroline Chatfield to EFSP, 23 July 1877), and fol. 41 (21 Feb. [1879?]. Maye Dilke addresses CWD as "Charley" (AM 43902, fol. 146 [17 March 1883?]). Prolific nicknaming was not unusual; see Lee, *Woolf*, 109–10, 164–65.

70. Nicholls, *Lost Prime Minister*, 12; AM 43904, fol. 204 [CWD to EFSP, 23 Jan. 1881]; see also Gwynn and Tuckwell, *Life of Dilke*, 2: 240–41, 566; GMT, "Rem.", A97.

71. EFSD claimed this room was sullied when VMC "fixed [it]*as the scene of some of her most horrible tales* [of adultery with CWD]" and CWD briefly wished to burn down the house; AM 118, fol. 140ff. (EFSD to ES, 28 Jan. 1886), and ch. 6 below.

72. Davidoff and Hall, *Family Fortunes*, pt. 1; see also Jane Rendall, *Origins of Modern Feminism: Women in Britain, France, and the United States, 1780–1860* (London: Macmillan, 1985), chs. 2 and 3.

73. EFSD, *French Painters*, 14; on the larger contexts, see Macleod, *Art and the Victorian Middle Class*, ch. 1, and Eric Gidal, "Passion Stamped on Lifeless Things: English Romanticism and the Poetics of the British Museum," Ph.D. dissertation, Department of English Language and Literature, University of Michigan, 1995.

74. Gwynn and Tuckwell, *Life of Dilke*, 1:6, 7, 9; Garrett, *Charles Wentworth Dilke*, 12; Jenkins, *Dilke*, 13–14, 15; Nicholls, *Lost Prime Minister*, 4–5. Wentworth was made a baronet in 1862 after earlier declining a knighthood; he was also Liberal M.P. for Wallingford for three years; Marchand, *Athenaeum*, 83n.

75. Macdonald claims few "educated young men" studied in Government Schools of Art (*Art Education*, 173); see also EFSD, "Art-Teaching and Technical Schools."

76. See Gillett, *Worlds of Art*; Yeldham, *Women Artists*; Macdonald, *Art Education*; Nunn, *Victorian Women Artists*, and Nunn, ed., *Canvassing: Recollections by Six Victorian Women Artists* (London: Camden Press, 1986); Jan Marsh, "Art, Ambition, and Sisterhood in the 1850s," and Sara M. Dodd, "Art Education for Women in the 1860s: a Decade of Debate," both in *Women in the Victorian Art World*, ed. Clarissa Campbell Orr (Manchester: Manchester University Press, 1995); Marsh and Nunn, *Women Artists*; Whitney Chadwick, *Women, Art, and Society* (London: Thames and Hudson, 1988); Claire Richter Sherman with Adele Holcomb, "Precursors and Pioneers (1820–1890)," in *Women as Interpreters of the Visual Arts*, ed. Sherman, (Westport, Conn.: Greenwood, 1981); 3–26; and Anthea Callen, *Angel in the Studio: Women in the Arts and Crafts Movement* (London: Astragal Books, 1979). For broader feminist conceptualizations of art history, see Roszika Parker and Griselda Pollock, *Old Mistresses: Women, Art, and Ideology* (New York: Pantheon, 1981), esp. chs. 2 and 3; Pollock, *Vision and Difference*, ch. 1; Lisa Ticknor, "Feminism, Art History, and Sexual Difference," *Genders* 3 (1988): 92–128; Germaine Greer, *The Obstacle Race* (New York: Farrar, Straus and Giroux, 1979); Linda Nochlin, *Women, Art, and Power, and Other Essays* (New York: Harper and Row, 1988). On the Slade, see Macdonald, *Art Education*, ch. 15; Gillett, *Worlds of Art*, 180–81; Nunn, *Victorian Women Artists*, 50–51; Michael Holroyd, *Augustus John: A Biography*, rev. ed. (Harmondsworth: Penguin, 1976), ch. 2; and Teresa Grimes, "Carrington," in Grimes, Judith Collins, and Oriana Baddeley, *Five Women Painters* (London: Lennard, 1989), 86–87; on later Victorian images of women artists, see Casteras, *Substance*, 41–42.

77. Cherry, *Painting Women*, esp. 55–57 and ch. 6, and Cherry, "Women Artists and the Politics of Feminism," in *Women in the Victorian Art World*, ed. Clarissa Campbell Orr (Manchester: Manchester University Press, 1995).

78. See Yeldham, *Women Artists*, 1:163–66, 169–73; Gillett, *Worlds of Art*, 137.

79. Taylor qtd. in Gillett, *Worlds of Art*, 139–40; Fox's daughter Eliza went on to an active

career as a painter, encouraged by her father, who allowed her to hold classes for drawing from the nude in his library; Grote qtd. in Gillett, *Worlds of Art*, 134; see also Yeldham, *Women Artists*, 1:12.

80. Ruskin, *Sesame and Lilies*, section 68; see also Casteras, *Images*, ch. 4.

81. Gillett, *Worlds of Art*, 135; cf. M. Jeanne Peterson, *Family, Love, and Work in the Lives of Victorian Gentlewomen* (Bloomington: Indiana University Press, 1989), 150–53.

82. Gillett, *Worlds of Art*, 156–57.

83. Earle, *Letters*, 89–93, and Memoirs , 203, 223–24, 235–39, 242–43, 249; on networks of female artists and "matronage," see Cherry, *Painting Women*, 102–4.

84. Frances Rosser Hullah, *Life of John Hullah, LLD.*, 2 vols. (London: Longmans, Green, 1886), 116–22. Hullah's biography of her husband, like many biographies by widows, includes fragments of autobiography; see Marilyn Yalom, "Biography as Autobiography: Adele Hugo, Witness of Her Husband's Life," in Bell and Yalom, eds., *Revealing Lives*, 53–64, and Bonnie Smith, "Historiography, Objectivity, and the Case of the Abusive Widow," in *Feminists Revision History*, ed. Anne-Louise Shapiro (New Brunswick: Rutgers University Press, 1994), 24–46. For Rosser, see also Yeldham, *Women Artists*, 1: 22; Rosser does not appear in Yeldham's list of women RA students (1:125), but a Frances Rossiter does, perhaps a misprint.

85. CWD, "Mem.,"4, 8. CWD adds that the women were such "intimate and mutually self-respecting friends that they afterwards voluntarily studied together upon the Continent"; if this trip occurred before EFS's marriage, it suggests a high degree of independence granted by their families. See also Cherry, *Painting Women*, 50.

86. Earle, *Letters*, 89–93.

87. F. Hullah, *John Hullah*, 123; John Hullah (1812–1884) was a Victorian music writer, teacher, and founder of singing schools, which he theorized as a mode of popular improvement and the instilling of social harmony. Frances Hullah contributed to *The Academy*, canvassed for Elizabeth Garrett Anderson's campaign for the London School Board in 1870, and was on the committee of the Central National Society for Women's Suffrage; *Women's Gazette and Weekly News*, 2 March 1889. Her texts are also very proud of her stepdaughter's artistic success. Theresa Villiers married Charles Earle, an Indian army officer, and wrote on gardening, vegetarianism, and "advice to the young"; she was the aunt of Constance Lytton. Her texts are ambivalent but impressed by the independence of younger women; see her Memoirs, 223–24.

88. Yeldham, *Women Artists*, 1:15; see also Macdonald, *Art Education*, 143, 146–48.

89. Qtd. in Yeldham, *Women Artists*, 1:12.

90. But see also Gillett, *Worlds of Art*, 168; Nunn, *Victorian Women Artists*, 174–86; Yeldham, *Women Artists*, 1: 284–91; and Angela V. John and Revel Guest, *Lady Charlotte: A Biography of the Nineteenth Century* (London: Weidenfeld and Nicholson, 1989).

91. Qtd. in Yeldham, *Women Artists*, 1:23; see also George Landow, *Victorian Types, Victorian Shadows: Biblical Typology in Victorian Literature, Art, and Thought* (London: Routledge Kegan Paul, 1980), esp. ch. 4.

92. Qtd. in Yeldham, *Women Artists*, 17.

93. Macdonald, *Art Education*, 147, qtg. Thackeray, *Heads of the People*, "The Artists" (1878).

94. Granville qtd. by Macdonald, *Art Education*, 147; see also 146–48; Callen, *Angel in the Studio*, 30; but cf. Yeldham, *Women Artists*, 1:14.

95. Macdonald, *Art Education*, 143, 146–48; see also Borzello, *Civilising Caliban*, 140, and ch. 2 passim. In 1847, the medal competitions were divided into sex-segregated categories to save male students the embarrassment of their frequent losses to women; Callen, *Angel in the Studio*, 28–29.

96. Nunn, *Victorian Women Artists*, 5.

97. Gillett, *Worlds of Art*, 142, qtg. Maurice, *Lectures to Ladies on Practical Subjects* (1857); see also Anna Jameson, qtd. in Denvir, *Early Nineteenth Century*, 98–101.

98. Callen, *Angel in the Studio*, 30; Gillett, *Worlds of Art*, 141.

99. Macdonald, *Art Education*, 158; Yeldham, *Women Artists*, 1:15; Gillett, *Worlds of Art*, 141–42. The School raised sufficient private funds to be reestablished in Bloomsbury; in 1862 the Queen patronized it and it was renamed the Royal Female School of Art ; Gillett, *Worlds of Art*, 263. Independence did not alter its emphasis on training designers, teachers, and commercial art workers; see Yeldham, *Women Artists*, 1:13–16, 19; Macdonald, *Art Education*, 135; and Nunn, *Victorian Women Artists*, 44–45.

100. *Art Journal* (1860), qtd. in Yeldham, *Women Artists*, 1:16.

101. Yeldham, *Women Artists*, 1:11, 19–27. The RA was opened by a well-coordinated campaign by women artists, but through the 1870s it remained difficult and in some years impossible for women to gain entry; Nunn, *Victorian Women Artists*, 46–47, 50–52; Gillett, *Worlds of Art*, 158–59, 179; Sidney C. Hutchinson, *The History of the Royal Academy 1768–1986*, second ed. (London: Robert Royce, 1986), chs. 10–12; Macdonald, *Art Education*, 175–76, and Cherry, *Painting Women*, 55–57.

102. Macdonald, *Art Education*, 172, 151, 159, 169, 201; Nunn, *Victorian Women Artists*, 48–50; Yeldham, *Women Artists*, 1:16; Pevsner, *Academies of Art*, 255.

103. Poynter qtd. by Nunn, *Victorian Women Artists*, 50, 52.

104. Other Government Schools of Design could also have offered such educations; see Hardman, *Six Victorian Thinkers*, 59.

105. CWD, "Mem.," 4. The other schools ranged in quality but had in common steep fees; EFS pursued her studies with a "slender purse"; CWD "Mem.," 8; see also Yeldham, *Women Artists*, 1:20–27; Cherry, *Painting Women*, 53–54, 58–62. By the 1870s, Ruskin turned against the South Kensington schools; see Kristine Otto Garrigen, " 'The splendidest May number of the *Graphic*': John Ruskin and the Royal Academy Exhibition of 1875," *Victorian Periodicals Review* 24 (1991): 22–33, 25; see also Robert Hewison, "Afterword: Ruskin and the Institutions" in Hewison, ed., *New Approaches to Ruskin: Thirteen Essays* (London: Routledge and Kegan Paul, 1981), 214–229.

106. Gilbert R. Redgrave, "The Lady Dilke Gift to the National Art Library," *The Library*, 2nd series, 7 (1906), 274; see also CWD, "Mem.," 7, and Ms. Don. e. 64, fol. 81 (CWD to F. G. Stephens, 30 Jan. 1905).

107. CWD, "Mem.," 6.

108. EFSD, "Art Teaching and Technical Schools," 236, 231, 233.

109. EFSD, "Art Teaching and Technical Schools," 232, 237, 241.

110. Chris Waters, *British Socialists and the Politics of Popular Culture*, 1884–1914 (Manchester: Manchester University Press, 1990).

111. Earle, *Letters*, 89; CWD, "Mem.," 4.

112. Qtd. in CWD, "Mem.," 8, 4.

113. CWD, "Mem.," 19, 8.

114. See Mss. Eng. lett. e. 93, fol. 89 (CWD to James Thursfield, 8 Jan. 1905) and fol. 91 (CWD to Thursfield, 10 Jan. 1905). AM 43918, fol. 50 (incomplete, official of South Kensington Board of Education to CWD, 30 Dec. 1904), claims records show that in 1859, "Miss E. Frances Strong passed and obtained a Good in Freehand and Object Drawing (two subjects)." CWD had EFS's winning drawings and claimed the official records did not show all the prizes she won or her full term of attendance. See also Macdonald, *Art Education*, ch. 11 and Appendix C.

115. CWD, "Mem.," 8, 9. On Mulready, see Jeremy Maas, *The Victorian Art World in Photographs* (New York: Universe Books, 1984), 84; Kathryn Moore Heleniak, *William Mulready* (New Haven: Yale University Press, 1980); Marcia Pointon, *Mulready* [from the 1986 exhibition "William Mulready: 1786–1863"] (London: Victoria & Albert Museum, 1986).

116. CWD, "Mem.," 23, citing EFSD, "Mulready"; see also PP 55, fol. 271f. (Pauline Trevelyan to EFSP, n.d. [1862]).

117. Gillett, *Worlds of Art*, 25–26; Heleniak, *Mulready*, 163–64; Eastlake, qtd. in Robertson, *Eastlake*, 118; Samuel Carter Hall, *Retrospect of a Long Life from 1815–1883* [1883], qtd. in Maas, *Victorian Art World*, 69–70. On women students and private lessons, see Cherry, *Painting Women*, 62.

118. EFSD, "Mulready," 346–47; CWD, "Mem.," 4, 8; see also Macdonald, *Art Education*, 29, 82, 98, and 174. Gillett, *Worlds of Art*, 181, notes that authorities in the Government Schools were inconsistent in allowing access to life-drawing.

119. Yeldham, *Women Artists*, 27, 29; Nunn, *Victorian Women Artists*, 52, 128; Macdonald, *Art Education*, 174–75; Gillett, *Worlds of Art*, 155–57; see also Hutchinson, *Royal Academy*, 118, 138, and Dodd, "Art Education for Women," 189.

120. Gillett, *Worlds of Art*, 176–77, 178, 268 n. 55, (qtg. Jackson, ed., *Professions and Professionalization*, 1970); see also Casteras, *Substance*, 45–46.

121. Hutchison, *Royal Academy*, 95–96, 103; Macdonald, *Art Education*, 29; Cherry, *Painting Women*, 55.

122. Mulock, *A Woman's Thoughts about Women* (1858), qtd. in Gillett, *Worlds of Art*, 152; Mulock's *Olive* (1850) is about a woman artist.

123. *Athenaeum*, 30 April 1859: 581; see also Cherry, *Painting Women*, 55–57.

124. Gillett, *Worlds of Art*, 178, 181; Hutchinson, *Royal Academy*, 118, 138.

125. EFSD, *French Painters*, 3–5, 15; cf. Adelaide Labille-Guiard, "Self-Portrait with Two Pupils" (1785), Metropolitan Museum of Art, New York City, #53.225.5.

126. EFSD, "Art Teaching and Technical Schools," 232.

127. CWD, "Mem.," 8, 88.

128. Gillett, *Worlds of Art*, 183; Robertson, *Eastlake*, 378; see also Heleniak, *Mulready*, ch. 5, esp. 153; and Frederic G. Stephens, *Memorials of William Mulready* (London: Sampson Low, Marston, Searle, and Rivington, 1890), 101.

129. CWD, "Mem.," 32, see also 88, and EFSD, "Mulready," 347; see also Ms. Don. e. 64, fol. 91 (CWD [dictated] to F.G. Stephens, 13 March 1905).

130. Elizabeth Varley Mulready exhibited 13 landscapes at the RA between 1811 and 1819; she was the noted but shadowy genre painter, "A. E. Mulready"; see Pointon, *Mulready*, 64, 96.

131. Pointon, *Mulready*, 64–68; cf. Maas, *Victorian Art World*, 183.

132. Maas, *Victorian Art World*, 183–84 (which doubts the tale about the model); Gillett, *Worlds of Art*, 268 n. 72, and 183; Heleniak, *Mulready*, 163–64; Pointon, *Mulready*, 69, 90.

133. EFSD, "Mulready," 346; EFSD, "Seamy Side," 422.

134. Trevelyan Papers, WCT 191 (EFSP to Pauline Trevelyan, 21 Jan. [1863?], and 30 July 1863); EFSP had gotten the news from "a sister artist a sculptor."

135. EFSD, "Mulready," 346, 349.

136. EFSD, "Mulready," 347, 351.

137. EFSD, "Mulready," 351.

138. F. Hullah qtd. in CWD, "Mem.," 4; see also AM 43903, fol. 1.

139. Lee, *Woolf*, 86.

140. Hullah qtd. in CWD, "Mem.," 4, and AM 43903, fol. 1; Lee, *Woolf*, 86; for "atmosphere of Italy," see Earle, *Memoirs*, 242; for "Signor," see also Watts's letters in AM 43908, fol. 6ff; Ellen Terry, *The Story of My Life* (New York: Schocken, 1982), 36; Ronald Chapman, *The Laurel and the Thorn: A Study of G. F. Watts* (London: Faber and Faber, 1945), chs. 4–6; and Macleod, *Art and the Victorian Middle Class*, 300–301.

141. Hullah qtd. in CWD, "Mem.," 4.

142. AM 43907, fol. 61 (M. E. Lewes [George Eliot] to EFSP, 17 Nov. 1873); fol. 63 (3 July 1874); fol. 64 (1 Dec. 1874)

143. Terry, *Story of My Life*, 33; Auerbach, *Ellen Terry*, ch. 2, esp. 84–87; Robert Bernard Martin, *Tennyson: The Unquiet Heart, a Biography* (Oxford: Oxford University Press, 1980), 407–9.

144. Julia Margaret Cameron, *Victorian Photographs of Famous Men and Fair Women*, ed. Roger Fry and Virginia Woolf, rev. ed., ed. Tristram Powell (1926; London: Chatto and Windus, 1992).

145. EFSD, *French Engravers*, 63; the engraving is by Jean-Georges Wille; for circulating female figures, see Marina Warner, *Monuments and Maidens: The Allegory of the Female Form* (New York: Athenaeum, 1985); see also Macleod, *Art and the Victorian Middle Class*, 186–90.

146. Alfred Tennyson, *Poetical Works of Tennyson* (London: Macmillan, 1899), 395–448.

147. CWD, "Mem.," 4–5, 19, 25. An element of tact may have been involved; Tennyson was a houseguest and came into the studio while EFS was there; see also AM 43907, fol. 2 (Leopold, Duke of Albany to EFSP, 21 Feb. 1872).

148. Alan Sinfield, *Alfred Tennyson* (Oxford: Blackwell, 1986), 164.

149. Debra Mancoff, *The Arthurian Revival in Victorian Art* (New York: Garland, 1990), 165, and " 'An Ancient Idea of Chivalric Greatness': The Arthurian Revival and Victorian History Painting," in Mary Flowers Braswell and John Bugge, eds., *The Arthurian Tradition: Essays in Convergence* (Tuscaloosa: University of Alabama Press, 1988); Pearce, *Woman/Image/Text*, ch. 7.

150. Mancoff, *Arthurian Revival*, 166, 232, and plates 52–54, 199, 242, 257–58, 174.

151. Christopher Ricks, headnote to "The Lady of Shalott" in Ricks, ed., *Tennyson: A Selected Edition Incorporating the Trinity College Manuscripts* (Berkeley: University of California Press, 1989), 18. Ricks confirms the relation between the "Lily Maid of Astolat" and the Lady of Shalott and quotes an ambiguous Tennyson: "The Lady of Shalott is evidently the Elaine of the *Morte d'Arthur* but I do not think that I had ever heard of the latter when I wrote the former." I am more concerned with iconographic similarities than textual sources; see, e.g., Mancoff, *Arthurian Revival*, pl. 54 and pl. 83. See also Brown University Department of Art, *Ladies of Shalott: A Victorian Masterpiece and Its Contexts* [exhibition catalogue] (Providence: Department of Art, Brown University, 1985); Karen Hodder, "The Lady of Shalott in Art and Literature," in Susan Mendus and Jane Rendall, eds., *Sexuality and Subordination: Interdisciplinary Studies of Gender in the Nineteenth Century* (Routledge, 1989), 60–88; and Pearce, *Woman/Image/Text*, ch. 4. These images also overlap with some Victorian Ophelias.

152. R. B. Martin, *Tennyson*, 414.

153. See Psomiades, "Beauty's Body," 33–35, esp. 34; Mancoff, *Arthurian Revival*, 166, 174–75, 232–33; see also Walkowitz, *City of Dreadful Delight*, 89.

154. Rosemary Mitchell, "A Stitch in Time? Women, Needlework, and the Making of History in Victorian Britain," *Journal of Victorian Culture* 1 (1996): 187; Cherry, *Painting Women*, 189–91; cf. Psomiades, "Beauty's Body," 34.

155. Dorothy Mermin, "The Damsel, the Knight, and the Victorian Woman Poet," in *Victorian Women Poets: A Critical Reader*, ed. Angela Leighton (Oxford: Blackwell, 1996), 201; Cherry, *Painting Women*, 190, 191; see also 80–81, on Emily Mary Osborn's *Nameless and Friendless*; cf. Loeb, *Consuming Angels*.

156. A. G. Temple qtd. in Macleod, *Art and the Victorian Middle Class*, 290.

157. Mavor, *Pleasures Taken*, 43–69; see also Cherry, *Painting Women*, 197–99; C. Rossetti, "In an Artist's Studio" and May Probyn, "A Model," both in Leighton and Reynolds, *Victorian Women Poets*.

158. EFSD, *French Engravers* 3, Plate 19 (facing 88), 2, 8–10, 15, 25, 37, 90, 95, 100, 151, 159, 167; EFSD, *French Painters*, 5, 11.

159. EFSD, *French Painters*, 14, 15.

160. GMT, "Rem.," A140.

161. EFSD, "The Secret," in *Shrine of Death*, 113, 114, 117, 118, 119, 120. See also EFSP, *Renaissance*, 2: 134–35 and ch. 5 below.

162. See also EFSD, "The Mirror of the Soul", in *BSL*, 237–60, esp. 254, 259–60.

163. Tennyson, "Lancelot and Elaine," *Poetical Works*, 399.

164. CWD, "Mem.," 5–6.

165. AM 43908, fol. 110 (John Ruskin to EFSD, 28 Jan. 1886).

166. Ruskin to Pauline Trevelyan, 28 August 1861, qtd. in R. Trevelyan, *Pre-Raphaelite Circle*, 174–75; Surtees, ed., *Reflections*, 123; ch. 3 below. See also Macleod, *Art and the Victorian Middle Class*, 169–70; Cherry, *Painting Women*, 99–100, 187–88; and Virginia Surtees, ed., *Sublime and Instructive: Letters from John Ruskin to Lousa, Marchioness of Waterford, Anna Blunden, and Ellen Heaton* (London: Michael Joseph, 1972).

167. Qtd. in CWD, "Mem.," 6.

168. CWD, "Mem.," 12, 9.

169. CWD, "Mem.," 12–13; emphasis mine.

170. CWD, "Mem.," 9 (CWD hastens to add that she later changed her mind about Russia); R. Trevelyan, *Pre-Raphaelite Circle*, 20, 27, 34; Macleod, *Art and the Victorian Middle Class*, 155; Cordrey, *Bygone Days*, 36.

171. CWD, "Mem.," 9; EFS did not attend the Brompton Oratory, built 1878–84, but may have attended the Catholic chapel served by the Institute of the Oratory since 1847 or a High Anglican church in the neighborhood; see also Earle, *Memoirs*, 242.

172. CWD, "Mem.," 10–12; for the discourses CWD was rejecting, see Elaine Showalter, *The Female Malady: Women, Madness, and English Culture* (New York: Pantheon, 1985).

173. AM 43932, fol. 137f.

174. CWD, "Mem.," 8, 11–12; she got off scot-free.

175. CWD, "Mem.," 10, 12, and 16–17; CWD claims his argument is also proven by comparing "the Prelude and several passages in the first book of 'Middlemarch' with passages still existing in the diaries and manuscripts of Miss Strong, penned before 1862"; he did not deposit these papers in an archive.

176. EFSP, *Renaissance*, 1:236; EFSD, "Of Love and Sorrow," in BSL, 165–66; ch. 5 below.

177. PP 140, fol. 10–11 (EFS to Rosa Tuckwell, n.d. [1861]); cf. Thomas Hardy, *Jude the Obscure* (1895; New York: Signet, 1961), 139.

178. Qtd. in CWD, "Mem.," 85; cf. EFSP, "Nicolas Poussin," 472.

179. AM 43907, fol. 143 (Frederic Leighton to EFSP, n.d. [1885]) and fol. 144 (Leighton to EFSP, 3 Feb. 1885).

180. Gwynn and Tuckwell, *Life of Dilke*, 1:146. AM 43902, fol. 213, gives a family tree; Katherine Mary Eliza Sheil was the daughter of Arthur Gore Sheil and Katherine Wise, "of the old Archbishop Wise Devonshire family"; Katie's mother left her about a thousand pounds a year; see also fol. 143 and Jenkins, *Dilke*, 77. She was a year older than CWD.

181. AM 43931, fols. 201–8; Jenkins, *Dilke*, 77–79. Pictures of Katie are in Gwynn and Tuckwell, *Life of Dilke*, facing 2:146; Nicholls, *Lost Prime Minister*, pl. 10; and AM 43902, fol. 156–57.

182. Jenkins, *Dilke*, 68–77, qtg. AM 43931; Gwynn and Tuckwell, *Life of Dilke*, 2:138–47; Virginia Cowles, *Edward VII and His Circle* (London: Hamish Hamilton, 1956), 99–106, 165–66; Nicholls, *Lost Prime Minister*, ch. 4.

183. CWD qtd. in Gwynn and Tuckwell, *Life of Dilke*, 2:147; see also AM 43932, fol. 35; CWD to Kate Field, qtd. in Nicholls, *Lost Prime Minister*, 59; marriage certificate in REND 10/14; see also Jenkins, *Dilke*, 78.

184. AM 43902, fol. 153 (Katie Dilke to CWD, n.d. [1872, 73, or 74]).

185. Gwynn and Tuckwell, *Life of Dilke*, 1:160; Nicholls, *Lost Prime Minister*, 60; see AM 43902, fols. 163–87; Browning is at fols. 165, 169, 170, 171, 180f; he gave an early reading of "Red Cotton Night-Cap Country" at one of Katie's soirees (see also Robert Secor, "Robert Browning and the Hunts of South Kensington," *Browning Institute Studies* 7 [1979], 115, 132); Mrs. Eustace Smith is at fol. 174 and 175f. The Dilkes frequently entertained groups of 8 to 10; guests ranged from Octavia Hill to Giuseppe Garibaldi; see Jenkins, *Dilke*, 82; Jalland, *Women, Marriage and Politics*, 194, 206; and AM 43932, fol. 18.

186. Gwynn and Tuckwell, *Life of Dilke*, 1:161, 163, 175–77; Jenkins, *Dilke*, 83–86; CWD, *The Fall of Prince Florestan of Monaco, by Himself* (London: Macmillan, 1874). Florestan is a Cambridge undergraduate who inherits the feudal principality of Monaco, whose chief, indeed only, source of revenue is its casino. After attempting secularizing and modernizing reforms, he concludes, "No system of government can be permanent which has for its opponents all the women, and for supporters only half the men; and any party will have for opponents all the women which . . . raises the flag of materialism. Women are not likely to abandon the idea of a compensation in the next world for the usage which too many of them meet with in this" (79).

187. AM 43902, fol. 52 (ts. copy, Ashton Dilke to CWD, 3 July 1872).

188. On CWD at university, see Nicholls, *Lost Prime Minister*, 8–10; Jenkins, *Dilke*, 21–31; Gwynn and Tuckwell, *Life of Dilke*, 1: 24–49; for his travels, see CWD, *Greater Britain*.

189. Jenkins, *Dilke*, 83; AM 43932, fol. 33; Gwynn and Tuckwell, *Life of Dilke*, 1: 180–81; AM 43932, fol. 78–79. On Katie's death, see also AM 43902, fols. 206, 209; Jalland, *Women, Marriage and Politics*, 171; and AM 43932, fol. 85. Katie's son, the fifth CWD, was known as Wentie. A shadowy figure in Dilke texts, he appears only once or twice in EFSP/D's texts and is unimportant to GMT's. Askwith says he was epileptic and "subnormal"; he spent time in a mental home in later life. CWD arranged for care but seems to have offered little attention; Wentie stayed with the Chamberlains in Highbury a great deal as a small child; attended school in Oxford and was sent to Rugby briefly after EFSP and CWD married, then to Germany; started at Trinity Hall, Cambridge, but left without a degree. He traveled and twice became involved with young women with whom marriage was blocked (in the first case, perhaps because "Miss Cohen" was Jewish). He married Florence Pearl Faithfull of New South Wales in 1915, and died aged 44, without children. See Askwith, *Lady Dilke*, 180–81; Jenkins, *Dilke*, 91, 135, 266, and Nicholls, *Lost Prime Minister*, 69, 297, 311

190. See AM 43902, fol. 210f., for letters of condolence. See also Gwynn and Tuckwell, *Life of Dilke*, 1: 181–83; Jenkins, *Dilke*, 89–91; AM 43932, fols. 84, 93; and Janet Oppenheim, *Shattered Nerves: Doctors, Patients, and Depression in Victorian England* (New York: Oxford University Press, 1991), 169.

CHAPTER THREE

1. CWD, "Mem.," 8; the engagement occurred c. 25 June 1861; PP 54, fols. 363f. and 365f. (Mary Roberts to MP). MP's account-book for 1861 shows "a ring for F." on June 27 (PP 42, 27 June 1861); his diary leaves off in November 1860 and resumes on the same page in Sept. 1862; PP 130, fol. 33. See also V. H. H. Green, *Oxford Common Room: A Study of Lincoln College and Mark Pattison* (London: Edward Arnold, 1957), 199–202.

2. Green, *Oxford Common Room*, 214; see also Green, *Love in a Cool Climate: The Letters of Mark Pattison and Meta Bradley, 1879–1884* (Oxford: Clarendon Press, 1985), 166, and Broughton, *Belinda*, 194.

3. E.g., Friedrich Max Muller to Jacob Bernays, 14 Dec. 1863, in *The Life and Letters of the Right Honourable Friedrich Max Muller*, ed. Georgina Max Muller, 2 vols. (London: Longmans, Green, 1902), 1: 272–73; see also MP, *Milton* (1879; London: Macmillan, 1909), 52–55.

4. Marcia Pointon, "Histories of Matrimony: J. E. Millais," in Pointon, ed., *Pre-Raphaelites Reviewed* (Manchester: Manchester University Press, 1989), 101–2.

5. Kingsbury Badger, "Mark Pattison and the Victorian Scholar," *Modern Language Quarterly* 6 (1945): 423–25.

6. Green, *Oxford Common Room*, 216; Green, *Love*, 167; PP 134, fol. 32 (MP diary, 30 Apr. 1883).

7. MP, *Mem.*; see also Askwith, *Lady Dilke*, 10.

8. Green, *Love*, 14–15; Green does consider the possibility of homoerotic attachments and

does not naturalize heterosexuality. On the regulation of Oxford marriages: until 1884, ordinary fellows of Colleges were unable to marry without forfeiting their fellowships; only heads of house could wed; see Linda Dowling, *Hellenism and Homoeroticism in Victorian Oxford* (Ithaca: Cornell University Press, 1994), 85; but at least two exceptions were made, in 1871, for Mandell Creighton of Merton and T. H. Green of Balliol (Beth Sutton-Ramspeck to VICTORIA Listserv, 21 July 1996). Glucker ("Case for Causaubon," 9) surmises that the blockage of MP's marriage until he became Rector accounts for the phrasing of Casaubon's letter to Dorothea Brooke in *Middlemarch*, as a remnant of MP's phrasing survives into Eliot's adaptation of a real letter, but the novel specifies that Dorothea and her sister are relative newcomers (2) and Casaubon is introduced to the sisters at the novel's beginning (4).

9. Askwith, *Lady Dilke*, 5, and ch. 2 passim.

10. PP 54, fol. 425ff (Frederick Shaw to MP, 14 Sept. 1861); see also fol. 437ff (Fox to MP, 20 Sept. 1861).

11. John Sparrow, *Mark Pattison and the Idea of a University* (Clark Lectures, Trinity College, Cambridge, 1965; Cambridge: Cambridge University Press, 1967), esp. 33–42; Green, *Oxford Common Room*; Green, *The Commonwealth of Lincoln College, 1427–1977* (Oxford: Oxford University Press, 1979); esp. 447–68; and Green, *Love*, esp. 9–15; Jo Manton, *Sister Dora: The Life of Dorothy Pattison* (London: Methuen, 1971). For MP's professional story, see also C. P. Snow, *The Masters* (London: Macmillan, 1951) and Ronald Knox, *Let Dons Delight, Being Variations on a Theme in an Oxford Common Room* (New York: Sheed and Ward, 1939), ch. 7 and notes.

12. These writers about the Pattisons and the Casaubons reforge links between MP and Eliot's failed scholar even as they dispute them; see, e.g., John Sparrow, letters to the editor on Richard Ellman,"Dorothea's Husbands," *Times Literary Supplement,* 16 March 1973; 4 May 1973, and 15 June 1973 [Ellman's essay in Ellmann, *Golden Codgers: Biographical Speculations* (Oxford: Oxford University Press, 1973)]; "An Oxford Caricature and Provocation," *Encounter* 33 (July 1972): 92–96; and replies to Gordon Haight's review of Sparrow, *Mark Pattison and the Idea of a University*, *Notes and Queries* 214 (November and December 1969). See also Manton, *Sister Dora*, 353–58, and Trev Lynn Broughton, "Impotence, Biography, and the Froude-Carlyle Controversy: 'Revelations on Ticklish Topics,' " *Journal of the History of Sexuality* 7 (1997): 502–36. MP's major works include *Isaac Casaubon, 1559–1614* (London: Longmans, Green, 1875); his study of Joseph Scaliger was unfinished.

13. The Bronte and Barrett stories are invariably cited in histories of the Pattisons; see, e.g., Green, *Commonwealth*, 424; Manton, *Sister Dora*, 28.

14. See EFSP, "Preface," to MP, Mem., 1885 edition, vi: "the writer expressly forbade the alteration of a word . . . not a line, not a word has been changed or destroyed," but asterisks indicate "omission[s] from the present edition . . . likely to wound the feelings of the living." Frank Pattison was probably given substantial right to suppress passages; no original manuscript survives.

15. I use "Gothic" extremely loosely, but see Michele Masse, *In the Name of Love: Women, Masochism, and the Gothic* (Ithaca: Cornell University Press, 1992); Alison Milbank, *Daughters of the House: Modes of the Gothic in Victorian Fiction* (New York: St. Martin's, 1992); Judith Halberstam, *Skin Shows: Gothic Horror and the Technology of Monsters* (Durham: Duke University Press, 1995); and Judith Wilt, "Love/Slave," [review essay] *Victorian Studies* 37 (1994): 451–60, esp. 458–59 on represented narrative in Gothic. On stories of paternal tyranny, see Sadoff, *Monsters of Affection*, and Cora Kaplan, "Wicked Fathers: A Family Romance," in Kaplan, *Sea Changes: Culture and Feminism* (London: Verso, 1986)

16. Davidoff, "Where the Stranger Begins," 207, 210, 209, 217.

17. *Sister Dora* (1977; dir. Mark Miller); Dorothy Tutin had the title role; Martin Connors and Jim Craddock, eds., *VideoHound's Golden Movie Retriever 1998* (Detroit: Visible Ink, 1998); Hardy, *Jude the Obscure*, 35.

18. All general information about the Pattisons from Manton, *Sister Dora*, esp. ch. 1–4, and Green, *Oxford Common Room*, ch. 4, unless specifically noted.

19. Manton, *Sister Dora*, 28; Green, *Oxford Common Room*, 85.

20. MP, *Mem.*, 24.

21. Manton, *Sister Dora*, 30.

22. Green, *Commonwealth*, 423.

23. Manton, *Sister Dora*, 26–29; Green, *Oxford Common Room*, 86; see also PP 56, fol. 244 (Mary Roberts to MP, 25 Apr. 1866).

24. MP, "Mem.," 19, 24–25.

25. Qtd. in Manton, *Sister Dora*, 29.

26. MP, "Mem.," 8, but cf. 125; see also Duncan Nimmo, "Learning Against Religion, Learning as Religion: Mark Pattison and the 'Victorian Crisis of Faith,' " in *Religion and Humanism: Papers Read at the Eighteenth Summer Meeting and Nineteenth Winter Meeting of the Ecclesiastical History Society*, ed. Keith Robbins (Oxford: Blackwell/Ecclesiastical History Society, 1981), 313.

27. MP, "Mem.," 13–25; Manton, *Sister Dora*, 30; Green, *Oxford Common Room*, 88.

28. Manton, *Sister Dora*, 29–30.

29. Green, *Oxford Common Room*, 169–70; Green, *Love*, 12; Manton, *Sister Dora*, 41, 81.

30. Green, *Oxford Common Room*, 93; by Green's account, the family saw Mark James as "disturbed" at least a year earlier; Manton, *Sister Dora*, 30, and Sparrow, *Mark Pattison*, 34, place the breakdown in June 1834. Two aunts, Mary Meadows and Eleanor Seward, lived nearby.

31. Manton, *Sister Dora*, 30–31; Anne Digby, *Madness, Morality, and Medicine: A History of the York Retreat* (Cambridge: Cambridge University Press, 1985).

32. Manton, *Sister Dora*, 31; Sparrow, *Mark Pattison*, 34–35, gives "nauseous" rather than "noisome" and "Established Church" for "Church of England".

33. Manton, *Sister Dora*, 31.

34. Qtd. in Manton, *Sister Dora*, 31–32; see also Green, *Oxford Common Room*, 93, 107.

35. PP 59, fol. 62f. (Jane Winn Pattison to MP, n.d.); see also Manton, *Sister Dora*, 31; MP, *Mem.*, 138.

36. Manton, *Sister Dora*, 32.

37. PP 59, fol. 59f. (Jane Winn Pattison to MP, n.d.); see also Green, *Oxford Common Room*, 107–8; 192–93; Manton, *Sister Dora*, 38–44.

38. MP, "Mem.," 117, emphasis in original; MP is writing of Easter 1833; note absence of his mother.

39. MP's diary, 28 Apr. 1878, qtd. in Green, *Oxford Common Room*, 86.

40. Francis Charles Montague, "Some Early Letters of Mark Pattison," *John Rylands Library Bulletin* 18 (January 1934), 157; cf. Manton's *Sister Dora*, passim, and Green, *Oxford Common Room*, 104–5. Green, *Love*, also appreciates gender as a structure inhabited by men as well as women.

41. See also Manton, *Sister Dora*, 38–40.

42. Davidoff, "Where the Stranger Begins," 209, 210; see also Janet Oppenheim, "A Mother's Role, A Daughter's Duty," *Journal of British Studies* 34 (1995), 209–10, 214–16.

43. Montague, "Early Letters," 159; cf. MP, *Mem.*, 157; see also Manton, *Sister Dora*, 38.

44. For tensions in Evangelicalism, see Rendall, *Origins*, ch. 3; Manton, *Sister Dora*, 38–41.

45. MP, *Mem.*, 59.

46. MP, *Mem.*, 46–49; emphasis added.

47. On Oxford homoerotics, see Dowling, *Hellenism*; Richard Dellamora, *Masculine Desire: The Sexual Politics of Victorian Aestheticism* (Chapel Hill: University of North Carolina Press, 1990); James Eli Adams, *Dandies and Desert Saints: Styles of Victorian Masculinities*, 75–105 (Ithaca: Cornell University Press, 1995); and ch. 5 below.

48. MP, *Mem.*, 46, 48, 49; see also Green, *Oxford Common Room*, 91–92.

49. MP, *Mem.*, 49, 53, 56; see also 68–69, 125. The decorum in question was heavily

aristocratic in origin, despite the marginal status of many Fellows; distinctions were visible in details of dress, precedence, and nomenclature; see J. Hunt, *Wider Sea*, 77–78, 80–84.

50. For MP and the Oxford movement, see Green, *Oxford Common Room*, 94–119; Fergal Nolan, "A Study of Mark Pattison's Religious Experience 1813–50" (D.Phil. thesis, Oxford, 1978); Nimmo, "Learning Against Religion"; Michael Pasko, "Mark Pattison's Course through the Oxford Movement," Ph.D. Dissertation, University of Illinois—Champaign-Urbana, 1964; and J. D. Holmes, "Newman, Froude, and Pattison: Some Aspects of their Relations," *Journal of the History of Religion* 4 (1966–67): 28–38. On names for the movement, see Owen Chadwick, *The Spirit of the Oxford Movement: Tractarian Essays* (Cambridge: Cambridge University Press, 1990), 135: "Tractarianism" (after the *Tracts for the Times*, i.e., the pamphlets in which ideas were formulated and disseminated), "the Oxford Movement" (for the centrality of Oxford dons, especially Pusey and Newman); "Puseyism" (after Edward Bouvier Pusey), and later "ritualism," "the Catholic Revival," and "Anglo-Catholicism." See also David Newsome, *Godliness and Good Learning: Four Studies on a Victorian Ideal* (London: Murray, 1961).

51. Green, *Oxford Common Room*, 94–95. On the homoerotics of Tractarianism, see Dellamora, *Masculine Desire*; Dowling, *Hellenism*; David Hilliard, "UnEnglish and Unmanly: Anglo-Catholicism and Homosexuality," *Victorian Studies* 25 (1982): 181–210; Adams, *Dandies*, 75–105; Robert Bernard Martin, *Gerard Manley Hopkins: A Very Private Life* (New York: HarperCollins, 1991), chs. 2 and 3; and Elaine Showalter, *Sexual Anarchy: Gender and Culture at the Fin de Siècle* (New York: Viking, 1990), 149.

52. MP, Mem., 326.

53. MP, Mem., 172, 174, 179; see also Nimmo, "Learning Against Religion," 313–14.

54. MP, Mem., 174–79.

55. MP, Mem., 171, 182.

56. Adams, *Dandies*, 90–91.

57. On MP's religious progress, see Nimmo, "Learning Against Religion," 311–24, and "Towards and Away from Newman's Theory of Doctrinal Development: Pointers from Mark Pattison in 1838 and 1846," *Journal of Theological Studies* 29 (1978): 160–62; Holmes, "Newman, Froude, and Pattison"; C. S. Emden, "Mark Pattison and J. A. Froude," *Oriel Papers* (1948): 176–87; and Chadwick, *Spirit*, 139, 141, 151.

58. MP, Mem., 172, 174, 171, 188–89, 208, 209.

59. Manton, *Sister Dora*, ch. 3, esp. 48–55; Green, *Oxford Common Room*, 105–8.

60. Green, *Commonwealth*, 424, fn.1.

61. Green, *Commonwealth*, 425.

62. Manton, *Sister Dora*, 56.

63. Qtd. in Manton, *Sister Dora*, 76.

64. Manton, *Sister Dora*, 58–59; see also Green, *Oxford Common Room*, 107–8.

65. Manton, *Sister Dora*, 58.

66. Manton, *Sister Dora*, 58; Green, *Oxford Common Room*, 104.

67. Qtd. in Manton, *Sister Dora*, 50. Strong-minded and outspokenly disapproving of her aunt's submission, Philippa had the advantage of being fatherless and she dominated her mother. Her logical mind and classical scholarship led her to Roman Catholicism. MP had been fond of her but after her conversion his diary expresses contempt and hatred for her Catholicism. Philippa wandered, living for a time in Paris; see Green, *Oxford Common Room*, 105, 114.

68. Manton, *Sister Dora*, 75; but see also 77.

69. MP, Mem., 182.

70. MP, Mem., 172, 174.

71. Manton, *Sister Dora*, 123–26; Green, *Oxford Common Room*, 192–93. MP and Eleanor seem to have refused to enter Hauxwell, and MP's refusal to attend the funeral brought criticism from Dora; MP immediately stopped writing her (Manton, *Sister Dora*, 125–26).

72. MP, Mem., 60, 55.

73. See Davidoff, "Where the Stranger Begins," 208.

74. See Manton, *Sister Dora*, passim, for Dora's career, esp. 37, 42–43, and 95 on nursing's appeal, and 131–32 for a suggestion that MP's support of Dora's departure was influenced by EFSP. See also Vicinus, *Independent Women*, chs. 2 and 3.

75. Qtd. in Green, *Oxford Common Room*, 303; see Manton, *Sister Dora*, chs. 18 and 19, for Dora's last years and death.

76. MP, *Memoirs*, 61 (directly following MP on Mark James as untruthful and self-inventing); see also 3; Margaret Lonsdale, *Sister Dora: A Biography* (London: C. Kegan Paul, 1880); see also Gertrude Leslie Mumford, "Sister Dora," in *Heroines of Modern Religion*, ed. Warren Dunham Foster (Freeport, NY: Books for Libraries Press, 1970) for Dora as saint.

77. W. Tuckwell, qtg. the "intimate friend" (perhaps T. F. Althaus), "Add. Quaed." to Tuckwell, *Reminiscences of Oxford*, *Oxford Magazine*, 21 June 1905, 411–13.

78. E.g., PP 54, fol. 477ff. (Rachel Stirke to MP, 21 Oct. 1861); see also Green, *Oxford Common Room*, 304, and Manton, *Sister Dora*, 68.

79. PP 137, fol. 1 (MP Diary, 29 Aug. 1856). See also Manton, *Sister Dora*, 127–28, and Davidoff, "Where the Stranger Begins," 215.

80. Manton, *Sister Dora*, 140–42. The letters on Fanny's breakdown are in PP 55*, a "secret" file removed from the larger Pattison collection by family pressure in 1917 and withheld from the public until c.1950. See BLR, d. 570 and ch. 4 below. See also PP 130, fol. 35f. (MP diary, 10 Oct. 1862 and following). Fanny was treated at Hammersmith by the renowned Dr. Forbes Winslow. Regarding her illness, I am reluctant to accept the judgment of her very judgmental family; "decoding" her transmitted story in cliched terms, as an hysterical manifestation of repressed eros by a parson's spinster daughter, would recapitulate her family's treatment. She may have been telling the truth or been engaging in conscious or unconscious displacement.

81. PP 130, fol. 4 (MP diary, [28 Dec. 1859]); PP 130, fol. 6v (MP diary, 4 [Jan.] 1860) and fol. 22 (11 June 1860), on Fanny's illnesses and their father's refusal to pay for any treatment; see also fol. 13v. and 14 (26 Jan. 1860).

82. For Fanny, see Manton, *Sister Dora*, 153, 213; Sarah also became an Associate Sister in the Christ Church Order in 1868; Manton, *Sister Dora*, 175. For MP's attempts to persuade Fanny, see PP 130, fol. 90 (MP diary, 9 Nov. 1874), fols. 93 [30 Nov. 1874] and 97 [31 Dec. 1874]; and Manton, *Sister Dora*, 280. For MP on Rachel's death, see PP 130, fol. 90 (MP diary, 9 Nov. 1874), fol. 90v. (12 Nov. 1874) and fol. 91 (13 Nov. 1874).

83. Mary married Canon R. E. Roberts of Richmond; Green, *Oxford Common Room*, 304. The Pattison daughters had taken part in local philanthropic activities when their father allowed— teaching and volunteer nursing—but these did not lead to paid employment. Several nervously considered becoming governesses; on governessing, see M. Jeanne Peterson, "The Victorian Governess: Status Incongruity in Family and Society," in *Suffer and Be Still: Women in the Victorian Age*, ed. Martha Vicinus (Bloomington: Indiana University Press, 1972); on employment, see Vicinus, *Independent Women*, ch. 1.

84. Elizabeth died in 1877; Green, *Commonwealth*, 424, fn. 2; there is no mention of her death in MP's diary.

85. Manton, *Sister Dora*, 94, citing sermon of 12 July 1857. MP's election in 1861 to the Rectorship of Lincoln did not change his sisters' situation, although he had claimed that his desire to become Rector in 1851 was partly motivated by a wish to help his "poor sisters"; see Manton, *Sister Dora*, 72–74; see also PP 136, fol. 52 (MP diary, 5 Jan. 1856).

86. PP 54, fol. 508f. (Jane Pattison to MP, 23 Nov. 1861); fol. 518f. (Jane Pattison to MP, 30 Nov. 1861).

87. MP did visit Hauxwell; see PP 130, fol. 43 (MP diary, 6 June 1864).

88. PP 130, fol. 62f (MP diary, 4–19 Jan. [1866]) MP resorted to Latin for his feelings

about his father's will: "iniquissimo . . . perfidiosi"; see also Green, *Love*, 108, and Manton, *Sister Dora*, 174–75.

89. Green, *Oxford Common Room*, 90; MP, Mem., 183–84.

90. MP's diary is incomplete and mutilated after Jane Winn Pattison's death on 4 Oct. PP 130, fol. 23ff (MP diary, 23 July 1860), despite the date, was written retrospectively, in the autumn; see also Manton, *Sister Dora*, 100–101, 106–8, 120–1.

91. PP 130, fol. 29ff (MP diary, 25 Nov. 1860); fol. 29v (MP diary, 26 Nov. 1860).

92. Green, *Oxford Common Room*, 200–202, on MP's election; see PP 54 (MP correspondence, 1861), esp. fol. 72 (23 Jan. 1861), a letter from Henry Strong. See also V. H. H. Green, *Lincoln College, Oxford* (pamphlet; Oxford: privately printed, n.d.) and PP 54, fol. 313 (Mary Roberts to MP, 18 April 1861).

93. PP 54, fol. 295ff. (Mary Roberts to MP, 23 March 1861); the cousin, "S. Watts," makes no further appearance, but see Manton, *Sister Dora*, 35 and 223. Mary was at Lincoln through June at least; see PP 54, fols. 326, 545 (Mary Roberts to MP, 18 May 1861).

94. PP 54, fol. 326, 545 (Mary Roberts to MP, 18 May 1861).

95. PP 54, fol. 333 (Mary Roberts to MP, 23 May 1861).

96. PP 54, fol. 335–47, passim. (Mary Roberts to MP, 27 May–5 June 1861). The "illness," a "frightful boil," "prevents her being able to put on her clothes" or walking and "from the pain and wakefulness . . . made her quite weak" (27 May). See also PP 54, fol. 346–47 (Mary Roberts to MP, 5 June 1861); fol. 372ff (Rachel Stirke to MP, 6 July 1861).

97. PP 54, fol. 365ff. (Dora Pattison to MP, 28 June [1861]); fol. 370ff (Rachel Stirke to MP, 29 June 1861); Rachel imagined EFS as brown-eyed (wrong) and "rather short and slim" (correct).

98. PP 54, fol. 365f. (Dora Pattison to MP, 28 June [1861]); fol. 370ff. (Rachel Stirke to MP, 6 July 1861); fol. 370ff. (Rachel Stirke to MP, 29 June 1861); see also Manton, *Sister Dora*, 127; and Margaret Homans, "Eliot, Wordsworth, and the Scene of the Sisters' Instruction," in Elizabeth Abel, ed, *Writing and Sexual Difference* (Chicago: University of Chicago Press, 1982). See PP 54, fol. 405ff (Rachel Stirke to MP, 12 Aug. 1861), for Rachel on her own marriage; see also fol. 372ff. (Rachel Stirke to MP, 6 July 1861).

99. PP 54, fol. 461ff (Mary Roberts to MP, 9 Oct. 1861).

100. CWD, "Mem.," 19.

101. Martin, *Hopkins*, 25–26.

102. Rachel Johnson, ed., *The Oxford Myth* (London: Weidenfeld and Nicolson, 1988); William S. Knickerbocker, *Creative Oxford: Its Influence in Victorian Literature* (Syracuse: University Press, 1925); Joseph Ellis Baker, *The Novel and the Oxford Movement* (Princeton: Princeton University Press, 1932); W. R. Ward, *Victorian Oxford* (London: Frank Cass & Co., 1965); Richard Symonds, *Oxford and Empire: The Last Lost Cause?* (New York: St. Martin's Press, 1986); Paul R. Deslandes, " 'The Foreign Element': Newcomers and the Rhetoric of Race, Nation, and Empire in 'Oxbridge' Undergraduate Culture, 1850–1920," *Journal of British Studies* 37 (1998): 54–90; E. G. W. Bill, *University Reform in Nineteenth-Century Oxford: A Study of Henry Halford Vaughn, 1811–1885* (Oxford: Oxford University Press, 1973); A. J. Engel, *From Clergyman to Don: The Rise of the Academic Profession in Nineteenth-Century Oxford* (Oxford: Clarendon Press, 1983); and Reba Soffer, *Discipline and Power: the University, History, and the Making of an English Elite, 1870–1930* (Stanford: Stanford University Press, 1994).

103. John Sutherland, "A Girl in the Bodleian: Mary Ward's Room of her Own," *Browning Institute Studies* 16 (1988), 169.

104. Susan Hitch, "Women," in *The Oxford Myth*, ed. Rachel Johnson (London: Weidenfeld and Nicolson, 1988), 85–100.

105. In 1959, the women's colleges were made "full colleges" in the University. Oxford began granting women degrees in 1920 but only this "final act of franchise" made Heads and

faculty of the women's colleges eligible for all University offices; Vera Brittain, *The Women at Oxford: A Fragment of History* (London: George G. Harrap, 1960); 238. See also Carol Dyhouse, *No Distinction of Sex: Women in British Universities, 1870–1939* (Bristol, Penn.: UCL Press, 1995); Annie M. A. H. Rogers, *Degrees by Degrees* (Oxford: Oxford University Press, 1938); Pauline Adams, *Somerville for Women: an Oxford College, 1879–1993* (Oxford: Oxford University Press, 1996); Gemma Bailey, ed., *Lady Margaret Hall: A Short History* (= *A Short History of Lady Margaret Hall*; Oxford: privately printed, 1923); Elizabeth C. Lodge, *Terms and Vacations*, ed. Janet Spens (Oxford: Oxford University Press, 1938); Penny Griffin, ed., *St Hugh's: One Hundred Years of Women's Education in Oxford* (London: Macmillan, 1986). On exclusion, see also Woolf, *Room of One's Own*, 112, and Sutherland, "Girl in the Bodleian," 170. For Cambridge, see Rita McWilliams-Tullberg, "Women and Degrees at Cambridge University, 1862–1897," in *A Widening Sphere: Changing Roles of Victorian Women*, ed. Martha Vicinus (Bloomington: Indiana University Press, 1977), 117–45; and Edward Shils and Carmen Blacker, eds., *Cambridge Women: Twelve Portraits* (Cambridge: Cambridge University Press, 1996).

106. Hitch, "Women," 90; Hitch distinguishes the exclusion of women from that of non-elite men; the latter was not a matter of policy. Katherine Bradley, "A Glimpse into Our Past—Forgotten Women of Oxford," *Lilith: Oxford Women's Magazine* 36 (October/ November 1987): 4–5, 15, notes the invisible presence of women's money in the men's colleges.

107. Hitch, "Women," 90, 85.

108. Virginia Woolf, "A Society" in Woolf, *Monday or Tuesday* (1921), reprinted in *The Complete Shorter Fiction of Virginia Woolf*, ed. Susan Dick (New York: Harcourt Brace Jovanovich, 1985), 124–36, esp. 121–22; Lee, *Virginia Woolf*, 282–83.

109. Arthur J. Engel, "Immoral Intentions: The University of Oxford and the Problem of Prostitution, 1827–1916," *Victorian Studies* 23 (1979): 79–107, esp. 84; see Bradley, "Glimpse," for some notable women of the town, including Sarah Cooper, the maker of "Frank Cooper" marmalade.

110. Burgon ended commiseratingly, "but you are not the worse off for [being permanently inferior]"; a contemporary caricature showed him ill in bed, hallucinating "siren-like women doctors and students of science"; Brittain, *Women at Oxford*, 69, 57. EFSP praised Burgon with faint damns: he was "a good creature, intensely narrow, full of faithful affections to Oxford," worth knowing for the exposure to opinions unlike one's own; PP 140, fol. 60f (EFSP to GMT, 17 Feb. 1884).

111. Hitch, "Women," 85–87: "Oxford sells things," and to sell Oxford to the most trans-atlantic audience, buildings, streets, and undergraduates are relentlessly reshaped; see also Ian Carter, *Ancient Cultures of Conceit: British University Fiction in the Post-war Years* (London: Routledge, 1990. On Oxford's male public space, see, e.g, Evelyn Waugh, *Brideshead Revisited: The Sacred and Profane Memories of Captain Charles Ryder* (Boston: Little, Brown, 1945), 58–59.

112. Paul Elmer More, "Oxford, Women, and God," in *A New England Group and Others* (London: Constable, 1912), 257–88.

113. Susan Leonardi, *Dangerous By Degrees: Women at Oxford and the Somerville College Novelists* (New Brunswick: Rutgers University Press, 1989), 6, 4. On intellectual women, see also Deirdre David, *Intellectual Women and Victorian Patriarchy: Harriet Martineau, Elizabeth Barrett Browning, George Eliot* (Ithaca: Cornell University Press, 1987), 1–26.

114. Bradley, "Glimpse," 5; Brittain, *Women at Oxford*, 42; Vicinus, *Independent Women*, ch. 4; Vera Farnell, *A Somervillian Looks Back* (Oxford: privately printed, 1948); on Clara Pater, see Jane Marcus, *Virgina Woolf and the Languages of Patriarchy* (Bloomington: Indiana University Press, 1987), 104; Michael Levey, *The Case of Walter Pater* (London: Thames & Hudson, 1978), 140–51.

115. Respectively, Bertha Johnson, Charlotte Symonds Green, Mary Augusta Arnold Ward, and Louise von Glehn Creighton (whose daughter, Gemma Bailey, was the historian of Lady Margaret Hall). See also Oppenheim, "Mother's Role," 227–28; and Noel Annan, "The Intel-

lectual Aristocracy," in *Studies in Social History: A Tribute to G. M. Trevelyan*, ed. J. H. Plumb (London: Longmans, Green, 1955).

116. Somerville College Gift-Book, 24 (entry dated 1883), Somerville College Library. Stella's work was "a large engraving (framed)." See also AM 43908, fol. 91 (Madeleine Shaw-Lefevre [Principal of Somerville] to EFSP, n.d. [ca. Apr. 1883]).

117. W. Tuckwell, *Reminiscences*, 8–9; see also J. E. C. Bodley, review of EFSD, BSL, *Athenaeum*, 3 June 1905, 679–80, and ch. 6 below. "Jack" Burton flourished in the 1830s; see also Brittain, *Women at Oxford*, 18. On marking women's achievements as public or private, see Rosemarie Bodenheimer, "Ambition and Its Audiences: George Eliot's Performing Figures," *Victorian Studies* 34 (1990): 7–34, esp. 8–15.

118. Peterson, *Family, Love, and Work*, 150–53; cf. Jalland, *Women, Marriage, and Politics*, 260–62, and Angie Acland's unpub. memoirs in Mss. Acland; see also her ms. annotations to the photographs in Ms. Don. [Acland] d. 14.

119. Josephine Butler, *Recollections of George Butler*, 2nd ed. (Bristol: Arrowsmith, n.d. [1893]), 86–116, 118, esp. 94–103; see also Judith R. Walkowitz, *Prostitution and Victorian Society: Women, Class, and the State* (Cambridge: Cambridge University Press, 1980), 116; and Barbara Caine, *Victorian Feminists* (New York: Oxford University Press, 1992), 65–66.

120. See Creighton, *Memoir*, ch. 4; John Sutherland, *Mrs Humphry Ward, Eminent Victorian, Pre-eminent Edwardian* (Oxford: Clarendon Press, 1990), ch. 6; Brittain, *Women at Oxford*, 31, 206–7; Janet Courtney, *An Oxford Portrait Gallery* (London: Chapman and Hall, 1931), 216, 218–19. The Oxford High School for Girls, founded in 1875, also lured progressive families to North Oxford.

121. Ruskin to Pauline Trevelyan, 28 Aug. 1861, qtd. in R. Trevelyan, *Pre-Raphaelite Circle*, 174–75; see also Surtees, ed., *Reflections*, 123.

122. Engel, *Clergyman to Don*, 5–6, n. 5; Ruskin qtd. in R. Trevelyan, *Pre-Raphaelite Circle*, 174–75.

123. George Eliot, "Woman in France: Madame de Sablé" in *The Essays of George Eliot*, ed. Thomas Pinney (London: Routledge & Kegan Paul, 1963), 3; Margaret Jeune, diary entry for 11 June 1861, from Margaret Jeune Gifford, ed., *Pages from the Diary of an Oxford Lady* (1932), qtd. in Harriet Blodgett, *Centuries of Female Days: Englishwomen's Private Diaries* (New Brunswick: Rutgers University Press, 1988), 115.

124. Askwith, *Lady Dilke*, 48; see also Green, *Oxford Common Room*, 306.

125. On clergy wives, see Davidoff and Hall, *Family Fortunes*, 123–25.

126. W. Tuckwell, *Reminiscences*, 6–10; PP 54, fol. 425ff. (Frederick Shaw to MP, 14 Sept. 1861).

127. Qtd. in Blodgett, *Centuries*, 110, 159–61, 198.

128. "Oxford Bells" in Woods, *The Collected Poems of Margaret L. Woods* (London: John Lane, 1914), 73–86.

129. Margaret Woods to Rhoda Broughton, qtd. in Cole, "Rhoda Broughton," Appendix 1, lxxxviii–lxxxvix.

130. Hippolyte Taine, *Sa Vie et Sa Correspondence*, 3rd ed., 4 vols. (Paris: Hachette, 1902–1907) 3: 150–51 (26 May 1871); see also GMT "Rem.," A31.

131. Jackson, *Ingram Bywater*, 20fn.

132. CWD, "Mem.," 16–17; see also 87; the whereabouts of these "diaries and manuscripts" are unknown.

133. AM 43932, fol. 137ff. NB: these memoirs, largely incorporated into Gwynn and Tuckwell's *Life of Dilke*, cannot be construed as "private"; the text's voice assumes a public readership. On *Middlemarch* and proposal letters, cf. Askwith, *Lady Dilke*, 15–16fn., and Glucker, "Case for Casaubon," 16–17.

134. Eliot, *Middlemarch*, 27, 28, 32. See also Lotte Hamburger and Joseph Hamburger, *Con-*

templating Adultery: The Secret Life of a Victorian Woman (New York: Fawcett Columbine, 1991), 30–35; nonfictional letters of proposal could test the outer limits of pretentiousness.

135. Oliphant, *Autobiography*, 277.

136. Charlotte Bronte, *The Professor* (Oxford: Blackwell, 1931), *Shirley* (Oxford: Clarendon Press, 1979), and *Villette*, ed. Mark Lilley (Harmondsworth: Penguin, 1979); Mrs. Alfred Sidgwick, *The Professor's Legacy* (London: J.M. Dent and Sons, n.d.); Louisa May Alcott, *Little Women* (New York: Modern Library, 1983); Anton Chekhov, *Uncle Vanya*, trans. and ed. Michael Frayn (New York: Methuen, 1994). See also Nina Auerbach, *Communities of Women: An Idea in Fiction* (Cambridge: Harvard University Press, 1978), 55–75; Ann B. Murphy, "The Borders of Ethical, Erotic, and Artistic Possibilities in *Little Women*," *Signs* 15 (1990), esp. n. 1 and 578–79. An American novel, Harold Frederic's *The Damnation of Theron Ware* (1896; Lincoln, Neb.: University of Nebraska Press, 1985), inverts this plot: a young married man is drawn to a woman who is learned and possessed of secret knowledges, but as in Henry James's *The Portrait of a Lady*, ed. Leon Edel (Boston: Houghton Mifflin, 1963), a Europeanized woman dangerously emblematizes culture and worldliness, not scholarship or institutionalized pedagogy.

137. Barbara Hardy, "The Miserable Marriages in *Middlemarch*, *Anna Karenina*, and *Effi Briest*," in *George Eliot in Europe*, ed. John Rignall (Aldershot: Scolar Press, 1997), 64.

138. *Essays and Reviews* was a volume of religious history and biblical criticism, denounced as anti-Christian; contributors included MP and Benjamin Jowett. See Basil Willey, *More Nineteenth Century Studies: A Group of Honest Doubters* (London: Chatto and Windus, 1956); Ieuan Ellis, *Seven Against Christ: A Study of Essays and Reviews* (Leiden: E.J. Brill, 1980); M. Francis, "The Origins of *Essays and Reviews*: An Interpretation of Mark Pattison in the 1850s" *Historical Journal* 17 (1974): 797–811; Nimmo, "Learning Against Religion," 316–17; and Josef Altholz, *Anatomy of a Controversy: The Debate over Essays and Reviews, 1860–64* (Aldershot: Scolar, 1994).

139. See Murphy, "Borders of Possibility," 578–79, 583, and Bronte, *Professor*.

140. Ruskin to Pauline Trevelyan, 28 Aug. 1861, qtd. in R. Trevelyan, *Pre-Raphaelite Circle*, 174–75; Surtees, ed., *Reflections*, 123. Glucker makes much of MP's treatment of Milton's marriage and discussion of Milton's views on divorce in MP, *Milton*; Glucker, "Case for Casaubon," esp. 16–17; see also MP, *Milton*, 52–53. Broughton's *Belinda* parallels the self-infatuated Professor Forth and Milton, including Forth's irritation that Belinda is not able to write Greek characters for him; see *Belinda*, 132–34. On the "Milton's daughter" motif, see Sandra Gilbert and Susan Gubar, *The Madwoman in the Attic: The Woman Writer and the Nineteenth-Century Literary Imagination* (New Haven: Yale University Press, 1979), part 3. On MP's *Milton*, see John Kijinski, "John Morley's 'English Men of Letters' Series and the Politics of Reading," *Victorian Studies* 34 (1991), 205–10.

141. Jebb to "C.L.S" (Caroline Lane Slemmer), 26 July 1873, in *Life and Letters of Sir Richard Claverhouse Jebb*, ed. Caroline Jebb (Cambridge: Cambridge University Press, 1907), 163–65.

142. Eliot, *Middlemarch*, 28.

143. PP 140, fol. 10–11 (EFS to Rosa Tuckwell, n.d.).

144. R. Trevelyan, *Pre-Raphaelite Circle*, 184, qtg. EFS to Mary Anne Eaton in letter forwarded from Eaton to Pauline Trevelyan.

145. Askwith, *Lady Dilke*, 18–19. Like EFS, Rose is aesthetic, plays the violin, and has more conventional sisters; M. Ward, *Robert Elsmere*, 12, 13, and 111; see also Sparrow, *Mark Pattison*, 19–23, and William S. Peterson, *Victorian Heretic: Mrs. Humphry Ward's Robert Elsmere* (Leicester: Leicester University Press, 1976), 151–52: "[I]n chapter 36 of the *Elsmere* MS [in the Honnold Library, Claremont, California], Langham tries to envision a life with Rose at Oxford, and the picture he conjures up is nearly identical to Mrs. Pattison's unhappy experiences there" (232, n. 26). But see also Mary Arnold [Mrs. Humphry] Ward, *A Writer's Recollections* (London: W. Collins, 1918), chs. 6 and 7, and Sutherland, "Girl in the Bodleian" and *Mrs. Humphry Ward*, ch. 3.

146. See Peterson, *Victorian Heretic*, and Valerie Sanders, *Eve's Renegades: Victorian Anti-Feminist Women Novelists* (London: Macmillan, 1996). But see also Jane Lewis, *Women and Social Action in Victorian and Edwardian England* (Stanford: Stanford University Press, 1991), ch. 4.

147. Ward, *Robert Elsmere*, 214–15, 216–17, 219, 218, emphases added.

148. GMT, "Rem.," A43, A272.

149. Woolf, "More Carlyle Letters," in *The Essays of Virginia Woolf*, ed. Andrew McNeillie, 6 vols. (New York: Harcourt Brace Jovanovich, 1986–), 1: 258.

150. See Josephine Butler, *Recollections*; Walkowitz, *Prostitution*, 116; Nancy Boyd, *Three Victorian Women Who Changed Their World: Josephine Butler, Octavia Hill, Florence Nightingale* (New York: Oxford University Press, 1982); Caine, *Victorian Feminists*, chs. 5 and 6; and David Rubinstein, *A Different World for Women: The Life of Millicent Garrett Fawcett* (New York: Harvester Wheatsheaf, 1991); see also Sylvia Strauss, "*Traitors to the Masculine Cause*": *The Men's Campaigns for Women's Rights* (Westport, Conn.: Greenwood Press, 1982) and Angela V. John and Claire Eustance, eds., *The Men's Share? Masculinities, Male Support, and Women's Suffrage in Britain, 1890–1920* (London: Routledge, 1987).

151. Qtd. in Gifford Lewis, *Eva Gore Booth and Esther Roper: A Biography* (London: Pandora, 1988), 50.

152. Hullah, *John Hullah*, 51–52; John Hullah had been married to another musician, "Miss Foster"; their daughter Caroline attended Queen's College, London, and studied art, including a stint with Holman Hunt. When Frances Rosser married Hullah, MP performed the ceremony: "the most melancholy wedding (one excepted) at which I was ever present"; PP 130, fol. 61 [MP diary, 15 Dec. 1865]).

153. Barbara Caine, *The Sisters of Beatrice Webb* (Oxford: Oxford University Press, 1986), 84–85; and Deborah Epstein Nord, *The Apprenticeship of Beatrice Webb* (Ithaca: Cornell University Press, 1985), 104–110; see also Walkowitz, *City of Dreadful Delight*, ch. 5.

154. Woolf, "Two Women" (review of Stephen, *Emily Davies and Girton College*), in *Essays*, ed. McNeillie, 4: 61–66.

155. On artists' marriages, see Cherry, *Painting Women*, 38–44.

156. Dellamora, *Masculine Desire*, esp. chs. 3 and 8; Dowling, *Hellenism*.

157. CWD, "Mem.," 17, 18, 19–20; see also Mss. Eng. lett. e. 93, fol. 103 (CWD to Thursfield, n.d. [c. March 1905]): "I'm going to 'put back' babelike (Dorothea) wh I change to childlike on yr hint. On thought I prefer babelike . . . What babelike seems to me to suggest the blind-puppy side of Dorothea?"

158. EFSP, *Renaissance*, 1:349.

159. EFSD, "Idealist Movement," 644–45 ; for positivism, see T. R. Wright, *The Religion of Humanity: The Impact of Comtean Positivism on Victorian Britain* (New York: Cambridge University Press, 1986); Mary Pickering, *Auguste Comte: An Intellectual Biography* (Cambridge: Cambridge University Press, 1993) and "Angels and Demons in the Moral Vision of Auguste Comte," *Journal of Women's History* 8 (1996): 10–40.

160. EFSD, "Idealist Movement," 644–46, 649.

161. But see also EFSD, "The Secret," and "A Vision of Learning"; both in EFSD, *Shrine of Death*, 37–56, and ch. 4 below.

162. "The Physician's Wife," in EFSD, *Shrine of Death*, 40–56; 41, 42, 43, 51, 54–55, 56. See also AM 43906, fol. 32f. (CWD to EFSP, 3 March 1885), and CWD, "Mem.," 93–95.

163. "Silver Cage," in EFSD, *Shrine of Death*, 27–35, 30, 31.

164. "Shrine of Death," in EFSD, *Shrine of Death*, 11–24, 13, 16, 23; see also Askwith, *Lady Dilke*, 19. See EFSD, "A Vision of Learning," and EFSP on Goujon's caryatids: "mysterious figures . . . eternal witness in their brooding quiet. . . . the burden of a riddle never to be read . . . on their lips, desire never to be fulfilled enchant[ing] their sight . . ." in *Renaissance*, 1: 192–93. See also Emily Wilding Davison, "The Price of Liberty," qtd. in Vicinus, *Independent Women*, 277.

165. CWD, "Mem.," epigraph; cf. 133, the epigraph EFSD chose for BSL, "I have loved to

hear my Lord spoken of; and where I have seen the print of his shoe in the earth, there I have coveted to set my foot too." See also Walkowitz, *City of Dreadful Delight*, 89.

166. ESFD, "Shrine of Death," 23; EFSD, "Parables of Life," 539–41.

167. Woolf, "More Carlyle Letters," 1: 261.

168. EFSP, *Renaissance*, 2: 35–37. The painting, now in the Louvre, is reproduced in Andre Chastel, *French Art*, vol. 2: *The Renaissance, 1430–1620* [henceforth Chastel, *French Art: The Renaissance*], trans. Deke Dusinberre (New York: Flammarion, 1994), 219. Cousin receives as much or more attention as any artist in EFSP's *Renaissance*—all of ch. 1 of vol. 2 and repeated appearances in ch. 2.

169. See Margaret L. King, "The Religious Retreat of Isotta Nogarola (1418–1466): Sexism and Its Consequences in the Fifteenth Century," *Signs* 3 (1978): 807–22; Elizabeth Cady Stanton, *The Woman's Bible* (1895–99; Boston: Northeastern University Press, 1993); Honnor Morten, *From a Nurse's Note-book* (1899), qtd. in Vicinus, *Independent Women*, 1; Virginia Woolf, "George Eliot," *The Common Reader*, 1st series (1925; New York: Harcourt Brace Jovanovich, 1953), 176. See also Francis Mason, "The Newer Eve: The Catholic Women's Suffrage Society in England, 1911–1923," *Catholic Historical Review* 72 (1986): 620–38; VMC (see ch. 6) was involved with this organization.

170. EFSP, *Renaissance*, 1: 20, 2: 35–37.

171. EFSP, *Renaissance*, 2: 36.

172. EFSP, *Renaissance*, 2: 37–38; see also 2:52.

CHAPTER FOUR

1. Lyn Haill and Janet Prowting, compilers, *The Invention of Love* program notes, Royal National Theatre, London, 1998; see also Vicinus, *Independent Women*, 195–96.

2. I am indebted to Cora Kaplan for this formulation; see also Sally Mitchell, *The Fallen Angel: Chastity, Class, and Women's Reading, 1835–1880* (Bowling Green: Bowling Green University Popular Press, 1981) and Ellen Bayuk Rosenman, "Spectacular Women: *The Mysteries of London* and the Female Body," *Victorian Studies* 40 (1996), 35–36.

3. See Sedgwick, *Tendencies*, 23–51.

4. Susan Lowndes, ed., *Diaries and Letters of Marie Belloc Lowndes, 1911–1947* (London: Chatto and Windus, 1971), 69–70.

5. Meredith to Julia Stephen, 25 July 1892, in *The Letters of George Meredith*, ed. C. L. Cline, 3 vols. (Oxford: Clarendon Press, 1970).

6. PP 118, fol. 62f. (EFSP to ES, 30 March 1881); "Oh!" is underlined three times, and "Hell" twice. Cf. Woolf's "beak of brass" in *To The Lighthouse* (New York: Harcourt Brace Jovanovich, 1955), 58–59.

7. In BLR, d. 570, undated and unnumbered item in GMT's hand.

8. See Coral Lansbury, *The Old Brown Dog: Women, Workers, and Vivisection in Edwardian England* (Madison: University of Wisconsin Press, 1985); see also Elaine Shefer, *Birds, Women, and Cages in Victorian and Pre-Raphaelite Art* (New York: P. Lang, 1989) and Hardy, *Jude the Obscure*, 209, 264.

9. AM 43946 (CWD, ms. memoir), fol. 4ff.; ch. 1 above.

10. In PP 60, fols. 55–128f., virtually every letter contains attempts to justify expenses; see also EFSP letters to ES, e.g., PP 118, fol. 236f., 22 Jan. 1880.

11. CWD, "Mem.," 24, 31.

12. The only reference to illness between her marriage and 1867 is PP 56, fol. 304f. (EFSP to MP, 6 Sept. 1866).

13. PP 140, fol. 6f. (EFSP to Rosa Tuckwell, 19 Feb. 1868); EFSP mentions an "instrument," which had been "inserted" and must remain for some months. See PP 188, fol. 24f. (EFSP to ES, 9 Aug. 1875): "my swelling is an abscess in course of formation in the left lip." Someone

has attempted to modify this to read "hip"; see also PP 60, fol. 61f. (EFSP to MP, 9 Aug. 1875). These descriptions are consistent with infections of the Bartolin's glands.

14. PP 60, fol. 84f. (EFSP to MP, 16 Dec. 1875) hints at recurrent "swellings" and (perhaps) irregular bleeding; see also AM 43906, fol. 89f. (EFSP to CWD, 11 June 1885); see also PP 118, fol. 28f. (EFSP to ES, 14 Dec. 1875): EFSP claimed she only slept well during her periods; at other times "the blood seems (I fancy) to go on getting disordered, & nasty, & I cannot sleep." See Elaine Showalter and English Showalter, "Victorian Women and Menstruation," in *Suffer and Be Still: Women in the Victorian Age*, ed. Martha Vicinus (Bloomington: Indiana University Press, 1972), 38–44.

15. The only hints that EFSP may have ever thought herself pregnant are some cryptic notes in PP 137, an 1865 travel diary of MP's cited by Askwith, *Lady Dilke*, 54fn. Askwith construes the Greek characters for "kata," followed two and a half months later by "kata arch" [arch = first or beginning], as denoting a missed period and the renewal of menstruation, as after a miscarriage, but "kata" may have, inconsistently, denoted *catamenia* [menstruation].

16. PP 54, fol. 491f. (Edward Howard to MP, 27 Oct. 1861) is the rare exception.

17. GMT, "Rem.," A103, A171; CWD, "Mem.," 62, 100; cf. Askwith, *Lady Dilke*, 53–54.

18. PP 118, fol. 22 (EFSP to ES, n.d. [August 1875]); emphasis EFSP's.

19. Acton to Mary Gladstone, qtd. in Owen Chadwick, *Acton and Gladstone* (London: Athlone Press, 1976), 53–54; Michael Sadleir, *Things Past* (London: Constable, 1944), 109–111: Sadleir's EFS is "a girl who wrote books about French painting in order to earn a little pin-money . . . jump[ed] at an academic alliance of some distinction, and gladly shut her eyes to the manifest foibles of her future husband"; cf. Maccoll, "Rhoda Broughton."

20. See Lorna Duffin, "The Conspicuous Consumptive: Woman as an Invalid," in *The Nineteenth-Century Woman: Her Cultural and Physical World*, ed. Duffin and Sara Delamont (New York: Barnes and Noble, 1978), 26–56; Miriam Bailin, *The Sickroom in Victorian Fiction: The Art of Being Ill* (New York: Cambridge University Press, 1994); and Athena Vrettos, *Somatic Fictions: Imagining Illness in Victorian Culture* (Stanford: Stanford University Press, 1995).

21. PP 140, fol. 6 (EFSP to Rosa Tuckwell, 19 Feb. 1868). The bells may condense Oxford (see Woods, "Oxford Bells") and/or domestic bell-ringing.

22. PP 60, fol. 55f. (EFSP to MP, 3 July 1875).

23. CWD, "Mem.," 32; see also PP 140, fol. 14f. (EFSP to Rosa Tuckwell, 11 Jan. 1870).

24. AM 43932, fol. 137f.

25. At Wildbad, EFSP was treated by a Dr. Burckhardt, who had previously cared for Angie Acland; Angie Acland's memoirs, in Mss. Acland, fol. 49; PP 118, fol. 22 (EFSP to ES, n.d.). For EFSP's movements between July and November 1875, see fols. 24–32.

26. See Pemble, *Mediterranean Passion*, ch. 2.

27. GMT, "Rem.," A162; CWD, "Mem.," 59 and facing illustration.

28. GMT, "Rem.," A148. PP 140, fol. 90f. (EFSD to W. Tuckwell, 23 Jan. 1888), half-jokingly claims her principles are "in theory only plain living and high thinking."

29. PP 118, fol. 24f. (EFSP to ES, 9 August 1875); emphasis EFSP's.

30. PP 60, fol. 61f. (EFSP to MP, 9 August 1875). This was written the same day as the letter to ES saying she did not feel responsible for MP's feelings.

31. PP 56, fol. 303ff. (EFSP to MP, 31 Aug. 1866).

32. PP 60, fol. 80f. (EFSP to MP, 23 Nov. 1875).

33. PP 60, fol. 61f. (EFSP to MP, 9 Aug. 1875); emphasis EFSP's.

34. Messick, "Trial of Writing," assisted my thinking about texts that stage other texts.

35. PP 118, fol. 22f. (EFSP to ES, n.d. [Aug.1875]).

36. PP 118, fol. 36f. (EFSP to ES, 22 Jan. 188?); fol. 28f. (EFSP to ES, 14 Dec. 1875).

37. PP 118, fol. 48f. (EFSP to ES, 20 Nov. 1880).

38. PP 118, fol. 24f. (EFSP to ES, 9 Aug. 1875); emphasis EFSP's.

39. Mss. Acland d.167, fol. 1 (F.E.D. Acland to Angie Acland, 16 Sept. 1896).

40. Rosemarie Bodenheimer, *The Real Life of Mary Ann Evans: George Eliot, Her Letters and Fiction* (Ithaca: Cornell University Press, 1994), 251, 242; see also Nina Auerbach, *Romantic Imprisonment: Women and Other Glorified Outcasts* (New York: Columbia University Press, 1986), 171–83.

41. AM 43907, fols. 30–79f. contains Eliot's letters to EFSP, 10 August 1869 to 29 May 1879; they are generally signed "M.E. Lewes" but see fol. 64 (1 Dec. 1874) for one signed "Madre. Mostly addressed to "My dear Mrs Pattison," they include endearments (fol. 32f. [6 Nov. 1869]; fol. 63f. [3 July 1874]; fol. 51f. [21 Nov. 1871]). Eliot stresses her own age, "ancient" and "aged"; fol. 36f. (21 Feb. 1870); fol. 53 (5 Sept. 1872). See also Bodenheimer, *Real Life*, 231.

42. AM 43907, fol. 36f. (George Eliot to EFSP, 21 Feb. 1870); see also fol. 65f. (3 Jan. 1875), fol. 70 (3 Mar. 1876); fol. 75 (25 May [1877?], and Gordon Haight, ed., *Selections from George Eliot's Letters* (New Haven: Yale University Press, 1985), 376.

43. On Moreau, see CWD, "Mem.," 50–51, 59–61. She "was a substantial person in all senses of the epithet" as well as a "loving" attendant; Moreau had worked for some of the "great families in the South of France . . . and as *femme de confiance* with the French dressmaker of the Imperial family at St. Petersburg," and attended some of EFSP's friends as a "travelling maid." Her niece became EFSD's maid in London and was at her deathbed. See also GMT, "Rem.," A29, and PP 118, fol. 149 (EFSD to ES, 5 Feb. 1886) and fol. 155 (8 Feb. 1886).

44. Mss. Bywater 58, fol. 179f (ES to Ingram Bywater, 7 Aug. 1884).

45. AM 43907, fol. 78f. (George Eliot to EFSP, 20 Feb. 1879); fol. 68 (18 Oct. 1875); fol. 68f. (18 Oct. 1875), fol. 67 (16 July 1875); fol. 72 (18 Feb. 1877); fol. 53f. (George Eliot to EFSP, 5 Sept. 1872); fol. 72f. (18 Feb. 1877); fol. 68f. (18 Oct. 1875); and fol. 55f. (16 Dec. 1872); and Bodenheimer, *Real Life*, 251.

46. ES to CWD, 18 Aug. 1885, qtd. in CWD, "Mem.," 96.

47. Margaret J. Tuke, *A History of Bedford College for Women, 1849–1937* (London: Oxford University Press, 1939), 108–10; Ms. Don. d. 14, facing fol. 37 (Angie Acland's annotations to a photograph of ES).

48. For "good friend," see ES's letter to a newspaper, clipping in Bodleian Library at GA Oxon b. 10, for "excellent as ladies are," see pamphlet, "Extract from a Leading Article in the *Oxford Journal* of January 21, 1871," at GA Oxon b. 10. See also Patricia Hollis, *Ladies Elect: Women in English Local Government, 1865–1914* (Oxford: Clarendon Press, 1987), 148–50.

49. PP 118, fol. 36f. (EFSP to ES, 22 Jan. 1880).

50. Rogers, *Degrees by Degrees*, 5; Brittain, *Women at Oxford*; and Farnell, *Somervillian Looks Back*, 4; ES's bequest of 750 pounds was used to build a "Hostel," the "Eleanor Smith Cottage." ES also contributed cash and furniture; Somerville College Gift-Book, 1–4, 20, 24, 44, 62, 78, 82, 92.

51. Reid to Martineau and Bostock, qtd. in Tuke, *Bedford College*, 316; see also 3, 16, 105, 318.

52. Tuke, *Bedford College*, 16, 94, 99–103, 108, 109, 135, 162, 169, 173, 299–322. The College's council and committees included John Hullah, Frances Kensington, Madeleine Shaw-Lefevre, Emma Lingen, Charles Kegan Paul, Anna Swanwick, and MP's niece, Jane Stirke Newton-Robinson. ES left Bedford seven hundred pounds.

53. Tuke, *Bedford College*, 108–10; see also GMT, "Rem.," A147; and Vanda Mortan, *Oxford Rebels: The Life and Friends of Nevil Story Maskelyne, 1823–1911: Pioneer Oxford Scientist, Photographer, and Politician* (Gloucester: Sutton, 1987).

54. PP 139, fol. 3f. (EFSP to James Thursfield, 24 March 1873); AM 43904, fol. 15f. (CWD to EFSD, 9 Feb. 1880); Tuke, *Bedford College*, 110.

55. Tuke, *Bedford College*, facing 145.

56. Ms. Don. d. 14 (photos taken between 1891 and 1900, with mss. annotations).

57. On Skene, see Peterson, *Victorian Heretic*, 62, and Edith C. Rickards, *Felicia Skene of Oxford: A Memoir* (London: John Murray, 1902).

58. Despite the terms of Emily Weedon Strong's will, MP was apparently able to control the funds as Mrs. Strong's trustee; see PP 118, fol. 42 (EFSP to ES. 23 Aug. 1880): "an old cousin of my godmother . . . if she intends to give me anything she shld be warned not to repeat the mistake of my mother. . . ." See PP 118, fol. 40 (EFSP to ES, 17 Mar. 1880) for an instance of ES as "banker."

59. Sadleir's ES is a figure of Victorian repression whom he pits against the "advanced" Rhoda Broughton; *Things Past*, 92–93. See also T. W. Cole, "Rhoda Broughton," D.Phil. thesis, St. Anne's College, University of Oxford, 1964, 150.

60. Mss. Bywater 58, fol. 179f. (ES to Ingram Bywater, 7 Aug. 1884); Mss. Eng. lett. d. 191, fol. 11f. (ES to C.H. Pearson, 6 Oct. 1881).

61. R. S. Rait, *Memorials of Albert Venn Dicey* (London: Macmillan, 1925) 25, 33; Dicey met ES in 1854; see also Richard A. Cosgrove, *The Rule of Law: Albert Venn Dicey, Victorian Jurist* (Chapel Hill: University of North Carolina Press, 1980), 13. Frank Dicey, Albert's brother, was an artist friend of EFSP.

62. See PP 118, fol. 90f. (EFSP to ES, 1 Feb. 1884).

63. PP 118, fol. 30f. (EFSP to ES, 9 Nov. 1876).

64. PP 118, fol. 74f. (EFSP to ES, 23 Mar. 1882). There is no way to know what the "utmost folly" signified—flight, flirtation, adultery, or suicide? A largely incoherent letter to MP suggests EFSP had been linked to "A.C.O." by gossip she encouraged but insists such gossip was baseless (PP 57, fol. 407, A.C.O. to MP). EFSP's relationship with Robert Browning can be read as a flirtation, but he reacted in startled tones when EFSP implied he was suggesting anything; see W. H. T. Armytage, "Robert Browning and Mrs. Pattison: Some Unpublished Letters," *University of Toronto Quarterly* 21 (1952): 179–92, and Mermin, "Some Sources"; cf. Maccoll, "Rhoda Broughton," 32. Askwith considers EFSP's relationship with Eugene Muntz a flirtation; *Lady Dilke*, 87–88, 100–101, 134–35.

65. PP 118, fol. 90f. (EFSP to ES, 1 Feb. 1884).

66. Trevelyan Papers, WCT 191 (EFSP to Pauline Trevelyan, 30 July 1863); see also EFSP to Pauline Trevelyan, 3 July [1865], 5 Sept. 1864, 20 Jan. 1965, and 21 Jan. [1865?]; and undated (c. 1865) letter noting that EFSP is "one of the Lady Patronesses" of the Radcliffe Infirmary. See also Ward, *Writer's Recollections*, 104–5.

67. Trevelyan Papers, WCT 191, EFSP to Pauline Trevelyan, 30 July 1863; emphasis EFSP's. The reference to her "old master" is not Mulready but someone in Oxford.

68. R. Trevelyan, *Pre-Raphaelite Circle*, 184–85, 206–7; Askwith, *Lady Dilke*, 29–31; CWD, "Mem.," 24

69. Rait, *Dicey*; Cosgrove, *Rule of Law*; but Dicey supported women's education and was a founder of Newnham College.

70. See Carroll Smith-Rosenberg, "The Female World of Love and Ritual: Relations Between Women in Nineteenth-Century America," in Smith-Rosenberg, *Disorderly Conduct: Visions of Gender in Victorian America* (New York: Oxford University Press, 1985), for the classic account of women's supportive cultures; see Deirdre d'Albertis, " 'Bookmaking Out of the Remains of the Dead': Elizabeth Gaskell's *The Life of Charlotte Bronte*," *Victorian Studies* 39 (1995), 3.

71. EFSD, "Physician's Wife," in *Shrine of Death*, 55–56; a drawing of the grave by EFSD faces the title page of this collection.

72. See Angela Carter, *Nothing Sacred: Selected Writings* (London: Virago, 1982), 197–99.

73. Angie Acland, unpublished ms., Ms. Don. d. 14, facing fol. 38.

74. C. Peterson, *Determined Reader*, 194, 195, and 189–90; George Eliot, *The Mill on the Floss*, ed. A.S. Byatt (Harmondsworth: Penguin, 1979), book 4, ch. 3; Barry Qualls, *The Secular Pilgrims of Victorian Fiction: The Novel as Book of Life* (Cambridge: Cambridge University Press, 1982).

75. CWD, "Mem.," 10.

76. EFSD, "Idealist Movement," 651; cf. CWD, "Mem.," 10–11, 21–22.

77. EFSD, "Idealist Movement," 652.

78. EFSD, "Of Love and Sorrow," in BSL, 166, probably written after 1895; EFSD, "Idealist Movement," 651; cf. CWD, "Mem.," 10–11, 21–22. See also EFSP, "Salon of 1876," 495.

79. Priscilla Robertson, *An Experience of Women: Pattern and Change in Nineteenth-Century Europe* (Philadelphia: Temple University Press, 1982), 177; Rose, *Parallel Lives*, 103; see also Hardy, *Jude the Obscure*, 213.

80. Elizabeth Wolstenholme Elmy, *The Criminal Code in its Relation to Women* (1880), qtd. in Susan Kingsley Kent, *Sex and Suffrage in Britain, 1860–1914* (Princeton: Princeton University Press, 1987), 92.

81. Lee Holcombe, *Wives and Property: Reform of the Married Women's Property Law in Nineteenth-Century England* (Toronto and Buffalo: University of Toronto Press, 1983); Mary Lyndon Shanley, *Feminism, Marriage, and the Law in Victorian England, 1850–1895* (London: Tauris, 1989).

82. Acton, *Functions and Disorders of the Reproductive System* (1857), qtd. in Robertson, *Experience of Women*, 179.

83. For feminist responses, see Walkowitz, *City of Dreadful Delight*, ch. 5 and Kent, *Sex and Suffrage*, esp. ch. 3, and 93–94; Jan Lambertz, "Feminists and the Politics of Wife-Beating," in *British Feminism in the Twentieth Century*, ed. Harold Smith (Amherst: University of Massachusetts Press, 1990); Lucy Bland, "Marriage Laid Bare: Middle-class Women and Marital Sex c. 1880–1914," in *Labour and Love: Women's Experience of Home and Family, 1850–1914*, ed. Jane Lewis (Oxford: Blackwell, 1987). See also Mary Hartman, *Victorian Murderesses: A True History of Thirteen Respectable French and English Women Accused of Unspeakable Crimes* (New York: Schocken, 1977), 34ff. and "conclusion."

84. Hardy, *Jude the Obscure*, esp. 208 and 228; see also Vera Brittain, *Honourable Estate: A Novel of Transition* (New York: Macmillan, 1936).

85. PP 60, fol. 91 (EFSP to MP, 21 Jan. 1876); all quotations, until further notice, from this letter.

86. MP's letter of response can be partially reconstructed by reference to PP 60, fol. 128f. (EFSP to MP, n d. [Jan. 1876). PP 130, MP's diary for the relevant period, is sketchy and contains no entries for Jan. 1876.

87. PP 60, fol. 128f. (EFSP to MP, n.d. Jan. 1876).

88. PP 60, fol. 128f. (EFSP to MP, n.d. Jan. 1876).

89. PP 60, fol. 128f. (EFSP to MP, n.d. Jan. 1876).

90. PP 60, fol. 93f. (EFSP to MP, 27 Jan. 1876); again, cf. Hardy, *Jude the Obscure*, 210–11.

91. PP 132, fol. 16v (MP diary, 1 June 1879), fol. 17v (9 June 1879); PP 118, fol. 28f. (EFSP to ES, 14 Dec. 1875).

92. EFSP, "Carstens," 78.

93. EFSP, "Nicolas Poussin," 473.

94. EFSD, "Silver Cage," in *Shrine of Death*, 27–35, 30, 31. See also EFSD, "Parables of Life," 538.

95. Richard D. Altick, ed., *Robert Browning: The Ring and the Book* (New Haven: Yale University Press, 1981), book 5, ll. 573–84, 603–9, 612–13. The Count is defending himself for murderously assaulting Pompilia. Browning's poem was published in 1868/69; "Silver Cage" was written in 1882 (AM 45665, fol. 9v); cf. also Charlotte Bronte, *Jane Eyre*, ed. Mark Schorer (Boston: Houghton Mifflin, 1959), 357.

96. EFSD, "Silver Cage," 32–33, 34–35.

97. EFSD, "Physician's Wife," in *Shrine of Death*, 40, 41, 42, 43, 51, 54–55, 56.

98. EFSD, "Idealist Movement," 650, 651, 652; some passages also appear in EFSD, BSL, 145, 166–67; see also CWD, "Mem.," 117–18.

99. EFSD, "Idealist Movement," 652, 653. See Thomas Laqueur, "Orgasm, Generation, and the Politics of Reproductive Biology," in Laqueur and Catherine Gallagher, The Making of the Modern Body: Sexuality and Society in the Nineteenth Century (Berkeley: University of California Press, 1987), esp. 35. I am indebted to Claudia Koonz for help in thinking about these issues. For EFSP on the claims of "nature" on women, see EFSP, review of Michelet, Nos Fils and Esquirol, L'Emile du dix-neuvième siècle.

100. EFSD, "Idealist Movement," 650, 651; cf. CWD, "Mem.," 10–11, 21–22, and AM 43932, fol. 137ff., esp. 145–55 and 173–83.

101. CWD, "Mem.," 19, 27, 18, 41, 26; emphasis added; cf. GMT, "Rem.," A26, and AM 43907, fol. 8ff. (Charles Newton to EFSP, 22 Feb. 1872). See also PP 140, fol. 87 (EFSD to GMT, n.d.); and Ward, Writer's Recollections, 105.

102. CWD does not note that Hellenistic studies were strongly coded as masculine; see Prins, Victorian Sapphos; Frank Turner, The Greek Heritage in Victorian England (New Haven: Yale University Press, 1981); Richard Jenkyns, The Victorians and Ancient Greece (Cambridge: Harvard University Press, 1980); Dellamora, Masculine Desire; G. W. Clarke, ed., Rediscovering Hellenism: The Hellenic Inheritance and the English Imagination (Cambridge: Cambridge University Press, 1989); Dowling, Hellenism; and Joseph Kestner, Mythology and Misogyny: The Social Discourse of Nineteenth-Century British Classical Subject Painting (Madison: University of Wisconsin Press, 1989).

103. CWD, "Mem.," 121–22.

104. See, e.g., EFSD, French Architects, ch. 4; see also ch. 7 below.

105. CWD, "Mem.," 21, 10; EFSD, "Idealist Movement," 651.

106. EFSD, "Physician's Wife," in Shrine of Death, 54–55.

107. Vicinus, Independent Women, 157–62, 187–210, and Frank Mort and Lynda Nead, "Sexuality, Modernity, and the Victorians," Journal of Victorian Culture 1 (1996), 128–29. For examples, see Jalland, Women, Marriage and Politics, 102–9; Betty Askwith, Two Victorian Families (London: Chatto and Windus, 1971); see Hardy, Jude the Obscure, 221, for unwanted marital sex as the worst adultery. On adultery and representation, see Tony Tanner, Adultery in the Novel: Contract and Transgression (Baltimore: Johns Hopkins University Press, 1979).

108. The letters are quite mutilated but some excisions may have been aimed at political gossip.

109. AM 43908, fol. 28 (Caroline Chatfield to EFSP, 23 July 1877) and fol. 41 (21 Feb. [1879?]: Chatfield tactlessly admires EFSP's Renaissance: "[I] can scarely believe it to be written by a woman."

110. AM 43903, fol. 129 (CWD to EFSP, n.d. [May 1878]); AM 43904, fol. 59 (CWD to EFSP, 25 April 1880), signed "ZZ." For "Dear Lady," see AM 43904, fol. 144 and 156 (CWD to EFSP, 8 Sept. and 11 Oct. 1880).

111. AM 43906, fol. 124f. (CWD to EFSP, n.d. [13 Aug. 1885?]. Askwith, Lady Dilke, 118n. thinks "Tots" referred to EFSD's stature (from Hottentot) and guesses that Hoya came from Hoya carnosa, a waxplant with white petalled flowers, in a reference to EFSD's complexion. A hoya is also a kind of bulldog, perhaps an allusion to EFSD's stubbornness. See also fol. 161 (EFSD to CWD, n.d. [after 1896]), in which the salutation and the signature are drawings of cats.

112. No consistency is notable until after EFSP married CWD. The earliest use of "Emilia" I found is a letter of 20 Jan. 1865 to Pauline Trevelyan, signed "Emilia Francis S. Pattison"; in other letters to Trevelyan, EFSP signs herself "EFSP," "E. Francis Pattison," "E.F. Pattison," and "Piggy" (EFSP to Pauline Trevelyan, 20 Jan. 1865); one letter (19 Sept. [1864 or 65]) concludes with a small drawing which looks like a guinea pig. In letters to ES, EFSP mostly used "F.S.P.," "E.F.S.P.," and sometimes simply "F." until 1880 and some letters are unsigned. EFSP's letters to Emily Thursfield (PP 140, fol. 21f., 2 Dec. 1880; PP 118, fol. 56f. [11 Feb. 1881], fol. 58f. [23 Mar. 1881], and fol. 74f. [23 Mar. 1882]) are signed "Emilia F.S.P.," "Em. F.S.P.," and "Emilia F.S.P."; letters to MP are almost invariably signed "F."

113. AM 43903, fol. 1; see also AM 43906, fol. 121 (CWD to EFSP, n.d. [c. 13 Aug. 1885]. "Fussie" or "Lady Fussie" was a nickname was used by GMT and later by CWD's son; GMT, "Rem.," ch. 18.

114. EFSP, *Renaissance*, 1: 121; see also 2: 108–9.

115. Margaret Drabble, ed., *Oxford Companion to English Literature*, 5th ed. (Oxford: Oxford University Press, 1985), s.v. "Emilia," "Two Noble Kinsmen," "Fletcher, John," and "Canterbury Tales." For EFSP on Chaucer, see BSL, 140.

116. Lisa Jardine, "Canon to the Left of Them, Canon to the Right of Them," in *The War of the Words: The Political Correctness Debate*, ed. Sarah Dunant (London: Virago, 1995): 97–115.

117. Drabble, ed., *Oxford Companion*, s.v. "Sandra Belloni."

118. Somerville Gift Book, 28f., Somerville College Library.

119. Drabble, ed., *Oxford Companion*, s.v. "Vittoria."

120. Fragment, PP 140, fol. 40 (EFSP to ? [CWD], n.d., c. Feb./Mar. 1881).

121. See Cora Kaplan, "Introduction" to Elizabeth Barrett Browning, *Aurora Leigh*, ed. Kaplan (London: The Women's Press, 1983); see also Ellen Moers, *Literary Women: The Great Writers* (New York: Doubleday, 1977), 173–210; Sandra Gilbert, "From *Patria* to *Matria*: Elizabeth Barrett Browning's *Risorgimento*," *PMLA* 99 (1984): 194–209; and Gill Frith, "Playing with Shawls: George Eliot's Use of Corinne in *The Mill on the Floss*," in *George Eliot in Europe*, ed. John Rignall (Aldershot: Scolar Press, 1997), 225–39, esp. 226–27; see also ch. 5 below.

122. Eliot, *Middlemarch*, 134, 136; AM 43907, fol. 79f. (George Eliot to EFSP, 29 May 1879).

123. Garrett, *Charles Wentworth Dilke*, 94, 180–88; AM 43902, fol. 286 (CWD to W. Dilke [great-uncle William], 22 July 1865); Gwynn and Tuckwell, *Life of Dilke*, 2: 567 (in ch. 61, written by W. Tuckwell).

124. David Perkins, ed., *English Romantic Writers*, 1038–46; ll. 14–17, 130, 525, 53–59; see also introductory note and ll. 41–52; see also Hardy, *Jude the Obscure*, 243, and Peterson, *Determined Reader*, 220–21.

125. Gwynn and Tuckwell, *Life of Dilke*, 1: 181, 182, 183; AM 43932, fol. 84; Jenkins, *Dilke*, 90, 92, 183; AM 43932, fol. 93; see also Oppenheim, *Shattered Nerves*, 169.

126. Gwynn and Tuckwell, *Life of Dilke*, 1:17–18.

127. Jenkins, *Dilke*, 24fn., qtg. AM 43930, fol. 134; CWD found Millicent Garrett Fawcett particularly insensitive; AM 43932, fol. 87.

128. AM 43932, fol. 94; AM 43932, fol. 94; Jenkins, *Dilke*, 91, and 24fn.

129. AM 43932, fol. 102.

130. AM 43932, fol. 137f.; AM 43940, fol. 115f.

131. CWD, "Mem.," 21.

132. AM 43932, fol. 137f. CWD returned to church attendance and "[his] sceptical frame of mind . . . was modified in 1874, and came to an end in 1875"; Jenkins claims CWD described himself as a "primitive Christian" but gives no source; Dilke, 91, 24fn.

133. Jenkins, *Dilke*, 94–95.

134. AM 43905, fol. 175 (CWD to EFSP, 3 Jan. 1883).

135. Gwynn and Tuckwell, *Life of Dilke*, 1: 199–200; the guests included Eliza Lynn Linton and Margaret Oliphant; AM 43932, fol. 115; Gwynn and Tuckwell, 1: 230; AM 43903, fol. 38f. (CWD to EFSP, [24 Aug. 1876]); and fol. 21 (CWD to EFSP, 26 Aug. 1875). CWD lamented that as a "a politician with only a grandmother" to act as hostess, he could not entertain women at his own dinner-parties.

136. But CWD could be indebted to her expertise and friendship with artists; see AM 43908, fol. 21 (Edward J. Poynter to EFSP, 1 June 1875), and fol. 41 (Norman Maccoll to EFSP, 20 Feb. 1879).

137. Jenkins, *Dilke*, 95, 113; AM 43903, fol. 110–20; AM 43904, fol. 64 (CWD to EFSP,

29 April 1880); see also Esther Simon Skolnick, *Leading Ladies: A Study of Eight Late Victorian and Edwardian Political Wives*, 325, 331, 338—39, 342—43, 346, 383.

138. PP 118, fol. 38f. (EFSP to ES, 10 Feb. 1880); the last word is cut away from the original but must be "opinion" or a synonym; see also fol. 48f. (EFSP to ES, 21 Nov. 1880): "I found on long discussion last month that he is fully agreed in what I wrote to you was the result of all the study of Ireland I went through last winter, so much so that he thought he had communicated with me!" and AM 43903, fol. 110—19 (CWD to EFSP, Feb. and Mar. 1878).

139. CWD, "Mem.," 53—54; AM 43903, fol. 83 [CWD to EFSP, 3 June (1877?)]; PP 118, fol. 36f. (EFSP to ES, 22 Jan. 1880).

140. AM 43903, fol. 30—32, 3 undated letters (CWD to EFSP; EFSP to CWD; CWD to EFSP); see CWD, "Mem.," 45—48 on their disagreements: "On 'reform of the Royal Academy' I was an extreme Radical, who thought her Toryfied by her surroundings."

141. AM 43904, fol. 174 (EFSP to CWD, 24 Nov. 1880); cf. AM 43905, fol. 173 (EFSP to CWD, 2 Jan. 1883). See also Jalland, *Women, Marriage, and Politics*, chs. 7 and 8; Caine, *Destined to Be Wives*, ch. 9; and Peterson, *Family, Love, and Work*, ch. 6.

142. AM 43903, fol. 150 (CWD to EFSP, 11 Dec. 1878); see also AM 43905, fol. 239 (CWD to EFSP, 7 Nov. 1883).

143. AM 43906, fol. 70 [CWD to EFSP, 5 May 1885]; AM 43906, fol. 102 (CWD to EFSP, n.d. [30 June 1885]); cf. AM 43903, fol. 19 (CWD to EFSP, n.d. [1875]).

144. AM 43903, fol. 3 (CWD to EFSP, n.d. "c. 28 Mar. 1875"); fol. 180 (CWD to EFSP, 8 Mar. 1879); CWD, "Mem.," 45—46. Their temporary disagreemen was on adult vs. "limited" (women's) suffrage; see ch. 6 below.

145. See Rose, *Parallel Lives*, ch. 3; Strauss, "Traitors," 28—36; Olive Banks, *The Biographical Dictionary of British Feminists*, Vol. 1: 1800—1930, s.v. "Mill, John Stuart," and "Taylor, Harriet"; Susan Groag Bell, "The Feminization of John Stuart Mill," in *Revealing Lives: Autobiography, Biography, and Gender*, ed. Bell and Marilyn Yalom (Albany: State University of New York Press, 1990), 81—92; Mary Lyndon Shanley, "Marital Slavery and Friendship: John Stuart Mill's *The Subjection of Women*," in Shanley and Carole Pateman, eds., *Feminist Interpretations and Political Theory* (Cambridge: Polity Press, 1991; and Hardman, *Six Victorian Thinkers*, ch. 4. There is no record that EFSP met Mill; Harriet Taylor died in 1858 but CWD and EFSD knew her daughter, Helen Taylor.

146. Jenkins, *Dilke*, 42—43, 44. See also AM 43929, fol. 98; Gwynn and Tuckwell, *Life of Dilke*, 1:168.

147. Mill has been doubted by immediate readers and virtually all later commenters, including, most egregiously, Freud, qtd. in P. Rose, *Parallel Lives*, 125. Rose participates in this project of "cutting Harriet down to size" too; see ibid., 132—134; cf. Hardman, *Six Victorian Thinkers*, 80, and Bell, "Feminization," 85—86. Robert Browning has also been doubted by a tradition of criticism, only recently emended; see Angela Leighton, *Elizabeth Barrett Browning* (Bloomington: Indiana University Press, 1986), ch. 1, and 93—95, 97—99; see also Moi, *Simone de Beauvoir*, ch. 2.

148. See also P. Rose, *Parallel Lives*, 103; 123—24.

149. Strauss, "Traitors," 29; Hardman, *Six Victorian Thinkers*, 77—78, 81—82; Banks, "Taylor, Harriet"; Bell, "Feminization," 85—90; Mill, *Autobiography*, qtd. in Strauss, "Traitors," 28, and P. Rose, *Parallel Lives*, 133. See also David Halperin, "Why is Diotima a Woman?" in Halperin, *One Hundred Years of Homosexuality and Other Essays on Greek Love* (New York: Routledge, 1990), 113—51; and Hardman, *Six Victorian Thinkers*, 74, 85—86.

150. Bell, "Feminization," 87—92.

151. Margaret Forster, *Elizabeth Barrett Browning: A Biography* (New York: Doubleday, 1989); see also Leighton, *Elizabeth Barrett Browning*, ch. 5.

152. See Strauss, "Traitors," 31.

153. Hardman, *Six Victorian Thinkers*, 78–79, 81; Strauss, "Traitors," 31; P. Rose, *Parallel Lives*, 120–22.

154. Hardman, *Six Victorian Thinkers*, 81; P. Rose, *Parallel Lives*, 122–23; Shanley, "Marital Slavery"; Bell, "Feminization," 84, qtg. Mill, *Autobiography*, original draft.

155. PP 118, fol. 52f. (EFSP to ES, 23 Mar. 1881): EFSP may be collapsing Anne Hathaway Bradley's views with MB's self-diagnosis in a letter EFSP saw. On discourses of hysteria, see Showalter, *Female Malady*, and Jan Goldstein, "The Uses of Male Hysteria: Medical and Literary Discourse in Nineteenth-Century France," *Representations* 34 (1991): 134–65, esp. 139–40.

156. PP 118, fol. 52f. (EFSP to ES, 23 Mar. 1881); PP 140, fol. 21f. (EFSP to Emily Thursfield, 2 Dec. 1880).

157. PP 118, fol. 48f. (EFSP to ES, 21 Nov. 1880); fol. 62f. (EFSP to ES, 30 Mar. 1881).

158. PP 118, fol. 52f. (EFSP to ES, 23 Mar. 1881); fol. 109f. (EFSP to ES, 4 Aug. 1884): "we made a very distressing discovery in [MP's diary] . . . wh leads one to think he perhaps had good reason for telling me it 'was his duty to provide for [Meta],' " hinting that MP's legacy was compensation for "ruining" MB.

159. PP 118, fol. 181 (EFSD to ES, 16 Mar. 1886).

160. PP 118, fol. 36f. (EFSP to ES, 22 Jan. 1880).

161. EFSP, "Palissy," 189; see EFSP, review of H. Morley, *Clement Marot*, in which EFSP rends Morley for alleging confusing the Marguerites (cf. Morley, letter of self-defence, *Academy*, 1 July 1871, 328); see also EFSP, *Renaissance*, 1: 355, 30.

162. John Kucich, *Repression in Victorian Fiction: Charlotte Bronte, George Eliot, and Charles Dickens* (Berkeley: University of California Press, 1987).

163. EFSP, *Renaissance*, 1: 18–19.

164. EFSP, *Renaissance*, 1: 201–4.

165. EFSP, *Renaissance*, 1: 18–19, 20. EFSP's text is familiar with the "coarser" images.

166. EFSP, "Art and Morality," 79.

167. AM 43906, fol. 136f. (EFSD to CWD, 8 Apr. 1886).

168. PP 140, fol. 37f. (EFSP to GMT, 23 Nov. 1881). EFSP is quoting from memory; I have not identified the poem.

169. EFSD, "Mirror of the Soul," in *BSL*, 240–41.

170. AM 43932, fol. 137f.; cf. Hardy, *Jude the Obscure*, 210–11.

171. AM 43906, fol. 53ff. (EFSP to CWD, 16 April 1885).

172. See PP 118, fol. 36f. (EFSP to ES, 22 Jan. 1880).

173. EFSP, *Renaissance*, 1:19–20, 238–39, and 356; see also the cunning syntax of EFSD on scandals' sales value in *French Engravers*, 94.

174. AM 43904, fol. 95 (CWD to EFSP, n.d. [May/June 1880]).

175. AM 43904, fol. 95 (CWD to EFSP, n.d. [May/June 1880]). EFSP misremembers the title (as "Effie's Wish") and protagonist's name (Ellie), and misquotes these lines:

> . . . I will have a lover,
> Riding on a steed of steeds:
> He shall love me without guile,
> And to him I will discover
> The swan's nest among the reeds. (st. 4)

Ellie's imagined lover, despite wealth, talents, nobility, and physical charms,

> . . . will not prize
> All the glory that he rides in,
> When he gazes in my face:

He will say, 'O Love, thine eyes
Build the shrine my soul abides in,
And I kneel here for thy grace!' " (st. 5–7).

Robert Browning, ed., *A Selection from the Poetry of Elizabeth Barrett Browning*, 5th ed. (1873), 5–8; see also Dorothy Mermin, "Barrett Browning's Stories," *Browning Institute Studies* 13 (1985), 105; and Leighton, *Barrett Browning*, 95–96.

176. EFSD, *French Engravers*, 11–12, 15; EFSD is quarrelling with George Sand's "Lettres d'un Voyageur"; "enchanted isle" is Vigée LeBrun qtd. by EFSD.

177. See AM 43906, fol. 83f. (EFSP to CWD, n.d. [beginning of letter missing; c. May/June 1885]). The "cottage" at Dockett Eddy was not finished until March 1885, after EFSP's departure for India, but that would not preclude a visit to a nearly-finished house; Gwynn and Tuckwell, *Life of Dilke*, 1:482–83; 2:90–91; AM 43905, fol. 118 [CWD to EFSP, 23 April 1882]).

178. Colin Eisler, "The Six Lives of an Art Historian," in *Women as Interpreters of the Visual Arts*, ed. Claire Richter Sherman (Westport, Conn.: Greenwood Press, 1981) 161, qtg. EFSP, *Renaissance*, 1: 203; Eisler reproduces the drawing, which faces 202 in EFSP's volume.

179. EFSP, *Renaissance*, 1: 206.

180. For CWD's reaction to MP's courtesy, see AM 43904, fol. 164f. (CWD to EFSP, 19 Nov. 1880); and PP 118, fol. 48f. (EFSP to ES, 21 Nov. 1880); see also AM 43911, fol. 125f. (MP to CWD 2 Dec. 1880); for "fancyman," see Green, *Love*, 56; for the "other man," see PP 122 (MP to MB, 20 Aug. 1881), and Askwith, *Lady Dilke*, 92; for "wishes me dead," see Green, *Commonwealth*, 489fn. (qtg. PP 124, fol. 185v).

181. Green, *Love*, 250–51.

182. Dowling, *Hellenism*; see also Martin, *Women and Modernity*, 73.

183. Green's *Love* is the most important account; see also Green, *Oxford Common Room*, and Askwith, *Lady Dilke*, chs. 8 and 9. Sparrow's *Mark Pattison*, ch. 2, has an arch tone that places it in the genre Green deplores. Transcriptions my own unless noted.

184. PP 131, fol. 22 (MP diary, 14 Mar. 1878); PP 132, fol. 31 (MP diary, 4 Nov. 1879). See also Green, *Love*, 9. "Daisy" Bradley later married H.G. Woods, sometime fellow and President of Trinity College; see p. 96 above; MB's sister Jessica married Courtenay Ilbert, later famous in British-Indian politics. See also PP 132, fol. 29v [MP diary, 26 Oct. 1879]); this entry is about MB's presence at tea; its immediate predecessor (24 Oct.) says MP has revised his will to leave "away from F. . . . above £5000," but would cancel the codicil "should F. come back to me." EFSP underlined MB's name and drew a line connecting the passages.

185. See Green, *Love*, 28fn.; PP 132, fol. 13 (MP diary, 25 April 1879); and PP 131, fol. 23ff. See also PP 136, fol. 20 (MP diary, 18 Sept. 1848, a transcription from Bronte, *Jane Eyre*, 210). See also Askwith, *Lady Dilke*, 78; PP 132, fol. 11 (MP diary, 16 April 1879); and Barbara Caine, "Beatrice Webb and the Woman Question," *History Workshop Journal* 14 (1982), 27. For MP's on MB's mental abilities, see Green, *Commonwealth*, 488, and PP 132, fol. 50v (MP diary, 28 Feburary 1880).

186. Augustus Hare, *The Story of My Life* (London: George Allen, 1896) 1:303–90, passim; and abridged account, *The Years with Mother*, ed. Malcolm Barnes (London: Century Publishing, 1984), 64, 65, 82–83. See also Green, *Love*, 1–3.

187. Hare, *Story of My Life*, qtd. in Green, *Love*, 7fn. Hare's autobiography is a compilation of ghost stories, and the Bradley family story invites association with Nicholas Abraham, "Notes on the Phantom: A Complement of Freud's Metapsychology," in Abraham and Maria Torok, *The Shell and the Kernel*, ed. and trans. Nicholas Rand (Chicago: University of Chicago Press, 1994), but Charles Bradley's placement of ghosts in his children's psyches is conscious and precise.

188. Green, *Love*, 3–4, 5; PP 119, fol. 97f. (MB to MP, 22 July 1880).

189. See PP 119, fol. 203f. (MB to MP, 16 Oct. 1880); fol. 28f. (MB to MP, n.d. [c. April

15 1880]); fol. 198f. (MB to MP, 14 Oct. 1880); and Green, *Love*, 7. MP and EFSP disputed MB's economic position in his diary, but MB, while single, had limited access to funds nominally her own; see PP 134, fol. 30 (MP diary, 13 April 1883).

190. PP 119, fol. 28 (MB to MP, n.d.); PP 119, fol. 140f. (MB to MP, 10 Sept. 1880).

191. Green, *Love*, 23−25.

192. For "Dearest Meta!" see PP 119, fol. 7 (MP to MB, 14 Feb. 1880); for "nothing left," see fol. 13f. (MP to MB, 3 March 1880); for "I can't expect more" and following, see fol. 66 (MP to MB, 11 July 1880).

193. PP 119, fol. 26f. (MP to MB, 19 April 1880); even MB thought MP's response to her enforced yachting slightly over the top; see fol. 28f. (MB to MP, 19 April 1880).

194. PP 119, fol. 11f. (MP to MB, 17 Feb. 1880); cf. PP 118, fol. 36 (EFSP to ES, 22 Jan. 1880). On Mary, see also PP 119, fols. 42 (MP to MB, 28 May 1880), 43 (MP to MB, 2 June 1880), 45f. (MB to MP, n.d. [summer 1880]), 49f. (MB to MP, 2 June 1880), 52f. (MP to MB, 3 June 1880), 53f. (MP to MB, 12 June 1880), 64 (MP to MB, 4 July 1880), and 66f. (MP to MB, 11 July 1880).

195. PP 119, fol. 124f. (MB to MP, 29 Aug. 1880); fol. 203 (MB to MP, 16 Oct. 1880).

196. PP 119, fol. 140f. (MB to MP, 10 Sept. 1880). Unluckily, this letter was opened and almost certainly read by EFSP; she wrote a note to MP on the back of it; see Green, *Love*, 46. For "unique mixture," see ibid., 59, and PP 119, fol. 248f. (MB to MP, 8 Dec. 1880).

197. For Jeannie Stirke, PP 119, fol. 100 (MP to MB, 27 July 1880); see also fol. 120f. (MP to MB, 20 Aug. 1880); PP 133, fol. 17 (MP diary, 6 Sept. 1880); and PP 119, fol. 134f. (MP to MB, 6 Sept. 1880).

198. See PP 119, fol. 53f. (MP to MB, 12 June 1880); fol. 169f. (MP to MB, 27 Sept. 1880); fol. 187f. (MP to MB, 8 Oct. 1880).

199. PP 119, fol. 144 (MP to MB, 12 Sept. 1880). MB's reply and fol. 155f. (MP to MB, 19 Sept. 1880) alludes to having confided his "secret sorrow."

200. PP 119, fol. 148f. (MB to MP, 14 Sept. 1880); fol. 237f. (MB to MP, 28 Oct. 1880); fol. 241 (MP to MB, 31 Oct. 1880).

201. PP 119, fol. 198f. (MB to MP, 14 Oct. 1880).

202. PP 119, fol. 248 (MB to MP, 8 Dec. 1880); PP 119, fol. 244f. (MP to MB, 1 Dec. 1880); Green, *Love*, 63.

203. PP 133, fol. 36 (MP diary, 8 March 1881); Green, *Love*, 32; despite MB's contempt for her, her stepmother showed kindness in the affair.

204. PP 133, fol. 21v (MP diary, 1 Nov. 1880); see PP 119, e.g., fol. 136f. (MP to MB, 9 Sept. 1880).

205. Green, *Love*, 61; PP 119, fol. 201 (MP to MB, 15 Oct. 1880); fol. 203 (MB to MP, 16 Oct. 1880); Green, *Love*, 63, qtg. MB to MP, 10 Feb. 1881.

206. PP 140, fol. 21 (EFSP to Emily Thursfield, 2 Dec. 1880): "I am told she has given her family a great deal of trouble by repeated & violent sets at men of all sorts & sizes & . . . several Oxford friends object to going to Lincoln whilst she is there . . . [MB] can hardly be a fit companion for a very young & very impressionable girl [like GMT]."

207. See EFSP's letters to ES, 1880−1884 (in PP 118) for occasional references to MB. Although often irritated and sometimes "very angry" over MP's conduct (e.g., PP 126, fol. 98f. [MP to MB, 1 April 1884]), EFSP never seems to have suspected MP of anything but foolishness until after his death; see PP 133, fol. 46 [MP diary, 16 June 1881]); and PP 134, fol. 6 (MP diary, 19 Nov. 1882) and fol. 13 (23 Dec. 1882).

208. PP 133, fol. 35v (MP diary, 5 Mar. 1881); see also Cole, "Rhoda Broughton"; and as Tamie Watters, "An Oxford Provocation," *Encounter* 36:4 (April 1971): 34−42 (and subsequent correspondence); on Broughton, see also Watters, preface to Broughton, *Belinda*; Ethel Arnold, "Rhoda Broughton as I Knew Her," *Fortnightly Review* 114 (August 1920): 262−78; Sadleir, *Things*

Past, ch. 6; Amy Cruse, *The Victorians and Their Reading* (Boston: Houghton Mifflin, 1935); and Marilyn Wood, *Rhoda Broughton (1840–1920): Profile of a Novelist* (Stamford, Lincs.: Paul Watkins, 1993).

209. PP 133, fol. 36v (MP diary, 11 Mar. 1881); for Laffan, see PP 60, fol. 138ff. (May Laffan [later Noel-Hartley] to MP, n.d. 1882–24 Oct. 1882).

210. See Cole, "Rhoda Broughton"; Watters, "Preface." MP had Jeannie Stirke read *Belinda* to him (PP 134, fol. 21v [MP diary, 3 Mar. 1883]) and had himself announced on a visit to Broughton as "Professor Forth"; "Protests fr. her that she didn't mean it—but!"; fol. 32, 30 April 1883.

211. Broughton, *Belinda*, 54–55; Passerini, *Autobiography*, 7.

212. Lang, *Old Friends*, 123–34.

213. Green, *Love*, 62–63.

214. E.g. PP 126, fol. 139f. (MP to MB, 2 Jan. 1884); PP 126, fol. 119 (MB to MP, 26 April 1884), fol. 127 (MP to MB, 29 April 1884).

215. PP 126, fol. 146 (MB to MP, 3 June 1884); emphasis mine.

216. PP 126, fol. 146f. (MB to MP, 3 June 1884). The poem is the address of a drowned sailor or voyager, first to the ghost or memory of the mathematician Archytas, then to the passing stranger, asking for ritual burial; it is a protest against the waste of death, which ravages even the brilliant and heroic, and of horror at neglect of the dead; Horace, *Odes*, trans. James Michie (London: Folio Society, 1987), book 1, ode 28.

217. PP 118, fol. 105ff. (EFSP to ES, 30 July 1884); GMT, "Rem.," A55. In its obituary of EFSD, the *Cotton Factory Times* of 28 Oct. 1904 recounted: "Mrs. Pattison was quick to profit by her intellectual environment. She studied classics under her husband's guidance with such success that in his last illness the fastidious scholar's greatest solace was to hear his wife construe Horace by the hour." There are very few sources from whom the writer could have "learned" this.

218. PP 130, fol. 73 (MP diary, following entry for 24 Nov. 1873); see also fol. 77 (10 Mar. 1874): "O spare me a little, before I go hence . . ."; and PP 133, fol. 50v (MP diary, 23 June 1880). For MP's long-standing health problems, see, e.g., PP 136, fol. 4f. (MP diary, 28 July 1848), and fol. 11 (17 Aug. 1848). See also Pat Jalland, *Death in the Victorian Family* (Oxford: Oxford University Press, 1996); and Sarah Webster Goodwin and Elisabeth Bronfen, eds., *Death and Representation* (Baltimore: Johns Hopkins University Press, 1993).

219. Green, *Love*, 128 (qtg. PP 123, MP to MB, 1 Jan. 1882); PP 130, fol. 65 (MP diary, compendium entry for summer 1871).

220. See PP 134, passim, for MP's symptoms; and fol. 59 (29 Nov. 1883) for Tuckwell's diagnosis: "degeneration of one of the valves of the heart." See also PP 118, fol. 104f. (EFSP to ES, 26 July 1884) and PP 140, fol. 14f. (EFSP to Rosa Tuckwell, 11 Jan. 1870).

221. PP 118, fol. 40f. (EFSP to ES, 17 Mar. 1880); fol. 46 (EFSP to ES, 12 Oct. 1880); fol. 81f. (EFSP to ES, 4 Dec. 1883). See fol. 79f. (EFSP to ES, 25 Nov. 1885) for EFSP's summary of the doctors' views; on her own health, see PP 134, esp. fol. 57 (MP diary, 15 Nov. 1883); and PP 118, fol. 79–84 (EFSP to ES, Nov.–Dec. 1883), esp. fol. 84f. (EFSP to ES, 30 Dec. 1883).

222. PP 134, fol. 61 (MP diary, compendium entry for Jan–May 1884); see also fol. 62v (May 1884); fol. 65 (13 June and following, 1884); PP 126, fol. 141–45 (MP to MB, 3 June 1884); fol. 153 (MP to MB, 11 June 1884).

223. See PP 118, fol. 118 (EFSP to ES, 8 Jan. 1884): EFSP overrides ES's suggestion that MP does not want her in Oxford and adds "& also this is how his father behaved each time a daughter was absent from Hauxwell."

224. For "first movement of irritation," see PP 118, fol. 86f. (EFSP to ES, 8 Jan. 1884); cf. PP 126, fol. 58f. (MP to MB, 3 Feb. 1884); for "tenderness and sympathy," see PP 118, fol. 90f. (EFSP to ES, 1 Feb. 1884).

225. EFSD, "Physician's Wife," in *Shrine of Death*, 47, 54.

226. See PP 126, fol. 58f. (MP to MB, 3 Feb. 1884); fol. 71 (MP to MB, 19 Feb. 1884); fol. 79 (MP to MB, 22 Feb. 1884).

227. PP 134, fol. 65 (MP diary, 13 June 1884); Green, *Love*, 223–24.

228. For EFSP's offer, see PP 118, fol. 98f. (EFSP to ES, 10 July 1884); for "one perfect thing," see fol. 94f. (EFSP to ES, 8 July 1884).

229. PP 118, fol. 94f. (EFSP to ES, 8 July 1884).

230. PP 118, fol. 98 (EFSP to ES, 10 July 1884).

231. EFSD, *French Architects*, 107–15; Anna Collot is on 113–14.

232. PP 118, fol. 81 (EFSP to ES, 4 Dec. 1883).

233. CWD, "Mem.," 87; emphasis mine.

234. PP 126, fol. 154 (MP to MB, 29 June 1884).

235. PP 118, fol. 100 (EFSP to ES, 15 July 1884); fol. 104f. (EFSP to ES, 26 July 1884).

236. EFSD, *French Engravers*, 83.

237. PP 118, fol. 96 (EFSP to ES, 9 July 1884); fol. 104f. (EFSP to ES, 26 July 1884); Stirke quotation at fol. 105 (EFSP to ES, 30 July 1884).

238. PP 118, fol. 107 (EFSP to ES, 2 Aug. 1884); fol. 109 (EFSP to ES, 4 Aug.1884); fol. 107f. (EFSP to ES, 2 Aug. 1884); fol. 115 (EFSP to ES, 11 Dec. 1884); see also Mss. Bywater 546, fol. 410 (Frank Pattison to Ingram Bywater, 3 August 1884). For Smith's reactions, see Mss. Bywater 58, fol. 179f. (ES to Ingram Bywater, 7 August 1884); ES continues, "So many wished to show affection & respect by going down to Harrogate & they naturally feel aggrieved at the one person who felt neither trying to forbid their coming." See also fol. 177 (William Ward Fowler to Ingram Bywater, 31 July 1884).

239. Mss. Bywater 58, fol. 179f. (ES to Ingram Bywater, 7 August 1884)

240. EFSP, *Renaissance*, 2: 224–25; 1: 96.

241. Askwith, *Lady Dilke*, 115; see also Mrs. Huth Jackson qtd. in GMT, "Rem.," A56, A70, A56.

242. PP 118, fol. 109 (EFSP to ES, 4 Aug. 1884).

243. GMT, "Rem.," A56, A68–70. MP had ignored EFSP's probable rapid remarriage and insisted she should need the money the books would fetch. She gave Somerville, besides books, several bookcases and dressers, a huge set of "white china desert [sic] plates," a brass chandelier, a carpet, and other cabinetry; Somerville College Gift-book, 28, 30.

244. PP 118, fol. 109 (EFSP to ES, 4 Aug. 1884). MP's will left little away from EFSP— small legacies to servants, his brother Frank, Ingram Bywater, T.F. Althaus, his godsons Mark Stebbing and Edgar Strong, his goddaughter Edith Nettleship, the bequest to MB, and a hundred pounds each to Jeannie and Mary Stirke. The estate was proved at £45,561; after legacies and death duties, EFSP inherited ca. £39,000.

245. Green, *Love*, 232–33; PP 118, fol. 115 (EFSP to ES, 11 Dec. 1884) and fol. 113 (EFSP to ES, 21 Aug.t 1881); see also fol. 76f. (EFSP to ES, 14 April 1882). Jeannie appears not to have attended Somerville; GMT's sister Marian did attend, probably at EFSP's expense (GMT, "Rem.," A53); on Bishop Otter's College (in Chichester), see ibid., A66–67. For the Royal Academy, see AM 43907, fol. 143 (Frederic Leighton to EFSP, n.d. [1885]) and fol. 144 (Leighton to EFSP, 3 Feb. 1885).

246. EFSD, "The Last Hour," in BSL, 266–67.

247. EFSD, "Vision of Learning," in *Shrine of Death*, 59, 60, 64, 66–67, 63, 68–72, 73, 74, 76. Note biblical reference: three days later the woman returns to the man who had been in a grave; this passage also overlaps with EFSP, "Palissy," 189. Note also the emphasis on the city's dreary climate, contrasted to a South of heat, light, herbs, and pines; cf. EFSP, "Carstens," 78: "free spirits . . . [stretch] out wild white arms, and mak[e] fantastic curves expressive of un-definable desire . . . But . . . fall prone . . . shrinking, cowering . . . , sucked in by the damp

earth already reeking with such vapours. . . . dead in the city of [their] . . . dreams. . . ." Cf. Hardy, *Jude the Obscure*, 387–88.

248. Roy Jenkins, *Victorian Scandal: A Biography of the Right Honourable Gentleman, Sir Charles Dilke* (New York: Chilmark Press, 1965), 5.

249. BLR, d. 570, fol. 2, MP to "Principal Librarian Bodleian," 8 June 1884; MP to Bodleian, 13 June, 1884; NB: the papers in BLR, d.570 are inconsistently numbered and bound. The selected letters became PP 60; fol. 54 is a note by MP: "F.'s letters from Nice 1875–76."

250. BLR, d. 570: A.V. Dicey to James Thursfield, 7 Nov. 1896; Thursfield to EFSD, 10 Nov. 1896; EFSD to Thursfield, 12 Nov. [1896]; Thursfield to GMT, 17 July 1911; Thursfield to GMT, 17 July 1911; 20 July 1911; and 31 Oct. 1915. CWD tried to get the letters from Thursfield when he was writing his "Memoir" of EFSD, but it is not clear if Thursfield agreed; see BLR, d. 570, CWD to Thursfield, 2 Jan. 1905. The collection, deposited in 1927, is now PP 118; fols. 1–21, on the acquisition of the papers, have been relocated to BLR 501/208.

251. BLR, d. 570: H. Craster, memo, 31 Oct. 1913; "H.E.C." [Craster], memos, 16 Sept. and 12 Sept., 1913.

252. BLR, d. 570: Falconer Madan, memo, 11 Jan. 1913; Bywater to Craster, 15 Nov. 1914.

253. BLR, d. 570: GMT to Craster, 18 Nov. 1936; James Thursfield to GMT, 31 Oct. 1915. Thursfield had earlier warned GMT to be careful about Mary Eustace Smith in case of litigation; Thursfield to GMT, 6 Aug. 1911.

254. BLR, d. 570: T.C.D. Gamblin [?] to Dr. Cowley, 3 Mar. 1926.

255. BLR, d. 570: T.F. Althaus to [illeg.], 9 Oct. 1927. The Bodleian did not grant "indiscriminate" access; Alan Harris of G. Bell and Sons was given access to the papers with the support of Althaus but a letter reminded him, "the Pattison letters are of a very intimate character . . . the Library authorities are not at all likely to sanction their publication" (BLR, d. 570: Harris to A.E. Cowley, 1 Dec. 1927; Cowley to Harris, 6 Dec. 1927).

256. BLR, d. 570: GMT to Craster, 12 May 1936.

257. GMT, "Rem."; PP 141 (MP to GMT, tss. copies; originals in AM 44886).

258. BLR, d. 570: Jane A. Newton-Robinson to H.E. Craster, 27 Oct. 1936, 17 July 1937, 2 July 1937, and 17 Oct. 1936.

269. Liddell, *Almond Tree*, 285 (emphasis in original); see also Sparrow, *Mark Pattison*, 30fn.

CHAPTER FIVE

1. My distinctions between the novel and textual depictions of the theatrical and spectacular are extremely fragile; see Jacqueline Rose, "George Eliot and the Spectacle of the Woman," in Rose, *Sexuality in the Field of Vision* (London: Verso, 1986), 104–22, esp. 108, 114; Martin Meisel, *Realisations: Narrative, Pictorial, and Theatrical Arts in Nineteenth-Century England* (Princeton: Princeton University Press, 1983), and Rosenman, "Spectacular Women." For Victorian texts which wrestle with the relations between sculpture, painting, narrative, and lyric, see John Stuart Mill, "What Is Poetry?" in *Victorian Prose and Poetry*, ed. Lionel Trilling and Harold Bloom (New York: Oxford University Press, 1973), 82–83; and, appropriately, Mill on "The Lady of Shalott" in "Tennyson's Poems," in Mill, *Autobiography and Literary Studies*, ed. John M. Robson and Jack Stillinger (Toronto: Toronto University Press, 1981), 397–418.

2. See Auerbach, *Ellen Terry*; Thompson, *Queen Victoria*; and Munich, *Queen Victoria's Secrets*, 4–6. Of the wider literature on theatricality and selfhood in the nineteenth century: see John Kucich, *The Power of Lies: Transgression in Victorian Fiction* (Ithaca: Cornell University Press, 1994), 28; Joseph Litvak, *Caught in the Act: Theatricality in the Nineteenth-Century English Novel* (Berkeley: University of California Press, 1991), xii; and Auerbach, *Private Theatricals*. See also Barbara Bodichon, "Objections to the Enfranchisement of Women Considered" (1866), qtd. in A. Burton, *Burdens of History*, 91.

3. Oscar Wilde, *The Picture of Dorian Grey*, in *The Picture of Dorian Grey and Other Writings by Oscar Wilde*, ed. Richard Ellman (New York: Bantam Books, 1982).

4. Steedman, *Landscape*, 37–38.

5. The most notable exposition is Walkowitz, *City of Dreadful Delight*.

6. Landy and Villarejo, *Queen Christina*, 27–28; see also Peter Brooks, *The Melodramatic Imagination: Balzac, Henry James, Melodrama, and the Mode of Excess* (New York: Columbia University Press, 1985).

7. See EFSD, "Idealist Movement," 643–56; see also David Norbrook, "The Life and Death of Renaissance Man," *Raritan* 8 (1989), 91.

8. EFSP, *Renaissance*, 1: 40, 54, 62, 84, 92, 163–64, 360, 229–30; see also 1: 122, 285, and 2: 139–40, 174–75; see also EFSP, "Nicolas Poussin," 476.

9. EFSD, *French Architects and Sculptors*, 13, 19.

10. EFSP, *Renaissance*, 2:135–36.

11. Riviere's essay reprinted in Victor Burgin, James Donald, and Cora Kaplan, eds., *Formations of Fantasy* (London: Methuen, 1986); Judith Butler, *Gender Trouble: Feminism and the Subversion of Identity* (New York: Routledge, 1990), and Butler, "Critically Queer," *GLQ: A Journal of Lesbian and Gay Studies*, 1 (1993): 17–32. See also Mary Anne Doane, "Film and the Masquerade: Theorizing the Female Spectator," in Doane, *Femmes Fatales: Feminism, Film Theory, Psychoanalysis* (New York: Routledge, 1991); Luce Irigaray, *This Sex Which Is Not One*, trans. Catherine Porter (Ithaca: Cornell University Press, 1985), 76; cf. Anne McClintock, *Imperial Leather: Race, Gender, and Sexuality in the Colonial Contest* (New York: Routledge, 1995), 62–64; and Naomi Schor, *Bad Objects: Essays Popular and Unpopular* (Durham: Duke University Press, 1995), 52–54.

12. "Histrionic theory of gender" from Diane Dugaw, *Warrior Women and Popular Balladry, 1650–1850* (Cambridge: Cambridge University Press, 1989), 11.

13. Butler warns of this danger; see her "Critically Queer."

14. Jane Gaines, "Costume and Narrative: How Dress Tells the Woman's Story," in Gaines and Charlotte Herzog, eds., *Fabrications: Costume and the Female Body* (New York: Routledge, 1990), 204, summarizing Thomas Elsaesser, "Tales of Sound and Fury: Observations on the Family Melodrama" (1985).

15. Ward, *Writer's Recollections*, 103. Ward is recalling the period between 1868 and 1872. The name "Mrs Pat" was applied to EFSP in the 1860s but for Ward's readers it would also conjure the actress Mrs. Patrick Campbell. On Ward in Oxford, see Sutherland, *Mrs Humphry Ward*, chs. 3 and 6; Peterson, *Victorian Heretic*; Enid Huws Jones, *Mrs. Humphry Ward* (London: Heinemann, 1973); and Virginia Woolf, "The Compromise"(1923), in *Essays*, ed. McNeillie, 3: 380–84.

16. Ward, *Writer's Recollections*, 102, 104.

17. GMT, "Rem.," A24; Maccoll, "Rhoda Broughton," 30–31; CWD, "Mem.," 19; Bodley, review of EFSD, BSL. On Victorian furniture, see Gerald Reitlinger, *The Economics of Taste: The Rise and Fall of the Objets d'Art Market since 1750* (New York: Holt Rinehart and Winston, 1963), chs. 5 and 6.

18. Penny, "Vertiginous" [review of Bruno Pons, *Grands Decors francais*, Katie Scott, *The Rococo Interior*, and Marianne Roland Michel, *Chardin*], *London Review of Books*, 12 Dec. 1996, 8–9; see also Macleod, *Art and the Victorian Middle Class*, 277; EFSD, *French Furniture*, passim; *French Architects*, ch. 2, esp. 7, 9, and 11.

19. Taine, *Vie et Correspondence*, 3: 149 (5 June 1871); 3: 147 (4 June 1871); Taine on Oxford men qtd. in Diderik Roll-Hansen, "The *Academy*, 1869–79: Victorian Intellectuals in Revolt," *Anglistica* 8 (1957), 168–69; for EFSP on Taine, see AM 43908, fol. 1 (EFSP to Rosa Tuckwell, 26 May 1871).

20. *Who Was Who* (1897–1916); CWD, "Mem," 26, 19.

21. Askwith, *Lady Dilke*, 97; see also Anthony Powell, "The Bowra World and Bowra Lore,"

in *Maurice Bowra, a Celebration*, ed. Hugh Lloyd-Jones (London: Duckworth, 1974), 90–105; see also PP 133, fol. 96v (MP Diary, 19 Oct. 1882).

22. See Soffer, *Discipline and Power*, and Symonds, *Oxford and Empire*.

23. Lee, *Woolf*, 86–87; see also 201–7, 235, and 271.

24. Leopold, the eighth child of Victoria, attended Oxford; EFSP may have met him through Henry Acland, his doctor; for EFSP's correspondence with Leopold (or his secretary, R. H. Collins), see AM 43907, fol. 1–18ff. (21 Feb. 1872–5 Mar. 1883); Leopold died in 1884. For Browning's letters to EFSP, see AM 43907, fol. 82–115 (April 1875 n.d. [c.1876]), and Armytage, "Robert Browning"; see also Mermin, "Some Sources," 84; and CWD, "Mem.," 39. EFSP quit "dealing" after she became a regular critic but still acted without profit as a kind of broker for some artists and friends.

25. CWD, "Mem.", 21, 18; see also AM 43908, fol. 8 [Newton to EFSP, 22 Feb. 1877]; Newton's wife was an artist who exhibited an "Elaine" in 1863 and may have been EFS's contemporary at South Kensington; Mancoff, *Arthurian Revival*, 174.

26. Ward, *Writer's Recollections*, 103–4; see also Engel, *Clergyman to Don*.

27. Huws Jones, *Mrs. Humphry Ward*, 37.

28. See Engel, *Clergyman to Don*; More, "Oxford, Women, and God"; Bodley, review of EFSD, BSL, 679.

29. Max Beerbohm, *Zuleika Dobson* (New York: Dodd, Mead, 1911).

30. Courtney, *Oxford Portrait Gallery*, 216, 218–19; Brittain, *Women at Oxford*, 45; cf. Georgina Battiscombe, *Reluctant Pioneer: a Life of Elizabeth Wordsworth* (London: Constable, 1978), 54–58; see also Maxine Berg, *A Woman in History: Eileen Power, 1889–1940* (Cambridge: Cambridge University Press, 1996), and Woolf, *A Room of One's Own*, 17.

31. Ward, *Writer's Recollections*, 152–53; AM 43908, fol. 306, newspaper picture of EFSP and Millicent Garrett Fawcett at a women's suffrage meeting, dated by miscellaneous hands between 1872 and 1878; CWD, "Mem.," 43–44; Bradley, "Glimpse"; Sheila Lewenhak, *Women and Trade Unions: An Outline History of Women in the British Trade Union Movement* (New York: St. Martins Press, 1977), 70; *Women's Union Journal*, July 1881, 70, 115; Sept. 1881, 89–90; Jan. 1883, 2; and Dec. 1884, 107–10; and AM 43918, fol. 51ff. (M. Nettleship to CWD, n.d.).

32. EFSP, *Renaissance*, 1; 25–26, 19–20, 29–30, 50, 57; J. Butler, *Recollections*, 94–103.

33. Eliot, "Woman in France," 9.

34. PP 130, fol. 72 (MP diary, 23 Nov. 1873); fol. 92v (MP diary, 25/26 Nov. 1874); *egkuklo* to move in a circle; *egkuklios* = a circular [as a letter or pamphlet]; *ta egkuklia* also signifies "the common things" or the surrounding world as opposed to the interior life; for MP's pride in EFSP's "cleverness," see, e.g., PP 132, fol. 19v (MP diary, 28 July 1879); for EFSP's artistic studies and "art friends," see PP 132, fol. 16v (MP diary, 1 June 1879) and fol. 17v (9 June 1879; for MP "stigmatizing" EFSP's " 'bohemian' friends," see PP 118, fol.28f. (EFSP to ES, 14 Dec. 1875).

35. Bertha Johnson, "The First Beginnings, 1873–1900," in Bailey, ed., *Lady Margaret Hall*, 28–30; Courtney, *Oxford Portrait Gallery*, 219; Brittain, *Women at Oxford*, 45–46.

36. PP 134, fol. 8v (MP diary, 29 Nov. 1882) has MP presiding over a meeting of the Oxford branch of the Women's Protective and Provident League; PP 131, fol. 26 (MP diary, 11 April 1878), MP moves a women's suffrage resolution; see Brittain, *Women at Oxford*, 44–45. Louise Creighton reports a suffrage meeting at which Lydia Becker spoke held at Lincoln in the early 1870s; Creighton, *Memoir*, 89; see also CWD "Mem.," 43; cf. ibid., 20.

37. Hullah, *Life of John Hullah*, 140; Church qtd. in Green, *Oxford Common Room*, 265; Tom Stoppard, *The Invention of Love* (London: Faber and Faber, 1997), 9; see also Thomas Seccombe and H. Spencer Scott, eds., *In Praise of Oxford: An Anthology in Prose and Verse*, 2 vols. (London: Constable, 1911), 2: 650.

38. Qtd. in Green, *Oxford Common Room*, 265 and *Commonwealth*, 483; see also William Ward Fowler, *Reminiscences* (Holywell, Oxford: priv. printed, 1921), 26–27.

39. MP was by the 1880s, "a sort of troglodyte . . . practically invisible to the ordinary member of the University"; Charles Oman, *Memories of Victorian Oxford and of Some Early Years* (London: Methuen, 1941), 210.

40. Fowler, *Reminiscences*, 26–27; see also Lionel Tollemache, *Old and Odd Memories* (London: Edward Arnold, 1908), 179; and John Morley, "On Pattison's Memoirs" (1885) in Morley, *Nineteenth Century Essays*, ed. Peter Stansky (Chicago: University of Chicago Press, 1970), 321, and 324–25.

41. Qtd. in Askwith, *Lady Dilke*, 78; cf. EFSP, *Renaissance*, 2:5.

42. Green, *Love*, 28, citing PP 119, fol. 13 (MP to MB, 3 March 1880).

43. Thomas Wright, *Life of Walter Pater* (London; Everett and Co., 1907), 252–53; Gosse, *Critical Kit-Kats* (1896), qtd. in Badger, "Mark Pattison," 441; see also Stoppard, *Invention*, 9.

44. PP 141, tss. copies of MP to GMT (originals in British Library): 27 Feb. 1879; 22 Sept. 1881; 3 Jan. 1882; 19 April 1882; 13 Mar. 1883; 16 June 1882; see also GMT, "Rem.," A48–53.

45. Rosebery qtd. in Green, *Oxford Common Room*, 308 n1.

46. W. Minto, ed., *Autobiographical Notes of the Life of William Bell Scott . . . and Notices of his Artistic and Poetical Circle of Friends 1830–1882*, 2 vols. (London: James R. Osgood, McIlvaine, and Co., 1892), 2: 67.

47. Askwith, *Lady Dilke*, ch. 5; Peterson, *Victorian Heretic*, 65–73; Ward, *Writer's Recollections*, 102–11; for pleasures in gardens, see EFSP, *Renaissance*, 1: 22–24.

48. Henry James to William James, 29 April 1869, in *Henry James Letters*, ed. Leon Edel, 2 vols. (Cambridge: Harvard University Press, 1974, 1975), 1: 111.

49. Sparrow, *Mark Pattison*, 9, qtg. "an honorary fellow of Lincoln who had it from one of the undergraduates who were at the party"; see also Askwith, *Lady Dilke*, 23.

50. Green, *Commonwealth*, 483, and *Oxford Common Room*, 266; no source given.

51. Taine, *Vie et Correspondence*, 3: 150–51 (26 May 1871); see also Paul Bourget, "Sensations d'Oxford: Notes de Voyage," *La Nouvelle Revue* 24 (1883), 565–66, for this trope.

52. Henry James to William James, 29 April 1869, in Edel, ed., *Henry James Letters*, 1:111; cf. James's innocently and unself-consciously emancipated American young women. For James's romantic view of Oxford, see Knickerbocker, *Creative Oxford*, 1–2.

53. Oliphant, *Autobiography and Letters*, 277; Bell Scott, 1864 letter to Pauline Trevelyan, qtd. in R. Trevelyan, *Pre-Raphaelite Circle*, 208–9; "artificiality and "heartlessness" are R. Trevelyan's.

54. Qtd. in Green, *Oxford Common Room*, 308 n1.

55. Johnson's diary for 1876, qtd. in Janet Trevelyan, *The Life of Mrs Humphry Ward* (New York: Dodd, Mead, 1923), 28; Johnson, "The First Beginnings," 29.

56. See Mary Poovey, *The Proper Lady and the Woman Writer: Ideology as Style in the Works of Mary Wollstonecraft, Mary Shelley, and Jane Austen* (Chicago: University of Chicago Press, 1984).

57. Francesca M. Wilson, *Rebel Daughter of a Country House: The Life of Eglantyne Jebb, Founder of the Save the Children Fund* (London: Allen and Unwin, 1967), 25–26, 29–31, 33–34, 36, 92; Caroline Jebb, ed., *Life and Letters of Sir Richard Claverhouse Jebb* (Cambridge: Cambridge University Press, 1907), 156–57 [letter of 29 Jan. 1872]); see also 98–99; for Jebb as a pro-suffrage M.P., see *Women's Suffrage Record*, Dec. 1903; as a boy, Jebb was taught by William Tuckwell.

58. Jebb, *Life and Letters*, 163–65 (letter of 20 July 1873).

59. Ward, *Writer's Recollections*, 104–5.

60. The known surviving paintings of EFSP are by Pauline Trevelyan and Laura Capel Lofft (discussed below) and Charles Camino; CWD also cites paintings by Bell Scott and "an unidentified artist, 'J.P.' perhaps Portaels the Belgian'," dated 1864 and 1865 respectively; CWD,

"Mem.," 23–25. On framing, see Helena Michie, *The Flesh Made Word: Female Figures and Women's Bodies* (Oxford: Oxford University Press, 1987), 9, 102–23, esp. 103–7.

61. Ward, *Writer's Recollections*, 109–10.

62. R. Trevelyan, *Pre-Raphaelite Circle*; Macleod, *Art and the Victorian Middle Class*, 171–72; and Robin Ironside, "Pre-Raphaelite Paintings at Wallington," *Architectural Review* 92 (Dec. 1942): 147–49.

63. CWD, "Mem.," 24; CWD describes the dress as "of the Venetian colour revival, inaugurated by Dante Rossetti and his friends." The painting is in the National Portrait Gallery, London, Reg. No.1823A; see also R. Trevelyan, *Pre-Raphaelite Circle*, 206, and EFSP, *Renaissance*, 1: 255, and 1: 36.

64. Photograph dated by CWD as 1862, AM 49612(b), item 1.

65. Hélène Cixous, "The Laugh of the Medusa," trans. Keith Cohen and Paula Cohen, in Elizabeth Abel and Emily Abel, eds., *The Signs Reader: Women, Gender, and Scholarship* (Chicago: University of Chicago Press, 1983) 296.

66. Janet Todd, *The Sign of Angellica: Women, Writing and Fiction 1660–1800* (London: Virago, 1989), 1, 2, 9, 10; Todd is arguing specifically about the eighteenth century.

67. Rivière, "Womanliness"; Doane, "Film and Masquerade"; Butler, *Gender Trouble* and "Critically Queer."

68. Wilde, *Dorian Grey and Other Writings*, 8.

69. For overviews, see Moe Meyer, ed., *The Politics and Poetics of Camp* (New York: Routledge, 1994), and David Bergman, ed., *Camp Grounds: Style and Homosexuality* (Amherst: University of Massachusetts Press, 1993).

70. Qtd. in Margaret Talbot, "Dressed to Thrill," *Lingua Franca* 1:4 (1991), 19.

71. Jonathan Dollimore, "Shakespeare, Cultural Materialism, Feminism, and Marxist Humanism," *New Literary History* 21 (1990), 489. I am also indebted to the papers and discussion at at "The Wilde Thing" conference, Princeton University, 6 April 1991.

72. See, e.g., Joan Nestle, ed., *The Persistent Desire: A Femme-Butch Reader* (Boston: Alyson, 1992) and Elizabeth Lapovsky Kennedy and Madeline D. Davis, *Boots of Leather, Slippers of Gold: The History of a Lesbian Community* (New York: Routledge, 1993).

73. Talbot, "Dressed to Thrill," 19.

74. For Gallop as controversial, see her *Feminist Accused of Sexual Harrassment* (Durham, N.C.: Duke University Press, 1997).

75. Frith, "Playing with Shawls," 228–29.

76. GMT, "Rem.," A140; see EFSP, *Renaissance*, 1: 63, on dress as "a serious and complex business."

77. EFSP, "Salon of 1876," 495; the painting is Laurens's "The Ghost of Marianne appearing to Herod the Great," and the female figure is "swathed and bound in graveclothes."

78. EFSP, "Nicolas Poussin," 476.

79. See ch. 7 below, and Wallace K. Ferguson, *The Renaissance in Historical Thought* (Cambridge, Mass.: Harvard University Press, 1948); Clio 17 (1988), special issue on the Renaissance in Victorian culture, esp. John R. Reed, "The Victorian Renaissance Self." On Oxford, male homoeroticism, and aesthetic discourse, see Dellamora, *Masculine Desire*, esp. ch. 8, and *Apocalyptic Overtures: Sexual Politics and the Sense of an Ending* (New Brunswick, N.J.: Rutgers University Press, 1994), ch. 2; Alan Sinfield, *The Wilde Century: Effeminacy, Oscar Wilde, and the Queer Moment* (New York: Routledge, 1994), 89, 132–34; see also Dowling, *Hellenism*; but cf. Joseph Bristow, *Effeminate England: Homoerotic Writing after 1885* (New York: Columbia University Press, 1995), 20.

80. John Addington Symonds, "A Problem in Greek Ethics" (1901) and "A Problem in Modern Ethics" (1896) in *Sexual Heretics: Male Homosexuality in English Literature from 1850–1900*, ed. Brian Reade (London: Routledge, 1970) and *The Renaissance in Italy*, 4 vols. (1875–86; reprinted in 2 vols., New York: Modern Library, 1935); Walter Pater, *Studies in the History of the Renaissance* (1873; Chicago: Academy Chicago, 1977. For Symonds, see also Phyllis Grosskurth, *John Addington*

Symonds, *A Biography* (London: Longmans, 1964); Bristow, *Effeminate England*, ch. 4; and Peter Allan Dale, "Beyond Humanism: J. A. Symonds and the Replotting of the Renaissance," *Clio* 17 (1988): 109–137. For Pater, see also Dellamora, *Masculine Desire*, chs. 5 and 9, esp. 134–35, and *Apocalyptic Overtures*, ch. 3; and Levey, *Case of Walter Pater*. On both Symonds and Pater, see Adams, *Dandies*, ch. 5. For Wilde, see Richard Ellman, *Oscar Wilde* (New York: Knopf, 1988), ch. 2 and 81, 156–57, 165–66; see also Philip E. Smith II and Michael S. Helfand, eds., *Oscar Wilde's Oxford Notebooks: A Portrait of Mind in the Making* (Oxford: Oxford University Press, 1988).

81. Dellamora, *Masculine Desire*, 147–66.

82. I am indebted to two unpublished and untitled essays on ekphrasis by Jean Borger.

83. W. J. T. Mitchell's crucial "Ekphrasis and the Other," *South Atlantic Quarterly* 91 (1992): 695–719; see also Gidal, "Passions Stamped."

84. EFSP, *Renaissance*, 1: 195–96, 198 (but cf. 1: 20); see also EFSP, "Nicolas Poussin," 476, on the fountain and the *Diane*. The work ESFP calls the *Fons Nyphium* is also known as the Fontaine des Nymphes or Fontaine des Innocents; for photographs and drawings, see Pierre du Colombier, *Jean Goujon* (Paris: Editions Albin Michel, 1949), plates 5– 9 and 78; Paul Vitry, *Jean Goujon* (Paris: Librairie Renouard, 1911), 53, 57, 65, 73; and Henry Jouin, *Jean Goujon* (Paris: Librairie de l'Art, n.d. [1904]), 49–57. See also Chastel, *French Art: The Renaissance*, 200–218.

85. EFSP, *Renaissance*, 1: 201–4; for Diane de Poitiers, see also 1: 105–6, and 119 on violence to her dead body. For the *Diane*, see du Colombier, *Goujon*, plate 43; Vitry, *Goujon*, 85; Jouin, *Goujon*, 71–73, and Chastel, *French Art: The Renaissance*, 175. See also EFSP, "Germain Pilon," 75; the *Diane* is also invoked in comparison to a fictional woman in EFSD, *French Engravers*, 124. Ironically, the *Diane*'s attribution has been questioned and some scholars suggest that Pilon— whom EFSP's texts excoriate—had a hand in its design; see Chastel, *French Art: The Renaissance*, 205, 208.

86. EFSP, *Renaissance*, 2: 240–43; see also 2: 246–47 for the faïence as the product of a "peculiar" and "individual" taste, "slender and fragile force," "thin and sinewy energy," "wonderful acuteness of nerve," which give it "elaborate," "dainty precision" with undertones of "sobriety"; "it perished in perfection." See also EFSP, "Nicolas Poussin," 476 on the faïence's triumphant liminality.

87. Peter Wollen, "The Same Old Solotaire" [review of Oscar Wilde and Aubrey Beardsley, *'Salome' and 'Under the Hill'* and Chris Snodgrass, *Aubrey Beardsley: Dandy of the Grotesque*], *London Review of Books*, 4 July 1996, 22; see also Marjorie Garber, *Vested Interests: Cross-Dressing and Cultural Anxiety* (New York: Routledge, 1992); Corinne Blackmer and Patricia Juliana Smith, "Introduction," to Blackmer and Smith, eds., *En Travesti: Women, Gender Subversion, and Opera* (New York: Columbia University Press, 1995); and Rosenman, "Spectacular Women," 46–47.

88. PP 118, fol. 28ff. (EFSP to ES, 14 Dec. 1875); PP 118, fol. 68ff. (EFSP to ES, 24 Jan. 1882); PP 118, fol. 36ff. (EFSP to ES, 22 Jan. 1880); emphasis added. See also AM 43906, fol. 89ff. (EFSP to CWD, 11 June 1885). "I devoutly hope to never see the other place again." "The other place" can be an undergraduate circumlocution by which Oxonians refer to Cambridge and vice versa; it can also be a polite phrase for hell.

89. Walburga Paget, *Embassies of Other Days*, 2 vols. (London: Hutchinson, 1923), 2: 340, 377.

90. EFSP, *Renaissance*, 1: 15, 2: 119–21; see also 2: 147, 160.

91. CWD, "Mem.," 22–23, allegedly quoting a "notebook" EFSP kept in Oxford.

92. One can dominate that which one can't get over, over, pass through, or clear; EFSP to Eugene Muntz, qtd. in CWD, "Mem.," 55; see also AM 43907, fol. 79f. (George Eliot to EFSP, 29 May 1879).

93. Kucich, *Power of Lies*, 4, 26, 33–34; for a useful comparison, see Robert Nye, *Masculinity and Male Codes of Honor in Modern France* (New York: Oxford University Press, 1993).

94. Cora Kaplan, " 'Like a Housemaid's Fancies': The Representation of Working-Class Women in Nineteenth-Century Writing," in *Grafts: Feminist Cultural Criticism*, ed. Susan Sheridan

(London: Verso, 1989), 57; see also Woolf, "Two Women," in *Essays*, ed. McNeillie, 4: 61–66.

95. On aristocratic women, see Leonore Davidoff, *The Best Circles: Society, Etiquette and the Season* (London: Croom Helm, 1973); Jalland, *Women, Marriage, and Politics*, esp. chs. 4, 7, and 8; Frances Brooke, countess of Warwick, *Life's Ebb and Flow* (London: Hutchinson, 1929); and Angela Lambert, *Unquiet Souls: A Social History of the Illustrious, Irreverent, Intimate Group of British Aristocrats Known as "The Souls"* (New York: Harper and Row, 1984). The cultural and political place of the aristocratic in British cultural has been much debated; see Martin J. Wiener, *English Culture and the Decline of the Industrial Spirit, 1850–1980* (Cambridge: Cambridge University Press, 1981); Perry Anderson, *English Questions* (London: Verso, 1992); Tom Nairn, *The Enchanted Glass: Britain and its Monarchy* (London: Century Hutchinson, 1988); and David Cannadine, *The Decline and Fall of the British Aristocracy* (New Haven: Yale University Press, 1990) and *Aspects of Aristocracy: Grandeur and Decline in Modern Britain* (New Haven: Yale University Press, 1994).

96. Sinfield, *Wilde Century*, 55, 70–72, 74.

97. See also Sarah Street, *British National Cinema* (New York: Routledge, 1997), 41, and Sue Harper, *Picturing the Past: the Rise and Fall of the British Costume Film* (London: British Film Institute, 1994), 26–27.

98. Qtd. in Sinfield, *Literature, Politics, and Culture*, 25; see also EFSP, *Renaissance*, 1: 191.

99. EFSP, *Renaissance*, 1: 190–91; 2: 19–21; 2: 286; 1:168; see also 2 : 20–21and 2: 293–95; a drawing of the Cousin figure is the frontispiece to EFSP's volume.

100. EFSP, *Renaissance*, 1: 73; Kaplan, "Like a Housemaid's Fancy," esp. 58; Margaret Maynard, " 'A Dream of Fair Women': Revival Dress and the Formation of Late-Victorian Images of Femininity," *Art History* 12 (1989): 322–24. Those recalling EFSP in Oxford could be influenced by these later discourses. See also Laurel Bradley, "From Eden to Empire: John Everett Millais's *Cherry Ripe*," *Victorian Studies* 34 (1991): 179–203, and "Evocations of the Eighteenth Century in Victorian Painting," Ph.D. dissertation, New York University, 1986.

101. For residual, see Williams, "Base and Superstructure."

102. Sinfield, *Wilde Century*; Bristow, *Effeminate England*; see also Adams, *Dandies*; on class cross-dressing, see Garber, *Vested Interests*.

103. Sinfield, *Wilde Century*, 71–78; Babuscio, "Camp," qtd. ibid., 156.

104. Sinfield, *Wilde Century*, 74–75, 156; see also Andrew Ross, *No Respect: Intellectuals and Popular Culture* (New York: Routlege, 1989), 144–47, and Bristow, *Effeminate England*, 103.

105. Sinfield, *Wilde Century*, 74; Bristow, *Effeminate England*, 103, on camp deployments of a depoliticized aristocracy; Sinfield and Dellamora suggest that in some texts—e.g., Wilde's *Picture of Dorian Grey*—men's performativity is purchased or poached as if in a zero-sum relationship to women's; Dellamora in dialogue with Ed Cohen, "Wilde Thing" conference; Sinfield, *Wilde Century*, 74. See Showalter, *Sexual Anarchy*, 170, 173, 176–77, on the troubled relations between male homosexual aesthetes and "New Women."

106. PP 118, fol. 72f. (EFSP to ES, 15 Feb. 1882); on open secrets, see Eve Kosofsky Sedgwick, *The Epistomology of the Closet* (Berkeley: University of California Press, 1992).

107. Cf. Bourget, "Sensations d'Oxford," 593–97; see also Virginia Woolf, *Three Guineas* (New York: Harcourt Brace Jovanovich, 1938), 18–21; Jane Marcus, "No More Horses: Virginia Woolf on Art and Propaganda," *Women's Studies* 4 (1977): 264–90; Carter, *Ancient Cultures of Conceit*, and especially Alan Bennett, *Writing Home* (London: Faber and Faber, 1994), 19–20.

108. EFSP, "Jehan Goujon," 24; see also EFSP, *Renaissance*, 2: 180–81.

109. EFSD, *Art in the Modern State*, 1–2.

110. Eisler, "Six Lives," 174, 164.

111. EFSD, *Art in the Modern State*, 2–6, 144–45.

112. EFSP, *Renaissance*, 1: 302.

113. EFSD, *French Architects*, 13, 21.

114. CWD, "Mem.," 96, 97, 99.

115. CWD, "Mem.," 99.

116. PP 118, fol. 68f. (EFSP to ES, 24 Jan. 1882); for "intense enjoyment . . ." see fol. 64ff. (EFSP to ES, 29 Sept. 1881); see also fol. 68f. (EFSP to ES, 24 Jan. 1882); PP 118, fol. 28ff. (EFSP to ES, 14 Dec. 1875); see also EFSD, "Vision of Learning," in Shrine of Death, 57–76; on the South, see Pemble, Mediterranean Passion, 12–13, 53–54, and Paul Fussell, Abroad: British Literary Travelling Between the Wars (Oxford: Oxford University Press, 1981).

117. EFSP, Renaissance, 2: 105–6.

118. EFSP, Renaissance, 2: 180–81; 1: 198, 201–2; EFSP, "Jehan Goujon," 24; see also EFSD, French Architects, 127.

119. Shari Benstock, Women of the Left Bank: Paris, 1900–1940 (Austin: University of Texas Press, 1986).

120. Frith, "Playing with Shawls," 226; PP 140, fol. 40 (EFSP to ? [CWD], n.d. [Feb./Mar. 1881] very mutilated); see also Gill Frith, "Embodying the Nation: Gender and Performance in Women's Fiction," New Formations 27 (1995–96): 98–113; Moers, Literary Women, 173–210; Orr, "Corinne Complex," 89–92; Davidoff and Hall, Family Fortunes, 161; Schor, Bad Objects, 162; and Leighton, Victorian Women Poets, 30–34. See EFSP, Renaissance, 1: 34, 73, on the prestige of the foreign.

121. Schor, Bad Objects, 162; Schor quotes "land of the living dead" from Margaret Waller, The Male Malady.

122. Stella Cottrell, "The Devil on Two Sticks: Francophobia in 1803," in Patriotism: The Making and Unmaking of British National Identity, ed. Raphael Samuel, vol. 1: History and Politics (London: Routledge, 1989), 259–74; Linda Colley, Britons: Forging the Nation 1707–1837 (New Haven, Conn.: Yale University Press, 1992), 24–25, 33–35, 88, 90–91, 251–52; and Margaret Hunt, "Racism, Imperialism, and the Traveler's Gaze in Eighteenth-Century England," Journal of British Studies 32 (1993): 333–57.

123. Cottrell, "Devil on Two Sticks," 260, 265–68.

124. Eliot qtd. in Levey, Case of Walter Pater, 77; see also Kijinski, "Morley's 'English Men of Letters,' " 209, 214, 219, 221; and Meisel, Realisations, 17–72.

125. Cottrell, "Devil on Two Sticks," 265–66; Roy Gridley, The Brownings and France: A Chronicle with Commentary (London: Athlone Press, 1982).

126. See Levey, Case of Walter Pater, 77.

127. See Lee, Woolf, 96.

128. Paul Blount, George Sand and the Victorian World (Athens, Georgia: University of Georgia Press, 1979); Walkowitz, Prostitution and Victorian Society, 123.

129. See, e.g., Henry James, The Ambassadors, ed. R. W. Stallman (New York: Signet/NAL, 1960).

130. EFSP, "Nicolas Poussin," 476–77; EFSP, Renaissance, 1:256, 258–59, 290; see also 1: 36, 61, and 2:158; cf. Orr, "Corinne Complex," 96.

131. EFSP was in the avant-garde as a fencing woman; see Lee,Woolf, 95; fencing also linked her to CWD; Jenkins, Dilke, 116–17. For French plays, see Roger Lancelyn Green, ed., The Diaries of Lewis Carroll, 2 vols. (London: Cassell, 1954), 1:77; Askwith, Lady Dilke, 26; and Taine, Vie et Correspondance, 3: 146–47.

132. Paget, Embassies, 2: 340, 377, describing EFSP in Rome in 1881; see also Sinfield, Wilde Century, 76–77.

133. Stephen Gwynn, Saints and Scholars (London: Thornton Butterworth, 1929), 81; see also Askwith, Lady Dilke, 115.

134. See DFM, 18 Nov. 1892, qtg. Paris correspondent for Truth on her "eighteenth-century air and physiognomy."

135. MP, review of John de Soyres, ed., The Provincial Letters of Pascal, The Academy 452 (1 Jan.

1881): 1; see also Althaus, "Recollections of Mark Pattison," 37; Margaret Jeune (diary, 11 June 1861), qtd. in Blodgett, Centuries, 115; Eliot, "Woman in France," 3, 5; see also Eliot, "Silly Novels," 186–220; Gillian Beer, George Eliot (Bloomington: Indiana University Press, 1986), 32–40; and Jennifer Uglow, George Eliot (New York: Pantheon, 1987), 72–73, 75.

136. Eliot, "Woman in France, 7, 8–9.

137. On the précieuses, see Dorothy A. L. Backer, Precious Women: A Feminist Phenomenon in the Age of Louis XIV (New York: Basic Books,1974); Carolyn Lougee, Le Paradis des Femmes: Women, Salons, and Social Stratification in Seventeenth-Century France (Princeton: Princeton University Press, 1976), 7; Bonnie Anderson and Judith Zinsser, A History of Their Own: Women in Europe from Prehistory to the Present, 2 vols. (New York: Harper and Row, 1988), esp. 2: 103–5; Eliot, "Woman in France," 44–45.

138. Eliot, "Woman in France," 45.

139. Cf. Juliet Dusinberre, Virginia Woolf's Renaissance: Woman Reader or Common Reader? (Iowa City: University of Iowa Press, 1997), 1–39.

140. Qtd. by Jackson, Ingram Bywater, 59; Le Figaro was noted for gossip, scandal, and racy prose.

141. Pemble, Mediterranean Passion, 40, 43–46.

142. "Art-Work of Lady Dilke," 439–40, 442–43. The writer deplores EFSD's failure to restrict her energies because women of genius should confine themselves; "the less extended the area in which ['that small band of Englishwomen who . . . have proved that feminine intellect, in its highest development, is on a par with that of man'] have worked, the greater the excellence of their achievement" (439). See also Eliot, "Woman in France," 6: "Madame de Sévigné remains the single instance of a woman who is supreme in a class of literature which has engaged the ambition of men."

143. On Bodley, see P. H. Bodley, " 'For Remembrance'," ts., MS. Eng. misc. d. 357; J. R. Shane Leslie, Memoir of J. E. C. Bodley (London: Jonathan Cape, 1930); Ellman, Wilde, 38–39, 58–59, 84, 177–78; and ch. 6 below.

144. Bodley, review of EFSD, BSL, 679–80.

145. Bodley, review of EFSD, BSL, 679–80; see also CWD, "Mem.," 120.

146. EFSD, Art in the Modern State, 144–45; see also EFSD, French Painters, ch. 3.

147. Bodley, review of EFSD, BSL, 680.

148. Eliot, "Woman in France," 5.

149. Philippa Pullar, Frank Harris (London: Hamilton, 1975), 109.

150. EFSD, French Architects, 17.

151. Malcolm Elwin, Victorian Wallflowers: A Panoramic Survey of the Popular Literary Periodicals (1934; reprint ed., Port Washington, N.Y.: Kennikat Press, 1966), 291, 311; and Cruse, Victorians and Their Reading, esp. 327–30.

152. Nancy Mitford, The Blessing (New York: Random House, 1951), 11–13; Mitford, of course, needed entertain no doubts about her own aristocratic lineage.

153. Norman MacKenzie and Jeanne MacKenzie, eds., The Diary of Beatrice Webb (London: Virago, 1982) 1: 294.

154. Eisler, "Six Lives" and Askwith, Lady Dilke, seem unsettled by EFSD's class-enactments.

155. Vicinus, Independent Women, 263–64; see also Lisa Tickner, The Spectacle of Women (Chicago: University of Chicago Press, 1988).

156. Kuhn, Family Secrets, 1.

157. Ann Snitow, "A Gender Diary," in Conflicts in Feminism, ed. Marianne Hirsch and Evelyn Fox Keller (New York: Routledge, 1990); see also Denise Riley, Am I That Name?: Feminism and the Category of "Women" in History (Minneapolis: University of Minnesota Press, 1988).

158. For the main currents within Victorian feminism, see Phillippa Levine, Feminist Lives in Victorian England: Private Roles and Public Commitment (Oxford: Basil Blackwell, 1990) and Victorian

Feminism, 1850–1900 (London: Hutchinson, 1987); Barbara Caine, *Victorian Feminists* (Oxford: Oxford University Press, 1992); and Jane Rendall, ed., *Equal or Different: Women's Politics 1800–1914* (Oxford: Basil Blackwell, 1987); on debates about sexual difference and morality, see Susan Kingsley Kent, *Sex and Suffrage in Britain, 1860–1914* (Princeton: Princeton University Press, 1987), and Lucy Bland, *Banishing the Beast: English Feminism and Sexual Morality 1885–1914* (London: Penguin, 1995).

159. See, e.g., PP 118, fol. 42f. (EFSP to ES, 23 Aug. 1880).

160. On the long-running larger issue, see also Susan Gubar, "Feminist Misogyny: Mary Wollstonecraft and the Paradox of 'It Takes One to Know One'," *Feminist Studies* 20 (1994): 453–73.

161. EFSD, *French Architects*, 45.

162. EFSP, *Renaissance*, 1: 235–37.

163. EFSP, "Germain Pilon," 75; see also EFSP, *Renaissance*, 1: 89, and 1: 250–51. For Pilon, see Chastel, *French Art: The Renaissance*, 200–218.

164. EFSD, *French Painters*, 53–57; Diderot qtd. on 56; on Pompadour, see also EFSD, *French Engravers*, 2, 95, 137–38 and passim.

165. EFSP, *Renaissance*, 2:69 (referring to Antoine Vérard, *La Bible des Poètes* [1493]).

166. EFSD, *French Engravers*, 121; see also EFSP, review of Michelet and Esquirol.

167. ESFD, "Of Love and Sorrow," 165–66; see also EFSD, *French Architects*, 63–64.

168. ESFD, "Of Love and Sorrow," 165–66.

169. Phyllis Grosskurth, *The Woeful Victorian: A Biography of John Addington Symonds* (New York: Holt Rinehart, and Winston, 1964), 84; see also Walkowitz, *City of Dreadful Delight*, 87–93.

170. Qtd. in Macleod, *Art and the Victorian Middle Class*, 282; see also Mavor, *Pleasures Taken*, ch. 2.

171. For Smith Paterson and the League, see Lewenhak, *Women and Trade Unions*, 56–57; Harold Goldman, *Emma Paterson: She Led Women into a Man's World* (London: Lawrence and Wishart, 1974); Sarah Boston, *Women Workers and the Trade Union Movement* (London: Davis-Poynter, 1980); Norbert Soldon, *Women in British Trade Unions, 1874–1976* (Dublin: Gill and Macmillan, 1978); Rosemary Feurer, "The Meaning of Sisterhood: The British Women's Movement and Protective Legislation, 1870–1900," *Victorian Studies* 31 (Winter 1988): 233–60; Gladys Boone, *The Women's Trade Union Leagues in Great Britain and the United States* (1942; New York: AMS Press, 1968); Robin Miller Jacoby, "Feminism and Class Consciousness in the British and American Women's Trade Union Leagues," in *Liberating Women's History*, ed. Berenice Carroll (Urbana: University of Illinois Press, 1976), 137–61; Teresa Olcott, "Dead Centre: The Women's Trade Union Movement in London, 1874–1914," *London Journal* 2 (1976): 33–50; Mary Drake McFeely, *Lady Inspectors: The Campaign for a Better Workplace, 1893–1921* (Oxford: Basil Blackwell, 1988); Anne Phillips, *Divided Loyalties: Dilemmas of Sex and Class* (London: Virago, 1987), 83, 88, 96–98; Barbara Drake, *Women in Trade Unions* (1920; London: Virago, 1984); Barbara Hutchins, *Women in Modern Industry* (London: London: G. Bell and Sons, 1915); Mary Agnes Hamilton, *Mary Macarthur, A Biographical Sketch* (London: Leonard Parsons, 1925), and Margaret Bondfield, *A Life's Work* (London: Hutchinson, 1951). There are entries on the major figures in the WTUL in Banks, *Biographical Dictionary*, and Joyce Bellamy and John Saville, eds., *The Dictionary of Labour Biography* (London: Macmillan, 1974–1979); Paterson is also discussed in Dale Spender, *Women of Ideas (and What Men Have Done to Them)* (London: Ark/Routledge Kegan Paul, 1982), 456–62. See also Paterson's obituary and letters following, in *Women's Union Journal*, vol. 11, no. 131 (Dec. 1886), 111–18.

172. EFSD, "Benefit Societies."

173. EFSD, "Benefit Societies," 852–53. See also EFSD, "Trades-Unions for Women," esp. 227; Levine, *Victorian Feminism*, 112–13; and A. B.[Annie] Marland-Brodie, "The Late Lady Dilke. A Fine Tribute," *Cotton Factory Times*, 4 November 1904.

174. See also EFSD, "Trades-Unionism for Women."

175. EFSD, "Benefit Societies," 519; GMT, "Rem.," A141.

176. GMT, "Rem.," A141; cf. CWD, "Mem.," 115, quotes EFSD using the same phrase in an 1898 speech at Bristol; see also *Women's Union Journal*, Dec. 1886, 111–18; "Like another woman of strong will and original character, who was adored by those she benefited [footnote in original: Sister Dora], she found it easier to do everything herself. . . ."

177. Bronte, *Villette*, 307.

178. Bronte, *Villette*, 307–8; cf. Bronte, *Jane Eyre*, 358; these female doublings recalls the doubled figure of Emily Weedon Strong and Kitty Davis in EFSD's other political origin story.

179. Emma Smith Paterson, *Labour News*, 1874, qtd. in WPPL, first *Annual Report* (1875).

180. *Women's Union Journal*, 16 September 1889; account of speech given in Dundee on 3 September; note that EFSD claims kinship with working-class women on their (purported) feelings for her.

181. For a middle-class masquerade, see Nord, *Apprenticeship*, 165–70.

182. *Women's Trade Union Journal*, vol. 11 (1886).

183. EFSD, "Trades Unionism for Women," 52.

184. "Lady Dilke on Trades Unionism," *Women's Union Journal*, 15 January 1890.

185. EFSD, "Trades Unionism for Women," 52–53; see also CWD, "Mem.," 112–13.

186. Marland-Brodie, "Late Lady Dilke."

187. Hamilton, *Mary Macarthur*, 43.

188. See Janet Courtney, *The Women of My Time* (London: Lovat Dickson, 1934), 142–50; GMT, "Rem.," A104; Marland-Brodie, "Late Lady Dilke."

189. Mackenzie and Mackenzie, eds., *Diary of Beatrice Webb*, 1: 294; see also GMT, "Rem.," A230; for Boileau, see AM 43918, fol. 94f. (Margarete Boileau to CWD, 27 May 1905).

190. GMT, "Rem.," A192, 150, 82. For Abraham (later Mrs. H. J. Tennant), see McFeely, *Lady Inspectors*, passim, and Courtney, *Women of My Time*, 127–28. For Smith, see GMT, *Constance Smith, A Short Memoir* (London: Duckworth, 1931), 9–11, 24–25, and below. See also Banks, *Biographical Dictionary*, and Bellamy and Saville, *Dictionary of Labour Biography*, both s.v. "Tuckwell, Gertrude M."

191. GMT, "Rem.," A90; GMT need not disown her own family; after EFSD's death, Rosa and William lived with CWD; see also AM 49611, fol. 17f. (EFSD to Rosa Tuckwell, 2 Mar. 1886).

192. GMT, "Rem.," A243, A84–85.

193. See, e.g., Lewis, *Women and Social Action*, 9–24, 302–11, for an overview of these issues; see also Ellen Ross, *Love and Toil: Motherhood in Outcast London, 1870–1918* (New York: Oxford University Press, 1993), 15–21; and Susan Pederson, *Family, Dependence, and the Origins of the Welfare State: Britain and France, 1914–1945* (New York: Cambridge University Press, 1993).

194. EFSD's colleagues in social reform were also mostly middle-class, including Alice Westlake, an early schoolboard member; Mary Jeune, who wrote about poor children; and Mary Arnold-Forster, daughter of an Oxford don married to a Tory M.P; see GMT, "Rem.," A84, A72, 73, 79; Hollis, *Ladies Elect*; Mary Jeune, "Holidays for Poor Children," *The New Review* 2, no. 12 (May 1890), 455–465; and AM 43941, fol. 319 for Arnold-Forster. Edith Simcox and Margaret Bondfield are more complex; see Simcox, "Autobiography of a Shirt Maker," ms. in Bodleian Library, Oxford, Eng. misc. d. 494, and K. Mackenzie, *Simcox and Eliot*; Lewenhak, *Women and Trade Unions*, 70–72, 77; Boston, *Women Workers*, 331; Bondfield, *A Life's Work*; see also Marland-Brodie, "Late Lady Dilke."

195. Hamilton, *Mary Macarthur*, 27.

196. See Lewenhak, *Women and Trade Unions*, 74–75; McFeely, *Lady Inspectors*, 14–15, 24; and Adelaide Anderson, *Women in the Factory: An Administrative Adventure, 1893–1921* (London: John Murray, 1922).

197. McFeely, *Lady Inspectors*, 14–15, 23–27; Deborah Thom, "The Bundle of Sticks: Women,

Trade Unionists, and Collective Organization before 1918," in *Unequal Opportunities: Women's Employment in England 1800–1918*, ed. Angela V. John (Oxford: Basil Blackwell, 1986), 274–75; EFSD, "Seamy Side," esp. 421.

198. 1894 speech by EFSD, qtd. in Drake, *Women in Trade Unions*, 37.

199. EFSD, "Trade Unions for Women," 238–39.

200. EFSD speech qtd. in CWD, "Mem.," 112.

201. For "evils far deadlier," see EFSD, "Trades Unionism for Women," 47–48; for "the hearth," see EFSD, "Trades-Unions for Women," 238, and Lewenhak, *Women and Trade Unions*, 91.

202. See CWD, "Mem.," 115–16.

203. See also Walkowitz, *City of Dreadful Delight*, 268 n. 101.

204. EFSD, "Appeal for Shoreditch"; see also the WTUL's response to W. T. Stead's "The Maiden Tribute to a Modern Babylon," "The 'Pall Mall Gazette' Revelations," *Women's Union Journal*, Aug. 1885: ". . . the general prevalence of vice is due, not so much to vicious tendencies, as to poverty and ignorance. . . . these can only be removed by associated effort, by combination among the workers. . . ." The League even surmises, against Stead's implication of older working-class women as procuresses, that trade union membership would make older women more responsible and less desperate.

205. EFSD, "Appeal for Shoreditch," 16–17.

206. EFSD, "Great Missionary Success," 679; cf. Gauri Viswanathan, "Coping with Colonial India: The Christian Convert's Rights of Passage in Colonial India," in *After Colonialism: Imperial Histories and Postcolonial Displacements*, ed. Gyan Prakash (Princeton: Princeton University Press, 1995), 183–210.

207. See also A. Burton, *Burdens of History*, and her, "A 'Pilgrim Reformer' at the Heart of the Empire: Behrami Malabari in Late-Victorian London," *Gender and History* 8 (1996): 175–96.

208. CWD, "Mem.," 31, but cf. 93–95; for a hilarious castigation of portraits of Bernhardt, see EFSP, "Salon of 1876 (Third Notice)," 517. On caricature and gender, see Auerbach, *Woman and the Demon*, 196–97.

209. GMT, "Rem.," A70.

210. EFSP, "Jehan Goujon," 24.

211. Green, ed., *Diaries of Lewis Carroll*, 1: 77; also quoted in Askwith, *Lady Dilke*, 26.

CHAPTER SIX

1. Oscar Wilde, "An Ideal Husband," in Wilde, *Dorian Grey and Other Writings*, 318.

2. See Walkowitz, *City of Dreadful Delight* and *Prostitution*; see also Walkowitz, Myra Jehlen, and Belle Chevigny, "Patrolling the Borders: Feminist Historiography and the New Historicism," *Radical History Review* 43 (1989), 30; Jeffrey Weeks, *Sex, Politics, and Society: The Regulation of Sexuality since 1800* (London: Longman, 1981), 86–89, and *Coming Out: Homosexual Politics in Britain from the Nineteenth Century to the Present* (London: Quartet Books, 1977), 19, 21; Frank Mort, *Dangerous Sexualities: Medico-Moral Politics in England Since 1830* (New York: Routledge Kegan Paul, 1987); Hartman, *Victorian Murderesses*; Gail Savage, " 'The Wilful Communication of a Loathsome Disease': Marital Conflict and Venereal Disease in Victorian England," *Victorian Studies* 34 (1990): 35–54, and "The Divorce Court and the Queen's/King's Proctor: Legal Patriarchy and the Sanctity of Marriage in England, 1861–1937," *Historical Papers/Communications historiques* 1989: 210–227; Martha Vicinus, "Lesbian Perversity and Victorian Marriage: The 1864 Codrington Divorce Case," *Journal of British Studies* 36 (1997): 70–98. Both kinds of trials were sites of display for the secrets of class; see Angus McLaren, *A Prescription for Murder: The Victorian Serial Killings of Dr. Thomas Neill Cream* (Chicago: University of Chicago Press, 1993) and Julie English Early, "Technology, Modernity, and 'the Little Man': Crippen's Capture by Wireless," *Victorian Studies* 39 (1996): 309–37.

3. Gertrude Campbell sued for judicial separation on the grounds that her husband had infected her with venereal disease; see Savage, " 'Wilful Communication'," 36; G. H. Fleming, *Victorian "Sex Goddess": Lady Colin Campbell* (Oxford: Oxford University Press, 1990); John Juxon, *Lewis and Lewis* (London: Collins, 1983), ch. 19; and H. Montgomery Hyde, *A Tangled Web: Sex Scandals in British Politics and Societ* (London: Constable, 1986), ch. 4. On the "Maiden Tribute," see Deborah Gorham, "The 'Maiden Tribute' Re-examined: Child Prostitution and the Idea of Childhood in Late-Victorian England," *Victorian Studies* 21 (Spring 1978): 353–79; Walkowitz, *Prostitution*, epilogue; and *City of Dreadful Delight*, chs. 3 and 4. The Cleveland Street scandal (1889–90) involved male homosexuality and prostitution; see Weeks, *Coming Out*, 19, 21; and H. Montgomery Hyde, *The Cleveland Street Scandal* (New York: Coward, McCann, and Geoghegan, 1976). See also Ed Cohen, *Talk on the Wilde Side: Towards a Geneaology of a Discourse on Male Sexualities* (New York: Routledge, 1993). On melodrama, see Walkowitz, Jehlen, and Chevigny, "Patrolling the Borders," 30, and Brooks, *Reading for the Plot*.

4. Walkowitz, Jehlen, and Chevigny, "Patrolling," 30; see also Walkowitz, *City of Dreadful Delight*, 7.

5. Jenkins, *Dilke and Victorian Scandal*; Askwith, *Lady Dilke*. See also Marysa deMoor, "An Honourable Gentleman Revisted: Emilia Strong Pattison's Noted Entry into the World of Sir Charles Wentworth Dilke and the *Athenaeum*," *Women's Writing* 2 (1995): 201–19.

6. J. Enoch Powell, *Joseph Chamberlain* (London: Thames and Hudson, 1977); Robert Rhodes James, *Rosebery: A Biography of Archibald Philip, Fifth Earl of Rosebery* (London: Weidenfeld and Nicolson, 1963), 352–56 (cf. S.[tephen] W. Roskill,"Introduction." *Catalogue* to the Roskill-Enthoven-Dilke Papers [REND], Cambridge: Churchill College Archives Centre, 1974); Nicholls, *Lost Prime Minister*, xvii, citing Kenneth Baker in the *Daily Express*, 2 June 1994.

7. Eric J. Watson, "George Joseph Smith, 1915" (1922), reprinted in *Famous Trials*, selected by John Mortimer, original ed. Harry Hodge and James H. Hodge (Harmondsworth: Penguin, 1984), 262.

8. REND 13; Roskill, "Foreword," iii–viii.

9. Lowndes, ed., *Diaries and Letters*, 116; Belloc Lowndes was a friend of VMC.

10. Malot, *Vices Français*; see also Askwith, *Lady Dilke*, 172–74, and PP 118, fol. 230 (EFSD to ES, 15 June 1887). The only known copy of *Josey* belongs to Roy Jenkins; for the photograph of VMC, see Jenkins, *Dilke*, 224.

11. PP 118, fol. 230 (EFSD to ES, 15 June 1887).

12. Betty Askwith, *A Tangled Web* (London: Victor Gollancz, 1960); Granada Television, *The Dilke Case* (broadcast 1960; see Jenkins, *Victorian Scandal*, 6); and Michael Dyne-Bradley, *The Right Honourable Gentleman* (London: Samuel French, 1966). Copyrighted as *An Element of Truth* in 1962, the play was first performed, as *The Right Honourable Gentleman*, on 28 May 1964 at Her Majesty's Theatre, London, with Anthony Quayle, Mary Law, and Anna Massey; reviews and clippings in REND 13/1. A second dramatization was included in a Granada television series on "Victorian Scandals" circa 1988; thanks to Angela V. John and Peter Martland. Cf. McLaren, *Prescription*, 163 fn. 60.

13. Charles Kingston, *Society Sensations* (New York: E. P. Dutton, 1922), 112–26; see also Juxon, *Lewis and Lewis* , 203–21; Hyde, *Tangled Web*, 111–26.

14. See Mort and Nead, "Sexuality, Modernity," 119–21, and William A. Cohen, *Sex Scandal: The Private Parts of Victorian Fiction* (Durham, N.C.: Duke University Press, 1996), 11–12.

15. On plotting, see also Halberstam, *Skin Shows*, 119–20.

16. Thanks to Gail Savage for confirming the absence of official transcripts of divorce cases. The major competing published accounts are pamphlets: F. W. J. Henning, *Crawford v. Crawford (The Queen's Proctor Intervening). Evidence Taken on the Hearing, with Notes* (London, 1886) and *The Crawford Divorce Case (Second Edition), Containing Important Facts Disclosed Since the Trial* (London, 1886), and W. T. Stead, "Has Sir Charles Dilke Cleared his Character? An Examination of the Report of the

Alleged Commission" (London, 1891), and "Deliverance or Doom? or, The Choice of Sir Charles Dilke, containing The National Protest, The Judge's Summing-Up, and The Truth About the Alleged 'Persecution' " (London, 1892) incorporating material originally published in the *Pall Mall Gazette* in 1886. Henning's and Stead's "transcripts" of the court proceedings are not only incomplete but annotated and prefaced with strongly pro- or anti-Dilke statements. (Henning also published *Josey*, the English version of Malot's pro-Dilke *Vices Français*.) See also *A Complete History of the Crawford Divorce Case (Illustrated)*, published by G. Purkness (London, n.d.), which is highly condensed and omits the material from the first trial re-presented in the second; a copy is in REND 12/15. See also Stephen Roskill's correspondence with Francis Bywater, 24 June-21 July 1976, in REND 13/6. On the competition of published accounts, see also Lowndes, ed., *Diaries and Letters*, 114–15. For the larger history, see Lawrence Stone, *The Road to Divorce: England, 1530–1987* (Oxford: Oxford University Press, 1990) and Allan Horstman, *Victorian Divorce* (New York: St. Martin's Press, 1985).

17. My account draws on Jenkins, *Dilke*, chs. 11–16, and Askwith, *Lady Dilke*, chs. 13–17, supplemented by material listed in the previous note, and ms. material in REND and the British and Bodleian Libraries. See also Nicholls, *Lost Prime Minister*, ch. 11.

18. Jenkins, *Dilke*, 217; Askwith, *Lady Dilke*, 137; Henning, *Crawford v. Crawford*, 9; photograph of the letter in AM 49612B, fol. 37. See also Anthea Trodd, *Domestic Crime in the Victorian Novel* (New York: St. Martin's Press, 1989), 130–31, and Susan David Bernstein, *Confessional Subjects: Revelations of Gender and Power in Victorian Literature and Culture* (Chapel Hill: University of North Carolina Press, 1997).

19. Henning, *Crawford v. Crawford*, 9.

20. For the Smith family, see Roskill, "Introduction," v–viii, and REND 7/1. There were ten Smith children: William Henry (b. 1856); Margaret Mary [Maye] (b. 1857, m. Ashton Dilke; m. William Russell Cooke; d. 1914); Helen Mary (b. 1858, m. Robert H.C. Harrison); Olive Mary (b. 1860, m. Thomas W. Barron); Eustace (b. 1861, m. Ellen Gertrude Hawkes); Virginia Mary (b. 1862, m. Donald Crawford; div. 1886); Ida Mary (b. 1864, m. R. C. Priestly); Rosalind Mary [Linda] (b. 1866, m. Ernest Enthoven); Clarence Dalrymple (b. 1868, m. Cicely Forster); and Launcelot Eustace (b. 1869, m. ?). On overlapping social worlds, see also Francis Bywater, "Cardinal Manning and the Dilke Divorce Case," *Chesterton Review* 18 (1992): 539–53, 541. For Maye Dilke's feminism, see, e.g., Mrs. Ashton Dilke, *Women's Suffrage* (London: Swan Sonnenschein, 1885), and Sandra Stanley Holton, *Suffrage Days: Stories from the Women's Suffrage Movement* (New York: Routledge, 1996), 73–74, 81.

21. REND 13/1, 1–2; Marion Rawson was the daughter of VMC's sister Linda. See also REND 12/2, ts. copy of Maye Smith to Olive Smith, Jan. 1876.

22. Macleod, *Art and the Victorian Middle Class*, 291–93, 474–75, and plate 55 on 294, Leighton's "Mary 'Eustacia' Dalrymple Smith." See also Walter Crane, *An Artist's Reminiscences* (London: Methuen, 1907), 164, 166, and Timothy Wilcox, "The Aesthetic Expunged: The Career and Collection of T. Eustace Smith, MP," *Journal of the History of Collections* 5 (1993): 43–57. For EFSP on Leighton, see her "Sir Frederic Leighton,"and "Five Paintings by Leighton." See also AM 43902, fol. 174, 175f., and AM 43932, fol. 18.

23. See, e.g., PP 56, fol. 299f. (Sibella Crawford to EFSP, 28 Aug. 1866) and PP 133, fol. 2 (MP diary, 5 and 6 May 1880).

24. Green, *Love*, 127–28; PP 123, fol. 192ff. (MB to MP, 16 May 1882) and fol. 199 ff. (MP to MB, 19 May 1882). This letter, dictated to GMT, denounces EFSP's failure to perceive this marital identity of interests: " 'She' is in great force . . . there is no escape from her consuming egotism . . . about me or my concerns or doings she never enquires or knows. . . ." EFSP is thus a pernicious influence; "I should be afraid to ask Jeannie [Stirke] as the girl would be exposed to an influence which would not be wholesome for her."

25. Green, *Love*, 183; PP 125, fol. 98ff. (MB to MP, 8 July 1883).

26. Jenkins, *Dilke*, 209, 157, 211–12.

27. AM 43906, fol. 16ff. (EFSP and CWD correspondence, 29 Aug. 1884–7 Sept. 1885), esp. fol. 66ff. (EFSP to CWD, 30 April 1885) (she read the first drafted chapter of *Art in the Modern State* to Mountstuart Grant-Duff the previous day and the first two chapters are nearly complete); and fol. 44ff. (EFSP to CWD, 10 Mar. 1885), and fol. 53ff. (EFSP to CWD, 16 April 1885): Julia Mount-Duff "cried over The Physician's Wife" and Mountstuart was "*astonish*[ed] at the suffering these stories bring before him" (emphasis EFSP's). CWD was reading the stories by March 1885, and setting them above EFSP's *Claude Lorrain*, "just as [George Eliot's] Scenes of Clerical Life were greater than Daniel Deronda or Middlemarch"; fol. 36ff. (CWD to EFSP, 3 March 1885). AM 45665, fol. 9v., undated list by EFSD, gives dates from 1865 to 1885 for the composition of the stories in *Shrine of Death*. See also PP 118 (EFSP to ES, 1884–85 *passim*).

28. AM 43906, fol. 49ff. (EFSP to CWD, 11 April 1885): "they are the outcome of a past in wh the present has no share"; see also GMT, "Rem.," A56, A70.

29. AM 43906, fol. 47ff. (EFSP to CWD, 26 March 1885). Suffering from dysentery on the voyage, she was dosed with laudanum, bismuth, quinine, and iron, and ate only "half-cooked" eggs and rare meat.

30. AM 43906, fol. 49ff. (EFSP to CWD, 11–13 April 1885). EFSP analogizes her journey to "a story of Jules Verne" followed by "Arabian Nights"; CWD replied: "[Tots] says she is as fit to settle Burmah as [illeg.] Why of course [she] is fit to settle Burmah or any other country! Another bit is about [her] being carried off by fairies. Why not. I'm sure the fairies wd be good fairies & wd only bring [her] lovingly to Zz & then [he] wd look after them if they *weren't* good" (AM 43906, fol. 70ff. [CWD to EFSP, 5 May 1885]).

31. AM 43906, fol. 53ff. (EFSP to CWD, 16 April 1885); fol. 56ff. (EFSP to CWD, 21 April 1885). See also fol. 23ff. (CWD to EFSP, 31 Dec. 1884): their future life will be "in an east wind out of doors like [illeg.] in the famous mistral picture," not "a merely warm and placid comfort."

32. AM 43906, fol. 68ff. (EFSP to CWD, 7 May 1885); fol. 72ff. (EFSP to CWD, 11 May 1885); fol. 100 (EFSP to CWD, 27 June 1885). See also AM 43906, fol. 23ff. (CWD to EFSP, 31 Dec. 1884).

33. See Jalland, *Women, Marriage, and Politics*, ch. 8, and Shkolnik, *Leading Ladies*.

34. AM 43906, fol. 81ff. (CWD to EFSP, 28 May 1885).

35. AM 43906, fol. 44ff. (EFSP to CWD, 10 Mar. 1885).

36. AM 43906, fol. 72ff. (EFSP to CWD, 11 May 1885).

37. AM 43906, fol. 75f. (EFSP to CWD, [?] May 1885).

38. AM 43906, fol. 109f. (CWD to EFSP, 20 July 1885). For earlier anonymous letters and fear of conspiracy, see Jenkins, *Dilke*, 220, and Askwith, *Lady Dilke*, 127.

39. AM 43906, fol. 109–111 (CWD to EFSP, "20th" and 21st" [July 1885]; mutilated and first page missing).

40. EFSP's letters and telegrams to CWD do not survive; for CWD's responses, see AM 43906, e.g., fol. 119f. (CWD to EFSP, 12 Aug. 1885); see also Jenkins, *Dilke*, 223.

41. AM 43906, fol. 112Ff (CWD to EFSP, n.d.): "if you marry me the choice will be between taking on yourself a name of shame or a name of infamy if I fight," but he has faith that she "will be supremely happy in my name & adoration"; similarly, "Of course my happiness depends absolutely on you, but don't *pretend* for my sake. If you don't feel that I am worthy and true don't say you do merely to keep me alive"; AM 43906, fol. 115ff. (CWD to EFSP, n.d.), mutilated.

42. AM 43906, fol. 115f. (CWD to EFSP, n.d.) and fol. 117ff. (CWD to EFSP, 6 Aug. 1885). The "Ruskin" was EFSP's *Sesame and Lilies*, given or lent to CWD. CWD's quotations of de Staël are primarily from *The Influence of the Passions*; she was "absolutely noble" and, at her best, the

equal of Tacitus; see AM 43932, fol. 105. EFSD included de Staël's *L'Allemagne* in her "Best Hundred Books."

43. CWD, "Mem.," 95.

44. REND 7/1 (CWD to Maye Dilke, n.d. [Aug./Sept. 1885]).

45. GMT, "Rem.," A57; but GMT later admits CWD and EFSP were engaged before VMC's confession (A71).

46. J. R. Shane Leslie, "Virginia Crawford, Sir Charles Dilke, and Cardinal Manning," *Dublin Review* 513 (1967), 179; Leslie says only that CWD "hoped to marry" EFSP; see also Leslie, *Memoir of Bodley*, 41. See also P. H. Bodley, "For Remembrance," fol. 104 [J. Bodley to Mary Bodley, 22 May 1880] and 104v. [J. Bodley to Mary Bodley, 24 May 1880]).

47. The judge was Charles Parker Butt; CWD was represented officially by Sir Charles Russell and advised unofficially by Sir Henry James; Jenkins, *Dilke*, 235, 236–38; see also Bywater, "Cardinal Manning," 543, and Savage, "Willful Communication," 38.

48. Henning, *Crawford v. Crawford*, 12; see also AM 43906, fol. 113f. (CWD to EFSP, n.d.): the allegation of homosexuality ("& a mess of other charges supported by conspiracy and perjured evidence") caused CWD to consider letting the case go uncontested. Bywater, "Cardinal Manning," 549, gives a different account of Rogerson's role.

49. Askwith, *Lady Dilke*, 158 and note; REND 13/1, 2.

50. Henning, *Crawford v. Crawford*, 10, 11.

51. Honoré Balzac, *A Woman of Thirty, and A Start in Life*, trans. Ellen Marriage (Philadelphia: Gebbie, 1900); thanks to Janine Hartman. CWD read "all of Balzac" in 1874/75 (AM 43932, fol. 102), and EFSD included three Balzac titles in her "Best Hundred Books."

52. Balzac, *Woman of Thirty*, 29–33, 84, 105, 107–8, 109.

53. Henning, *Crawford v. Crawford*, 12.

54. Foucault, *History of Sexuality: Introduction*, 105.

55. Walkowitz, *City of Dreadful Delight*, 81–120; Gorham, "Maiden Tribute."

56. See Askwith, *Lady Dilke*, 151–52; Jenkins, *Dilke*, 240–44; Walkowitz, *City of Dreadful Delight*, 126; *Pall Mall Gazette*, March and April 1886. See also AM 49611, fol. 134–57, misc. correspondence, 1 Feb.–12 Mar., 1895.

57. See Savage, "Divorce Court," and " 'Wilful Communication,' " 52 n. 9.

58. I am indebted to Kim Lane Scheppele for suggesting this line of thought.

59. Savage, "Divorce Court," 214; quotation is from Lord Redesdale.

60. The judge was Sir James Hannen; the Queen's Proctor was represented by Sir Walter Phillimore. The jury was a "special jury," drawn from the City, with a higher property qualification than in ordinary court.

61. Jenkins, *Dilke*, 261–62.

62. PP 118, fol. 170ff. (EFSD to ES, 25 Feb.1886).

63. Henning, *Crawford v. Crawford*, 11.

64. Stead, "Deliverance or Doom," 34–35.

65. Stead, "Deliverance or Doom," 38. See also *Liverpool Daily Post*: "Woman against woman, Mrs. Crawford brought a charge so startling that people were naturally inclined to rush to the conclusion that it must be true since it appeared to go beyond the bounds of mere imagination"; 6 Mar. 1891; see also 9 Mar. 1891.

66. Matthews qtd. in Stead, "Deliverance or Doom," 30.

67. Jenkins, *Dilke*, 326–28.

68. CWD won the seat by 175 votes and lost it by 176; Jenkins, *Dilke*, 226–27, 259.

69. Jenkins, *Dilke*, 330.

70. Bywater, "Cardinal Manning," 546–48, for an account of VMC's conversion. VMC published on topics from French women's legal rights to D'Annunzio to the organization of charity in Canada, in the *Month, Catholic World*, the *Dublin Review*, the *Fortnightly Review*, and contributed to

Catholic feminist papers and discussions. Her books and pamphlets include: *A Key to Labour Problems* (1896); *Saint Clotilda* (1898); *Studies in Foreign Literature* (1899); *Fra Angelico* (1900); *Raphael* (1902); *Studies in Saintship* (1903); *The Legends of the Saints* (1907); *Ideals of Charity* (1908); *Switzerland Today* (1911); *Venice* (1910); *The Church and the Worker Before and After the Encyclical 'Rerum Novarum'* (1916); *Catholic Social Doctrine, 1891-1931* (1933); *Josephine Butler* (1928); *The Institute of the Assumption* (1941); and *Frederic Ozanam, Catholic and Democrat* (1947).

71. Stead, "Has Dilke Cleared His Character?", 15.

72. See Roskill, "Foreword"; Leslie, "Virginia Crawford," and Bywater, "Cardinal Manning," 549-50.

73. Macleod, *Art and the Victorian Middle Class*, 294; see also Holton, *Suffrage Days*, 74.

74. VMC rarely spoken of the case in private either; see Bywater, "Cardinal Manning," 548-50; but see REND 13/1, p. 2: R. E. Enthoven records Marion Rawson's claims that Donald Crawford was a domestic tyrant, making "a most almighty row" about VMC being seen in public with a young man, her brother, and that Donald was impotent, a belief Rawson says was shared by the whole family. Enthoven quotes Rawson, "Virginia always wanted a child and told [me] that if she had had children 'nothing that happened would have happened.' " Donald Crawford remarried, aged 77, in 1914; that marriage, to Lilian Moncrieff, was also childless.

75. Qtd. in Stead, "Deliverance or Doom," 31.

76. Henning, *Crawford v. Crawford*, 74; see also Gillian Swanson, "Good-Time Girls, Men of Truth, and a Thoroughly Filthy Fellow: Sexual Pathology in the Profumo Affair," *New Formations* 24 (1995): 122-54.

77. Stead, *Deliverance or Doom*, 6.

78. Cottrell, "Devil on Two Sticks," 260, 265, 267.

79. Stead, qtd. in Walkowitz, *City of Dreadful Delight*, 126, 281 n. 23.

80. Walkowitz, *City of Dreadful Delight*, 281.

81. On CWD's class position, see ch. 2 and Nicholls, *Lost Prime Minister*, xxiii. CWD's youthful republicanism is not explicitly engaged in the texts I have examined but may have operated less to remove the taint of the aristocratic than to reiterate his transgressions of lines.

82. This pattern continued in the twentieth century: Askwith's *Lady Dilke* assumes unremitting sexual activity on the part of Victorian men and annexes virtually every woman CWD knew as a probable mistress. "Sophistication" about Victorian sexual hypocrisy can be oddly similar to the "Victorian" sexual ideologies purportedly transcended; Askwith's men are predators and working-class women passive sexual objects: Askwith assumes CWD slept with Fanny Grey Stock, despite her sworn statements that he had not, because she was a servant and therefore at his command; Askwith asserts that Stock was not telling the truth when she said she refused to testify in court for *private reasons of her own* unconnected with the case, and dismisses the possibility that Stock might have her own stories (*Lady Dilke*, 159-65, 169-71).

83. There are hints in the Dilke papers that Rogerson had been an "intimate friend" of CWD's *grandfather*, a story the Dilkes were not willing to produce; see PP 118, fol. 189ff. (EFSD to ES, 9 April 1886). For EFSD and Rogerson, see AM 49455. The Rogerson subplots combine Collins's *The Woman in White* (New York: Bantam Books, 1985) with George Meredith's *Diana of the Crossways* (New York: Modern Library, 1977), which was itself "based on" a scandal involving Caroline Norton; Rogerson claimed her brothers, one of whom was Donald Crawford's solicitor, had her unlawfully confined for madness, causing a mental breakdown, while her brothers later charged CWD both with squandering her investments *and* unlawfully using inside information drawn from his government connections to increase her dividends.

84. Letter from "H." to *Women's Herald*, 23 July 1892; letter from Mary Marles Thomas, relaying resolution of Carmarthen Women's Liberal Association, *Women's Herald*, 2 July 1892.

85. Stead, "Deliverance or Doom," 25.

86. *Woman's Journal* (Boston), 2 July 1892, 211; thanks to Robert Johnston. VMC was born

before CWD's first liaison with Mary Eustace Smith. See also Nicholls, *Lost Prime Minister*, 200–201, for an account of a very odd twentieth-century pro-Dilke version of this theme.

87. See Caine, *Victorian Feminists*, 211, 213, 221–34; see also Kent, *Sex and Suffrage*, ch. 7; Margaret Jackson, *The Real Facts of Life: Feminism and the Politics of Sexuality c. 1850–1940* (London: Taylor and Francis, 1994), and Bland, *Banishing the Beast*.

88. *Women's Herald*, 18 June 1892.

89. Resolution proposed by Mary Costelloe and passed by Southern Counties Women's Liberal Associations Conference, reported in *Women's Herald*, 2 May 1891; resolution passed by Bristol Women's Liberal Association, *Women's Herald*, 1 Aug. 1891.

90. Stead, "Deliverance or Doom," 26–29.

91. E. Edith Walker, speech to Ladies' National Association, 18 March 1891, qtd. in *Women's Herald*, 21 March 1891, and Walker, letter to *Women's Herald*, 4 April 1891.

92. *Woman's Journal*, 2 July 1892, 211.

93. *Women's Gazette and Weekly News*, 15 December 1888.

94. *Women's Penny Paper*, 25 May 1889, qtd. in Linda Walker, "Party Political Women: A Comparative Study of Liberal Women and the Primrose League, 1890–1914," in *Equal or Different? Women's Politics, 1800–1914*, ed. Jane Rendall (Oxford: Basil Blackwell, 1987), 177.

95. The WLF was engaged in a number of internal debates centered on the relationships between women's political organizations, the political parties, the suffrage movement and its internal divisions, and the social purity movement. Several Dilke allies, especially Eliza Orme, were among the minority in the WLF who wished to emphasize links to the Liberal Party.

96. Sylvia Pankhurst, *The Suffragette Movement: An Intimate Account of Persons and Ideals* (London: Virago, 1972), 205; see also Holton, *Suffrage Days*, 88, 101. On suffrage strategies and principles, see Constance Rover, *Women's Suffrage and Party Politics in Britain, 1866–1914* (London: Routledge and Kegan Paul, 1967); Sandra Stanley Holton, *Feminism and Democracy: Women's Suffrage and Reform Politics in Britain 1900–1918* (Cambridge: Cambridge University Press, 1986), 5, and "Manliness and Militancy: The Political Protest of Male Suffragists and the Gendering of the 'Suffragette' Identity," in Claire Eustance and Angela V. John, eds. *The Men's Share?, Masculinities, Male Support, and Women's Suffrage in Britain, 1890–1920* (London: Routledge, 1987), esp. 117–19; and Claire Hirschfield, "Fractured Faith: Liberal Party Women and the Suffrage Issue in Britain, 1892–1914," *Gender and History* 2 (1990): 173–97.

97. MacKenzie and MacKenzie, eds., *Diaries of Beatrice Webb*, 1: 160, 294; see also Walker, "Party Political Women," 176–77, and Nord, *Apprenticeship*. Webb's position vis-à-vis the Dilkes was overdetermined by her own unhappy affair with Chamberlain; perhaps by rumors that her father, Richard Potter, had had an affair with Eustacia Smith; and by the complexities of middle-class socialism; see Caine, *Destined to Be Wives*, 21.

98. AM 49611, fol. 134–57, misc. correspondence of 1 Feb. through 12 March, 1895. The deferrred irony of EFSD's disinvitation is John Profumo's long and noted association with Toynbee Hall after his sexual-political fall.

99. Philippa Levine, *Victorian Feminism 1850–1900* (London: Hutchinson, 1987), 159.

100. For other lost friends, see MS. Eng. letters e. 93, fol. 89f. (CWD to James Thursfield, 8 Jan. 1905), fol. 155 (Thursfield to CWD, n.d. [1905]), and Jackson, *Memoirs*, 41.

101. AM 47911, fol. 65f. (EFSP to Cyril Flower, 2 Feb. 1885); AM 47938, fol. 28 (Constance Flower's diary, 3 Feb. 1885).

102. Anthony S. Wohl, " 'Dizzi-Ben-Dizzi': Disraeli as Alien," *Journal of British Studies* 34 (1995): 375–411; see also Jonathan Freedman, "Henry James and the Discourses of Antisemitism," in *Between 'Race' and Culture: Representations of 'the Jew' in English and American Literature*, ed. Bryan Cheyette (Stanford: Stanford University Press, 1996), 62–83. See also AM 43903, fol. 220 (EFSP to CWD, 9 May 1879): EFSP muses on the irreducible "otherness" of Jews. See Nicholls, *Lost Prime Minister*, 293, on CWD's opposition to the infamous 1905 Aliens Act.

103. R. W. Davis, *The English Rothschilds* (Chapel Hill: University of North Carolina Press, 1983) claims Flower's elevation to the peerage was a triumph of mediocrity; cf. E. F. Benson, *Final Edition* (London: Hogarth, 1988), 46–53, 57; see also Macleod, *Art and the Victorian Middle Class*, 279, 284, 298–99, and appendix. For Flower's friendship, see AM 47911, fol. 73 (25 Jan. 1886), fol. 75 (29 Jan. 1886), and fol. 80 (23 Feb. 1886); AM 43908, fol. 244 (Battersea to EFSD, 14 Oct. 1897) and GMT, "Rem.," A92.

104. Blodgett, *Centuries*, 203, 221–22; Constance Flower [Lady Battersea], *Reminiscences* (London: Macmillan, 1922) and *Waifs and Strays* (London: Arthur L. Humphreys, 1921).

105. Benson, *Final Edition*, 50; Blodgett, *Centuries*, 77.

106. Flower, *Reminiscences*, 439–40; Walker, "Party Political Women," 176–77, 188.

107. AM 47938, fol. 38f. (Constance Flower diary, 12 Jan. 1886). Other texts complicate any solid positioning of Constance's loyalties; her writings position her mother, Louisa de Rothschild, as her great love and an ally in moral battles against Cyril (see Blodgett, *Centuries*, 91–92, 224), but cf. Benson, *Final Edition*, 50–51; see also Lowndes, ed., *Diaries and Letters*, 70.

108. Stead, *Deliverance or Doom?*, 6–8.

109. Acts of the Apostles, 5:1–11; David Lyle Jeffrey, gen. ed., *A Dictionary of Biblical Tradition in English Literature* (Grand Rapids: Eerdmans, 1992), and Paul J. Achtemeier, gen. ed., *Harper's Bible Dictionary* (San Francisco: Harper and Row, 1985), s.v. "Ananias" in both. Ananias and Sapphira "held back" a portion of God's due, and Stead suggested the Dilkes were holding back truth from him. He recycled the motif in Stead, "The Sins of Ananias and Sapphira," *Welsh Review* 1 (1892): 321–28; reprinted as pamphlet (London, n.d. [c. 1891]).

110. Stead, *Deliverance or Doom?*, 9–13, esp. 10, 12.

111. Stead, *Deliverance or Doom?*, 21.

112. Qtd. in Ann Thwaite, *Edmund Gosse: A Literary Landscape 1849–1920* (London: Secker and Warburg, 1984), 265; thanks to Michael Gibson for this reference.

113. See also *Liverpool Daily Post*, 9 March 1891.

114. R. Pankhurst qtd. in S. Pankhurst, *Suffragette Movement*, 70; Holyoake in DFM, 3 April 1891, "What A Veteran Reformer Says"; see also Holton, *Suffrage Days*, ch. 4, esp. 73–74.

115. S. C. Cronwright Schreiner, ed., *The Letters of Olive Schreiner, 1876–1920* (1924; rep., Westport, Conn.: Hyperion Press, 1976), 220–21 (Schreiner to Stead, n.d., 1896?); see also 204, 206, and AM 43908, fol. 189 (Olive Schreiner to EFSD, 17 Mar. 1891).

116. *Women's Herald*, 10 Jan. 1891; see also Holton, *Suffrage Days*, 74.

117. I am grateful to Geoff Eley for helping me with this point. For the tradition of "the argument from virtue," see Anna K. Clark, "The Rhetoric of Chartist Domesticity," *Journal of British History* 31 (1992): 62–88.

118. See "Aliquis," [W. A. Hunter, LL.D., MP for Aberdeen], "Sir Charles Dilke and His Accusers" pamphlet, 1904, but reprinted from earlier *Northern Daily News* (Aberdeen); DFM, 15 April 1892.

119. PP 118, fol. 218ff (EFSD to ES, 10 Nov. 1886).

120. PP 118, fol. 218f. (EFSD to ES, 10 Nov. 1886); see also PP 118, fol. 166 (EFSD to ES, 23 Feb. 1886). EFSP, *Renaissance*, 2: 8 and 2: 105, contrasts the Virgin's deep grief with the "hysteric agony" of Mary Magdalen and the "indifferent, half-selfish curiosity" of women looking on; see also EFSD, *French Architects*, 101, on another sexually bad woman playing Magdalen.

121. AM 49611, fol. 42ff. (EFSD to unknown, 6 May 1886); see also Askwith, *Lady Dilke*, 158 and 158n. For EFSD and Stead, see AM 43907, fol. 248–83 (Stead to EFSD and EFSD's notes).

122. Askwith repeats this interpretation in both *Lady Dilke*, 153–54, 168, and *Tangled Web*, 75–79.

123. *Dwarf*, 10 Feb. 1891; 10 Mar. 1891; on Tranby Croft, 17 Feb. 1891; on the Russell case, 8 Dec. 1891.

124. Jenkins, *Victorian Scandal*, 359–60. See also the anti-Dilke Henry James, qtd. in Askwith, *Lady Dilke*, 142.

125. Qtd. in Jenkins, *Dilke*, 350–54, and *Victorian Scandal*, 6, 350–54. See also Leslie, *Memoir of Bodley*, 44; Rhodes James, *Rosebery*, 182–88; REND 13/1, 3; and Stead, *Deliverance or Doom?*, 19.

126. See Leslie, *Memoir of Bodley*, 45; Leslie, "Virginia Crawford," and P. H. Bodley, "For Remembrance"; R. V. C. Bodley, "The Man Who Insulted King Edward," *The Sunday Times*, 5 January 1969.

127. Qtd. in Leslie, *Memoir of Bodley*, 45; see also AM 43967, fols. 1,10, 15 (Bodley to GMT, 1912, with notes by GMT) and GMT, "Rem.," A91; Bodley also resented being "cheated" of his rightful position as biographer of Manning (Leslie, *Memoir of Bodley*, 45, and Bywater, "Cardinal Manning," 548–49). Like EFSD and VMC, Bodley's later career was in representing France to the English; Bywater, "Cardinal Manning," 550–51, and J. R. Shane Leslie, *The Film of Memory* (London: Michael Joseph, 1938), 208.

128. Leslie, *Memoir of Bodley*, 41–42, 45; Bodley to CWD, 27 Sept. 1887, qtd. in Jenkins, *Dilke*, 351.

129. Leslie, *Memoir of Bodley*, ch. 1. On Bodley and Chamberlain, see GMT, "Rem.," A92; and AM 43967, fol. 10ff. (Bodley to GMT, 28 June 1912); see also Jenkins, *Dilke*, 354–58; Francis Bywater, "Chamberlain and the Dilke Case," ts. in REND 13/6, and attached correspondence between Bywater and Stephen Roskill; and Richard Jay, *Joseph Chamberlain: A Political Study* (New York: Oxford University Press, 1981), 352–56. This plot crosses the Rosebery plot; Rosebery was threatened by sexual scandal via his private secretary; see Neill Bartlett, *Who Was That Man? A Present for Mr Oscar Wilde* (London: Serpent's Tail, 1988), 147.

130. AM 49611, fol. 42ff. (EFSD to unknown, 6 May 1886).

131. Bodley to Mary Bodley, 23 Jan. 1886, qtd. in P.H. Bodley, " 'For Remembrance'," fol. 175v.; Bodley, qtd. in Leslie, *Memoir of Bodley*, 45. But see AM 49611, fol. 42 (EFSD to unknown, 6 May 1886).

132. Thanks to Angela V. John for finding and sharing this letter; original in the Fales Library, Elmer Holmes Bobst Library of New York University, Elizabeth Robins Papers, series 2, subseries 3, box 7, folder 14.

133. For trivialization of male sexual activity by some Dilkeites, see Lowndes, ed., *Diaries and Letters*, 115.

134. Jenkins, *Dilke*, 11, and ch. 10.

135. Leslie, "Virginia Crawford," 177; VMC's will; and Roskill, "Foreword."

136. Macleod, *Art and the Victorian Middle Class*, 293–94, 475.

137. Jenkins, *Dilke*, 12.

138. See also G. M. Young, *Victorian England: Portrait of an Age* (New York: Doubleday, 1964), 259; and Thomas William Heyck, *The Dimensions of British Radicalism: The Case of Ireland, 1874–1895* (Urbana: University of Illinois Press, 1974), 160.

139. See Banks, *Biographical Dictionary*, s.v. "Dilke, Charles Wentworth"; Gwynn and Tuckwell, *Life of Dilke*, 2: 6–7, 17, 469, 353; Jenkins, *Victorian Scandal*, 53–54; Strauss, "Traitors," 185, 188–89, 190; Ray Strachey, *The Cause: A Short History of the Women's Movement in Great Britain* (1928; London: Virago, 1978), 118, 274; more broadly, see also John and Eustance, eds., *The Men's Share?.* Cf. Nicholls, *Lost Prime Minister*, 312.

140. Huws Jones, *Mrs. Humphry Ward*, 38; Lowndes, ed., *Diaries and Letters*, 115.

141. Jenkins's eleventh chapter (after ch. 10, "Mr. Gladstone's Successor?") is "Mrs. Crawford Intervenes," in both *Dilke* and *Victorian Scandal*.

142. See Richard Price, "Historiography, Narrative, and the Nineteenth Century," *Journal of British Studies* 35 (1996): 220–56, esp. 221–32.

143. Qtd. in Nicholls, *Lost Prime Minister*, 312.

144. See Nicholls, *Lost Prime Minister*, chs. 14–18; Gwynn and Tuckwell, *Life of Dilke*, vol. 2.

145. Jenkins, *Dilke*, 226–27, 259.

146. CWD won the Forest in 1892 by 5360 to the Tory's 2520; subsequent margins were larger.

147. DFM, 23 May 1890; 10 April 1891.

148. See Jenkins, *Dilke*, 381; PP 118, passim, esp. fol. 161 (EFSD to ES, 20 Feb. 1886), fol. 178 (11 March 1886), and fol. 170 (25 Feb. 1886) and fol. 174ff. [3 March 1886]) on Nonconformist support for CWD. But cf. Mss. Eng. lett. 174, fol. 80ff. (CWD to Bodley, 1890, "21st"). Broadhurst 1889 speech to Dundee trades leaders, qtd. in DFM, 15 May 1891.

149. See also Eugenio Biagini, *Liberty, Retrenchment and Reform: Popular Liberalism in the Age of Gladstone, 1860–1880* (Cambridge: Cambridge University Press, 1992), 358 n. 282; cf. deMoor, "Honourable Gentleman," 206.

150. DFM, 10 July 1891; 4 Sept. 1891; 16 Oct. 1891; 27 Nov. 1891.

151. DFM, 1 April 1892, citing speech by CWD to Fulham Women's Liberal Association, 28 March 1892. On CWD's refusals of Scottish ad Welsh constituencies, see Mss. Eng. lett. d. 174, fol. 80 [CWD to Bodley, 1890, "21st," no month]).

152. Jenkins, *Dilke*, 383; Mss. Eng. lett. d. 174, fol. 80 (CWD to Bodley, 1890, "21st"); DFM, 22 July 1892.

153. Reprinted in DFM, 27 Aug. 1897. On CWD's relations with the ILP, especially Keir Hardie, see David Howell, *British Workers and the Independent Labour Party, 1888–1906* (Manchester: Manchester University Press, 1983), 270, 368, 371; see also GMT, " Rem.," A169–70.

154. Stead qtd. in Jenkins, *Dilke*, 381, 383; CWD qtd. in Gwynn and Tuckwell, *Life of Dilke*, 2: 284.

155. For "Gladstonian in the extreme," see DFM, 6 Jan. 1888; on the Forest, see C. E. Hart, *The Industrial History of Dean* (Newton Abbot: David and Charles, 1971); Chris Fisher, *Custom, Work, and Market Capitalism: The Forest of Dean Colliers, 1788–1888* (London: Croom Helm, 1981); Fisher and and John Smethurst, " 'War on the Law of Supply and Demand': The Amalgamated Association of Miners and the Forest of Dean Colliers, 1869–1875," in Royden Harrison, ed., *Independent Colliers: The Coal-Miner as Archetypal Proletarian Reconsidered* (Hassocks: Harvester, 1978). On Samuelson, see DFM, 6 June, 27 June, 4 July, 18 July, 26 Sept., 12 Dec., and 19 Dec.1890; for Rowlinson and the miners, see, e.g., 2 May 1890 or 16 Jan. 1891.

156. DFM, 9 March 1888, 23 May 1890. Price, "Historiography," 232, warns against reading newspapers as expressing working-class views; my focus is on DFM's representations of class.

157. John R. Cook, *Dennis Potter: A Life on Screen* (Manchester: Manchester University Press, 1995), 8–9.

158. DFM, 27 March 1891.

159. DFM, 26 June 1891.

160. DFM, 15 July 1892.

161. DFM, 26 June 1891.

162. DFM, 3 July 1891 and 13 Nov. 1891. Hughes allegedly called pro-Dilke Forest Nonconformists "a handful of ill-informed men"; *Methodist Times*, qtd. in DFM, 1 April 1892.

163. See, e.g., DFM, 17 Jan. 1890; 28 Nov. 1890; 13 Nov. 1891; for "Torquemada," 11 Dec. 1891.

164. DFM, 19 Dec. 1890.

165. DFM, 18 Nov. 1892.

166. DFM, 17 Jan. 1890; see also 13 Nov. 1891 and 28 Nov. 1890.

167. DFM, 13 Nov. 1891, 11 Dec. 1891; Blake, letter in DFM, 4 Dec. 1891.

168. DFM, 27 May 1892.

169. DFM, 15 July 1892; 2 Sept. 1892.

170. Qtd. in DFM, 5 Aug. 1892.

171. DFM, 5 Aug. 1892.

172. GMT, "Rem.," A120; PP 118, fol. 254ff. (EFSD to ES, n.d. [1892]; see also AM 43980, passim (EFSD's letters to people in Cinderford); Gwynn and Tuckwell, Life of Dilke, 2:284.

173. Lewenhak, Women and Trade Unions, 70; see also Women's Union Journal, July 1881, 70, 115; Sept. 1881, 89–90; Jan. 1883, 2; and Dec. 1884, 107–10, which reprints EFSP's "address" to the Oxford WPPL; AM 43918, fol. 51ff. (M. Nettleship to CWD, n.d.), and Cole, "Rhoda Broughton," 191. See also ch. 5 above, esp. note 171.

174. EFSD, "Trades-Unions for Women," 228.

175. People's Journal of Dundee, 7 Sept. and 14 Sept. 1889; for other EFSD speeches, see, e.g., People's Journal for Perthshire, 31 Aug. 1889; Newcastle Daily Leader, 7 Sept. 1891; Norfolk News (Norwich), 8 Sept. 1894.

176. DFM, 12 Feb. 1892, qtg. T. B. Fox of Newnham (Glos.), chair of meeting at Longhope, 8 Feb. 1892; speech by the (Baptist) Reverend Sidney Elsom, qtd. in DFM, 17 April 1891; DFM, 10 April 1891 (EFSD speech in Manchester, meeting presided over by the Bishop of Manchester).

177. For EFSD's travels and work for the League, see Women's Union Journal, 1886–1904, passim, and the League's annual reports for accounts of each year's major tours and financial contributions. The Dilkes contributed from CWD's money and EFSD's inheritance from MP, upwards of five to six hundred pounds a year, sometimes considerably more—in direct funds, by payment of EFSD's secretary, and by paying the costs of their own tours and expenses at the TUC. See also Soldon, Women in British Trade Unions, 27.

178. Drake, Women in Trade Unions, 16–17; obituary of Paterson, Women's Union Journal, 114.

179. MacKenzie and Mackenzie, eds., Diary of Beatrice Webb, 2: 20–21.

180. Women's Union Journal, 15 September 1890.

181. See Boston, Women Workers, 35; Soldon, Women in British Trade Unions, 36, 37; Jill Liddington and Jill Norris, One Hand Tied Behind Us: The Rise of the Women's Suffrage Movement (London: Virago, 1978), 38, 79, 134, 158; Women's Union Journal, 15 July 1890, 52.

182. See Drake, Women in Trade Unions, 37, qtg. an 1894 speech by EFSD.

183. See Lewenhak, Women and Trade Unions, 78–80; Women's Union Journal, 15 March 1890, 22 (account of EFSD's remarks at a meeting in Glasgow). Debates on protective legislation continued to split the League, but see Soldon, Women in British Trade Unionism, 36, citing Women's Trade Union Review, July 1893. EFSD's support for protective legislation was often for measures that regulated conditions or limited long shifts of night work. But Feurer, "Meaning of Sisterhood," 254, sees EFSD's position as a "rejection," of "freedom of contract, open labour market, sex antagonism, self-help, and anti-statism." See also Thom, "Bundle of Sticks," 272–73.

184. Soldon, Women in British Trade Unions, 40; but see EFSP's address to the Oxford WPPL, in Women's Union Journal, Dec. 1884, 109: working-class women "must learn to . . . to rely upon youselves, to fight your own difficulties, to look for no other saviour than your united forces."

185. EFSD, "Trades Unions for Women," 233, 234.

186. Thom, "Bundle of Sticks"; Phillips, Divided Loyalties, 82–87; Levine, Victorian Feminism, 118–123; Feurer, "Meaning of Sisterhood." See also Angela V. John, By The Sweat of Their Brow: Women Workers at Victorian Coal Mines (London: Routledge Kegan Paul, 1984); Sonya Rose, Limited Livelihoods: Gender and Class in Nineteenth-Century England (Berkeley: University of California Press, 1992), ch. 3, esp. 70–71; and Elizabeth Roberts, Women's Work, 1840–1940 (Cambridge: Cambridge University Press, 1995).

187. Women's Trade Union Journal, July 1877, EFSP speech at the League's annual meeting; also in Boston, Women Workers; cf. Soldon, Women in British Trade Unions, 28–29. See also Women's Union Journal, (July 1881), 70.

188. Soldon, Women in British Trade Unions, 35–36.

189. GMT, "Rem.," A142.

190. GMT, "Rem.," A142.

191. Drake, *Women in Trade Unions*, 27.

192. *Women's Union Journal*, 15 Jan. 1890, 3.

193. EFSD, "Trades Unionism for Women," 47–48. See also "The 'Pall Mall Gazette' Revelations," *Women's Union Journal*, Aug. 1885, 61–62.

194. *Women's Union Journal*, 16 September 1889, 70; account of speech given in Dundee on 3 September.

195. EFSD, "Trade Unions for Women," 238.

196. See EFSD, "Woman Suffrage in England." EFSD argues, with no prescience at all, that the woman's suffrage movement has stalled. See also CWD, "Woman Suffrage and Electoral Reform" (pamphlet; The People's Suffrage Federation, London, 1910). On the politics of suffrage, see Holton, *Feminism and Democracy*; Liddington and Norris, *One Hand Tied*, esp. 180; Strauss, "Traitors," 189–90; and Pankhurst, *Suffragette Movement*, 70, 96, 205. On the WTUL and suffrage, see Liddington and Norris, *One Hand Tied*, 15, 135–36, 180–81, and Thom, "Bundle of Sticks," 265–66.

197. *Women's Herald*, 19 December 1891, letter from Millicent Garret Fawcett.

198. Pankhurst, *Suffragette Movement*, 96.

199. GMT, "Rem.," A352; see also GMT, *Constance Smith*, 17.

200. *Yorkshire Daily Post*, 8 September 1904.

201. For "Second Member," see e.g., DFM, 7 Oct. 1892, 30 Dec. 1892; Gwynn and Tuckwell, *Life of Dilke*, 2: 284; see also Jenkins, *Dilke*, 385–86.

202. Ben Turner, "An Appreciation," *Cotton Factory Times*, 28 October 1904.

203. *Yorkshire Daily Post*, qtd. in *Liverpool Daily Post*, 18 March 1891.

204. *Birmingham Daily Post*, 14 September 1891.

205. AM 43918, fol. 73f. (Bodley to CWD, 21 March 1905).

206. Qtd. in CWD, "Mem.," 127, translation mine; original, dated "1897" by another hand, AM 43908, fol. 227ff. See also AM 43918, fol. 70 (Marie-Thérèse Ollivier to CWD, 16 Feb. 1905).

207. PP 118, fol. 153ff. (EFSD to ES, 8 Feb. 1886).

208. PP 118, fol. 132f. (EFSD to ES, 4 Oct. 1885); fol. 142ff. (EFSD to ES, 29 Jan. 1886); fol. 232 (EFSD to ES, 10 Jan. 1887).

209. PP 118, fol. 232 (EFSD to ES, 10 Jan. 1887); see also fol. 161 (EFSD to ES, 20 Feburary 1886); fols. 166 (23 Feb. 1886) and 170 (25 Feb. 1886); fol. 180 (n.d.) for Westlake's report; and fol. 212ff. (7 July 1886): when CWD lost his seat "the faces of the workmen [were] grievous & . . . strong men shed tears . . ."; see fol. 216 (15 Sept. 1886) for anti-Dilkeism as middle-class.

210. PP 118, fol. 174ff. (EFSD to ES, 3 Mar. 1886).

211. For "dirty dishonourable" Stead, see AM 49611, fol. 131 (EFSD to James Thursfield, 11 July 1889); Mss. Eng. Lett. d. 187, fol. 104ff. (EFSD to C. H. Pearson, 30 Aug. [1891?]).

212. AM 49611, fol. 122ff. (EFSD to Mrs. Chesson, 24 Nov. 1888); copy of missing original.

213. PP 118, fol. 132f. (EFSD to ES, 4 Oct. 1885).

214. PP 118, fol. 135 (EFSD to ES, 23 Dec. 1885); emphasis EFSD's; fol. 140ff. (EFSD to ES, 28 Jan. 1886).

215. PP 118, fol. 232F (EFSD to ES, 10 Jan. 1887).

216. See AM 49611, fol. 35, for draft of a letter, probably to Stead, in EFSD's hand.

217. PP 118, fol. 142 (EFSD to ES, 29 Jan. 1886); fol. 218f. (EFSD to ES, 10 Nov. 1886).

218. AM 49611, fol. 122ff. (EFSD to Mrs. Chesson, 24 Nov. 1888); copy of missing original.

219. PP 118, fol. 252f. (EFSD to ES, 30 Jan. 1888).

220. PP 118, fol. 153ff. (EFSD to ES, 8 Feb. 1886); see also Rhoda Broughton to George Bentley, 19 Feb. 1886, qtd. in Cole, "Rhoda Broughton," 184.

221. Ms. Eng. lett. e. 93, fol. 91 (CWD to James Thursfield, 10 Jan. 1905). One instance illustrates both the difficulty of appraising how friendships were affected and the extremely small social world the principals inhabited: relations between EFSD and Theresa Earle seem to have cooled after the case, perhaps because Earle was not willing to swear that CWD had been at her home on a specific date (Askwith, Lady Dilke, 156–57 and note) and perhaps also because Earle's cousin Therese Harcourt was a devoted anti-Dilkeite who interrupted her husband's long friendship with CWD after the trials. See also Lowndes, ed., Diaries and Letters, 70.

222. Ms. Eng. lett. e. 93, fol. 89f. (CWD to James Thursfield, 8 Jan. 1905); on Julia Grant-Duff, see also PP 118, fol. 224ff. (EFSD to ES, 8 Mar. 1887).

223. AM 43919, fol. 21f. (Julia Grant-Duff to CWD, 6 Feb. 1906) and fol. 283f. (Constance Flower to CWD, 8 Dec. 1907); fol. 93 (CWD to James Thursfield, 26 Jan. 1905). For Gladstone see AM 47911, fol. 93ff. ("W.E.G." [Gladstone] to unknown [CWD?], 10 Aug. 1889).

224. GMT, "Rem.," A85.

225. GMT, "Rem.," A86, A88; but see E. F. Benson, As We Were (London: Longman's, Green, 1930), 136–38.

226. Gwynn and Tuckwell, Life of Dilke, 2: 368–86. CWD spent "half his income on social work and on the aboriginal Societies and native races"; GMT, "Rem.," A88–89, A249; see also Nicholls, Lost Prime Minister, 306–9; EFSD, "Great Missionary Success," and "Coming Elections in France."

227. GMT., "Rem.," A90.

228. GMT, "Rem.," A60–63, 65–67.

229. GMT, "Rem.," A140, A87, A88, A89, A91, A93–94, A144, A92–93.

230. GMT, "Rem.," A85.

231. Raymond Williams, Culture and Society, 1750–1950 (London: Penguin, 1963), conclusion.

232. GMT, "Rem., A79, A81, A60–67, A72, A73, A84–85, A88–94, A189, A243, A126.

233. GMT, Constance Smith, A24–25, A27.

234. GMT, Constance Smith, 24–25; "Rem.," A98–102; Gwynn and Tuckwell, Life of Dilke, 2: 518–19. For McKenna, see GMT, "Rem.," A83; see also A84, A157, A126. CWD was noted for his generosity to men of all parties, from Tories to Sidney Webb; see A121–22; see also A170.

235. Askwith, Lady Dilke, 178–81, 116n; Gwynn and Tuckwell, Life of Dilke, 2:91, 324; GMT, "Rem.", A96.

236. Gwynn and Tuckwell, Life of Dilke, 324 and 324n., 325, 326, and photograph facing 326.

237. Gwynn and Tuckwell, Life of Dilke, 2:240–41; GMT, "Rem.," A97.

238. Gwynn and Tuckwell, Life of Dilke, 2: 240–41, 566; GMT, "Rem.," A97.

239. GMT, "Rem.," A97, A230–31; Gwynn and Tuckwell, Life of Dilke, 2:547.

240. Gwynn and Tuckwell, Life of Dilke, photograph facing 2:324; GMT, "Rem.," A98; Askwith, Lady Dilke, 178.

241. Gwynn and Tuckwell, Life of Dilke, 2: 323.

242. Gwynn and Tuckwell, Life of Dilke, 2: 324, 319; see also GMT, "Rem.," A149, and PP 140, fol. 92ff. (n.d., clipping from "D.C.," probably Daily Chronicle, with mss. "corrections").

243. GMT, "Rem.," A103.

244. GMT, "Rem.," A189.

245. CWD, "Mem.," 123; GMT, "Rem.," A228.

246. GMT, "Rem.," A253.

247. EFSD's will, Somerset House, London.

248. MacKenzie and MacKenzie, eds., *Diaries of Beatrice Webb*, 1: 294; AM 43918, fol. 94f. (Margarete Boileau to CWD, 27 May 1905).

249. GMT, "Rem.," A145; GMT, *Constance Smith*, 15; Hamilton, *Mary Macarthur*, 21, 27–28; see also Pamela Graves, *Labour Women: Women in British Working-Class Politics, 1918–1939* (Cambridge: Cambridge University Press, 1994).

250. GMT, "Rem.," A148; GMT, *Constance Smith*, 14–17, 24, 26, and passim. According to GMT, Smith had fallen in love with a man with whom she studied Greek, who died before they could marry, and work was partly consolation. Jane Harrison invited her to collaborate in historical work, but her "vocation was for work which would build up a better future," and she investigated women's conditions in London's sweated trades. She was a dedicated Christian. GMT and her brother later lived with a woman named Jennet Lush, in whose house she died in 1951 (GMT will, Somerset House, London).

CHAPTER SEVEN

1. For the *Britannica* entries, see Gillian Thomas, *A Position to Command Respect: Women and the Eleventh Britannica* (Methuchen, N.J. and London: Scarecrow Press, 1992); the title of Thomas's work is a quotation from EFSD (74); see CWD, "Mem.," 26–27. See also deMoor, "Honourable Gentleman," for EFSD's writing for the *Athenaeum*.

2. Eisler, "Six Lives," 147; see also Askwith, *Lady Dilke*, chs. 4 and 20; and Roll-Hansen, "The *Academy*," 153.

3. CWD, "Mem.," 18.

4. Eisler, "Six Lives," 160.

5. EFSP, review of Tyrwhitt, qtd. in CWD, "Mem.," 28

6. Unsigned review of Pater, *Imaginary Portraits*, *Athenaeum*, 24 June 1887, 824–25, reprinted in *Walter Pater: The Critical Heritage*, ed. R. M. Seiler (London: Routledge & Kegan Paul, 1980), 165–67.

7. I make no arguments for the accuracy of EFSP/D's claims about the Renaissance, especially not about the Renaissance as a site of feminist desire. For contrasting feminist appraisals, see Joan Kelly, "Did Women Have a Renaissance?" in Renate Bridenthal and Claudia Koonz, eds., *Becoming Visible: Women in European History*, 2nd ed. (Boston: Houghton Mifflin, 1982), and Constance Jordan, *Renaissance Feminism: Literary Texts and Historical Models* (Ithaca: Cornell University Press, 1990).

8. CWD, "Mem.," 117–18; for overlapping passages, see EFSD, BSL, 145, 166–67.

9. EFSD, *Renaissance*, 1:339; on cross-gender identification, see, e.g., Carol Clover, *Men, Women, and Chainsaws: Gender in the Modern Horror Film* (Princeton: Princeton University Press, 1992).

10. GMT, "Rem.," A26.

11. EFSD, "Idealist Movement," 643. Augustine's phrase is "O to love, O to go, O to die to the self, O to reach [or arrive at] God"; I am profoundly indebted to Catherine Brown and Yopie Prins for help with this passage. See also EFSD, "Of the Spiritual Life," in EFSD, BSL, 145–46.

12. "Idealist Movement," 644, 650. See also EFSD, "Best Hundred Books," for de Sales.

13. EFSD, "Idealist Movement," 650, 648.

14. EFSD, "Idealist Movement," 651; cf. CWD, "Mem.," 21–22.

15. EFSD, "Idealist Movement," 651.

16. EFSD, "Idealist Movement," 651–52.

17. EFSD, "Idealist Movement," 651.

18. On the Renaissance in the nineteenth century, see Ferguson, *Renaissance*; Peter Burke,

Culture and Society in Renaissance Italy, 1420–1540 (London: B.T. Batsford, 1972), 1–21; J. B. Bullen, "The Idea of the Italian Renaissance in English Culture, 1800–1900," Ph.D. thesis, University of Cambridge, 1975; David Norbrook, "Life and Death of Renaissance Man," *Raritan* 8:4 (1989): 89–110; Jacob Korg, ed., *Clio* 17:2 (1988), special issue on the Renaissance in Victorian culture. See also Dale, *The Victorian Critic and the Idea of History* (Cambridge: Harvard University Press, 1977), and Alan Johnson, "Inventing the Italian Renaissance in Early Victorian England," *Victorians Institute Journal* 15 (1987): 37–45. On MP, see M. L. Clarke, *Classical Education in Britain, 1500–1900* (Cambridge: Cambridge University Press, 1959), 101, 102, 116–17.

19. EFSD, "Idealist Movement," 652, 653.

20. EFSD, "Idealist Movement," 653.

21. Eliot, *Middlemarch*, 135.

22. EFSD, "Idealist Movement," 653. See also Sandra M. Den Otter, *British Idealism and Social Explanation: A Study in Late-Victorian Thought* (Oxford: Oxford University Press, 1996).

23. EFSD, "Idealist Movement," 655, 652, 654.

24. EFSD, "Idealist Movement," 655, 652.

25. EFSP, "Nicholas Poussin," 474.

26. EFSP, review of Pater, *Renaissance*; see also Roll-Hansen, "*Academy*," 172.

27. EFSP, *Renaissance*, 1: 32.

28. For "shock" and "anarchy," see EFSD, "Idealist Movement," 650, and CWD, "Mem.," 10.

29. EFSP, *Renaissance*, 1: 10.

30. EFSP, "Poussin," 475.

31. EFSP, *Renaissance*, 1: 13.

32. EFSP, "Art and Morality," 78, 79.

33. EFSP, "Nicolas Poussin," 474.

34. EFSP, *Renaissance*, 1: 18–19; EFSD, *Art in the Modern State*, 2.

35. EFSP, "Art and Morality," 66–83, 78, 79; see EFSD, *French Architects*, 47.

36. EFSP, *Renaissance*, 1: 18–19.

37. AM 43908, fol. 110 (Ruskin to EFSD, 28 Jan. 1886); fol. 132 (Ruskin to EFSD, 24 Mar. 1887).

38. For Victorian medievalisms, see, e.g., *Browning Institute Studies* 8 (1980), esp. Helene E. Roberts, "Victorian Medievalism: Revival or Masquerade?," 11–44; for Carlyle's medievalism, see his *Past and Present* (1843; Boston: Houghton Mifflin, 1965); for Morris's, see especially *News from Nowhere, or, An Epoch of Rest: Being Some Chapters from a Utopian Romance* (1890; New York: Cambridge University Press, 1995) and *A Dream of John Ball* (London: Reeves and Turner, 1888); for an influential female medievalism, see Adele M. Holcomb, "Anna Jameson (1794–1860): Sacred Art and Social Vision," in *Women as Interpreters of the Visual Arts*, ed. Claire Richter Sherman (Westport, Conn.: Greenwood Press, 1981), 93–121.

39. EFSD, *French Architects*, 31, 148; for Victorian discourses of skill and beauty, see also Gagnier, *Subjectivities*, 70–73.

40. EFSD, *Renaissance*, 1: 67; 2: 249–94; EFSP, "Bernard Palissy."

41. EFSD, *Art in the Modern State*, 222.

42. EFSP, "Nicolas Poussin," 472.

43. EFSD, *French Architects*, 34, 38, 42, 54, 59, 72, 109, 146; see also EFSD, *French Painters*, 2, 16.

44. EFSD, *French Architects*, 42.

45. Ellman, *Wilde*, 81, 156–57, 165–66.

46. EFSD, *Art in the Modern State*, 222; see also 1, 3–5, 137, 220.

47. EFSD, *French Architects*, 7; see also 24, 34, 90, and EFSD, *French Painters*, 2, 14.

48. EFSP, "Nicolas Poussin," 472.

49. EFSP, "Nicolas Poussin," 475.

50. EFSP, "Nicolas Poussin," 472.

51. EFSP, "Bernard Palissy," 189.

52. EFSP, "Nicolas Poussin," 477.

53. EFSP, "Nicolas Poussin," 472.

54. EFSP, review of Ruskin, Lectures and Catalogue, 305, emphasis added.

55. EFSP, Renaissance, 1:18–19.

56. EFSP, Renaissance, 1:18–19.

57. EFSP, Renaissance, 1:18–19.

58. EFSD, French Architects, 7, 24, 26, 33, 44.

59. EFSP, review of Ruskin, Lectures and Catalogue, 305–6.

60. For the genre érotique, see EFSD, French Architects, 106, 141.

61. People's Journal for Dundee, 14 Sept. 1889; EFSD speech to meeting of millworkers in Glasgow, 9 Sept. 1889.

62. EFSP, Renaissance 1: 14; People's Journal for Dundee, 14 Sept. 1889; EFSD speech to meeting of millworkers in Glasgow, 9 Sept. 1889.

63. EFSP, Renaissance, 1: 14.

64. Qtd. in CWD, "Mem.," 121–22; see also Renaissance, 2: 295; EFSD, Art in the Modern State, 2.

65. EFSP, Renaissance, 2: 295.

66. EFSD, "Trades Unions for Women," 51–52.

67. CWD, "Mem.," 28.

68. EFSP, "Art and Morality," 81.

69. C. Drury E. Fortnum, review of EFSP, Renaissance, qtd. in Askwith, Lady Dilke, 72–73fn. Fortnum also claims EFSP is wrong in her assessment of Villon: when women overstep propriety, they still fail as scholars.

70. CWD, "Mem.," 46–48; CWD had insisted Zola's subjects were too disgusting, but EFSP outflanked him by a comparison certain to provoke his filial loyalties: "She said that if she had been 'reviewing Keats' on [his] first appearance . . . she might have [thought him] 'unwholesome reading' " and "to her, some of what were supposed to be the finest of the poems of Keats and Shelley seemed to occupy much the same position that Zola's books held with me; and the fact that on the one side we found 'goddesses and peacock's feathers' and on the other side 'gin in courts,' made 'little difference.' "

71. EFSP, "Art and Morality," 70, 72–75, 82.

72. EFSP, Renaissance, 2: 122–23.

73. EFSP, "Use of Looking at Pictures."

74. EFSP, "Art and Morality" 82. EFSP instances Gautier's Mademoiselle de Maupin and "the cruder animalisms" of Whitman's Leaves of Grass, along with the "grotesque obscenities" of Callot and the extremes of "mutilations" and sufferings of Gustave Doré and Holbein the elder. For the wider context, see Kate Flint, "Moral judgment and the language of English art criticism, 1870–1910," Oxford Art Journal 6:2 (1983): 59–66

75. EFSP, "Nicolas Poussin," 472.

76. EFSP, "Germaine Pilon," 75.

77. EFSP, "Summer Exhibition of the Society of French Artists," 204.

78. EFSP, "Eighth Exhibition of the Society of French Artists," 500.

79. EFSP, "Summer Exhibition of the Society of French Artists," 204.

80. EFSP, review of Ruskin, Queen of the Air; also in Ruskin: The Critical Heritage, ed. J. L. Bradley (London: Routledge Kegan Paul, 1984), 316–18.

81. EFSP, review of Ruskin, *Lectures and Catalogue,* 305; see also EFSP, "Art and Morality."

82. CWD, "Mem.," 28.

83. EFSD, review of Tyrwhitt, qtd. in CWD, "Mem.," 28; also qtd. in Eisler, "Six Lives," 158.

84. Trevelyan Papers, WCT 191 (EFSP to Pauline Trevelyan, 20 Jan. 1965). The Dudley Gallery picture was an interior with seven figures. In stressing the virtues of "modern" art, EFSP was agreeing with Trevelyan's denunciation of "mere antiquarian costume pictures," opposed to true Pre-Raphaelite "real men & women . . . full of character & invention" (PP 55, fol. 271f. [Pauline Trevelyan to EFSP, n.d. (1862)]).

85. EFSP, "Eighth Exhibition of the Society of French Artists," 500.

86. EFSP, "Carstens," 76.

87. EFSP, "Exhibition of the Royal Academy of Arts" (1872).

88. EFSD, *French Architects,* 47; EFSP, *Renaissance,* 1:202.

89. EFSP, *Renaissance,* 1: 1, 2.

90. Eisler, "Six Lives," 170; Askwith, *Lady Dilke,* 197–98.

91. EFSD, *French Architects,* vi.

92. CWD, "Mem.," 41, 27, 121–22.

93. EFSP, review of Pater, *Renaissance,* in Seiler, ed., *Pater,* 166.

94. EFSP to Eugene Muntz, qtd. in CWD, "Mem.," 20–21: "Sometimes I think (too) that the best use one could make of one's own life would be to devote oneself to knowing all, to make oneself [to be made] master—at least in general significance—of all that the human spirit has conquered in all fields [on all grounds];—but, I'm forty years old, and it's too late."

95. Qtd. in CWD, "Mem.," 54–55.

96. EFSD, "Of the Spiritual Life," BSL, 145, 151; EFSD gives the passage on Socrates in Italian: *e resta la figura piu originale della storia dello spirito umano;* I give CWD's translation; CWD, "Mem.," 232, note A.

97. EFSD, "Of Love and Sorrow," in EFSD, BSL, 164, 162; EFSD's essay refuses some possible meanings in citing Teresa; see Jill L. Matus, "Saint Teresa, Hysteria, and *Middlemarch,*" *Journal of the History of Sexuality* 1:2 (October 1990): 215–40, and Corinne Blackmer, "The Ecstasies of Saint Teresa: The Saint as Queer Diva from Crashaw to *Four Saints in Three Acts,*" in Blackmer and Patricia Juliana Smith, eds., *En Travesti: Women, Gender Subversion, and Opera* (New York: Columbia University Press, 1995).

98. EFSD, "Of the Spiritual Life," BSL, 152, 170, 154, 164, 151; cf. EFSD, "Idealist Movement," 656; see also CWD, "Mem.," 102, qtg. "private notebook" of EFSD's for 1887: ". . . is the contemplative life more perfect than the practical? Either by itself is but a half-life, and the ideal must be placed in the *satisfaction of all the energies*" (emphasis mine).

99. On the emergence of art history as a professional field, see Michael Podro, *The Critical Historians of Art* (New Haven: Yale University Press, 1982); Michael Ann Holly, *Panofsky and the Foundations of Art History* (Ithaca: Cornell University Press, 1984), ch. 1; Flint, "English Critical Reaction," esp. chs. 2–4, and Sherman, ed., *Women as Interpreters.* On historical professionalism and gender, see Natalie Zemon Davis, "Gender and Genre: Women as Historical Writers, 1400–1820," in *Beyond Their Sex: Learned Women of the European Past,* ed. Patricia Labalme (New York: New York University Press, 1980), 153–75; Maxine Berg, "The First Women Economic Historians," *Economic History Review* 45 (1992): 308–29, and *A Woman in History;* Nancy Cott, *A Woman Making History: Mary Beard Through Her Letters* (New Haven: Yale University Press, 1990); Ellen C. DuBois, "Making Women's History: Historian-Activists of Women's Rights, 1880–1940," *Radical History Review* 49 (1990): 61–84; Bonnie Smith, forthcoming.

100. Frederick Wedmore, review of EFSP, *Claude Lorrain,* qtd. in Askwith, *Lady Dilke,* 197.

101. Askwith, *Lady Dilke,* 198.

102. Pater qtd. by Katherine Bradley in T. and D. C. Sturge Moore, eds., *Works and Days: From the Journal of Michael Field* (London: John Murray, 1933), 137; EFSP, review of Pater, *Renaissance*; see also Roll-Hansen, *"Academy,"* 172.

103. Conlon, "Walter Pater," 168–69. Conlon attempts to have it both ways, as he also defends Pater's scholarship and contends that EFSP "and her contemporaries" misjudged Pater by regarding the absence of scholarly apparatus and documentation as evidence of "misrepresentation." EFSP's review did not merely voice suspicions but pointed out errors of fact.

104. Conlon, "Walter Pater"; Dale, *Victorian Critic*, 189–90.

105. Conlon, "Walter Pater"; Dale, *Victorian Critic*, 189–90. On naming: Seiler, *Pater*, 71, perhaps as egregiously, chummily calls her "Emilia" but overgenerously attributes to her a career as "a scholar at Oxford" *before* her marriage to MP, i.e., in her teens.

106. CWD, "Mem.," 20, 26–27; Ward, *Writer's Recollections*, 105.

107. CWD, "Mem.," 41; EFSD qtd. by CWD, "Mem.," 27; PP 140, fol. 87 (EFSD to GMT, n.d.).

108. MP, *Essays*, 2 vols., ed. Henry Nettleship (New York: B. Franklin, 1889); Nimmo, "Learning Against Religion," 315.

109. PP 141, tss. copies of MP to GMT, 13 Mar. 1883.

110. EFSD, *Art in the Modern State*, 28; EFSD, "Idealist Movement," 644; EFSP, *Renaissance*, 2: 293.

111. See Morley, "On Pattison's Memoirs," 338, but see also Nimmo, "Learning Against Religion," 320, 321–22; CWD also gives MP some credit for EFSP's engagement in women's trades-unionism; "Mark Pattison's diatribes on the uselessness of mere monasticism . . . turned his wife from speculative theology to more human forms of devotion"; CWD, "Mem.," 43.

112. Hugh Lloyd-Jones, *Blood for the Ghosts: Classical Influences in the Nineteenth and Twentieth Centuries* (London: Duckworth, 1982), ch. 1; see also Nirad C. Chaudhuri, *Scholar Extraordinary: The Life of Professor the Rt. Hon. Friedrich Max Muller, P.C.* (London: Chatto & Windus, 1974), 213–16; Clarke, *Classical Education in Britain*, 126; Sparrow, *Mark Pattison*, ch. 4; see also Stoppard, *Invention*, 15.

113. Lloyd-Jones, *Blood for the Ghosts*, ch. 1. See also MP, *Suggestions on Academical Organisation, with Especial Reference to Oxford* (New York: Arno Press, 1977); John Kenyon, *The History Men: The Historical Profession in England since the Renaissance* (London: Weidenfeld and Nicolson, 1983), 166–67, Sofer, *Discipline and Power*, R. Symonds, *Oxford and Empire*, and Engel, *Clergyman to Don*. Some of MP's contemporaries noted that his argument that the true purpose of a university was research was not assisted by his relatively small output when he did no teaching at all and few of his duties as Rector; William Ward Fowler, *Reminiscences* (Holywell, Oxford: priv. printed, 1921), 57–58; and Raymond H. Coon, *William Ward Fowler: An Oxford Humanist* (Oxford: Blackwell, 1934); Mandell Creighton to James Thursfield, 14 Dec. 1872, in *The Life and Letters of Mandell Creighton*, ed. Louise Creighton (London: Longmans, Green, 1904) 1:134–35; and, more generously, John Morley, qtd. in Knickerbocker, *Creative Oxford*, 106. See also Stoppard, *Invention*, 48–49.

114. Noel Annan, "Major Barbara at Work," *New Statesman*, 14 July 1967: 52.

115. Anthony Grafton, "Mark Pattison," *American Scholar* 52: 2 (Spring 1983): 229–36; 230, 233, 235, 236. See also Grafton, *Joseph Scaliger: A Study in the History of Classical Scholarship*, vol. 1: *Textual Criticism and Exegesis* (Oxford: Clarendon Press, 1983), 186, 190, and 227.

116. EFSP, "Max Schasler, History of Aesthetic," 267.

117. EFSP, review of Pater, *Renaissance*, in Seiler, ed., *Pater*, 165–66; cf. Macleod, *Art and the Victorian Middle Class*, 272.

118. EFSP, *Renaissance*, 1:28; see also Pemble, *Mediterranean Passion*, 153–55.

119. EFSD, *Renaissance*, 1:, 13–14, 12, 23, 26, 28,41, 49, 50, 57, 62, 83.

120. EFSP, *Renaissance*, 1: 15–16, 17; 2: 150, 283.

121. Stoppard, *Invention*, 49.

122. EFSD, "Idealist Movement," 652–54, 655.

123. EFSP, *Renaissance*, 1:18–19.

124. For opposed feminist uses of the language of ingestion, see Nina Auerbach, "Engorging Patriarchy," in Shari Benstock, ed., *Feminist Issues in Literary Scholarship* (Bloomington: Indiana University Press, 1987), 150–60, and bell hooks, "Eating the Other," in hooks, *Black Looks: Race and Representation* (Boston: South End Press, 1992), 21–39.

125. Epigram to EFSP, *Renaissance*, from La Fontaine; trans. by Eisler, "Six Lives," 160.

IDENTIFIED WORKS BY
E. F. S. PATTISON/DILKE

Based in part on Claire Richter Sherman, *Women as Interpreters of the Visual Arts* (Westport, Conn.: Greenwood Press, 1981), 177–80; see also Marysa deMoor, "An Honourable Gentleman Revisted: Emilia Strong Pattison's Noted Entry into the World of Sir Charles Wentworth Dilke and the *Athenaeum*," *Women's Writing* 2 (1995): 201–19. Does not include reprints in American journals.

AS E. F. S. PATTISON

Books

Claude Lorrain, Sa vie et Ses Oeuvres. Bibliothèque International d'Art. Paris: T. Rouam, 1884.
The Renaissance of Art in France. 2 vols. London: C. Kegan Paul and Co., 1879.

Articles and Titled Reviews

"Address" to Oxford Women's Provident and Protective League. *Women's Union Journal*, December 1884: 109.
"Art and Morality." (Review of Laprade, *Le Sentiment de la Nature avant le Christianisme* and *Le Sentiment de la Nature chez les Modernes*). *Westminster Review*, n. s. 35 (January 1869): 66–83.
"Art Books." Three parts. *Academy* 7 (1 May 1875): 460–62; *Academy* 8 (30 October 1875): 460–62; (20 November 1875): 535.
"Bernard Palissy, the Potter." *Portfolio* 1 (1870): 189–91.
"Caldecott's Illustrations to *Bracebridge Hall*." *Academy* 11 (20 January 1877): 58.
"Carstens." *Portfolio* 1 (1870): 76–80.
"A Chapter of the French Renaissance." *Contemporary Review* 30 (August 1877): 466–80.
"The Collection of M. Gambart at Les Palmiers, Nice." [Unsigned] *Athenaeum* (26 August 1876): 276–78.

"Edward J. Poynter, R.A." *Magazine of Art* 6 (April 1883): 245–51.

"Eight Miniatures by Jean Cousin(?)." *Academy* 2 (15 November 1871): 516.

"Eighth Exhibition of the Society of French Artists." *Academy* 5 (2 May 1874): 500.

"The Exhibition of the Royal Academy of Arts."*Academy* 3 (15 May 1872): 184–85.

"Exhibition of the Société des Beaux-Arts, Nice." *Academy* 11 (14 April 1877): 328–29.

"Five Paintings by Frederic Leighton, R.A." *Academy* 5 (28 March 1874): 351.

"Fragonard and His Decorative Paintings at Grasse." *Academy* 14 (10 August 1878): 149–50.

"French Chateaux of the Renaissance." *Contemporary Review* 30 (October 1877): 579–97.

"Germain Pilon." *Portfolio* 2 (1871): 72–75.

"The Glass Paintings of Jean Cousin at Sens." *Academy* 24 (22 December 1883): 423.

"Grimm's *Select Essays*." [Review of Grimm, *Zehn ausgewahlte Essays zur Einfuhrung in da Studium der modernen Kunst*.] *Academy* 3 (1 April 1872): 124–25.

"Herman Reigel, Cornelius." [Review of Riegel, *Cornelius, du Meister der deutschen Malerei*.] *Academy* 2 (15 February 1871): 129–30.

"The Holbein Controversy." *Academy* 2 (1 November 1871): 492–93.

"The International Exhibition: Paris, 1878." Six parts. *Academy* 13 (1 June 1878): 493–94; (15 June 1878): 538–40; (22 June 1878): 563–65; *Academy* 14 (6 July 1878): 20–21; (20 July 1878): 70–72; (2 August 1878): 122–24.

"Jean Cousin." *Academy* 4 (15 January 1873): 26.

"Jehan Cousin." *Portfolio* 2 (1871): 7–9.

"Jehan Goujon." *Portfolio* 2 (1871): 22–24.

"Max Schasler, History of Aesthetic." [Review of Schasler, *Aesthetik als Philosophie des Schonen und der Kunst*.] *Academy* (15 July 1872): 266–67.

"Nicolas Poussin." *Fortnightly Review*, n.s. 11 (April 1872): 472–77.

"Notes from Paris." Two parts. *Athenaeum* (17 May 1879): 641; (24 November 1879): 671–72.

"The Painter of the Dead (Jean Paul Laurens)." *Magazine of Art* 7 (September 1884): 51.

"The Picture by Piero della Francesca." *Academy* 6 (22 August 1874): 219–20.

"Recent Works on Voltaire." [Review of Desnoiresterres, *Voltaire et la Société Française au XVIIIe Siècle*; Strauss, *Six Lectures on Voltaire*; and Morley, *Voltaire*.] *Academy* (15 August 1872): 301–2.

"The Royal Academy." Three parts. *Academy* 23 (12 May 1883): 334–35; (19 May 1883): 353–54; (26 May 1883): 372–74.

"The Salon of 1876." Three parts. *Academy* 9 (13 May 1876): 463–65; (20 May 1876): 494–96; (27 May 1876): 516–17.

"The Salon of 1877." Four parts. *Academy* 11 (12 May 1877): 422–23; (19 May 1877): 445–46; (2 June 1877): 494–95; (9 June 1877): 518–19.

"The Salon of 1879." Five parts. *Academy* 15 (24 May 1879): 463–64; (31 May 1879): 484–85; (7 June 1879): 505–6; (14 June 1879): 528–29; (21 June 1879): 547–49.

"The Salon of 1880." Three parts. *Academy* 17 (15 May 1880): 370–71; (22 May 1880): 389–90; (5 June 1880): 427–28.

"The Salon of 1881." Four parts. *Academy* 19 (14 May 1881): 360–61; (28 May 1881): 399–400; (4 June 1881): 418–20; (11 June 1881): 439–40.

"The Salon of 1882." Four parts. *Academy* 21 (6 May 1882): 327–28; (13 May 1882): 344–45; (20 May 1882): 365–67; (3 June 1882): 401–3.

"Sir Frederic Leighton, P.R.A." In *Illustrated Biographies of Modern Artists*. Ed. Francois G. Dumas. Paris, 1882.

"The Studios." Seven parts. *Academy* 7 (20 February 1875): 202–3; (27 February 1875): 228–29; (6 March 1875): 251; (13 March 1875): 277–78; (20 March 1975): 304–5; (27 March 1875): 330–31; (3 April, 1875): 357–58.

"Summer Exhibition of the Society of French Artists." *Academy* 3 (1 June 1872): 204–5.

"Tissot On the Imagination." [Review of Tissot, *L'Imagination, ses bienfaits, et ses égarements, surtout dans le domaine du merveilleux.*] *Saturday Review* 28 (10 July 1869): 56–58.

"The Use of Looking at Pictures," *Westminster Review* n.s. 44 (October 1873): 415–23.

Encyclopedia Articles

All in *Encyclopaedia Britannica.* 9th ed. Edinburgh: Adam and Charles Black, 1880.

"Jean Antoine Houdon."

"Jean Auguste Dominique Ingres."

"Jean Baptiste Greuze."

"Jean Francois Millet."

Other Reviews

Burty, ed., *Lettres de Eugene Delacroix. Academy* 18 (11 September 1880): 192.

Desnoiresterres, *Voltaire et Genève. Academy* 9 (8 January 1876): 25–26.

Dumas, ed., *Salon illustré de 1879. Academy* 17 (27 March 1880): 239–40.

Gonse, *Eugene Fromentin, peintre et écrivain. Athenaeum* (23 July 1881): 118–19.

Gower, *Three Hundred French Portraits Representing Personages of the Courts of Francis I, Henry II, and Francis II, by Clouet . . . from the originals at Castle Howard, Yorkshire. Academy* 10 (7 July 1876): 18.

Hamerton, *Thoughts About Art. Academy* 5 (24 January 1874): 101.

Inventoire général des richesses d'art de la France, vol. 1, *Monuments réligieux. Academy* 13 (23 March 1878): 265–66.

Jahrbuch der koniglichen preussischen Kunstsammlungen. Athenaeum (3 Janaury 1880): 26.

Landseer, *Life and Letters of William Bewick, (Artist). Academy* 2 (15 October 1871): 471.

Menard, *L'Art en Alsace-Lorraine. Academy* 10 (7 October 1876): 365–66.

Michelet, *Nos Fils,* and Esquirol *L'Émile du dix-neuvième siècle. Academy* 1 (9 July 1870): 250–51.

H. Morley, *Clement Marot and Other Studies. Academy* (1 June 1871): 279–80.

Muntz, *Raphael: sa vie, son oeuvre, et son temps. Academy* 19 (29 January 1881): 85–86.

Passavant, *Raphael of Urbino and His Father, Giovanni Santi. Academy* 3 (1 January 1872): 6.

Pater, *Studies in the History of the Renaissance. Westminster Review* n.s. 43 (April 1873): 639–41. Also in Seiler, ed., *Pater.*

Petroz, *L'Art et la critique en France depuis 1822. Academy* 11 (10 March 1877): 213–14.

Poynter, *Ten Lectures on Art. Academy* 16 (27 September 1879): 235–36.

Robertson, *A Critical Account of the Drawings by Michel Angelo and Raffaelo in the University Galleries, Oxford,* and Burlington Fine Arts Club Catalogue, *Raphael Sanzio and Michel Angelo Buonarotti. Academy* 2 (22 October 1870): 6–7.

Ruskin, *Lectures on Art and Catalogue of Examples. Academy* (10 September 1870): 305–6.

Ruskin, *Queen of the Air.* Unsigned. *Westminster Review,* n.s. 36 (October 1869): 663–36. Also in Bradley, ed., *Ruskin.*

Thausing, *Die Votiv Kirche in Wien. Academy* 17 (24 January 1880): 71–72.

Tyrwhitt, *A Handbook of Pictorial Art. Saturday Review* 26 (22 August 1868): 261–63.

Wedmore, *Studies in English Art. Academy* 10 (16 December 1876): 591–92.

Weekes, *Lectures on Art Delivered at the Royal Academy. Academy* 17 (12 June 1880): 443.

AS E. F. S. DILKE

Books

Art in the Modern State. London: Chapman and Hall, 1888.

The Book of the Spiritual Life, with a Memoir of the Author by the Rt. Hon. Sir Charles W. Dilke,

Bt., M.P. London: John Murray, 1905. Revised ed., without memoir or photographs, London: John Murray, 1911.

French Architects and Sculptors of the Eighteenth Century. London: George Bell, 1900.

French Engravers and Draughtsmen of the Eighteenth Century. London: George Bell, 1902.

French Furniture and Decoration in the Eighteenth Century. London: George Bell, 1901.

French Painters of the Eighteenth Century. London: George Bell, 1899.

The Shrine of Death and Other Stories. London: George Routledge, 1886.

The Shrine of Love and Other Stories. London: George Routledge, 1891.

Articles, Stories, and Reviews

"Address" to meeting in Dundee, 3 September 1889. *Women's Union Journal* (September 16, 1889): 70.

"Address" to meeting in Glasgow. *Women's Union Journal* (15 March 1890): 22.

"The Adventures of Beelzebub." *Universal Review* 6 (January–April 1890): 223–41.

"Art-Teaching and Technical Schools," *Fortnightly Review* n.s. 47 (February 1890): 231–41.

"Ary Renan." *Athenaeum* (11 August 1900): 194.

"Benefit Societies and Trades Unions for Women." *Fortnightly Review* n.s. 45 (June 1889): 852–56; also in *Women's Gazette and Weekly News* (15 June 1889): 519, 522.

"Chardin et ses ouevres à Potsdam et à Stockholm." Three parts. *Gazette des Beaux-Arts* 22 (1 September 1899): 177–90; (1 October 1899): 333–42; (1 November 1899): 390–96.

"Christophe (Ernest Louis Aquilas)." *Art Journal* 46 (1894): 40–45.

"The Coming Elections in France." *Fortnightly Review* n.s. 46 (September 1889): 334–41.

"France's Great Military Artist (Edouard Detaille)." *Cosmopolitan* 11 (September 1891): 515–24.

"France Under Richelieu." *Fortnightly Review* n.s. 38 (December 1885): 752–67.

"France Under Colbert." *Fortnightly Review* n.s. 39 (February 1886): 209–20.

"The Great Missionary Success." *Fortnightly Review* n.s. 45 (May 1889): 677–83.

"The Idealist Movement and Positive Science. An Experience." *Cosmopolis* 7 (September 1897): 643–56.

"The Industrial Position of Women." *Fortnightly Review* n.s. 54 (October 1893): 499–508.

"Introduction." *Objets d'art at Hertford House* (the Wallace Collection), by E. Molinier. London: The Wallace Collection, 1903.

"Jean-François de Troy et sa rivalité avec François Le Moine." *Gazette des Beaux-Arts* 21 (1 April 1899): 280–90.

"Lady Dilke on Trades Unionism for Women," *Women's Union Journal* 15, no. 168 (January 15 1890): 3 (adumbration of EFSD, "Trades-Unionism for Women").

"L'art français au Guildhall de Londres en 1898." *Gazette des Beaux-Arts* 20 (1 October 1898): 321–36.

"Le Boudoir de la Marquise de Serilly au Musée de South Kensington." Two parts. *Gazette des Beaux-Arts* 20 (1 July 1898): 5–16; (1 August 1898): 118–28.

"Les coustou: Les chevaux de Marly et le tombeau du Dauphin." Two parts. *Gazette des Beaux-Arts* 25 (1 January 1901): 5–14; and (1 March 1901): 203–14.

"Letters of Antoine Watteau." *Athenaeum* (29 September 1900): 408

"Madame Renan." *Athenaeum* (2 June 1894): 709.

"Mulready." *Fortnightly Review* n.s. 52 (September 1892): 346–51.

"The Next Extension of the Suffrage." *Universal Review* 4 (May–August 1889): 371–79.

Obituary of Emma Smith Paterson. [Unsigned.] *Women's Union Journal,* December 1886: 111–118.

"Parables of Life." *Universal Review* 5 (September–December 1889): 535–50.

"Preface." *Women's Work,* by A. Amy Bulley and Margaret Whitley. London: Methuen, 1894.

"Randolph Caldecott." *Art Journal* 47 (1895): 138–42, 203–8.

Review of Pater, *Imaginary Portraits, Athenaeum,* 24 June 1887, 824–25. Also in Seiler, ed., *Pater.*

"The Royal Academy of Painting and Sculpture in France." *Fortnightly Review* n.s. 40 (November 1886): 605–16.

"Samuel Strong and the Georgia Loyalists," *Annual Transactions of the United Empire Loyalists' Association of Ontario* 3 (1899–1900): 23–28.

"S.A.R. the Duc d'Aumale." *Athenaeum* (15 May 1897): 650–51.

"The Seamy Side of Trades Unionism for Women," *New Review* 2, no. 12 (May 1890), 418–22.

"The Starved Government Department." *New Review* 4 (January 1891): 75–80.

"Trades Unionism Among Women." Coauthored by Florence Routledge. *Fortnightly Review* n.s. 49 (May 1891): 741–50.

"Trades-Unionism for Women." *New Review* 2 (January 1890): 43–53.

"Trade Unions for Women." *North American Review* 153 (August 1891): 227–39.

"Woman Suffrage in England." *North American Review* 164 (February 1897): 151–59.

"Women and the Royal Commission." *Fortnightly Review* n.s. 50 (October 1891): 535–38.

INDEX